D0867227

EUROPEAN HISTORICAL DICTIONARIES
Edited by Jon Woronoff

1. *Portugal,* by Douglas L. Wheeler. 1993
2. *Turkey,* by Metin Heper. 1994
3. *Poland,* by George Sanford and Adriana Gozdecka-Sanford. 1994
4. *Germany,* by Wayne C. Thompson, Susan L. Thompson, and Juliet S. Thompson. 1994
5. *Greece,* by Thanos M. Veremis and Mark Dragoumis. 1994.

Historical Dictionary
of
GERMANY

by
WAYNE C. THOMPSON
SUSAN L. THOMPSON
JULIET S. THOMPSON

European Historical Dictionaries, No. 4

The Scarecrow Press, Inc.
Metuchen, N.J., & London
1994

British Library Cataloguing-in-Publication data available

Library of Congress Cataloging-in-Publication Data

Thompson, Wayne C., 1943-
Historical dictionary of Germany / by Wayne C. Thompson, Susan L.
Thompson, Juliet S. Thompson.
p.   cm. -- (European historical dictionaries; no. 4)
Includes bibliographical references.
ISBN 0-8108-2869-3 (alk. paper)
1. Germany--History--Dictionaries.   I. Thompson, Susan L.
II. Thompson, Juliet S., 1971-   . III. Title.   IV. Series.
DD84.T48   1994
943'.003--dc20   94-5673

To Katie

CONTENTS

EDITOR'S FOREWORD

Few countries have undergone as many metamorphoses as Germany. Surely one of the most spectacular was the reunification of "West" and "East" Germany in 1990, with their once radically different political, economic, and social systems. This new Germany, strategically placed and looming large in population and economic clout, will be a key player in a new, broader Europe. To learn more about it, one could hardly have a better introduction than this historical dictionary. It amply covers the collapse of the German Democratic Republic, the absorption of the new Länder in the Federal Republic of Germany, the problems this has caused, and also the positive achievements.

But this book concentrates not only on the new Germany. It takes a close look at many of the older Germanys as well. It reaches back beyond the postwar settlement to the Nazi era, the Weimar Republic, the unification engineered by Bismarck, and so on to the earliest times. These periods are described in specific entries and in an extensive chronology which contains a dozen maps. Other entries introduce significant persons, places, events, institutions, and cultural developments. Numerous photographs are included to aid the reader. While much ground is covered in this very comprehensive volume, one of its major contributions is a formidable bibliography that can direct interested readers to more detailed sources of information.

The *Historical Dictionary of Germany* was written by Wayne C. Thompson, Susan L. Thompson, and Juliet S. Thompson. Wayne is a specialist on German affairs and a professor of political science at the Virginia Military Institute; he has written numerous articles, monographs, and books, including *In the Eye of the Storm: Kurt Riezler and the Crises of Modern Germany* (University of Iowa Press, 1980) and *The Political Odyssey of Herbert Wehner* (Westview Press, 1993). Susan teaches German at Mary Baldwin College. They have studied and taught in Germany and return for frequent visits. Juliet is an editor and Ph.D. candidate at Old Dominion University in Norfolk, Virginia, who went to school in Germany and also returns often. With Wayne's focus on politics, history, and economics, Susan's interest in culture and literature, and Juliet's collaboration on all aspects of the book, including primary responsibility for the chronology, bibliography, and style, they make an excellent team.

Jon Woronoff
Series Editor

ACKNOWLEDGMENTS

The authors are deeply indebted to a number of persons and institutions whose help was indispensable for the completion of this challenging project. Heinrich Bortfeldt helped write the entries on the Party of Democratic Socialism (PDS) and the collapse of the Socialist Unity Party (SED). Both he and his wife, Karin, gave us tips and information to improve some of the entries. Robert Youngblood helped us recall the major contemporary eastern and western German writers who should be included. Michael Bunch began the tedious work of constructing the bibliography and chronology, and we were able to build on his foundations. Suzanne Thompson is responsible for transforming our computer files into the kind of camera-ready copy which we could never have produced on our own. Larry Bland gave us advice on the presentation of visuals in the book and helped us make corrections. The Virginia Military Institute's (VMI) Office of Information Services was always ready to help us solve any menacing computer mysteries.

We owe special thanks to the libraries of Washington and Lee University (W & L) and the Virginia Military Institute in Lexington. Barbara Brown of W & L permitted us to use closed, air-conditioned carrels, without which we could not have worked during the summer of 1992. Janet Holly of VMI's Preston Library conducted computer bibliographical searches which enabled us to produce a bibliography as up-to-date as possible. The VMI Research Committee provided some funding for a research trip to Germany to work in the University of Freiburg library. The library of the American Institute on Contemporary German Studies in Washington, D.C., helped us find information we needed for the chronology and bibliography. Finally, we owe thanks to four institutions which gave us permission to use photos and maps in their possession: Philip Stryker and Stryker-Post Publications provided us with all the maps and some of the photos for this book. The German Information Office in New York not only lent us photos, but it provided us with countless pieces of information for the entries which we could find nowhere else. The Presse- und Informationsamt der Bundesregierung in Bonn kindly gave us permission to use photos from its files, as did the George C. Marshall Library in Lexington, Virginia.

ABBREVIATIONS AND ACRONYMS

ADN	General German News Agency (Arbeitsgemeinschaft der öffentlich-rechtlichen Rundfunkanstalten Deutschlands)
AICGS	American Institute for Contemporary German Studies
AJV/ML	Marxist-Leninist Workers' Youth Association (Arbeiterjugend Vereinigung/Marxist-Leninist)
APO	Extra-Parliamentary Opposition (Ausserparlamentarische Opposition)
ARD	Association of Public Broadcasting Corporations (Arbeitsgemeinschaft der öffentlich-rechtlichen Rundfunkanstalten Deutschlands)
ASJG	Autonomous Socialist Youth Group (Autonome Sozialistische Jugendgruppe)
BDA	Federation of German Employers' Associations (Bundesvereinigung der Deutschen Arbeitgeberverbände)
BDI	Federal Association of German Industry (Bundesverband der Deutschen Industrie)
BENELU	Belgium, Netherlands, Luxembourg
BfV	Federal Office for the Protection of the Constitution (Bundesamt für Verfassungsschutz)
BHE	Bloc of Expellees and Disenfranchised (Bund der Heimatvertriebenen und Entrechteten)
BMFT	Federal Ministry for Research and Technology (Bundesministerium für Forschung und Technologie)
BND	Federal Intelligence Service (Bundesnachrichtendienst)
BRD	Federal Republic of Germany (Bundesrepublik Deutschland, for which "BRD" is an officially unacceptable abbreviation)
BSA	League of Socialist Workers (Bund Sozialistischer Arbeiter)
BVP	Bavarian People's Party (Bayerische Volkspartei)
BWK	League of West German Communists (Bund Westdeutscher Kommunisten)
CDU	Christian Democratic Union (Christlich

	Demokratische Union)
CGGP	Conference Group on German Politics
CSCE	Conference on Security and Cooperation in Europe
CSU	Christian Social Union (Christlich-Soziale Union)
DA	Democratic Awakening (Demokratischer Aufbruch) and Democratic Alternative (Demokratische Alternative), two different parties
DAAD	German Academic Exchange Service (Deutscher Akademischer Austauschdienst)
DAF	German Labor Front (Deutsche Arbeitsfront)
DAG	German Salaried Employees' Union (Deutsche Angestellten-Gewerkschaft)
DARA	German Space Agency (Deutsche Agentur für Raumfahrt-Angelegenheiten)
DASA	German Aerospace, Inc. (Deutsche Aerospace AG)
DBB	German Civil Servants' Federation (Deutscher Beamtenbund)
DBP	Democratic Farmers' Party (Demokratische Bauernpartei)
DDP	German Democratic Party (Deutsche Demokratische Partei)
DDR	German Democratic Republic (Deutsche Demokratische Republik)
DFD	Democratic German Women's League (Demokratischer Frauenbund Deutschlands)
DFP	German Forum Party (Deutsche Forum Partei)
DGB	German Trade Union Federation (Deutscher Gewerkschaftsbund)
DIHT	German Industry and Trade Congress (Deutscher Industrie- und Handelstag)
DKP	German Communist Party (Deutsche Kommunistische Partei)
DLR	German Aerospace Research Establishment (Deutsche Forschungsanstalt für Luft- und Raumfahrt, formerly DFVLR)
DNVP	German National People's Party (Deutschnationale Volkspartei)
DP	Displaced Person and German Party (Deutsche Partei)
DPA	German Press Agency (Deutsche Presse Agentur)

DPS	Democratic Party of the Saar (Demokratische Partei des Saarlandes)
DSU	German Social Union (Deutsche Soziale Union)
DVB	German Farmers' Union (Deutscher Bauernverband)
DVP	German People's Party (Deutsche Volkspartei)
DVU	German People's Union (Deutsche Volksunion)
EC	European Community
ECSC	European Coal and Steel Community
EDC	European Defense Community
ESA	European Space Agency
EURATOM	European Atomic Community
FAU	Free Workers' Union (Freie Arbeiterinnen-Union)
FAU/AP	FAU Anarchist Party (FAU/Anarchistenpartei)
FAU/R	FAU Council Communists (FAU/Räte)
FDGB	Free German Trade Union Federation (Freier Deutscher Gewerkschaftsbund)
FDJ	Free German Youth (Freie Deutsche Jugend)
FDP	Free Democratic Party (Freie Demokratische Partei, "Liberals")
FÖGA	Federation of Violence-Free Action Groups (Föderation Gewaltfreier Aktionsgruppen)
FRG	Federal Republic of Germany (Bundesrepublik Deutschland)
GAL	Green-Alternative List (Grün-Alternative Liste)
GCML	George C. Marshall Library, Lexington, Virginia
GDP	All-German Party (Gesamtdeutsche Partei)
GDR	German Democratic Republic (Deutsche Demokratische Republik, DDR)
GESTAPO	Secret State Police (Geheime Staatspolizei)
GIC	German Information Center, New York, New York
GIM	Group International Marxists (Gruppe Internationale Marxisten)
GNP	Gross National Product
GPBHE	Refugee Party (See BHE)
GSA	German Studies Association
GVP	All-German People's Party (Gesamtdeutsche Volkspartei)
HJ	Hitler Youth (Hitlerjugend)
IAA	International Workers' Association (Internationale Arbeiter-Assoziation)

IG	Industry Union (Industrie Gewerkschaft)
IMF	International Monetary Fund
INF	Intermediate-Range Nuclear Forces
ISA	International Socialist Workers' Organization (Internationale Sozialistische Arbeiterorganisation)
KB	Communist League (Kommunistischer Bund)
KBW	Communist League of West Germany (Kommunistischer Bund Westdeutschlands)
KPD	Communist Party of Germany (Kommunistische Partei Deutschlands)
KPD-ML	Communist Party of Germany-Marxist Leninist (KPD-Marxist-Leninist, later simply KPD)
KVP	People's Police in Military Installations (Kasernierte Volkspolizei)
LDP	Liberal Democratic Party (Liberaldemokratische Partei)
LDPD	Liberal Democratic Party of Germany (Liberaldemokratische Partei Deutschlands)
LfV	Land Office for the Protection of the Constitution (Landesamt für Verfassungsschutz)
LTTE	Liberation Tigers of Tamil Ealam
MBB	Messerschmitt-Bölkow-Blohm
MG	Marxist Group (Marxistische Gruppe)
MfS	Ministry for State Security (Ministerium für Staatssicherheit--Stasi)
MLPD	Marxist-Leninist Party of Germany (Marxistisch-Leninistische Partei Deutschlands)
NATO	North Atlantic Treaty Organization
NPD & NDPD	National Democratic Party of Germany (Nationaldemokratische Partei Deutschlands), two different parties
NSDAP	National Socialist Workers' Party of Germany (Nationalsozialistische Deutsche Arbeiterpartei, or NAZI)
NVA	National People's Army (Nationale Volksarmee)
OECD	Organization for Economic Cooperation and Development
OEEC	Organization for European Economic Cooperation

OKW	Supreme Command of the Armed Forces (Oberkommando der Wehrmacht)
OMGUS	Office of Military Government U.S.
ÖTV	Public Service, Transport and Transportation Union (Öffentlicher Dienst, Transport und Verkehr)
PDS	Party of Democratic Socialism (Partei des Demokratischen Sozialismus)
PIB	Presse- und Informationsamt der Bundesregierung
PKK	Workers' Party of Kurdistan
PPA	Progress Presse-Agentur
RAF	Red Army Faction (Rote Armee Fraktion)
RIAS	Radio in the American Sector
RZ	Red Cells (Rote Zellen)
SA	Storm Division (Sturmabteilung)
SAG	Socialist Workers' Group (Sozialistische Arbeitergruppe)
SAP	Socialist Workers' Party (Sozialistische Arbeiterpartei)
SD	Security Service (Sicherheitsdienst)
SDI	Strategic Defense Initiative
SDS	Socialist German Student Federation (Sozialistische Deutsche Studentenschaften)
SED	Socialist Unity Party of Germany (Sozialistische Einheitspartei Deutschlands)
SEW	Socialist Unity Party of West Berlin (Sozialistische Einheitspartei West Berlins)
SI	Socialist Initiative (Sozialistische Initiative)
SMAD	Soviet Military Administration in Germany
SPD	Social Democratic Party of Germany (Sozialdemokratische Partei Deutschlands)
SPP	Stryker Post Publications
SPS	Social Democratic Party of the Saar (Sozialdemokratische Partei des Saarlandes)
SRP	Socialist Reich Party (Sozialistische Reichspartei)
SS	Protective Squad (Schutzstaffel)
Stasi	State Security (Ministerium für Staatssicherheit, MfS)
SZOG	Soviet Zone of Germany
TLD	Trotskyist League of Germany (Trotsky Liga Deutschlands)

UniBW	Universities of the Federal Armed Forces (Universitäten der Bundeswehr)
USPD	Independent Social Democratic Party (Unabhängige SPD)
VAT	Value Added Tax (Umsatzsteuer)
VDS	Association of German Student Bodies (Verband Deutscher Studentenschaften)
VOPO	People's Police (Volkspolizei)
VS	Association of German Writers (Verband Deutscher Schriftsteller in der IG Medien)
VSP	United Socialist Party (Vereinigte Sozialistische Partei)
WAV	Economic Reconstruction League (Wirtschaftliche Aufbauvereinigung)
WEU	Western European Union
ZDF	Second German Television (Zweites Deutsches Fernsehen)

MAPS AND ILLUSTRATIONS

The Federal Republic of Germany. The *Länder* of Mecklenburg-Western
Pomerania, Saxony-Anhalt, Brandenburg, Thuringia, and Saxony as well as the
eastern part of Berlin were in the Soviet occupation zone and the German
Democratic Republic, 1945-90. The Oder and Neisse rivers form the post-1945
border with Poland. (*Source:* Stryker-Post Publications.)

INTRODUCTION

Few people of the world have such a rich and varied past as do the Germans. Yet theirs is a history full of mountains and valleys. Without German science, theology, philosophy, music, literature, and the other arts, Western civilization would have been left with gaping holes. But Germans have known times of shame and destitution so deep and dark that many could not be sure that the sun would ever shine again.

German history is one of religious, class, and territorial division. Otto von Bismarck once said that Italy was merely a geographical concept, but he could have said exactly the same about Germany. For many centuries there existed the fiction of a unified, almost universal German empire stretching from the North Sea to Sicily. Yet, until 1871 Germany was, in fact, a highly fractured scene of independent and rival kingdoms, principalities, ecclesiastical states, and independent cities. Even though most of their subjects spoke one of hundreds of German dialects, few considered themselves Germans; rather they felt themselves to be Saxons, Bavarians, Prussians, Rhinelanders, or Frankfurters. When political unity finally came in 1871, many Germans were left outside the new German Empire, such as the German-speaking Swiss and Austrians. This unity lasted only three-quarters of a century and ended in disgrace and destruction. Two Germanys emerged from the ashes of the war, both being founded in 1949. One is the Federal Republic of Germany (FRG or "West Germany"), which has a capitalist economy and western-style democracy. It belongs to the North Atlantic Treaty Organization (NATO) and European Community (EC). The other was the German Democratic Republic (GDR or "East Germany"), which had a centrally planned communist economy and was basically a one-party, non-democratic police state created by and modeled after the Soviet Union, which maintained 380,000 troops in the country. Not until the Berlin Wall came tumbling down on November 9, 1989, did reunification become possible; on October 3, 1990, Germany became one country again, and that date is now celebrated as the national holiday.

Germany is populated by a dynamic, talented, and imaginative people who for centuries have defied definition. Two thousand years ago, the Roman historian Tacitus called the Germanic tribes (which later migrated to most other parts of Western and Eastern Europe) warlike, but until the 20th century the Germans brought war to other nations far less frequently than did others. Germans were deeply involved in tragic

Germans celebrate reunification in front of Brandenburg Gate, midnight,
October 3, 1990. (*Source:* PIB.)

wars in the 20th century, and even in 1950, the U.S. High
Commissioner for Germany, John J. McCloy, joked: "Just give me a
brass band and a loudspeaker truck. Then let me march from Lake
Constance in the South to Kiel up North, and I will have an army of a
million men behind me, all eager-eyed." He was badly mistaken.
Contemporary Germany is, in fact, a country in which pacifist sentiment
is perhaps stronger than in any other European or North American
country. One young German noted with pleasure and with some
exaggeration that "Europeans have always wanted a pacifist Germany;
well, now they have one!" Indeed, a major source of American irritation
toward post-war Germany was the unwillingness of many Germans to
defend themselves.

The French-Swiss writer, Madame de Staël, described the Germans
almost 200 years ago as a pacific, poetic and romantic people, but
Germans also acquired a reputation for diligence and order. German

politics has often been described as romantic and irrational. But it was a German statesman (Bismarck) with whom one most directly associates the term *Realpolitik,* which describes a carefully measured, rational policy based on a realistic assessment of a nation's interests, goals, and means. The Germans' road to democracy was bumpy and they made several wrong turns. But today Germany is one of the world's most stable and tolerant democracies, about which former Chancellor Willy Brandt could say in the early 1970s: "Germans can again be proud of their country."

Germans are still somewhat haunted by their history. No people tries so hard to come to grips with its own past, and almost no one is more critical of Germany and its past than is the German himself. The Germans' critical eye to their own past has brought some undeniable benefits to the present. It has helped to harden both the democratic consensus and the determination to bend over backwards to respect and protect human rights and dignity.

Cliches are never more than half-truths, but those relating to Germans are much more in need of revision than those about most other peoples. Germany is a country in the process of rapid change. This is partly because of industrialization familiar to Americans and other Western Europeans. In part it is due to a lingering reaction to their own experience under Hitler, a dictator almost universally regarded outside and inside Germany as the most evil and brutal individual in recorded history. One can witness change in Germans' attitudes on politics, social problems, religion, and work, as well as in almost all German societal institutions, including the family and the schools. The process of integrating the former GDR, which had been ruled by a Communist dictatorship for 40 years, is altering Germany even further.

PEOPLE AND GEOGRAPHY

The Germans constitute the largest nationality in Europe west of Russia, where there are more than 1.5 ethnic Germans still living. The FRG has close to 80 million inhabitants after absorbing 17 million East Germans. With an area of 137,691 square miles (357,050 square kilometers), it is a very densely populated country, with 250 inhabitants per square mile. The only European countries where the people live more closely together are the Netherlands and Belgium. Its population is unevenly dispersed, though. The most thickly settled part is the Ruhr-

Rhine area around Düsseldorf, Cologne (Köln), Dortmund and Essen (a conglomeration of cities and heavy industry often called "Ruhr City"). Other large urban concentrations are the Rhine-Main area around Frankfurt, the Rhine-Neckar area around Mannheim and Ludwigshaven, the Swabian industrial concentration around Stuttgart, as well as the cities of Berlin, Leipzig, Dresden, Bremen, Hamburg, Hanover, Nuremberg and Munich. There are, however, very thinly settled areas in the Northern German Plain, the Eifel Mountain region, the Upper Palatinate, the Bavarian Forest, and the peripheral areas adjacent to the earlier border with the GDR. Those latter areas on both sides of the former dividing line are experiencing rapid growth in unified Germany as they become the new heartland.

The FRG has experienced a rapid flight from farms into cities and towns; the rural population dropped from 23 percent in 1950 to less than 5 percent today. But about half of all Germans live in towns or villages of less than 20,000 inhabitants. Unlike countries such as France, Britain, Italy or Denmark, no single German city dominates the political, cultural and economic life of the entire country although Berlin may gradually assume this position in the 21st century. Berlin again became the official capital after reunification on October 3, 1990. The temporary seat of government remains Bonn (pop. 300,000), but parliament voted in June 1991 to move it to Berlin over a ten-year period. The German population is not growing; the FRG has one of the lowest birth rates in the world.

Germany has for centuries been called the "land of the middle" because it occupies the heart of Europe. This is a major reason why other European powers have often sought to keep Germany divided and weak. It has no natural frontiers, and the North German Plain, which is interspersed with hills, remains an ideal invasion route. Only the Alpine foothills in the southeast offer uninviting terrain for invading commanders. Because the altitude rises from the North Sea to the Alps, most of Germany's rivers, which provide the country with an excellent inland waterway system, flow north and empty into the North Sea via the Rhine, Ems, Weser and Elbe Rivers. The only exception is the Danube, which flows southeast toward the Black Sea; in 1992 the final canal linking the Rhine and Danube Rivers was completed. This opened up a navigable inland waterway from the North Sea to the Black Sea.

The visitor to Germany now looks in vain for physical traces of the pauperized and demolished land which in 1945 began to dig itself out from under a pile of rubble. In the western part one sees a highly prosperous country with a well-fed, well-clothed, well-cared-for and predominantly middle-class people. Germans in the eastern part will enjoy roughly the same prosperity by the end of the century. The FRG is ribboned by highly modern highways traveled by millions of private automobiles. Its modern cities in the West show few signs of urban blight, but cities in the East manifest their four decades of mindless and tasteless urban renewal or neglect. It is an economic giant in the world and now operates in European politics with far more confidence, effectiveness and respect than almost any other nation dreamed would be possible after Germany's total collapse in 1945.

The FRG has even become a less tense and far more pleasant place to live. With high incomes in the West, a short (38.5 hour or less) work week and a commitment to "quality of life," Germans have become world champion travellers abroad. When they stay home, they enjoy swimming pools, tennis courts, saunas and "free time centers," which have proliferated everywhere. Their cities contain museums, concert halls and pedestrian zones filled with sidewalk cafes, street-shows and pleasant street life. When the University of Reading in Britain made a study of European cities in 1986, it considered such factors as social and environmental conditions, the state of the urban economy, per capita income, unemployment, net migration and supply of hotel bedrooms (as a measure of how many people visit them). The study concluded that the top two cities were Frankfurt and Munich. Eleven of the top 20 cities in Europe were western German, and not a single western German city figured among the bottom 20. Germans are increasingly enjoying their comfortable lives with a spontaneity which invites a much closer look at this modern country.

During its entire existence as a state, the FRG has not faced a single truly serious challenge to its legitimacy. This stands in stark contrast to the Weimar Republic, which was born into crisis and never extricated itself from it. In its 40 years of life, the western German regime made remarkable strides to win the approval and support of its citizens. The challenge now is to win eastern Germans' support as well and to make them feel like "first-class citizens." A 1991 poll revealed that 90 percent of them considered themselves to be "second-class citizens" in their new country, and a third of their western countrymen agreed.

Sensible observation of the FRG, combined with an examination of relevant public opinion surveys, indicates that the western German political culture has changed considerably since 1945 and that the FRG is a stable and democratic country with a politically interested, informed, involved and tolerant citizenry. Immediately after the war, after excessive political mobilization and propaganda under Hitler, Germans tended to withdraw from public affairs and to seek refuge in private and family circles. Citizens in the GDR tended to do the same, seeking their own personal niches. Now Germans in both parts are no less active in public or political affairs than their counterparts in older democracies such as the U.S. and Holland. In terms of party membership, attendance at political gatherings and especially voting, they are even more active than those counterparts.

A few facts help demonstrate Germans' overall satisfaction with their regime, at least in the western part. In 1951, 90 percent of all adult West Germans believed that Germany had been better off during an earlier German regime, and a third even favored restoration of the Hohenzollern monarchy; but, by 1976, 90 percent thought they were better off under the present regime, and almost no one wanted the restoration of the monarchy. This is due to many western citizens' positive experience under democracy. Their country has had a high level of accomplishment. Prosperity and the expanded social welfare system smoothed class conflicts and allowed all groups in the society more benefits from the system and a greater opportunity to advance. The FRG is a functioning democracy in which some Germans are asking what kind of democracy the FRG should have, not whether the FRG should remain a democracy. The criticism that Germans have become very materialist is certainly valid. But while materialism might be rejected in principle (but seldom in practice) by some leftists and intellectuals, it has no doubt made the FRG far more governable and respected as a political democracy.

FOREIGN AND DEFENSE POLICY

Over the years the FRG became more independent and critical of the U.S. Washington was absorbed during the 1960s and early 1970s with Vietnam and a new relationship with the Soviet Union and China. The FRG increasingly shouldered political responsibilities and exercised diplomatic flexibility throughout the world. It has also witnessed a diminution in Europe of French, British, and American influence, as well as a disappearance of Soviet power. Because of its past, the FRG always preferred a low-key, quieter diplomacy that would be least likely to arouse fear or envy in other countries. It is now less restrained by the embarrassing German past. However, long-standing habits die hard, and reunification has not changed the FRG's low-key approach in a fundamental way. Nevertheless, the cliche that the FRG is an "economic giant and a political dwarf" is outdated.

In his first policy statement in the all-German Bundestag, Chancellor Helmut Kohl pledged that "there is no comfortable niche in international politics for us Germans, and we must not shirk our responsibility." The united nation will, he promised, not be a "restless *Reich.*" A new Germany in a new kind of Europe has emerged, and it is realistic that the continent's largest and richest democracy will have to bear more responsibility in a world without a Soviet Union and in which American predominance declines. This is not a role which Germany seeks, but one which is thrust upon it. This was confirmed by a *Spiegel* poll a few weeks after reunification: only 23 percent of Germans believed their country should be a major power in Europe, and 47 percent opposed it. In the spring of 1991 another poll showed that 71 percent backed the government's assurances that German reunification must primarily be seen as an impetus for the political union of Europe.

The new Germany displayed its willingness to use its new political clout in December 1991, when it muscled its EC partners into recognizing the independence of the Yugoslav republics of Slovenia and Croatia, despite serious misgivings in London, Paris, Washington, and the UN. It was especially noteworthy that Bonn did not even reply to a formal U.S. request to withhold such recognition. Then, in 1992, it asked the EC to grant the German language equal status with English and French in meetings and documents, even though surveys show that Germans are more likely to speak foreign languages than any other EC citizens except the Dutch. Since reunification German is the most widely spoken language in the EC and is experiencing a revival in eastern Europe. Said one German diplomat: "We have the size and the importance now to work in our own language."

It was to be expected that for a while, Germany would be preoccupied with the mounting problems and costs of its reunification and the rebuilding of eastern Germany's bankrupt economy. It did not want to be distracted and was inclined to continue to hide behind its constitutional ban on using force for anything but defending its own territory or its NATO allies. Some politicians and legal scholars argue that this does not prevent Bonn from joining international alliances such as the coalition in the Persian Gulf in 1991, but this question remains to be settled.

ECONOMY AND THE PROBLEMS
OF INTEGRATING THE EAST

The FRG deserves its reputation as an economic giant. It has the strongest economy in Europe, is economically the most important member of the EC, and has one of the world's hardest currencies. It is the biggest exporter in the world. Its economic activity is guided by the principle of the social market economy. This means that while it does not permit unrestrained economic competition whatever the social costs, it does openly advocate and support liberal (free) world trade.

The FRG has a number of economic assets which have made it one of the world's most prosperous democracies. It is located in the middle of Europe and has an excellent net of road, rail, water, and air connections which tie it to all the world's major markets. Largely because a great part of its industry was destroyed or dismantled during and after the Second World War, the western part has ultra-modern plants and equipment, as will the eastern part by the end of the century. It also continues to enjoy a tradition of efficiency and quality production and service. When the victors wanted to place the loser's goods at a disadvantage after the First World War, they required the words "Made in Germany" to be stamped in English on all German products. However, this measure boomeranged: German goods and services were of such high quality that purchasers did not avoid, but instead sought goods with those words stamped on them.

Germany's prosperity is vitally important for political reasons. The danger that a disappearance of economic success could threaten democratic values applies more or less to all Western countries. But in the case of Germany it applies to a far greater extent. Its first real experiment with democracy during the interwar years was rocked from the beginning by staggering economic problems. The fact that an economic depression had left more than six million Germans out of work was a major reason why the Weimar Republic fell in January 1933. The FRG was able to win and maintain legitimacy in the eyes of its own citizens largely through its almost stunning economic accomplishments, often called an "economic miracle." Now it faces the daunting challenge of absorbing a bankrupt, unproductive socialist economy in its eastern lands, whose people had been deprived of prosperity for four decades. It has proven to be more difficult than expected.

Germany's reunification in 1990 presents the FRG with awesome difficulties and challenges which threaten the peace and stability of German society and tax the imagination of German leaders. In a way, the problems are even greater than when the FRG had to rebuild a devastated land after 1945. During the 12-year Nazi regime, Germany had maintained the institutional infrastructure of a market economy, private property, a private sector legal code, and an administrative sector which understood the market system. Eastern Germans could not fall back on such continuity in 1990.

During 40 years of Communist rule, the economy was continuously plundered, first by the Soviet occupiers in the form of war reparations, and then by the Socialist Unity Party of Germany (SED), who let the country's capital stock, housing, transportation network, communications systems, and environment degenerate. Enterprises had no resources of their own for investment; profits were sent to the central government, which was stingy in returning money for modernization. The economy was planned from the top, and the country was largely isolated economically from the capitalist world. Trade of generally shoddy goods was on a state-to-state basis and directed primarily toward the GDR's Communist partners in Eastern Europe and the Soviet Union. This "command economy" created hopeless bottlenecks and shortfalls and robbed individuals and firms of the opportunity to apply their own initiative and creativity to improve their economic situation. Only 5 percent of the workforce worked independently in repair shops, small stores, and restaurants. Citizens and trade unionists were nurtured to be passive, obeying the leaders at the top in return for a guaranteed job and income, which was the highest in the communist world.

Thus, when western Germans woke up from the initial euphoria of reunification, they found an economy in the East where roughly half the workforce in the average company was unproductive, a majority of the companies were uncompetitive in the world market, a third of the country's production had traditionally been exported to countries in the East which could no longer pay for poorly made and overpriced eastern German goods, most of the property used for industry and farming had been taken out of private hands, environmental neglect had reached crisis proportions, and citizens had huge pent-up consumer expectations they hoped would be gratified immediately. Perhaps worst of all, citizens had forgotten over the past four decades how a market system, a private company, and a western legal system operate.

It was in this setting that Chancellor Kohl, who like most German politicians genuinely underestimated the economic difficulties involved in the unparalleled merger of two so different economic systems and who wanted to win the first all-German federal elections in December 1990, announced that "no one will be worse off" after unity. Such unjustified optimism rapidly instilled disappointment, pessimism, cynicism, fear, deep unrest and rage among eastern Germans when they soon experienced the worst economic collapse in Germany since the Great Depression in 1929-33. Within a month after reunification, eastern German industrial output and employment (including short-time work) had fallen by more than a third and was getting steadily worse.

Why did this economic collapse occur? On July 1, 1990, the western *Deutschmark*, one of the world's hardest currencies, was introduced in the GDR at an exchange rate of one-to-one, even though experts estimated the east mark to have only a quarter of a west mark's value. The Kohl government regarded this as a political necessity to keep the momentum of unity going, but it made no economic sense. Eastern Germany's former communist trading partners could no longer buy its goods priced in west marks, so a third of its customers disappeared. These markets could not be replaced in the West because of the low quality of eastern products. The problem was further aggravated by the fact that East Germans themselves wanted to buy higher quality western goods, rather than goods produced in their own part of Germany. Thus, demand for their products declined even further, while western Germany's economy boomed because of the huge demand in the East.

Production costs rose because pay was in a more valuable currency while output was going down. At the same time, wages also rose as East Germans desired to have the same pay level as their countrymen in the West. Within a year of monetary union wages had risen 50 percent to 80 percent in many eastern firms, and East Germans' pay had risen to about half that in the West and was steadily going up. These raises occurred despite a drastic cut in productivity; therefore, eastern companies' competitive advantage from cheap labor was destroyed. Run-down East German companies which have to pay employees at western German wage levels cannot produce goods at prices that people are willing to pay. By mid-1991 fewer than one in ten companies in the East was economically viable. Barring a rise in productivity, the higher wages climb, the more employees have to be laid off to meet the payroll. But to increase productivity enough to pay high wages, companies need to be dramatically modernized. That is, they desperately need investment, but this is perhaps the greatest disappointment.

It was expected that western companies would invest heavily in the East and thereby cushion the shock of transition to a capitalist economy, but several factors held them back. The first is precisely the fact that eastern enterprises are not economically viable. Investors do not want to buy companies which lose money, have antiquated equipment, bloated workforces, unrealistically high wage levels compared with productivity, and environmental liabilities which could bankrupt an investor. East German firms were so careless in polluting the air, soil and water that the clean-up costs are staggering. Legal changes were necessary to relieve new owners of the responsibility for a firm's past pollution. East German factories used high-polluting energy sources, such as brown coal, which must be replaced with cleaner fuels at high cost. In many cases it is cheaper to create new companies rather than to take over problem-ridden old ones. Finally, the infrastructure needed for modern business was outdated: a 1920s vintage telephone and communications system, an absence of modern and pleasant office space, a road network which has barely been maintained since Hitler's time, and a largely non-computer-literate workforce.

A second problem was a complicated jumble of property claims resulting from earlier expropriations by the Nazis, the Soviets, and the SED. Property taken and redistributed by the Soviets between 1945 and 1949 is not to be returned to former owners, in contrast to confiscations before and after, with some qualifications. More than a million claims to such property were filed, but the litigation is complicated and time-consuming. This is especially true since local and Land government administrations are understaffed and practically bankrupt. Also many East German judges were removed because of their earlier collaboration with the Communist state. By mid-1992 only about 5 percent of the claims had been settled.

Investors are naturally fearful of time- and cost-consuming litigation involving property claims, and they are therefore inclined to wait until such problems are sorted out before sending in their money. Realizing the difficulty, the Bonn government, working together with the eastern Land governments, finally agreed that property could be sold to investors rather than returned to prior owners (who would be compensated) if this were necessary to create jobs. Bonn wished to protect jobs not only in order to quiet fears and unrest in the East, but in order to prevent a massive migration of East Germans into the West. Most want to remain in eastern Germany, but in 1991 an estimated 10,000 persons a month, often those with dynamism and badly-needed skills, moved westward, and this continued in 1992. Several hundred thousand more commute up to eight hours per day to work in the West.

A further problem in stimulating economic activity is that eastern Germans are understandably mystified by the intricate complexity of western German laws and regulations which have been introduced into the East. Anxious East Germans who are suddenly having to live under totally different and unfamiliar rules are buying hastily published paperbacks with titles like *Your Rights as a Tenant, Your Rights as an Employee,* and *How to Deal with the Tax System.* Few know how a capitalist business works and how to start one up. They lack management and financial know-how and are unprepared to dive into a free-market system. Leipzig's mayor spoke of "a whole society far more complicated than any of us realized; everything here is new." Investors, as well as ordinary East Germans, are dismayed to see that management in struggling East German firms, at least below the top level, is still largely the same as during the Communist era. There are doubts not only about how much those managers know about a capitalist system, but also how much they believe in it. Although they may be well educated and experienced, their presence is a psychological blow to those East Germans who had dreamed of starting anew.

To help guide the transition from an unproductive socialist economy to a modern capitalist one, a Trust Agency (*Treuhand*) holding company was established. Its job after unity was to try to privatize at reasonable prices and as quickly as possible the huge empire of former East German state assets. It also had to divide up state assets among the various levels of government, distribute liquidity cash, supervise the restructuring of companies not yet fit for sale, and prevent the creation of monopolies. No agency could accomplish such a massive task easily. It became a scapegoat for the downturn in the eastern economy and for capitalism's slow start. Amid mounting protests against unemployment and soaring costs for rent, energy, and transportation, its chairman, Detlev Rohwedder, was assassinated in his Düsseldorf home. His violent death eliminated the last hopes that the merger of two unequal parts into one harmonious whole could be done without upheaval.

In the meantime, the Bonn government sought ways to speed up the recovery. This was an unaccustomed challenge because West Germany had created its economic prosperity and strength by slow, steady, balanced growth, not by quick action, as is being demanded for the East, which produces only 10 percent of the FRG's GNP. It allots about DM 100 billion (ca. $60 billion) annually for a variety of subsidies. The Kohl government subjected itself to intense criticism in the West for raising taxes in 1991 to help rebuild the East's economy after promising before the federal elections not to do that; they included a 7.5 percent surcharge on income and corporate taxes, higher social security levies, and hefty tax increases on gasoline and cigarettes. This was the largest tax hike in German history. Its commitments, combined with the $11 billion in aid to fight the war in the Gulf and $9 billion (which some consider to be a mere "downpayment") to pay for the withdrawal of Soviet troops from Germany, caused Bonn's government deficit to balloon to 5 percent of GNP, a level higher than the equivalent figure in the U.S. during the Reagan presidency. However, because the German savings ratio is three times the U.S. level, Bonn can draw on those larger domestic savings to help finance the budget without borrowing abroad. To make its economic picture a bit worse, the FRG began experiencing trade and current accounts deficits.

ONE GERMAN CULTURE?

Germany is politically and legally unified. But the two sides have not yet formed a harmonious whole, and the resentments which separate West from East are deep. For decades Germans on each side of the Wall had assumed that they were basically the same, speaking the same language, reading the same literature, sharing the same historical and cultural traditions. They thought they knew and understood each other, but they were wrong. Germans are not psychologically unified, and a sense of national solidarity is lacking to complete the reunification process. *Ostpolitik* expert Egon Bahr remarked at the time of unity that "we Germans got married in a hurry and enjoyed it. Now we must get to know each other. Normally it is the other way around, but, then, what is normal in Germany?" Former Foreign Minister Hans-Dietrich Genscher, who himself grew up in Halle in the GDR, liked to tell the joke about the *Ossi* (eastern German) saying that "We are one people!", to which the *Wessi* (western German) replies: "So are we!"

Many western Germans believe they have inherited an unknown, problem-ridden country populated by German-speaking strangers. Eastern Germans, in turn, are baffled by the new Germany of which they are now a part and had expected more sympathy from westerners than they have gotten. They are stunned to see how little remains of the society in which they grew up. Western German laws and traditions are so much the norm that many easterners agree with psychologist Margit Venner: "This is not unification, it's an annexation!" President Richard von Weizsäcker always says it best: "We cannot deny how much divides us still. . . . The form of unity has been determined: now we must give it substance."

Visually the two parts are beginning to look more like each other. Although the East is still drab and polluted by comparison, it is undergoing a face-lift. Facades of shops are being freshly painted and city streets refurbished. Stores are bountifully stocked with consumer goods, and western firms, banks, and gasoline stations are opening branches everywhere. But anyone visiting both parts of Germany hears an earful about the other and quickly realizes that misunderstandings abound: *Ossis* are allegedly petty bourgeois, narrow-minded, provincial, ungrateful despite their outstretched palms, and want all the benefits of capitalism now despite the fact that they are lazy (a dubious notion given the fact that eastern Germans created 300,000 new businesses in the first seven months of unity!). By contrast, *Wessis* are seen to be rich snobs, arrogant, inconsiderate, insensitive, egotistical, distrustful, and less kind toward children. Many eastern Germans suffer from an inferiority complex toward western Germans, whom they find to be more decisive, independent, more open to the world, more confident, and more able to achieve and to master problems.

The economic disparity is enormous, although it will narrow dramatically within a decade. In 1992, eastern Germans earned half as much as western Germans in an economy with about 40 percent of the real output per worker. Per household the easterners had half as many cars (to say nothing about the low quality of East German automobiles, which are rapidly disappearing), deep freezers, and color televisions, 7 percent as many telephones, and a seventh as many automatic washing machines. In 1991, the average East German household had financial assets valued at DM 20,000 versus DM 100,000 in the West. The Bundesbank noted that "the financial situation of the population in the new federal states is similar to the situation in western Germany in the early 1970s." They had only 27 square meters of living space per inhabitant (compared with 35.5 in the cramped West) in decrepit housing, 40 percent of which was built before the First World War. Although about 42 percent of East German housing was privately owned before 1989, the bad effects of rent control and centralized allocation were visible. The poor condition of housing was the price East Germans had to pay for having to spend only 3 percent of their disposable income on it. Finally, toxic pollution and poor medical delivery kept East Germans' life expectancy lower than in the West: 69 years for men and 75 years for women, compared with 70 and 77 years in the West respectively.

One should not dwell exclusively on the differences. Eastern and western Germans voted in much the same way in 1990, and many polls the same year revealed similar opinions after reunification. Both prize the same thing--high income. A total of 71 percent of Germans saw the environment as the top priority, with 82 percent of eastern Germans and 87 percent of westerners favoring increased spending in that area. Both sides rejected any suggestion of increased spending on the military, although rising crime, drug use, violence against foreigners, and soccer hooliganism prompted 40 percent of eastern Germans, but only 22 percent of westerners, to desire more respect for state authority, and 65 percent and 25 percent respectively to want greater police presence. Two-thirds of Germans in both parts were "proud to be German," although western Germans had a greater sense of being European than did their eastern countrymen, who had been kept largely isolated. They generally agreed who their favorite nationalities are: French, American, and Austrian, although the easterners put the Austrians ahead of the Americans. They also disliked the same peoples--Poles, Turks, and Gypsies, although eastern Germans' antipathy was somewhat stronger. Asked what country should be the new Germany's model, 40 percent said Switzerland, because of its "wealth and independence," and 29 percent said Sweden; only 6 percent, 8 percent, and 2 percent respectively cited the U.S., France, and Britain as their models.

The FRG faces daunting challenges, and Germany has not yet found a consensus for bearing the political and economic costs of unity. Social and economic conditions in the new Germany are more polarized than in the old West Germany, and the political environment is less settled and predictable. But the problems are relatively minor compared with those it faced in the 1940s and 1950s. With a dynamic economy in the

West, a sterling track-record for achievement, and a well-trained work force in the East, Germany will succeed despite much uncertainty. Unrest in the East will be worrisome, but it will not derail democracy in the FRG. As a fully sovereign, unified nation, it will show more independence in its foreign policy, but it will be a conscientious partner in the restructuring of NATO, at the same time that it promotes a unified Europe and some form of European defense identity.

Berlin Wall, February 20, 1990 (*Source*: PIB)

CHRONOLOGY OF IMPORTANT EVENTS IN GERMANY

9 A.D.: Arminius (Hermann) practically decimates the Roman occupation forces in the Teutoburg Forest.

800: Charlemagne is crowned emperor in Rome.

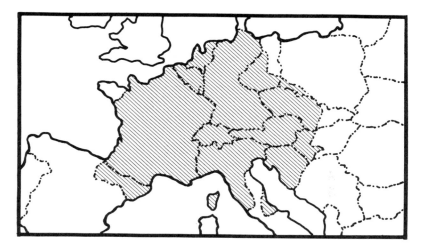

Charlemagne's Empire in 814 (*Source:* SPP.)

814: Charlemagne dies in Aachen.

843: Under the Treaty of Verdun, Charlemagne's grandchildren divide up the empire. Lothar receives the central, Charles the Bold the western, and Ludwig the German the eastern territories.

870 to ca. 900: Formation of the duchies of Franconia, Saxony, Bavaria, Swabia, and Lorraine.

911: Upon the extinction of the Carolingians, Conrad of Franconia becomes king of Germany.

919: The Saxon Duke Henry I is elected king. The Saxon dynasty rules Germany until 1024.

955: Otto I defeats the Hungarians at Lechfeld near Augsburg.

962: Otto I is crowned emperor in Rome and is recognized by Byzantium.

968: Creation of the archbishopric of Magdeburg as the center of the colonizing movements to the East

1024-1125: The Salian dynasty

1075: Beginning of the "investiture" dispute between the Emperor and the Pope (*i.e.*, who had the right to appoint bishops). It is settled by the Concordat of Worms in 1122.

1096: Beginning of the First Crusade

1138-1259: The Hohenstaufen dynasty

1180: Friedrich I (Barbarossa) outlaws the Saxon Duke, Henry the Lion.

1190: The Teutonic Order is founded in Akko. In the 13th and 14th centuries it dominates vast territories along the Baltic coast.

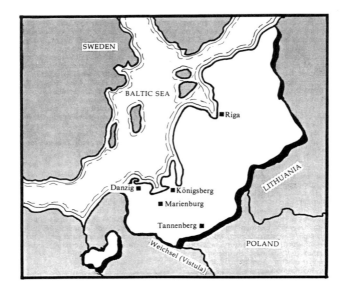

The German Order of Knights at its pinnacle. (*Source:* SPP.)

1235: Emperor Friedrich II proclaims the Peace of Mainz, the first imperial law in the German language.

1256-73: The Great Interregnum

1273: Rudolf of Habsburg becomes king of Germany. He increases his power by his victory over King Ottocar II of Bohemia.

1293: Lübeck becomes the leading city of the Hanseatic League.

1348: The first German university is founded in Prague, which Charles IV makes the permanent capital of the empire.

1348-52: The Plague ("Black Death")

1356: The Golden Bull lays down the rules for the election of the king, who is to be elected in Frankfurt and crowned in Aachen.

1370: Victory of the Hanseatic League over the Danes

1400: King Wenceslaus is removed from the throne by the electors because of incapacity.

1417: The Hohenzollern Friedrich I, burgave of Nuremberg, becomes elector of Brandenburg.

1452: Last coronation of a German emperor in Rome (Friedrich III)

1493: Peasant uprising on the upper Rhine

1495: Proclamation of the "Eternal Peace" at the Diet of Worms

1499: Switzerland breaks away from the empire

1517: Martin Luther proclaims his 95 Theses; beginning of the Reformation

1522-23: Uprising of the knights

1524-25: Peasants' war

1529: The Turks lay siege to Vienna.

1546-47: Emperor Charles V defeats the Protestant princes and towns allied against him.

1555: The Peace of Augsburg after which the princes determine the religion of their territories

1618: A protest by Bohemian Protestants in Prague marks the beginning of the Thirty-Years War, which ends in 1648 with the Peace of Westphalia, concluded at Münster and Osnabrück.

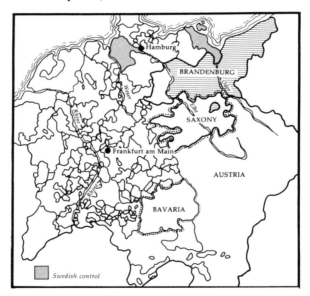

The extremely fragmented Holy Roman Empire after the Treaty of Westphalia: 1648. (*Source:* SPP.)

1663-1806: The "permanent imperial diet" meets at Regensburg. This is a congress of representatives of the princes and towns of the empire.

1683: Repulsion of the second Turkish attack on Vienna, and the first German emigrants leave Krefeld for America.

1697: Prince August the Strong of Saxony becomes the King of Poland.

1701: The elector Friedrich III of Brandenburg crowns himself King Friedrich I of Prussia in Königsberg.

1717: Introduction of general compulsory education in Prussia

1740-42: First Silesian War between Prussia and Austria

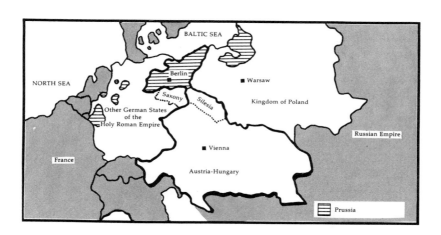

Middle Europe in 1740 when Maria Theresia (22) became Empress of Austria and Friedrich the Great (28), King of Prussia. (*Source:* SPP.)

1744-45: Second Silesian War

1756-63: The Seven-Year War in which Prussia faces Austria, France, Russia, Sweden, and most of the imperial electors

1792: Beginning of the war against revolutionary France

1806: Dissolution of the Holy Roman Empire of the German Nation

1807: Beginning of the Stein-Hardenberg reforms in Prussia

1813: Battle of the Nations at Leipzig

1814-15: Congress of Vienna

1815: Holy Alliance between Russia, Austria, and Prussia to suppress liberal movements

1834: Founding of the German Customs Union

1835: First German railway between Nuremberg and Fürth

1848-49: Revolution in Germany; Frankfurt National Assembly

1850: Introduction of the three-class electoral system in Prussia

1861: Founding of the German Progressive Party

1862: Otto von Bismarck becomes Prime Minister of Prussia

1863: Founding of the General German Workers' Association, the predecessor of the Social Democratic Party of Germany (SPD)

1864: Prussian-Austrian victory over Denmark

1866: War between Prussia and Austria; dissolution of the German Confederation

July 19, 1870, to February 26, 1871: Franco-Prussian War

September 2, 1870: Battle of Sedan

January 18, 1871: Founding of the unified German empire by proclamation in Hall of Mirrors, Versailles, with Bismarck as first chancellor

1872-80: Bismarck's "Kulturkampf" against the Catholic Church

October 21, 1878: Anti-Socialist Law enacted

1882: Tripartite alliance with Austria and Italy

1883-89: Enactment of progressive social security legislation

March 9 to June 15, 1888: Upon Wilhelm I's death, Kaiser Friedrich reigns 99 days and is succeeded at his death by Wilhelm II.

March 20, 1890: Dismissal of Bismarck

1890-1894: Imperial Chancellor Leo von Caprivi

1894-1901: Imperial Chancellor Chlodwig Prince zu Hohenlohe-Schillingsfürst

1900-1909: Imperial Chancellor Bernhard Prince von Bülow

October 28, 1908: Daily Telegraph Affair

1909-1917: Imperial Chancellor Theobald von Bethmann Hollweg

1912-1913: Balkan Wars

1914-1918

June 28, 1914: Assassination of Austrian Archduke Ferdinand in Sarajevo

July 1914: European diplomatic crisis which results in outbreak of the First World War

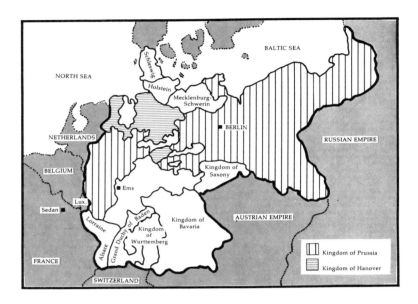

The unification of Germany, 1871, showing only the major states and areas. (*Source:* SPP.)

August 13, 1914: Germany declares war on Russia and France and enters the First World War.

August 23-31, 1914: Battle of Tannenberg

September 6-9, 1914: Battle on the Marne

May 7, 1915: Sinking of the Lusitania

February 21 to December 1916: Battle of Verdun

February 1, 1917: Germany declares unrestricted submarine warfare.

April 6, 1917: The U.S. enters the First World War against Germany.

July 19, 1917: Reichstag Peace Resolution

March 3, 1918: Peace of Brest-Litovsk

October 3, 1918: Prince Max of Baden becomes chancellor, and a German offer to cease fire is made.

October 26, 1918: A new constitution is proclaimed, and Erich Ludendorff is dismissed.

October 28, 1918: Sailors mutiny in Kiel.

November 7, 1918: Revolution in Munich

November 9, 1918: Kaiser abdicates and Scheidemann proclaims a republic

November 10, 1918: Kaiser flees to Holland; General Groener secretly discusses cooperation with Friedrich Ebert

November 11, 1918: Armistice signed in Compiègne

Adolf Hitler joins crowd on Munich's ODEONSPLATZ cheering the outbreak of war. (*Source:* GCML, Lexington, Virginia.)

December 16-20, 1918: Mass meeting of the workers and soldiers soviets

December 30, 1918: Foundation of Communist Party of Germany (KPD) and of Stahlhelm League

Combatants in First World War, 1915. (*Source:* SPP.)

1919-1932

January 5, 1919: Mass demonstration in Tiergarten in Berlin. Founding of German Workers' Party, which is later renamed the National Socialist Workers' Party of Germany (NSDAP or Nazi). Hitler is member number five.

January 5-12, 1919: Heavy fighting in Berlin

January 15, 1919: Murder of Karl Liebknecht and Rosa Luxemburg

January 19, 1919: Elections to a National Assembly to be held in Weimar, and a republican majority results. Assembly convenes February 6.

February 11, 1919: Friedrich Ebert (SPD) elected president

February 13, 1919: Philipp Scheidemann (SPD) becomes chancellor and the head of the "Weimar Coalition" (SPD, Center, DDP).

March-April 1919: Heavy fighting in Berlin, Ruhr, and central Germany

April 7-May 2, 1919: Soviet republic in Munich

June 21, 1919: Gustav Bauer (SPD) becomes chancellor.

June 28, 1919: Germany signs the Treaty of Versailles, which goes into effect on January 10, 1920.

August 11, 1919: The Weimar Constitution goes into effect.

March 13-17, 1920: Kapp Putsch in Berlin

March 27, 1920: Hermann Müller (SPD) becomes chancellor.

March-May 1920: Uprising in the Ruhr. The Red Army in Germany is destroyed by the Reichswehr.

June 6, 1920: First Reichstag elections; "Weimar Coalition" loses its majority for the rest of the Weimar Republic.

June 25, 1920: Konstantin Fehrenbach (Center) becomes chancellor.

March 1921: Communist uprisings in Saxony and Hamburg

May 10, 1921: Joseph Wirth (Center) becomes chancellor.

August 18, 1921: One American dollar is worth 550 marks.

Minister President Scheidemann and his wife go to the National Assembly in Berlin. (*Source:* PIB.)

August 26, 1921: Matthias Erzberger, who is held responsible for Versailles Treaty, is murdered by secret right-wing "Organization Consul."

April 16, 1922: Treaty of Rapallo

June 24, 1922: Assassination of Walter Rathenau

November 22, 1922: Wilhelm Cuno (independent) becomes chancellor.

December 31, 1922: One American dollar is worth 7,500 marks.

January 11, 1923: The French occupy the Ruhr, and until September 26, 1923, Germans practice "passive resistance." The French begin to withdraw July 14, 1925, and are completely out on June 30, 1930.

May 24, 1923: One American dollar is worth 54,300 marks.

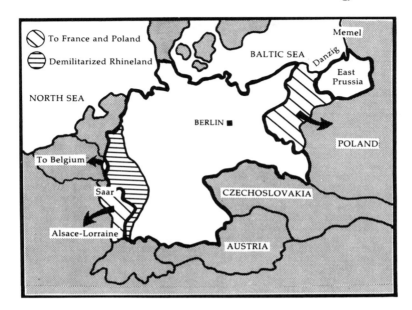

German territorial agreements with the Allies following First World War. (*Source:* SPP.)

June 11, 1923: Berlin streetcar ticket costs 600 marks.

August 13, 1923: Gustav Stresemann (DVP) becomes chancellor.

September 3, 1923: Berlin streetcar ticket costs 400,000 marks.

September 26, 1923: Policy of passive resistance in Ruhr is ended.

October-November 1923: Separatist movements in the Rhineland

November 8, 1923: Hitler putsch attempt in Munich

November 15, 1923: One American dollar having reached the value of 4,200 billion marks, a currency reform introducing the Rentenmark makes one dollar worth 4.2 Rentenmarks, and inflation is ended.

November 30, 1923: Wilhelm Marx (Center) becomes chancellor.

April 1, 1924: Hitler is sentenced to five years of fortress arrest.

August 29, 1924: Dawes Plan is accepted by Reichstag.

January 15, 1925: Hans Luther (independent) becomes chancellor.

February 24, 1925: Hitler is released from prison after having dictated *Mein Kampf.* Nazi party is refounded.

February 28, 1925: President Friedrich Ebert dies.

April 26, 1925: General von Hindenburg is elected Reich president.

October 16, 1925: Treaty of Locarno

April 24, 1926: German-Soviet Friendship Treaty

May 26, 1926: Wilhelm Marx again becomes chancellor.

September 8, 1926: Germany enters League of Nations.

December 10, 1926: Foreign Minister Stresemann receives Nobel Peace Prize.

August 1927: First Nazi rally in Nuremberg

June 28, 1928: Hermann Müller again becomes chancellor.

May 1, 1929: *Blutmai* (Blood May), the Communist uprising in Berlin

July 9, 1929: Hitler, Hugenberg, and Seldte unite to oppose the Young Plan.

October 3, 1929: Gustav Stresemann dies.

October 25, 1929: New York stock market crash sparks world economic depression.

March 30, 1930: Heinrich Brüning (Center) becomes chancellor.

June 30, 1930: Last French troops leave German soil.

September 14, 1930: Reichstag elections in which Nazis increase their seats from 12 to 107 and emerge as second strongest party.

January 1931: Unemployment reaches five million.

October 11, 1931: Creation of Harzburg Front, which unites right-wing parties and groups

October 1931: National Socialist student organization gains a majority in the Union of German Students.

January 1932: Unemployment reaches six million.

April 10, 1932: Hindenburg is reelected president.

April 13, 1932: Brüning bans SA and SS.

May 30, 1932: Hindenburg dismisses Brüning.

Hitler at Third Party Congress in Nuremberg, 1929. (*Source:* GCML, Lexington, Virginia.)

June 1, 1932: Franz von Papen (Center) becomes chancellor.

June 14, 1932: SA and SS are again legalized.

July 9, 1932: Conference of Lausanne results in end of reparations.

July 20, 1932: Prussian Government of Braun and Severing are dismissed.

July 31, 1932: In Reichstag elections Nazis decline, but still win 37.5 percent of votes and 230 seats.

September 12, 1932: Von Papen dissolves the Reichstag.

October 1932: Unemployment reaches 7.5 million.

November 3, 1932: Berlin transport strike in which Nazis and Communists collaborate.

November 6, 1932: In Reichstag elections the Nazis lose two million votes and 34 seats, but Communists gain 42, leaving a parliamentary majority in the hands of two parties opposed to the Weimar Republic and liberal democracy.

December 3, 1932: General von Schleicher becomes chancellor.

1933-1939

January 4, 1933: Hitler meets von Papen.

January 30, 1933: Hitler is named chancellor.

February 27, 1933: Reichstag Fire

March 23, 1933: Enabling Law

May 2, 1933: Trade unions are dissolved.

July 20, 1933: Concordat between Germany and Vatican

October 14, 1933: Germany leaves the League of Nations.

January 26, 1934: German-Polish non-aggression pact

June 30, 1934: Liquidation of SA and other opponents of Hitler's regime in "Röhm Putsch"

August 2, 1934: President von Hindenburg dies.

March 16, 1935: Universal male military service is reintroduced.

September 15, 1935: Anti-Jewish "Nuremberg Laws" and beginning of systematic persecution of Jews

1936: Olympic Games in Berlin. Exhibit of "degenerate art"

March 7, 1936: Wehrmacht occupies the Rhineland.

October 25, 1936: Berlin-Rome Axis

November 25, 1936: Anti-Comintern Pact with Japan

March 12, 1938: German troops march into Austria and annex it (*Anschluss*).

September 29, 1938: Munich Conference and annexation of Sudetenland, which is occupied by German troops on October 1

November 9, 1938: Crystal Night attack on Jews

March 15, 1939: German troops invade and conquer Czechoslovakia.

May 22, 1939: "Pact of Steel" military alliance between Germany and Italy

August 23, 1939: German-Soviet non-aggression pact

September 1, 1939: Germany's attack on Poland, which signals the beginning of the Second World War

September 3, 1939: Britain and France declare war on Germany.

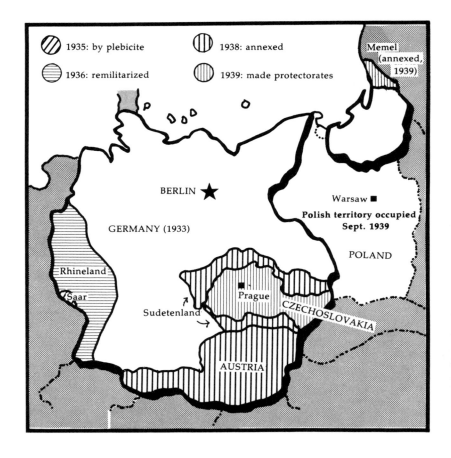

German Expansion, 1935-39. (*Source:* SPP.)

1940-1945

April 9, 1940: Germany occupies Denmark and Norway.

May 10, 1940: Germany attacks France, which agrees to a cease-fire on June 22, 1940.

German soldiers marching through the Arc de Triomphe, Paris. (Mauritius, Black Star. *Source:* GCML, Lexington, Virginia.)

August 13, 1940: Germany launches air attack in "Battle of Britain."

March 30, 1941: General Rommel's Afrikakorps attacks in North Africa. The Allies land on November 7, 1942 to oppose him, and the German and Italian forces in Africa capitulate on May 13, 1943.

April 6, 1941: Germany begins invasion of Yugoslavia and Greece.

June 22, 1941: Germany invades the Soviet Union.

December 11, 1941: Germany declares war on the United States.

January 20, 1942: Wannsee Conference initiates the "final solution" of Jews.

May 30-31, 1942: First major Allied bombing attack against Cologne

January 25, 1943: At the Casablanca Conference, President Roosevelt and Prime Minister Churchill demand Germany's "unconditional surrender."

February 2, 1943: End of Battle of Stalingrad, which began on November 19, 1942, and capture of General Paulus' entire Sixth Army, signalling the beginning of the end for the Third Reich

February 18, 1943: Goebbels declares "total war" in the Berlin Sportpalast.

June 6, 1944: Landing of Allies on the Normandy beaches

July 20, 1944: Failed assassination attempt against Hitler

September 22, 1944: President Roosevelt withdraws his previous written approval of Morgenthau Plan.

October 11, 1944: First Soviet military break-through in East Prussia

September 12, 1944: In the London Protocol among the U.S., UK, and USSR, the future occupation zones of Greater Berlin are delimited, and the foundations for the Four-Power status of Berlin are created. On November 14, France is included in the treaty.

December 16, 1944: Beginning of German Ardennes offensive, which fails after initial successes

February 4-11, 1945: Allied commanders at the conference of Yalta decide on measures to end the war and on dividing conquered Germany into occupation zones. The movement of Poland's western border and the addition of France as a fourth occupying power are agreed upon.

April 19, 1945: Due to the initiative of Kurt Schumacher, Social Democrats decide at a meeting in Hanover to refound the SPD.

April 25, 1945: American and Soviet troops meet at Torgau on the Elbe.

April 26, 1945: U.S. Joint Chiefs of Staff send a directive, JCS 1067, to the supreme commander of the American occupying forces, General Eisenhower, explaining the fundamental goals of the military government in Germany. The order still contains elements of the Morgenthau Plan.

April 30, 1945: Hitler's suicide in the Reich Chancellery bunker; the "Reich government" he put into place under Grand Admiral Dönitz begins effort to rescue as many soldiers and civilians as possible by bringing them westward.

May 2, 1945: Stalin announces complete conquest of Berlin.

May 4, 1945: Signing at General Montgomery's headquarters in Lüneburg of capitulation of German armed forces on the British front, Denmark, and the Netherlands

May 7, 1945: The unconditional surrender of German military forces is signed at Eisenhower's headquarters in Reims.

May 9, 1945: The German surrender is repeated at the Soviet headquarters in Berlin-Karlshorst.

June 5, 1945: The Berlin Declaration: German governmental power is transferred to the governments of the four Allied forces--U.S., USSR, Great Britain and France. Germany is divided into four zones of occupation. All four Allied forces occupy greater Berlin, and the Kommandatura is established. Agreement on control mechanism in Germany. Creation of the Allied Command Council with seat in Berlin. Decisions pertaining to Germany as a whole must be unanimous.

June 11, 1945: Legalization of the KPD in Berlin.

Col. Gen. Gustaf Jodl signs unconditional surrender at Reims, France. (Photo by U.S. Army Signal Corps. *Source:* GCML, Lexington, Virginia.)

Desolation in Germany, 1945. (National Archives. *Source:* SPP.)

June 17, 1945: Founding of the Rhineland CDU in Cologne.

July 17-August 2, 1945: The Potsdam Conference of the Big Three: Truman (U.S.), Churchill (Great Britain), who was replaced by Attlee after July 28, and Stalin (USSR). France joins the Potsdam Protocol on August 4, 1945.

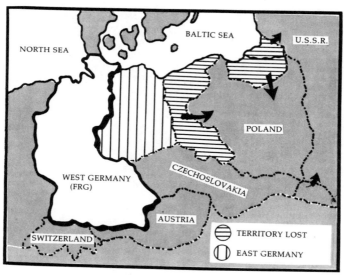

Germany after the Second World War. (*Source:* SPP.)

From August 27, 1945: Democratic parties are permitted at the district level in the three western zones. In the American sector the parties are permitted from August 27 on, in the British sector from September 15 on, and in the French sector from December 12 on.

September 19, 1945: Formation of Bavaria, Greater Hesse and Wurttemberg-Baden (later Baden-Wurttemberg) through proclamations of the U.S. military government

October 10, 1945: Creation of the CSU in Würzburg, Bavaria

November 20, 1945, to October 1, 1946: The top 24 war criminals are tried at Nuremberg. The leadership elite of the Nazi party, the Gestapo, SD, and SS are declared criminal organizations. Trials of lawyers, SS doctors, concentration camp commandants, diplomats, generals, industrialists, and leading officials follow.

Nazi defendants at Nuremberg Trial. (Photo by U.S. Army Signal Corps. *Source:* GCML, Lexington, Virginia.)

November 21, 1945: Americans create the Radio in the American Sector (RIAS) in Berlin.

November 30, 1945: The Four-Power agreement to establish three air corridors between Berlin and the other Western occupation zones is confirmed by the Allied Control Council.

1946-1949

January 20, 1946: First free German elections since 1933 are held in the American zone (Municipal elections).

April 21-22, 1946: The KPD and SPD join to form the Socialist Unity Party (SED) in the Soviet Zone of Occupation (SZOG).

May 9-11, 1946: The first SPD party congress in the three western zones elects Kurt Schumacher chairman.

Wilhelm Pieck, Otto Grotewohl, and Walter Ulbricht at congress to form SED. (*Source:* GIC, New York.)

May 25, 1946: U.S. military governor, General Lucius D. Clay, orders the temporary halt of reparations deliveries to the Soviet Union because the latter does not deliver food to the western zones, as had been agreed.

July 17, 1946: Soviet Foreign Minister Molotov describes the Neisse line as the permanent border between Germany and Poland.

July 29, 1946: The British government accepts the American proposal to unify their zones.

September 6, 1946: In Stuttgart, U.S. Secretary of State James F. Byrnes gives a speech about the necessity of an economically unified Germany, the revival of German economic strength, and the strengthening of German responsibility in politics and economics.

October 1, 1946: The verdict of the Nuremberg Trials is rendered: 12 death penalties, seven prison sentences, and three acquittals.

December 22, 1946: Annexation of the Saarland into the French customs and economic sphere.

January 1, 1947: Official establishment of Bizonia, which was a merger of the American and British zones into one united economic area.

February 25, 1947: Prussia is dissolved by law no. 46 of the Allied Control Council. On July 23, 1952, all Länder in the GDR are abolished, and a unitary state is created.

March 1, 1947: The Länder of the American zone are granted increased legislative, executive and judicial powers.

March 10 to April 24, 1947: In Moscow the fourth foreign ministers' conference fails in part because of disagreement on the Germany question. The Soviets stick with their demands for a unified German state, maintenance of the Oder-Neisse border, a share in the control of the Ruhr area, the return of the Saarland to Germany, reparation of ten billion dollars, and the dissolution of Bizonia. France desires the separation of the Ruhr and the Saarland from Germany. Britain and the U.S. demand a build-up of Germany through economic unity and correction of the Oder-Neisse line.

April 22-25, 1947: Founding congress in Bielefeld of the Federation of German Trade Unions (DGB) in the British zone

June 5, 1947: In a speech at Harvard University, U.S. Secretary of State George C. Marshall recommends that Europeans join in a mutual economic recovery program. This was the seed of the Marshall Plan.

June 6-8, 1947: Conference of Ministers President in Munich to discuss economic, food, and refugee problems. Disagreement over the agenda prompts the premature departure of the delegation from the Soviet zone, signalling the division of Germany.

July 17, 1947: U.S. government sends new guidelines to military governor Lucius Clay to replace those issued in 1945. The new objectives are the development of a German sense of responsibility in the Länder, a limitation of the dismantling of industries to those which produce weapons, an eventual increase in the standard of living, and an end to the German need for economic subsidies.

November 25 to December 15, 1947: At the fifth conference of foreign ministers in London, no agreement is reached concerning a peace treaty with Germany. Secretary of State Marshall rejects reparations from current German production.

March 1, 1948: The "Bank Deutscher Länder," later the Bundesbank, is founded in Frankfurt am Main.

March 20, 1948: Marshall Sokolovski boycotts the Allied Control Council in protest against the six-power conference in London and the anti-Soviet alliance of the Western European Union (WEU). Four-Power control of Germany comes to an end.

June 20, 1948: Currency reform in the western zones: Each person is paid DM 40, and the Reichsmark is replaced by the Deutsche Mark at a rate of 10:1.

June 23, 1948: The separate "Deutsche Mark der Deutschen Notenbank" is introduced to the Soviet zone.

June 24, 1948: The western Allies prevent a Soviet attempt to extend to West Berlin the currency reform the USSR had initiated in its zone of occupation. The Soviet Union begins a total blockade of land and waterways leading to the western sectors of Berlin and cuts off the supply of energy. The U.S., supported by the UK, begins the Berlin Airlift to support the city on June 26, 1948; it lasts until September 30, 1949.

July 3, 1948: The police stationed in military installations (Kasernierte Volkspolizei--KVP) is created as a forerunner of the National People's Army (Nationale Volksarmee--NVA).

August 10-23, 1948: Constitutional Convention at Herrenchiemsee in Bavaria

September 1, 1948: The Parliamentary Council begins its work in Bonn. Dr. Konrad Adenauer is elected council president.

December 8, 1948: After the division of Berlin is sealed by the undemocratic election of Friedrich Ebert, Jr., as mayor of the Soviet sector of Berlin on November 30, the new (west) Berlin city assembly unanimously elects Ernst Reuter mayor of (west) Berlin.

December 11, 1948: The Free Democratic Party (FDP) of the three western zones is founded in Heppenheim.

April 4, 1949: The North Atlantic Treaty Organization (NATO) is founded in Washington.

April 22, 1949: The Ruhr statute is put into effect. Coal and iron production in the Ruhr is to be internationally controlled by the western occupying powers and the Benelux nations.

May 8, 1949: The Parliamentary Council passes the Basic Law (Grundgesetz) 53 to 12. The military governors accept it on May 12.

May 10, 1949: Bonn is chosen as the temporary seat of government.

May 12, 1949: The Soviet Union lifts the Berlin Blockade.

May 23, 1949: The Basic Law is ceremoniously presented in the final session of the Parliamentary Council and takes effect immediately.

June 20, 1949: The Allied High Commission replaces the military government. High Commissioners are John McCloy (U.S.), André François-Poncet (France), and Sir Brian Robertson (U.K.).

July 7, 1949: The first German Bundestag and Bundesrat convene.

July 12, 1949: The Federal Assembly elects Theodor Heuss federal president.

July 15, 1949: Konrad Adenauer of the CDU is elected federal chancellor. His first cabinet, serving from July 20, 1949, to October 20, 1953, is a coalition government consisting of the CDU/CSU, the FDP, and the DP.

August 14, 1949: Elections to the first German Bundestag. Voter turnout is 78.5 percent; the CDU/CSU receives 31 percent and the SPD 29.2 percent.

First cabinet of Konrad Adenauer (middle). To Adenauer's right is Economics minister Ludwig Erhard. (*Source:* GIC, New York.)

September 21, 1949: The three High Commissioners recognize the Federal Republic of Germany (FRG) by receiving the chancellor and his cabinet at Petersberg.

October 7, 1949: The German Democratic Republic (GDR) is founded. On the same day, the FRG government releases a statement denouncing the government in the Soviet zone as unlawful because it was not chosen in a free election. For the same reasons, the Allied High Commission on October 10 declares the Soviet zone government incapable of representing the central part of Germany.

October 31, 1949: The FRG becomes a member of the Organization for European Economic Cooperation (OEEC), whose assignment is to implement the Marshall Plan.

November 22, 1949: Petersberg Agreement

December 15, 1949: The U.S. and FRG agree on economic cooperation. The FRG is required to use Marshall Plan aid in economic and agricultural reconstruction.

The 1950s

March 16, 1950: British opposition leader Churchill rises in the House of Commons as the first leading politician to support German rearmament.

March 25, 1950: The USSR grants the GDR sovereignty.

May 1, 1950: The rationing of food is discontinued in the FRG.

May 15, 1950: Communique of the three western Allied foreign ministers at the London Conference: Germany should step-by-step rejoin the community of free European people. When this has been accomplished, Germany should be freed of the control to which it has been subjected, and the Allied forces should recognize German sovereignty as was agreed upon in the Occupation Statute. A committee to study the Occupation Statute is to be established. The peaceful reunification of Germany remains the ultimate goal of

Allied policy, and they agree upon steps that should precede the reunification.

July 6, 1950: The GDR and Poland sign an agreement in Görlitz recognizing the Oder-Neisse line as their common border.

July 20-24, 1950: At the third party congress of the SED, a Central Committee is created. On July 25, 1950, Walter Ulbricht is elected general secretary of the Central Committee.

August 18, 1950: The FRG chancellor demands German defensive troops as a counterpart to the GDR People's Police.

September 12-18, 1950: A conference of western Allied foreign ministers in New York announces a new Germany policy, which espouses the FRG's claim to sole representation of Germany (Alleinvertretungsanspruch) and a West German armed contribution to the defense of Europe.

September 26, 1950: The Atlantic Pact in New York decides on the creation of a joint army. Germany should be in the position to assist in the defense of Western Europe.

October 26, 1950: The federal government makes Theodor Blank, CDU, responsible for questions regarding allied occupation forces. This office, "Dienststelle Blank," is the forerunner of the FRG defense ministry.

January 1951: The Allied High Commission declares the end of the program to dismantle industries.

March 16, 1951: Creation of the federal border troops.

April 18, 1951: Treaty founding the European Coal and Steel Community (ECSC). Consisting of France, Italy, the FRG, and the Benelux nations, it is to replace the Ruhr Statute and the Ruhr Authority as a first step toward European integration.

May 2, 1951: The FRG becomes a full member of the European Council. The Saarland remains an associated member.

July 9, 1951: Great Britain ends its state of war with Germany, and the British Commonwealth states follow suit. France follows on July 13, the U.S. on October 19, 1951.

December 9, 1951: In a referendum in Wurttemberg-Baden, Wurttemberg-Hohenzollern, and Baden a majority of 69.7 percent votes to create the Land Baden-Wurttemberg.

March 10, 1952: Stalin proposes to the western powers the reunification and armed neutrality of Germany (Stalin note).

March 25, 1952: The western powers answer the Stalin note: free all-German elections are the precondition for peace talks.

March 26, 1952: Germany Treaty (Bonn Conventions)

April 9, 1952: Stalin sends a second note to the western powers in which he agrees to a free all-German election under Four-Power, not UN, control. The positions of both sides remain the same in further notes (May 24, July 10, and August 23 to September 23). The western powers doubt the seriousness of Stalin's offer and, in agreement with the Bonn government, reject neutrality.

May 26, 1952: The GDR sets up prohibited zones along its border with the FRG.

August 2, 1952: The FRG joins the International Monetary Fund (IMF).

August 20, 1952: Kurt Schumacher, the first SPD chairman, dies. Erich Ollenhauer is elected his successor on September 27.

September 10, 1952: A restitution agreement between the FRG and Israel is signed, as well as with the Jewish Claims Conference.

October 7, 1952: Introduction of military rank and new uniforms for the People's Police in military installations (KVP). The GDR's border police had been under the control of the Ministry for State Security since May 16, 1952.

March 5, 1953: Stalin dies. Georgi M. Malenkov succeeds him.

June 16, 1953: In East Berlin, construction workers strike against the raising of work quotas. On June 17, an uprising takes place in East Berlin and the GDR. Worker protests develop into demonstrations against the SED government. The bloody rebellion is crushed by Soviet troops and the state of emergency is annulled on July 11. On August 4, the FRG declares June 17 the Day of German Unity, which serves as the national holiday until German unification on October 3, 1990, which replaced June 17.

Uprising in East Berlin, 1953. (*Source:* GIC, New York.)

June 25, 1953: The Bundestag passes a new law requiring parties to obtain at least 5 percent of the votes in an election or to win an electoral constituency directly, in order to receive seats in the Bundestag. On July 8, 1953, the electoral system of the "second ballot" is introduced.

September 6, 1953: Elections for the second Bundestag. The CDU/CSU wins 45.2 percent of the votes, the SPD 28.8 percent, and the FDP 9.5 percent. On October 20, Adenauer presents his coalition consisting of the CDU/CSU, FDP, DP and GB/BHE.

March 25, 1954: The Soviet Union recognizes GDR sovereignty.

July 23, 1954: Otto John, previously president of the Federal Office for the Protection of the Constitution (BfV), announces his defection to the GDR in a radio speech from East Berlin.

October 23, 1954: Paris Treaties, by which FRG is admitted to NATO and the WEU

April 20, 1955: The U.S. and the FRG agree on the termination of occupation government, as well as on a treaty regarding the presence of foreign troops in the FRG.

May 5, 1955: The Paris Treaties take effect. The FRG receives sovereignty, joining the WEU on May 7 and NATO on May 9. The occupation statute is thereby terminated with the exception of a few special Allied rights concerning deployment of troops, the status of Berlin, German reunification, and a peace treaty.

May 14, 1955: The GDR, Albania, Bulgaria, Poland, Romania, Czechoslovakia, Hungary, and the USSR form the Warsaw Pact. The GDR officially joins on January 27, 1956.

July 24-27, 1955: Soviet leader Nikita Khrushchev proclaims the two-state doctrine during a visit to the GDR, whereby German reunification is to be a German matter, and the political accomplishments of the GDR must remain untouched.

September 8-14, 1955: Chancellor Adenauer leads a delegation to Moscow. The FRG and the Soviet Union agree to return German prisoners of war, and this agreement is unanimously passed by the Bundestag on September 23, 1955. The first prisoners of war arrive in Germany on October 7. On December 20, Germany officially reopens diplomatic relations with the Soviet Union after 14 years.

September 20, 1955: Soviet recognition of the GDR sovereignty is enshrined in a treaty.

September 22, 1955: The federal government announces the Hallstein Doctrine, declaring that the FRG regards as an unfriendly act any country's (except the Soviet Union's) establishment of diplomatic relations with the GDR, and such a country must expect retaliation from the FRG. The Hallstein Doctrine is legalized on December 9, 1955.

January 2, 1956: First Bundeswehr units commence service.

January 18, 1956: The GDR passes laws establishing the National People's Army (NVA) and the Ministry for National Defense. The People's Police stationed in barracks is dissolved and merged into the NVA, which becomes a partner in the Warsaw Pact on January 29.

July 21, 1956: Introduction of conscription in the FRG for all men between the ages of 18 and 45; the right to conscientious objection is maintained. The law does not apply to West Berlin.

August 17, 1956: The Constitutional Court in the FRG declares the Communist Party of Germany (KPD) unconstitutional at the conclusion of a five-year trial. The party is dissolved and its funds confiscated; it is reconstituted later as the German Communist Party (DKP).

October 27, 1956: A treaty with France settles the Saarland problem. It is to be politically annexed to the FRG on January 1, 1957, with economic annexation following by the end of 1959. The Franco-

German Saar treaties are unanimously accepted by the Bundestag on December 14, 1956.

February 6, 1957: The Bundestag confirms Berlin as the capital of Germany.

April 1, 1957: The first West German draftees are called up. Discussions begin regarding the arming of the Bundeswehr with delivery systems for nuclear weapons.

September 15, 1957: In the elections to the third Bundestag, the CDU/CSU receives 50.2 percent of the votes; this is the only time in the FRG's history that a single party receives an absolute majority. On October 29, 1957, the third Adenauer government takes office, with the small DP in the coalition.

October 3, 1957: After the death of Otto Suhr (SPD), Willy Brandt (SPD) is elected mayor of West Berlin.

October 19, 1957: The FRG breaks diplomatic relations with Yugoslavia, which had recognized the GDR. The Hallstein Doctrine is applied for the first time.

January 1, 1958: The EEC and EURATOM treaties come into force with the FRG as a founding member.

September 14, 1958: President Charles de Gaulle and Chancellor Adenauer meet for the first time.

November 10, 1958: Outbreak of the Berlin Crisis; Khrushchev demands the revision of the Potsdam Agreement.

November 27, 1958: Khrushchev delivers an ultimatum: the Soviet government declares the rights of the western powers in Berlin to have been forfeited. It demands that West Berlin be given the status of a free city within six months or Soviet rights in Berlin will be turned over to the GDR.

March 18, 1959: The SPD reveals its Germany Plan, proposing the creation of a demilitarized, nuclear-free, tension-free Germany in Central Europe.

March 19, 1959: The Soviet Union again recognizes the Western Allies' rights in Berlin.

July 1, 1959: The Federal Assembly in Berlin elects Heinrich Lübke as the second president of the FRG.

August 26, 1959: Dwight D. Eisenhower is the first American president to visit the FRG.

September 15-27, 1959: Khrushchev retracts the Berlin ultimatum of 1958 at talks with Eisenhower at Camp David and advocates the peaceful coexistence of East and West.

November 13-15, 1959: In an extraordinary party congress at Bad Godesberg, the SPD adopts a new party program, the Godesberg Program, which renounces Marxist objectives.

The 1960s

April 14, 1960: The collectivization of GDR agriculture is completed as all farmers join the production collectives.

June 30, 1960: Herbert Wehner explains the new SPD foreign policy in an important speech before the Bundestag which establishes the basis for a bi-partisan foreign policy in the FRG and for the SPD's ability to rule.

September 7, 1960: GDR president Wilhelm Pieck dies. On September 12 the office of GDR president is eliminated. The People's Chamber (Volkskammer) establishes a State Council and elects Walter Ulbricht chairman.

March 18, 1961: Franz-Josef Strauss is elected chairman of the Christian Social Union (CSU).

April 23, 1961: Herbert Wehner declares the SPD's willingness to form a coalition with the CDU, but at the CDU party congress on April 25 Chancellor Adenauer declines all cooperation with the SPD.

June 15, 1961: At an international press conference in East Berlin, GDR State Council chairman Ulbricht demands the neutralization of West Berlin. He denies reports regarding GDR intentions to build a wall around East Berlin.

August 3-5, 1961: Warsaw Pact leaders give the GDR permission to block all escape routes to West Berlin.

August 13, 1961: The GDR closes its borders with the FRG and begins the construction of the Berlin Wall. The outflow of refugees from the GDR is stopped. On October 27, American and Soviet tanks confront each other at Checkpoint Charlie in Berlin.

Construction of Berlin Wall, 1961. (*Source:* GIC, New York.)

September 17, 1961: Elections are held for the fourth Bundestag. The CDU/CSU wins 45.4 percent, the SPD 36.2 percent, and the FDP 12.8 percent. At 85, Konrad Adenauer is reelected on November 7 chancellor for the fourth time, and on November 14, a CDU/CSU-FDP coalition takes office. The FDP demands as a condition the resignation of Adenauer, since it fought the election battle with the slogan "For the CDU--without Adenauer."

January 24, 1962: The GDR introduces conscription.

August 17, 1962: Eighteen-year-old East Berlin construction worker Peter Fechter is shot while trying to escape over the Wall. This provokes consternation and uneasiness in West Berlin and the FRG.

October 26, 1962: The "Spiegel Affair." After a report critical of a NATO maneuver was published in the Hamburg news magazine *Der Spiegel,* the federal prosecutors arrest several members of the staff, including editors Rudolf Augstein and Conrad Ahlers.

November 26, 1962: Federal Minister Paul Lücke and Herbert Wehner meet to discuss a possible coalition between the CDU and SPD, but it is clear on December 5 that a grand coalition under Adenauer cannot materialize. On December 14, his fifth cabinet, a coalition between the CDU/CSU and the FDP, is sworn in.

January 22, 1963: Chancellor Adenauer and President de Gaulle sign the Elysée Treaty in Paris, regulating future Franco-German cooperation.

June 23-26, 1963: President John F. Kennedy visits the FRG and West Berlin. A sentence from the speech he delivers to the crowds at the Schöneberg city hall becomes world famous: "All free people, wherever they may live, are citizens of Berlin, and therefore as a free man I am proud to say, I am a Berliner!"

July 15, 1963: In a speech at Tutzing, Egon Bahr announces a new concept of German policy toward the East: "change through rapprochement."

October 11, 1963: Konrad Adenauer resigns as chancellor.

October 16, 1963: Ludwig Erhard (CDU) is elected chancellor.

December 18, 1963: The West Berlin Senate concludes an agreement with the GDR to permit West Berliners to visit East Berlin around Christmas and New Year's. By 1966, three more such pass agreements had been arranged, and in 1972 a Traffic Treaty was signed.

February 15-16, 1964: After the death of Erich Ollenhauer, Willy Brandt, mayor of West Berlin, is elected chairman of the SPD at an extraordinary party congress.

June 12, 1964: The Soviet Union and the GDR sign a treaty of friendship and support on the basis of a "three-nation theory," which considers West Berlin an independent political entity. The borders of the GDR are guaranteed to be inviolable.

June 26, 1964: The Western powers reject the three-nation theory.

September 9, 1964: The GDR government permits its citizens of retirement age to travel to the West.

November 28, 1964: The National Democratic Party of Germany (NDP) is founded. It becomes a reservoir of right-wing discontent.

March 25, 1965: The statute of limitations for National Socialist crimes is extended.

April 7, 1965: Soviet and GDR authorities block land and water routes to West Berlin.

May 5, 1965: The East German State Council, the Cabinet Council, and the National Council of the National Front proclaim that a reunified Germany must be socialist.

May 13, 1965: Israel and the FRG begin diplomatic relations. In response, several Arab nations break relations with the FRG.

August 19, 1965: At the conclusion of the Auschwitz trials in Frankfurt, mild sentences are announced, provoking strong protests in Germany and abroad.

September 19, 1965: Elections to the fifth Bundestag result in the CDU/CSU receiving 47.6 percent of the votes, the SPD 39.3 percent, and the FDP 9.5 percent. On October 20, Ludwig Erhard (CDU) is reelected chancellor, and on the 26th his second cabinet, a coalition of the CDU/CSU and the FDP, is sworn in.

February 11, 1966: The Central Committee of the SED sends an open letter to the SPD proposing an exchange of speakers. The executive committee of the SPD responds on March 19 with its conditions. The negotiations are not successful; a federal law allowing free passage for SED dignitaries would have to be passed, and SED representative Albert Norden cancels his trip to Hamburg in protest.

March 21-23, 1966: Ludwig Erhard replaces former chancellor Adenauer as CDU chairman at the fourteenth CDU party congress.

October 1, 1966: Albert Speer, leading architect of the Third Reich and from 1942 to 1945 minister of mobilization and war production, and Baldur von Schirach, Third Reich youth leader and governor of Vienna from 1940, are released from the Berlin war crime prison Spandau after serving their sentences.

October 27, 1966: FDP minister resigns from Erhard's cabinet. A majority of the FDP decides to end the governing coalition prematurely. New negotiations with the CDU/CSU break down.

November 6, 1966: In Hesse Landtag elections the NPD wins 7.9 percent of the votes and eight seats in the Hesse legislature. On November 20, it wins 7.4 percent of the votes in Landtag elections in Bavaria.

November 30, 1966: Chancellor Erhard announces his resignation.

December 1, 1966: Baden-Wurttemberg's Minister President Kurt Georg Kiesinger (CDU) becomes chancellor, and he begins building a grand coalition between the CDU/CSU and the SPD. Willy Brandt (SPD) is named vice-chancellor and foreign minister.

Architects of the Grand Coalition, Herbert Wehner (left) and Kurt Georg Kiesinger. (*Source:* PIB.)

December 14, 1966: As the new minister of all-German affairs, Herbert Wehner explains that diplomatic recognition of the GDR will only be possible when that country is democratically legitimate.

January 31, 1967: The FRG resumes diplomatic relations with Romania, thereby giving up the Hallstein Doctrine. Open controversy begins between the SED and the Romanian Communist Party.

February 20, 1967: The GDR People's Chamber passes a law introducing separate GDR citizenship.

May 10, 1967: GDR Minister President Willi Stoph sends a letter to Chancellor Kiesinger. In a return letter, the chancellor declares himself prepared to discuss the normalization of relations between both German governments.

January 29/30, 1968: At the FDP party congress in Freiburg im Breisgau, Walter Scheel is named party chairman to succeed Erich Mende.

March 26, 1968: The GDR People's Chamber approves a new constitution. A referendum is held on April 6; according to the SED figures, 94 percent approve of the constitution, which takes effect on April 8.

April 2, 1968: Two department stores in Frankfurt are burned to the ground. Andreas Baader, Thorwad Proll, Horst Söhnlein, and Gudrun Ensslin are arrested on suspicion of arson. The destructive act signals the division between APO and terrorists.

April 11, 1968: Rudi Dutschke, chairman of the Socialist Student Association (SDS), is seriously wounded in an assassination attempt. The incident provokes bloody riots all over the FRG. The subsequent Easter student uprisings are the high point of the "Expropriate Springer" campaign.

May 27, 1968: The three Western powers declare that Allied restrictions will be lifted if a German emergency law goes into effect. On May 30, the Bundestag passes the new emergency law, which is to be invoked in time of war, catastrophe, or whenever the constitution itself is threatened. The law, the 17th amendment to the Basic Law, goes into effect on June 28.

September 22, 1968: The German Communist Party (DKP) is founded to replace the forbidden KPD.

October 12-27, 1968: For the first time two separate German teams participate in the Olympic Games at Mexico City.

October 28, 1968: Brandt announces the FRG's willingness to accept the existence of the GDR as a second German state and to respond to the GDR on the basis of equality of rights.

February 26-27, 1969: President Richard Nixon visits the FRG and West Berlin and stimulates discussions on a lessening of tensions in Berlin.

March 5, 1969: In West Berlin, the Federal Assembly elects Minister of Justice Gustav Heinemann (SPD) federal president with 512 of 1023 votes. The CDU/CSU candidate, Gerhard Schröder, receives 506 votes.

May 30, 1969: In a modified Hallstein Doctrine, the federal government announces that any additional act recognizing the GDR will be considered an unfriendly act.

August 4, 1969: The statute of limitation for murder is extended to 30 years so that further National Socialist crimes can be pursued.

September 28, 1969: In elections to the sixth Bundestag, the CDU/CSU receives 46.1 percent of the votes, the SPD 42.7 percent, and the FDP 5.8 percent. From September 29 to October 15, the FDP conducts coalition negotiations with both the SPD and the CDU/CSU. SPD chairman Willy Brandt announces his party's intentions to take over the leadership of the federal government and to construct a coalition with the FDP. The FDP agrees on October 3. On October 21, the Bundestag elects Brandt chancellor with 251 votes, and on October 22, the Brandt/Scheel coalition of SPD and FDP is sworn in.

October 28, 1969: Chancellor Willy Brandt announces in the Bundestag the most comprehensive reform program in postwar German history. He declares himself prepared to engage in negotiations on the basis of equal status with the GDR under the concept "two states, one nation" in Germany.

The 1970s

March 19, 1970: Chancellor Brandt and the chairman of the GDR Council of Ministers, Willi Stoph, meet in Erfurt, GDR, to discuss relations between the two Germanys. East German crowds cheer enthusiastically for Brandt, thereby embarrassing GDR leaders. On May 21, they meet in Kassel for further talks.

GDR Minister President Willi Stoph (left) receives Chancellor Willy Brandt in Erfurt. (*Source:* PIB.)

April 5-11, 1970: Brandt visits the U.S. President Nixon assures American support of Brandt's eastern policy (*Ostpolitik*).

July 31, 1970: The Basic Law is changed to lower the voting age to 18.

August 11-13, 1970: Brandt visits the Soviet Union. On August 12, the Moscow Treaty is signed between the two countries, calling for the renunciation of violence and the recognition of existing European borders.

November 14, 1970: The SPD refuses all contact with the DKP.

December 7, 1970: Chancellor Brandt and Premier Cyrankiewicz sign the Warsaw Treaty. The treaty builds a foundation for the normalization of German-Polish relations by recognizing the Oder-Neisse line as the border between Poland and Germany.

December 17, 1970: Ulbricht denies the future possibility of a unified German nation because a German socialist nation has already been established in the GDR.

January 23, 1971: The first ethnic German immigrants from Poland arrive in the FRG.

January 31, 1971: Telephone contact between East and West Berlin is reestablished after 19 years.

May 3, 1971: Ulbricht is pressured to resign as First Secretary of the SED Central Committee. Erich Honecker succeeds him.

September 3, 1971: The Four-Power (Quadripartite) Agreement concerning Berlin is signed by the U.S., U.K., France, and the USSR.

October 4-5, 1971: Rainer Barzel becomes the new CDU chairman. His deputy is Helmut Kohl. On November 29 Barzel is elected CDU/CSU chancellor candidate.

October 20, 1971: Chancellor Brandt wins the 1971 Nobel Peace Prize for his eastern policy.

October 25-27, 1971: The FDP adopts the Freiburg Theses at its party congress. Karl-Hermann Flach becomes general secretary.

December 17, 1971: FRG State Secretary Egon Bahr and GDR State Secretary Michael Kohl sign an agreement on transit traffic between the FRG and West Berlin.

January 6, 1972: In a speech before NVA soldiers, Honecker describes the FRG as an imperialist foreign country.

February 23-25, 1972: The Bundestag begins debates on the eastern treaties. CDU leader Rainer Barzel's call for a constructive vote of no-confidence on February 27 is not heeded.

March 29, 1972: The GDR government allows the Berlin Agreement to take effect earlier than planned, permitting West Berliners to travel to East Berlin.

April 23, 1972: With the retirement of Wilhelm Helms of the FDP, the social-liberal coalition loses its majority in the Bundestag.

April 26, 1972: Egon Bahr and Michael Kohl successfully conclude negotiations for a traffic treaty between the FRG and GDR.

April 27, 1972: The CDU/CSU attempt to defeat Chancellor Brandt by means of the FRG's first constructive vote of no-confidence fails. Rainer Barzel would have been elected chancellor.

May 11, 1972: Attack on the fifth American Army headquarters in Frankfurt. Colonel Paul A. Bloomquist is killed, and 13 others are injured. The "Kommando Petra Schelm" claims responsibility.

May 17, 1972: The CDU/CSU decides to abstain in the vote for the eastern treaties. The Bundestag ratifies the treaties anyway; the Moscow Treaty is passed with 248 votes for, 10 against, and 238 abstentions, while the Warsaw Treaty is ratified with 248 for, 17 against, and 231 abstentions. A declaration of unanimous support for the eastern treaties is passed with 491 votes for and five abstentions.

May 24, 1972: The U.S. Army European headquarters in Heidelberg are attacked, and three soldiers are killed. A commando of the Red Army Faction (RAF) claims responsibility.

June 3, 1972: The Moscow Treaty, the Warsaw Treaty, and the Berlin Quadripartite Agreement, which had been ratified by the Bundestag on May 17, 1972, go into effect. The West Berlin Senate and the GDR government agree to a traffic treaty which permits West Berliners to visit the GDR and East Berlin.

August 16, 1972: Official negotiations dealing with the foundations of FRG-GDR relations begin.

August 26 to September 11, 1972: The twentieth Olympic Games take place in Munich and Kiel. On September 5-6, members of the Palestinian organization Black September mastermind an assassination strike against the Israeli team in Munich's Olympic Village. Eleven Israeli athletes, one policeman, and five terrorists are killed.

September 1, 1972: GDR authorities declare closed areas and protective strips along the border with the FRG. The ministry of defense permits GDR border troops to shoot when necessary.

November 19, 1972: Early elections to the Bundestag take place, the first after the voting age had been lowered to 18. For the first time, the SPD emerges as the largest party, winning 45.8 percent of the votes, the CDU/CSU 44.9 percent, and the FDP 8.4 percent. On December 14, the Bundestag reelects Brandt as chancellor, and on December 15 the second SPD/FDP cabinet, led by Brandt and Scheel, is formed.

December 10, 1972: Heinrich Böll wins the Nobel Prize for Literature in Stockholm.

December 21, 1972: State Secretaries Egon Bahr and Michael Kohl sign the Basic Treaty. It calls for recognition of Four-Power responsibility in Berlin, inviolability of borders, limitation of any one German government's jurisdictional claims to the territory of that sovereign state and not to all of Germany, exchange of permanent liaison representatives to each other's capitals, maintenance of intra-German trade, and UN membership for both countries.

March 8, 1973: The GDR refuses to grant any form of reparation payment to Israel for German crimes committed during the Third Reich.

May 11, 1973: After controversial debates, the Basic Treaty with the GDR is ratified by the Bundestag. It takes effect on June 21.

May 30/31, 1973: Wolfgang Mischnick (FDP) and Herbert Wehner (SPD) meet with Erich Honecker in East Berlin.

June 7-11, 1973: Brandt is the first chancellor to visit Israel.

June 12, 1973: The minister president of Rhineland-Palatinate, Helmut Kohl, becomes the new CDU chairman after the retirement of Rainer Barzel. Kurt Biedenkopf becomes the new general secretary.

July 1, 1973: A new law places civilian service on an equal basis with military service.

July 31, 1973: A Constitutional Court in Karlsruhe rules that the Basic Treaty with the GDR is compatible with the Basic Law.

September 3, 1973: For the first time, journalists from the FRG are accredited in the GDR.

September 18, 1973: The FRG and the GDR are admitted to the UN.

September 24 to October 1, 1973: From Moscow, Herbert Wehner criticizes the *Ostpolitik* of the government and the chancellor.

October 1, 1973: The universities of the federal armed forces open in Hamburg and Munich.

October 3, 1973: The People's Chamber elects Willi Stoph chairman of the State Council and Horst Sindermann chairman of the Ministerial Council.

December 11, 1973: The FRG opens diplomatic relations with Czechoslovakia. This Prague Treaty annuls the Munich Agreement of September 29, 1938.

January 1, 1974: The GDR begins using "DDR" car stickers instead of the FRG's "D."

April 25, 1974: Günter Guillaume, Chancellor Brandt's personal aide, is arrested under suspicion of espionage for the GDR. On December 15, 1975, he and his wife Christel are sentenced to thirteen years in prison. In 1981, Guillaume is handed over to the GDR in a spy exchange.

April 25, 1974: A German-American Agreement is signed providing for compensation of American costs for stationing troops in the FRG.

May 2, 1974: The GDR's and FRG's permanent representations commence their work in Bonn and East Berlin. Chiefs of these missions are assigned on December 18, 1975.

May 6, 1974: Chancellor Brandt resigns in connection with the Guillaume affair. On May 9, at Brandt's suggestion, the SPD nominates Helmut Schmidt as its chancellor candidate for the May 16 election in the Bundestag. Schmidt is elected chancellor, and the social-liberal coalition continues.

May 15, 1974: Walter Scheel is elected by the Federal Assembly to succeed Gustav Heinemann as federal president. Scheel wins 530 votes with 5 abstentions, while the CDU/CSU candidate, Richard von Weizsäcker, receives 498 votes. Scheel takes office July 1.

September 4, 1974: The U.S. opens diplomatic relations with the GDR.

September 27, 1974: The People's Chamber amends the GDR constitution, eliminating the term "German nation" effective October 7.

October 1, 1974: At the FDP party congress in Hamburg, Hans-Dietrich Genscher is chosen to succeed Scheel as FDP chairman.

January 20, 1975: After the retirement of Otto Winzer, Oskar Fischer is chosen as GDR foreign minister.

February 27, 1975: Peter Lorenz, chairman of the Berlin CDU, is kidnapped by the terrorist group "June 2 Movement."

April 24, 1975: The FRG's embassy in Stockholm is attacked by members of the "Holger Meins Kommando," and two diplomats are killed. The FRG government rejects the group's demands. On July 20, 1977, the superior Land court in Düsseldorf sentences four terrorists guilty of this attack to life in prison.

Helmut Schmidt is sworn in as chancellor by Bundestag President Annemarie Renger. (*Source:* GIC, New York.)

June 19, 1975: The CDU/CSU chooses Helmut Kohl, Rhineland-Palatinate minister president and CDU chairman, to be chancellor candidate.

August 1, 1975: After two years of negotiations in Geneva and Helsinki, the CSCE final act is signed. On July 28, the SED Politburo and the Council of Ministers empower Erich Honecker to sign the act. Talks between Helmut Schmidt and Honecker take place on the fringes of the CSCE ceremony.

October 7, 1975: The GDR's twenty-sixth anniversary is celebrated as a national holiday. The USSR and the GDR sign a treaty of friendship, cooperation, and mutual assistance to last 25 years.

October 28 to November 2, 1975: Helmut Schmidt is the first German chancellor to visit the People's Republic of China. He meets with Mao Tse-tung.

November 10-15, 1975: Walter Scheel is the first federal president to visit the Soviet Union.

February 19, 1976: Second reading and final vote in the Bundestag on the agreements with Poland. The treaties are passed by 276 votes to 191. Fifteen opposition representatives vote for the treaties.

March 30, 1976: State secretaries Dietrich Elias of the FRG postal ministry and Manfred Calov of the corresponding DDR ministry sign government agreements dealing with mail and telecommunications as well as an administrative agreement opening the way for the installation of direct telephone dialing.

May 9, 1976: Ulrike Meinhof is found dead in her Stuttgart-Stammheim cell.

May 18-22, 1976: The ninth SED party congress in East Berlin accepts a new program and party statute. Erich Honecker is elected general secretary.

July 24, 1976: Tension between the FRG and the GDR increases because of serious border incidents in which, among other things, GDR border patrols fire their weapons.

October 3, 1976: In Bundestag elections the CDU/CSU wins 48.6 percent of the votes, the SPD 42.2 percent, and the FDP 7.9 percent. On December 15, 1976, the Bundestag reelects Helmut Schmidt chancellor with a SPD/FDP coalition holding a slim majority.

November 16, 1976: During a tour in the West, GDR authorities deprive singer Wolf Biermann of his citizenship and prevent him from returning to the GDR. On November 3, author Rainer Kunze had been expelled from the GDR Writers' Union and, like other opposition authors, moves to the FRG on July 14, 1977.

November 26, 1976: Willy Brandt becomes chairman of the Socialist International. Robert Havemann, world-famous scientist and critic of the GDR government, is placed under house arrest.

January 11, 1977: The People's Police begins to prevent GDR citizens from visiting the FRG's permanent representation in East Berlin because GDR dissidents are seeking refuge there.

February 27, 1977: In an interview with *Saarbrücker Zeitung*, Erich Honecker acknowledges that approximately ten thousand GDR citizens had filed applications for emigration. He says that general travel freedom could be permitted only after the FRG recognizes GDR citizenship.

March 7, 1977: The CDU party congress in Düsseldorf confirms Helmut Kohl as party chairman. Heiner Geissler becomes general secretary, succeeding Kurt Biedenkopf.

April 7, 1977: Federal Attorney-General Siegfried Buback and his driver are murdered in broad daylight by RAF terrorists.

July 30, 1977: Jürgen Ponto, chairman of the Dresdner Bank, is shot in his Taunus villa by terrorists attempting to kidnap him. Involved in this bloody act is Susanne Albrecht, daughter of close friends of Ponto. She is later given refuge in the GDR.

August 23, 1977: GDR regime critic Rudolf Bahro is arrested and sentenced to eight years in prison because of his book *The Alternative in Eastern Europe* which could only be published in the FRG. Revocation of citizenship and immigration to the FRG follows in 1979.

October 13, 1977: Palestinian terrorists hijack a Lufthansa jet to force the release of incarcerated RAF terrorists. On October 18, a special commando of the federal border patrol, GSG 9, forces its way into the hijacked plane in Mogadishu, Somalia, and frees all hostages. On the same day, terrorists Baader, Ensslin and Raspe, who had been imprisoned for life, commit suicide in their Stuttgart-Stammheim cells.

October 19, 1977: The corpse of Hanns-Martin Schleyer is found in Mulhouse, France, 44 days after his abduction. A major search is started for 16 known terrorists believed responsible for the murders of Buback, Ponto, and Schleyer. On April 29, 1991, Silke Maier-Witt, who was arrested in the GDR in August 1990, is charged with participation in the Schleyer murder.

March 9, 1978: The three federal intelligence services, MAD, BND and BfV, are placed by law under parliamentary control.

April 7, 1978: President Carter shocks the Schmidt government by deciding to delay indefinitely the production of neutron weapons.

May 4-7, 1978: Soviet leader Leonid Brezhnev visits the FRG. A long-term agreement is signed providing for close economic cooperation on big projects such as energy development, transport network, and mechanical engineering.

May 5, 1978: Baden-Wurttemberg Minister President Hans Filbinger denies accusations brought against him concerning his activity as lawyer and judge during the Third Reich. Pressured by his fellow CDU party members, he resigns on August 7 and is replaced by Lothar Späth, also CDU.

August 26 to September 3, 1978: GDR cosmonaut Sigmund Jähn flies on a Soviet mission and becomes the first German in space.

September 1, 1978: Introduction of military education in grades nine and ten of GDR schools.

November 29, 1978: A new FRG-GDR traffic agreement provides for the completion and improvement of highway and waterway connections to West Berlin.

January 22-27, 1979: The third channel of German television shows the American TV film "Holocaust" in four parts, unleashing an emotional discussion in the FRG.

March 17-18, 1979: Founding of the Greens in Frankfurt.

April 11, 1979: Working conditions for Western correspondents in the GDR are tightened, making all planned interviews subject to approval.

April 26, 1979: The Constitutional Court strengthens the previously existing judicial rulings on the use of National Socialist emblems. Whoever sells toys or model airplanes with Nazi symbols is liable for punishment.

May 23, 1979: Karl Carstens, CDU, is elected federal president and takes office July 1.

May 24, 1979: Bavarian Minister President Franz-Josef Strauss demands to be the CDU/CSU chancellor candidate for the 1980 Bundestag elections. The CSU regards the nomination of Lower Saxony's Minister President Albrecht as a hostile sign. Therefore, on July 2, the CDU/CSU Bundestag parliamentary group selects Strauss to be the Union's candidate.

July 3, 1979: The Bundestag abolishes the statute of limitations for murder, enabling newly discovered Nazi crimes to be prosecuted.

July 10, 1979: For the first time, terrorist activities by right-wing extremists are registered in the intelligence report presented by Interior Minister Gerhard Baum. On September 13, the superior court of Celle sentences six young neo-Nazis to prison terms varying from four to 11 years. This trial is the first targeting right-wing extremists.

September 5, 1979: The FRG and GDR sign an energy treaty in Leipzig.

October 7, 1979: The Greens receive their first mandate to a Land parliament following elections in Bremen in which they received 6.8 percent of the votes.

December 12, 1979: The NATO dual-track decision to station medium-range missiles in Germany and other European NATO countries is adopted, but they must first be the subject of arms control negotiations between the U.S. and Soviet Union.

The 1980s

January 1, 1980: The GDR is elected to be a member of the UN Security Council for a two-year term.

January 13, 1980: At their congress in Karlsruhe the Greens declare themselves to be an FRG-wide party.

January 17, 1980: General Gert Bastian is relieved of his command of the Twelfth Panzer Division because of his criticism of the NATO dual-track decision.

January 30, 1980: The Nuremberg right-wing paramilitary "Wehrsportgruppe Hoffmann" is outlawed.

April 23, 1980: The Soviet invasion of Afghanistan prompts the Bundestag to follow the U.S. lead in declaring a boycott of the Olympic Games in Moscow.

May 6, 1980: Riots break out in Bremen at a public military celebration honoring the Bundeswehr's 25th year in NATO.

September 26, 1980: Since 1964, 13,000 political prisoners of the GDR were prematurely released due to special efforts by the Bonn government, and 30,000 GDR citizens emigrated to the FRG to reunite with family.

September 26, 1980: Thirteen people are killed and 219 wounded by a right-wing terrorist bombing at the Munich Oktoberfest.

October 5, 1980: In the elections to the ninth Bundestag, the CDU/CSU receives 44.5 percent of the votes, the SPD 42.9 percent, and the FDP 10.6 percent. On November 5, the Bundestag reelects Helmut Schmidt chancellor heading an SPD/FDP coalition.

May 16-17, 1981: To put pressure on his own party, Helmut Schmidt threatens to resign as chancellor if the SPD does not support the NATO dual-track decision. On May 29-31, Hans-Dietrich Genscher also threatens to resign if his FDP does not support it.

August 31, 1981: At U.S. Air Force headquarters in Ramstein, a terrorist bombing injures two Germans and 18 Americans.

September 15, 1981: The "Gudrun Ensslin Kommando" attempts to assassinate the supreme commander of the U.S. Army in Europe, General Kroesen, in Heidelberg.

October 10, 1981: The peace movement organizes a mass demonstration in Bonn against the NATO dual-track decision, with 300,000 demonstrators participating. On October 13, the visit of American Secretary of State Alexander Haig sparks a battle between the police and demonstrators opposing nuclear armament.

December 11-13, 1981: Schmidt visits the GDR. Talks with state and party leader Honecker take place on the Werbellinsee and the Döllnsee. During the visit, martial law is declared in Poland.

January 27, 1982: Interior Minister Baum bans the neo-Nazi People's Socialist Movement of Germany for its increasing militancy and similarities to the banned Nazi party.

February 14, 1982: A forum of 5,000 supporters of the East German peace movement meets at the Kreuz (Cross) Church in Dresden.

February 24-25, 1982: In Paris, Chancellor Schmidt and French President Mitterrand agree to revive the political and security cooperation called for in the Franco-German Treaty of 1963.

April 19-23, 1982: The SPD party congress in Munich calls for a social democratic economic policy. The SPD also criticizes its coalition partner, the FDP, thereby further weakening the cohesion of the governing coalition.

June 9-11, 1982: President Ronald Reagan visits the FRG and West Berlin during his ten-day trip to Europe. A NATO summit meeting takes place in Bonn, where 400,000 to 500,000 people participate in renewed peace demonstrations.

September 9, 1982: In his State of the Nation address to the Bundestag, Schmidt demands that the FDP commit itself unmistakably to the ruling coalition.

September 17, 1982: The four FDP ministers, Hans-Dietrich Genscher, Gerhart Baum, Otto Graf Lambsdorff and Josef Ertl, resign from the Schmidt cabinet. Chancellor Schmidt constructs an SPD minority cabinet and calls for early Bundestag elections.

September 20, 1982: The CDU/CSU and the FDP begin coalition negotiations and decide to unseat Chancellor Schmidt by means of a vote of no-confidence in the Bundestag on October 1.

October 1, 1982: The Bundestag elects Helmut Kohl the sixth chancellor.

October 13, 1982: Chancellor Kohl delivers his government statement supporting the NATO dual-track decision and better relations with the GDR.

November 5-7, 1982: At the FDP party congress in West Berlin, chairman Hans-Dietrich Genscher faces strong intra-party criticism. Prominent members leave the party, such as FDP General Secretary Günter Verheugen, who resigns on September 29.

November 10, 1982: Leonid Brezhnev dies. Federal president Karl Carstens meets with Honecker on the fringes of the mourning ceremonies in Moscow.

December 17, 1982: Chancellor Kohl brings about the dissolution of the Bundestag by calling for a no-confidence vote which is designed so that he loses. New elections are set for March 6, 1983.

February 20, 1983: In Dresden 100,000 demonstrators call for peace.

March 6, 1983: In the early elections for the tenth Bundestag, the CDU/CSU receives 48.8 percent of the votes, the SPD 38.2 percent, and the FDP 6.9 percent. The Greens enter the Bundestag with 5.6 percent. On March 29, Helmut Kohl is elected chancellor and continues the CDU/CSU-FDP ruling coalition. Rainer Barzel becomes Bundestag president.

June 8, 1983: Roland Jahn, member of the Jena peace group, is forced to emigrate to the FRG. He is the twentieth peace movement activist to be forced out of the GDR.

June 25, 1983: During Vice President George Bush's visit to Germany commemorating the 300th anniversary of organized German emigration to the United States, riots protesting U.S. security policy break out in Krefeld, from where the first emigrants started.

September 1, 1983: Members of the peace movement blockade the U.S. depot at Mutlangen, protesting against the deployment of Pershing II missiles in the FRG.

September 15, 1983: The mayor of Berlin, Richard von Weizsäcker, meets with Erich Honecker at the Niederschönhausen Palace in East Berlin. The meeting is the first of its kind in the history of the divided city.

September 28, 1983: The GDR begins demolishing its automatic shooting devices along the inter-German border, a process which will not be finished until November 30, 1984.

December 6, 1983: The federal government bans the Action Front National Socialists/National Activists, the largest neo-Nazi organization in the FRG.

January 24, 1984: GDR citizens who fled to the FRG's permanent representation in East Berlin are permitted to emigrate.

February 13, 1984: Kohl and Honecker meet in Moscow the night before the funeral ceremony of Soviet leader Yuri Andropov, who died on February 9.

March 8, 1984: An SPD parliamentary delegation visits the GDR People's Chamber in East Berlin. This meeting is the first official discussion between parliamentarians from both German states.

May 10, 1984: Following Moscow's lead, the GDR's Olympic committee refuses to allow East German athletes to participate in the Los Angeles Olympic Games.

May 23, 1984: Richard von Weizsäcker (CDU) is elected Carstens' successor as federal president by a large majority. Luise Rinser, the Greens' candidate, receives 68 votes. He takes office July 1.

June 15, 1984: The People's Chamber follows SED directives and elects Egon Krenz and Günter Mittag as representatives to the State Council.

June 26, 1984: Bonn's permanent representation in East Berlin is closed after more than 50 GDR citizens try to force their emigration by fleeing there. It is reopened with increased security after five weeks.

September 22, 1984: Helmut Kohl and François Mitterrand hold hands in silence at the Verdun military cemetery to commemorate the victims of both world wars.

December 13, 1984: Forty GDR refugees waiting in the FRG's embassy in Prague for their visas to the West begin a hunger strike. Genscher meets with them. The last six return to the GDR on January 15, 1985 after they are promised immunity.

1984: The increasing dissatisfaction of GDR citizens with the political and economic conditions in their country is manifested by the growing number of applications for emigration; 35,000 are permitted to emigrate to the FRG.

March 10, 1985: Soviet leader Constantine Chernenko dies. Mikhail Gorbachev becomes the new general secretary. Once again, Kohl and Honecker meet for discussions during the funeral ceremonies.

April 18, 1985: In his state of the nation address, Chancellor Kohl supports the Strategic Defense Initiative (SDI), but he leaves the question of FRG participation open. Not until March 19, 1986, do Kohl and U.S. defense minister Caspar Weinberger agree on German participation in SDI.

May 1, 1985: President Reagan visits the FRG and, together with Chancellor Kohl, goes to the military cemetery at Bitburg. The visit provokes harsh criticism, since members of the Waffen-SS are also buried at the cemetery.

June 11, 1985: The largest spy exchange since 1945 takes place on the Glienicker Bridge between Potsdam and West Berlin.

June 25, 1985: The Saar is the first Land to lift the Extremists' Decree. Active members of the DKP and the NPD are no longer barred from civil service.

August 1985: Thirty-four young GDR citizens, including priest Rainer Eppelmann, use the world youth games in Moscow as an opportunity to write a protest letter demanding more freedom of speech and assembly in the GDR.

August 22, 1985: The BfV announces the disappearance of Hans Joachim Tiedge, who was its official responsible for counter-intelligence against the GDR. The incident develops into one of the largest spy scandals in postwar German history. Heribert Hellenbroich, the leader of the BND, is forced to retire due to the Tiedge affair.

October 16, 1985: In Hesse the SPD and the Greens form a coalition with Joschka Fischer of the Greens as minister for environment and energy.

October 30, 1985: A German-organized space mission involving the American space shuttle Challenger is launched.

November 1, 1985: The last mine is removed from the inter-German border.

February 6, 1986: The Ministry for State Security (Stasi) is awarded the Karl Marx medal and the SED banner of honor for its "exemplary fulfillment of duty in the interest of the entire working class."

February 11, 1986: On the Glienicker Bridge between West Berlin and Potsdam, three western spies and Soviet regime critic Anatoly Shcharansky are turned over to the West. In return, the U.S. and the FRG hand over five Eastern agents.

February 17, 1986: Horst Sindermann, president of the GDR Peoples' Chamber arrives in Bonn for a four-day visit. He is the highest-ranking East German official ever to visit the FRG.

February 25, 1986: The chairman of the SPD's parliamentary group, Hans-Jochen Vogel, rejects the demand of the SPD's left-wing to eliminate from the Basic Law the requirement to seek German unity.

April 5, 1986: A bomb attack on the West Berlin disco "La Belle," a place frequented by American soldiers, kills two and injures 200. The American government believes the attack was instigated by Libya and on April 15 bombs the Libyan leader's headquarters in Tripoli. On April 23, the FRG demands that Libya reduce its embassy staff in Bonn by half and makes entry into the FRG more difficult for Libyan citizens.

May 6, 1986: After 12 years of negotiations, a culture agreement is signed by both German states.

May 17-19, 1986: More than 300 people, including 157 policemen, are wounded at a Wackersdorf facility for the re-enrichment of uranium in the heaviest rioting yet.

May 26, 1986: The GDR demands that all accredited Western diplomats in East Berlin show their diplomatic passports rather than the previously required employment identification when crossing the border into West Berlin. France, the U.S., and the U.K. perceive this action as a violation of the Four-Power status of Berlin and threaten to sever diplomatic relations with the GDR if their diplomats are affected. The GDR retracts the measures in June.

July 7, 1986: In an interview, the chancellor protests the GDR policy of allowing asylum seekers to flee into the FRG via West Berlin.

On September 18, the GDR tightens travel regulations and dams the flood of such asylum seekers.

July 9, 1986: Siemens manager Karl Heinz Beckurt and his chauffeur, Eckhard Groppler, are murdered by a remote control bomb device in Strasslach near Munich.

October 7, 1986: Despite many protests, Brokdorf on the lower Elbe becomes the first German nuclear power plant to be activated after the Chernobyl disaster.

October 10, 1986: G. Braunmühl, head of the Foreign Office's political division, is murdered on a Bonn street by RAF terrorists.

October 16, 1986: The FRG is again chosen to serve in the UN Security Council for two years, as it had been in 1976.

November 11, 1986: The Constitutional Court rules that sit-ins in front of military installations are punishable.

January 4, 1987: At the CDU meeting in Dortmund, Helmut Kohl characterizes the GDR as a regime which keeps 2,000 political prisoners in prisons and concentration camps. The GDR permanent representation in Bonn officially protests the term "concentration camp."

January 25, 1987: In the elections to the eleventh Bundestag, the CDU/CSU receives 44.3 percent of the votes, the SPD 37 percent, the FDP 9.1 percent, and the Greens 8.3 percent. This is the worst CDU/CSU election performance since 1949. Nevertheless, on March 11, Helmut Kohl is elected chancellor, and the CDU/CSU-FDP coalition continues to rule.

February 5, 1987: GDR spy chief Markus Wolf voluntarily retires from the Ministry for State Security as head of its espionage operations. When the GDR collapses in 1989, he flees to the Soviet Union but returns to Germany in the summer of 1991 to face legal charges against him.

February 16, 1987: The Bonn municipal court finds FDP party leaders Otto Graf Lambsdorff and Hans Friderichs guilty of tax evasion and fines them DM 180,000 and DM 61,500, respectively. Eberhard von Brauchtisch receives a penalty of two years probation and a fine of DM 555,000. This "Flick Affair" tarnishes the image of the FRG's major parties.

March 23, 1987: Willy Brandt resigns as SPD chairman as a result of his suggestion to make a Greek national, Margarita Mathiopoulos, who is not a party member, the new SPD spokesperson.

March 25, 1987: For the first time two Bundeswehr officers are invited to observe East German and Soviet military maneuvers.

May 25, 1987: The census runs smoothly, despite calls for boycotts and isolated cases of attacks on census takers.

May 28, 1987: West German private pilot Matthias Rust lands his Cessna on Moscow's Red Square. Two days later, Defense Minister Sergei Sokolov and Air Defense Chief Alexander Koldunov are forced to resign. On September 4, the Soviet Supreme Court sentences Rust to four years hard labor. He is pardoned on August 3, 1988, and expelled from the Soviet Union.

June 9, 1987: Despite the presence of a large number of policemen, approximately 3,000 people in East Berlin's Unter den Linden demand the destruction of the Wall, call for freedom, and chant praise for Gorbachev.

June 12, 1987: President Reagan visits Berlin in honor of its 750th anniversary and demands: "Mr. Gorbachev, tear down this wall!"

June 14, 1987: At a special SPD party congress, Willy Brandt is named honorary chairman for life, a post created specially for him. Hans-Jochen Vogel becomes the new party chairman.

July 17, 1987: The GDR abolishes the death penalty on the occasion of its 38 years of existence.

GDR leader, Erich Honecker (left) is received by Chancellor Helmut Kohl. (*Source:* GIC, New York.)

August 17, 1987: Rudolf Hess, former deputy of Hitler, dies at age 93, and Spandau prison in Berlin is razed.

August 27, 1987: The SED and SPD publish a common report in which, for the first time, they try to work through the ideological differences between Social Democrats and Communists and develop a long-term plan for cooperation.

September 7-11, 1987: Erich Honecker becomes the first GDR leader to visit the FRG in the history of the two Germanies.

September 12, 1987: The news magazine *Der Spiegel* accuses Schleswig-Holstein Minister President Uwe Barschel (CDU) of having the top SPD candidate for the upcoming Land elections trailed and watched. Under pressure by the FDP and the public,

Barschel resigns on September 25. On October 11, he is found dead in a Geneva hotel from a toxic overdose.

January 17, 1988: GDR security forces arrest 120 people during demonstrations commemorating the sixty-ninth anniversary since Rosa Luxemburg and Karl Liebknecht were killed. Demonstrators display signs quoting Luxemburg: "Freedom is also the freedom of those who think differently." Fifty-four people are expelled from the GDR.

February 11, 1988: West Berlin Mayor Eberhard Diepgen meets with Honecker in East Berlin. They announce improvements in East-West travel and visits.

February 25, 1988: Soviet troops in the GDR begin the withdrawal of intermediate-range nuclear missiles in Bischofswalde.

March 1, 1988: Inhabitants of West Berlin are henceforth permitted to spend one night in East Berlin when on a day trip.

March 3, 1988: For the first time in ten years, a meeting occurs between government and Lutheran Church leaders in the GDR.

May 18, 1988: Rupert Scholz, West Berlin senator for federal affairs, becomes the new defense minister. His predecessor, Manfred Wörner, is sworn in as NATO general secretary on July 1.

August 15, 1988: The GDR opens diplomatic relations with the EC.

August 28, 1988: Seventy people die in a three-plane crash at an air show at the American Air Force base in Ramstein. More than 300 people are injured. The accident spawns serious political debate over such air shows and low-level flying.

September 27-29, 1988: After talks with Mikhail Gorbachev in Moscow, Erich Honecker advocates Gorbachev's policy of *perestroika*. However, Honecker fails to put the policy into practice.

October 3, 1988: Franz-Josef Strauss, CSU chairman and Bavarian minister president, dies of a heart attack. Former federal finance minister, Max Streibl, becomes the new Bavarian minister president, and Theo Waigel the party chairman and federal finance minister.

November 11, 1988: Bundestag president Philipp Jenninger, CDU, resigns in the wake of criticism of his speech commemorating the fiftieth anniversary of the Crystal Night assault on Jews. Former family minister, Rita Süssmuth, is elected as the new Bundestag president on November 25.

November 20-24, 1988: First visit of an official European Parliament delegation to the GDR's People's Chamber.

January 11, 1989: Twenty GDR citizens leave the FRG's permanent representation in East Berlin, where they had been for a year, waiting to leave the country. They are promised immunity and the reevaluation of their travel applications.

February 9, 1989: The right-wing extremist National Rally, led by Michael Kühnen, is banned because of its unconstitutional goals.

March 6, 1989: A treaty for a city partnership between Bonn and Potsdam is drafted.

March 28-29, 1989: High-ranking officers of the Bundeswehr and the NVA meet in Hamburg for discussions.

May 2, 1989: Hungary rips down the electrified fence along the Austrian border, opening an escape route to the West.

May 17, 1989: In GDR municipal elections, the government announces that the combined parties of the National Front had won 98.85 percent of the vote. Opposition and church leaders accuse the government of falsifying the election results, a charge which was later substantiated after the collapse of the GDR.

May 23, 1989: Federal president Richard von Weizsäcker is reelected with 86.2 percent of the vote.

June 7, 1989: In East Berlin the Stasi breaks up a demonstration protesting the falsification of the May 7 election results.

June 8, 1989: The GDR People's Chamber proclaims its support for China's use of force in quelling the democratic movement in that country, after *Neues Deutschland* had done the same on June 5.

June 12-15, 1989: Gorbachev is warmly received in Bonn. At the end of his visit, he explains in a press conference that the Berlin Wall can disappear as soon as the conditions which prompted its construction no longer exist.

July 7, 1989: At the first East Bloc leaders' conference in Bucharest, Romania, Gorbachev acknowledges each socialist state's right to develop on its own.

July 25, 1989: Hungary announces that hundreds of East Germans had sought refuge at the FRG's embassy in Budapest.

August 8, 1989: The FRG's permanent representation in East Berlin is closed to visitors because 131 GDR citizens are there demanding the right to emigrate. On August 13, the Bonn embassy in Budapest closes due to overcrowding; 180 GDR citizens are waiting there for visas. More and more East Germans take advantage of the "green border" between Austria and Hungary to flee to the West.

August 10-11, 1989: The West German airline, Lufthansa, and the GDR line, Interflug, open inter-German air traffic with connections from Frankfurt to Leipzig and Leipzig to Düsseldorf.

August 19, 1989: In a "Great Escape" more than 900 East Germans flee from Hungary to Austria.

September 1, 1989: The FRG government rejects an SPD proposal to accept the western Polish border as final, while underscoring its continued support of the 1970 Warsaw Treaty.

September 2, 1989: More than 3,500 East Germans wait in Hungarian camps for permission to leave for the West. A conference of Lutheran Church leaders drafts a letter demanding social reform in the GDR.

September 4, 1989: Hundreds of people demonstrate for more travel freedom in front of the Nikolai Church in Leipzig.

September 10-11, 1989: Hungary opens its borders to all GDR citizens, explaining that the multi-national CSCE Accords nullify a 1969 bilateral agreement with the GDR not to permit each other's country to be used as an escape route. Thousands of GDR citizens arrive in Bavaria. The New Forum is created in East Berlin.

September 10, 1989: Hungary permits GDR refugees at the FRG embassy in Budapest to emigrate.

September 11, 1989: New Forum, led by Bärbel Bohley and Jens Reich, holds its founding conference in the GDR; on September 21 its September 19 request for official recognition is rejected on the grounds that its members are "enemies of the state."

September 12, 1989: Another citizens' movement, "Democracy Now," led by Konrad Weiss and Wolfgang Ullmann, demands in its founding proclamation a "democratic restructuring" of the GDR.

September 30, 1989: Foreign Minister Genscher visits the FRG's Prague embassy. 7,000 refugees leave for the West from Prague and Warsaw. In the days that follow 15,000 people arrive in the FRG in cars and specially chartered trains and planes.

October 1, 1989: With Honecker's permission, some 1,500 refugees from the GDR at the FRG's embassy in Warsaw leave for the West, joined by more from Prague. As the "freedom trains" pass through the GDR, more refugees jump aboard.

October 2, 1989: The first of many weekly Monday mass demonstrations following peace services in the Nikolai Church takes place.

October 4, 1989: Rioting erupts in Dresden as 5,000 persons storm the railway station and try to board refugee trains for the FRG. Saxony's SED chief, Hans Modrow, approves of force to restrain the crowd.

October 7, 1989: Official celebration of the fortieth anniversary of the founding of the GDR. Gorbachev is the honored guest and tells SED leaders that "he who comes late is punished by life." Nevertheless, Honecker praises orthodox communism and gives no hint that he intends to reform the GDR. Tens of thousands of people demonstrate all over the GDR against the SED regime, and Police arrest more than 1,000.

October 7, 1989: The SPD is refounded in the GDR, with Ibrahim Böhme as its leader.

October 8, 1989: Hans Modrow agrees to talks with the opposition.

October 9, 1989: "Monday Demonstration" in Leipzig: 100,000 people chant, "We are the people!" and "Gorby help us!" Further large-scale demonstrations follow in other cities. The demonstrations are renewed in Leipzig on October 16.

October 17, 1989: Honecker secretly orders force to be used to suppress the protesters, but Egon Krenz flies to Leipzig and reportedly countermands the order.

October 18, 1989: After holding the reins of power for 18 years, Honecker is removed from office and is succeeded by Krenz.

November 1, 1989: Krenz consults with Gorbachev in Moscow and endorses *perestroika*. On November 3, he cleans house in the old Politburo, removing Kurt Hager, Erich Mielke, Hermann Axen, Alfred Neumann, and Erich Mückenberger.

November 4, 1989: Approximately one million people demonstrate in East Berlin. Czechoslovakia opens its border, permitting thousands of East Germans to flee to the West. By November 6, about 30,000 East Germans escape through Czechoslovakia.

Berliners chisel away the penetrated wall. (*Source:* PIB.)

November 5, 1989: The GDR government proposes a new travel law, but the opposition groups insist that such reforms are insufficient, prompting the cabinet to resign the following day.

November 8, 1989: The Politburo resigns, and Hans Modrow (SED) becomes the new Minister President.

November 9, 1989: The GDR ends travel restrictions and opens its borders. The people of East and West Berlin sing, dance, celebrate and embrace on top of the Berlin Wall. Many chisel away pieces of the "ugliest edifice in the world."

November 10, 1989: Chancellor Kohl interrupts his trip to Poland and, together with other politicians, speaks to Berliners in front of the "Schöneberger Rathaus" and at the "Gedächtniskirche" in West Berlin.

November 11, 1989: Lothar de Maizière becomes chairman of the CDU-East, and on November 18 he becomes Modrow's deputy.

November 13, 1989: Modrow is elected president of the GDR Council of Ministers.

November 17, 1989: The Ministry for State Security is liquidated and replaced by the Office for National Security.

November 23, 1989: Procedures to expel Honecker from the SED are begun, and on December 3 he and 11 others are expelled.

November 28, 1989: Chancellor Kohl presents a ten-point program in the Bundestag to overcome the division of Germany and Europe, the final step toward German unity to be taken in five years.

December 1, 1989: The GDR's parliament removes the SED's monopoly on power from the text of the constitution, and on December 3 Krenz, the Politburo, and the entire Central Committee resign. Three days later Krenz relinquishes his last post as Chairman of the State Council. On January 21, 1990, he is expelled from the SED-PDS.

December 2-3, 1989: Presidents Bush and Gorbachev meet in Malta, and the main topic is the German question.

December 6, 1989: All political prisoners in the GDR are given amnesty.

December 7, 1989: The first of 16 "Round Table" discussions between the government and opposition groups takes place; the final meeting is on March 12, 1990.

December 9, 1989: Gregor Gysi is elected SED leader. He announces that "I don't want to rescue the party; I want to construct a new one." On this same day the Council of Europe meets in Strasbourg. Heads of government and state confirm Germany's right to self-determination and declare that a unified Germany should be embedded in an integrated Europe.

December 12, 1989: Secretary of State James Baker meets with Chancellor Kohl in West Berlin and Modrow in Potsdam to discuss the events in Germany.

December 19, 1989: Kohl and Modrow meet in Dresden, where Kohl addresses a large gathering of people.

December 22, 1989: The Brandenburg Gate in Berlin is reopened.

December 24, 1989: The visa and minimum daily exchange requirements for West Germans visiting the GDR are abolished, enabling 380,000 West Germans and 765,000 West Berliners to visit the GDR during Christmas; 2.4 million East Germans visit the West.

The 1990s

January 3, 1990: Alliance '90 is formed as an electoral alliance of several reform groups, and it makes this public on February 6.

January 20, 1990: The German Social Union (DSU) is founded.

January 29, 1990: The Monday demonstration in Leipzig demands immediate unification of Germany.

February 5, 1990: Formation of a "Government of National Responsibility" with Modrow as Prime Minister and members from the SED-PDS, CDU, LDPD, SPD, and other new parties and groups. On the same day, Helmut Kohl attends the meeting at which Democratic Awakening, the CDU, and the CSU agree on an election alliance called "Alliance for Germany."

February 7, 1990: The FRG government announces that it is ready for negotiations with GDR leaders to establish economic union, and it creates a cabinet committee "German Unity."

February 10, 1990: Chancellor Kohl and Foreign Minister Genscher meet in Moscow with Gorbachev, who assures the Germans that they may live together in one state.

February 12, 1990: A demonstration in Leipzig calling for German unity opens with the national anthem of the FRG.

February 13-14, 1990: Prime Minister Modrow visits Bonn and is not received warmly. Chancellor Kohl suggests negotiations on an economic and monetary union.

February 14, 1990: The foreign ministers of the four victorious powers and of the two German states agree to begin formal talks on German unity ("2 plus 4" talks).

February 15, 1990: In Paris, Kohl briefs Mitterrand on his talks with Gorbachev and on the current developments in Germany.

February 21, 1990: All party parliamentary groups in the GDR People's Chamber agree to German unification.

February 24-25, 1990: Chancellor Kohl meets with President Bush at Camp David and stresses that the security alliance and friendship with the U.S. are of fundamental importance to unified Germany.

March 14, 1990: Democratic Renewal chairman Wolfgang Schnur admits that he had been a paid collaborator of Stasi and resigns from all public and party offices. Chancellor Kohl is cheered by 300,000 at an election gathering in Leipzig.

March 18, 1990: The first free elections are held in the GDR. The "Alliance for Germany" (CDU, CSU and Democratic Awakening) wins, but falls short of an absolute majority.

April 5, 1990: Constituent meeting of the first freely-elected People's Chamber in the GDR. The physician Sabine Bergmann-Pohl is elected speaker of the parliament and also assumes responsibility as acting head of state for the GDR.

April 12, 1990: For the first time in its history, the People's Chamber in the GDR elects a democratic government. A grand coalition is formed consisting of the "Alliance for Germany," the Liberals, and the SPD. Lothar de Maizière is elected prime minister of the GDR.

April 19, 1990: In his policy statement, de Maizière declares a commitment to German unity. He admits that East Germans share guilt for the crimes of the Third Reich, and on April 23 the People's Chamber allocates DM 6.2 million for Holocaust victims.

April 23, 1990: Citizens of Karl-Marx-Stadt vote in a referendum to change the city's name back to Chemnitz.

April 28, 1990: EC leaders welcome German unification at a special meeting in Dublin and prepare the way for integrating the GDR in the EC upon achievement of German unity.

May 5, 1990: The foreign ministers of the two German states, France, the U.S., U.K. and USSR meet in Bonn for an initial round of "2 plus 4" talks on the foreign policy aspects of German unity.

May 6, 1990: Local elections held in the GDR and show the CDU continues to be the strongest party.

May 9, 1990: The western German Federation of Trade Unions (DGB) decides to liquidate its East German equivalent, the FDGB.

May 14, 1990: The federal and Land governments make DM 115 billion available in a "German Unity Fund" for four and a half years.

May 16-17, 1990: In Washington, Chancellor Kohl thanks President Bush for his support at the "2 plus 4" talks, particularly in regard to achievement of full sovereignty.

May 18, 1990: The treaty between the FRG and GDR establishing a monetary, economic and social union is signed in Bonn by the governments of the two states; the Bundestag ratifies the treaty on June 21 and the Bundesrat on June 22.

June 6, 1990: RAF terrorist Susanne Albrecht is arrested in East Berlin, and on June 14 four more terrorists who had been harbored in the GDR are arrested in Frankfurt an der Oder.

June 8, 1990: Kohl and Bush meet in Washington and emphasize that full NATO membership of the united Germany is indispensable.

June 12, 1990: The first joint session of the East and West Berlin city governments

June 17, 1990: In a joint session in East Berlin, the Bundestag and the People's Chamber commemorate the June 17, 1953 uprising in the GDR.

June 21, 1990: The Bundestag and People's Chamber approve identically worded resolutions on the border between the united Germany and Poland. They announce their willingness to reaffirm the definitive nature of the border on the basis of an international treaty.

June 27, 1990: The governments of the FRG and GDR approve a reciprocal agreement on the elimination of border checks along the intra-German border as of July 1, 1990.

July 1, 1990: The monetary, economic, and social union enters into force. East Germans go to exchange offices and, under most circumstances, exchange their East German marks for West German marks at a rate of 1:1.

July 14-16, 1990: Chancellor Kohl visits the Soviet Union and reaches an agreement with President Gorbachev that the united Germany shall have full sovereignty, therefore will be able to decide freely its alliance membership in the future, and will reduce its armed forces to 370,000 soldiers. The Soviet Union agrees to withdraw its forces from the GDR by the end of 1994 in return for Bonn's financial assistance in paying, retraining, transporting, and rehousing the returning Soviet troops.

July 17, 1990: In the "2 plus 4" talks in Paris the six foreign ministers, joined by the Polish foreign minister, agree on principles for establishing the definitive borders of the unified Germany.

July 22, 1990: The People's Chamber passes a law establishing Länder in the GDR. Under this law five states are to be formed, and eastern and western Berlin will combine to form a sixth.

August 19, 1990: The eastern SPD leaves the de Maizière government and reunites with the SPD in the West on September 27.

August 23, 1990: The People's Chamber resolves to accede to the FRG on October 3, 1990.

August 31, 1990: The Unification Treaty between the FRG and GDR is signed at the Crown Prince Palace in Berlin by Interior Minister Schäuble and State Secretary Krause.

September 12, 1990: Talks among the foreign ministers in Moscow are concluded. The Treaty on the Final Settlement with Respect to Germany ("2 plus 4" Treaty) is signed.

September 19, 1990: The People's Chamber ratifies the Unification Treaty, followed by the Bundestag on September 20. On September 21, the Bundesrat holds its final deliberation on it.

October 1, 1990: Merger of CDU-East and CDU-West. Kohl is elected party chairman, and de Maizière deputy party chairman.

October 1, 1990: The document suspending Four-Power rights is signed in New York, and at midnight the next day the Four-Power status of Berlin expires.

October 3, 1990: The GDR accedes to the FRG in accordance with Article 23 of the Basic Law and thereby becomes subject to the Basic Law. Five new states are formed in the territory of the former GDR: Brandenburg, Mecklenburg-Western Pomerania, Saxony, Saxony-Anhalt, and Thuringia, with united Berlin forming a sixth. Chancellor Kohl declares in a message to foreign governments that the German borders are fixed forever.

October 4, 1990: The first session of the Bundestag with the 144 deputies delegated by the People's Chamber is held in the Berlin Reichstag building. The new federal ministers are sworn in, and Chancellor Kohl delivers the policy statement. On October 5 the Bundestag ratifies the "2-plus-4" Treaty; ratification by the U.S. Senate follows on October 11.

Leaders witness reunification. Hans-Dietrich Genscher, Hannelore Kohl, Helmut Kohl, Richard von Weizsäcker, and Lothar de Maizière. (*Source:* PIB.)

October 12, 1990: The Bundesrat meets, and for the first time, plenipotentiaries of the five new states participate in an advisory capacity.

October 14, 1990: Elections to the Land parliaments are held in the five new eastern Länder.

November 9, 1990: The FRG signs a friendship treaty with the Soviet Union.

November 14, 1990: The FRG signs a treaty with Poland officially fixing their mutual border along the Oder-Neisse Line.

December 2, 1990: The first all-German Bundestag elections are held. The CDU/CSU and FDP renew their governing coalition under Helmut Kohl, who is reelected as chancellor on January 16, 1991.

December 2, 1990: An arrest warrant is issued for Erich Honecker, who is being sheltered in the Soviet military hospital in Beelitz near Berlin.

December 15, 1990: Lothar de Maizière resigns as deputy CDU party chairman because of allegations that he cooperated with the Stasi.

January 21, 1991: Foreign Minister Genscher warns against anti-Americanism after protest marches against the Gulf War to liberate Kuwait from Iraq take place in several cities.

January 29, 1991: Beginning in Berlin of the trial of former GDR trade union leader and Politburo member, Harry Tisch, accused of embezzlement and misusing DM 104 million in trade union funds.

February 1, 1991: Foreign Minister Genscher states that the FRG government is ready to make the necessary amendment to the Basic Law to enable German military to cooperate in UN actions.

March 1, 1991: To help pay the costs of German unification taxes are increased on mineral oil, cigarettes, insurance premiums, and individual and corporate income.

March 6, 1991: Bonn officials are stunned to learn that the Soviet Defense Minister Dmitri Yazov visits Soviet forces in Weimar without notifying the German government in advance. This is a violation of Germany's sovereignty, as is the transfer of Erich Honecker in a Soviet military plane to Moscow on March 13, despite a German arrest warrant against him.

March 15, 1991: United Germany gains complete sovereignty when the Soviet government delivers the ratified 2-plus-4 "Treaty on the Final Settlement with Regard to Germany."

April 1, 1991: Detlev Rohwedder, head of the Treuhand, is murdered by RAF terrorists at his home in Düsseldorf.

April 21, 1991: In Chancellor Kohl's home Land of Rhineland-Palatinate, his CDU is defeated in Land elections for the first time in 44 years. The SPD takes power.

April 23, 1991: The Constitutional Court in Karlsruhe rules that the nationalization of property in the Soviet Zone of Occupation between 1945 and 1949 is constitutional and that landowners who were expropriated during that time have a claim to compensation, but not to restitution.

May 12-13, 1991: Approximately 300 fundamentalist Greens leave the Green Party and create a new one, the "Ecological Left."

May 21, 1991: Former GDR Prime Minister Willi Stoph, Defense Minister Heinz Kessler, Secretary of the Defense Council Fritz Treletz, and another Defense Council member, Hans Albrecht, are arrested in Berlin on charges of having given border guards the order to "shoot-to-kill" escapees.

June 20, 1991: The Bundestag votes narrowly to move the seat of government back to Berlin, although some ministries and federal offices will remain in Bonn.

July 18, 1991: The Berlin Prosecutor's Office brings charges of abuse of power against Günter Mittag, former Politburo member in charge of the GDR economy.

July 19, 1991: Charges are brought against the last GDR spy chief, Werner Grossmann, but on July 29 they are dropped by the Berlin Chamber Court which considers it unconstitutional to prosecute former GDR espionage officials, when their counterparts in the FRG are not subject to punishment.

August 14, 1991: The federal cabinet adopts a legislative draft to rehabilitate and compensate victims of punishment for political crimes in the former GDR.

August 18, 1991: The remains of Prussian King Friedrich Wilhelm I and Friedrich II (the Great) are transferred from Hohenzollernburg near Hechingen in Baden-Wurttemberg to Brandenburg to be reburied in Potsdam. Friedrich Wilhelm was interred in the Friedenskirche at the edge of Sanssouci Park, and his son, Friedrich, on the upper castle terrasse, in accordance with his wish.

August 26, 1991: After 44 years a unified *Duden* is again published.

November 14, 1991: The Bundestag passes a law permitting people who were subject to surveillance by the Stasi in the former GDR to examine their files and identify their harassers or denunciators. Access was opened on January 1, 1992.

January 15, 1992: The FRG announces diplomatic recognition of Slovenia and Croatia, forcing other EC countries to do the same.

January 20, 1992: A Berlin court convicts two former East German border guards in the killing of a GDR citizen as he attempted to flee to the FRG in February 1989. The guard who shot was imprisoned three-and-one-half years for manslaughter.

February 10, 1992: Trial begins in Berlin against Erich Mielke, former GDR Minister of State Security. He is charged with the murders of two policemen on August 9, 1931, when Mielke was only 23 years old. Other crimes are investigated, and he returns to court November 12, 1992.

April 5, 1992: In Land elections in Baden-Wurttemberg and Schleswig-Holstein, the governing parties suffer large losses, while parties on the far right make strong gains, winning more than enough votes to gain seats in the Land parliaments.

May 17, 1992: Hans-Dietrich Genscher resigns as foreign minister, a post he had held exactly 18 years. He is replaced by Klaus Kinkel.

June 14, 1992: In the first plebiscite in a new eastern German Land, the citizens of Brandenburg approve a new constitution.

July 15, 1992: The FRG government approves the deployment of a destroyer and three reconnaissance planes to the Adriatic Sea to help monitor the UN embargo against Serbia and Montenegro.

July 29, 1992: Erich Honecker is forced to return to Germany to face charges of manslaughter, corruption, and breach of trust. The manslaughter charges stem from his having personally supervised the construction of the Berlin Wall, where 350 deaths had occurred. His luck ran out when the Soviet Union collapsed in December 1991, and he fled to the Chilean embassy in Moscow to avoid extradition to Germany to face charges. He is put on trial on November 12, 1992.

August 22, 1992: Right-wing youth gangs, sporting swastikas and shouting neo-Nazi slogans and cheered on by some bystanders, attack an asylum hostel in Rostock and battle police for several days. This is followed on August 29-30 by similar attacks in Cottbus and two other towns in Brandenburg and by a bombing of a memorial in Berlin to Holocaust victims. Such attacks continue thoughout the autumn despite official condemnation and numerous demonstrations in German cities against anti-foreigner and anti-Semitic violence.

September 16, 1992: Israeli Prime Minister Yitzhak Rabin visits an exhibition in the "Jewish Barracks" in Sachsenhausen on the oppression of Jews during the Third Reich. This is the first time an Israeli leader visited a German concentration camp. Ten days later, the barracks are gutted by arson, becoming the third Berlin-area memorial to Jewish Holocaust victims damaged in recent weeks.

September 24, 1992: Germany and Romania agree to repatriate each other's citizens residing illegally in the other. It is part of efforts to stem the flow of illegal asylum-seekers to Germany. On the same day, legendary East German spymaster, Markus Wolf, who headed the foreign service of the GDR's Stasi secret police, is charged with espionage and treason.

September 25, 1992: The Rhine-Main-Danube Canal is completed.

October 8, 1992: Willy Brandt dies. Thousands turn out for his state funeral in Berlin on October 17.

October 19, 1992: The bodies of Green politicians Gerd Bastian and Petra Kelly are found in their Bonn apartment; they had been dead for several weeks. Evidently Bastian shot Kelly and then himself.

November 8, 1992: A mass rally in Berlin involving 300,000 persons condemning anti-foreigner violence is brought to a halt by an estimated 500 anarchist protesters, who hurl eggs, paint bombs, and angry chants.

November 12, 1992: Trial begins for Erich Honecker in Berlin. The terminally ill former SED chief is joined on the stand by other top SED leaders. They are the only leaders in the ex-Soviet empire to face justice in a Western court.

November 17, 1992: The SPD overwhelmingly approves a proposal to tighten Germany's liberal asylum laws and clear the way for German soldiers to take part in U.N. peace-keeping (though not in combat) missions by agreeing to amend the constitutional ban on military activity outside the NATO area.

December 7, 1992: The major parties agree to scrap the absolute guarantee of political asylum for refugees.

December 10, 1992: German Alternative becomes the second neo-Nazi group in two weeks to be banned. On December 16, the federal government orders intelligence surveillance of the Republicans to determine whether they fit the legal definition of "anti-democratic," which would permit the government to ban them also.

January 11, 1993: U.N. Secretary General Boutros-Ghali tells German leaders that the world needs "Germany's full participation" in every type of U.N. military operation.

January 12-13, 1993: The trial of Erich Honecker is suspended. Berlin's Constitutional Court rules that "it violates respect for human rights to keep in jail an accused person who is suffering from an incurable illness." He joins his family in Chile. On January 27, a higher court overrules the Berlin Constitutional Court and orders that the trial proceed to a formal end with or without Honecker, who remains in Chile, a country with no extradition agreement with Germany. On April 13, 1993, the manslaughter prosecution of Honecker is formally ended for health reasons.

February 6, 1993: For economic reasons the Kohl government announces sharp cuts in the Bundeswehr, perhaps to 300,000 troops by 1996.

March 13, 1993: The federal government and the 16 Länder agree upon a "Solidarity Pact" to continue financing the reconstruction of eastern Germany.

March 23, 1993: The Berlin and federal governments announce that the asbestos contaminated Palace of the Republic site of the GDR parliament, built on the spot where the Kaiser's city castle had been located, would be razed and replaced by a Foreign Ministry building. Some East Berliners protest this decision.

March 24, 1993: To demonstrate that united Germany is willing to assume new responsibilities, the Kohl government announces that German aircraft will join in airlifting food and medical supplies to Bosnia.

April 8, 1993: The Constitutional Court approves of German military participation in U.N. enforcement of a "no-fly" zone over Bosnia, which begins April 12. The German airmen serving on crews of NATO AWACS reconnaissance planes are the first German soldiers to take part in combat missions since 1945.

April 21, 1993: The Bundestag approves of Bosnian mission, as well as of sending 1,640 troops on a humanitarian aid program to Somalia. Foreign Minister Kinkel says the end of the Cold War terminates the German conception of a military only for defense purposes. The first Bundeswehr troops leave for Somalia May 12.

April 26, 1993: The Holocaust Memorial Museum opens in Washington D.C. The German government, worried that the exhibition would damage the country's democratic image, offers to pay for an exhibit on postwar Germany. The offer is rejected. Nevertheless, German archivists provide the museum with many original Holocaust materials.

May 3, 1993: SPD leader Björn Engholm resigns amid revelations that he gave false testimony in the 1987 Barschel affair, which had brought him to power. On the same day, metal workers begin the first legal strike in eastern Germany in more than 60 years. Employers accept most of their demands.

May 4, 1993: GDR spymaster Markus Wolf goes on trial for treason. Calling the case absurd and political, he asks: "What country am I supposed to have betrayed?" He is found guilty December 6.

May 26, 1993: Amidst a violent confrontation between police and demonstrators, the Bundestag revokes the constitutional guarantee of asylum to any politically oppressed person, to take effect July 1. Polls show 70% of Germans favor this.

May 27, 1993: Hans Modrow is convicted of rigging a 1989 election in the GDR, the first verdict rendered by a court in reunified Germany against a top East German official.

May 28, 1993: The Constitutional Court declares most abortions illegal in all parts of Germany.

May 29, 1993: A right-wing extremist burns a house in Solingen, killing five Turks. This is the worst of thousands of anti-foreigner attacks since 1990 and provokes the first major violent response by Germany's 1.8 million Turks.

June 13, 1993: In the first-ever internal referendum of 900,000 SPD members, Rhineland-Palatinate Minister President Rudolf Scharping was elected national SPD chairman. On June 21 he announced that he would be the SPD chancellor candidate in the 1994 Bundestag elections.

June 23, 1993: The Constitutional Court rules that the Bundeswehr may continue its mission in Somalia. U.N. Secretary General Boutros-Ghali visits Bonn the same day and thanks the German government and people for their contribution to U.N. activities.

August 6, 1993: Germany's first Jewish Gymnasium (high school) in 50 years opens its doors in Berlin. This follows by seven years the creation of a Jewish elementary school in the city.

September 7, 1993: A poll commissioned by the chancellor's office to determine the effects of highly publicized right-wing extremism and xenophobic attacks in Germany reveals that more than half of all American respondents fear a return of Nazism in Germany, and 41% believe that unified Germany is a danger to European peace. Nevertheless, mutual esteem is expressed: three out of four Germans and Americans said they like each other.

September 16, 1993: Three top officials of the former GDR, Heinz Kessler, Fritz Steletz, and Heinz Albrecht, all ex-members of the National Defense Council, are convicted of manslaughter and receive jail sentences in connection with the deaths of Germans escaping to the West. Willi Stoph and Erich Mielke are declared too ill to stand trial, but on October 27 Mielke is convicted of murdering two policemen in 1932.

October 3, 1993: Germans celebrate the third anniversary of their national unification in a somber mood. Six million Germans are unemployed, crime is soaring, the federal deficit is at an all-time high, labor-management relations have degenerated, Berlin's bid for the 2000 Olympic Games is rebuffed, and the FRG is uncertain about its role in the post-Cold War world. Journalist Christoph Bertram of *Die Zeit* concludes that Germans are worn down by "the enormous, exhausting experiment of German unification."

October 12, 1993: The Constitutional Court upholds the Maastricht Treaty on European Union, which goes into effect November 1. It rejects 20 legal challenges that the treaty violates German sovereignty and the principles of a democratic state. On October 29, Frankfurt is chosen as the site for a future European central bank.

The
Dictionary

Konrad Adenauer (left) with Gerhard Schröder (*Source*: PIB)

ABORTION. The issue of abortion has been as contentious and emotional as in the U.S. and other European countries. The SPD-FDP governing coalition responded to demands of women's groups and liberal politicians in the early 1970s to reform the law, Paragraph 218, which banned abortions as a criminal offense. In April 1974, the Bundestag narrowly passed a bill permitting abortion during the first three months of pregnancy if the doctor and mother agreed. However, the CDU/CSU (q.v.) governed Länder and 193 CDU/CSU Bundestag members appealed to the Constitutional Court for a judicial review of the law. The Court overturned the reform law as unconstitutional, but at the same time it declared that abortions could be performed within 12 weeks of conception in cases where the mother's condition would be threatened by the pregnancy. In practice, this meant that women who sought abortion in Catholic Länder in the south, particularly Bavaria, were normally denied it by doctors, whereas women in the northern SPD-ruled Länder could more easily get permission. In East Germany abortions were free on demand. When German reunification (q.v.) came in 1990, eastern and western Germany retained their own abortion laws, leaving abortion legal in the East and basically illegal in the West. On June 26, 1992, the Bundestag majority tried to end this anomaly by voting to let women decide on an abortion in the first 12 weeks of pregnancy after submitting to a non-binding medical counseling session. But, in August 1992, the Constitutional Court (q.v.) sided with Bavaria and 247 Bundestag members, including Chancellor Helmut Kohl (q.v.), by blocking the change from taking effect. This issue continues to split Germany along geographic and gender lines, with the East, North, and women generally favoring liberalized abortion, and the Catholic South favoring more restrictions.

ADENAUER, KONRAD (1876-1967). Mayor of Cologne (1917-33 and again in 1945), CDU chairman (1946-66), chancellor (1949-63). Known as "der Alte" (the old man), Adenauer was frequently compared to Herbert Wehner of the SPD (qq.v.). Both were strong-willed, authoritarian, overbearing, and experienced experts in political tactics and maneuvering, who successfully and resolutely pursued their political objectives. They were committed democrats who were often accused of acting undemocratically and heavy-handedly within their parties. They were masters of power politics although power in itself was not the ultimate goal for either of them. Both had been outsiders during the Third Reich (q.v.) although Adenauer's emigration was of the "inner" type, meaning that he had remained inside Germany after tuning the Nazis out. Both were relatively lonely people. They were unquestionably the strongest men within their respective parties and were seen as capable of moving their parties in whatever direction they wanted. They could be ruthless toward their political opponents, and then bury the hatchet when political expediency required them to do so.

In October 1963, Adenauer stepped down as chancellor. He had served for thirteen years, as many years as the Weimar Republic had lasted, and one more than Hitler's "Thousand-Year Reich." He bequeathed to his country stability and prosperity unknown in German history. The social market economy (q.v.) had made capitalism, democracy, and social welfare compatible. The political culture had been thoroughly transformed and infused with democratic values. The extremes of left and right found no foothold in the new republic, whose Basic Law (q.v.) had become almost universally accepted and respected by its citizens. He left his countrymen a legacy of hope, freedom, and respect abroad. He anchored the FRG in the West, strongly supported the steps toward building a united Europe, and crowned his foreign policy achievements with a rapprochement with France which served as the two-headed pillar for that united Europe. (See also FEDERAL REPUBLIC OF GERMANY, FOUNDATION.)

ADENAUER, AND FORMER NAZIS.   Some Germans found Adenauer to be too lenient toward former Nazis (q.v.) and all too willing to hire for top positions men with brown-tainted careers, such as his right-hand man Heinrich Globke, who had written the commentaries for the Nuremberg Jewish Laws. Adenauer, whom nobody suspected of ever having Nazi inclinations, spoke of the problem of creating a new democracy with persons who had been either too old or too young to have been politically active during Hitler's rule. "We can't use those in between because they were in the [Nazi] party." Even the SPD (q.v.) found it expedient to show leniency toward those who had turned away from National Socialism. Several Christian Democrats with whom they had to work during the Grand Coalition (q.v.) had embarrassing pasts, including Chancellor Kiesinger (q.v.), who had worn an SS uniform and worked in the propaganda section of the foreign ministry.

ADORNO, THEODOR (1903-1969).   Director of Institute for Social Research in Frankfurt am Main.

AGADIR CRISIS (1911) see EMPIRE, FOREIGN POLICY

AGRICULTURE. Agriculture is fairly efficient in the West, which was able to produce about three-fourths of western Germany's food needs. This is remarkable, considering that before the war the western part of Germany was predominantly industrial, whereas the eastern part was the country's agricultural bread basket. The main crops are flour and feed grains, potatoes, sugar beets, vegetables, fruits and wine, and most farmers also raise livestock, mostly cattle. Government-sponsored land consolidation schemes have raised the number of large and medium-sized farms considerably, although small farms still predominate in the West. Cooperatives, which link together about three-fourths of the western farms, strengthen small farmers' competitiveness. Western German farmers exercise impressive political clout; they have been able to prevent the Bonn government in GATT negotiations from accepting freer trade in agriculture, which the Americans especially demand.

   Agriculture was collectivized in East Germany in 1958, creating large collective farms and fields. Many former owners retained title to their land, but it was non-negotiable and therefore worthless to them. In the GDR (q.v.) 12 percent of the work force was engaged in agriculture, compared with only 5 percent in western Germany. Farmers in the East enjoyed certain privileges, compared with their countrymen in industry: they escaped the worst pollution, many had their own homes and private plots, they were heavily subsidized, and they enjoyed the time off and sick leave that private farmers in the West do not have. Despite the large scale of their farms, East German farmers produced only 40 percent as much per capita as their western German counterparts, although they had made the GDR self-sufficient in food. Like everybody else in the East, farmers are undergoing a tortured transition to other jobs or to a forgotten form of private agriculture. The former collective farms are strangled with debt.

AHLEN PROGRAM (CDU) see SCHUMACHER, KURT

AHLERS, CONRAD (1922-1980). SPD, leader of the press office and state minister (1969-72). (See also SPIEGEL AFFAIR.)

ALBRECHT, HANS see HONECKER, ERICH

ALBRECHT, SUSANNE see TERRORIST GROUPS

ALL-GERMAN LEAGUE (ALLDEUTSCHER VEREIN). Along with the German Colonial Society and the "Fleet League," the All-German League mounted a powerful propaganda campaign after 1890 to support Germany's efforts to become a world power and to build a fleet commensurate with that striving. Their goals were not always observed by the government, but their influence in public opinion became a major consideration in the minds of Germany's rulers.

ALL-GERMAN PARTY (GESAMTDEUTSCHE PARTEI--GDP). This party arose to represent the views of German refugees from the East, but it received only 2.8 percent of the votes in the 1961 Bundestag elections and then disappeared.

ALL-GERMAN PEOPLE'S PARTY (GESAMTDEUTSCHE VOLKSPARTEI--GVP). In August 1950, Gustav Heinemann resigned as CDU (qq.v.) federal interior minister and founded this party, which had only one objective--to prevent German rearmament. He and those who supported this party argued that rearmament was not only immoral, but it also made German reunification (q.v.) more difficult to achieve. Like the philosopher, Karl Jaspers (q.v.), Heinemann believed that Germany should set a high moral example to the rest of the world after the crimes of the Third Reich (q.v.). This party was short-lived, but it helped create the backing and momentum for the anti-rearmament movement, especially the "Ohne-mich" (q.v.) campaign.

ALLEMANN, FRITZ RENE see JASPERS, KARL

ALLIANCE FOR GERMANY (ALLIANZ FÜR DEUTSCHLAND) see DEMOCRATIC AWAKENING; REUNIFICATION

ALLIANCE OF FREE DEMOCRATS. An East German non-communist party at the time of the GDR (q.v.) elections on March 18, 1990, which won 5.28 percent of the votes. It was sponsored by the FDP (q.v.) and was a combination of three small Liberal parties--German Forum Party (DFP), Liberal Democratic Party (LDP), and eastern FDP.

ALLIANCE 90 (BÜNDNIS 90). This is an electoral union of New Forum, the citizens' group " Democracy Now," and "Initiative Peace and Human Rights," all groups of East Germans who had been active in the 1989 revolutionary movement from the start. It wanted, at least temporarily, to preserve the GDR's (q.v.) independence. In the March 18, 1990 elections it won only 2.9 percent of the votes. In the December 1990 Bundestag elections, it won seats because of the special rules applying to that election alone. (See also ELECTIONS 1990; GERMAN DEMOCRATIC REPUBLIC; GREENS.)

ALLIED CITY COMMAND FOR BERLIN. This was created after the Second World War (q.v.) to facilitate Four-Power control over Berlin. However, the outbreak of the Cold War exacerbated the serious differences between the victorious Western Allies and the Soviet Union, which left the Allied City Command for Berlin on June 16, 1948. Thereupon, the three Western Allies created a Three-Power Command, which approved the election of Ernst Reuter (q.v.) as mayor of West Berlin in December 1948. Since November 20, 1948, Friedrich Ebert (q.v.) functioned as mayor of the eastern sector of Berlin controlled by the Soviet Union. In 1949, East Berlin was declared to be the capital of the newly-formed GDR (q.v.).

ALLIED CONTROL COUNCIL (ALLIERTER KONTROLLRAT). On November 14, 1944, the U.S., U.K., and Soviet Union, joined later that month by France, agreed that after Germany's defeat sovereign power in that country would be exercised by the supreme commanders of the four victorious Allies. This was confirmed at the Potsdam Conference (q.v.) in July 1945. Each commander would be supreme in his own country's zone of occupation, and an Allied Control Council in Berlin, which was first presented to the public on August 30, 1945, would deal with questions involving all of Germany, such as voiding Nazi laws, denazification (q.v.), demilitarization, dismantling of industries as reparations (q.v.), and the creation of a unified economy. Major problems were that all decisions had to be unanimous, and the Control Council had no executive power of its own. It was dependent on the individual commanders to carry out its decisions. It was further weakened by the emergence of the Cold War and the resulting distrust among the Allies, by differences even among Western Allies as the French had different views than the U.S. and U.K., and finally by divergent developments in the four zones. The last meeting was on March 20, 1948, when the Soviet representative stormed out in protest against the policies of the other three powers. (See also ALLIED OCCUPATION.)

G.I. surrounded by German children. (Photo by U.S. Army Signal Corps. *Source:* GCML, Lexington, Virginia)

ALLIED HIGH COMMISSION (ALLIIERTE HOCHKOMMISSION). The Petersberg Agreement (q.v.), signed on November 22, 1949, nullified both the occupation statute and the Allied High Commission, which was composed of civilian officials from the victorious powers who had replaced the supreme military commanders as representatives of their respective countries in Germany.

ALLIED OCCUPATION OF GERMANY. The Soviet Union and Poland annexed large chunks of German territory in the East, and Germany was reduced to about three-fourths its prewar size. What remained of Germany was divided into four occupation zones: the Soviet zone was former East Germany; the British zone was in the North; the French zone was in the Southwest and the American zone was in Bavaria, Hesse and the port of Bremerhaven in the North. Berlin was also divided into four sectors. Full power was in the hands of the four Allied commanders, who bore enormous burdens in bringing order to the chaos, feeding the population, reestablishing a tolerable economic situation and creating political conditions which would make impossible the return of National Socialism.

The Allies tried to work together, and the United States even pulled its troops out of Saxony and Thuringia in July 1945 in order to honor its agreement on occupation zones established at Yalta in February 1945. Also in July, the leaders of the three major Allies--the Soviet Union, the United States and Great Britain--met at Potsdam, outside of Berlin, to discuss Germany's future. France had not taken part in the Yalta Conference and, to the ire of General de Gaulle, was not invited to the Potsdam meeting.

There were many disagreements on details, but the three basically agreed that Germany should be denazified (q.v.), that the Oder-Neisse (q.v.) frontier would at least temporarily be the border between Germany and Poland, that Germans in Hungary, Czechoslovakia and Poland would be transferred to Germany, that Germany would be required to pay reparations (q.v.) as long as these payments would "leave enough resources to enable the German people to subsist without external assistance," that "during the period of occupation Germany shall be treated as a single economic unit," that the German political structure would be decentralized, and finally that German political life should be reconstructed on a democratic basis.

It soon became obvious that Allied cooperation was impossible, given the differing definitions of such terms as "democratic" and the four victors' greatly different security and political objectives in Europe. The Allies' disharmony was West Germany's opportunity and permitted it to rise quickly from the ashes of defeat. Talks involving the political and economic future of Germany stalled, and American soldiers became impatient to go home. Toward the end of 1945 there were spontaneous GI demonstrations in Paris and Frankfurt which left no doubt in the minds of American leaders that the large part of the three million U.S. soldiers in Europe had to be demobilized very quickly. GIs were sent back to the U.S. at a stunningly fast rate; clearly a long occupation of Germany was not among American plans. Nor was a permanent feeding and economic subsidy of a part of the German people among those aims. Despite the agreements at Potsdam, Germany was not operating as an economic unit. It had become increasingly clear to U.S. leaders that the resulting prolongation of German poverty and economic stagnation would not only greatlyharm Germany's neighbors, who were traditionally dependent upon trade with Germany, but would perhaps make Germany vulnerable to communist appeals.

American leaders soon became convinced that U.S. policy should shed all its punitive aspects and shift toward wholehearted support of the democratic potential in Germany. The former aspects had been advocated by President Roosevelt's treasury secretary, Henry Morgenthau, who had wished forcefully to change Germany from an industrialized nation back to an agrarian society. His proposals had never become official U.S. policy, but elements of it had been incorporated in the official American occupation guideline, JCS 1067. However, U.S. Secretary of State James Byrnes announced in Stuttgart on September 6, 1946 a significant change in U.S. policy. In the opera house of that bombed-out city, he aimed to quiet German fears by assuring them that "as long as an occupation force is required in Germany the army of the United States will be part of that occupation force." He went on to propose a greater measure of German self-government and, as a first step, the merging of the American and British zones. A British observer commented on the dramatic effect of this speech: "At the time they were spoken these were bold words and they came to the millions of Germans who had heard or read them as the first glimmer of dawn after a long, dark night. Their moral impact was incalculable." (See also OFFICE OF MILITARY GOVERNMENT U.S.)

ALSACE AND LORRAINE see FRANCO-PRUSSIAN WAR

ALTDORFER, ALBRECHT (1480-1538). A contemporary of Dürer and Grünewald (qq.v.), Altdorfer was known as the master of the Danube School. He is mainly recognized for his landscapes, the most famous being *The Battle of Arebela*. He also did woodcuts and engravings.

ALTMEIER, PETER see LAND PRINCES

AMERICA, GERMAN ATTITUDES TOWARD AND EXODUS TO. One of the many consequences of the seemingly perpetual war and religious strife was that many beleaguered sects, such as the Mennonites, Quakers and Dunkers, decided to seek their peace and happiness in the New World. There they could escape the political and religious hierarchy, as well as the earthly corruption into which the European nobility had apparently fallen. The first German immigrants to America tended to settle in New York, Maryland and Virginia, but in 1681 William Penn established the first religiously free state in Pennsylvania. The German exodus to Pennsylvania began with 13 Mennonite families from Krefeld in Westphalia, who landed in Philadelphia on October 6, 1683, a day still celebrated in some parts of the United States as "German Day." They created Germantown on the outskirts of Philadelphia. They were followed by the Moravians, so-called because they came from the Hapsburg province of Moravia, and the Amish (erroneously called Pennsylvania "Dutch") from the area of Bern, Switzerland, who have retained to this day, in large part, most aspects of a life style characteristic of pious Germans in the 17th century, including the Bern dialect of German.

Not all Germans found in America the "quiet, honest and God-fearing life" of which they had dreamed, but their reports back to Germany helped open the flood gates for further waves of refugees from religious persecution in the 18th century. One Protestant group from the area of Brunswick set sail in 1707 for New York, but unfavorable winds forced them to land in Philadelphia. They decided to settle in New Jersey, which in 1733 became the home of an immigrant named Johann Peter Rockefeller, who founded one of the world's richest families. By 1776 there were more than 250,000 Germans living in the thirteen colonies. Germany's religious quarrels were America's gain.

The American Revolution had sparked the imagination of many literate Germans. The Americans were celebrated as the "Hellenes of our time," who, by challenging the exclusive rule of the "breed of the nobility," had shown feudal Europe the way to "sweet equality." The greatest German poet of all time was Johann Wolfgang von Goethe, who along with Friedrich Schiller (qq.v.) was the greatest advocate of both the impetuous Storm and Stress (q.v.: a literary age when writers rebelled against the restraints of classicism and the enlightenment) and the restrained Classical period in German literature during the second half of the 18th and early part of the 19th centuries. Goethe wrote in *Poetry in Truth* that the youthful United States was "a magnificent country," "a magnet for the eyes of the whole world." He wrote "America, your lot is fairer than ours." In 1781, Friedrich Klopstock wrote a hymn to the new nation entitled "The Present War." It said, among other things, "You are the rose dawn of a great new day . . . that will last for centuries." Two years later an anonymous poet gave expression to the popular feeling: "The nations of all Europe will respond with echoes of this holy victory."

As was the case after Hitler (q.v.) jolted Germany with his brutal intolerance after 1933, America greatly profited from the events which shook Germany in 1848-49. Revolutionaries and sympathizers fled by the thousands to the United States, which had been one of the few countries in the world to send a message of encouragement to the Frankfurt Parliament. These German exiles brought their ideals and their zeal with them, and many of them spoke out elegantly against slavery, streamed into the new Republican Party and fought mainly on the side of the North during the Civil War. Frederick Hecker organized an all-German regiment for Lincoln; the young Graf (Count) Ferdinand von Zeppelin (q.v.) made his first ascent in a balloon in America and acted as an aerial observer for the North in the Civil War.

The former leaders of the Baden Revolutionary Army, Franz Siegel and Carl Schurz (q.v.), fought for the North. Siegel led an army in the Battle of New Market on May 15, 1864 against Confederate units which included the Virginia Military Institute corps of cadets. Partly because of the young cadets' legendary bravery, Siegel's forces were badly beaten. Schurz was a particularly towering figure among the "1848ers." He campaigned for Lincoln in the 1860 election, was named by the winner as ambassador to Madrid, but he resigned this post later in order to return to America to command a division in the Union Army. Under President Rutherford B. Hayes he was Secretary of the Interior and introduced civil service reform and advocated the integration of the Indians into American society.

The end of the American Civil War stimulated even greater numbers of Germans to seek a better life in America. In the years between 1866 and 1896 Germans were the largest immigrant group to go to America, reaching a peak of a half million in 1882, or more than two-thirds of all immigrants in that year. In fact, Germans led in overall immigration between 1820 and 1920, and in 1907 alone 1.3 million Germans arrived in the United States. Most settled in the quadrangle of New York-Minneapolis-St.Louis-Baltimore, where they established German communities with their own schools, newspapers, churches, hospitals and clubs. They also opened breweries and beer gardens. Their habit of engaging in more pleasant Sunday activities, such as sponsoring band contests, festivals, or simply walking with the family or chatting in a beer garden, contributed to lightening the Sunday severity found all too often in 19th century America.

AMERICA, GERMAN PERCEPTIONS OF. Perhaps nothing is more noticeable for visitors to the FRG than the attachment of Germans, especially youth, to virtually anything which is American. On the radio, one hears far less German music than American and British. As a form of protest against the massive influence of American culture, there was a tendency among youths in the "alternative scene" to avoid English expressions and to insist upon German-language music. By 1986 this "new wave" had run its course in rock music, and the trend was back to English lyrics. Only two out of the top 30 singles were sung in German, even though a third of the songs had been produced in German-speaking countries. For young singers, sales outside of Germany were more important than nationalist urges. Even the CDU's 1990 electoral campaign was sung in English: "Feel the power, touch the future, reach the heart!"

There is seldom an evening in which an American television show cannot be seen. Jeans, T-shirts and jogging shoes are worn by young Germans, who crowd into fast-food chains such as McDonald's and Burger King, found in every city of any size. Their parents often shop in large supermarkets or shopping centers or fill their cars' tanks at gasoline stations which seem to offer everything from groceries and magazines to car washes. American slang has mightily invaded the German language, and young people, businessmen and scholars seldom express themselves for long without using some English words. But, unlike many French, most Germans do not seem to be distressed by this linguistic invasion.

The *Financial Times* quoted the deputy editor of the daily *Die Welt,* who discovered that one could write German articles while using hardly any German words: "Unser Way of Life im Media Business ist hart, da muss man ein tougher Kerl sein. Morgens Warm-up und Stretching, dann ein Teller Corn Flakes und ein Soft Drink oder Darjeeling Tea, dann in das Office--und schon Brunch mit den Top-Leuten, meeting zum Thema: Sollen wir die Zeitung pushen mit Snob Appeal oder auf Low Profile achten? Ich habe den Managern ganz cool und businesslike mein Papier presentiert: Wir müssen News powern und erst dann den Akzent auf Layout und Design legen, auf der Front Page die Headline mehr aufjazzen und die Deadline beachten. Für jede Story brauchen wir ein starkes Lead. Der Cartoon muss gut plaziert sein. Das Editorial muss Glamour und Style haben, unsere Top Priority bleibt: Action und Service!"

Many German protest movements, such as those against war, for women's and minorities' rights and in favor of environmental protection, are largely based on American examples. Never have more Germans visited the United States than in the 1980s and 1990s. Scholars and students especially find it important to work or study for a time in the U.S.

Despite the undeniable and seemingly irresistible attraction which many Germans have toward aspects of American culture, many observers, including some Germans, have noted anti-Americanism in the FRG. But, in fact, only among the militant leftist circles does this come blatantly to the surface. Anti-American sentiments are largely silent among a part of the politicized youth and left-leaning intellectuals. Anti-Americanism, to the extent that it exists, should not be confused with criticism directed against certain American policies, such as high military budgets or tacit support for authoritarian regimes in the Third World, policies which are also criticized within the U.S. Nor should anti-Americanism be seen in terms of a general aversion to the U.S. or its people.

Criticism of America is more a general way of expressing anti-capitalist, anti-growth attitudes. It involves cultural rejection of a scientific and technical civilization which the U.S. seems to represent. It is also an outgrowth of a conflict between generations. On the one hand is an older generation in the West which admired American democracy and prosperity and which has never forgotten the Marshall Plan (q.v.) and the U.S. defense of West Berlin in the late 1940s and 1950s. One TV journalist said at the time of reunification: "We had help from the Americans, who had thought carefully about what should become of Germany, and this enabled us to make something of ourselves." Chancellor Kohl (q.v.) frequently told campaign audiences in the East that if they had been occupied by the Americans, their lives would have been as democratic and prosperous as in the West. On the other hand, a younger generation grew up amidst material prosperity and talk of detente. Their political consciousness was shaped at a time when the shock waves of severe racial tension in American cities, the Vietnam War and Watergate were being felt outside the U.S. In East Germany much propaganda had been directed against America, but polls reveal very little anti-Americanism there.

More than anything else, anti-Americanism means protest against the prevailing culture of the westernized FRG. It is linked with longings, observable in other Western European countries and the U.S. as well, to drop out of a highly competitive, urbanized society oriented toward comfort, economic prosperity and individual success, and to adopt so-called alternative forms of living which are poorly defined. Thus, anti-Americanism is less a political call to arms against the U.S. than it is a code word for a change of values among a part of contemporary German younger people which embodies a conflict among several cultures within the FRG itself.

Anti-Americanism is statistically almost invisible. How little overall impact anti-American tendencies have on the West German population is revealed by virtually every opinion poll which seeks to measure it. Opinion polls have consistently indicated that more Germans would want to emigrate to America if they had to leave their own country than to any other country in the world, and that more would want to be Americans than any other nationality, if, in some hypothetical situation, they could no longer be Germans.

One frequently hears cliches in Germany about Americans: that they always chew gum, wear their pants too short, generally dress tastelessly (in loud colors, plaid pants, and Bermuda shorts), are fanatic joggers and sport addicts. Some Germans find that many Americans are overweight, uncultured, slightly naive and politically uninformed about the rest of the world, even though Americans have an almost missionary desire to spread the American way of life. Yet, opinion polls reveal different, more positive descriptions of Americans: that they have a good business sense, are individualistic, energetic, patriotic, progressive and technically talented. Less than a fifth of all Germans consider Americans to be ill-mannered or ruthless, and only 4 percent consider them to be insecure.

Except in certain areas where there are large concentrations of American soldiers, Americans and Germans mingle rather well with each other although there are differences between them. Like some other European nationalities, Germans tend to be more private than Americans. They often do not know their neighbors and are more apt to put fences around their houses to ensure their privacy. They also observe certain social conventions which slow down the development of intimate social contact. For instance, the German language has two different words for "you." The German says *Sie* if he wants to keep formal and at a distance and *Du* if he wants to be more familiar. The English equivalent of a formal "you," "Thee," fell into disuse years ago, even among small religious sects which had retained it. In Germany, colleagues who have worked with each other for years might still address each other as *Herr* (Mr.), *Frau* (Mrs.) or *Fräulein* (Miss). There is no German equivalent to Ms.!

Europeans, including Germans, are uncomfortable about answering such personal questions when one first meets as where one works, for whom one voted, or how one acquired a certain painting or piece or furniture in his abode, questions which the American generally feels free to ask in order to open a conversation. This is not to say that Germans do not form firm friendships. They certainly do, even if it takes longer to do so. But while Germans seem to like the more relaxed American manner, they do generally recognize and mildly criticize the superficial aspect of Americans' personal interaction. Unlike most Americans, Germans tend not to call other people by their first names and to use casual expressions like "drop by sometime," unless they really mean it and wish to give an unmistakable signal of friendliness to a person.

AMERICAN INSTITUTE FOR CONTEMPORARY GERMAN STUDIES (AICGS). Located in Washington D.C. and affiliated with Johns Hopkins University, the AICGS is a major hub for scholarly contacts between Americans and German leaders. Its goals are to help develop a new generation of American scholars with a thorough knowledge of the political, economic, societal, and cultural dimensions of Germany and to deepen the American public's understanding of German affairs. Its director is Robert Gerald Livingston, whose deputy is Jackson Janes.

ANDERSON, LALA see MARLEEN, LILI

ANSCHLUSS. This word refers to the union of Germany and Austria in 1938. After the First World War (q.v.), the German portion of the collapsed Austro-Hungarian Empire wanted to join Germany, but this was forbidden by the victorious Allies in the Treaties of Versailles (q.v.) and St. Germain. There was agitation for unity in Austria during the 1920s, and Germany supported this when the Austrian, Adolf Hitler (q.v.), became German chancellor in 1933. In February 1938, Hitler requested a meeting with Austria's Chancellor Kurt von Schuschnigg at Berchtesgaden to demand concessions for Austrian Nazis (q.v.). When Schuschnigg tried to delay Hitler by a plebiscite to underscore Austrian independence, Hitler issued an ultimatum on March 11, 1938, demanding the resignation of Schuschnigg, who was replaced by the Austrian Nazi, Arthur Seyss-Inquart, who invited the German army to occupy Austria, which it did on March 12, 1938. Seyss-Inquart declared the union of the two countries the next day. On April 10, the Nazis conducted a plebiscite which showed, according to Nazi figures, 99.75 percent in favor of the union.

ANTI-COMINTERN PACT (1936). On November 25, 1936, Germany and Japan agreed to oppose international communism. Italy joined the Pact in November 1937. Japan's price was recognition of its puppet regime in Manchuria. In September 1940, these three countries became the initial signatories of the Tripartite Pact (q.v.). (See also BERLIN-ROME AXIS.)

ANTI-SEMITISM. Conscious of the magnitude of the crimes that Germans committed against Jews during the Third Reich (q.v.), the post-war German democracy has always forbidden any public expression of anti-Semitism. The taboo against voicing anything critical of Jews was demonstrated by the fact that Shakespeare's *Merchant of Venice* was not shown in the FRG for years. Other plays, such as Rainer Fassbinder's *Garbage, the City and Death*, were prevented from opening because of unacceptable anti-Semitic language used. The FRG has not hidden the horrors of the Holocaust (q.v.) from school curricula, has provided restitution (q.v.) to Jewish victims of Nazism, and made every effort to support the state of Israel diplomatically. In general, the 40,000 or so Jews who reside in the FRG since the war have not suffered discrimination and indignity. In 1993, Stasi (q.v.) records were uncovered which revealed that in the 1960s and 1970s East German agents in the FRG had manipulated leftist groups, Jews, intellectuals, and Nazi sympathizers in a campaign to discredit Bonn by persuading the world that West Germany remained a hotbed of racism and revanchism.

It was an understandable shock to Jews in and out of Germany to see the defacement of Jewish monuments and memorials become almost commonplace in the wake of reunification (q.v.), especially in the autumn of 1992. In September, the former Sachsenhausen concentration camp in Oranienburg near Berlin, including the "Jewish Barracks," was set on fire ten days after the first visit ever to a concentration camp by an Israeli prime minister. In October, vandals damaged a Jewish cemetery for slave laborers at the Ueberlingen labor camp, a satellite of Dachau near Munich, and the Ravensbrück concentration camp for women was firebombed. When right-wing youth threw Molotov cocktails into hostels for foreigners in Rostock, the Berlin-based Central Council for Jews in Germany issued a statement that the cheering by bystanders was reminiscent of the popular support Hitler (q.v.) had received in 1933. Jerzy Kanal, chairman of the Jewish Community of Berlin, said the Rostock violence reminded many Jews of the infamous Crystal Night in 1938. He noted that "the entire Jewish community is disturbed. We could hardly have imagined that such a thing is again possible today in Germany."

Such racist outrages occur in many European countries, but in Germany the combination of historical memory and severe economic unrest arouses particular international interest in such things. Although Chancellor Kohl (q.v.) called the attacks "a disgrace for our land," his government was unable to do much about them. The common thread between the wave of hostility toward foreigners and the pre-1945 anti-Semitism in Germany is the search for scapegoats for social misfortune. The most visible targets for the economically discontented are now the refugees who pour into Germany. But violence-prone hoodlums in Germany know that the best way to get international publicity is to deface Jewish shrines and spout anti-Semitic slogans. This does not diminish the embarrassment and shame for such acts. But the political culture of the FRG cannot be compared to that of the Weimar Republic or the Third Reich (qq.v.). The leader of Germany's Jewish community, Ignatz Bubis, was right when he screamed at anarchists pelting President von Weizsäcker (q.v.), who was pleading for tolerance: "I am ashamed of what has happened here. We are not in 1938, but in 1992!"

(See also GALINSKI, HEINZ; HOLOCAUST; NATIONAL DEMOCRATIC PARTY OF GERMANY; NUREMBERG LAWS; RESTITUTION TO JEWS.)

ANTI-SOCIALIST LAW see BISMARCK, DOMESTIC POLICY

APEL, HANS (1932-). SPD, federal finance minister (1974-78) and defense minister (1978-82).

APPEASEMENT POLICY see MUNICH AGREEMENT

ARMED FORCES, FEDERAL see BUNDESWEHR

ARMINIUS (18/16 B.C.-19/22 A.D.). A Germanic tribal chief, later known to Germans as Hermann. (See ROMANS IN GERMANY.)

ARNOLD, KARL see LAND PRINCES

ART NOUVEAU (JUGENDSTIL). The name originated from the journal *Jugend* (meaning "Youth") established in Munich in 1896. It was a reaction at the turn of the century to mass production and the ugliness of industrialization and included architecture, painting, drama, interior decor, and literature. It is characterized by excessive ornamentation, unusual lines, and themes of nature and animals.

ARTICLE 48 (PRESIDENTIAL DECREE POWER) see WEIMAR REPUBLIC

ARTICLE 231 (WAR GUILT CLAUSE). This clause in the Versailles Treaty (q.v.) assigned all guilt for the outbreak and conduct of the First World War (q.v.) to Germany and its allies. It was incomprehensible even to many Germans who were willing to admit that Germany was partly responsible, and it became a hated symbol of Germany's post-war humiliation which played into the hands of right-wing political groups which wished to profit from Germany's dissatisfaction. (See also VERSAILLES TREATY.)

ASSOCIATION OF PUBLIC BROADCASTING CORPORATIONS (ARD) see RADIO AND TELEVISION

AUGSBURG, PEACE OF (1555). The new Protestant faith spread quickly throughout northern Germany and Scandinavia. By 1555, about four-fifths of all Germans had embraced the new belief. In that year the Peace of Augsburg was reached which recognized that the Protestant faith had an equal status with the Catholic and that each territorial prince and free city would decide which faith should be practiced by all residents under their control. *Cuius regio, eius religio* ("whoever rules chooses the religion") was the formula for a kind of religious freedom which was restricted to the rulers. Those subjects who could not accept their rulers' preference had to move to another territory or city, and thousands of Germans did just that. Thus, the religious division of Germany was sealed for centuries. (See also THIRTY-YEARS WAR.)

AUGSTEIN, RUDOLF (1923-). Publisher of *Der Spiegel*. (See also SPIEGEL AFFAIR.)

AUSCHWITZ LIE see NATIONAL DEMOCRATIC PARTY OF GERMANY

AUSSERPARLAMENTARISCHE OPPOSITION (EXTRA-PARLIAMENTARY OPPOSITION--APO) see GRAND COALITION

AUSTRIAN STATE TREATY (1955) see NORTH ATLANTIC TREATY ORGANIZATION

AUSTRO-PRUSSIAN WAR (1866) see BISMARCK, OTTO VON

AUTONOMOUS ANARCHIST GROUPS OF THE UNDOGMATIC LEFT. These groups renounce strict organizational structures and are extremely divided over aims and whether to utilize violent or non-violent action in order to change society. Their numbers grew in the last years of the 1980s. They maintain "Info-Stores" and "Libertarian Centers" in more than 50 cities. They were generally skeptical of the collapse of the GDR and of communism in Eastern Europe, seeing in it a "capitalist reunification" and a capitulation to the blackmail of multinational corporations. The diverse autonomous anarchist groupings within the undogmatic New Left tend to be tiny, loosely organized, short-lived and prone to violence. They attract several thousand predominantly young people, who engage in "solidarity actions" to support third-world liberation movements. But their contacts with like-minded left-extremist groups outside the FRG were sporadic and generally limited to specific actions. (See FEDERATION OF VIOLENCE-FREE ACTION GROUPS; FREE WORKERS' UNION; and SPONTIS.)

-B-

BAADER, ANDREAS (1944-1977) and BAADER-MEINHOF BAND see TERRORIST GROUPS

BACH, JOHANN SEBASTIAN (1685-1750). Bach was the most famous member of a family from Eisenach which produced six generations of musicians. Bach occupied various musical posts before becoming the court musical director at Köthen in Anhalt. He was appointed choirmaster at St. Thomas' Church, Leipzig, and city music director in 1723, a post he maintained until his death. He wrote numerous orchestral works, suites, and concertos, as well as violin and keyboard concertos. His vocal works include over two hundred cantatas for ecclesiastical use, two secular works and great choral masterpieces like the Christmas and Easter Oratorios and St. Matthew and St. John Passions.

BADEN, PRINCE MAX (MAXIMILIAN ALEXANDER FRIEDRICH WILHELM) VON (1867-1929). When he became chancellor on October 3, 1918, it was the first time in German history a new government was formed with the participation of parliament. Constitutional reforms were introduced which included the voting system, ministerial responsibility to parliament, and control of the armed forces by the government, not by the Kaiser. The latter accepted all these changes but refused to abdicate. Therefore, Max simply announced the abdication on November 9, ordered his aides to begin phoning the newspapers, and resigned on the same day after handing over power to Friedrich Ebert (q.v.). (See also EBERT, FRIEDRICH; REVOLUTION IN GERMANY.)

BAEUCHLE, HANS-JOACHIM (SPD) see WIENAND AFFAIR

BAHR, EGON KARL-HEINZ (1922-). SPD minister for special tasks (1972-74), of economic cooperation (1974-76). A key aide of

Chancellor Willy Brandt (qq.v.) and chief negotiator with the SED. (See also CHANGE THROUGH RAPPROCHEMENT; OSTPOLITIK.)

BAHRO, RUDOLF (1935-). He joined the SED (q.v.) in 1954 and studied philosophy at Humboldt University from 1954-59, after which he pursued the normal career in the SED apparatus. He was a socialist who held numerous middle-level posts in the GDR (q.v.) and grew increasingly critical of those who directed the GDR economy. His dissertation on the formation of specialists in state enterprises was rejected in 1975 on the grounds that it lacked the proper "scientific foundations." The 1968 Warsaw Pact invasion of Czechoslovakia prompted him to begin work on *The Alternative in Eastern Europe*, which was strongly critical of the GDR's system of economic planning and central control. Bahro maintained in this book that the GDR regime had become frozen into a centralized, dictatorial bureaucracy which stifled creativity and economic efficiency. The solution, he argued, was democratization which would make the government answerable to the people. In August 1977, shortly after the book was published in the West, Bahro was arrested and convicted allegedly for betraying state secrets. He served two years of an eight-year sentence. In part thanks to a broad international campaign, he was released and deported to the FRG in 1979. There he became a Green (q.v.) politician, directing his criticism against his newly adopted country.

BANGEMANN, MARTIN (1934-). FDP general secretary from 1973.

BANK DEUTSCHER LÄNDER see BUNDESBANK

BANKELSÄNGER (BENCH SINGER). This is a street singer or "walking newspaper" of the 18th and 19th centuries who sang ballads recounting crimes and catastrophes such as fires, shipwrecks, and mine disasters and then sold posters of a sort (*Schilder*) which illustrated the ballad. The word appeared first in 1709 and refers to the elevated position of a singer standing on a bench.

BARBAROSSA (1122-1190). Emperor Friedrich I was from the Swabian dynasty of Staufen, which from 1138 ruled Germany for about a century. Known as Barbarossa because of his red beard, Friedrich was a strong monarch from the moment he ascended the throne in 1152 at the age of 30. He was a handsome and imposing man, intelligent and well-educated. A highly charismatic figure who attracted loyalty and devotion like a magnet, he was a model knight whose martial skills he continued to display by participating in tournaments until age 60. Despite a determined challenge within Germany by the Saxon duke, his aims were clear: supremacy in northern and central Italy without suppressing the Italian cities' freedoms, and continued influence over the papacy without directly controlling Rome. He wanted to crown his reign with a triumphant crusade, but after forging a mighty army and guiding it toward the Holy Land, he drowned in a river in Saleph in Asia Minor.

After his death a legend was circulated by bards throughout Germany that the red-bearded emperor was not really dead, but instead had sunk into a magic slumber within the mountain of Kyffhäuser, sitting on an ivory throne, his head resting on a marble table. He would leave Kyffhäuser only when his land signaled that it needed his help; if, however, all was in order, ravens would fly around the mountain, and Barbarossa would return to his sleep for another hundred years.

BARBIE, KLAUS. Known as the "Butcher of Lyon" for the atrocities he supervised as Nazi (q.v.) chief in that French city during the German occupation in the Second World War (q.v.), he was captured in Latin America and sentenced to life in prison by a French court in July 1987.

BARLACH, ERNST (1870-1938). Son of a doctor who is best known as a sculptor, graphic artist, dramatist and novelist. He studied art in Dresden, Hamburg and Paris. His style was inspired by a trip to Russia in 1906. His brooding search for God and the somberness of his vision are reflected in his expressionistic figures reminiscent of medieval times. Although he received numerous honors, Barlach's art was regarded as degenerate by the Nazis (q.v.), and his works were destroyed or impounded in 1937. Barlach's most important literary works were written when he was over forty. He received the Kleist Prize for Literature in 1924.

BARMEN DECLARATION (1934) see CONFESSING CHURCH

BAROQUE. This term applies to a 17th century style of painting, architecture, sculpture, music and literature and is derived from the Portuguese word, *barocco,* which means an irregularly shaped pearl. Its features are bombastic, dynamic, inflated, and superlative. Its ornateness and rich expression show a preoccupation with the yearnings of man for a higher spiritual existence. Ornamental devices such as the metaphor, simile, symbol, and allegory were employed to heighten the effect of the literary work. German literature made rapid progress thanks to Martin Opitz's book containing prescribed rules and patterns for courtly and religious poetry. Andreas Gryphius is one of the most outstanding poets and tragic dramatists of this period.

BARSCHEL, UWE (1944-1987). In 1987, revelations appeared that this young CDU minister president of Schleswig-Holstein had used dirty tricks, such as having anonymous tips concerning his challenger's (Björn Engholm, q.v.) sex life and tax payments given to the press during the Land election campaign. After denying the allegations and winning the election, it became clear that he had indeed used such tricks. Barschel committed suicide in Switzerland and unleashed emotional soul-searching in the FRG over political campaign practices. This scandal also hurt Gerhard Stoltenberg (q.v.), leader of the Schleswig-Holstein CDU (q.v.). In May 1988, the SPD took power in Kiel.

BARTH, KARL. Born in 1886 in Basel, Barth worked in Bonn, where he was a prominent figure in existentialism and crisis theology. Summing up his views in *The Knowledge of God and the Service of God* (1938), he argued that crisis lies in the triumph of faith over reason. Philosophy is opposed to faith. In his dialectical theology, God is transcendent, insofar as man cannot know the divine mind. Also, man can only trust God for salvation and for the truth of the Christian revelation. The chaos of human affairs demonstrates how helpless man is in dealing with life.

BARZEL, RAINER (1924-). CDU minister for all-German questions (1962-63), for inner-German relations (1982-83), party chairman (1971-73), CDU chancellor candidate 1972, Bundestag president (1983-84). (See also ELECTIONS 1972; POLITICAL PRISONERS; WIENAND AFFAIR.)

BASIC LAW (GRUNDGESETZ). The Basic Law serves as the FRG's constitution. It reflects several objectives which the founders hoped to achieve: individual freedom, political democracy, stability (to prevent a repetition of the Weimar experience), built-in safeguards against the emergence of another dictatorship, and links with some aspects of the German political tradition. In contrast to the U.S. Constitution, which has a Bill of Rights attached at the end, the Germans placed guarantees for unalienable rights and liberties and the protection of life in the first 20 articles of the Basic Law. Also in contrast with the U.S. document, the Basic Law explicitly grants Germans, who had never experienced a successful democratic revolution, the right of revolution. Article 20 reads in part: " . . .all Germans shall have the right to resist any person or persons seeking to abolish the constitutional order, should no other remedy be possible." (See also DEMOCRACY ON GUARD; FEDERAL REPUBLIC OF GERMANY, FOUNDATION; OVERCOMING THE PAST; PARLIAMENTARY COUNCIL.)

BASIC TREATY (GRUNDLAGENVERTRAG--1972). Treaty between two Germanys. (See OSTPOLITIK.)

BASIS DEMOKRATIE. Term to describe a grass-roots approach to democracy, in which the rank-and-file within the parties and citizens' groups outside them have an important input into policy making. (See also CITIZENS' INITIATIVES.)

BASTIAN, GERT (1923-1992). A soldier in the Second World War (q.v.), he became a Bundeswehr (q.v.) general who was relieved from his command because of his opposition to the Dual-Track Decision and who became a major spokesman for the peace movement (q.v.). He also served in the Bundestag as a Green deputy from 1983-87. Like Petra Kelly (q.v.), he opposed the Green practice of rotating their representatives in the Bundestag. Both became increasingly isolated within the party and reclusive in their private lives. On October 19, 1992, their bodies were found in the house they shared in Bonn. According to the police, Bastian shot Kelly in her sleep and then himself. (See also KELLY, PETRA.)

BATTLE OF THE NATIONS, LEIPZIG (1813) see FRENCH REVOLUTION

BAUDISSIN, W. GRAF VON (1907-) see BUNDESWEHR

BAUHAUS. A comprehensive art school founded in Weimar in 1919 under the official directorship of Walter Gropius (1883-1969). Bauhaus (from the German, *bauen*, to build) offered courses in architecture, music, drama, and painting. It stressed the interdependence of the plastic arts under the primacy of architecture and craftmanship. Notable teachers were Lyonel Feininger (1871-1956), Vasily Kandinsky (1866-1944) and Paul Klee. The Bauhaus was moved to Dessau and then to Berlin where it was closed by the Nazis in 1933. In 1937 the "New Bauhaus" was opened in Chicago with L. Moholy-Nagy (1895-1946) as its director.

BAUHAUS, ULRICH see GUILLAUME AFFAIR

BAUM, GERHART RUDOLF (1932-). FDP (q.v.), federal interior minister from 1977.

BAVARIA PARTY (BAYERNPARTEI). A regional party that survived for a while after the foundation of the FRG, it was able to win a few seats in the first Bundestag.

BAVARIAN PEOPLE'S PARTY (BAYERISCHE VOLKSPARTEI-- BVP). This was the Bavarian affiliate of the Catholic Center Party (q.v.) and the forerunner to the CSU (q.v.).

BAYREUTH. A town in Bavaria best known for the Wagner festival held each summer in the Festspielhaus built by Bavarian King Ludwig II in 1872-76.

BEAMTER (OFFICIAL) see CIVIL SERVICE LAW

BEBEL, AUGUST (1840-1913). SPD politician and co-founder with Wilhelm Liebknecht (q.v.) of the Social Democratic Workers' Party in Eisenach in 1869. He soon became its chairman. In 1875, he also co-founded the Socialist Workers' Party of Germany in Gotha, which became the forerunner of the Social Democratic Party (SPD, q.v.). In 1871, he gained a seat in the new German Reichstag. He strongly opposed war credits, the annexation of Alsace-Lorraine, and Bismarck's foreign policy (q.v.) in general. These positions gained him and his party the reputation of "enemies of the empire" and unreliable. In 1872, he and Liebknecht were imprisoned for two years. He demanded both political and economic equality. He became the government's chief critic after passage of the Socialist Law, arguing that thousands of Social Democrats were being thrown into jail because of their convictions. Despite his strong Marxist convictions, he always advocated the peaceful achievement of SPD objectives, in contrast to such comrades as Rosa Luxemburg (q.v.). He remained SPD leader until his death. (See also BISMARCK, OTTO VON; SOCIAL DEMOCRATIC PARTY OF GERMANY.)

BECK, LUDWIG (1880-1944) see TROTT ZU SOLZ, ADAM VON

BECKER, JUREK (1937-). Son of a Jewish worker who grew up in a ghetto in Poland and later in the concentration camps Ravensbruck and Sachsenhausen. From 1945 he lived in East Berlin where he studied philosophy and worked free-lance for film and television. He received the Heinrich Mann Prize for Literature for his first novel, *Jacob the Liar*, which has been translated into many languages and made into a film. He was expelled from the GDR (q.v.) in 1979 after he protested the earlier eviction of Wolf Biermann (q.v.). After stays in the U.S. and West Berlin he became the city scribe for Bergin-Enkheim.

BECKMANN, MAX (1884-1950). Influenced by the darkest period of Nazi (q.v.) tyranny, this independent and forceful painter expressed cruelty and human suffering with timeless visions of the horrors of his generation. His work was condemned as "degenerate" by Hitler (q.v.).

BEETHOVEN, LUDWIG VAN (1770-1827). Born in Bonn and bullied by his father to become another Mozart, he left school at age eleven and eventually became a court musician. He followed Haydn (q.v.) to Vienna where he remained the rest of his life. Brusque with a difficult personality, Beethoven rejected the system of patronage and became a free-lance musician. After he became completely deaf in 1819, he produced his most powerful and important works. He is considered to be the most original of all German composers, as well as the first "subjective" composer. He wrote nine symphonies for the orchestra, choral works (the Ninth Symphony), stage works and chamber music.

BEHAIM, MARTIN see RENAISSANCE

BELLETRISTIK. This is the German term for fictional as opposed to non-fictional writing.

BENN, GOTTFRIED (1886-1956). This physician wrote poetry while serving in both world wars. He returned to private practice in East Berlin where he continued his poetic activity, experimenting with linguistics and earning a European reputation as one of the greatest and most influential expressionist poets. He was a physician who dissected man with a disgust reaching nihilism. (See also WEIMAR CULTURE.)

BERGHOFER, WOLFGANG (1943-). SED, PDS (qq.v.), mayor of Dresden (1986-90), Berghofer was convicted in February 1992 of election fraud, along with former SED chief in Dresden, Werner Moke. They were charged with rigging the municipal elections in the GDR on May 7, 1989. (See also PARTY OF DEMOCRATIC SOCIALISM.)

BERGMANN-POHL, SABINE (1946-). Elected CDU president of the GDR People's Chamber on April 5, 1990, and as such she exercised the functions of head of state.

BERLIN BLOCKADE (1948-1949). The "Cold War" which resulted from the severe differences between the Soviet Union and the Western Allies ultimately helped seal Germany's division, but it also offered the three Western zones the chance to regain a large part of German sovereignty. The sense that the Western Allies and the West Germans had important common objectives was stimulated by the communist seizure of power in February 1948 in Czechoslovakia, although the country had functioned since 1945 as a parliamentary democracy.

Especially revealing was the blockade of all road and rail routes to Western Berlin from June 1948 until May 1949. This was in response to increasing political and economic unity among the three Western zones, most visible in the currency reform. No doubt the Soviets expected that the Western Allies could be forced to relinquish their rights in Berlin and to abandon the city. The American response was to organize an aerial supply line between the Western zones and the besieged city. This seemingly impossible task (which even included transporting coal!) sparked American and West German imagination and admiration. Several hundred American and British aircraft carried up to 12,000 tons of supplies to Berlin each day. The success of this heroic operation, combined with the effect of adverse world opinion, forced the Soviets to lift the blockade and further cemented West German-American solidarity.

BERLIN, CONFERENCE OF (November 1884 - February 1885). This was a meeting of representatives of 15 nations convened by Otto von Bismarck (q.v.) to ease the tension among the European powers caused by the partition of Central Africa. It gave Bismarck an opportunity to cooperate with France, which had been defeated in the Franco-Prussian War (q.v.).

BERLIN, CONGRESS OF (1878). This was an international conference in June and July convened by Bismarck to establish a balance in southeastern Europe acceptable to the great powers. Among the agreements were the creation of an autonomous principality of Bulgaria, confirmation of the independence of Serbia, Montenegro, and Romania, recognition of Russia's possession of the Caucasus and of Austria-Hungary's right to occupy Bosnia-Herzogovina.

BERLIN TO BAGHDAD RAILWAY. A German company with backing from the government received a concession in 1899 to build a railway from Constantinople to the Persian Gulf. Because German financial interests already dominated the rail net in Central Europe and the Balkans, this project was called the "Berlin-to-Bagdad Railway." It caused friction with the Russians, French, and British which were pacified by early 1914. But only a small line of track had been laid when the First World War (q.v.) broke out, and the project was abandoned.

BERLIN TREATY (1926) see WEIMAR REPUBLIC

BERLIN WALL. Erected on August 13, 1961, it was subsequently "improved" in the 1960s. To the west, a wall of concrete slabs was erected and capped by a wide cylindrical pipe to prevent an easy grip. Behind it was a "death strip" approximately 50 meters wide containing barricades, detectors, watch towers, and guard dogs on long leads. To the east the border was also sealed by a wall so that eastern Germans would not be able to see the barrier as easily as could westerners. The areas adjoining the wall were off limits, and even East Germans living close to it, as well as their families and friends, were required to have special permits or identification to go into the restricted areas. The official demolition of the wall began on June 13, 1990, and the segments were brought to large depots around Berlin and recycled for use in road construction.

BERLIN-ROME AXIS. Between 1936 and 1945, Nazi Germany and fascist Italy were allies. In 1936, the two countries agreed to the "October Protocols" calling for a loose understanding of collaboration. On May 22, 1939, this was upgraded to a formal alliance between the two partners, the so-called "Pact of Steel." (See also ANTI-COMINTERN PACT; TRIPARTITE PACT.)

BERNHARDI, FRIEDRICH VON. In 1912, this retired German general published *Germany and the Next War*, which by 1914 had been released in nine editions and had been translated into almost all major languages in the world, including Japanese. Bernhardi noted that the Germans "have reached a crisis in our national and political developments" and therefore had "the duty to make war." "War is a biological necessity of the first importance, a regulative element in the life of mankind which cannot be dispensed with. . . . Without war, inferior or decaying races would easily choke the growth of healthy, budding elements, and a universal decadence would follow." This book revealed how openly many Germans were already talking about the coming war, and it strengthened many nationalist elements' conviction that an aggressive German policy was right, even if it led to war.

BERNSTEIN, EDUARD (1850-1932). The father of "revisionism" in the SPD (q.v.), Bernstein argued in the late 19th and early 20th centuries that the SPD should seek evolutionary, not revolutionary change in Germany. His moderate, gradualist approach to winning power through elections was anathema to the radicals within his party, but it was very important for the reformed SPD after 1945. (See also KAUTSKY, KARL; SOCIAL DEMOCRATIC PARTY OF GERMANY.)

BESSERWESSI. The Society for German Language chose this word as the "most characteristic" word of 1991. It combines *besser* meaning better with *Wessi*, a derogatory word for western Germans, and is a play on *Besserwisser* or "know-it-all." The winning word for 1992 was *Politikverdrossenheit* (Disaffection with Politics).

BETHMANN HOLLWEG, THEOBALD VON (1856-1921). Imperial chancellor (1909-17) caught between conflicting demands from the Kaiser, armed forces, Reichstag, and public opinion. (See also EMPIRE FOREIGN POLICY, FIRST WORLD WAR; SEPTEMBER PROGRAM.)

BEUMELBURG, WERNER see WEIMAR CULTURE

BIEDENKOPF, KURT HANS (1930-). General secretary of the CDU (1973-77), minister president of Saxony (1990-). A brilliant debater and independent-minded Christian Democrat, he became an influential spokesman for the needs of the eastern Länder after reunification. (q.v.)

BIEDERMEIER. A term referring to a period of literature (1815-1848) and also to a style of decoration and painting in post-Napoleonic Germany, particularly by painters such as Carl Spitzweg (q.v.) and Moritz von Schwind, who emphasized small idyllic details of everyday life. Albert Lortzing's operas are also a product of this period. Biedermeier literature suggests non-controversial topics considered to be apolitical, idyllic, conservative and banal, written during a time of political suppression. This was appropriate for the times. In the three decades following the Congress of Vienna (q.v.) in 1815, Germans were intellectually as divided as ever. The Biedermeier era was a time of relative peace and security in which the bulk of Germans passively accepted the existing political and social orders. Ordinary Germans did not look very far beyond their family and village lives.

BIERMANN, WOLF (1936-). This writer, poet, and composer is the son of a communist dock worker who was killed in Auschwitz in 1943. Wolf moved from Hamburg to East Berlin in 1953. In 1960, Biermann published his first songs which criticized the East German regime. Undaunted by his expulsion from the SED (q.v.), his protest songs continued until they were then banned in 1965. While on tour in the West in 1976, he was finally expelled as an "enemy of the state" and his GDR citizenship was revoked. His case became a symbol of the GDR's repression. Many writers and artists emigrated as a result. He now lives in Hamburg, where he writes and sings and views himself and as a "contemporary critic of world history."

BILDUNGSROMAN. This is a type of novel in which the chief character, after a series of false starts and wrong choices, is led to follow the right path and to develop into a mature, well-balanced individual. This type of novel is more common in German literature than in French or English.

BISMARCK, OTTO VON (1815-1898). Prussian minister president (1862-72 and 1873-90), imperial chancellor (1871-90). During the two decades following the events of 1848-49, Prussia (q.v.) not only steadily increased its industrial base and power, but it moved aggressively to establish the preconditions for German unity under Prussian domination. One step was the submission by the new king, Wilhelm I, of a bill to reorganize and double the size of the army, a measure hotly opposed by a majority in Prussia's lower house. The majority did grant a large sum to

Otto von Bismarck (*Source:* SPP.)

strengthen the existing army units, but when Wilhelm simply used this money to finance his desired reorganization, the parliament refused to grant any more funds until the king canceled his unauthorized army reform. The result was such a serious deadlock and tension that the king reportedly considered resigning. Only a person of extraordinary skill could lead Prussia out of this crisis. That man was Bismarck.

Bismarck's background and reputation seemed to be just what a conservative king like Wilhelm I would have wanted. An East Elbian aristocrat, his disdain for scholarly things and his youthful love of beer-swilling and disorderly conduct had caused him to be banished from the city limits of Göttingen where he had been sent for an unsuccessful year of university study. Yet, since 1850 he had gained much diplomatic experience, first as the Prussian representative to the parliament of the German Confederation in Frankfurt, then as an envoy in St. Petersburg and Paris. These assignments helped him broaden his scope beyond Prussia and conclude that Prussia should become the heart of a unified Germany without Austria. Already in 1856 he had written "Germany is clearly too small for us both . . . In the not too distant future we shall have to fight for our existence against Austria . . . since the course of events in Germany has no other solution."

Appointed Prussian chancellor in 1862, Bismarck was unsuccessful in persuading parliament to accept the king's plans for reforming the army. For a while he simply ignored parliament, but he knew that he could not continue to do so forever. Thus, he decided to initiate a bold foreign policy that would capture the imagination of nationalists and liberals alike and ultimately achieve German unity. The success of this policy won the admiration of many of his countrymen for generations to come.

Bismarck's first years as chancellor of Prussia were ones of armament and war. In 1864, 1866 and 1870, he conducted short but significant wars against Denmark, Austria and France. The war conducted by both Prussia and Austria against Denmark in 1864 over Danish control of the predominantly German-populated territories of Schleswig and Holstein gave Prussian commanders useful battlefield experience. The Prussian victory at Düppel in Jutland also stimulated patriotic feeling in Prussia and in other German states. It weakened liberal opposition to the army reform bill and inclined more and more Germans to look to Prussia for leadership.

It is hardly surprising that the joint administration of Schleswig-Holstein agreed upon by the Prussian and Austrian victors did not go well. Friction was inevitable, and Bismarck was very astute in exploiting it to force a showdown with Austria, which would never have peacefully acquiesced to his designs for German unity. In mid-1866 Bismarck ordered Prussian troops to occupy Holstein, and after declaring the German Confederation dissolved, he declared war on Austria. It lasted only seven weeks. With new breech-loading rifles that had just been used so successfully in the American Civil War, and with the capacity to move their troops to the battlefield on new railroads, the far better prepared Prussians were able to deliver a stinging defeat to the Austrian and Saxon armies at the Battle of Königgrätz. This victory eliminated Austria from the soon-to-be unified Germany.

In July 1867, a North German Confederation composed of 22 German states north of the Main River came into existence, with the king of Prussia as its president. Bismarck's very moderate treatment of the defeated Austrian Empire enabled Prussia to gain in Austria a trustworthy ally for a half century. When, in 1870, Prussia launched its final war to establish German unity, Austria did not support that last active opponent to a united Germany: France. (See FRANCO-PRUSSIAN WAR.)

BISMARCK, ALLIANCE SYSTEM. The limited wars against Denmark, Austria, and France were models of the primacy of political over military objectives. Military actions ceased the moment Bismarck's political objectives were achieved. Faced with demands to crush entire armies or to humiliate defeated enemies through triumphant marches through their capitals, Bismarck always insisted that the business at hand was the conduct of Prussian (q.v.) or German politics, not an attempt to administer "justice" or to humiliate or destroy great powers. Bismarck strove after 1871 to protect what Germany had gained. Above all, he guarded Germany's most vital interest, the European center. He did not allow Germany's attention to be dangerously diverted by numerous colonial adventures. He once said, pointing to a map of Europe: "Here is Russia and here is France, and here we are in the middle. That is my map of Africa."

To ensure Germany's protection, Bismarck built up one of the most complicated and delicate alliance systems ever known in peacetime. He saw Germany threatened from two sides and sought to eliminate this threat by preventing the French and Russians from forming a coalition against Germany. He accomplished this by maintaining friendly relations with Britain, by isolating France diplomatically, and by establishing a "Dual Alliance" with Austria in 1879 and the "Reinsurance Treaty" among Austria, Russia and Germany in 1887. The latter obligated Germany to stand by whichever partner was attacked by the other, thereby discouraging potential aggression from either Austria or Russia. Bismarck did not regard this treaty as incompatible with the Dual Alliance with Austria because in neither agreement was Germany obligated to aid any aggressor. Of course, one factor gave Bismarck great flexibility: he alone could determine guilt for any outbreak of hostilities, and this decision would always have been in accordance with German national interests.

The legacy which Bismarck left Germany was not all positive. His alliance system was exceedingly complicated, and he failed to train successors to continue the policy. His followers, who wished to simplify the alliance system, did not renew the Reinsurance Treaty in 1894. Also, his style of *Realpolitik* (q.v.) demanded great skill, the sober and unimpassioned recognition of the limits of power, the exercise of moderation and the respect of other nations' vital interests.

His successors often imperfectly understood his policies, and they tended to remember the gestures of his statecraft and not its substance. Bismarckian *Realpolitik,* if understood only in fragments, could be a dangerous inheritance for any nation.

BISMARCK, DOMESTIC POLICY. The legacy which Bismarck left German domestic politics was not entirely positive. The German Empire had the outward appearance of being democratic. However, while some other European countries, such as England and France, were in the process of becoming more democratic in practice, Germany was not. It remained a country in which the most important decisions were made by people who were not elected and not directly subject to popular or parliamentary control. Bismarck's skill as a politician prevented a process of democratic reform from gaining any momentum.

The chancellor, like many of his countrymen, felt uncomfortable about political and cultural pluralism in Germany. This was especially revealed in laws which Bismarck introduced to limit the influence of the Catholic Church and the SPD (q.v.). His campaign against the Catholic Church, called the *Kulturkampf* ("Culture Struggle" q.v.), was similar to campaigns conducted in many European countries in the 19th century to limit the Church's influence over education and other social affairs. Bismarck also resented the growth of the Catholic Center Party (q.v.) and suspected that the Vatican was trying to stir up opposition to the Imperial government among the Polish minority within Germany and among the other Catholic countries in Europe. A series of laws whittling away at the Church's privileges was passed starting in 1873, but these laws unleashed such an outcry among Catholics and Protestants alike that Bismarck was forced to repeal most of them by 1881.

The leader was also unable to view German socialists as loyal citizens because of their Marxist revolutionary program and their talk of internationalism. He blamed the socialists for two unsuccessful assassination attempts against the Kaiser in 1877, and in October of the following year he succeeded in persuading parliament to pass an Anti-Socialist Law forbidding all associations which aimed to subvert the existing order or which showed "socialist tendencies." This law forced the SPD to operate underground, crippled the growing labor unions, deprived socialists of the customary protection of the law and drove many of them into exile abroad. Like the laws against the Catholic

Church, this also backfired and actually stimulated an increase in the membership and overall strength of the SPD.

At the same time, Bismarck linked these repressive measure with progressive social welfare laws to help the needy and working classes. The first social insurance laws were introduced in 1881, and in 1883 there came a Sickness Insurance Law, one-third of the premiums for which were to be paid by the employers, and an accident insurance financed entirely by the employers. In 1889, old-age disability insurance financed by employees, employers and the government was introduced. These laws were far in advance of those of any other nation and were the model for the National Insurance Act of 1911 in Britain; not until the 1930s were such programs introduced in the United States by the federal government. Even today, Germans are very proud of their social welfare legislation.

BITBURG CEREMONY (1985) see KOHL, HELMUT and OVERCOMING THE PAST

BITTERFELD MOVEMENT. In 1959, a group of GDR (q.v.) writers launched a literary movement, endorsed by SED leader Walter Ulbricht (qq.v.), calling for writers to put themselves in the shoes of workers by spending some time working in factories or on collective farms before trying to write about life in the GDR. The movement also urged workers to try their hand at writing. However, little came of this.

BIZONIA. The year 1947 saw the end of any possibility that the four victorious Allies could work together in harmony and good faith. The failure of the foreign ministers conference in Moscow in April, the refusal of the Soviet Union to allow itself or those countries under its domination to accept Marshall Plan (q.v.) assistance, the breakdown in June of a meeting of all German Land government chiefs in Munich, and the founding in October of the Cominform in Moscow, designed to coordinate a communist propaganda offensive against the "imperialism of the United States and its Western Allies," all reflected a degeneration of East-West relations.

The year 1948 brought no improvement. In February, the British and Americans created a sort of economic government, which was joined in the summer by the French zone (except the Saar, which was not reunited with Germany until 1957 following a plebiscite). This union, at first called "Bizonia," tightened the links which had already emerged between the two zones. This new body brought together leading German political figures, who began discussing the future German government and thereby established an early foundation for the FRG. Leaders of Bizonia elaborated the future guiding West German economic principle of the "social market economy" (q.v.). Bizonia used the Marshall Plan (q.v.) assistance to improve its citizens' well-being.

BLANK, THEODOR (b. 1905) and DIENSTSTELLE see BUNDESWEHR

BLAUE REITER, DER (THE BLUE RIDER). This was an early 20th century art movement in Munich named after a painting of the same name by Russian painter Vasily Kandinsky. The emphasis was on the emotional and psychological properties of color, line, and shape on canvas prompted by subconscious feelings.

BLOC OF EXPELLEES AND DISENFRANCHISED (BUND DER HEIMATVERTRIEBENEN UND ENTRECHTETEN--BHE). This was one of several refugee parties founded after 1945. The BHE was created in Schleswig-Holstein in 1950 and won 23.4 percent of the votes in its Land election that year to become the second largest party behind the SPD. In 1951, it became a national party. It was weakened by the fact that its top leaders were former Nazis (q.v.). By the end of the 1950s it had been largely absorbed by the CDU (q.v.).

BLOC PARTIES. A term referring to the non-communist parties in the GDR which continued to exist after the formation of the SED (qq.v.) but which collaborated with the Communist-dominated SED in a National Front. They did not include the SPD, which was forced to meld with the KPD (qq.v.) to form the SED. These bloc parties emerged from the German Revolution (q.v.) of 1989 tainted by their earlier collaboration and were treated with some suspicion in both parts of Germany. (See also GERMAN DEMOCRATIC REPUBLIC.)

BLOCH, ERNST (1885-1977). A philosopher and writer, Bloch received a professorship in philosophy at the University of Leipzig, but he had to stop teaching there in 1957 because of political pressure from the SED (q.v.). Four years later he moved to Tübingen in the FRG. A main theme in all his writings was always "the upright human position."

BLOOD AND SOIL (BLUT UND BODEN). A Nazi (q.v.) concept that an organic *Volk* (people) is bound together by blood ties and common roots in a specific territory. Such a concept excluded Jews and other nationalities.

BLÜCHER, GEBHARD VON (1742-1819). A Prussian soldier who fought in the last battles of the Seven Years War (1756-63) and in the campaigns against the French revolutionary armies, he continued to resist Napoleon even after the fall of Berlin in 1806. He was prominent in the 1813 campaign against the French alliance, winning a decisive victory on the Katzbach in Silesia. He fought in the Battle of Leipzig, during which campaign he was made a marshal, and in 1814 he led the Prussian army into France and the heart of Paris. When Napoleon escaped his enforced exile in Elbe, Blücher was given command of the Army of the Lower Rhine. Although wounded by his own cavalry at Ligny, he arrived at Waterloo two days later with reinforcements at a critical time in the battle. In 1814, he was made Prince of Wahlstadt. (See also FRENCH REVOLUTION.)

BLUE ANGEL (DER BLAUE ENGEL). A film produced by Josef von Sternberg in 1929 starring Marlene Dietrich (q.v.) based on the novel, *Professor Unrat*, by Heinrich Mann (q.v.). It was the foundation for one of the most remarkable collaborations between director and star in cinema history.

BLÜM, NORBERT (1935-). CDU specialist for social affairs and minister in the Kohl (q.v.) government.

BÖCKLER, HANS (1875-1951). Chairman of the DGB (1947-51) and effective advocate of co-determination (q.v.). The DGB awards a prize bearing his name to persons strongly supportive of the labor movement.

BOHLEY, BÄRBEL (1945-). A painter and graphic designer, she was spokesperson for the "Women for Freedom" and was arrested several times. She resisted her deportation to the West and was one of the founders of the "New Forum," which was created on September 11, 1989. (See also GERMAN DEMOCRATIC REPUBLIC, COLLAPSE.)

BÖHME, IBRAHIM (1944-). Founder and chairman of the SPD in the GDR (qq.v.) from February to March 1990, but he was forced to resign because of allegations of earlier collaboration with the Stasi (q.v.).

BÖLL, HEINRICH (1917-1985). This former soldier and prisoner of war returned to Germany in 1945 and began his studies in Cologne, where his writing career began. He is considered the best-known author at home and abroad who ever wrote in the FRG. His first novels deal critically and ironically with the social problems of postwar Germany. Catholicism and its role in society is a central theme in his work. An outspoken anti-militarist and critic of the FRG, Böll was the sixth German to receive the Nobel Prize for Literature in 1972. His worldwide success is also due to the simplicity of his language which makes it easily translatable. Böll and his wife Annemarie translated many English authors into German, among them George Bernard Shaw. (See also OVERCOMING THE PAST.)

BONHOEFFER, DIETRICH VON (1906-1945). A young theologian and university lecturer at the time of Hitler's takeover of power in 1933, Bonhoeffer became a leading exponent of the Confessing Church (q.v.). He served for a while as pastor of the German Protestant Church in London before returning to Germany. He was arrested and sent to Flossenburg concentration camp. In the final days of the war, on April 9, 1945, he and other prominent prisoners were executed. His writings continue to be read for their message about the responsibilities of Christians in the face of unjust rule.

BONN CONVENTIONS (GERMANY TREATY/DEUTSCHLAND VERTRAG, 1951) see REARMAMENT

BOOK BURNING. In Berlin and other German university cities the Nazis (q.v.) and their sympathizers publicly burned books on May 10, 1933, under the pretext that they were "un-German." Among the authors whose books were burned were Heinrich Mann (q.v.), Sigmund Freud, Karl Marx (q.v.), Carl von Ossietzky (q.v.), Kurt Tucholsky (q.v.), and Erich Kästner (q.v.).

BORCHERT, WOLFGANG (1921-1947). Borchert worked in a bookstore and then as an actor before he was drafted and sent to the front at the age of twenty. He was arrested twice for his pacifism and returned home in 1945 a very sick man. In his short stories and texts he makes the reader conscious of the collapse of values of the "lost generation." He died shortly before the premiere of his successful drama, *Out in the Cold (Draussen vor der Tür)*.

BORMANN, MARTIN (1900-?). Director of Nazi Party chancellory and Hitler's secretary (1941-45); disappeared from Hitler's bunker in Berlin at the end of the war; believed to have died in Latin America.

BÖRNE, LUDWIG see LIBERALISM

BORTFELDT, HEINRICH (1950-). A former researcher for the GDR central committee's elite Academy of Social Sciences, Dr. Bortfeldt wrote ground-breaking books on the transition of the SED to PDS (qq.v.) and on the United States' role in the German reunification process.

BRAHMS, JOHANNES (1833-1897). Brahms came from Hamburg and was a composer and pianist during the Romantic period. He wrote symphonies, concerts, chamber music, piano works and choral compositions and more than 200 songs. He was considered by his good friend, Schumann (q.v.), to be "a genius." He excelled in variation forms and after Bach (q.v.) was considered a master of counterpoint. *A German Requiem* is the best known work of this very successful composer. (See also EMPIRE CULTURE.)

BRANDENBURG see PRUSSIA

BRANDENBURG GATE. This is the only remaining town gate in Berlin. It was built from 1788 to 1791 by Carl G. Langhans who designed it after the *Propylaea* in Athens as Berlin's *Arch de Triumph*. Surmounted by the "Quadriga of Victory" (q.v.), the Gate was heavily damaged in the Second World War (q.v.). It was repaired under Russian occupation in 1956, and the recast chariot and horses again faced East. The Gate, closed off from 1961-89, was a symbol of a divided Germany until the Berlin Wall (q.v.) fell on November 9, 1989. On December 22, 1989, the Gate reopened and is once again the heart and symbol of Berlin.

East Germans demonstrate at Brandenburg Gate, 1953. (*Source:* GIC.)

Brandenburg Gate and Berlin Wall. (*Source:* GIC.)

BRANDT, WILLY (1913-1992). Adopted *nom de guerre* for Herbert Frahm. Mayor of West Berlin (1957-66), foreign minister (1966-69), chancellor (1969-74), chairman of SPD (1964-87). Brandt was born Herbert Frahm in Lübeck, the illegitimate son of a salesclerk. He learned his socialist convictions from his grandfather, and he became active in socialist groups during his youth. In 1930, he joined the SPD (q.v.). When the Nazis (q.v.) came to power in 1933, he took the name "Willy Brandt." He operated underground for a few months, and just as the Nazis were about to arrest him, he fled on a fishing boat to Norway via Copenhagen. He became a Norwegian citizen, studied history, and spent a half year in Berlin in 1936 disguised as a Norwegian student, but operating as leader of an underground socialist resistance group. His Norwegian was so good that when the Germans occupied Norway in 1940, he donned a Norwegian military uniform, was captured, and spent a month in a POW camp before being released by his unsuspecting captors. He went to Sweden, where he was a journalist active in the resistance movement. In 1945, he returned to Norway, where he entered the foreign service with a posting to Berlin in 1947 as a uniformed military press attaché. In the same year, he reapplied for his German citizenship, of which the Nazis had stripped him. When he received it in 1948, he went to work for West Berlin Mayor Ernst Reuter (q.v.). By the time he died of intestinal cancer in 1992, he had exercised influence on the center stage of international politics longer than any other contemporary politician.

As long as he was in politics, he was haunted by his past as an anti-Nazi, who had lived the war years outside of Germany and who had returned to Germany after the war wearing a Norwegian officer's uniform. After the 1965 election, Brandt sat down to write a book, *Draussen (Outside)*, an account of his activities: "I was not against Germany; I was against its despoilers. I didn't break with Germany, rather I was moved by concern for our nation. I didn't choose the easy way, rather I risked my neck more than once." He would have been gratified by what Chancellor Helmut Kohl (q.v.) called him at the time of his death in 1992: "A German patriot, European and world citizen simultaneously." President Richard von Weizsäcker (q.v.) praised his "humanity, his visionary power and his certain instinct for peace in Germany, for reconciliation with former enemies and for the restoration of the German name....He changed the Germans' relationship with the world, as well as the world's to Germany."

As Mayor of West Berlin in the 1950s, he had gained worldwide attention because of the dramatic confrontation between East and West in the middle of that city. In the early 1960s a leadership troika composed of Herbert Wehner (q.v.), Fritz Erler (q.v.), and Brandt took shape in the SPD. Ollenhauer (q.v.), who represented an earlier generation of Social Democrats and who had supported the move away from ideology and toward modernization, had to be nudged aside gradually; he did not possess the charisma and ability to appeal to the mass of voters. He lacked the passion and spark for politics, and he did not possess the sharp mind and industriousness which some powerful colleagues demanded. Most fatal, he generally buckled under criticism. In August 1960, Brandt, who was already popular and internationally famous, was selected as the new chancellor candidate for the 1961 elections. The SPD's previously uncovered flank--in foreign policy--was converted into a protected flank. There were several key figures, including Carlo Schmid, Erler, Wehner and Brandt, who had been working on rejuvenating the leadership against the resistance of the party executive.

For an entire decade Brandt had opposed SPD leaders in Bonn and had been one of the most outspoken proponents of the reform course. He had spent little time in the capital and had no significant following in SPD headquarters in Bonn. He had grown up in the working-class movement, but he had become a critical intellectual. He had spent much time abroad in the anti-Hitler resistance, spoke foreign languages, and exuded youth, dynamism, and progress when compared with Adenauer (q.v.). Brandt had yet another plus: he and Erler were respected in Washington, and both had good rapport with the man who was elected president in 1960: John F. Kennedy. In the U.S., Brandt was the only German politician who equaled Adenauer in terms of popularity in public opinion. No longer would the CDU/CSU be able to contend that an SPD chancellor would endanger relations with the U.S. partner.

Brandt had a real talent to think with precision, to persuade through discussion, to integrate and bring about consensus, to mobilize and instill enthusiasm and loyalty among followers and voters, and to represent Germany well in the world through his dignity, cosmopolitanism, foreign language skills, loyalty as a partner, and chairmanship of the Socialist International. Unlike Wehner, Brandt had no consuming commitment to politics or a party for which he would sacrifice all personal happiness and private life. Brandt loved life outside of politics and liked alcohol, female company (which accelerated his fall as chancellor), and off-color jokes. Brandt could seem to be warm and approachable and the kind of person who had many friends. However, those who knew him found the opposite to be true. Up close he was shy, aloof, and inclined toward silence. He reportedly had no real friends and did little to show warmth and sympathy to people who had helped him. He forgot names and birthdays, and he quickly dropped people whom he no longer needed. He found it morbid to visit sick and dying comrades at their bedside.

In 1969, the SPD and FDP won a razor-thin victory in parliamentary elections, and Brandt became chancellor. The 1972 election was a personal triumph for him. It was the only one he had personally won for his party; he was at the zenith of his political career. But not every Social Democrat was pleased with his performance as chancellor and party chairman. There were some who found that he was too apathetic about his duties; the most powerful and most dangerous of his critics were Wehner and Helmut Schmidt (q.v.), the party's two vice-chairmen. Thus, Brandt was given little opportunity to bask in the warmth of his victory; a year and a half later, he found himself evicted from the chancellor's bungalow. His complacency and aloofness grew more pronounced after receiving the Nobel Peace Prize in 1973 for his government's *Ostpolitik* (q.v.). Peter Koch wrote that Brandt's always strong self-confidence and secret sense of superiority over others began to manifest themselves toward the outside: "He demanded respect, even in his own family circle." More and more Social Democrats began speaking derisively of the "peace chancellor" as "Zeus" or "heavenly father." The FRG's political system requires an active chancellor who participates fully in the shaping of the government's policies; Brandt had largely let go of the reins. After stepping down as chancellor in 1974, Brandt remained chairman of the SPD until 1987. When the Berlin Wall (q.v.) came down in 1989, he was an inspirational figure on the scene encouraging the steps toward German reunification (q.v.).

BRAUER, MAX (1887-1973). SPD mayor of Altona (1924-33), first mayor of Hamburg (1946-53 and 1957-61). (See also LAND PRINCES.)

BRAUN, EVA (1912-1945). Hitler's consort and bride in the final hours of his life. (See also THIRD REICH.)

BRAUN, OTTO (1872-1955). SPD politician who ruled Prussia as minister president with only short interruptions from 1920 until 1932. His government was considered the strongest bulwark of democracy during the turbulent Weimar era. (See also WEIMAR REPUBLIC.)

BRAUN, WERNHER VON (1912-1977) see ROCKETS

BRECHT, BERTOLD (1898-1956). This controversial literary giant and son of a successful factory owner actually began his career as a medical student in Munich from 1917-21. He began writing verse and prose as early as 1914 for his hometown newspaper in Augsburg. Brecht wrote more than 40 plays and became world famous with *The Threepenny Opera* (1928). *Mother Courage and Her Children* (1941) dealt with the ravages of war. His collections of poetry, short stories, calendar tales and essays reflect the writings of a keen observer, a social critic and satirist who clearly sided with the proletariat. Brecht left Germany in 1933, living first in Denmark and Sweden and finally in the U.S., where he stayed until 1947. He returned to East Berlin and, together with Helene Weigl, founded the Berliner Ensemble in 1949 with which he remained closely connected until his death in 1956. His epic theater (*Episches Theater*) required the audience to be critically detached, relaxed and thus able to reflect on the lessons presented on the stage. Songs were interspersed to alienate the spectator from the stage reality. Epic theater was to instruct and at the same time evoke critical thinking. His use of satire and his radical political consciousness and racy, hard hitting verse produced some of the most exciting dramatic art of the 20th century. (See also VERFREMDUNGSEFFEKT.)

BRENTANO, HEINRICH VON (1904-1964). CDU, chairman of CDU/CSU Bundestag parliamentary group (1955-61), foreign minister.

BREST-LITOVSK, PEACE OF (1918) see RUSSIAN REVOLUTION

BREUEL, BIRGIT (1937-). President of Treuhand (q.v.).

BROCKDORFF-RANTZAU, ULRICH COUNT VON (1869-1928). Foreign minister (1918-19), ambassador to Soviet Union (1922-28).

BROKDORF. Nuclear plant outside of Hamburg and scene of violent battles between police and anti-nuclear protesters. In the summer of 1988, the new SPD (q.v.) energy minister of Schleswig-Holstein canceled its operating license, but this decision was reversed by the federal environmental minister, Klaus Töpfer.

BRÜCKE, DIE (THE BRIDGE). An early 20th century art movement organized in Dresden by a group of German painters, it symbolized the unity of nature and emotion.

BRÜNING, HEINRICH (1885-1970). Center Party, chancellor (1930-32). Having made a name as an economics specialist, he was appointed chancellor on March 29, 1930 by President von Hindenburg (q.v.) with no participation of the Reichstag. His cabinet was composed of experts who were not bound to parties in the Reichstag either. Supported by the president, he ruled by using the emergency decree powers provided by Article 48 of the Weimar Constitution. Unfortunately, his total reliance on this and ignoring of parliament undermined that same constitution. His main goal was to end the reparations (q.v.) payments instead of combatting unemployment. Known in the streets as the "Hunger Chancellor," he lost the confidence of Hindenburg and was forced to step down on May 30, 1932. He later emigrated to the U.S., where he taught economics at Harvard University and maintained contacts with the German resistance movement. (See also HITLER, SEIZURE OF POWER; WEIMAR REPUBLIC.)

BUBACK, SIEGFRIED (1920-1977). Chief federal prosecutor, assassinated by terrorists. (See TERRORIST GROUPS.)

BUBIS, IGNATZ see ANTI-SEMITISM

BÜCHNER, GEORG (1813-1837). Büchner was a forerunner of realistic drama who died of typhoid at the age of 24 while living as a political refugee in Switzerland. Of all Büchner's works only *Dantons Tod* was published in his lifetime. Büchner did not come into his own until the 20th century. His appeal lies in his questioning scrutiny of all forms of convention and positive beliefs. *Woyzeck* and his Novella *Lenz* are two of his most important works.

BÜLOW, BERNHARD HEINRICH MARTIN PRINCE VON (1849-1929). Imperial chancellor (1900-09). Son of Bernhard Ernst von Bülow, Bismarck's (q.v.) foreign minister from 1877 to 1879, he served as ambassador in Rome (1894) and foreign minister (1897). Lacking convictions, he was weak, and he tended to be dominated by others, especially by Foreign Office Counselor Holstein and Admiral Tirpitz (q.v.). He was able to maintain himself in office for nine years because he had learned how to flatter the Kaiser, which was the secret to any chancellor's influence under Wilhelm II (q.v.). His relations with the Kaiser deteriorated because of Wilhelm's tendency to act independently in foreign affairs, sometimes with disastrous effects. One such example was the *Daily Telegraph* Affair in October 1908, when he created public embarrassment by boasting to that British newspaper that he had influenced the outcome of the Boer War. This affair marked a diminution in the Kaiser's influence over German policies. Bülow resigned in 1909, but he again became ambassador to Rome in 1914 where he attempted unsuccessfully to dissuade Italy from changing sides in the war.

BUNDESBANK (FEDERAL BANK). The powerful and prestigious Federal Bank, located in Frankfurt, is perhaps the world's most independent central bank and, some say, the closest equivalent to a central bank for the entire EC (q.v.). It is charged with issuing Germany's legal tender, regulating the circulation of money and the supply of credit to industry, determining the discount and Lombard rates and required minimum reserves for banks, and defending the value of the currency against inflation. Remembering how political manipulation of the Reichsbank had helped cause the hyperinflation in the 1920s, the FRG's founders ensured that the new central bank would be impervious to government pressure. In fact, it was already independent since the bank had been founded as the Bank Deutscher Länder in 1948 when there was no German government. Members of the federal government may attend its council meetings, but they have no vote. While not bound by instructions from the government, the bank must support its general economic policy, as well as advise and provide information to the government. In some matters, such as the fixing of exchange rates, the government can overrule it. Indeed, Karl Otto Pöhl (q.v.) resigned as president in 1991 because the chancellor had not heeded his advice on German monetary unification. All presidents of the Land central banks are on its Central Bank Council, as well as up to ten directors appointed for eight-year terms upon recommendation by the federal government.

BUNDESGRENZSCHUTZ. Federal border police. One of its elite units, the GSG 9, is responsible for anti-terrorist actions.

BUNDESWEHR (FEDERAL ARMED FORCES). With Germany in ruins by 1945, there was little thought in anyone's mind of placing the Germans back into uniform. Anti-war sentiment was strong, and the controversy over entering NATO (q.v.) and reintroducing conscription was so intense and emotional that it is a wonder that the young democracy survived it. A mass movement known by the slogan "ohne mich" ("without me") enjoyed widespread support. In a 1950 opinion poll, 70 percent of males at Bonn University vowed never to put on a military uniform. A 1955 opinion survey revealed that while 40 percent of the respondents were in favor of a West German army, 45 percent (and 71 percent of those identifying with the Social Democratic Party-- SPD) were opposed. It was in this charged atmosphere that the Bundeswehr was born.

Much attention was paid to creating the right kind of military. In 1950, Konrad Adenauer (q.v.) appointed Theodor Blank to shape a new "army of democrats" operating under democratic military statutes, resolutely accepting civilian control, and committed to the defense of parliamentary democracy. *"Dienststelle Blank"* sought to reduce, if not eliminate, the tension between democratic values and military necessities. It "presented civil and military worlds as integrated, and mutually reinforcing." Thus, service in the military would not be a radical break from civilian life. These goals were to be ensured by a new concept: *Innere Führung* (inner leadership), elaborated by General W. Graf von Baudissin. As a "citizen in uniform," with the emphasis on the first word, the soldier has rights which he sustains through participation and initiative. He is an autonomous moral being who can "balance the claims of subordination against the demands of conscience." A soldier's morale is best when he can exercise his rights. It is assumed that a soldier performs better when he understands the political values for which he fights. Finally, in a technical army, self-discipline is more important than blind obedience. Leaders issuing orders to highly-specialized soldiers must apply modern management techniques to achieve maximum efficiency. *Innere Führung* is crucial for the thinking soldier. It helps explain the character, curriculum and civilian appearance of the Bundeswehr Universities (q.v.).

Reunification (q.v.) and the collapse of the Soviet empire in central Europe profoundly affected the size and the mission of the Bundeswehr. It remains the largest NATO land army in Europe and also contains a formidable air force and a small navy which operates in the North and Baltic Seas. Soon after reunification the Bundeswehr began a unique effort of merging two formerly hostile armies into one. About 25,000 professional East German soldiers who are judged to be reliable defenders of Germany's democratic order are becoming a part of a combined force which, in compliance with an agreement made with the Soviet Union in July 1990, will number 370,000 troops. The same agreement specifies that no western German units will be deployed on former GDR (q.v.) territory until the Soviet Union has withdrawn its 375,000 troops by the end of 1994 (later moved up by four months), and that no foreign troops and nuclear weapons will ever be stationed there. Germany retains its conscript army, and males in both parts of Germany are required to perform 12 months of military service, unless they are judged to be conscientious objectors, in which case they must perform alternative civilian duty. Almost all German units are assigned to NATO, the supreme commander of which is always an American general. According to Article 115 of the Basic Law (q.v.), the FRG can order its army to fight only in case of defense, a situation which applies, according to the North Atlantic Treaty, when any NATO country is attacked by an outside power. (See NORTH ATLANTIC TREATY ORGANIZATION.)

BUNDESWEHR OMBUDSMAN (WEHRBEAUFTRAGTER). This position was created in 1959. The ombudsman is appointed by the Bundestag for a five-year term and makes an annual report to parliament. Any member of the Bundeswehr can complain directly to this official, who can then investigate matters. The existence of this office underscores the principle that a soldier in the FRG is a "civilian in uniform," who does not belong to a separate caste or to a "state within a state."

BUNDESWEHR UNIVERSITIES (UniBW). The Bundeswehr's (q.v.) creation in 1956 presented such daunting challenges that its leaders postponed the sensitive question of officer education. The primary emphasis was placed on equipment, integration with allied forces, recruitment of officers and non-commissioned officers who had prior military experience and training, as well as on implementing the concepts of *Innere Führung* and "citizen in uniform." By the late 1960s the issue of officer education had to be faced. This was an extraordinarily bad time for it. The FRG was in tumult, and there was a growing "extra-parliamentary opposition" in the streets. The Vietnam War hardened anti-military feelings among West Germans. In 1968, only 22 percent of respondents believed that a soldier has more social prestige than a civilian, and 59 percent were of the opposite opinion. Unlike the Prussian lieutenant, who, in the words of historian Friedrich Meinecke, "went through the world like a young god," the Bundeswehr officer met with widespread rejection, or at least indifference. The effect of such resentment against the military profession obviously hampered officer recruitment. The late 1960s were also times of experimentation and reform, and the entire educational system was being reexamined. A reform-minded SPD-FDP government assumed power in 1969 with Helmut Schmidt (qq.v.) as defense minister. Unlike many Social Democrats, he was an expert in military matters and was more interested in improving the performance of the Bundeswehr than in setting limits on it.

On October 1, 1973, West Germany's first military universities opened their doors in Hamburg and Munich to officers and officer cadets. Such an event would have been accepted as quite normal in most other countries, where military academies of one kind or the other have long been a fixture in the system of higher education. This was not the case in the FRG, a young country which, because of the German past, has serious reservations about the very idea of military power and armed forces. The founding of the military universities became the subject of intense public controversy regarding what role the military should play in a new democratic society and what kind of education its soldiers need. A new kind of Germany carefully created a new kind of military universities. One observer noted in 1971: "An educational instrument is being created which must be sharply controlled if it is not to fall into the wrong hands and serve purposes hostile to the society." The creation of the Universities of the Bundeswehr was an experiment to break from the past.

One of the Bundeswehr's greatest needs was to improve the training and education of its soldiers in all ranks, an issue which had been under discussion throughout the 1960s. What problems did the Bundeswehr face? The first was that traditional German military training was geared toward efficiency. This had been undeniably successful on the tactical and operational (though not on the strategic) levels. But this ultimately led to a kind of overspecialization and narrow-mindedness which tended to isolate the officer corps from German society. The culmination of this process was the super-professional, elitist *Reichswehr*, which was not a reliable instrument for the democratic objectives of the Weimar Republic (q.v.). The Bundeswehr's concepts of "citizen in uniform" and *Innere Führung* were not compatible with a system of training based almost exclusively on military efficiency.

Further, it was having increasing difficulty in recruiting officers. The FRG was a prosperous society, and the Bundeswehr had to compete for talent by offering more educational opportunities. This was especially true after 1969 when the SPD-FDP dramatically widened the doors of the *Gymnasien* and universities, which held the keys to higher paying, prestigious jobs. This meant that fewer high school graduates (*Abiturienten*) were willing to consider the military as a career. At the same time, technical requirements for both military and civilian professions were becoming more similar and the need to integrate military and civilian training more obvious. In 1967, 63 percent of all officers had received the *Abitur*, but only 5.5 percent (16.7 percent of the generals) had studied at the university. The reform was aimed at serving both sectors' needs.

While the birthrate in the FRG plummeted, important social changes were also taking place. Since the Bundeswehr had always tried to integrate the armed forces into society, it was inevitably affected by these changes. Anti-military sentiments and cynicism toward all national security concerns were strong, and patriotism and national loyalty were no longer accepted by most young Germans, particularly in the heady years of the student rebellions during the late 1960s and 1970s. The policy of detente further weakened the conviction that military force was ever appropriate or even related to maintaining peace. These changes in attitudes made military leadership more difficult; to gain authority over troops, a leader had to convince young Germans that their military service was important. This required that officers be more educated in social sciences and pedagogy, as well as in technical subjects.

By the late 1960s, statistics demonstrating the shortfalls in recruitment had become compelling. The Bundeswehr needed 30,000 long-term officers. But, in 1969, only 1,000 officer candidates entered, half the number needed. In combat units of the army, recruitment of officers fell as much as 70 percent short of what was needed. Most applicants were interested in serving only two to four years. Also, fewer career officers were needed than 12-year officers. Since the latter would leave the military at age 30-40, they would need a civilian profession in order to survive. Helmut Schmidt ordered a complete examination of the inner structure of the Bundeswehr, including the military training and education of all ranks. To deal with the problem of recruiting talented officer candidates, he appointed on July 11, 1970, a "Commission for the Reordering of Training and Education in the Bundeswehr," chaired by Professor Thomas Ellwein (SPD) and composed of 25 members, including soldiers of all ranks, civil servants and experts from independent groups.

Once the decision to proceed with the founding of the two UniBw in Hamburg and Munich was made in Bonn on June 29, 1972, all speed records were broken putting them into operation. The *Hamburger A bendblatt* reported in a headline that "The *Bundeswehr* University Is Shooting out of the Ground!" In March 1972, work began in Hamburg, and in October 1973 the first students arrived. Students enjoy most of the freedoms of civilian universities and do not wear uniforms. Professors are civilians who have complete academic freedom, and the curricula have to conform to the academic standards set by the Länder of Hamburg and Bavaria. Despite some problems, such as compressing a rigorous university education into a maximum of four years, the two military universities have been a success. They did not create a "state within a state." There are no signs that officers in the FRG resent their democratically elected political leaders. Nor is there evidence that the Bundeswehr tries to wield undue political influence, even though it does act as an interest group to bring its own views to the attention of parliament and politicians. Officers regard themselves as fully included in the everyday political dealings of a democratic and pluralistic society. The officer corps is no longer as homogeneous as earlier, and their political opinions are largely within the democratic spectrum of the three traditional major parties, the CDU/CSU, SPD and FDP. Military service in the FRG has little effect on soldiers' political views. After the reunification of Germany, the Bundeswehr continues to face major challenges in legitimizing and maintaining a modern and credible military force in a society which is ultra-sensitive to all things military.

BURGFRIEDEN see EBERT, FRIEDRICH

BUSCH, WILHELM (1832-1908). This artist and comic poet studied art in Düsseldorf, Antwerp and Munich after starting as a mechanical engineer. In Munich he gained recognition for his comic illustrations which appeared in two weeklies. At the age of 32 he returned to Wiedensahl, his birthplace, to live with his widowed sister and three nephews who often inspired his work. During this time he published *Max und Moritz*, his most famous work. His specialty was satire in humorous verse accompanied by large numbers of drastic and grotesque line drawings. Much of his pungent satire was directed against the Catholic Church and the complacency of the older Germany.

BYRNES, JAMES F. (1879-1972). U.S. secretary of state (1945-47), see ALLIED OCCUPATION OF GERMANY

-C-

CAPRIVI, GEORG LEO COUNT VON (1831-1899). Imperial chancellor (1890-94).

CARLSBAD ACTS AND CONSERVATIVE REACTION. After 1815, there was an ultra-conservative reaction led by the governments of Prussia and Austria, a development which sorely disappointed many Germans, especially the youth. Many had hoped during the wars of liberation from French domination that Germany would become democratic and united. Indeed, they believed that the despotic power of the individual German sovereigns could be broken by creating a unified Germany. Until the 1860s the aims of unity and freedom went hand in hand. Nowhere were these hopes stronger than at the universities, where idealistic students formed highly politicized fraternities under the banner of "honor, freedom, fatherland." The fraternity members dressed in clothing fashionable in Germany in much earlier days, and their colors were black, red and gold, which had been the colors of volunteers during the wars of liberation, and which thereafter became the symbolic colors of republicanism in Germany. They are the colors of the FRG today.

In 1817 the fraternity at the University of Jena sponsored a mass assembly at Wartburg Castle for persons from all over Germany on the fourth anniversary of the Battle of Leipzig and the 300th anniversary of Luther's Reformation. Thousands came, and passionate speeches were given calling for individual liberty, constitutional government and

German unity. Reactionary policies of the leading German states were criticized. At the end of this nationalistic rally, the father of the popular gymnastic associations, Friedrich Ludwig Jahn, organized a particularly unfortunate ceremony which was repeated 116 years later in Berlin: not only the symbols of authority, such as a pigtail and a Prussian corporal's cane, but "un-German" books were thrown into a huge bonfire.

Among the books thrown into the flames were those of a playwright, August von Kotzebue. Two years later a deranged and fanatical theology student assassinated him, calling him a "traitor of youth." This senseless act was just what the leaders of most German states needed to declare the "Carlsbad Acts" in 1819. They called for rigid censorship, prohibition of any political activity directed against the authoritarian order in most states, the outlawing of fraternities (which continued to operate underground), and close scrutiny and supervision of the universities. The Prussian king dismissed all his reformist ministers, and Prussia and Austria remained the centers of conservative reaction.

CAROLINIAN EMPIRE. It is doubtful that a German nation would ever have emerged if a Carolinian empire had not taken shape after Roman rule had effectively ended. This far-flung empire, comprising 80 percent of Germanic peoples and encompassing some speaking Latin-based languages in the West, reached its peak under Charlemagne ("Charles the Great") who ascended the throne in 768 A.D. During his rule the empire extended from northwestern Europe south to Rome and from Hungary to northern Spain. Charlemagne was a leader of extraordinary personal qualities who spent half his time in the saddle holding his vast territory together. His empire survived only a few years after his death in 814. It was divided in 817 into the Kingdoms of East and West Franconia and Lorraine. After bitter and complicated inheritance quarrels, two realms faced each other along roughly the same line as the present border between Germany and France. By 843 this border had become more or less fixed, and in the year 925 it became firmly established. Only in the East could subsequent German expansion take place.

Although Charlemagne's huge empire had been considerably reduced after his death, he had created the indispensable foundation for the formation of a German nation and a German consciousness. There were no other geographic, racial, cultural or strictly linguistic factors which could have pulled Germany together without Charlemagne's political and military acumen. During his reign some persons began to refer to the tongues spoken in the Eastern part of the empire as "Deutsch" (*Doich*)--German, a word derived from "*Diutisk,*" meaning "common" or "popular." In the following three centuries more and more inhabitants of what is now Germany developed a consciousness of being German.

CARSTENS, KARL (1914-92). CDU, law professor, federal president (1979-84). Carstens studied law and became a member of the Nazi party. After serving as a Wehrmacht officer from 1939 to 1945, he became a law professor and held many public offices. He became chairman of the CDU parliamentary group in 1973 and president of the Bundestag from 1976 to 1979. Despite criticism for earlier Nazi party membership, he was elected federal president in 1979, a post he held until 1984. He was well known for seeking contact with the population, especially through his hobby of hiking. During his presidency, he hiked all the way across the FRG, logging almost a thousand miles.

CARTEL OFFICE (KARTELLAMT) see DECARTELIZATION

CASSIRER, ERNST (1874-1945). A Neo-Kantian active in Breslau, Marburg, and Berlin, Cassirer was interested in the relationship between Kantianism and science, which he treated in *Problem of Knowledge* (1906). Later he studied symbolic forms in general and argued that the categories used for organizing knowledge and experience in any given age express the specific needs of that age.

CATHOLIC LEAGUE see THIRTY-YEARS WAR

CENTER PARTY (ZENTRUM). This was the Catholic political organization in the German Empire and Weimar Republic (qq.v.). It was founded in 1871 by Ludwig Windhorst to protect Catholic interests against Bismarck's (q.v.) policies, which focused on the interests of Prussia's Protestant majority. It especially opposed Bismarck's Culture Struggle (q.v.), but it supported the chancellor's repressive policies against the Social Democrats in the 1880s. From 1893 to 1907 it was the strongest party in a coalition with the Conservatives, but as nationalism became a growing force, it gradually lost influence to nationalist groups. Under the leadership of Matthias Erzberger (q.v.), it guided a Peace Resolution through the Reichstag which advocated a negotiated peace without annexations. Among its notable members in the Weimar Republic were Brüning (q.v.) and von Papen (q.v.). Like all other rival parties, it was outlawed by the Nazis (q.v.) in 1933, but as a political force it reemerged after the war to become a part of the CDU/CSU (q.v.). (See also BISMARCK DOMESTIC POLICY; WEIMAR REPUBLIC.)

CENTRAL POWERS. This originally referred to Germany, Austria-Hungary, and Italy after the formation of the Triple Alliance (q.v.) in 1882. After Italy defected in 1914, it generally referred to Germany and Austria-Hungary, as opposed to the "Entente Powers" of Britain, France, and Russia.

CHANGE THROUGH RAPPROCHEMENT (WANDEL DURCH ANNÄHERUNG). The SPD did not merely follow along behind the CDU/CSU initiatives toward the GDR (qq.v.), even though it was supporting all government moves to improve relations with the East. On July 15, 1963, Willy Brandt's (q.v.) most intimate German policy adviser, Egon Bahr (q.v.), gave a speech in the Bavarian city of Tutzing, which was memorable mainly because of two phrases: "*Wandel durch Annäherung*" and "policy of small steps." He did not recommend diplomatic recognition of "the so-called GDR," nor would he and Brandt do so until the end of 1969. Walter Ulbricht (q.v.) publicly opposed such a strategy; his obstinacy prompted the Soviet Union to support his removal in 1971.

CHAOTICS (CHAOTEN) see SPONTIS

CHARLEMAGNE (KARL DER GROSSE) (747-814 A.D.) see CAROLINIAN EMPIRE

CHECKPOINT CHARLIE. This checkpoint separating East and West Berlin got its name from the American alphabet. After border fortifications were erected through Berlin and across Germany in 1961, President John F. Kennedy ordered U.S. forces to create three checkpoints in order that they could exercise their right of free access to Berlin at any time as stipulated in the Quadripartite Agreement. Checkpoint Alpha was in Helmstedt, Lower Saxony between the FRG and GDR (qq.v.); Bravo was the crossing between West Berlin and the

GDR; Charlie connected East and West Berlin. As of 1962 Checkpoint Charlie was the only crossing point for foreigners visiting Berlin. It was removed in 1990.

CHILDREN'S UNION ERNST THÄLMANN (GDR)   see FREE GERMAN YOUTH

CHRISTIAN DEMOCRATIC UNION (CDU)--CHRISTLICH DEMOKRATISCHE UNION) / CHRISTIAN SOCIAL UNION (CSU)-- CHRISTLICH-SOZIALE UNION.) The CDU, which is linked in parliament and in federal elections with its Bavarian sister party, the CSU, is the first successful political party in German history which did not rest on a single confessional or class base. It is a union of diverse groups who after the Nazi (q.v.) catastrophe wanted to put Christian principles back into political life and take ideological rigidity out of it. They wished to give Germany a moral and democratic rebirth. Adenauer's economics minister, Ludwig Erhard (qq.v.), introduced a brand of capitalism with social conscience (called the "social market economy") which brought not only prosperity, but a broad net of social assistance for the uprooted, the hungry, the unemployed, the old and the sick.

Germans are very proud of their generous social legislation, and the creation of the FRG's modern social net is primarily the work of the CDU/CSU; the SPD-FDP (qq.v.) coalition only tightened this net in a few places during the 1970s. It is thus a democratic, reform-oriented party, which attracts votes primarily from Catholics, independent business people, white-collar employees and civil servants. It would not be considered a conservative party in the U.S., even though it does win the votes of most conservatives in Germany. However, this does not weaken or embarrass the CDU/CSU since almost all conservatives in the FRG, in contrast to the Weimar Republic (q.v.), support the democratic system. For years the party grappled with the problem of how to put aside the internal struggles within its talented and experienced leadership in order to present a picture of unity.

Catholic Bavaria is the FRG's most conservative state, and the CSU is therefore also conservative. The CSU, which especially appeals to Catholics, rural and small-city dwellers, craftsmen, small business groups and, increasingly, those in the service industries, easily wins land elections in Bavaria (though not in Munich, the state capital).

After Franz Josef Strauss' (q.v.) death in 1988, Theo Waigel (q.v.) assumed the leadership of the party.

At the time of German reunification in 1990, the Union parties controlled many major cities and four out of five of the new Länder in eastern Germany (the exception being Brandenburg). But, by mid-1991, they had lost power in all western German Länder but Bavaria and Baden-Wurttemberg, where the CDU's powerful minister president, Lothar Späth, was forced to resign because of financial impropriety. Before Germany's dramatic move toward unity, it appeared that Kohl's (q.v.) party, which was ridden with dissatisfaction about what appeared to be a bumbling chancellor, was heading for defeat in the December 2, 1990, federal elections. However, Kohl instinctively knew that, faced with the challenges of melding two Germanys into one, German voters would choose that leader who was decisive and exuded confidence that future problems could be solved. Therefore, the Union parties adopted the slogans, "Yes to Germany! Yes to the Future!" At each of its election rallies, a campaign song was sung in English: "Feel the power, touch the future, reach the heart!" The governing CDU-CSU-FDP coalition won 55 percent of the votes and actually performed better in the East than in the West. The CDU-CSU captured 44 percent of the votes and 319 seats.

The CDU's standing in the East was troubled after the election by the cabinet resignation of the GDR's last prime minister, Lothar de Maizière (q.v.). As a lawyer and high lay official in the East German Protestant Church, he was shown to have maintained contacts with the Stasi (q.v.) from 1981 to 1988. He maintained that these were necessary for his efforts to defend his clients and church. He was cleared of allegations that he had actually spied for the Stasi, but he was forced to relinquish his party vice-chairmanship to another eastern German, Angela Merkel. Other leaders of the old eastern CDU, one of the bloc parties (q.v.) which had cooperated with the Communists, were gradually forced out of their posts. Every major ministerial post in Kohl's government, as well as the highest representational positions, such as the presidency and vice-presidency of the Bundestag, remained in westerners' hands; only minor cabinet posts, such as transport, were awarded to easterners. (See also ELECTIONS, FEDERAL (1990).)

CHRISTIAN DEMOCRATIC UNION, EAST   see DEMOCRATIC AWAKENING

CHRISTIAN SOCIAL UNION (CSU) see CHRISTIAN
DEMOCRATIC UNION

CITIZENS' INITIATIVES (BÜRGERINITIATIVEN). In 1968-69 the
first such groupings, which were independent of political parties and
other organizations, sprang up. The spark came from perceived
problems in such areas as education (q.v.), transportation, city planning,
and environmental protection. In the beginning they were loosely
organized and rather amateur in their action, but they rapidly became
more sophisticated and effective. Some were able to slow down or stop
the construction of nuclear power plants, such as Whyl, Kalkar, and
Brokdorf (q.v.). The rapid growth of these initiatives in the 1970s and
1980s caused many Germans to ask whether the political system had
failed, rulers had overlooked the interests of citizens, and traditional
parties had become unable to express the will of the citizens. These
groups have not led to a change in the constitutional order established
by the Basic Law (q.v.), but they have affected the political system and
parties. They have forced the parties to deal with new topics and to pay
closer attention to movements outside the party landscape. (See also
GREENS; PARTIES.)

CIVIL SERVICE LAW. Although this was enacted in 1937 during the
Third Reich, it was drafted during the Weimar Republic (qq.v.). In June
1950, it was re-enacted without substantial modifications as the Federal
Civil Service Law. The 1950 law establishes the legal basis for civil
service and retains the earlier Prussian division of state personnel into
officials (*Beamter*), public employees (*Angestellten*), and workers
(*Arbeiter*). An important emphasis in the FRG law is the duty of the
civil servant to be loyal to the Basic Law (q.v.). The highest level, the
officials, are not permitted to strike, and their disputes are dealt with by
Administrative, not Labor, Courts. Their interests are represented by the
German Officials' Federation (DBB), while the public employees are
organized in the German Employees' Union (DAG), and the workers by
an industrial trade union, the Public Service, Transport and
Transportation (ÖTV). (See also EXTREMIST DECISION.)

CIVILIAN SERVICE (ZIVILDIENST or ERSATZDIENST). The
FRG's Basic Law (q.v.) guarantees the right of conscientious objection.
Therefore, even after the creation of the Bundeswehr (q.v.), those young
German males who can demonstrate that they could not serve in the

military for reasons of conscience are permitted to perform alternative civilian service instead. Authorities are very liberal in granting this privilege, and Germany has more conscientious objectors than any other NATO country. Many hospitals, clinics, and social services have become dependent upon their work.

CLASSICISM (1788-1805). German Classicism refers mainly to the work produced by Goethe and Schiller from 1795-1805 when they formed the most important friendship in German literature. Both abandoned the passion of the Storm and Stress (q.v.) for the restraint and formality of classical literature and its serious content and strict rules. Relying on Greek and Roman models, literature was to reflect the wholeness of life and show a harmony between the individual, who must first find inner freedom, and his world of which tragedy was a recognized part. Inner freedom must first be achieved before one can function in one's society. A "beautiful soul" provided the moral instincts for one's actions and thus a more humane ideal culture toward which one strove. Goethe's *Iphigenie* (1787) in her truthfulness and purity embodied the "beautiful soul." *Torquato Tasso* (1790), *Wilhelm Meisters Lehrjahr* (1795), *Hermann und Dorothea* (1797), and *Faust* (1808, 1832) are Goethe's most important works during this period. Schiller's most famous works are *Don Carlos* (1787), *Wallenstein* (1799), and *Maria Stuart* (1800).

CLAUSEWITZ, KARL VON (1780-1831). A Prussian general and military theorist, he entered the Prussian army in 1792, served in the Rhine campaigns of 1793-94, became an instructor in the German War School in 1809, and helped Generals Gneisenau and Scharnhorst (qq.v.), from whom he learned much of his military science, to introduce army reforms. When the Prussian king entered an alliance with Napoleon in 1812, Clausewitz, like many Prussian officers, resigned his commission, joined the Russian army, and fought in the engagements which defeated Napoleon's Grand Army in Russia. He subsequently fought in the wars of liberation from Napoleon, serving as chief of staff of the third Prussian corps in the Battle of Waterloo (1815).

In 1818, he was promoted to general and appointed director of the War School. In that position he developed his theories on war, elaborated most persuasively in his unfinished masterpiece, *Vom Kriege (On War)*, published posthumously in 1833 and soon translated into most European languages. He broke from tradition by refusing to produce a rigid system of strategy. Instead, he attempted to identify the factors that decide success in war, emphasizing the importance of psychological and accidental factors that cannot be calculated precisely. He hoped that his writings would help students develop a theoretically founded military judgment and be able to weigh all relevant factors in a given situation. Strategy, he argued, should aim at the enemy's forces, his resources, and his will to fight. Defensive warfare is politically and militarily stronger than the offensive. The most memorable contribution from *On War* is his argument that "war is nothing but a continuation of political intercourse" by different means. That is, war has meaning only insofar as it serves higher political objectives; it is not an end in itself. He died of cholera in 1831. (See also FRENCH REVOLUTION.)

CLAY, LUCIUS DuBIGNON (1897-1978). Military Governor of American Occupation Zone (1947-49). (See also ALLIED OCCUPATION; CURRENCY REFORM.)

CO-DETERMINATION (MITBESTIMMUNG). Worker co-determination was introduced while the Christian parties were in power, but the SPD (q.v.) wanted to expand it. A 1972 law broadened the responsibility of works councils in allocating employee benefits and improving working conditions. But it proved much harder to gain acceptance for a scheme that would have granted workers equality with management in economic decision-making. The business community resisted it fiercely, and the FDP (q.v.) saw it as too great a sacrifice of economic freedom. The partners reached tentative agreement on a compromise draft in early 1974. It increased the number of non-management personnel in the board rooms, but management would still retain the upper hand. (See also LABOR; SCHMIDT, HELMUT.)

COLLECTIVE GUILT. This is guilt applied to an entire people. It is difficult to defend from the legal, ethical, and international legal point of view. After 1945, the entire German people were frequently referred to as collectively responsible for Nazi (q.v.) crimes, a view that the Protestant Church and the FRG's first president, Theodor Heuss (q.v.), rejected. (See also DENAZIFICATION; OVERCOMING THE PAST.)

COMMITTEE FOR JUSTICE. In June 1992, this was formed as a grassroots movement designed to unite eastern Germans and make western Germans wake up to the troubled transition of the former GDR since German reunification (qq.v.). It is based on the conclusion that the large parties are not sufficiently receptive to the plight of eastern Germans, and that the western German political system has failed eastern Germans. The group met with almost universal rejection from the established political parties. This committee is intended to exert supra-parliamentary pressure on politicians. The leading founders are PDS chairman Gregor Gysi (q.v.) and Peter-Michael Diestel (CDU). Diestel was the GDR's last interior minister, and he lost favor in Bonn because he voiced sympathy for the plight of Stasi (q.v.) agents. He was head of the CDU (q.v.) parliamentary group in Brandenburg when he was forced to resign because of a possibly shady financial deal involving the purchase of a house, and because of his statements about the Stasi. The two were joined in the founding by 69 prominent persons from both parts of Germany, including Stefan Heym and Gottfried Forck (qq.v.). Brandenburg's Minister President Manfred Stolpe (q.v.) described the founding of this group as a "last warning" to complacent western German politicians.

COMMUNISM IN GERMANY. Communism is a spent force in Germany, condemned to political irrelevance. In the 1990s, German Communists are in the throes of crisis. Only the Party of Democratic Socialism (PDS, q.v.) is a credible electoral and parliamentary force; it alone is in the Bundestag. The German Communist Party (DKP, q.v.) in the western part of Germany remains as irrelevant as ever. It was badly battered by the collapse of communism in the GDR (q.v.), to which it was always uncritically servile. It suffered great losses in membership and capacity for action; the cut-off of funds from the GDR shattered its party organization, and its leaders no longer enjoy the confidence of the activists. It also lost its theoretical bearings. The KPD, the Spartakist-Workers' Party, and Independent SPD (USPD) were reborn in the GDR during the closing months of that sinking regime in 1990. They offer socialist alternatives to the capitalist system, but all are negligible political forces. Only the highly diverse collection of Marxist-Leninist, Trotskyite, anarchist and autonomist sects, which had maintained independence from the ruling Communist parties in East Berlin and Moscow, remain stable. They are deeply divided ideologically, impotent at election time, and have only a minuscule following, but they can make their presence known in demonstrations, squatting, and terrorist actions. They are poised to try to take advantage of the many problems stemming from uncertainties growing out of the German reunification process. All in all, following the collapse of communism in the Soviet Union and Eastern Europe, the future of Communist parties in Western Europe, including Germany, is extremely bleak. They are in deep shock and are searching in vain for stable new ground under their feet. (See also GERMAN COMMUNIST PARTY; PARTY OF DEMOCRATIC SOCIALISM.)

COMMUNIST LEAGUE (KOMMUNISTISCHER BUND--KB). The KB's headquarters are in Hamburg, where about half of its ca. 400 followers live. Demanding "confrontation with the state" and abolition of the "capitalist republic," it has considerable influence within the Green-Alternative List (GAL). The KB publishes a monthly *Arbeiterkampf* (Worker Struggle), which has a circulation of about 5,000. The "Group Z" split from the KB in 1979 and joined the Greens (q.v.), with many of its members rising to top positions in the Greens' federal and Land organizations. The KB militantly opposed German unity, claiming that Germany had no right to self-determination and that unity was an attempt to establish Germany as a major power which threatens other countries.

COMMUNIST MANIFESTO (1848) see MARX, KARL.

COMMUNIST PARTY OF GERMANY (KOMMUNISTISCHE PARTEI DEUTSCHLANDS--KPD) see COMMUNISM; GERMAN COMMUNIST PARTY; REVOLUTION, GERMAN

CONCENTRATION CAMPS. This term was first coined during the Boer War in South Africa, when the British interned Boer civilians from 1900 to 1902 to prevent them from helping the guerrillas. In Germany, the "Soviet Republic of Bavaria," led by Kurt Eisner in 1919, interned its enemies at Dachau, outside of Munich. The Nazis (q.v.) created their first concentration camps at Oranienburg (near Berlin) and Dachau, and by 1939 the number had grown to six, containing 21,000 prisoners. The role of the camps as places to intern the regime's opponents changed after the war began. They greatly increased in number and became primarily extermination camps for Jews and other unwanted minorities. Most notorious were Auschwitz and Belsen in Poland and Buchenwald (near Weimar). Some camps provided slave labor for German industry. Germany's allies, such as Hungary and

Rumania, also had concentration camps. After France was conquered by Germany, the Vichy Republic established internment camps for resistance fighters and Jews. Although they never were death camps for mass extermination of people, they were way-stations to such camps for many unfortunate victims. (See also NAZI REPRESSION.)

CONCERTED ACTION (KONZERTIERTE AKTION--1967-1977). This was a tripartite framework for consultation between government, industry, and unions. The objective was to influence non-government actors' economic decisions by providing them with as much information as possible on the state of the economy. (See also GRAND COALITION.)

CONCORDAT (1933). On July 8, 1933, the Vatican signed a Concordat with the Hitler (q.v.) regime, recognizing it and agreeing to restrictions on political and social Catholic organizations in Germany. In return, the Nazis (q.v.) promised to guarantee freedom of religion, the protection of Church bodies, the right to the dissemination of pastoral letters, and the preservation of parochial schools. Although many German Catholic priests and lay persons opposed this accord, the Church in Germany paid a high moral and political price. Even though from the very beginning the Nazis repeatedly violated the agreement, it made clear-cut confrontation with the regime impossible. Some Catholic leaders opposed certain Nazi policies, such as Hitler's euthanasia program in 1941, which Count Galen, the Bishop of Münster decried. Thousands of priests and laymen were sent to concentration camps and prisons, and members of the Catholic workers' movement worked with the Kreisau Circle (q.v.) and participated in the efforts to overthrow the Hitler regime. Nevertheless, in contrast to the Protestant Church, the Catholic never issued a proclamation of guilt in 1945 or initiated a critical discussion of its activities during the Third Reich (q.v.). The Pope's dubious role during the Hitler era was dramatized by Rolf Hochhuth's (q.v.) play, *The Deputy*, in 1963. (See also CONFESSING CHURCH; STUTTGART CONFESSION OF GUILT.)

CONFERENCE GROUP ON GERMAN POLITICS (CGGP). This facilitates the exchange of ideas and information among hundreds of American scholars generally working on German politics.

CONFERENCE ON SECURITY AND COOPERATION IN EUROPE (CSCE) see SCHMIDT, HELMUT

CONFESSING CHURCH (BEKENNENDE KIRCHE). Within the Protestant Church, the Nazis (q.v.) encouraged the "German Christians" movement, which was oriented toward the Nazis' leadership principle and ideology of the *Volk*. This movement was intended to culminate in a non-denominational German "National Church," and it found many adherents within the Protestant Church and especially among theologians in the universities. In September 1933, Ludwig Müller, an army chaplain and confidant of Hitler (q.v.), was elected "Reich Bishop" at a national synod in Wittenberg dominated by the "German Christians."

In opposition to this Nazi movement, the Confessing Church resistance effort grew out of a group of Protestants around Martin Niemöller (q.v.) who created an "Emergency League of Clergymen" (*Pfarrernotbund*) in early 1934. At its Barmen Confession Synod in late May 1934, it asserted itself as the legal Protestant Church and sharply challenged the "German Christians." The Nazis banned the Barmen Declaration. Confessing Church pastors were watched by the Gestapo and often arrested in the pulpit, and writings were confiscated. Members were routinely prevented from preaching, and they were arrested, deported, and sentenced to long terms in concentration camps (q.v.). But the movement was never crushed, and Church representatives repeatedly made public protests against the deportation of Jews, Hitler's euthanasia program, and the existence of concentration camps (q.v.). (See also CONCORDAT; RESISTANCE TO HITLER; STUTTGART CONFESSION OF GUILT.)

CONGRESS OF VIENNA (1814-1815). Following the final defeat of Napoleon, the statesmen at the Congress of Vienna were tired of revolution and were interested in restoring much of what had existed a quarter of a century earlier. None wanted a unified Germany and none wanted the dissolution of their own states. Their chief objective was to protect Europe from a renewal of the kinds of shocks and challenges which had come out of France. None talked of popular sovereignty, and all spoke of legitimate monarchy. In the end, Prussia gave up some land to a newly-created Kingdom of Poland, but received the northern part of Saxony, Swedish Pomerania and the island of Rügen, as well as territory in the Rhineland and Westphalia. These new territories were separated from the rest of Prussia by Hanover, Braunschweig, and Hesse-Cassel, but they placed it along a common border with France. Its job was one which was performed earlier by Austria--to prevent France, whose 1789 borders remained practically unchanged, from threatening central Europe. As a result of the settlement, Prussia grew into Germany, while Austria grew out of Germany toward Northern Italy and the Balkans. The mineral resources in upper Silesia and the Rhineland provided Prussia with the potential to become the greatest industrial power in Germany and ultimately in Europe.

The Congress of Vienna had no interest in a unified Germany, but it did create a German Confederation to replace the old empire which had died a quiet death almost a decade earlier. The Confederation was a loose association of 35 sovereign German principalities (including the five kingdoms of Prussia, Hanover, Bavaria, Wurttemberg and Saxony) and four free cities. Its sole institution was a Federal Parliament (Bundestag) in Frankfurt, whose chairman was always an Austrian and whose delegates were not elected, but were appointed by the member states. In other words, it was a diplomatic organization, not a real parliament. It was dominated by Austria and Prussia, whose main goal by now was to prevent all change. They were not alone.

The violent events which had shaken Europe in the past quarter century had left many Germans and non-Germans alike longing for peace, order and authority. All members of the Confederation pledged, however, to introduce constitutions, which, if they were observed, would have placed limits on rulers. Such constitutions never saw the light of day in most German states until more than three decades later. This included Prussia and Austria, where absolutism was quickly restored and which joined with Russia in a "Holy Alliance" in 1815 to suppress signs of revolution anywhere in Europe. Only in southern Germany were constitutions introduced which established limited monarchies and brought more citizens into political life. The most shining example was Baden, where the first signs of parliamentary democracy in Germany became visible.

CONSCIENTIOUS OBJECTION (WEHRDIENSTVERWEIGERUNG, often incorrectly referred to as KRIEGSDIENSTVERWEIGERUNG) see ARMED FORCES; OVERCOMING THE PAST; PEACE MOVEMENT

CONSERVATIVE PARTY (KONSERVATIVE PARTEI) see GERMAN REICH PARTY

CONSOLIDATION LAW (1950). This reenacted the earlier Judicature Act in the newly created FRG. It created a Federal High Court in Karlsruhe to replace the former Reich Court (*Reichsgericht*) in Leipzig. The creation of the Federal Constitutional Court (q.v.) in 1951 and a European Court of Justice in 1957 expanded the possibilities of legal appeal provided by the Judicature Act. The Local Court is increasingly becoming a general court of first appeal.

CONSTITUTION OF THE FEDERAL REPUBLIC OF GERMANY see BASIC LAW

CONSTITUTIONAL COURT (VERFASSUNGSGERICHT). To underscore their commitment to the principles in the Basic Law (q.v.), the FRG's founders, with the full support of the Allied occupation authorities, created this court. It has the power of judicial review and therefore is the final arbiter in constitutional questions. With two chambers located in Karlsruhe, it reviews legislation, adjudicates disputes between the national and Land (q.v.) political institutions, rules on questions concerning individual rights, and can even ban groups or parties if it believes their activities are not in harmony with the principles of the Basic Law. The court has a clearly political character, as the selection of the justices reveals: half of the 16 justices are chosen by the lower house of parliament (Bundestag) and half by the upper house (Bundesrat, which ensures that Land interests are not overlooked). The court is administratively independent and cannot be impeached by the parliament. It has not been afraid to lock horns with the government. All parties in disputes before this powerful court, including the national government, have always complied with its decisions.

CONSTRUCTIVE VOTE OF NO-CONFIDENCE see WENDE

COUNCIL OF ELDERS. This is the steering committee of the Bundestag responsible for scheduling debates, setting the legislative agenda, making committee assignments, and generally coordinating all Bundestag activities. It is composed of the leadership of the Bundestag and representatives of the parliamentary groups (q.v.), and its chairperson is the Bundestag president. The Bundestag president, who is nominated by the largest party in the governing coalition, and the vice-presidents, who are nominated by the other major parties in the Bundestag, constitute another executive body, the Presidium, which deals with routine administrative matters of the Bundestag.

COUNCIL OF EXPERTS (SACHVERSTÄNDIGENRAT). Created in 1963, this panel of five economists issues an annual report on the state of the economy and criticizes specific economic and fiscal policies of the federal government.

COUNCIL OF PEOPLE'S REPRESENTATIVES. Body headed by Friedrich Ebert (q.v.) to which Chancellor Max von Baden (q.v.) handed over power on November 9, 1918, the day the Kaiser abdicated and the German republic was declared. (See also REVOLUTION IN GERMANY.)

COUNTER-CYCLICAL ECONOMIC COUNCIL (KONJUNKTURRAT) see LAW ON STABILITY AND GROWTH

COUNTER-REFORMATION see THIRTY-YEARS WAR

CRYSTAL NIGHT (KRISTALLNACHT, November 9-10, 1938) see NAZI REPRESSION

CULTURE STRUGGLE (KULTURKAMPF). This refers to Bismarck's (q.v.) conflict with the Catholic Church from 1871-87. He feared that the Church was demanding that Catholics be primarily loyal to it, rather than to the state. He was also alarmed by the formation of the Catholic Center Party (q.v.), which was consistently opposed to Prussia. The Prussian "Falk Laws" of 1873 resulted in the complete subordination of the Catholic Church to state control. Many priests went to prison for opposing this. Most Catholic rights were restored in 1887. (See also BISMARCK DOMESTIC POLICY.)

CURATORIUM INDIVISIBLE GERMANY (KURATORIUM UNTEILBARES DEUTSCHLAND). In order to keep interest in German unity alive, Jacob Kaiser (q.v.), Thomas Dehler, and SPD Chairman Erich Ollenhauer (q.v.) founded this organization in 1954. Federal President Theodor Heuss (q.v.) approved it as an official bipartisan organization. Its members sought to emphasize that the FRG's integration with the West would not divert attention from the goal of reunification (q.v.). With its headquarters in Bonn, it was active in sponsoring high-level conferences through the 1980s until unity was achieved in 1990. Its long-serving chairman was Johann Baptist Gradl, a Christian Democrat from East Germany.

CURRENCY. Deutsche Mark, also introduced in eastern Germany on July 1, 1990. Germans had very negative experiences with devastatingly high inflation during the Weimar Republic (q.v.). It pauperized and radicalized many people and handicapped the newly created democracy almost from the beginning. Therefore, after 1949 the FRG has placed a very high priority on protecting the value of its money by controlling inflation. The Bundesbank (q.v.) assumes the main responsibility for this. The desire to maintain the stability of their currency makes many Germans leery of a unified European currency, even though the Kohl government accepted the goal to create one. Selected dollar values show how the D-Mark has appreciated: On March 6, 1961, the Mark was revalued 4.75 percent, making one dollar worth DM 4. In 1971 the dollar's link to gold was cut; this ended fixed exchange rates, and currencies were thereafter "floated," finding their values on exchange markets according to "supply and demand." On March 1, 1978, the dollar sank for the first time below the two DM level; on January 3, 1980, it fell to DM 1.7; on September 1, 1992, it dropped below DM 1.40, a record low. Since German prosperity is heavily dependent upon the export of goods and services, its exporters must constantly improve quality, service, and efficiency in order to offset the effects of one of the world's hardest currencies. This was especially difficult for firms in eastern Germany, whose pre-reunification customers in the East could hardly pay for eastern German goods in D-Mark after 1990. (See also WEIMAR REPUBLIC.)

CURRENCY REFORM (1948). West German economic recovery got an important shot in the arm from a bracing currency reform in mid-1948 through which the increasingly worthless *Reichsmark* was replaced by a new *Deutschmark*. Every German started at the same point, with only 40 marks in his pocket. This reform was followed by a scrapping of all rationing and price controls--a bold move widely criticized at the time, but one which the chairman of the Bizonal Economic Council, Professor Ludwig Erhard (q.v.), and the U.S.

occupation governor, General Lucius Clay (q.v.), considered essential. They proved to be right. Suddenly goods reappeared in the stores and markets. One witnessed a disappearance of the black market, whose more treasured items had come from the U.S. military post exchanges (PXs). For a while Germans had a *de facto* "cigarette economy," in which American cigarettes, not old German Reichsmarks, were the country's actual currency. After several years, many Germans could actually begin smoking cigarettes again rather than hoarding them as a money substitute! The economic improvement was so dramatic that in 1949 Erhard's party could enter the first West German elections with the convincing slogan *Es geht wieder!* ("It's working again!")

CUSTOMS UNION (ZOLLVEREIN, 1834). This was established in 1834 by all German states except Austria, Hanover, Mecklenburg, Oldenburg, Holstein and the Hansa Cities (q.v.). This far-sighted move which created a unified inland market not only became the cornerstone for a united Germany 37 years later, but it became an important model years later for the EC (q.v.). The German Customs Union greatly stimulated the industrialization of Germany, whose population at the time was three-fourths agricultural. At the same time it diminished the position within Germany of Austria and enhanced the economic predominance of Prussia.

GIs trying to control the black market, which thrived until currency reform. (*Source:* Army signal corps and GCML, Lexington, Virginia.)

-D-

DAHRENDORF, RALF (1929-). Former sociologist at University of Konstanz and author of the seminal book, *Society and Democracy in Germany*. After serving as an FDP (q.v.) member of the Bundestag and parliamentary secretary in the foreign office (1969-70), he became a member of the EC (q.v.) Commission in Brussels and in 1974 director of the London School of Economics. After being knighted, Sir Ralf was named warden of St. Antony's College in Oxford. (See also JASPERS, KARL.)

DAILY TELEGRAPH AFFAIR (1908). In an interview with this British newspaper, published on October 28, 1908, Kaiser Wilhelm II was seeking to diminish British fears of Germany's plans to build a powerful blue-water navy and to present himself as a lover of peace. But he combined historical distortions with offensive flattery, and the conclusion was that he advocated sheer force in international relations. His clumsy diplomacy caused a storm of protest in both countries and practically led to Wilhelm's abdication. It diminished his political influence. (See also BÜLOW, BERNHARD.)

DAIMLER, GOTTFRIED (1834-1900). A scientist, he invented a practical gasoline-burning internal-combustion engine in 1886, fitting it into a car the following year. This idea grew into the prestigious Mercedes-Benz automobiles and other vehicles.

DANZIG (NOW GDANSK IN POLAND). Located at the mouth of the Vistula River, this German-inhabited city was Poland's only seaport from the 15th century until 1793, when Prussia annexed it. The Treaty of Versailles (q.v.) made it a free city to provide Poland with an outlet to the sea, along with a new port at Gdynia, located in the "Polish Corridor" which connected the main part of the country with the sea. The Nazis (q.v.) gained control of the Danzig Senate in 1933, and the Nazi leader there proclaimed the union of the city with Germany. This act was one of the sparks for the outbreak of the Second World War (q.v.). The Russians captured the city in March 1945 and handed it over to the Poles who expelled the entire German population.

DATA PROTECTION (DATENSCHUTZ). Because of increasing concern about the misuse of data and the names of innocent persons stored in intelligence computer systems, the federal and Länder parliaments created commissioners for data protection and passed laws restricting the use of information in the data banks. It was concern over the possible misuse which caused emotional and widespread opposition to the 1980 census which could not be conducted until 1987. (See also OVERCOMING PAST.)

DÄUBLER-GMELIN, HERTA. Elected first deputy of SPD Bundestag parliamentary group in December 1991.

DAWES, CHARLES and PLAN (1924) see WEIMAR REPUBLIC

DE BRUYN, GÜNTER (1926-). Born in Berlin, de Bruyn was a soldier and prisoner of war before he finally settled in the GDR (q.v.). He had a variety of work experiences and became a full-time writer in 1963. His short stories are admired for their social criticism. Collective and individual guilt are popular themes in his stories.

DE STAEL, MADAME DE see INTRODUCTION

DECARTELIZATION. The victorious Allies insisted after 1945 that the German economy as a whole be so reconstructed that power would be taken away from the cartels, the interlocking groups of industrial leaders which many people considered to have been heavily responsible for Hitler's (q.v.) acquisition of power and conduct of warfare. Many German business leaders were also interested in decartelization, reasoning that if German industry were to be successful in the postwar world, it would have to adapt to foreign, particularly American methods, which required open markets and a rejection of cartels. The Germans created a Cartel Office (*Kartellamt*) in West Berlin which still functions to prevent the formation of these interlocking groups.

DEGENERATE ART (ENTARTETE KUNST). This was a Nazi (q.v.) conception applied to virtually all non-representational painting, sculpture, and graphic art. Exhibitions of this art were held in Munich and other cities in 1936, but they were so well attended that the Nazis got scared and closed them. A number of public monuments were destroyed or defaced. Many of the artists were forced to emigrate.

DEHLER, THOMAS (1897-1967). FDP, federal justice minister (1949-53), chairman of FDP parliamentary group (1953-57), vice-president of the Bundestag (1960-67). (See CURATORIUM.)

DEMOCRACY NOW (DEMOKRATIE JETZT) see ALLIANCE 90

DEMOCRACY ON GUARD. The new republic was to be strengthened by being a "democracy on guard" (*streitbare Demokratie*). Critics of the almost universally defamed Weimar Republic noted that Hitler (qq.v.) had gained power while following the rules of what some persons had considered to be the "most democratic constitution" in the world. The permissive Weimar constitution, which was neutral and "value-relative," had enabled extremists on both the left and right to use the liberties it guaranteed to undermine the democratic order. By contrast, the FRG's Basic Law (q.v.) was to be for certain values, and to be bound to a value-oriented political system. After the moral vacuum of the Hitler era, the new *Rechtsstaat* (q.v.) was to have as its core value "the dignity of man." No law, administrative act, or legal judgment was to be in contradiction to this value system.

There is considerable wisdom in the decision to create a "democracy on guard," but there are many problems in attempting to achieve this goal. Activist measures to try to protect the democratic order by clamping down hard on groups which the government brands as threats to the constitution open Bonn's leaders to charges that they themselves are the real threats to civil liberties. For instance, remembering that the Nazi party had been permitted to operate freely, Article 21 of the Basic Law requires that all political parties "conform to democratic principles." Those which "according to their aims and the conduct of their members, seek to impair or abolish the free democratic basic order or jeopardize the existence of the FRG are unconstitutional." Few people complained when a rowdy right-wing party, called the Socialist Reich Party (SRP), was outlawed in 1952. But when the Communist Party (KPD, q.v.) was banned in 1956, a chorus of protest arose, alleging that this followed the dangerous path trodden by the rabidly anti-Communist Hitler. Some critics found the ban "primitive" and "reactionary." Nothing had changed, they argued. Another example is the Extremists Decision (q.v.), drafted by ex-Chancellor Brandt (q.v.) and the Land governments to control the rebellious student protesters. Government fears were strengthened when radicals, such as Rudi Dutschke, began speaking in the late 1960s about a "long march through the institutions." Remembering the Weimar Republic as a "democracy without democrats," which had far too few civil servants who were prepared or inclined to defend the republic, the Basic Law in 1949 stipulated that all applicants for the civil service must guarantee that they are prepared actively to support the free and democratic order at all times.

DEMOCRATIC AWAKENING (DEMOKRATISCHER AUFBRUCH-- DA). Founded on December 16-17, 1989, and led by Wolfgang Schnur (q.v.) until March 1990, this party was supported by the western CDU (q.v.). Since the eastern CDU had been one of the "bloc parties" (q.v.) which had worked with the Communists in the SED, the Bonn CDU was hesitant to work with it. In preparation for the March 18, 1990, GDR elections (q.v.), the old eastern CDU was combined with the new DA and new German Social Union (DSU) to form the "Alliance for Germany." This non-communist alliance barely missed winning an absolute majority, and it therefore formed a coalition with the SPD to administer the demise of the GDR.

DEMOCRATIC FARMERS' PARTY (DEMOKRATISCHE BAUERNPARTEI--DBD). In order to mobilize East German voters who by 1949 had still not been attracted to the SED or the bloc parties (qq.v.), which were no more than satellites of the SED, the latter cultivated two new parties, the DBD and the National Democratic Party of Germany (NDPD). The DBD was intended to attract a rural population which had traditionally been hostile to the Communists. The NDPD directed its appeal to former Nazis (q.v.), army officers, and others who were tainted by their activities in the Third Reich (q.v.).

DEMOCRATIC GERMAN WOMEN'S LEAGUE (DEMOKRATISCHER FRAUENBUND DEUTSCHLANDS--DFD) see WOMEN'S LEAGUE

DEMOCRATIC PEOPLE'S PARTY (DEMOKRATISCHE VOLKSPARTEI--DVP, 1945) see FREE DEMOCRATIC PARTY

DENAZIFICATION. The victorious powers in 1945 were determined to exterminate the Nazi (q.v.) bacillus so that the past could never repeat itself and to punish those who had borne responsibility in the Hitler (q.v.) regime. But the Allies had no clear idea on exactly what the essence of Nazism had been and how to change the Germans. At the Potsdam Conference they agreed to strive for "democracy" and "justice." But the elasticity of these concepts in the minds of such ideologically divided Allies made American diplomat George Kennan admit that "I can remember no political document which could have depressed me more."

Nor were the minority of Germans who dealt with this problem unified. Those from the Kreisau (q.v.) and July 20 circles believed that the purging and punishing should be done by the Germans themselves, by means of a restored *Rechtsstaat* (q.v.,"State of Law"), and should be limited to the top Nazis. Many Social Democrats, who had opposed the Enabling Act (q.v.) in 1933 and who had been active in the resistance (q.v.), sought a broader purge aiming at a change of elites and of the economic structures. They had revolutionary expectations. The Communists, who had also paid a heavy price in the resistance, especially after Hitler had broken the Non-Aggression Pact and invaded the Soviet Union, also wanted large-scale expropriations of property and radical purges. However, they wished to leave the "small Nazi party comrade" alone to gain his support for the new communist order. It is no wonder that so many Germans were dissatisfied in the end with the process of denazification.

The victorious Allies could all agree, as could most Germans at the time, that the highest surviving Nazi leaders be placed on trial in Nuremberg from November 1945 to October 1946, where most were sentenced to death or long prison terms. The judges there established that any members of certain groups declared criminal could be brought to trial in the separate zones of occupation to determine guilt for war crimes and crimes against peace and humanity. The Reich government and the general staff were not declared to be illegal. Mere membership in tainted organizations was not enough to convict a person, but could be grounds for a trial in which his actual participation in a specific crime had to be proved. The western Allies and most Germans themselves wanted any actions against suspected Nazi criminals to follow established legal procedures. Proving such participation by millions of Germans in legal proceedings with the right of appeal became a hopelessly daunting task, but it was nevertheless attempted.

The process of rooting out Nazis proved to be a cumbersome, perplexing and unmanageable task. It was so complex and was based on such a maze of often contradictory texts and directives that any summary of it is extremely difficult. By the time it was terminated, it was widely believed to have been a colossal failure, and German support for it dwindled steadily. The Americans showed the most energy and enthusiasm (some would say "naivete"), while the Soviets revealed a somewhat greater interest in facilitating a revolution than in punishing former Nazis. The French and British began by following the American lead before growing more skeptical.

The first step was to intern people who were subject to "automatic" arrest because of the posts they had held or organizations to which they belonged. By the end of 1946 the Americans had locked up 95,000 persons, the British 64,000, the French 19,000, and the Soviets 67,000. These figures do not include a great number who had been already released. Mass dismissals from jobs were ordered, and in the American zone anybody who had belonged to the Nazi party or any organization connected with it was barred from practicing a profession or craft other than manual labor or a subordinate position. About a third of those in the public service was dismissed, and in some parts of the American zone the percentage of top or mid-level civil servants was much higher: three-fourths in Hesse, almost all in Nuremberg, and 295 out of 302 judges in the Bamberg region. Two out of three teachers in the American zone were fired.

It soon became apparent that such massive dismissals threatened the entire country with economic and administrative breakdown and could not be maintained. There were simply too few people who could take the place of those who were fired. The victors faced a conflict of two important goals: to root out all Nazis and to get the German economy on its feet. This became especially urgent as the cooperative spirit with the Soviet Union crumbled and the contours of the Cold War began to take shape. Perhaps the most notorious case was that of Alfred Krupp, who had been sentenced at Nuremberg to 12 years in prison for utilizing slave labor, but was freed after only three in order to get his steel works producing again.

General George Patton grumbled out loud, and Major General Ernest Harmon admitted: "I can't stand the Krauts, but it's one thing to make them understand who won the war, and another to get them through the winter without food and coal....One can't have the railways operated by shopkeepers and the factories led by shoe-shine boys." Dozens of American occupation officers had to be threatened with court martial if they continued to resist applying the denazification guidelines. Polls taken among both Germans and American occupiers at the time revealed that many Germans still believed that Nazism was good in theory and would have been good in practice if it had not been for the war. Surprisingly many American soldiers in Germany agreed with this view.

With the entire effort threatening to collapse, a new procedure had to be introduced in 1946, which for the first time involved the help of the German Land governments. The new and highly controversial "Law for the Liberation from National Socialism and Militarism," which became a target for newly founded parties in the Western zones, created a monstrous process, requiring 13 million (out of 17 million) Germans in the American zone alone to fill out a questionnaire, from which it would be determined into which of five categories they should be placed. This questionnaire became the subject of a best-selling satire written by Ernst von Solomon, *Der Fragebogen*.

A gigantic apparatus had to be built up to process these questionnaires. In 545 courts, 22,000 Germans worked on the cases, which required trials and the possibility of appeal, of which there were many. The case load grew to 950,000 and was impossible to deal with. In the end, only 1,654 ex-Nazis were declared to be "heavily burdened" (*hauptbelastet*), and the overwhelming majority were declared merely to have been slightly involved or only "tag-alongs" (*Mitläufer*); 95 percent of those dismissed from the public service returned to their jobs, albeit after a delay. A major problem was that denazification was linked with rehabilitation, which Germans sarcastically called a *Persilschein* (a certificate of Persil, a soap powder). Therefore, anybody who was cleared had convinced the court and himself that he had not been responsible for what had happened during the Third Reich. This made the question of national guilt very problematic. Many Germans could disclaim any guilt by pointing out that "I was cleared by a court of law!"

In the Soviet Zone there were also mass dismissals of public servants and teachers, sparing for the most part the lower level Nazis. Interested primarily in a revolution, the Soviets expropriated private property and established a dictatorship of their satellite party, the KPD, later the SED (q.v.). They were little concerned about the legalities of their actions, as was indicated by an order from Walter Ulbricht (q.v.) to farmers in Sachsen-Anhalt who were uneasy about seizing private land without a law authorizing it: "That is all simple: you take the land from the landowner, and that is the first step toward a democratic order....A law? If the farmers here decide to take the land, that is their democratic right." When the farmers still desired a law, Ulbricht responded: "Well

OK, if you need a law, we will create one so that you can conduct this entirely orderly (*ganz ordentlich*)."

The idea of socializing the economy in order to break the power of the capitalists who had supported Hitler was widely popular in all zones and among many Christian Democrats as well as Social Democrats. Many persons believed that it was the capitalist economic system which had been responsible for the Nazi takeover and that it had to be rooted out of Germany as well. But this possibility of massive nationalizations and decartelization (q.v.) in the Western zones was overtaken by events and the desire to put the German economy back on its feet. The Americans never had much taste for it anyway. Backing away from such fundamental economic changes opened up another vulnerable flank for critics, who bemoaned a golden opportunity lost. SPD leader Kurt Schumacher (q.v.), who died in 1952 of ailments acquired during 12 years in concentration camps, spoke bitterly of the "lost opportunity."

In February 1948, the Soviets ended denazification in their zone, and the Western powers also decided to terminate their programs quickly and generously. They handed the whole responsibility over to the Land governments in the fall of 1948, which were under severe political pressure from below to end the whole process. Despite popular dissatisfaction, the new West German government continued, unifying the procedure and dealing with the question of who could be reinstated and who could not. It was a contentious political issue, with the Christian parties pushing for a reinstatement of most persons, while the SPD (q.v.) opposed any mass return to normalcy. In May 1951, almost all persons who had not been declared by a court to be unfit for public service were allowed to go back to work. This elicited howls of "renazification." However, a large part of the tainted officials in the upper and middle levels had been kept out of their jobs for six years, thereby clearing the way for new and younger persons to move up in the civil service.

West German courts began ending their legal action against Nazi war criminals altogether in the late 1980s. It had long become too difficult to find enough witnesses or proof to prosecute suspects. But it had been politically impossible at various times to allow the normal statute of limitations to go into effect. By 1987, 91,000 people had been prosecuted in West Germany, and 6,479 sentences had been meted out: 12 death sentences until 1950, when the death penalty was abolished, 160 life sentences, and 6,192 prison terms. The Western Allies issued

5,025 penalties under their own authority, including 806 death sentences.

The GDR renounced all guilt by arguing that Nazism had been the product of capitalism and was thus the responsibility of the capitalist part of Germany. Not until the non-communist government of Lothar de Maizière (q.v.) took office in April 1990, a mere half year before the disappearance of the GDR, did the leaders of the GDR admit sharing guilt for the crimes committed in the Third Reich, especially against Jews. This confession was de Maizière's first act as prime minister, and his government is no doubt the first in history to begin its work with a public apology. Until the early 1990s Austria stubbornly stuck to its claim that it was Nazi Germany's first victim, a claim supported by Allied policy during the war. But from the very beginning the FRG took the position that a people cannot sneak away from its own history. Even if an entire people cannot be burdened with collective guilt (q.v.) for everything which the Nazis had done, West German leaders accepted the notion that the Third Reich and all the crimes which had been committed under it are a part of German history, and that the German people as a whole must answer for it. There can never be a "zero hour" (q.v.) when a sharp break with the past can be made, and West Germany accepted the German past with all the positive and negative consequences which went with it. In Richard von Weizsäcker's (q.v.) words, "there was no 'zero hour,' but we had the chance of a new beginning. We used it as best we could."

It would appear that everything possible had been done to ferret out the real Nazis and to show good faith in compensating the victims generously, to the extent that one can ever truly compensate for loss of life. But the Federal Republic was never able to convince everyone that justice had been done and that its roots had not in fact been poisoned by the Nazi past. A string of embarrassing revelations bolstered this view. For example, Adenauer's (q.v.) state secretary and closest adviser from 1953 to 1963 was Hans Globke. A former high official in Hitler's interior ministry, Globke had allegedly helped draft a portion of the anti-Jewish laws.

In 1966, Kurt Georg Kiesinger (q.v.), a decent and modest southern German, became chancellor. But he had served Propaganda Minister Joseph Goebbels as deputy director of the radio department of the Reich foreign office. He did not deserve the public slap he received from Beate Klarsfeld (q.v.), but it was not easy to respond to novelist Günther Grass' (q.v.) open letters to him asking: "If a former Nazi can become chancellor, not only the petty hanger-on of former times but also a youngster for whom the Third Reich is ancient history can vote National Democrat with a clear conscience." Other reports in 1970 revealed that half of the 15,000 magistrates and judges in the FRG had held positions in the Nazi era. No member of the judiciary has been prosecuted for crimes committed during the Hitler era.

In 1977, Hans Filbinger, the very picture of the gentle *Landesvater* (father of his state), was forced to resign as minister president (governor) of Baden-Wurttemberg as a result of a press campaign led by author Rolf Hochhut (q.v.). Filbinger had recommended in his doctoral dissertation four decades earlier that "racial inferiors" should be put to death and dangerous "moral criminals" be emasculated. It was also reported that he had signed death sentences for teenage naval deserters in the final days of the war. His public denials of these charges proved to be lies. His presence in the Bundestag on the occasion of President Weizsäcker's speech commemorating the fortieth anniversary of the fall of the Hitler regime was, in some Germans' view, a serious blunder. In January 1993, Dr. Hans-Joachim Sewering of Dachau, the former president of the Federal Physicians' Chamber, was elected president of the World Medical Association. But he was forced to withdraw when it was revealed that, as a member of the Nazi Party and SS, he had signed an order to send a 14-year-old girl to her death in a euthanasia center.

In May 1992, a Stuttgart court sentenced 80-year-old former SS sergeant, Josef Franz Schwammberg, to life in prison for abetting in the murder of hundreds of Jews in the forced labor camps of Rozwadov and Przemysl. He fled to Argentina after the war, where he was arrested in 1987 and extradited to Germany in May 1990. The director of the Central Office for the Prosecution of Nazi Crimes in Ludwigsburg, Alfred Streim, noted that since the end of the war 163 life sentences have been given to Nazi criminals in western Germany; none was executed because the Basic Law (q.v.) forbade the death penalty in 1949. Some 6,200 persons were imprisoned. The GDR passed sentences against 12,900 persons. Streim said that "in the future, there will probably be no more big Nazi trials."

Revelations of high officials with a tainted past may indicate how successful the FRG was in integrating people who once went astray. It may show how persons can change their convictions to become sincere democrats. Also, they may not have been in a position to order that crimes be committed. But many Germans would agree with Stuttgart historian, Eberhardt Jäckel, who said: "Whether these and other men were personally guilty is not the point. It was bad for German democracy, and it set a bad example to the younger generation, that people with *any* kind of Nazi record should have been given such posts. Adenauer and the other CDU leaders should have been more scrupulous."

The controversial denazification programs of the occupation powers required that those Germans who had held positions of obvious authority or influence under the Nazis be jailed, fined or demoted. Others, such as civil servants, teachers, journalists or industrial leaders, most of whom had no choice about joining the Nazi Party, were at least temporarily removed from their jobs. In the end, all the elites under the previous regime had been deprived of their status, except church leaders. It is questionable whether the denazification measures were strictly necessary at all. Defeat and utter destruction under the leadership of Hitler had been the best antidote to Nazism. Although it took several more years to convince many Germans that even the general idea of National Socialism had been wrong, their approval of the concrete form which Nazism had taken had disappeared almost completely by the end of the war.

The German Army was completely disbanded, and when a Federal Army was created in 1956, the military's influence and prestige in political and social life had been almost entirely eliminated. The various classes had not been eradicated, but they had been brought more closely together during the Third Reich and the aftermath of the war. Germans now mingled more easily with one another. Although an end to hostilities brought no political revolution or social upheaval, as had been the case in 1918, the quiet social and political revolution which culminated in 1945 was much more far-reaching than that of 1918. Germans were now divided territorially, but they were no longer so divided domestically. The old conservatives had been discredited, and the romanticism of war, assertiveness in the world, and ideas about German national unique superiority had been extinguished. Ideologies had little appeal anymore, and most Germans had become convinced that a flight from the much debunked "bourgeois values," including especially parliamentary democracy within a rule of law, solves no problems and can bring immense suffering to human beings. Many Germans emerged from the war politically apathetic, but important changes in their political attitudes had occurred which would augur well for a new German democracy.

DETTKE, DIETER (1941-). SPD, author of a book on superpower relations, Dr. Dettke served for many years under Eugen Selbmann as the foreign policy adviser to the SPD Bundestag parliamentary group. After a brief stint in the Foreign Office, he has subsequently served for many years as the director of the Washington office of the Friedrich Ebert Foundation (q.v.), where he has made a major contribution in bringing Americans into contact with leading Social Democrats.

DEUTSCHE ALTERNATIVE and DEUTSCHE LIGA see PARTIES, RIGHT-WING

DEUTSCHLAND, DEUTSCHLAND ÜBER ALLES (SONG) see ELECTIONS 1972 and LIBERALISM

DIEPGEN, EBERHARD (1941-). CDU, mayor of Berlin in the 1990s.

DIESEL, RUDOLF (1858-1913). A scientifically trained engineer from Germany's Technische Hochschulen (technical universities), Diesel invented the engine bearing his name. His inventive work was in part motivated by social concerns, the desire to produce a small power source that would reinvigorate the artisan class. A poor businessman, he went bankrupt and ended his own life.

DIESTEL, PETER-MICHAEL (1952-) see COMMITTEE FOR JUSTICE

DIETRICH, MARLENE (1901-1992). An actress, she became an instant success in her first film, *The Blue Angel* (q.v.). Adamantly opposed to Hitler (q.v.), she refused his invitation to return to Berlin, which she had left in 1930. She became a Hollywood star and American citizen in 1939, entertained the Allied troops in the Second World War (q.v.), and returned to Berlin after the war wearing an American army uniform. Many Germans considered her a traitor. When she visited Berlin in 1960, she was met by demonstrators chanting "Marlene Go Home!" She never set foot in Germany again and said: "I want to be buried in France, leave my heart in England, and to Germany--nothing!" She died in her Paris apartment and was returned to Berlin to be buried beside her mother. Thousands lined the streets to say good-bye, and the Green party (q.v.) placed a wreath on her grave with the words: "You were the real Germany." (See also WEIMAR CULTURE.)

DILTHEY, WILHELM (1833-1911). Dilthey elaborated a positivistic idealism. He based philosophy on inner experience. The purpose of philosophy is to elevate the inner motives of a culture to consciousness of themselves and to a realization of their goals. Knowledge embraces both thought and the entire psychic life. In *Introduction to the Sciences of the Spirit* (1883), he distinguished between natural sciences and the sciences of the spirit. The latter deal with immediate reality, values, and norms, with reality as it appears in history and society, and with systems of culture. What we see in the phenomena of the external world is an opposite and correlate of ourselves. (See also EMPIRE CULTURE.)

DIRECT DEMOCRACY see WEIMAR REPUBLIC

DIX, OTTO (1891-1969). Best known for his depiction of the horrors of war which he experienced in the First World War (q.v.), Dix was a social critic whose scenes of human suffering and moral decadence shocked his public. He taught at the art academy in Dresden until he was dismissed by the Nazis (q.v.). He retreated to the romantic landscapes of Swabia before returning to his expressionistic style with its large, bold effects.

DÖBLIN, ALFRED (1878-1957). A physician turned author, Döblin studied at the Universities of Freiburg and Berlin and later practiced in the slums of eastern Berlin after 1918. A Jew and active Social Democrat, Döblin fled to France after Hitler (q.v.) came to power, and in 1940 he escaped to the U.S. and converted to Catholicism in the same year. In 1945, he returned to Germany as a military officer and eventually settled in Paris in 1951. Döblin was acutely aware of the vulnerability of the individual against the forces of society. His 1929 expressionist novel, *Berlin Alexanderplatz*, depicts the uphill struggle of an ex-convict to rehabilitate himself. He wrote many more novels and essays dealing with political, social and literary themes.

DOHNANYI, KLAUS VON (1928-). SPD, federal minister for education and science (1972-74), state minister and parliamentary secretary in Foreign Office (1979-81), Mayor of Hamburg.

DÖNITZ, KARL (1891-1980). Supreme commander of German Navy (1943-45), Hitler's (q.v.) successor as Reich president and supreme commander of armed forces in closing days of Second World War (q.v.).

DORNBERGER, WALTER R. see ROCKETS

DÖRRIE, DORIS (1955-). This filmmaker from Hanover studied drama and film in the U.S. and Munich. After several documentary and children's made-for-television films, she made her first feature film, *Straight for the Heart,* in 1983. Her entertaining ironic exploration of the male mystique, *Männer,* established her reputation as one of the finest contemporary filmmakers. She is the author of two novels and two collections of short stories. (See also FILM.)

DREGGER, ALFRED (1920-). CDU, Member of Bundestag since 1972 and of CDU Executive Committee. Served as CDU parliamentary group chairman during Kohl (qq.v.) government.

DRESSLER, RUDOLF (1940-). In December 1991 he was elected SPD (q.v.) deputy chairman of Bundestag parliamentary group.

DROSTE-HÜLSDORFF, ANNETTE VON (1797-1848). She is considered the finest lyric poetess in the history of German literature. Firmly rooted in her region (Westphalia) and her Catholicism, she wrote with realistic observation and deep psychological insight. *Die Judenbuche* (*The Jew's Beech Tree*) is her best novel and deals with crime, ignorance, and racial prejudice.

DUAL ALLIANCE WITH AUSTRIA (1879) see BISMARCK ALLIANCE SYSTEM

DUCHAC, JOSEF see VOGEL, BERNHARD

DUDEN. This dictionary of rules, grammar and spelling written by Konrad Duden in 1880 has been newly revised to become an all-German publication. The GDR (q.v.) had its own version since 1947. There are now over 115,000 entries including some 5,000 new ones with loan words like "lifestyle" and "Dönerkabab," a Turkish sandwich. After German reunification (q.v.) in 1990, the first common *Duden* in four decades was published.

DÜHRING, K. EUGEN (1833-1921). A lawyer and lecturer on philosophy and economics, he had to give up academic work because of blindness. Starting with an early expression of his views in *Natural Dialectic* (1865), he argued that reality is what appears in our experience. Although the intellect constantly tries to create continuity and infinity, reality only appears in finite units. Nature produces beings that act and enjoy their existence, and pain and cruelty are elements in the satisfactions of life. He believed in moral progress. Contemplation of the order of the universe creates universal affection in one's mind. That affection replaces traditional forms of religion.

DÜRER, ALBRECHT (1471-1528). As the first artist outside of Italy to gain an international reputation, the well-traveled Dürer knew many of the leading humanists and artists of his time. As a master of the graphic arts, he was trained as a goldsmith before taking up painting, print making, and woodcuts. His *Self Portrait, Praying Hands,* and *Hare* are easily identifiable. This "Leonardo of the North" from Nuremberg illustrated books and circulated prints on single sheets, thus making art available to people of ordinary means. His self-portraits, correspondence and diary give us an accurate account of his life and times. (See also RENAISSANCE.)

DUTSCHKE, RUDI (1940-1979) see DEMOCRACY ON GUARD and GREENS

DWINGER, EDWIN ERICH see WEIMAR CULTURE

-E-

EBERT, FRIEDRICH (1871-1925). SPD chairman (1913-19), Reich president (1919-25). Ebert was born into poverty, the son of a Heidelberg tailor. His profession was saddle making, and he had also worked in his earlier years as a bartender. He entered the Reichstag in 1912, and when the war broke out in 1914, he supported the *Burgfrieden* ("peace in the fortress") which called for all German parties to unify behind the war effort. Nevertheless, he opposed the policies of annexation and advocated a generous peace. On November 9, 1918, he was appointed the last imperial chancellor; when his predecessor, Prince Max von Baden (q.v.), advised him to take the German Empire into his heart, Ebert answered: "I have lost two sons for this Empire." He sought to end the revolutionary unrest and to have a national assembly elected which would write a democratic constitution for Germany. However, his pact with the supreme military command on November 10, 1918, to reestablish order, including the use of the armed forces and Free Corps against workers, were thenceforth decried by leftists as a betrayal of the working class and the revolution. On February 11, 1919, the National Assembly elected him president (renewed for three years on October 24, 1922). He tried to be a good president for all the Germans. He confessed at the time he was sworn in that "I am a son of the working class and grew up in the world of socialist thought and am inclined to deny neither my origin nor my convictions." In 1924 he even had to appear in court to testify against these charges, causing such strain on him that he died on February 28, 1925, of an appendix infection. (See also REVOLUTION IN GERMANY; WEIMAR REPUBLIC.)

EBERT, FRIEDRICH (1894-1979).   SPD, then SED, son of former President Ebert. Mayor of East Berlin (1948-61).

ECOLOGICAL LEFT/ALTERNATIVE LIST see GREENS

ECONOMIC COUNCIL (KONJUNKTURRAT) see TAXATION

ECONOMIC MIRACLE (WIRTSCHAFTSWUNDER) see ERHARD, LUDWIG

ECONOMIC RECONSTRUCTION LEAGUE (WIRTSCHAFTLICHE AUFBAUVEREINIGUNG--WAV). This was a small party which emerged temporarily during the post-1945 occupation period.

ECONOMY, ENERGY. In no sector is the FRG's dependence upon imports so critical as in energy, especially oil, which accounts for 35.6 percent of the FRG's needs. The precipitous fall in the price of oil (and in the value of the U.S. dollar) was an economic boon during Kohl's (q.v.) chancellorship and was an important reason for his government's reelection in 1990. Most of its natural gas, which provides 15 percent of the FRG's energy, must be imported. The only significant domestic energy source is coal, from which 37 percent of the FRG's energy is derived. It accounts for about 28 percent of the West's needs and a far higher percentage of the East's. However, German coal must be subsidized since its extraction costs are higher than the costs of importing foreign coal. Alternative forms of energy, including hydroelectric power, account for only 2 percent of energy consumption.

Although conservation measures have had some success, total energy consumption continues to rise. The government had planned to cope with this through nuclear power, which in 1985 accounted for a third of West Germany's electricity. The FRG already has more than a dozen nuclear power plants. Their numbers were to have been increased, but in 1992 nuclear power provided only 10 percent of the country's energy. Planners were almost stopped in their tracks by the intense domestic protest to the construction of nuclear power plants and of facilities for the reprocessing and storage of nuclear wastes. By 1991, the FRG government had shut down all the Soviet-designed reactors in the East because they failed to meet safety standards. The economics ministry proposed that two modern plants be built on the sites of former reactors at Stendal, as well as at Greifswald, where a meltdown almost occurred in the mid-1970s.

Currently Germany can use French reprocessing facilities and temporarily store wastes at the power stations, but this is not a permanent solution. The inability to expand nuclear power generation at a more rapid rate and to develop alternative sources, despite the fact that many government research subsidies are devoted to energy-related projects, prevents the FRG from improving the structural weaknesses of its energy position. It has succeeded in reducing its dependence on oil imported from the Persian Gulf; its main supplier now is the U.K. It remains the highest per capita importer of energy and food of any major industrialized country.

ECONOMY, FOREIGN TRADE. Foreign trade remains the essential pillar of the FRG's prosperity. It is one of the world's leading exporters, and exports account for over half of its manufacturing jobs. A third (compared with 12 percent in Japan) of its GNP is derived from exports, a fact which makes the FRG very sensitive to world economic climates. It has the advantage of not being overly reliant on the U.S. market, to which only 10 percent of its exports flow, versus 40 percent of Japan's and 75 percent of Canada's. Past export success has provided the FRG with investment capital, much of which is invested in the U.S. About 40 percent of all German foreign investments are made in the U.S., and only 18 percent in developing countries. The FRG is poor in natural resources, except for modest deposits of iron ore, of natural gas and especially of hard coal in the Ruhr and Saar regions, and of brown coal in the foothills of the Harz mountains, near Cologne, and in the East. In general, it must import raw materials and export finished goods. Since raw materials are usually priced on the international market chiefly in U.S. dollars, the FRG is very vulnerable to rises in the dollar's value.

ECONOMY, GOVERNMENT INTERVENTION. FRG governments have been more hesitant than many other Western European countries to intervene directly in the economy and to protect or prop up lame duck industries. Voices have sometimes been raised, especially by the labor unions, for protection against the extremely rapid rise of competitive Japanese exports into the FRG, which have created serious economic problems for the shipbuilding, steel, photo, and especially automotive industries.

The state participates in the ownership and management of some public services such as the telephone, rail and airline systems. The Kohl (q.v.) government moved very slowly to fulfil its promise to sell off a large part of its shares in private industry. Direct state aid to failing sectors in the West was significant in the coal, shipbuilding and electrical industries. The federal and state governments have given financial assistance to service, aerospace, computer, automotive and energy-related industries. The bulk of subsidies was paid to service industries, especially transport. For instance, the Federal Railway (*Bundesbahn*) receives one D-Mark in subsidy for every D-Mark it earns. The average farmer also receives handsome subsidies. The states are also involved in such pragmatic (not ideologically-inspired) intervention. For example, Bavaria offered BMW DM 190 million not to create a new plant in Austria. Baden-Wurttemberg also offered Daimler-Benz, the country's biggest company, DM 140 million to keep a new plant within the state. In fact, Baden-Wurttemberg devotes one-tenth of its budget to science and research facilities to enable its companies to stay ahead in technology. (See also PRIVATIZATION.)

EDELWEISS PIRATES see HITLER YOUTH

EDICT OF POTSDAM see PRUSSIA

EDUCATION. Reforms since the late 1960s have opened up the school system in the West to permit more working- and lower-class children better educational opportunities, as had already been done in the East. Traditional authoritarianism has disappeared in German schools. One sees very few traces of the former stern discipline. The school environment is relaxed, and pupils' relations with their teachers are often close and warm. Discussion and the free expression of opinion are generally encouraged.

Since education is a Land responsibility, there is considerable diversity in the school systems within the FRG. Roughly half of the children between the ages of three and six attend kindergartens, which are not a part of the state school system and for which fees are normally charged. All children at age seven enter a unified primary school (*Grundschule*), which they attend for four years (six in Hamburg, Bremen and Berlin). After this, children enter one of three different kinds of higher schools. As of 1990, a third of the girls and 40 percent of the boys (compared with two-thirds of both in 1969) complete a five-year short-course secondary school (*Hauptschule*) until age 15, followed by three years of part-time vocational school combined with on-the-job training. In an intermediate school (*Realschule*), 39 percent of girls and 33 percent of boys (compared with 24 percent and 20 percent in 1969) complete a course lasting six years leading to a graduation certificate (*mittlere Reife*) which permits persons to enter certain advanced technical schools and the medium levels of business and administration. Some continue on for a "limited" *Abitur* (called a *Fachabitur*), which then allows university-level study in a restricted number of subjects. The third kind of school, the *Gymnasium,* offers a more academically demanding nine-year course, aiming toward a diploma called the *Abitur,* which entitles one to enter the universities; 28 percent of all girls and 26 percent of boys (compared with 10 percent and 15 percent in 1969) attend *Gymnasien.*

For many years critics argued that such a tracked system merely hardened class distinctions within the society by favoring the children of civil servants, salaried employees and the independently employed. In contrast to workers, these groups traditionally encourage their children to enter the more academically demanding schools and to make financial sacrifices by entering their future jobs much later in life. On the other hand, one can argue that because German schools have only a 10 percent dropout rate, compared with about 25 percent in the U.S. and 45 percent in the U.K., and therefore prepare young Germans better for the work force, the school system actually narrows social and economic differences more effectively than in the U.S. and U.K.

Nevertheless, certain reforms have been introduced which are praised by some and severely criticized by others.

First, some pupils in advanced classes are given state financial support in order to reduce the monetary burdens for poorer families which longer schooling entails. Second, a "second educational path" was introduced for those pupils who later conclude that they made the wrong decision at age 11 concerning what higher school they should attend. This path involves demanding evening courses for three to six years, but diligent pupils with determination can receive *Realschule* or *Gymnasium* certificates and gain access to higher educational institutions. A third reform was the creation in some cities of "comprehensive schools" (*Gesamtschulen*). Like the American high school, the comprehensive school combines all pupils under one roof, but nevertheless permits some interior tracking for pupils with different interests and objectives. These schools were never widely accepted and are attended by only 5 percent of all pupils. Fourth, a far greater percentage of students has been allowed to attend the formerly elite *Gymnasium*, which is the crucial way-station towards the universities and well-paid, prestigious professions. Now, a fourth of student-age Germans study at the universities, compared with only 6 percent in 1950.

While the education system has been considerably opened up, criticism against it still abounds. Some argue that the reforms have left too many traditional elements in place. Others counter that the reforms have greatly lowered educational standards. Noting western Germany's economic success, some observers from abroad focus on four strengths of the German school system: First, secondary school pupils are educated according to their aptitudes. Second, they avoid over-specialization. They must show competence in at least 10 subjects before graduation and must achieve a minimum standard, judged by authorities from outside each school, in the core subjects of mathematics, science, German, and for all but the least able, a foreign language. Third, teachers are treated as members of the professional middle class, with high social status, the best pay in the world, tenure as civil servants, and a short school day from 8 AM to 1 PM. Fourth, future workers are given top training. Three-fourths of all graduates (almost all who are not going to the university) spend at least three years in a rigorous apprenticeship working for a quarter the normal pay under the guidance of a qualified "master." At the same time, they go a day or two a week to vocational schools learning the theory of their chosen trade; German companies pay 40 percent of the costs of such schools. They cannot get a good job until they have served their time as apprentices and have passed a difficult practical and theoretical examination. But the apprentice is paid year-round and has a guaranteed job when training is completed if he stays with the company.

East German schools always tried to narrow social differences by merging tracks within the old German educational system and giving pupils a "polytechnic" education: one which brings all pupils into the working world for practical experience. Unfortunately, those schools also included heavy doses of propaganda in their curricula. Therefore, after reunification (q.v.) in 1990 a shake-down began. Many schools were renamed so that their original names replaced their communist-inspired ones. Former textbooks were discarded and replaced by ones from the West. Courses on communist ideology were dropped, and the approach in civics and history courses was drastically altered. Former teachers who belonged to the SED (q.v.) had to fill out questionnaires and survive a screening process to continue teaching.

Once Russian was made an elective, rather than a required course, 90 percent of the pupils dropped it and picked up English instead. East Germans had never liked Russian, and very few ever mastered it despite the years they were compelled to study it. Studies in 1990 showed that their competence in English equalled that of Russian, even though their exposure to English in school had been scant. Of course, thousands of teachers of Russian had to be hurriedly retrained to teach English. A study of schools in both parts of Germany a few weeks after reunification revealed astonishing similarities in kids' attitudes and cast doubt on the effect of intense communist propaganda over 40 years. In both parts of Germany, children wanted an "interesting job," safe from economic ups and downs, and with maximum free time; both preferred free enterprise and believed that pay should be linked to performance; they were not interested in political activism; and English was their foreign language of choice.

The extremely rapid increase in pupils who finish the *Gymnasium* has led to serious overcrowding at the universities. Although more than 20 new universities have been built in the West since the mid-1960s, students have great problems being admitted to the programs and universities of their choice. Budget cuts prevented the universities from expanding their staffs to cope with the high numbers of students. Many students are dissatisfied with the lack of sufficient facilities and staff. This problem is exacerbated by the fact that the average student now spends 14 semesters at the university before taking final examinations, thereby strengthening the *ewiger Student* (eternal student) image. In order to offer an alternative to the crowded universities, the first private German universities were founded in Witten-Herdecke, Koblenz, and Ingolstadt. Modeled largely on American private colleges, the future of these sole private universities remains uncertain.

The uneasiness of the students is exacerbated by the increasingly restricted job market which awaits them after they finish their studies. Until well into the 1970s, an economically booming FRG, with expanding industries and financially strong and generous state treasuries, could absorb almost all university graduates. In 1974-75, for example, 85 percent of university graduates were given public service jobs. Those prosperous years have waned, and the paucity of jobs in the East darkens employment prospects even further. (See also BUNDESWEHR UNIVERSITIES.)

EDUCATION COUNCIL (WISSENSCHAFTSRAT). Consisting of the federal and Land ministers of education, this body meets to discuss matters of joint concern. It has standardized such things as teacher training, examinations, and school holidays, which are staggered in Germany so that all families with school children are not driving to their holiday destinations at the same time.

EHARD, HANS see LAND PRINCES

EHMKE, HORST (1927-). SPD, law professor in Freiburg, federal justice minister (1969), chief of chancellor's office and minister for special tasks (1969-72), and for research and technology (1972-74).

EICHENDORFF, JOSEPH VON (1788-1857). Eichendorff's early years on the family estate and his Roman Catholic religious faith are the two fundamental influences on one of the finest romantic poets in the history of German literature. His melodious poems dealing with the beauties of nature were expressed simply and sincerely. Many became folk songs (e.g. *Das zerbrochene Ringlein*) and inspired Robert Schumann (q.v.) to some of his best compositions (*Liederkreis*). In addition to the humorous tale, *Aus dem Leben eines Taugenichts (From the Life of a Good-for-Nothing)*, he translated religious dramas and authored a treatise on German literature from a strictly Catholic perspective.

EICHMANN, KARL ADOLF (1906-1962). Head of the "Jewish Desk" in the Bureau of Security (Reichssicherheitshauptamt), Eichmann organized the deportation of Jews to extermination camps in Poland. After the Second World War he escaped to Argentina, where he was captured by the Israeli secret service and taken to Israel to stand trial. He was executed in June 1962. (See also HEYDRICH, REINHARD; WANNSEE.)

EINSATZGRUPPEN see NAZI REPRESSION

EINSTEIN, ALBERT (1879-1955). Born in Ulm, Einstein was both a scientist and a philosopher. His theory of relativity changed the world, and his work led to reflections on the final meaning of experience. Because he was Jewish, he fled Nazi (q.v.) Germany and ended up at Princeton University. Toward the end of his life he published *Generalization of the Gravitational Theory*, a controversial book in which he tried to unify all physical phenomena under a single concept or law. Einstein was involved in the political affairs of his time, advocating complete world disarmament, a socialist society, limited world government, and a homeland for the Jews. (See also EMPIRE CULTURE.)

EISNER, KURT (1867-1919) see CONCENTRATION CAMPS

ELECTIONS, FEDERAL (1949). Nation-wide the SPD did poorly, garnering only 29.2 percent of the votes, falling behind the CDU (qq.v.), which was able to win 31 percent and patch together a coalition government with a one-vote majority. Since the "5 percent hurdle" did not yet apply, numerous small parties entered the Bundestag. Kurt Schumacher's (q.v.) SPD rejected a coalition government with the CDU on August 30, 1949. Despite their disappointing showing at the polls, the Social Democrats came within a whisker of ruling the new West German state and had to wait 20 years for the opportunity to take command.

ELECTIONS, FEDERAL (1953). The first real test for the voters' approval of the government's and opposition's foreign policy approaches came on September 6, 1953. This was one of the few West German elections in which foreign policy issues dominated the campaign. Konrad Adenauer (q.v.) was able to profit from Germans' disgust that the uprising in the GDR (q.v.) had been crushed. The CDU/CSU (q.v.) shot up from 31 to 45.2 percent, and its number of seats rose from 139 to 243, nearly an absolute majority. The results disappointed the SPD (q.v.), whose percentage of votes fell from 29.2 to 28.8 percent. The SPD's hope of mobilizing a majority of voters behind the goal of reunification (q.v.) as an immediate and urgent task was dashed. West Germans gave security a higher priority than unity. Adenauer's answer to the problem of security had been simple and easily comprehensible, whereas the SPD's concepts were too contradictory, incomplete, vague, and complicated to be persuasive. Many leading Social Democrats saw an urgent need to reexamine the party's security policy.

ELECTIONS, FEDERAL (1957). The SPD (q.v.) went into the federal parliamentary elections on September 15, 1957, confident that it could make significant gains. Opinion polls indicated that West Germans were not happy about the creation of the Bundeswehr (q.v.) or the stationing of American nuclear weapons on German soil. The SPD had opposed all of these. Polls also indicated that West Germans still desired to see Germany reunified, and the SPD had always publicly advocated that goal more vociferously than Adenauer's (q.v.) coalition. One month before the election the SPD hurled the slogan into the campaign: "Whoever votes CDU/CSU risks perpetual one-party domination, inflation, permanent division of our Fatherland, atomic bombs and atomic death." Adenauer hammered at a simple theme: "In the hard world of facts there were only two roads for the FRG: cooperation with the West or cooperation with the Soviets. Everything in between is not politics but illusion." He opposed all talk of neutrality or of weakening the Atlantic Alliance. He asked all Germans to think about the economic benefits his policy had brought to a people so recently impoverished. Above all, the FRG should attempt "no experiments" at this point in its development.

The election results stunned both the SPD and Adenauer. The CDU/CSU (q.v.) slogans, "No Experiments" and "You know what you have, therefore CDU" were embraced by a population that saw its prosperity and security guaranteed by Adenauer. The CDU/CSU vote rose from 44 to over 50 percent, giving it the first and only absolute majority in the Bundestag since the foundation of the FRG. The SPD enlarged its votes by only 2.6 percent to a total of 32 percent. This increase was mainly because the KPD (q.v.) had been outlawed in 1956 and had advised its supporters to vote SPD. After eight years of opposition this result jolted the party and set it on a course to change its party program and foreign policy.

ELECTIONS, FEDERAL (1961). Equipped with a new Godesberg Program tailored to West German society, a foreign and defense policy that would frighten neither voters nor allies, and a ruggedly handsome and modern 47 year-old SPD (q.v.) chancellor candidate, Willy Brandt (q.v.), to face the 85 year-old Konrad Adenauer (q.v.) at the polls, the SPD entered the 1961 elections a different party. It portrayed Brandt as a family man and a German equivalent of President John F. Kennedy. As much as possible, the SPD avoided the symbols of the past, such as the color red and hard-hitting rhetoric about the working class. The results indicated that the SPD's efforts to adjust its image and policies had begun to bear fruit. It gained 4.4 percent, moving from 31.8 to 36.2 percent of the total vote and from 169 to 190 seats in the Bundestag. The CDU/CSU (q.v.) lost its absolute majority and watched 5 percent of its voters desert to the FDP (q.v.), its own coalition partner, which had its best election yet. Compared to the federal election of 1957 the CDU's lead over the SPD was halved. But the combined votes of all the governing parties made it clear that a majority of voters was not yet ready for a fundamental change, especially in a time of crisis such as the one that existed since East German leaders had erected the Berlin Wall (q.v.) on August 21, less than a month before the elections.

ELECTIONS, FEDERAL (1965). Under severe attack in Bonn, Ludwig Erhard (q.v.), who had replaced Konrad Adenauer (q.v.) as chancellor in 1963, was still regarded outside the capital as the epitome of prosperity and continuity. His electoral slogan, "Sure is sure," was as effective as his predecessor's "No experiments!" He was also willing to play hardball against Willy Brandt (q.v.), whose fame as West Berlin's crisis mayor had largely evaporated. The SPD (q.v.) gained 12 seats and a million more votes than it had in 1961. It had made gains in areas and groups where it had traditionally been weak: in the Catholic Lands of Bavaria, Rhineland-Palatinate and the Saar, among practicing Christians of both confessions, and among women and the elderly. However, Erhard, the "people's chancellor," proved to be a formidable vote-getter. He added a million voters for his party and achieved the second best CDU/CSU (q.v.) performance since 1949, winning 47.6 percent of the votes, compared with 39.3 percent for the SPD.

ELECTIONS, FEDERAL (1969). The SPD's (q.v.) total membership had stagnated, it was slipping in Land elections, and many of its youth were in open rebellion against the SPD criticizing it for trying to stabilize rather than change the status quo. The CDU (q.v.) seemed to have recovered from its political difficulties under Ludwig Erhard (q.v.) and to have the wind at its back. Chancellor Kurt-Georg Kiesinger's (q.v.) popularity was soaring, while Willy Brandt's (q.v.) was plunging. But Brandt's party conducted the better campaign and reaped the rewards for it. The SPD was seen as more in step with the times and as the party of change, both in foreign and domestic policy. Frightened by the NPD (q.v.) on the right, Kiesinger had chosen what the CDU defined as a "nationalist conservative policy," in line with Franz Josef Strauss's (q.v.) promise that no party would overtake the CDU/CSU on the right. While many West Germans had become optimistic about the possibilities of detente, the policy being pursued by the new American president, Richard Nixon, Kiesinger adopted a harder anti-communist line toward Eastern Europe and the GDR, and he balked at signing the nuclear non-proliferation pact. Noting the popularity polls in his favor and the frequent description of the FRG as a "chancellor democracy," his slogan was: "It Depends on the Chancellor." By contrast, the SPD chose the slogans, "We Have the Right Men," feminism not having yet become a factor in West German politics, and "We Are Creating the Modern Germany." Foreign Minister Brandt campaigned as the cool, unflappable, prudent statesman, flying to the United Nations in New York to meet with the world's leaders, and, like the American president, speaking of detente and arms control. He promised to build on the foreign policy progress made in the past three years.

While Brandt was pulling himself up by his bootstraps, Economics Minister Karl Schiller (q.v.) was pulling his party to victory. His popularity parallelled that of Kiesinger. The main election issue turned out to be the pocketbook, as usual. It was Schiller who was widely viewed as the man whose wise fiscal and budgetary policies had lifted the FRG out of its recession, hardened the *Deutschmark,* and preserved the welfare system. The economics professor's catchy terms, such as "overcome the valley's floor," "recovery in moderation," "concerted action," "social symmetry," and "global steering," made the dismal science interesting again.

The SPD also benefitted from a new kind of campaigning organized by Günter Grass (q.v.), a persistent critic of Germany's past and all traces of it in the present. He mobilized 3,000 volunteers, including well-known writers, musicians, artists, and intellectuals, to tour the FRG and whip up support for what he called the "Es-Pe-De." Grass later wrote about his experiences in a book entitled *From the Diary of a Snail.* On election night, September 28, it was obvious that Wehner's strategy of making the SPD a "party capable of governing" through participation in the Grand Coalition (q.v.) had succeeded. While neither of the coalition partners won a clear majority, the CDU/CSU had lost almost 2 percent of their voters and three seats, down to 46.1 percent and 242 seats, but still the largest in the Bundestag. The SPD had advanced for the third straight time since the 1959 Godesberg Program, gaining 3 percent to 42.7 percent and 22 seats to a total of 224; in three elections, the SPD had improved its position by an impressive 10 percent, putting it barely behind the Union parties. The NPD (q.v.) suffered a setback from which it never recovered, falling .7 percent short of the required 5 percent to win any parliamentary seats. It quickly lost all its representation in the Land parliaments and sank into insignificance.

Perhaps the rudest shock was issued to the internally-divided FDP (q.v.), which plunged from 9.5 percent of the votes to only 5.8 percent; it lost 19 of its seats, retaining only 30. Its change of leaders and orientation as well as its support of a Social Democrat for president had prompted a massive exodus of members and cost it 40 percent of its voters. Every time the FDP made a major adjustment in its political orientation, it suffered frightful losses of members and voters; this also happened in 1982, when the FDP shifted its alliance partners from the SPD to the CDU/CSU. The stage was set for the FRG's first real change of regiment. A confident and unusually decisive Brandt declared that "We'll do it!": take the power the voters had offered.

ELECTIONS, FEDERAL (1972). On September 20, 1972, Willy Brandt (q.v.) called for a vote of confidence in the Bundestag. Since he wanted new general elections, he ensured its failure by ordering the members of the cabinet to abstain. President Gustav Heinemann (q.v.) was therefore compelled to dissolve the body and call new elections for November. This was yet another successful test of how strong the FRG's democratic political system had become. The center-left coalition had established a truly multiparty choice for the voters. Also, in a highly charged, polarized atmosphere, the first-ever use of Article 67 of the Basic Law (q.v.), permitting votes of no-confidence, the resignation of a chancellor, and the call for elections before the end of the full four-year legislative period demonstrated that, unlike the Weimar Republic (q.v.), the new democracy could deal with a situation in which a parliamentary majority had disappeared.

The SPD (q.v.) entered the campaign on the crest of a wave of popularity, largely as a result of its *Ostpolitik* (q.v.). Brandt addressed the enthusiastic delegates to the party's Dortmund congress on October 12 under a gigantic poster reading "Willy Brandt Must Remain Chancellor." The SPD's campaign focused on the chancellor himself, who exuded confidence, gentleness, and pride. Election posters with his smiling face bore the slogan: "Germans--We Can Be Proud of our Country," suggesting that the party's diplomatic offensive had improved the Germans' image in the world. The confident national pride was also expressed in the national colors--black, red, and gold--used on all SPD bulletins instead of the traditional red party color. The *"Deutschlandlied,"* which some people still mistakenly identified with exaggerated nationalism and Hitler, was played at some SPD rallies, something which would have been unthinkable only a few years earlier. The Social Democratic Voter Initiative, founded three years earlier by Günter Grass (q.v.) in order to mobilize support for the SPD, was active, with some notable new recruits, such as Heinrich Böll (q.v.) and prominent Catholics.

The CDU/CSU (q.v.) and its chancellor candidate, Rainer Barzel (q.v.), were on the defensive from the very start. Their calls to renegotiate the treaties aroused little interest, and their attempts to shift primary attention to the economy failed, despite the fact that the former super-minister, Karl Schiller (q.v.), had become the most celebrated defector after leaving the SPD for the CDU. The election was a plebiscite on *Ostpolitik* (q.v.). Shortly before the polling, the SPD benefitted from being able to unveil a draft treaty with the GDR (q.v.), from preparations for the admission of both Germanys to the United Nations, and from a helping hand from Moscow, which announced that three thousand Soviet Germans would be permitted to leave for the FRG.

More than 91 percent went to the polls on November 19 and gave the SPD the biggest vote ever: 45.8 percent and 230 seats. For the first time, the SPD became the largest party in the Bundestag, as the CDU/CSU fell to 44.9 percent and 225 seats. The FDP (q.v.) coalition partners jumped to 8.4 percent of the votes and gained 11 seats to a total of 41. Thus, the ruling coalition enjoyed a comfortable 46-seat majority in the Bundestag. The SPD made inroads among Catholic workers and into CDU/CSU preserves: rural areas and elderly women. Perhaps the most important signal for the future was that 60 percent of young voters supported the SPD. The election showed that the SPD was seen as a competent governing party.

ELECTIONS, FEDERAL (1976). The SPD-FDP (q.v.) government went into the 1976 federal elections boasting high personal income, social security, economic growth, and Western Europe's lowest inflation rate. Thus, the SPD believed that its electoral slogan, "Model Germany," was justified. The opposition called attention to the intra-SPD feuding and the rhetorical flights of the neo-Marxist minority within the party. It sensed growing dissatisfaction with the social-liberal coalition, as a string of losses in Land elections had shown. It adopted as its slogans "Freedom Instead of Socialism" (CDU) and "Freedom or Socialism" (CSU). Like many other Social Democrats, Chancellor Helmut Schmidt (q.v.) was sufficiently frightened that he stopped referring to himself as a "socialist" and began using "democratic socialist" instead. His CDU opponent, Helmut Kohl (q.v.), ran consistently behind in polls. However, a campaign centered around the popular Schmidt, whose support within the party was limited, could hardly spark the kind of enthusiasm among idealistic Social Democrats that Brandt had enjoyed in 1972. It was the "chancellor's bonus" that won the election for the SPD, which got 42.6 percent of the votes, down from 45.8 percent in 1972, and 214 seats, down from 225. The FDP also dropped .5 percent to 7.9 percent, and it won 39 seats, down from 41. This meant that the coalition had a majority of only ten seats. It hurt the SPD that it was no longer the largest party in the Bundestag. It had lost a million votes, including Catholic workers (probably because of abortion reform), women, and people under age twenty-four.

ELECTIONS, FEDERAL (1980). It was largely thanks to Helmut Schmidt's (q.v.) popularity and Franz Josef Strauss' (q.v.) lack of it outside of Bavaria that the SPD-FDP (qq.v.) coalition survived the October 1980 elections. Schmidt had carefully curried the favor of the business community by intensifying consultations with it and practicing financial restraint in office; businessmen feared that Strauss could upset social harmony by attacking the labor unions. The SPD entitled its electoral platform "Security for Germany," calling for reforms combined with fiscal restraint. But the election revolved around personalities far more than issues; it degenerated into one of the dirtiest in FRG history.

The SPD centered its campaign around the immensely popular Schmidt. Many Christian Democrats were unhappy because Strauss had threatened to end the traditional CSU support for the CDU (qq.v.) if he were not accepted as the Union candidate. Strauss and the CDU/CSU aimed their barbs at the SPD and Schmidt: "intellectual neutralism," "peacenik," "prophet of panic," "the party of capitulation," and "the Moscow faction." For the first time, an embarrassing tidbit about Schmidt's pre-war past was dug up: television film footage on August 15 showed him present at a trial in the courtroom of the infamous Nazi judge Roland Freisler in Berlin. Schmidt did not deny being there, but he said that he had been ordered to attend as a young lieutenant. Social Democrats were no more tender in their treatment of Strauss, calling him a man "without scruples," an "arsonist who was ready to set democracy ablaze," "incredibly uncontrolled" and thus "not qualified to govern this country."

As polls had predicted, the SPD-FDP coalition not only won reelection, it actually gained ground, winning what would seem like a far more comfortable 45 seat majority in the Bundestag. The SPD inched up to capture 42.9 percent of the vote and 218 seats, compared with 42.6 percent and 214 seats in 1976. The most dramatic gains were made by the FDP, which soared from 7.9 percent of the vote and 39 seats to 10.6 percent and 53 seats. Although many analysts had been predicting its demise, the FDP again appeared in the minds of voters to provide an important brake to extreme policy moves on the part of the larger parties. Some leftist Social Democrats voted for the rising Greens (q.v.), while some moderate Social Democrats actually supported the FDP in order to apply controls on their own party. The FDP's gains emboldened it to assert itself more forcefully within the governing coalition. When it thought that the SPD had gone too far in 1982, it abandoned it and brought the SPD government down. The CDU/CSU slipped in the polling from 48.6 percent of the votes and 243 seats in 1976 to 44.5 percent and 226 seats in 1980.

ELECTIONS, FEDERAL (1983). The elections were a disaster for the SPD and a resounding victory for Helmut Kohl's CDU (qq.v.). Distancing itself from Schmidt's policy on INF (q.v.) deployments, but ruling out any coalition or cooperation with the Greens (q.v.), the SPD dropped to 38.2 percent of the vote and only 193 seats, 25 fewer than before. This was the party's worst showing since 1961. It was driven back to its fortresses and core clientele, and it lost ground among groups it had worked a quarter of a century to attract. Its losses were greatest among young voters, many of whom voted for the Greens, who barely succeeded in clearing the 5 percent hurdle and entering the Bundestag as the first minor party to gain seats since 1957. For years to come, the SPD would try to woo those Green voters back. The FDP (q.v.) lost a third of its voters, but it hung on with 7 percent of the votes and 34 seats. Pledging to deploy new American medium-range missiles in the FRG and promising "less state, more market; fewer collective burdens, more personal performance; fewer encrusted structures, more mobility, self-initiative, and competition," the CDU/CSU made dramatic gains, capturing 48.8 percent of the votes and 244 seats, its second-best result ever. So convincing was its victory that Kohl's talk of a "*Wende*" (q.v.) having taken place after 13 years of SPD rule seemed credible and made the new opposition role for the SPD even more difficult to digest. In 1983, it had been swept from most Land governments and saw a jubilant CDU/CSU firmly in the saddle in Bonn and in Land capitals.

ELECTIONS, FEDERAL (1987). Helmut Kohl's CDU/CSU-FDP (qq.v.) won its second Bundestag election after taking the reins of power in 1982. However, the CDU/CSU dropped from 48.8 percent of the votes and 244 seats to 44.3 percent and 223 seats. The Kohl government's reelection demonstrated Germans' overall satisfaction with his rule, but talk of an absolute majority scared many potential voters into the arms of the FDP, which always played the role of moderating any government in Bonn. The FDP rose to 9.1 percent of the votes and 46 seats, up from 6.9 percent and 34 seats in 1983. The SPD (q.v.) entered the elections with a new chancellor candidate, Johannes Rau, a pragmatic, middle-of-the-road minister president in North Rhine-Westphalia. But the results showed the extent to which the SPD had deteriorated since the 1970s. It won only 37 percent of the votes and 186 seats. This was its worst showing since 1961. Meanwhile the Greens (q.v.) continued to grow, capturing 8.3 percent of the votes and 42 seats.

ELECTIONS, FEDERAL (1990). The first all-German election in 58 years was a plebiscite on unity, after the fact. Those parties which had seized the opportunity to bring it about were handsomely rewarded, and those which seemed petty and afraid and who cast doubt on unity were punished. With voter participation falling to a new low of 77.8 percent

(74 percent in the East), the governing CDU-CSU-FDP (qq.v.) coalition won 55 percent of the votes and actually performed better in the East than in the West. The CDU-CSU captured 44 percent of the votes and 319 seats. It won big in the former GDR (q.v.), where few Catholics live. Half of the East German workers voted CDU, and it was the preferred party for young voters in both parts of Germany. The FDP gained dramatically, winning 11 percent nation-wide and 79 seats. Its two top politicians, Hans-Dietrich Genscher and Wolfgang Mischnick (qq.v.), had grown up in the GDR and could therefore present themselves to voters as both easterners and westerners. That helps explain the FDP's 12.9 percent result in the East and the impressive harvest of party members there.

The SPD's (q.v.) chancellor candidate was Oskar Lafontaine (q.v.), who was almost killed when a deranged women slit his throat with a butcher knife. He harped on the problems and costs associated with reunification (q.v.) and was perceived as a prophet of doom. His leftist themes did not interest German voters in 1990, especially those in eastern Germany, who wanted prosperity within the FRG. *Die Zeit* called him "the wrong man at the wrong time," and the electoral disaster proved this. The SPD dropped to 33.5 percent of the vote and 239 seats. Its 35.7 percent in the West was well below its 1987 performance, and its 24.3 percent in the East, which had been the party's electoral fortress before Hitler's take-over, was shocking.

Grossly misreading the popular mood supporting unity and failing to unite their separate parties in both parts of Germany, western German Greens (q.v.) received only 4.8 percent of the votes in the West and were therefore ejected from parliament, to their shock and dismay. They were thrown back to the political fringe. Their spokesman noted sadly: "We fell under the wheels of German unification." An election coalition of eastern German Greens and Alliance 90, a collection of eastern German grassroots groups which organized the 1989 revolution, won 6 percent of the votes in the East (1.2 percent nation-wide) and eight seats under the special election law which applied only to the 1990 elections.

The PDS (q.v.) advocated a middle road between the discredited old-style communism in the East and capitalism in the West. Its slogan was "A Liking for the Left," and its leader was the only media star; Gregor Gysi was a witty, brilliant East Berlin lawyer. It formed a "Left List/PDS," of which it was the senior partner. This alliance garnered only .3 percent of the votes in the West and 11.1 percent in the East, for a total of 2.4 percent nationwide. For this election only, the 5 percent hurdle was waived for new parties, so the PDS was given 17 seats in the Bundestag. Gysi won a directly elected seat in East Berlin's Hellersdorf-Marzahn, a very unusual feat for a candidate from a small party.

ELECTIONS, GDR (March 18, 1990). As in 1949, the Social Democrats expected to win the first crucial free election in the GDR in March 1990, but when the votes were counted, the Christian Democrats had again carried the day, winning 40.9 percent of the votes; the East German equivalent to the CSU (q.v.), the German Social Union (DSU), won 6.3 percent. The SPD (q.v.) was disappointed to garner only 21.8 percent, while the Communists (renamed PDS, q.v.) were elated to receive 16 percent of the votes. East Germans had opted for the prosperity and freedom that the CDU offered, as well as fusion with the proven West German model, rather than to risk uncertain social experiments. In April 1990 Lothar de Maizière (q.v.) became prime minister at the head of a grand coalition of the CDU, SPD, and a number of smaller parties.

ELECTIONS LAW (1990). Because the December 2, 1990, Bundestag elections came only two months after German reunification (q.v.), eastern German parties had not yet had time to organize in the entire FRG. Therefore, for this election only the 5 percent minimum vote for any party to win seats was revised to allow any party to have seats which won 5 percent of the votes in either eastern or western Germany. This one-time change permitted both the PDS (q.v.) and the eastern Greens-Alliance 90 (q.v.) to win seats in 1990.

ELECTIONS, REFORM. The one great failure of the Grand Coalition (q.v.) was a reform that would have dramatically changed the political party landscape. Discussed was the introduction of the single constituency electoral system to replace the FRG's hybrid proportional representation system. The effect would have been that only two large parties, the SPD and the CDU/CSU, would survive, and all small parties, including especially the FDP (qq.v.), would be eliminated. The reform was not enacted, prompting many CDU/CSU politicians to accuse the SPD partner of betraying their agreement when entering the 1966 Grand Coalition in the first place.

ELECTORS see GERMAN EMPIRE

ELISABETH CHRISTINE VON BRAUNSCHWEIG (1715-1792) see FRIEDRICH II, THE GREAT

ELLWEIN, THOMAS see BUNDESWEHR UNIVERSITIES

ELYSEE TREATY (GERMAN-FRENCH TREATY) see FRANCO-GERMAN RELATIONS.

EMERGENCY COMMUNITY FOR PEACE IN EUROPE see SOVIET NOTES

EMERGENCY LEAGUE OF CLERGYMEN (PFARRERNOTBUND) see CONFESSING CHURCH

EMERGENCY POWERS ACT (NOTSTANDGESETZ, 1968). The Basic Law (q.v.) gives the government special powers if the basic democratic order is endangered. The chancellor may declare two kinds of emergency: to strengthen the military in a defense crisis or to boost police powers in times of civil unrest or natural disaster. As of 1992 neither power had ever been used. The government can shortcut the usual means of passing laws if the parliament is stalemated over an urgent matter. But the chancellor may do this only after he has called a vote of confidence on his rule. (See GRAND COALITION; OVERCOMING THE PAST.)

EMMA. This feminist magazine was founded in 1977 by a journalist Alice Schwarzer, who had been involved in the French women's movement while working in Paris.

EMPIRE, CULTURE AND SCHOLARSHIP. After 1871 imperial Germany exploded with artistic and scholarly creativity. Its universities and research laboratories became places where the most imaginative thinking in the world was being done. For instance, Wilhelm Konrad Röntgen discovered X-rays, Max Planck (q.v.) the quantum theory, and Albert Einstein (q.v.) the theory of relativity. Robert Koch did ground-breaking research on tuberculosis, cholera and sleeping sickness, Paul Ehrlich on syphilis and Rudolph Virchow on pathology. The work of such great professors as Theodor Mommsen and Heinrich von

Treitschke (q.v.) in history, Wilhelm Dilthey (q.v.) in philosophy, Ferdinand Tönnies (q.v.), Georg Simmel and Max Weber (q.v.) in sociology, and Adolf Wagner, Lujo Brentano and Werner Sombart in economics, is still admired today.

Berlin also gained a reputation as an exciting cultural center. There Johannes Brahms and Richard Strauss (qq.v.) composed their music. The sympathetic Prussian social critic, Theodor Fontane (q.v.), wrote his novels, focusing on the Prussia (q.v.) which he loved, but which he saw in decline. Also, after the opening of Die Freie Bühne (The Free Stage), such talented playwrights as Gerhard Hauptmann and Frank Wedekind (qq.v.) were able to introduce a new element of criticism and expressionism into the German theater. Unlike France then and today, Germany's culture and scholarship were not concentrated in the nation's capital, but were also distributed among such cities as Hamburg, Cologne, Leipzig, Munich and Frankfurt am Main. Despite the cultural creativity of the time, many educated Germans were gripped with a kind of cultural pessimism. They looked around themselves and saw what they considered to be excessive materialism and consumerism, values which they viewed as British and American. German spirit was in decline, they lamented, and many agreed with the philosopher Friedrich Nietzsche (q.v.), who in 1888 claimed "Germany is a spirit: for the past 18 years a contradiction in terms."

EMPIRE, FOREIGN POLICY. The robust and assertive foreign policy on which Wilhelm II (q.v.) embarked in the 1890s, when Germany enjoyed relatively good relations with the other major countries in the world, led Germany by 1914 into a diplomatic situation in which it felt encircled and distrusted. By building a powerful navy, pursuing colonial ambitions in Africa, and frequently brandishing the sword, Germany's rulers created more problems than they were able to solve.

Bismarck (q.v.) had kept the German Empire within the limits which were imposed upon it by its geographic position in the middle of Europe. He had avoided colonial adventures, which would only have antagonized the other European powers, especially Britain. However, supported by German public opinion, his successors changed this. By the turn of the century the German flag flew in Africa (Cameroons, Southwest Africa and Tanganyika), there was a tiny foothold in China and a smattering of Pacific islands (named, ironically, the Bismarck Archipelago).

In order to try to protect this usually unprofitable empire, Germany decided to build a battle fleet that would enable it to conduct a major naval war against the great powers. Kaiser Wilhelm II announced in 1898 "Our future lies on the water." This decision was a major factor in the deterioration of good relations between Britain and Germany. A German navy that challenged Britain, an island completely dependent upon open sea lanes, was bound to be destabilizing and to drive the English into the arms of Germany's potential enemies. Undoubtedly the chief influence on German naval thinking was Captain A.T. Mahan of the United States Navy. In *The Influence of Sea Power on History* he argued that mastery of the oceans is world domination and that any strong land power fighting against an amphibious master which also has land forces is destined to lose. Mahan visited Germany in 1893 and was received like a hero. He was invited to dine aboard the Kaiser's yacht. The ruler wrote in 1894 to a friend "I am just now not reading but devouring Captain Mahan's book and am trying to learn it by heart. It is on board all my ships and constantly quoted by my captains and officers."

What worried the British and the French was that Germany was willing to use its new navy. In mid-1911, Wilhelm sent a gunboat to Morocco's Atlantic port of Agadir in response to France's dispatching a military mission to Fez. France's action was a clear violation of the 1906 agreements of Algeciras, but the German overreaction to this move caused other Europeans to overlook this point. German bellicosity concerned Europe more than a questionable French interpretation of a treaty. Thereafter, German political calculation had always to include the possibility of a war with Britain, which was now firmly on the side of the Entente (France and Russia). The most vocal spokesman for impatient German nationalism was the Pan-German Union, about which Chancellor Bethmann Hollweg (q.v.) declared in 1912 in despair: "Politics cannot be made with these idiots!"

EMS TELEGRAM (1870) see FRANCO-PRUSSIAN WAR

ENABLING ACT (ERMÄCHTIGUNGSGESETZ). On March 23, 1933, the National Socialists and German Nationalists presented a law to the Reichstag transferring to Hitler (q.v.) all legislative power. All parties but the SPD (q.v.) approved this law which emasculated the Reichstag. (See also HITLER'S SEIZURE OF POWER.)

ENGELS, FRIEDRICH (1820-1895). Born in Germany of a well-to-do textile manufacturing family, Engels became the agent in Manchester for his father's business. There he studied Chartism, which proposed social reforms, and he wrote *The Condition of the Working Class in England* in 1844, as well as *The Origin of the Family* and *Private Property and the State*. He joined in polemics against contemporary philosophers. He regarded the state as an executive committee of the ruling class and therefore to be destroyed. His political and philosophical interests brought him into touch with Karl Marx (q.v.), who was living as an exile in Britain. He collaborated on the writing of *The Communist Manifesto,* participated in the revolutionary movement in Baden, and kept the Marx family financially solvent. From 1870 to 1883 he worked full time helping Marx with his writings and completed in 1894 Marx's unfinished *Das Kapital.*

ENGHOLM, BJÖRN (1939-). SPD federal minister for education and science (1981-82), minister president of Schleswig-Holstein (1987-), chairman of SPD (1991-1993). An urbane, cultured, moderate politician with close connections with the labor movement, Engholm was named SPD party chairman to unify the party after Oskar Lafontaine's (qq.v.) decisive defeat in the 1990 Bundestag elections. Amidst revelations that he gave false testimony in the 1987 Barschel affair, which had brought him to power, Engholm resigned. He was replaced as national party chairman by Rudolf Scharping (q.v.) who shares his pragmatic, moderate brand of social democracy. His successor as Schleswig-Holstein minister president is Heidi Simonis (1943-). (See also BARSCHEL, UWE; SOCIAL DEMOCRATIC PARTY OF GERMANY.)

ENLIGHTENMENT (AUFKLÄRUNG--1700-1785). A literary movement advocating a rational, unprejudiced, humanitarian, scientific and reformatory approach to life which followed a turbulent century of religious wars and absolutism. The movement was hostile to the Church, authoritarian institutions, and all sources of intolerance. Writers demanded well-defined genres, dramatic unities, avoidance of the unreal, clarity and good taste; all aimed at teaching and delighting the emerging bourgeois classes. Representative literary writers were Gottsched (1700-1766, q.v.), Bodmer (1698-1793, q.v.), Breitinger (1701-1776, q.v.), Haller (1708-1777, q.v.), Gellert (1715-1769, q.v.), Wieland (1733-1813, q.v.) and Lessing (1729-1781, q.v.) whose *Nathan der Weise* best summed up the doctrine of the Enlightenment. The ethical and aesthetic advances of the Enlightenment continued as an undercurrent through the Storm and Stress, Classical, and Romantic (qq.v.) periods of German literature.

ENSSLIN, GUDRUN (1940-1977) see TERRORIST GROUPS

ENTENTE POWERS. Britain, France, and Russia. (See also CENTRAL POWERS.)

EPPELMANN, RAINER (1943-). Pastor, pacifist, and last defense minister of the GDR (q.v.) in the non-communist government which took office in April 1990.

EPPLER, ERHARD (1926-). SPD, co-founder of GVP in 1952, federal minister for economic cooperation (1968-74), chairman of SPD Landtag parliamentary group in Baden-Wurttemberg (1976-80). An intelligent, idealistic Social Democrat who supported the peace movement and opposed the moderate policies of Helmut Schmidt (q.v.).

EQUALIZATION OF BURDENS LAW (LASTENAUSGLEICH, 1951). After the foundation of the FRG in 1949, a quarter of the West German population was refugees from the East. To satisfy them, the Adenauer (q.v.) government put this law into effect in 1951 which financially compensated refugees for lands and property they had lost in the East.

ERFURT CONFERENCE (1808). Napoleon staged this elaborate meeting with Czar Alexander I in the presence of the German princes in order to show the friendship he had established with the Russians 15 months earlier at Tilsit (q.v.). He wanted to use the Russians to persuade Austria to stay out of the war and to make a deal over Turkey. But the Czar had been informed of Napoleon's plans by Talleyrand and therefore refused to commit himself, thereby frustrating Napoleon's designs.

ERFURT PROGRAM (1891). At its party congress in Erfurt, the SPD (q.v.) not only adopted its present name, but also a party program consisting of two parts, which reflected the competing revolutionary and revisionist tendencies within this working-class party. One was an outline of social developments and long-run objectives expressed in Marxist terms. The other described more modest goals to be accomplished peacefully by parliamentary means. (See also BEBEL, AUGUST; SOCIAL DEMOCRATIC PARTY OF GERMANY.)

ERHARD, LUDWIG (1897-1977). CDU, federal economics minister (1949-63), chancellor (1963-66). Born in Fürth, Erhard fought in the First World War (q.v.) and pursued an academic career in Nuremberg until 1945, when he became a professor in Munich and economics adviser for the American military government. In 1945-46, he was Bavarian minister of trade and commerce and, from March 1948, director for administering the economy of Bizonia (q.v.), in which capacity he prepared for the 1948 currency reform (q.v.). He entered Konrad Adenauer's (q.v.) first cabinet as economics minister, a post he held until he replaced Adenauer as chancellor in 1963. More than any other politician, he developed the concept of "social market economy" (q.v.) and was a popular "electoral locomotive" for the CDU (q.v.). As chancellor, he led the CDU to victory in the 1965 elections, and he supported new initiatives for normalizing relations with states in the Warsaw Pact, to which his government sent a "peace note" on March 25, 1966, proposing a renunciation of force. However, this failed, in part because it did not include the GDR (q.v.). His government did not renounce the Hallstein Doctrine (q.v.). He and his foreign minister, Gerhard Schröder (q.v.), were called "Atlanticists" because of their advocacy of strong ties with the U.S. and NATO (q.v.), but this emphasis weakened the ties with France which Adenauer (q.v.) had established.

In many persons' opinion, Erhard had been a better economics minister than chancellor in a time when fears began to creep into Germans' minds about whether the FRG's "economic miracle" might have begun to run out of steam. Many viewed him as a transitional figure. CDU party chief Adenauer belittled him at every occasion ("I will bring him to null!"), and he became the butt of jokes in Bonn circles. He was accused of being indecisive and inexperienced in foreign affairs. Erhard admitted that "soon after I took office in 1963 I had the feeling that my party friends were no friends." He resigned as chancellor on November 30, 1966, and the next day his CDU/CSU-FDP government was replaced by the Grand Coalition (q.v.), led by Kurt-Georg Kiesinger (q.v.). He died on May 5, 1977, lauded as "the father of the economic miracle" and the symbol of the FRG's prosperity and social market economy.

ERLER, FRITZ (1913-1967). SPD, Member of the SPD Party Executive (1958-67), Deputy SPD chairman and leader of SPD Bundestag parliamentary group (1964-67). A brilliant reformer within the SPD (q.v.), Erler died of leukemia at the zenith of his political influence. (See also SED-SPD SPEAKER EXCHANGE.)

ERNST, MAX (1891-1976). He was a German-French painter from Cologne, who made the most important contribution to the Surrealist Movement. His work was imaginative and always experimental, and his use of collage was highly individual.

ERZBERGER, MATTHIAS (1875-1921). Center Party (q.v.) politician who led the German delegation at the cease-fire meeting at Compiègne on November 8, 1918, at which time French Marshal Foch delivered undiscussable conditions which Germany could either take or leave by November 11. Having no alternative, he signed, for which he was assassinated on August 21, 1921, by right-wing forces calling themselves "Organization Consul." (See also CENTER PARTY; VERSAILLES TREATY; WEIMAR REPUBLIC.)

EUROPEAN COMMUNITY (EC). After the Second World War (q.v.), Germany has always sought to regain legitimacy and overcome suspicion by being a low-keyed cooperative part of international organizations larger than itself, particularly NATO (q.v.) and the EC. In 1951 it joined with France, Italy, and the BENELUX countries to transfer a small part of its national sovereignty to a supranational organization, the European Coal and Steel Community (ECSC). Not only was it bold and far-sighted to share these important resources rather than to fight wars over them, but the ECSC gave these six nations the practice in economic cooperation needed to convince them that further moves to create a unified Europe could succeed.

They signed the Treaties of Rome in 1957 which created both the European Economic Community (EEC, frequently called the "Common Market") and EURATOM, which seeks to coordinate their atomic research and policy. Both came into existence in 1958 and joined with the ECSC to create a single organizational structure with headquarters in Brussels. A European Parliament is located in Strasbourg. To underscore the political objective and the fact that the three European Communities are managed by common institutions, they are increasingly referred to in the singular as the "European Community." This term avoids giving the impression that it is only economic in nature. By 1993, the EC had been joined by the United Kingdom, Ireland, Denmark, Greece, Spain and Portugal, embracing about 350 million people and commanding the largest GNP in the world. Because of its success, most other countries in eastern and western Europe are seeking admission.

The EC provides for the elimination of tariffs and customs among members, common tariff and customs barriers toward non-members, the free movement of labor and capital within the union, and equal agricultural price levels through the Common Agricultural Program (CAP). Its European Political Cooperation (EPC) seeks, without much success, to coordinate foreign policy. In 1987, the EC introduced the Single European Act, which spells out certain EC objectives, with 1992 as the target date: completion of the internal market, of an area without frontiers, and of more effective and democratic institutions, as well as progress toward economic and monetary union. In December 1991, member governments adopted the Maastricht Treaty calling for a common European currency by the end of the century, as well as a common foreign and defense policy. However, as the difficult ratification process in the member states showed, it is easier for European leaders to proclaim goals than it is to enact them. (See also FRANCO-GERMAN RELATIONS.)

EUROPEAN DEFENSE COMMUNITY (EDC) see REARMAMENT

EVANGELISCHE KIRCHE (PROTESTANT CHURCH) see RELIGION

EXILE LITERATURE. This term refers to the German-speaking writers who were forced to leave their homelands during the Nazi (q.v.) period in the 1930s and 1940s, such as Bertold Brecht, Anna Seghers, Heinrich and Thomas Mann (qq.v.). Their works, though varied, reflect the extraordinary circumstances under which they were conceived.

EXPRESSIONISM (1910-1925). This European artistic movement encompassed most art forms and included German literature. It was predominantly a reaction against Naturalism (q.v.) and Impressionism.

Popular themes were: the search for a new humanity, the battle between the generations (father and son), the conflict between the sexes, and in some cases, political activism. Their aim was to express the souls, the sensations, and the inner reactions of their heroes from the inside to the outside. Writers during this period produced poetry (Gottfried Benn), drama (early Brecht), and prose (A. Döblin, qq.v.). In art the painters used bold, vigorous brush work, emphatic lines, and bright colors to produce powerful canvases expressive of intense human feeling. *Der blaue Reiter* (qq.v.) and *Die Brücke* were two impressionist art movements whose experiments were short-lived. Notable artists were Emil Nolde, Max Beckmann, George Grosz, Käthe Kollwitz, Ludwig Kirschner, Gabriele Münter (qq.v.), and Max Pechstein.

EXTRA-PARLIAMENTARY OPPOSITION (AUSSERPARLAMENTARISCHE OPPOSITION--APO) see GRAND COALITION

EXTREMIST DECISION (*RADIKALENERLASS/BERUFSVERBOT*). Fear in the 1960s and 1970s that the growing Marxist-oriented approach to politics could weaken the theoretical underpinnings of liberal democracy and induce many citizens to misuse the free political order in order to destroy it, as had happened during Weimar, prompted the Social-Liberal coalition in January 1972 to adopt the Extremists Decision (known by its opponents as the "bar to profession"), which required security checks and could exclude non-democrats from the civil service. This was an attempt to serve the constitutional requirement that democracy be on guard against those who might attempt to misuse personal freedoms to undermine it. The Weimar Republic (q.v.) is often remembered as a "democracy without democrats," in which far too few civil servants were inclined to defend the government. Therefore, the Basic Law (q.v.) stipulates that all applicants must guarantee that they are prepared actively to support the free and democratic order at all times.

There was considerable wisdom in the framers' decision to create a "democracy on guard" (q.v.), but there are many problems in attempting to achieve this goal. As memories of Nazi terror fade, Germans find it more difficult to define convincingly democracy and democratic behavior. Few would argue with ex-Chancellor Helmut Schmidt's (q.v.) observation that a person who smears obscenities on Jewish grave stones does not belong in state service two weeks later. However, should a person who in his youth joined a radical movement which preached the destruction of pluralist, parliamentary democracy be considered an anti-democrat the rest of his life? This question of whether the Extremists Decision should be applied to former communists became relevant in eastern Germany, where many judges, professors, teachers, researchers, and civil servants have been removed from their jobs because they had been active members of the SED (q.v.). (See also DEMOCRACY ON GUARD.)

EYLMANN, HORST see POLITICAL PRISONERS

-F-

FALKENHAYN, ERICH VON (1861-1922). Prussian war minister (1913-15), chief of general staff (1914-16).

FALLERSLEBEN, HOFFMAN VON (1798-1874) see LIBERALISM

FAMILY, GERMAN. German society was already in a process of change when two different German societies were grafted together in 1990. For the third time since 1933, Germans in the East must adjust to a very different kind of society. From an earlier German society characterized by authoritarian behavior and institutions and by great social and economic differences among citizens has emerged in the West a predominantly middle-class society with widespread prosperity and with more opportunities, education and upward social mobility. Some of these changes are clearly reflected in important social institutions.

Particularly since the Second World War (q.v.), the authoritarian family structure has given way to a more relaxed family organization. This breakdown actually started during the Third Reich (q.v.), when children were mobilized in activities outside the family and were even encouraged to report on their parents' opinions and behavior, if they veered from Nazi (q.v.) ideology. One now sees more and more permissiveness in the contemporary German family, and it is also increasingly fashionable in middle and upper-middle class families for children to call their parents by their first names.

That this trend toward a less rigid family structure will probably continue is indicated by comparative polls. In 1953, a third of all young respondents between the ages of 13 and 24 indicated they would like to raise their children "exactly the same as I was raised." In 1975, the figure was only 14 percent. Also, 28 percent of young respondents indicated in 1951 that independence and free will were the values which should be stressed in the family, whereas 25 percent believed that obedience and deference were the most important values; in 1976, the corresponding percentages were 51 percent and 10 percent.

The combined effects of weaker religious beliefs, Marx's attacks on the family as "legalized prostitution," the former practice of favoring single mothers in the distribution of apartments, and the fact that 91 percent of women in the East worked, compared with only 51 percent in the West, contributed in eastern Germany to considerable family differences compared with the West. In the pre-unification GDR (q.v.) 32 percent of children were born out of wedlock, compared with 9 percent in the West. The divorce rate was a third higher in the East. Among the thousands of legal and social issues which had to be resolved before reunification (q.v.), very few were so controversial that no agreement was possible. The most celebrated example was abortion (q.v.), and the GDR's law permitting legal abortion on demand within three months was left in place there, while the West's more restricted Paragraph 218 applied in the old FRG. Polls after reunification revealed that 57 percent of East Germans still favored legal abortion on demand, compared with only 28 percent in the West. In June 1992, a narrow majority in the Bundestag voted to legalize abortions in all of Germany, but in August 1992 the Constitutional Court (q.v.) voted unanimously to block the change to a more liberalized abortion.

FASCHING.   This is the period of celebration before Lent which begins at the eleventh hour on the eleventh day of the eleventh month. Originally called "Shrove Tuesday," it is now *Karneval* in the Rhineland and *Fasching* in Southern Germany.

FASSBINDER, RAINER WERNER (1946-1982).   This former actor turned film maker was the dominating force in the New German Cinema (q.v.) of the 1970s. By the time he died at age 36 he had produced over 40 films. No one film is like the other, and each goes further than the last. Known for their freshness, experimentalism, and variety of subject matter, Fassbinder's films are a legacy of quality. (See also ANTI-SEMITISM; FILM.)

FECHTER, PETER. An 18-year old East German, he was the first to be shot along the Berlin Wall (q.v.). On August 17, 1962, Berliners on both sides of the wall watched the tragedy, unable to reach him as he bled to death in the "no man's land" between East and West Berlin.

FEDERAL ADMINISTRATIVE OFFICE see FEDERAL HIGHER AUTHORITIES

FEDERAL ALLIANCE OF GERMAN EMPLOYER ASSOCIATIONS (BUNDESVEREINIGUNG DER DEUTSCHEN ARBEITGEBERVERBÄNDE--BDA). The BDA covers all the chief sectors of the economy and is concerned with all aspects involved with employment, including social policy and wages. More than 80 percent of employers belong to the BDA, but the interests of the largest firms predominate. Sectoral employers' organizations make collective bargaining agreements, but the BDA ensures that the various agreements in different sectors are concerted and that no sector enters agreements which are out of line in terms of wages, hours, and co-determination (q.v.). Well-funded, the BDA can compensate sectors and firms shaken by industrial disputes.

FEDERAL ASSEMBLY (BUNDESVERSAMMLUNG) see PRESIDENT, FEDERAL

FEDERAL ASSOCIATION OF GERMAN INDUSTRY (BUNDESVERBAND DER DEUTSCHEN INDUSTRIE--BDI). The BDI represents the interests of German industry. It is broken down into 35 associations, and it embraces about 95 percent of the firms in the industrial sector. It tends to be identified with the interests of large business.

FEDERAL AUDITOR-GENERAL (BUNDESRECHNUNGSHOF). This is the Auditor-General for the FRG and is responsible for auditing the expenditure of federal ministries. Similar offices examine the expenditures of Land governments.

FEDERAL CIVIL SERVICE LAW (BUNDESBEAMTENGESETZ) see CIVIL SERVICE LAW

FEDERAL COMITY (BUNDESTREUE) DOCTRINE. This doctrine requires that each unit of the federation take account not only of its own interests, but also of the well-being of the whole when it formulates and implements policy.

FEDERAL HIGH COURT (BUNDESGERICHTSHOF) see CONSOLIDATION LAW

FEDERAL HIGHER AUTHORITIES (BUNDESOBERBEHÖRDEN). These authorities exist to relieve ministries of certain administrative duties. They are subordinated to a parent ministry and are responsible throughout the FRG for a specific function which requires special technical knowledge and independence from other policy areas. Many of these authorities are larger and more important than their parent ministries. Examples are the Federal Administrative Office which deals with citizenship questions, the Federal Insurance Office in Berlin which supervises medical insurance funds (*Krankenkassen)* for the ministry of labor and social affairs, and the German Meteorological Office in Offenbach, which handles weather forecasting for the transport ministry.

FEDERAL INSURANCE OFFICE see FEDERAL HIGHER AUTHORITIES

FEDERAL MINISTRY FOR RESEARCH AND TECHNOLOGY (BUNDESMINISTERIUM FÜR FORSCHUNG UND TECHNOLOGIE- -BMFT) see SPACE PROGRAM

FEDERAL REPUBLIC OF GERMANY (FRG)--BUNDESREPUBLIK DEUTSCHLAND, FOUNDATION OF (1949). The disagreements among the four occupation powers reached such an impasse that the three Western Allies decided in the summer of 1948 to permit German leaders in their three zones to write a constitution and to found a West German state. The Constituent Assembly met in Bonn on September 1, 1948, under the chairmanship of the elderly former mayor of Cologne, Konrad Adenauer (q.v.), and under the watchful eyes of the three occupation authorities. Things were finally settled by May 8, 1949, almost four years to the day since the capitulation of the Third Reich (q.v.).

What was created was seen to be strictly "for a transitional period," and the document was called a Basic Law (q.v.), not a constitution, a word which might connote something more permanent. The founders wrote into the preamble that they had acted on behalf of Germans living under Soviet occupation and that "the entire German people is called upon to accomplish, by free self-determination, the unity and freedom of Germany." Thus, West German leaders imposed upon themselves the obligation to bring the two parts of Germany back together, even though that goal seemed to be slipping farther and farther into the distant future.

On August 14, 1949, most of the eligible voters in West Germany went to the polls to elect their first parliamentary representatives. Adenauer's Christian Democratic Union (CDU, q.v.), along with the Bavarian Christian Social Union (CSU, q.v.), captured 31 percent of the votes, and the SPD (q.v.) 29.2 percent. Several other parties also won seats, and Adenauer was able to patch together a coalition government with only a one-vote majority, his own vote! Adenauer was to serve as West German chancellor until 1963, longer than the entire Weimar Republic (q.v.) had existed. This shrewd politician was seen by the voters as a comforting father-figure (*Der Alte*--"The Old Man"), who took a firmer control of West German politics than any other chancellor since. As a confident (some say authoritarian) ruler, he was able to place his imprint on the young democracy as no one since. The Soviet Union responded to the creation of the FRG by converting its occupation zone into the German Democratic Republic (GDR, q.v.), ruled by the communist-led SED (q.v.).

The FRG's new capital was not established in a major West German city such as Frankfurt am Main chiefly because such a seat might appear as a permanent capital city for a state which was expressly intended to be provisional. Instead, the sleepy Rhenish university town of Bonn was selected as the "temporary" seat of government, and an architecturally unattractive former teacher's college became the new parliament and governmental center. Some like to call it "the federal village." The new government ordered that the gutted Reichstag building, located a few meters within the Western sector of Berlin, be reconstructed so that it could again serve as the capitol of a reunified Germany. Work on the renovation was completed in the 1970s, and in 1991 the Bundestag voted to move the seat of government back to Berlin.

FEDERATION OF ACADEMIC FREEDOM (BUND FREIHEIT DER WISSENSCHAFT). Outraged by the chaos caused by student revolutionaries and their allies in the faculties of some universities during the 1960s and 1970s, this organization was formed to oppose the politicization of the universities, to defend academic freedom, and to block the assaults on the "achievement ethic" (*Leistungsprinzip*) and on rationality made by romantics in the student movement. Most of its members were conservatives, but some, such as political scientists Richard Löwenthal (West Berlin) and Kurt Sontheimer (Munich) were Social Democrats.

FEDERATION OF GERMAN GIRLS (BUND DEUTSCHER MÄDEL) see HITLER YOUTH

FEDERATION OF VIOLENCE-FREE ACTION GROUPS--GRASS-ROOTS (FÖDERATION GEWALTFREIER AKTIONSGRUPPEN--FÖGA). This organization has about 500 followers in ca. 80 groups and collectives. Its monthly *graswurzelrevolution* (Grass-Roots Revolution), with a circulation of 3,000, advocates a nonviolent revolution and creation of a decentralized society based on anarchy and self-administration to replace present state power. The aims are primarily antimilitarism, peace, and "social defense." Environmental protection, especially against nuclear power and reprocessing plants, is also important. It maintains an information and coordination center in Cologne.

FELFE, HEINZ. Felfe made his way into the West German intelligence agency, the Bundesnachrichten Dienst (BND), after the war, and by the time of his arrest in 1963 he had amassed a thorough knowledge of that organization's structure. That is why the Soviets desperately wanted his release from prison and why the FRG's government did not. In February 1969, Felfe was released to the GDR (q.v.), where he became a professor at the Humboldt University in Berlin. (See also POLITICAL PRISONERS.)

FEST, JOACHIM see HITLER WAVE

FEUCHTWANGER, LION (1884-1958). A liberal Jewish refugee who was forced to leave Hitler Germany, Feuchtwanger enjoyed international success as a dramatic critic and writer of Jewish plays and historical novels, such as *Jud Süss* (*Sweet Jew*). He founded the German weekly, *Der Spiegel*, in 1908. His home in California was a refuge to many other emigres such as Thomas Mann and Bertold Brecht (qq.v.).

FEUERBACH, LUDWIG A. (1804-1872). Living and working in Landshut, Berlin, and Erlangen, Feuerbach was inspired by both his study of natural science and Hegel. In *Essence of Christianity* (1841) he argued that religion is the consciousness of the infinity of man's own nature, and "God" is that infinity. The diverse aspects of the divine nature are a response to human needs. He therefore rejected revelation and sacraments.

FICHTE, JOHANN GOTTLIEB (1762-1814). A philosopher living and working in Rammenau, Jena, Leipzig, and Berlin, Fichte was the first great representative of the absolute idealistic school. He drew his inspiration primarily from Immanuel Kant's *Critique of Practical Reason* and *Critique of Pure Reason*. He concluded from the latter work that man lives by what he believes rather than by what he knows. Man's moral interests must take priority over his scientific interests; his chief concern must be the realization of his ethical obligations. Man's basic reality is his will, the true "thing-in-itself." His will is a microcosm of the whole universe, which is a moral order working out tasks on a grand scale. God is the absolute spirit immanent in the universe. At any time in history, this spirit expresses itself most fully in the leading culture of the age. Fichte argued that the disunited Germans, who had been conquered by Napoleon's Grande Armée, should unite and become the manifestation of the absolute. That is Germany's proper place in history. His 1808 *Addresses to the German Nation* had a profound impact on the nationalism which emerged in Germany.

FIGHT ATOMIC DEATH (KAMPF DEM ATOMTOD). In late 1957, George F. Kennan and Polish Foreign Minister Adam Rapacki had proposed plans for creating a nuclear-free zone in Central Europe that could be the prelude for a neutral, reunified Germany. Many Germans were intensely interested in these ideas. Adenauer (q.v.) and his government branded them "the end of freedom" and bruskly rejected them in January 1958. His government was working on plans to accept a possible NATO (q.v.) offer to arm the Bundeswehr (q.v.) with atomic weapons. This provoked an outburst of public protests. Despite the fact that the SPD (q.v.) had just lost a federal election by opposing Adenauer's foreign and defense policy, many Social Democrats thought that they had found a cause which would attract voters to the SPD without having to reform the party. Polls in 1958 indicated that more than 80 percent of West German respondents and even 70 percent of CDU/CSU (q.v.) supporters opposed the deployment of atomic launchers in the FRG. Therefore, on March 7, the SPD joined the extra-parliamentary movement composed of some FDP (q.v.) politicians, trade unionists, church leaders of both confessions, scientists, artists, pacifists, and other public personalities, who united under the banner of *Kampf dem Atomtod*, and warned: "The German people on both sides of the zonal border will be victims of certain atomic death in the event of a war between East and West." They demanded a referendum on the issue, even though there was no constitutional provision for that. Although the SPD had occasionally tried to strengthen its parliamentary opposition to German rearmament by joining brief public protests, this was the first time the party had made a major departure from parliamentary democracy to achieve its goals.

For several months large demonstrations took place in most major cities throughout the FRG. But the SPD's support for the movement quickly ran out of steam after the June 6 provincial elections in North Rhine-Westphalia, the largest Land in the FRG. The electoral trend continued to favor the CDU. Obviously, "Fight Atomic Death" had done nothing to change the West Germans' voting preferences. What it had done, however, was to generate even more accusations that the SPD was neutralist. It also strengthened the legacy of anti-nuclear sentiment in the SPD, which continued to plague the party. (See also PEACE MOVEMENT.)

FILBINGER, HANS (1913-) see DENAZIFICATION

FILM, POST-1945. Until the mid-1960s it appeared that the German reputation in film, established before the war by such directors as Fritz Lang (q.v.), Ernst Lubitsch, F.W. Murnau and G.W. Pabst, would be lost forever. The first two decades of postwar productions were mainly provincial, unproblematic entertainment films, which could be summed up in one German word: *Schmalz* (corniness). The need to compete with television for viewers helped keep the level of films low. Between 1956 and 1976, the annual production of German films and the number of cinemas dropped by 50 percent. Even today, a fourth of all films shown in the FRG comes from the U.S. and a fifth from Italy and France. Only a fifth comes from Germany itself, and fewer than 6 percent of all western German film viewers went to see them. Partly because of the 1968 Film Promotion Measures Act and a Film Promotion Agency, which channels state subsidies to producers of feature, documentary, short and youth films, a wave of creative film making, known as "the young German film," emerged in the 1960s.

German directors in this wave have succeeded in winning international recognition. They include Alexander Kluge, Volker Schlöndorff, Johannes Schaaf, the late Rainer Werner Fassbinder (q.v.), Hans Jürgen Syberburg, Bernhard Sinkel, Margarethe von Trotte (q.v.) and two directors who particularly like to place their films in American settings, Werner Herzog (q.v.) and Wim Wenders (q.v.). However, since they often fail to attract sufficiently large audiences, the federal government decided to curtail funding for heavily experimental and purely artistic films after 1983. Like their literary counterparts, German film directors tend to focus on the blemishes of Germany's social and political order. A refreshing exception is Doris Dörrie (q.v.), a self-assured young director. She went to the U.S. to become an actress, but instead studied film and theater in California and New York. In her box office success *Männer* (Men), the characters laugh about themselves and each other, and their laughter is contagious for the audience. She reflects the waning ideological inclinations of contemporary Germans: "I grew up with pop concerts, not with political discussions....The fact that I do not deal with big political themes is directly linked to that."

Eastern Germany's film future is uncertain. The Trust Agency announced in 1991 that it would try to save the DEFA film production studios in Potsdam-Babelsberg, and in 1992 it was sold to the French real estate and film producer, Compagnie Générale des Eaux (CGE), which plans to develop the famed-but-faded studio. Founded in 1946, it was the site of the entire GDR film industry and included a college for film and TV and an agency for film exports and imports. Before 1989 it had annually produced about 20 feature films, 25 TV films, 170 documentaries, and many animated films. CGE and Bertelsmann, the German media giant, plan to build a media city housing two German TV networks, a film academy, and the renovated DEFA studios, now headed by Volker Schlöndorff.

FINAL SOLUTION see NAZI REPRESSION

FINANCE PLANNING COUNCIL (FINANZPLANUNGSRAT) see LAW ON STABILITY AND GROWTH and TAXATION

FIRST WORLD WAR. There was general shock and indignation in all of Europe when Archduke Franz Ferdinand's assassination was announced. On July 5 and 6, 1914, Germany granted its ally, Austria-Hungary, a free hand to deal with the matter, and Russia (and indirectly France) gave the Serbians a similarly free hand. Only in the final days of the crisis did the German chancellor desperately try to regain control of the situation. Subsequent events revealed that German interests would have been better served by a tighter German rein on Austrian policy. However, in the eyes of German leaders, there appeared to be no alternative to their policy of allowing Austria to deal harshly with Serbia at this time. On July 28, Austria-Hungary declared war on Serbia, and two days later Russia made the critical decision to order general mobilization, thus indicating its unwillingness to allow the Austrian-Serbian war to remain localized. German leaders had for a long time made it clear that they perceived a Russian general mobilization to be a threat to Germany itself. When Russia refused to withdraw its call to arms, Germany sent a last warning to both Russia and France. When the German note remained unanswered by August 1, Germany declared war on Russia. It did not immediately declare war on France, but France mobilized its army anyway on August 1. With Russia, Germany and France carrying out general military buildups, a European war had become unavoidable. When Germany violated Belgian territory in order to gain easier access to France, Britain also entered the war, thereby transforming the European war, which Germany probably would have won, into a world war.

All the European powers shared responsibility for the outbreak of World War I. Some, such as Austria-Hungary and Serbia, bore the greatest responsibility. Germany, Russia and France must be blamed for not having sufficiently restrained their respective allies and thereby having allowed a local Balkan squabble (where there had already been two wars in 1912 and 1913) to ignite a world war. Britain bears the least responsibility for the war which came. Nevertheless, crowds of people in all belligerent countries greeted the outbreak of war with a gaiety which is usually reserved for carnival time. Two million German, more than a million French, a million British, a million Austrian, a half million Italian and countless Russian soldiers perished in the four-year blood-letting which followed. The war also destroyed the old Europe, and what could be pieced back together collapsed a mere two decades later.

Almost immediately after the start of hostilities, German troops knifed through Belgium and into France according to a carefully laid "Schlieffen Plan" (q.v.), but by mid-September at the Battle of the Marne, they had been stopped in their tracks before reaching Paris. For four years two opposing armies faced each other in trenches stretching from the English Channel to the Swiss border and protected by mazes of barbed wire, machine gun nests, mortar and heavy artillery batteries. Chemical warfare (gas) was also introduced during the grisly conflict. Occasionally massive attacks were launched against the opposing trenches which sometimes brought infinitesimal gains and always huge human losses. For instance, in the inconclusive Battle of the Somme in 1916, the Germans lost 650,000 men and the Allies 614,000.

It was a different story in the East, where warfare was highly mobile and brought huge gains and losses of territory. After an initial Russian advance into East Prussia, German forces scored stunning victories against the Russians at Tannenberg and the Masurian Lakes. Out of these victories was born the legend of military genius and invincibility which surrounded the victorious Generals Paul von Hindenburg and Erich Ludendorff (qq.v.) for the remainder of the war. By 1916 their authority over military and political questions alike exceeded even that of the Kaiser and the chancellor.

The German successes in the East enabled their armies to march right into the heart of Russia. Still, the badly shaken Czarist Empire managed to put up stiff resistance. It became clear to the Germans that the two-front war was a vice which could eventually crush Germany. This became especially apparent when the United States entered the war on the Allied side in the spring of 1917. President Woodrow Wilson had been determined to keep the Americans out of the war, but the Germans made several blunders which drew the U.S. into the conflict. A high official in the Foreign Office, Arthur Zimmermann, sent a telegram to the Mexican government promising territorial rewards north of the Mexican border if it would support Germany in the war. This telegram was intercepted by the Americans and understandably antagonized American leaders and public opinion. The most serious German mistakes involved naval warfare against neutral shipping. By the spring of 1915, German surface ships had been swept from all the major seas except the North and Baltic Seas. Because of the ever-tightening British blockade of the North Sea and English Channel outlets, the bulk of the German Navy, which had been built up with so much fanfare and political sacrifice, remained bottled up in Germany's northern ports. This blockade also brought increasing hunger and deprivation to the German population and gradually led German leaders to use submarines to strike at Allied shipping. Submarines were regarded as a particularly hideous weapon at the time since they torpedoed ships without warning and without any capacity to help survivors. A particular outcry had gone up in the U.S. when a large passenger liner, the Lusitania, was torpedoed off the coast of Ireland in mid-1915, with a loss of 1,198 lives, including 139 Americans. The indignation in America was such that the Germans promised not to repeat such attacks.

For a while German submarine activity died down, but by early 1917 Generals Hindenburg and Ludendorff, backed by their immense popularity, forced the adoption of unrestricted submarine warfare on the unwilling chancellor. The head of the German Admiralty misjudged the ultimate effect of America's entry into the war to be "exactly zero;" in any case, it was widely believed that Britain would be forced to its knees before Americans would arrive. Although the first American divisions did not arrive in France until almost a year later, the immediate boost to Allied morale and the military contribution made by American soldiers in the final months of the war were decisive in the defeat of Germany.

FISCHER, FRITZ and CONTROVERSY   see SEPTEMBER PROGRAM

FISCHER, JOSCHKA (1948-). A Green who brought the informality of tieless shirts and sneakers to ministerial circles in Hesse, Fischer was instrumental in forging a coalition with the SPD (q.v.) in Hesse in 1985 and became environmental minister. He was the first-ever Green minister. The coalition failed, but it was restored following the January 1991 Hesse elections, with Fischer, a committed "Realo," as deputy minister president and minister for environment, energy and federal affairs. He had begun his political career with the "Revolutionary Struggle" groups from 1968 to 1975 and was elected to the Bundestag in 1983 after becoming a Green. (See also GREENS.)

FIVE NEW FEDERAL LÄNDER (FÜNF NEUE BUNDESLÄNDER). After Germany became unified in October 1990, people were unsure how to refer to that part of Germany belonging to the "former GDR." Therefore, many used this clumsy formulation.

FIVE WISE MEN (FÜNF WEISEN) see TAXATION

FLAG.   Three horizontal stripes of black, red and gold. (See CARLSBAD ACTS.)

FLEET LEAGUE (FLOTTENVEREIN) see ALL-GERMAN LEAGUE

FLICK AFFAIR. In late 1981 the investigative weekly *Der Spiegel* began publishing documents linking the large Flick industrial corporation with sizable but secret financial contributions to politicians in the FDP, CDU/CSU, and SPD (qq.v.). The evidence suggested that the recipients had not declared these contributions, as the law required. Both Flick executives and some prominent politicians were indicted on the grounds that the latter had helped the firm evade federal taxes. In 1984, the FDP economics minister, Count Otto von Lambsdorff (q.v.) resigned in order to deal with charges that he was involved in the scandal. The legal proceedings ended inconclusively in 1987 with some partial convictions and suspended sentences. The scandal shook the integrity of the entire political establishment and put wind into the sails of the Greens (q.v.).

FONTANE, THEODOR (1819-1898).   A pharmacist turned correspondent, Fontane developed at an old age into one of the most alert and subtle novelists of his time. At age 59 he began writing the first of 14 novels which were completed in 20 years. His subject matter varies from his travel volumes about Mark Brandenburg and his historical novels about war to his conversational (*Der Stechlin*) and psychological (*Effi Briest*) novels, which gained him greatest fame. He portrays Berlin society with delicate irony, and depicts his characters with understanding and compassion. Fontane wrote two autobiographical works, poetry, and was also a drama critic. (See also EMPIRE CULTURE.)

FORCK, GOTTFRIED (1923-). As Bishop of the Protestant Church in Berlin-Brandenburg, this scrappy theologian frequently criticized the SED (q.v.) regime and society from the early 1980s. Above all, he opposed the militarization of the GDR (q.v.). It was thanks to Forck that the Church in Berlin made its rooms available to opposition groups.

FOREIGN EXTREMIST ORGANIZATIONS IN GERMANY. The FRG has many foreign extremist organizations which operate within the country. Their numbers grow as the FRG becomes a haven for more and more refugees from the Third World. The presence of so many visibly alien people creates domestic political tensions and provides a convenient scapegoat and target for right-wing German extremist circles. The BfV estimated that by 1990 about 54,300 foreigners belonged to Marxist extremist organizations (more than twice as many as belonged to corresponding right-wing extremist groups). The most active and violence-oriented is the orthodox-communist Workers' Party of Kurdistan (PKK). The Liberation Tigers of Tamil Ealam (LTTE) makes its presence felt, as do violent Irish, Palestinian, Iranian, Turkish and Yugoslavian groups.

FORMED SOCIETY (FORMIERTE GESELLSCHAFT). This is a concept which Chancellor Ludwig Erhard (q.v.) enunciated after his 1965 election victory. The social market economy (q.v.) had brought the FRG economic recovery. Now was the time for a new stage of social development he called the "formed society." This implies a rational, shaped, "fully formed" society in which organized political interests and their struggles are not bad, but actually aid social and economic progress. He wished to put his stamp on this new era and make certain that it served a free society and economy for the good of the German people. However, he was out of power in 1966, and this goal was largely forgotten.

FÖRSTER, ELISABETH see NIETZSCHE

FOURTEEN POINTS see VERSAILLES TREATY

FRAKTION see PARLIAMENTARY GROUP

FRANCO-GERMAN RELATIONS. Since its inception in 1949, the FRG has regarded its relationship with its former "perpetual enemy" France to be the cornerstone of a peaceful and united Western Europe. The two countries are each other's most important trading partners, their leaders meet on a regular basis, and they bend over backwards to get along with each other. Konrad Adenauer (q.v.), who as a Rhinelander was always skeptical of German nationalism and was oriented toward France, sought from the beginning of his chancellorship to achieve the

FRG's reconciliation with France, which would end the rivalries between the two peoples which had lasted for centuries. In the early 1950s, he worked together with French Foreign Minister Robert Schuman, whose Schuman Plan led to the European Coal and Steel Community (ECSC). Collaboration later in the 1950s led to the European Economic Community (EEC) and EURATOM in 1958; the three are collectively called the European Community (EC) (q.v.). When Charles de Gaulle became French president in 1958, there were bilateral tensions because of de Gaulle's hostility to supranational institutions. Nevertheless, on January 22, 1963, Adenauer and de Gaulle signed the Elysée Treaty, which obligated both countries to engage in permanent consultation and summit meetings twice a year at which questions of foreign, economic, defense, and culture policy would be discussed. A strengthened youth exchange was established. These semiannual meetings have continued ever since.

As a political heir to Konrad Adenauer, Helmut Kohl (q.v.) regards the FRG's relationship with France as vitally important. He also shares the views of many Western European leaders that the "European pillar" of NATO (q.v.) defense must be strengthened. In 1988, he supported the creation of the Franco-German Council on Security and Deterrence, which facilitates closer defense consultation and cooperation between the two countries. He also approved the creation of a Franco-German brigade, with headquarters in Böblingen, near Stuttgart. With the U.S. reducing its troop strength in Europe, especially in Germany, after the collapse of the Soviet Union, Kohl agreed to create a larger, corps-level unit with the French.

An example of an activity which gives German leaders an opportunity to tighten this important tie is in the FRG's space program (q.v.). Chancellor Kohl is especially inclined to support French space projects, although he is sometimes willing to say no, as he did when the French urged him to cooperate in building a spy satellite. The government's inclination to accept France's initiatives in space since 1962, when the FRG began funding space research and projects, to allow the French to take the lead, and not to push German-conceived projects strongly enough is sometimes criticized in Germany. An exasperated Bavarian industrialist reportedly remarked that "when cooperating with the French, the Germans are only permitted to build the outhouse."

FRANCO-PRUSSIAN WAR (1870-1871). With increasing nervousness the French looked east across the Rhine where Bismarck (q.v.) had created momentum toward German unity. Feverish French diplomatic activity in the south German states and Austria failed to create determined opposition to Prussia (q.v.). The crisis erupted in mid-1870 when the Prussian government announced that Prince Leopold of the House of Hohenzollern had accepted the Spanish throne, which had been vacant since 1868. As Bismarck (q.v.) well knew, the French would never tolerate a Hohenzollern on the Spanish throne, since they would then face a hostile dynasty on their eastern and southwestern borders. The French ambassador to Prussia, Benedetti, persuaded Wilhelm I at the spa Bad Ems that it would be a good idea to withdraw Leopold's candidacy. Wilhelm politely refused to assure the French diplomat that the Hohenzollern candidacy would not be renewed in the future. The king wired his description of the talks to Bismarck, who then published the telegram after intentionally shortening it in such a way that Wilhelm's reply to Benedetti seemed far more abrupt and impolite than it actually had been. The French were infuriated by this "Ems Telegram," and in an atmosphere of inflamed emotion, the government declared war on Prussia on July 19.

To France's surprise, the south German states immediately joined the Prussians in the war. The Prussians struck quickly and fatally. Smashing through Lorraine, the Prussian Army cut Paris off from the two main French armies and delivered a devastating blow to the French at Sedan on the Belgian border. By January 1871, all resistance ended. A humiliated France looked on as the German Empire was proclaimed in the Hall of Mirrors in the Palace of Versailles on January 18, 1871. For the first time in history, there was a united Germany. Bismarck was mistaken in acquiescing to pressures from the Kaiser, Prussian military leaders and others by imposing a harsh peace on a prostrate France. Germany annexed Alsace and most of Lorraine, with their advanced industry and rich iron deposits. Also, France was required to pay a very large indemnity and to allow German occupation troops to remain in France until the sum was paid. For the next half century, French policy would revolve around undoing these terrible losses, and the pigeons that German leaders had turned loose in 1871 would come back to roost with a vengeance in 1919. (See also BISMARCK, OTTO VON.)

FRANKFURT PARLIAMENT see REVOLUTION OF 1848

FRANKFURT, TREATY OF, PEACE OF (1871). Following the siege and capitulation of Paris, the Franco-Prussian War (q.v.) was ended by this treaty of May 10, 1871. France was forced to cede Alsace and part of Lorraine, including the fortresses of Didenhofen and Metz, and pay an indemnity of $1 billion within three years. The eastern departments of France were to remain occupied until payment had been made. Even though the French succeeded in paying this by gaining loans on international capital markets, the German terms infuriated the French and set a very bad precedent for subsequent peace terms in 1919. (See also BISMARCK, OTTO VON; VERSAILLES TREATY.)

FREE CONSERVATIVE PARTY (FREIKONSERVATIVE PARTEI) see GERMAN REICH PARTY

FREE CORPS (FREIKORPS) see REVOLUTION IN GERMANY

FREE DEMOCRATIC PARTY OF GERMANY (FREI DEMOKRATISCHE PARTEI--FDP, "LIBERALS"). After 1945, liberals sought to overcome the traditional division between right- and left-liberal party organizations, represented in the Weimar Republic by the DDP and DVP (qq.v.). They succeeded in this; in Wurttemberg and Baden Theodor Heuss (q.v.) and Reinhold Maier re-founded the Democratic People's Party (DVP). Attempts to create a Germany-wide liberal party failed when the Liberal Democratic Party of Germany (LDPD), founded in Berlin by Wilhelm Külz, spurned cooperation and focused on the Eastern Zone, where it became one of the "bloc parties" which cooperated with the SED (qq.v.). On December 11, 1948, the western liberal parties formed the FDP under Heuss' leadership. Nevertheless, the more conservative and nationalist wing of the party, which had formed the DVP in Weimar, sometimes clashed with those liberals from the DDP tradition. This was especially apparent in the debates over *Ostpolitik* (q.v.), when some conservative Free Democrats, such as Erich Mende (q.v.), left the party to join the CDU (q.v.).

For a long time, the FDP was the only small party to survive in the Bundestag. It has never received more than 13 percent of the vote, and at times it danced dangerously close to the 5 percent line. Yet the FDP plays a role in German politics far out of proportion to its size or voter strength. Only once (in 1957) has a party ever won an absolute majority of seats in the Bundestag. Thus, German governments must always be coalitions of two or more parties, and the FDP has been and remains linchpin for almost every governmental coalition. Since 1949 it has been excluded from only two cabinets.

The FDP sees itself as the heir to the traditional German liberal movement, which was always composed of two strains: a strong nationalist commitment and the protection of individual rights through minimizing state intervention in the economy and society. In the early 1970s, the nationalist strain largely left the party, so throughout the 1970s the FDP could be more comfortable in the center-moderate left coalition in Bonn. The FDP attracts most of its votes from the middle class mainly in urban areas. Like the SPD (q.v.), it has attracted some critical and confrontational elements which have become difficult or impossible for the party to digest.

From 1969 to 1982, the FDP was in the governing coalition with the SPD. However, it is economically more conservative than its former partner, and it increasingly disagreed with the Social Democratic medicine for coping with unemployment and the rising public debt. It sensed a conservative wind blowing in West Germany, and a string of electoral disasters in Land elections reminded it that it was in danger of being dragged down by the SPD. Therefore, in 1982 it decided to change partners, thereby enabling the Christian Democrats to rule in Bonn. The FDP was widely criticized for the way in which it brought the Schmidt (q.v.) government tumbling down. But its indispensable role as a moderating coalition partner was again recognized: In 1987 it was able to raise its 6.9 percent of the votes and 34 seats to 9.1 percent and 46 seats. In 1990 it won 11 percent nationwide and 79 seats. It won 12.9 percent in the East, thanks partly to Genscher and Wolfgang Mischnick (qq.v), who had grown up in the GDR and could present themselves as both easterners and westerners.

FREE GERMAN TRADE UNION FEDERATION (FREIER DEUTSCHER GEWERKSCHAFTSBUND--FDGB). The East German, SED-controlled trade union federation, its job was to secure workers' compliance to SED (q.v.) directives, rather than to protect workers from their employers. Discredited and bankrupt after the collapse of the GDR (q.v.), it died a slow death, since the more successful West German DGB (q.v.) refused to merge with it or support it.

FREE GERMAN WORKERS' PARTY see PARTIES, RIGHT-WING

FREE GERMAN YOUTH (FREIE DEUTSCHE JUGEND--FDJ). SED youth organization in GDR, founded by Erich Honecker (qq.v.) on March 7, 1946, as a nonparty organization, but its subordination to the SED was completed by 1952. Its tasks were the political organization, Marxist-Leninist ideological education, mass support of SED decisions, and provision of free-time activities and pre-military training of young people. It was supposed to provide the future SED cadre. According to official SED figures, it had around 2.2 million members, which constituted about 70 percent of young East Germans between the ages of 14 and 25. Younger children were organized in the Children's Union (*Kinderverband*) Pioneer Organization Ernst Thälmann.

FREE WORKERS' UNION (FREIE ARBEITERINNEN-UNION-- FAU). FAU has 200 members in 20 local groups and a headquarters in Cologne, is a member of the anarcho-syndicalist International Workers' Association (Internationale Arbeiter-Assoziation, IAA) and publishes a bimonthly *Direkt Aktion* in Dieburg. It founded *Schwarze Hilfe* (Black Help) to assist imprisoned anarcho-sydicalists, anarchists and autonomists. It also maintains contact with the international coordinating office of the anarchist Black Cross in London. The principles espoused by anarcho-sydicalists can be summarized as antistate, antiparliamentary, and antimilitary. FAU adherents oppose both Western capitalism and the "state capitalism" practiced in communist countries. Their supreme task, as they see it, is the revolutionary work in factories to create collective resistance against capitalism. They dream of a society characterized by decentralization and self-administration. There are some independent opposition FAU organizations which wish to work also outside the factory arena. They include the FAU Anarchist Party (FAU/AP) in Heidelberg, which occasionally publishes *Fanal*, and the FAU Council Communists (FAU/R) in Hamburg.

FREIBURG THESES. Adopted in 1971 by the FDP (q.v.), which was in a governing coalition with the SPD (q.v.) at the time, these had at their heart the concept of "reform capitalism." This was a victory for the view that economic market mechanisms had to be limited and restrained by social considerations.

FREIKAUF see POLITICAL PRISONERS

FREISLER, ROLAND (1893-1945). Nazi president of People's Court (1942-45), killed in Allied air raid. (See also ELECTIONS 1980; RESISTANCE TO HITLER.)

FRENCH REVOLUTION AND OCCUPATION OF GERMANY. While many Germans were inspired by American ideas and events, it was the French Revolution in 1789 which brought the spark of democratic revolution to Europe. Prussia (q.v.) had been a state well-ordered from above; France was now a nation whose most powerful inspiration came from below--from the people. Revolutionary France was able to fuse ideals, whose force had already been put into practice in America, with national power to an extent that no country on the continent of Europe could resist. The French Revolution was a declaration of war against the Old Europe. To underscore this, French revolutionary leaders promised in the early years of the revolution to help any people which rose up against despotic rulers, and Napoleon's Grand Army later carried the message through the heart of Europe and all the way to Moscow.

Some leading Germans greeted Napoleon and the French Revolution. The philosopher Friedrich Hegel (q.v.) called this mighty convulsion "the end of history." His compatriot Immanuel Kant (q.v.) admired the idealism of the French masses as did Friedrich Schiller (q.v.) whose admiration, like that of many others, diminished when the guillotine began doing its grisly work. Goethe (q.v.) went to meet Napoleon in Erfurt, where the Frenchman was greeted by the masses and princes with such flattery and servility that Talleyrand wrote disgustedly: "They kiss the hand which could destroy them today or tomorrow." In Germany, Napoleonic power was recognized and, for one reason or another, respected. Wherever it was not, Napoleon sent his armies, and by 1807 all German states had been compelled one by one to make peace with France.

French domination over most of Germany brought an enormous territorial reshuffling at the expense of the smaller territories, which he eliminated. He abolished all religious rule over sovereign territories, gave the medium-sized states more territory, and elevated Bavaria and Wurttemberg to kingdoms. In 1806 he grouped 16 middle-sized states, including Bavaria, Wurttemberg and Baden into a Rhenish League with one of Napoleon's brothers as the monarch, all under French protection. They were obligated to supply 64,000 troops to Napoleon, who assumed control over their armies. All were compelled to declare their exit from the German Empire, which thereby lost a third of its territory. Combined with Napoleon's defeat of the Austrians and Russians at the battle of Austerlitz, 60 miles (100 kilometers) north of Vienna in 1806, this spelled the end of the German Empire, which had existed for almost a thousand years, although it had been weak and very divided. Shortly thereafter, Emperor Franz II cast off the German imperial crown and the Holy Roman Empire of the Germans came to an end.

Napoleon's objective was clear: he wished to create states in Germany which were strong enough to support France but too weak to constitute a threat to it. The French occupiers were loved nowhere in Germany, and French rule was absolute, in the sense that all orders came from above. Yet it was in some respects very progressive and liberal. Everyone was equal before the law, class privileges were reduced or abolished, schools were taken over by the state, the legal systems were simplified, and the churches' active hand in politics was reduced or eliminated. This liberal influence was most lasting in the Rhineland, where it henceforth outweighed the absolutist tradition.

Prussia had made peace with Napoleon in 1795. This gave it a decade without war, but also permitted Napoleon a free hand in Germany. When Prussia finally had to act against France, it stood alone. At first Napoleon had been friendly toward Prussia in order to keep it out of any coalition directed against France. There was no need for such friendliness once Austria had been defeated, so Napoleon simply marched his troops through Prussia. When the Prussian King Friedrich Wilhelm III protested this, Napoleon unleashed his armies against Prussia, delivering humiliating defeats in the battles of Saalfeld, Jena, Auerstädt and Friedland.

At the end of October 1806, Napoleon led his troops into Berlin, where he declared his continental blockade against England. He also helped himself, as he did in every land which he dominated, to art treasures, including the four horses on top of the Brandenburg Gate (q.v.), and shipped them off to Paris. In the summer of 1807, Prussia was compelled to join France and Russia in the Peace of Tilsit (q.v.). This peace treaty permitted Prussia to continue existing as a state, but it lost half its territory, including all its lands west of the Elbe, and was forced to provide France with money and troops. In short order, Prussia had been reduced to an insignificant country completely in the hands of Napoleon.

After this devastating defeat, the Prussian king declared that the Prussian state must replace through intellectual and cultural strength what it had lost in material strength. He knew that Prussia had to reform and modernize itself, so he appointed such men as Baron vom Stein, Karl August von Hardenberg, Neidhart von Gneisenau, Gerhard von Scharnhorst and Wilhelm von Humboldt (qq.v.) to make all Prussian citizens, in Gneisenau's words, "free, noble and independent so that they believe they are part of the whole." Prussia now experienced a burst of reform activity, brought to a head by the misery of defeat. The overall strength of that country seemed to indicate the strength of the new ideas coming out of France. The social, political, military and educational reforms were not sufficiently democratic in the modern sense, and some of them were undone after 1815. But they were steps in the right direction, and they aroused much enthusiasm throughout Germany at the time. Serfdom was abolished, although serfs were obliged to pay for their emancipation by incurring debts or by ceding much land they had tilled to the former landowners. Thus, many Junker (q.v.) estates actually grew larger, and many former serfs became landless agricultural workers whose lot in life had improved very little, especially since the landowners still maintained control over the police and lower-level judiciary within their districts. Still, it was an important turning point which allowed peasants to win back much of what they had lost in 1525. Noblemen were allowed to practice bourgeois professions, such as law and commerce, and the bourgeoisie was permitted to acquire former knightly estates. Jews were granted social and economic equality, although they still did not gain equal political rights. The cities were given a greater measure of self-rule in that public officials were to be elected by all property owners. Right into the 20th century, local government in Prussia was admired throughout Europe, even though it stood in sharp contrast to the semi-absolutism in the countryside.

General Scharnhorst wrote in 1798 that "we will not be able to win battles until we learn like the Jacobins to awaken the community spirit." The model was the new French army, and the goal was to create an army motivated by patriotic spirit. All degrading punishments were abolished. Universal military service was introduced in order "to unify the army and the nation," and foreigners were no longer permitted to serve. Ability was to become the sole criterion for advancement, so the officer ranks were opened up to non-noblemen. The change was slow, but the percentage of commoners in the officer corps rose from 7 percent in 1806 to 21 percent by 1848.

The far-sighted minister of culture, Wilhelm von Humboldt, introduced educational reforms aimed at opening up the system to the talented from all classes. Elementary schools were created for all, and humanistic high schools (*Gymnasien*) were created for those destined to rise to higher positions. In 1810, the University of Berlin was created. This was the first university in Germany to combine free research and teaching, and it was permitted to administer itself in order to guarantee it continuing freedom.

From 1807 until 1812, the Germans had experienced a peace which was really more like a slow preparation for war. In 1812, the great part of Napoleon's Grand Army, which at the time included some 30,000 Bavarians, 30,000 Austrians and 20,000 Prussians, froze in the snows of Russia. German statesmen stuck their wet political fingers in the air and began to make secret preparations for a change of alliances. Napoleon feared that the worst was ahead of him. In mid-1813, he called the Austrian Chancellor Metternich to his headquarters in Dresden and announced that he "would not withdraw from a single inch of territory . . . I was brought up on the battlefield, and a man like me worries little about the lives of a million persons." Metternich asked icily why he said such a thing behind closed doors instead of announcing it from one end of France to the other. Napoleon replied: "It may cost me my throne, but I will bury the world underneath its rubble." Just 132 years later another defeated dictator who had brought war and destruction to all of Europe would say the very same thing from an underground bunker in Berlin.

Within four months after his meeting with Metternich, Napoleon's hold on Germany, Italy and Spain had been broken. He suffered a crushing defeat in late 1813 at the "Battle of the Nations" near Leipzig, a battle which brought a scarcely believable carnage: 70,000 Frenchmen and 52,000 allies lost their lives. On March 31, 1814, the Russian Tsar and the Prussian king marched into Paris at the head of their troops. The following year an English army under Wellington and a Prussian army under Generals Blücher (q.v.) and Gneisenau played the key roles in defeating Napoleon once and for all at Waterloo.

Napoleon's occupation of Germany was not a total disaster. He left the German nation far less fragmented than it had been before. About three hundred German states, cities and territories had been joined into fifty, and the Congress of Vienna (q.v.) would reduce that number even further. This paved the way for a united Germany in the future. The French also brought a valuable reform impulse. As in 1918 it was most unfortunate that democratic ideas had been brought into Germany by the troops of an alien occupation power. The French Revolution therefore ultimately created in the minds of many influential Germans enmity toward France and democratic ideas. Initially, some leading Germans greeted this momentous event, and in Mainz a revolutionary republic inspired by France was briefly established. However, the excesses of the Revolution became increasingly visible, and it progressed from civil war within France to an international struggle for power, largely on German soil. These excesses led some important Germans, such as Goethe and Schiller (qq.v.), to reject revolution as a valid means of change, and it therefore strengthened the traditional German allergy toward revolution. The bloody excesses in France also led many to doubt that the French Revolution was, in fact, a step in the direction of eliminating tyranny and social injustice.

The French occupation of Germany spawned German nationalism by enabling persons in all parts of Germany to put aside some of their local patriotism and struggle side-by-side to rid Germany of a foreign power. From then on, German nationalism became an increasingly important factor. Since no unified German state yet existed, German nationalism took on an idealistic and romantic character. Since it was born in reaction to a conqueror who seemed to understand how to achieve French national interests under the cover of high-sounding calls for "liberty, equality and fraternity," German nationalism and the struggle against alien rule became linked in the minds of far too many Germans with resistance against the ideals of the French Revolution, known in Germany as the "ideas of 1789." This unfortunate link helped conservative rulers throughout Germany to water down or undo reforms which Napoleon had introduced or promised before 1815. It also established in many German minds until 1945 a strong resistance to the ideas of democracy, equality, civil rights, popular sovereignty, mass participation in politics and representative government legitimized by the consent of the governed.

FRICK, WILHELM (1877-1946). Nazi interior minister (1933-43), Reich protector of Bohemia and Moravia (1943-45). Found guilty at the Nuremberg Trials (q.v.) and executed.

FRICKE, HEINZ. In 1992, the 66-year-old Fricke was appointed the music director of the Kennedy Center in Washington, D.C. The long-serving music director of the German State Opera in East Berlin, who is best known for his interpretation of the German repertoire, became the second eastern German music director to be attracted to the U.S. Kurt Masur (q.v.) of the Leipzig Gewandhaus was won earlier by the New York Philharmonic Orchestra.

FRIDERICHS, HANS (1931-). Banker and FDP minister of economics (1972-77). (See also FLICK AFFAIR.)

FRIEDRICH I, BARBAROSSA (1122-1190). German king and emperor (1152-90). (See BARBAROSSA.)

FRIEDRICH WILHELM (1620-1688). Great Elector (Kurfürst) of Brandenburg (1640-88). (See also PRUSSIA.)

FRIEDRICH I (1657-1713). King of Prussia (1701-13). (See also PRUSSIA.)

FRIEDRICH WILHELM I, THE "SOLDIER KING" (1688-1740). King of Prussia (1713-40). (See also PRUSSIA.)

FRIEDRICH II, THE GREAT (1712-1786). As a young man, Friedrich II was a sensitive, highly intelligent humanist, who composed flute concertos which are still played in concert halls, and who preferred all his life to use the French language. He even wrote thoroughly respectable poetry and essays in French. Most of his writings, which now fill 25 volumes, are in French rather than German, which he never learned to write without numerous mistakes. He was a close friend of the French philosopher and satirist Voltaire, whom he invited for prolonged visits to Berlin and Potsdam. In general, the young Friedrich was open to all the cultural, philosophical and liberal political ideas of his day. He was an enlightened man with a strong sense of taste, and his favorite residence in Potsdam, Sans Souci (French for "Carefree"), manifested his nature. He despised the absolutist government of his father, even if it was aimed at the good of the people. Once, at age 18 he even tried to flee his father's kingdom with a close friend, but they were caught and delivered back to an irate parent and placed in prison.

Friedrich the Great.(*Source:* SPP.)
Nell Cooke Byers

What should his father have done? Have the heir to the throne and his friend both hanged for treason? Disregard the law of the land and forgive both for a treasonous act? The father's solution: he had the friend executed for treason right in front of Friedrich's eyes! This paradoxical mixture of strict justice, mercy, and reason of state has troubled many people ever since.

Finally, at the age of 28, Friedrich II ascended to the throne in 1740. The young king's reaction to this event was characteristic: "How I abhor this job to which the blind coincidence of birth has condemned me!" Many persons saw in the new king the first philosopher to ascend a throne since the Roman Emperor Marcus Aurelius. Friedrich announced that "any man who seeks the truth and loves it must be treasured in any human society." Within the first week of his rule, he abolished torture in all cases but high treason. Throughout his 48-year reign, he demanded of every subject a strict performance of his duty. But he was always inclined to permit anything else which did not directly hurt the interests of the state. This tolerance was applied not only to religious practices, intellectual and artistic pursuits, but to personal behavior as well. For instance, when a case was reported of a cavalry officer caught committing a heinous act of sodomy upon his horse, Friedrich merely ordered that the poor man be transferred to the infantry!

After Friedrich became king, he put his flute away forever. Before he had been crowned, he had referred to a military uniform as "a gown of death," but afterwards he was scarcely ever seen wearing anything else. His transformation from a sensitive humanist to "the first servant of the state," as he later called himself, is one of the intriguing mysteries of history. Few would have ever guessed in 1740 that he would become known as "Friedrich the Great" as a result of his leadership. As king, he had become a lonesome figure with a tortured soul, inwardly unhappy, but restlessly active, working 18 hours per day.

He was always unkempt and ungroomed, and he loved nobody and was loved by nobody. He had especially troubled relations with women and preferred the company of men in his beloved San Souci palace in Potsdam. Against his will, he was pressured by his family to marry Elisabeth Christine von Braunschweig. He relented, but no sooner was the ceremony over than he packed her off to a separate palace and saw her only a few times the rest of his life. It need not be said that their marriage was childless.

The first half of his reign was a period of almost constant war, which at times seemed to threaten his country's very existence, but which in the end elevated Prussia (q.v.) to the rank of a great European power. The newly crowned king had just published an elegant attack on Machiavelli's immorality and duplicity in politics; within weeks Friedrich unleashed an unprovoked and unjustified attack on Austrian-owned Silesia. Certainly he was no more unscrupulous than most other rulers of the time. But in this and in almost all other wars during his reign, justice happened to be on the side of his enemies.

Friedrich later said that he had started what was known as "The War of the Austrian Succession" because "the satisfaction of seeing my name in the newspapers and later in history had seduced me." However, one should not take very seriously such remarks made by a cynic such as Friedrich. What really motivated him was a unique opportunity: in the same year he had become king--1740--a young and politically inexperienced woman, Maria-Theresia, had ascended the Austrian throne. He calculated that she would not have known how to respond to such a brazen act on Prussia's part. There were few Austrian troops in Silesia, so the venture promised to be a military cake-walk. Surprisingly, the young Austrian Empress rejected Friedrich's ultimatum to withdraw from the province, so the latter unleashed his troops in late 1740. The two armies clashed in furious battle at Mollwitz. Things looked so hopeless for the Prussians that the young ruler actually fled from the battlefield, an offense normally punishable by death. But he was saved by a Prussian victory later that day. Ultimately, two campaigns were necessary to secure Prussian domination of Silesia. By also taking a substantial portion of land from the Poles, Friedrich was able to unite East and West Prussia into a single territory. Friedrich tried to justify his action in 1743: "I hope those who will later judge me . . . will be able to differentiate in me the philosopher from the prince, the honorable man from the politician. I must confess that whoever is dragged into the mess [*Getriebe*] of high-level European politics finds it very difficult to preserve his own character frankly and honestly." He wrote that the art of politics appears in many ways "as the opposite of private morality." However, it is the morality of the princes, who "do only that which promises to be to their advantage. The Prince had no alternative to following the practice which authorizes deceit and the abuse of power."

His qualms were not such that he could resist the temptation in 1756 to swoop into Saxony and thereby become embroiled in a "Seven-Years War" with Austria, which lasted until 1763. Friedrich's troops met with initial success. He published Maria-Theresia's secret plans that were found in the Saxon state archives, which the Prussian troops had captured. These plans showed that the Austrian empress was by no means above duplicity when her state's interests were at stake. This war provided clear examples of the extent to which the fate of whole nations depended at that time upon the personal preferences and whims of their absolutist rulers. When the Russian Tsarina Elizabeth, daughter of Tsar Peter the Great, was informed that Friedrich had cracked a joke about her at the dinner table in Sans Souci, she exploded with rage, and joined Austria, France, Bavaria and Saxony in a war against Prussia. Her decision almost destroyed Friedrich's kingdom. Soon the Russians were at the gates of Königsberg, the French were approaching the Elbe, and the Austrians reentered Silesia. Friedrich tirelessly led his almost hopelessly outnumbered troops from one edge of his kingdom to the other, meeting first one enemy and then another. He was imaginative and bold, and his administration in Potsdam, which his predecessors had built up, worked like a perfectly constructed and oiled machine.

Though he received money from England, which as usual was very interested in weakening France, the Prussians stood alone against all the great European continental powers. Friedrich's army had lost almost all its artillery by late 1760. Berlin had fallen to the enemy, and England had stopped sending money to a ruler so near to defeat. But in early 1762 a wonder occurred. Tsarina Elizabeth died, and her successor, Peter III, was a glowing admirer of Friedrich the Great. He not only left the enemy coalition, he entered into an alliance with Prussia, thereby saving that country from certain defeat. Peter III was assassinated a year later, and his wife, who was later called Catherine the Great, quickly withdrew Russia from the war entirely. But by that time Austria was physically and financially exhausted and had to sue for peace in 1763. In the Peace of Hubertusburg, the situation seemed to revert to the status quo ante, with Prussia retaining Silesia and East Prussia and with Saxon independence being reestablished. But in reality this was a great triumph for Prussia. By maintaining itself successfully against three great powers in Europe, it won recognition as a great power in its own right. Prussia also learned that good relations with Russia were absolutely essential, and until 1890 such relations remained a primary goal of every Prussian leader.

Friedrich II was one of the most brilliant military leaders of all time. It has been said that one of Adolf Hitler's favorite films was about Friedrich the Great. It is unfortunate that the one lesson Hitler learned from the miraculous victory in 1763, was that an iron will and bitter determination not to surrender can ultimately carry the day, despite the enemy's overwhelming material and manpower superiority. His tragic attempt to repeat Friedrich's feat almost two centuries later brought indescribable death and misery to Germans and their neighbors.

After the war's end, Prussia under Friedrich the Great enjoyed 23 years of peace. It was nevertheless able to continue enlarging itself by participating with Russia and Austria in the partition of Poland. Seeing that Russia was perfectly willing to intervene militarily in Poland in order to prevent any strengthening of the Polish state, Friedrich suggested the first partition in 1772. Maria-Theresia had serious qualms about such a dastardly act of political immorality, and Friedrich gleefully reported later that "she wept, but she took." In 1793 and 1795 these three powers partitioned Poland again, creating a potentially dangerous domestic political situation within Prussia by making Poles a majority of all inhabitants within the borders of Prussia.

Friedrich II was called "the Great" during his own lifetime. This was not only because of his wars and his successful, but sometimes morally questionable foreign policy, but also because of his reforms, his intellectual and cultural achievements as a young man, and the kind of state which he helped create. The Prussian state was feared by its neighbors because it was militarily strong and prepared and because of its qualities as a state. It had an uncorrupted administration, an independent judiciary, and a state of law (*Rechtsstaat,* q.v.) in which there was more legal equality for all citizens than could be found in most other European states at the time. Journalists could write relatively freely, although Friedrich once had a newspaperman beaten who wrote uncomplimentary things about the king.

Prussia's tolerance toward all religions was considered in Europe to be a bad example during most of the 17th and 18th centuries. It was also tolerant toward the different nationalities within its own borders and toward enlightened learning of all kinds. By the standards of the 18th century, which are those which should be used to judge the state ruled by Friedrich the Great, Prussia was a modern and enlightened state. It was certainly no democracy, but enlightenment in politics at first meant basing the affairs of state on reason. This initially manifested itself in Europe in the form of absolutism, and France under Cardinal Richelieu was an early model. Not until the French Revolution, when a brand of enlightenment which stressed human rights and popular sovereignty and when the call of "liberty, equality and fraternity" caught fire in Europe, was Prussia challenged by a state and ideas which were clearly more modern than its own. Indeed, after Friedrich's death in 1786, the newly risen Prussia had only two more decades before it crumbled in the face of Napoleon's France.

FRIEDRICH WILHELM IV (1795-1861). King of Prussia (1840-61). (See also REVOLUTION OF 1848.)

FRIEDRICH (1831-1888). During the long reign of Kaiser Wilhelm I, some Germans hoped for an era of liberal reform after his death in 1888. But his son, Friedrich, who was known to favor such reforms, died of throat cancer only 99 days after his coronation.

FRIEDRICH, CASPAR DAVID (1774-1840). A Romantic painter blessed with the ability to convey a religious mood through his landscapes and seascapes that reveal the divinity of nature. He also painted religious subjects and architectural pictures of Dresden. (See also ROMANTICISM.)

FRIEDRICH EBERT FOUNDATION see STIFTUNGEN

FRIEDRICH NAUMANN FOUNDATION see STIFTUNGEN

FUNDIS see GREENS

FURRER, REINHARD see SPACE PROGRAM

-G-

GALEN, COUNT BISHOP OF MÜNSTER see CONCORDAT

GALINSKI, HEINZ (1912-1992). Chairman of the Central Council of Jews in Germany, a tax-supported organization which represents the 35,000 Jews who register their religion with the government, Galinski was an Auschwitz survivor. For 43 years he led Berlin's small Jewish community which has shrunk from 173,000 before the war to a combined total of about 8,500 in 1992. His father had fought for Germany in the First World War (q.v.) but was killed by the Gestapo in the Crystal Night pogrom in 1938. Employing a combative style, he forcefully reminded Germans of the Nazis' (q.v.) crimes and demanded that younger Germans prove their distance from the Holocaust (q.v.) by showing greater tolerance for foreigners living in Germany. (See also ANTI-SEMITISM; NAZI REPRESSION.)

GAUCH, JOACHIM (1940-).   A Protestant minister from Mecklenburg-Vorpommern harassed by the Stasi in the GDR (qq.v.), Gauch was one of the founders of the New Forum (q.v.). After reunification he was appointed federal commissioner in charge of administering Stasi files. (See also GERMAN DEMOCRATIC REPUBLIC; STASI.)

GAULEITER see NAZI PARTY

GAUS, GÜNTER (1929-). SPD, chief editor of *Der Spiegel* (1969-73), state secretary in federal chancellor's office (1973-74), permanent representative of FRG to GDR (1974-80), during which time he coined the term "niche society" (*Nichengesellschaft*) to describe the way East Germans fled politics by absorbing themselves in their own narrow private affairs.

GEISSLER, HEINRICH (HEINER) (1930-). General secretary of CDU (1977-89), minister for family, youth and health (1982-85). Geissler personifies the progressive and pragmatic wing of the CDU (q.v.) which counsels resistance against the clamorings of the right. He pointed to the electoral dangers of pandering to what he saw as marginal right-wing groups. Instead he argued for a policy reoriented toward the political middle and centered on a progressive social policy and support of *Ostpolitik* (q.v.). Since Adenauer (q.v.) stepped down as chancellor in 1963, there has been an uneasy alliance within the CDU between pragmatists like Geissler and a more conservative wing.

GELLERT, CHRISTIAN FÜRCHTEGOTT (1715-1769). He is best known for his verse fables with a moral and for his church hymns which attracted the attention of Beethoven (q.v.) and are still used today.

GEMEINSCHAFT (COMMUNITY). During the 19th and 20th centuries there was a shift in political thinking from the traditional, organic "community" to a more individualistic (some would say "alienating") "society" (*Gesellschaft*).

GENERAL GERMAN NEWS AGENCY (ALLGEMEINE DEUTSCHE NACHRICHTEN--ADN). Located in Berlin, this was the GDR's leading press agency. After reunification (q.v.), it continued to function.

GENERAL GERMAN WORKERS' UNION see LASSALLE, FERDINAND

GENIEZEIT (GENIUS TIME) see STORM AND STRESS

GENSCHER, HANS-DIETRICH (1927-). Chairman of FDP (1974-85), interior minister (1969-74), foreign minister (1974-92). Born in eastern Germany, Genscher fled to the FRG after completing his studies. He became one of the FRG's most successful and popular politicians. Upon his retirement as foreign minister (though not from active parliamentary and party politics) in May 1992, the *Neue Osnabrücker Zeitung* summed up his accomplishments and significance: "The farewell of the Halle native from the ministry that he ran for 18 years signifies one of the deepest personal upheavals in the history of the Federal Republic. Nothing can make this clearer than the unusual fact that he gave a political direction, even a political philosophy its name: Genscherism. This word stands for calculability, a feel for the accomplishable, but even more for the reconciliation of East and West with the objective of the restoration of German unity, which, together with Kohl, he so brilliantly achieved."

GERMAN ACADEMIC EXCHANGE OFFICE (DEUTSCHER AKADEMISCHER AUSTAUSCHDIENST--DAAD). The DAAD sponsors a wide range of research grants to fund research on German subjects. It has an office in New York.

GERMAN AEROSPACE RESEARCH ESTABLISHMENT (DEUTSCHE FORSCHUNGSANSTALT FÜR LUFT- UND RAUMFAHRT--DLR, FORMERLY DFVLR) see SPACE PROGRAM

GERMAN ALTERNATIVE (DEUTSCHE ALTERNATIVE--DA) see PARTIES, RIGHT-WING

GERMAN CHRISTIANS (NAZI) see CONFESSING CHURCH

GERMAN CIVIL SERVANTS' FEDERATION (DBB) see LABOR

GERMAN COLONIAL LEAGUE (DEUTSCHE KOLONIALGESELLSCHAFT) see ALL-GERMAN LEAGUE

GERMAN COMMUNIST PARTY (DEUTSCHE KOMMUNISTISCHE PARTY--DKP). The DKP was the successor to the outlawed Communist Party of Germany (KOMMUNISTISCHE PARTEI DEUTSCHLANDS)--KPD in West Germany. The KPD had been founded at the end of 1918 and played a major political role during the Weimar Republic (q.v.) until it was outlawed in 1933. It was always unswervingly loyal to the Soviet Union. After the war, the KPD sent two representatives (out of a total of 65) to the Parliamentary Council, which sat from September 1948 to May 1949 to produce a Basic Law (q.v.) for the FRG. In the end, the KPD decided to oppose the Basic Law, which came into effect in 1949. The SED (q.v.), which the KPD supported, assumed government in East Germany the same year.

In the first West German federal elections in 1949, the KPD won 5.7 percent of the votes and gained 15 members in the Bundestag. In the next election in 1953 its vote plummeted to 2.2 percent, far short of the minimum 5 percent required for seats in Bundestag. Until 1990, Communists never again won seats, and its percentage of votes declined steadily. The weakening popular support for the KPD merely increased its dependence upon a foreign patron, the SED in the GDR (q.v.). This dependence contributed to the Constitutional Court's (q.v.) outlawing of the KPD in August 1956. By the time the party was renamed the DKP and again legalized in 1968 (with new statutes and statements of purpose carefully crafted to be compatible with the Basic Law), two important developments had occurred: first, the party's membership had shrunk to about 7,000. Second, the tumultuous 1960s had produced in the FRG scores of radical and independent communist or radical leftist groups to compete with the orthodox parties. Because it remained slavishly pro-Moscow and pro-SED (which funded it handsomely), its voter support in the FRG remained minuscule. Except for its ability to provide logistic support for some protest demonstrations, it remained politically irrelevant in the FRG.

On January 5, 1991, representatives of the PDS (q.v.) and DKP met in Berlin and agreed to remain separate and competing parties, with neither dominating the other, although occasional cooperation could be considered. After 1989, the DKP had entered a crisis from which it will never recover. The collapse of Communist power and ideology in the GDR and the Soviet Union's encouragement of reform in Eastern Europe devastated the DKP, which had always been studiously servile to the SED and the Soviet rulers. The DKP's leadership was incapable of responding to the 1989 revolution which brought the party to the brink of fragmentation and bankruptcy.

It is an understatement to say that the DKP was overwhelmed by the peaceful revolution in the GDR and by German reunification (q.v.). A few die-hards asserted that it was a "betrayal of the working class" and "democracy flim-flam" when the "class enemy" is given free rein to eject Communists from power through elections. The minority wing seized the opportunity to convene a "Renewal Congress" in Frankfurt am Main in October 1989 to discuss the split within the DKP. The "renewers" decided to create their own structures which would enable them to prepare separately for the DKP's future congresses. They demanded a "break with the DKP's traditional socialism and party conceptions," the toleration of factions within the party, and the resignation of the entire leadership as a necessary precondition for the wing's further work within the DKP. They further decided to create their own office in Cologne and to publish a monthly information letter. Although the "renewers" had shaken the DKP to the roots, they were unable to take control of it because of some serious tactical errors. They could not create unity within their own ranks and were therefore unable to agree on a common policy for steering the party in a new direction.

Disaster struck the DKP in late November 1989: the SED announced the termination of all foreign currency support, which despite DKP denials had amounted to an estimated 50-70 million West marks annually sent through conspiratorial channels. SED subsidies had always been essential to financing the high costs of maintaining party headquarters in Düsseldorf, an office in Bonn, and more than 200 local offices, the production and distribution of propaganda materials, mass rallies, election campaigns, and subsidies to DKP affiliated or influenced organizations. DKP functionaries were kept on the payrolls of communist firms and travel agencies directed by the SED. The DKP had a few other financial sources, particularly membership dues and income from the sale of party publications. Clandestine subsidies from the SED were about three times higher than the DKP's revenues from within the FRG.

After 1989 the DKP had to operate completely on its own. No financial help could be expected from the Soviet Union. Contributions by GDR firms operating in the FRG dried up, and the split in the party prompted many members to leave or to stop making their contributions. In consequence, almost all of the party's bloated staff was dismissed-- about 500 people in all. In February 1990, the PDS paid "damages" amounting to DM 6 million to the DKP to alleviate the "social costs" of those functionaries who had lost their jobs. However, the money was misappropriated by the DKP, which used it to build up a new party apparatus of about 50 persons, rather than to distribute it among the unemployed comrades. What small funds remained were in the hands of the apparatus; the "renewers" got nothing. The party's publications were severely affected: the daily organ, *Unsere Zeit*, was converted to a weekly, and some other party publications were terminated; the DKP's news agency, Progress Presse-Agentur (PPA), and publishing house, Paul-Rugenstein-Verlag, were shut down. The latter's bankruptcy eliminated the vital prop for the DKP's most important publication aimed at domestic alliance partners: *Volkszeitung*. East German advertising in DKP publications disappeared.

The DKP is, as always, impotent and irrelevant. In May 1991, its membership stood at a dismal 8,500. In its former stronghold, Hamburg, it garnered an unimpressive 680 votes in the 1991 Land elections, behind virtually all other left-wing parties and groupings. Discredited by its complete dependence on the former SED and incapable of drawing any useful lessons from the collapse of East German socialism, the DKP feels itself to be increasingly isolated.

Despite *perestroika* it clings to tattered Leninist concepts. It is shunned by a PDS which is concentrating on its own survival and does not want to tarnish its fragile public image by associating with the orthodox DKP, which has, for all practical purposes, become a mere political sect. (See also COMMUNISM; GERMAN DEMOCRATIC REPUBLIC; PARTY OF DEMOCRATIC SOCIALISM.)

GERMAN CONFEDERATION (DEUTSCHER BUND 1815-1866) see CONGRESS OF VIENNA

GERMAN CONSERVATIVE PARTY/RIGHT PARTY. This was the first of a series of efforts to rally former Nazi (q.v.) party members, disillusioned veterans, officials who were removed from their jobs during denazification (q.v.), and other dissatisfied elements. In 1949, it won five seats in the first Bundestag elections, but it disappeared after the second elections in 1953.

GERMAN DEMOCRATIC PARTY (DEUTSCHE DEMOKRATISCHE PARTEI--DDP). Founded in 1918 at the end of the First World War, the DDP sought to preserve the liberal tradition established in Frankfurt's Paul's Church (q.v.) in 1848. It attracted most of the academics in Germany who advocated a democratic republic. Among its leaders were Friedrich Naumann, Hugo Preuss, and Max Weber (qq.v.), who worked out the democratic framework for the Weimar Constitution. The DDP, SPD, and Catholic Center Party formed the Weimar Coalition (qq.v.), which immediately declared support for the new republic. (See also WEIMAR REPUBLIC.)

GERMAN DEMOCRATIC REPUBLIC (DEUTSCHE DEMOKRATISCHE REPUBLIK--GDR). At first the Soviet Zone of Germany was governed by the Soviet Military Administration. But the Soviet authorities had long-range plans for Germany which involved re-educating the people and eventually winning them over to communism. German Communists who had spent the Nazi (q.v.) years in the Soviet Union were brought back, put in charge of local governments, and given control over the press, radio, and book publishing. Their instructions were to educate the people in anti-fascism and to gain their cooperation for Soviet occupiers. On April 30, 1945, Walter Ulbricht (q.v.) returned from the USSR in a Soviet aircraft and in June announced the reestablishment of the Communist Party of Germany

(KPD). It combined with the CDU, SPD (qq.v.), and Liberal Democrats to form an "Anti-fascist Democratic Bloc," which was soon dominated by the KPD. The Soviets had expected that the Communists' long record of anti-fascism would make the KPD popular among workers, but the latter clearly preferred the SPD. In April 1946, this prompted the forcible uniting of the two parties into a Socialist Unity Party (SED, q.v.), with Ulbricht as general secretary. The other parties declined in significance until they were little more than a facade.

In 1948, work on a new constitution began, and on October 7, 1949, the GDR came into being. Industry was nationalized and agriculture was collectivized, creating a state-controlled economy. SED domination was tightened through a pervasive state police (Stasi, q.v.) which spied on the citizenry and stifled dissent. On May 26, 1952, the border between the two Germanys was sealed by barbed wire, minefields, watchtowers, and free-fire zones.

Stalin's death in March 1953 and the gradual rise of a new Soviet leadership undermined the positions of all orthodox leaders in Eastern Europe. Although Stalinist from the beginning, Ulbricht managed to hold onto power until 1971. He faced occasional challenges to his leadership. Almost immediately after Stalin's death, the Politburo disregarded Ulbricht's will and adopted a "New Course" which moved toward greater political and economic pluralism. Buckling under reparations to the USSR, higher production quotas, and the lack of personal freedom, workers revolted on June 17, 1953, but Soviet forces brutally put down the insurrection. Until German reunification (q.v.) in 1990, this date was commemorated in the FRG as the "Day of German Unity." The revolt may have saved Ulbricht's career; the Soviets now backed him against the moderates, who found themselves removed from their positions of authority.

On January 29, 1956, the GDR joined hands militarily with the Soviet Union by creating a National People's Army (NVA) and joining the Warsaw Pact. In 1956, Soviet leader Nikita Khrushchev delivered a dramatic speech attacking the Stalinist heritage. This message emboldened Communist intellectuals in the GDR who wanted to make the SED more responsive to the people and to create a more popular, humane form of socialism. Their chief spokesman, Wolfgang Harich, was arrested and sentenced to ten years in prison. Other reformers were branded "revisionists" and forced to retreat.

Ulbricht met his most serious political challenge on August 13, 1961, when, backed by the Soviets, he authorized the sudden construction of a wall between West and East Berlin, where hundreds of thousands of East Germans had continued to flee. This sealed the last escape route and forced East Germans to come to terms with their plight and their government; there was no longer any alternative. This was the only instance in world history that a wall was erected to keep an entire people confined, rather than to keep enemies out. The constant drain on manpower, particularly skilled persons, had been an important economic reason for the wall. Despite the devastating blow it delivered to the international prestige of this socialist state which tried to present itself as the model for Germany's future, it led to greater prosperity in the GDR after 1961 and helped provide East Germans with the highest standard of living within the Soviet empire. Ten years later the Soviet Union concluded that its interests required closer relations between the two Germanys. When Ulbricht opposed this, he was replaced in 1971 by Erich Honecker (q.v.), a roofer who had grown up in the Saarland. In 1935, he had been jailed by the Nazis and spent ten years in a Berlin prison. After the war he became chairman of the Communist Free German Youth (q.v.). Following political training in Moscow, he oversaw the military and security services. He had opposed any form of "revisionism" and was totally loyal to the Soviet Union. He supported the erection of the Berlin Wall (q.v.) and was linked in 1990 with the orders to shoot to kill along the dividing line between East and West Germany.

When Mikhail Gorbachev launched his reformist policy of *perestroika* in 1985, Honecker and other members of the SED leadership resisted introducing it in the GDR on the grounds that the East German economy had already been reformed in the 1970s and was working well. Their rejection of a market economy was ideologically motivated. They argued that if the GDR adopted it, then there would be nothing to distinguish it from the FRG; consequently there would be no further justification for the GDR to exist as a separate state. They also resisted introducing more freedom in the political realm and even prevented the distribution of some free-thinking Soviet newspapers, such as the *Moscow News*. It was extremely embarrassing for a party which had been so servile to the Soviet Union to be in a position of having to resist its leadership. The SED found itself in a fatal dilemma from which it could never extricate itself.

GERMAN DEMOCRATIC REPUBLIC, COLLAPSE (1989-1990). In 1989 one of the most dramatic postwar developments began taking place before the very eyes of a stunned world public: German reunification (q.v.). In late summer a westward exodus commenced, as East German vacationers began crossing the newly opened border between Hungary and Austria. Budapest informed the irate East German leaders that the human rights agreements accepted at the Helsinki Conference in 1975 superseded earlier bilateral treaties preventing the free movement of peoples. The next avenue of escape was through Czechoslovakia. After thousands had taken refuge at the West German embassy in Prague, "freedom trains" took East Germans through the GDR into the West. The stampede grew when Czechoslovakia opened its western borders.

Under enormous stress, the GDR celebrated its fortieth and final anniversary on October 7, 1989. The SED's (q.v.) slogan for the event was "Ever Forward--Never Backward!" The prediction was accurate, but the Communist chiefs were badly mistaken about which direction was forward. The honored guest was Gorbachev himself, who at that time was the most popular political figure in both Germanys. However, rather than lend his prestige to the struggling East German leaders, he made it known that they would have to pay a high price if they did not learn the lessons of history and adopt timely reforms. He informed them that they could not expect the support of Soviet troops in the GDR to prop up their rule against the people. Without Soviet military backing Communist rule could survive nowhere in Germany.

This was a very important message in a country in which public demonstrations had been going on for some time. An umbrella opposition group, New Forum (q.v.), had come into existence a few weeks earlier, and huge demonstrations had spread to all major East German cities. Things came to a head on October 9 in Leipzig. Honecker reportedly issued an order to security forces to put down the demonstration by any means. Communist leaders in Leipzig, fearing a massacre such as had occurred in China the previous June, decided to prevent such a bloodbath in their city. With Kurt Masur (q.v.), director of Leipzig's Gewandhaus Orchestra, as spokesman, and joined by Protestant Church leaders, they issued an appeal for calm. They coupled this with a call for non-violence and "a free exchange of opinions about the continuation of socialism in our country." Such a dialogue would occur "not only in the Leipzig area, but with our national government."

On October 18, Honecker was ousted from power and replaced by Egon Krenz (q.v.).

The Berlin Wall (q.v.) came tumbling down on November 9. It is ironic that a wall which had been constructed in 1961 to keep East Germans in was opened in 1989 for the same reason! Within minutes millions of East Germans began pouring over the border. Germans, who for decades had suppressed displays of national feeling, experienced a deeply emotional outpouring. While millions sat in front of their televisions and wept, Berliners danced together on top of the Wall, embraced each other on the streets, and chiseled away at the ugly barrier. When word arrived at the Bundestag, many members, including some Greens (q.v.), stood up and spontaneously sang the third verse of the national anthem, which stresses "unity and justice and freedom." The rest of Europe looked on with mixed feelings, uneasily remembering a frightening German past, but stirred by the sight of people casting off their shackles and demanding freedom and self-determination.

Krenz proved to be only an interim figure. Unable to put an end to either the demonstrations or the continued emigration to the West, he promised "free, democratic and secret elections," a move toward a market economy, separation of party and state, freedom of assembly, and a new law on broadcasting and press freedom. He also appointed as prime minister Hans Modrow (q.v.) from Dresden, one of the very few East German Communists who was personally popular. Honecker was arrested, but he was released for health reasons and was soon taken under the wing of the Soviet Army in the GDR. Krenz could not save his party or himself, and he and the other members of the politburo resigned on December 3. Five days later, a special SED party congress met and installed Gregor Gysi (q.v.), a lawyer who had made a name for himself by defending dissidents and the opposition New Forum. Upon accepting the leadership, Gysi admitted that a complete break with Stalinism and a new form of socialism were needed and that the SED was responsible for plunging the GDR into crisis. Feeling betrayed, within two months hundreds of thousands of members left the party, which renamed itself the PDS (q.v.) in a futile attempt to escape the impending doom.

There was an outpouring of disgust and rage among East Germans as massive corruption on the part of their former leaders was revealed. They had enriched themselves while in office. Television broadcast images of the "proletarian" leaders' luxury compound in Wandlitz, estates with as many as 22 staff members, hunting lodges, deer parks, well-stocked wine cellars, satellite dishes for better reception of Western broadcasts. Their living standards had been totally removed from the meager everyday existence of normal GDR citizens long fed on exhortations for austerity. Even worse were revelations of shady financial dealings totalling millions of marks, involving illegal arms sales to Third World countries and foreign currency maneuvers, the profits of which ended up in personal Swiss bank accounts. Said one rank-and-file SED member: "We did not expect this of Communists and their creed of equality."

GERMAN DEMOCRATIC REPUBLIC, UPRISING (June 17, 1953). The most dramatic demonstration of how unjust East Germans viewed their regime to be came on June 17, 1953. The SED (q.v.) had seen trouble brewing before the explosion actually came. On June 9, Walter Ulbricht (q.v.), whose slavish devotion to every Soviet wish could no longer find a majority in the SED politburo now that Stalin was dead, announced that "a variety of mistakes had been made on the part of the SED and the government." A "new course" would be pursued involving an amnesty, as well as scaling down production norms, loosening travel restrictions, and dropping all compulsory measures against individual farmers and small private entrepreneurs.

However, before critics within the politburo could initiate reform, workers in East Berlin laid down their tools and took to the streets. By June 17, the strike and demonstrations had spread to other East German cities, and most of the country's laborers joined the general strike. The candle of hope flickered only briefly, and Soviet tanks and troops succeeded in crushing the uprising within a few days. Ulbricht was saved, and those politburo members who had contemplated reform, such as Rudolf Herrnstadt, chief editor of the official party organ *Neues Deutschland*, and Wilhelm Zaisser, minister of state security, were expelled from the politburo. The party apparatus was thoroughly purged down to the grass-roots level. Further motives for the uprising were the demand for Ulbricht's removal ("Away with the Spitzbart!") and other functionaries, free elections and a state of law, free movement between the two parts of Germany, and perhaps most important of all, reunification.

GERMAN EMPIRE. In 911 A.D., the eastern Franconian realm, created when the Carolinian empire (q.v.) was divided in 817, became the German Empire. "Empire," however, is a somewhat misleading word, since it connotes a centralized, unified power. In Germany there was a strong degree of unity, but until 1871 rule was by a multitude of heads of local states and independent cities. By the 11th century these states and cities had become the most powerful in Europe and were able to claim the title "Roman Empire." In the 13th century, this was dignified to the title "Holy Roman Empire," and, in the 15th century, "Holy Roman Empire of the German Nation." Its reach and power expanded and contracted, but it always retained certain organizational features: the highest nobility (usually called "electors") actually elected an emperor. Although this position was not hereditary as was the case with other European monarchies, there was a dynastic element in that, with very few exceptions, the new emperor had to be a blood relative of his predecessor. There was no capital city; he moved around continually, ruling from wherever he happened to be. He usually resided in various bishoprics or in a collection of buildings known as a *Pfalz*. As one can now see in the charming medieval city of Goslar in the Harz Mountains, the *Pfalz* contained a royal residence, buildings and stables for the emperor's retinue, at least one church or chapel and surrounding farms, mines and businesses from which he could derive his income. Since no taxes were levied, he was compelled to finance his activities from the various imperial estates throughout the empire. Finally, the major and minor nobility met infrequently in an imperial diet called the Reichstag, a body whose work cannot be compared to a modern democratic parliament, but one which displayed how much the emperor depended upon the lesser noblemen if he wanted to conduct a war, increase his revenues or the like.

Germany always has been a mixture of central and regional power, of unity and disunity. There were endless struggles over who should lead in the empire, and the emperor's actual power was never assured, even after he had been elected. He had to maintain a powerful army and forge delicate alliances among the rival dukes in the realm and powerful archbishops who ruled such important cities as Mainz, Cologne and Trier. This is why provinces and cities became much more important in Germany than in other countries. The German emperors focused their attention far beyond what is now the German-speaking world, particularly on Italy. In 962, the Pope crowned Saxon King Otto I emperor in St. Peter's Cathedral in Rome, a tradition which was to last over 500 years. This unique privilege, which was bestowed on no other ruler, entitled the German monarch to be called "emperor." It also gave the German Empire a universalistic claim to rule over the entire Western world as the protector of Christianity. This claim never became reality.

The special relationship which was established between the emperors and popes proved to be of questionable value for both. German emperors became embroiled in Italian and papal affairs for more than three centuries, a costly diversion from the more important task of creating a unified Germany. Emperors became active in papal selections and on occasion succeeded in driving popes right out of Rome. At the same time, popes often connived with Germany's enemies and bitterly fought against emperors' attempts to gain control of the Catholic Church within Germany. A showdown between the two occurred in 1077. Emperor Heinrich IV replaced Pope Gregory VII when the latter refused to permit Heinrich to appoint bishops and other high Church officials in Germany. Gregory struck back by taking away Heinrich's imperial crown, releasing all of Heinrich's subjects from their loyalty to the Emperor, and excommunicating him. The latter soon realized how much he had overreached his power and authority and felt compelled to go to the fortress of Canossa, where the Pope had sought protection. Dressed in the simple garb of a penitent, Heinrich pleaded three days for forgiveness. Then, with outstretched arms, he threw himself at the Pope's feet, who had no alternative but to forgive him. Heinrich's act of prostration at the feet of the Pope was a turning point in German history. Soon thereafter, a revengeful Heinrich drove Pope Gregory into exile and lonely death in southern Italy. For centuries the German emperors could always count the popes among their enemies, even though they continued to influence papal elections until about 1250.

The perennial activity of the emperors in Italy tended seriously to weaken their ability to contend with the domestic challenges to their authority. The German emperors' attention had become so fixed on Italy that the last Staufen emperor, Friedrich II, an erudite and far-sighted ruler, tried to rule the enormous empire from Sicily. Yet, by the time he died in 1250 and his successor, Conradino, had been executed in 1268, the German emperors could hardly pretend anymore to control large areas outside Germany. They had lost much of their power and influence within Germany as well. Due largely to the emperors' obsession with crusades and Italian campaigns, rather than for consolidating and increasing their power within Germany itself, a process of power erosion set in which left some free cities, several hundred German noblemen and the Church largely free of imperial control.

By 1268, no one could speak any longer of a powerful and supreme emperor over all of Germany. He could not call on the princes to support him in wartime without their approval; there was no common foreign policy, nor was there an imperial army. The only imperial laws which had any chance of being obeyed were those which had been approved by all three segments of the Reichstag--the "electors," the other princes, and the cities--which the emperor convened infrequently in Worms, Frankfurt, Regensburg, Augsburg or some other important city in southern Germany.

From the 13th century on, the parts of the empire predominated over the whole, the regions over the empire, the princes, kings and high clergy over the emperor. For six centuries the absence of any strong, centralizing power in Germany prevented the development of a unified German nation, as the French and English had been able to do. For six centuries, German politics was largely characterized by conflict among ruling houses. After 1438, the imperial crown practically became the sole possession of the House of Habsburg, and Austria gradually became the predominant German-speaking territory and one of the most powerful countries in Europe.

GERMAN EMPLOYEES' UNION (DEUTSCHE ANGESTELLTEN-GEWERKSCHAFT--DAG) see CIVIL SERVICE LAW

GERMAN EMPLOYERS' ASSOCIATIONS (BUNDESVEREINIGUNG DER DEUTSCHEN ARBEITGEBERVERBÄNDE)--(BDA) see LABOR

GERMAN FARMERS' UNION (DEUTSCHER BAUERNVERBAND--DVB). This organization claimed 750,000 members in 1991 and represents more than 90 percent of all Germans engaged in agriculture on a full time basis. Its influence in the FRG is great, largely because it is regarded very favorably in mass and elite opinion. The German public seems to accept the view that farmers perform an essential service in the economy as a whole and that it is vital to maintain the agricultural infrastructure. Helmut Kohl's (q.v.) long-serving agriculture minister, Ignaz Kiechle, was a prominent member of the DBV for an extended period of time.

GERMAN FATHERLAND PARTY (DEUTSCHE VATERLANDSPARTEI). On July 19, 1917, a majority in the Reichstag passed a Peace Resolution. To oppose this effort to achieve a "peace of understanding" with Germany's enemies, the Fatherland Party sprang into existence. It was founded and led by Admiral Tirpitz and Wolfgang Kapp (q.v.). Kapp led a right-wing putsch attempt in 1920. The party was supported by the Supreme Army Command and many German industrialists. The Peace Resolution represented one of the first steps in the direction of a parliamentary regime.

GERMAN FORUM PARTY (DEUTSCHE FORUM PARTEI--DFP) see ALLIANCE OF FREE DEMOCRATS

GERMAN HISTORICAL INSTITUTE. Located in Washington, D.C., this research and lecture institution serves as a forum for the interchange of scholarship and ideas on German history.

GERMAN INDUSTRY AND TRADE CONGRESS (DEUTSCHER INDUSTRIE UND HANDELSTAG--DIHT). The DIHT represents chambers of commerce, which are not obliged to join. It energetically speaks for business interests, particularly those of small and medium size.

GERMAN LABOR FRONT (DEUTSCHE ARBEITSFRONT--DAF). This was developed, under the direction of Robert Ley, as a Nazi alternative to labor unions, which were officially dissolved in May 1933. It aimed to take the confrontation out of workers' relations with the state and their employers. In effect, it was a means for subordinating workers to Hitler's (q.v.) goals.

GERMAN LEAGUE (DEUTSCHE LIGA) see PARTIES, RIGHT-WING

GERMAN NATIONAL PEOPLE'S PARTY (DEUTSCHNATIONALE VOLKSPARTEI--DNVP). A monarchist party, the DNVP nevertheless participated in some Weimar governments until its new chairman,

Alfred Hugenberg (q.v.), led the party into a right-radical, anti-Weimar position. (See also HARZBURG FRONT.)

GERMAN NATIONALISTS   see ENABLING ACT

GERMAN OFFICIALS' FEDERATION (DEUTSCHER BEAMTENBUND--DBB) see CIVIL SERVICE LAW

GERMAN PARTY (DEUTSCHE PARTEI--DP). A small party, which found its primary strength in the North, the DP joined Konrad Adenauer's (q.v.) governing coalition in 1949, along with the CDU/CSU and FDP (qq.v.), and remained a partner in the 1950s.

GERMAN PEOPLE'S PARTY (DEUTSCHE VOLKSPARTEI--DVP). In 1918, Gustav Stresemann (q.v.) founded the monarchist-inclined DVP, which distinguished itself clearly from the more leftist-liberal DDP (q.v.).

GERMAN PEOPLE'S UNION see PARTIES, RIGHT-WING

GERMAN PRESS AGENCY (DEUTSCHE PRESSE AGENTUR--DPA). Located in Hamburg, it is the FRG's leading press agency.

GERMAN PROGRESSIVE PARTY (DEUTSCHE FORTSCHRITTSPARTEI). In the revolutionary years 1848-49 political groupings emerged which developed into the first German parties. The German Progressive Party became the first party in German history to announce a party program at the time of its founding in 1861. From the very beginning, its work was extended to all of Germany, and its goals were German unification under Prussian (q.v.) leadership, the introduction of a constitutional regime, responsible government (meaning that ministers would be answerable to a parliament elected by the people), and the separation of church and state. The party had neither a party apparatus nor a high degree of organization; its leaders came from commerce and industry, the educated bourgeoisie, and liberal estate owners. In 1862, it won a majority of seats in the Prussian parliament and was in a serious controversy with the Prussian king and Bismarck (q.v.) concerning the budget for a reform of the army. (See also BISMARCK, OTTO VON.)

GERMAN REICH PARTY (DEUTSCHE REICHSPARTEI). In the years of reaction between 1849 and 1858, the Conservatives had the greatest influence. All Conservatives supported Bismarck's foreign policy and military victories, but a more moderate group that also favored a form of parliamentary government split off, calling itself first the "Free Conservative Party" and from 1871 the German Reich Party. This party should not be confused with a radical right-wing party of the same name, using the initials DRP, which emerged in 1946 and won 1.8 percent of the votes and five seats in the 1949 Bundestag election. In that year the Socialist Reich Party (SRP) broke away. It preached Nazi ideology (q.v.) and was organized according to the Nazi leadership principle. It was banned by the Constitutional Court (q.v.) as an offspring of the outlawed Nazi party.

GERMAN SALARIED EMPLOYEES' UNION (DEUTSCHE ANGESTELLTEN-GEWERKSCHAFT)-- (DAG) see LABOR

GERMAN SOCIAL UNION (DEUTSCHE SOZIALE UNION--DSU) see DEMOCRATIC AWAKENING; ELECTIONS, GERMAN DEMOCRATIC REPUBLIC

GERMAN SOCIALIST STUDENT FEDERATION (Sozialistische Deutsche Studentenschaften--SDS). This was the leading radical student organization in the 1950s and 1960s. It began as an organization linked to the SPD (q.v.), but the mother party severed these ties in 1961, and the SPD declared membership in the SDS to be incompatible with that in the SPD. In the 1950s its focus was opposition to Western integration and NATO (q.v.), but in the 1960s it shifted its criticism to the political system itself. By 1966, it was dominated by the authoritarian left. Its efforts to change society through street protests failed, and the organization was disbanded in 1970.

GERMAN-SOVIET NON-AGGRESSION PACT (1939). Signed by foreign ministers Ribbentrop (q.v.) and Molotov on August 23, 1939, its published terms included pledges to refrain from aggression against each other and to remain neutral if either country were involved in a war. However, there were secret clauses carving Eastern Europe up into spheres of influence. The Russians gained a free hand in Bessarabia, Eastern Poland, Latvia, Estonia, and Finland, and Germany was to have Lithuania and the rest of Poland. On September 28, 1939, another secret accord delivered Lithuania to the Soviet sphere, and Germany extended its sphere further into Poland. This was a prelude to Hitler's (q.v.) invasion of Poland on September 1, 1939, which unleashed the Second World War (q.v.). The pact became void when the Germans attacked the Soviet Union on June 22, 1941. The Soviet Union did not publicly acknowledge these secret clauses until after Mikhail Gorbachev came to power in 1985, and the GDR (q.v.) leadership also denied the existence of these clauses.

GERMAN SPACE AGENCY (Deutsche Agentur für Raumfahrt-Angelegenheiten--DARA) see SPACE PROGRAM

GERMAN STUDENT BODY ASSOCIATIONS (VERBAND DEUTSCHER STUDENTENSCHAFTEN--VDS). Calling for a "Democratization of the Universities," this organization joined with other radicalized student organizations in the late 1960s to reintroduce the ideology of radical Marxism. They were greatly influenced by the American protest movements of the time, including the anti-war campaigns everywhere in the U.S. and the "Free Speech Movement" in Berkeley.

GERMAN STUDIES ASSOCIATION (GSA). The GSA is an American umbrella organization for all disciplines studying German affairs. It sponsors an annual conference and publishes the *German Studies Review*, which contains articles and book reviews in English and German.

GERMAN TRADE UNION FEDERATION (DEUTSCHER GEWERKSCHAFTSBUND--DGB) see LABOR

GERMAN YOUNG PEOPLE (DEUTSCHES JUNGVOLK) see HITLER YOUTH

GERMANY PLAN (DEUTSCHLANDPLAN, 1959). The dramatic last attempt to achieve unity by the traditional method was the "Germany Plan." It was the culmination of SPD efforts to establish a foreign policy alternative to the Adenauer (qq.v.) government. Such a final effort was made even more urgent by a prolonged crisis in Berlin in 1958. The Soviet leaders issued an ultimatum that Berlin become a "free city" and that both Germanys be recognized as sovereign states.

With no wall sealing off the GDR (q.v.), refugees poured across the demarcation line in Berlin. The influx put pressure on the FRG to find some kind of settlement to the German problem that would stop this. The Four Powers were preparing to meet again in Geneva in 1959, and the plan's author, Herbert Wehner (q.v.), wanted them to agree to discuss German unity seriously. He also worried that they might change the status of West Berlin, after the GDR had incorporated the eastern part of Berlin and began calling "Berlin" its capital. The ultimate aim of the plan was reunification in a step-by-step process and "within the framework of a Four-Power settlement on European security and the German question." Within a "zone of relaxed tension," including both Germanys, Poland, Czechoslovakia, and Hungary, all foreign troops and nuclear weapons would be withdrawn and limits set on national forces inside the zone. The U.S., USSR, and all other interested states would guarantee the defense of the zone by means of a collective security agreement. The states within it would no longer need NATO (q.v.) and the Warsaw Pact to guarantee their security, so they could withdraw from these alliances. The "disengagement" of armies on German soil would create "more favorable conditions" for settling the knotty political problems. The two German states would gradually intensify their cooperation and come together in four stages. Both would send an equal number of delegates to an all-German conference to discuss internal German matters. An equal number of deputies would then be elected in each part of Germany to serve in a parliamentary council to decide common communications, transportation, and economic policy, to be followed by legislation on taxes, currency, tariffs, and social policy. They would ultimately draft a law for electing an assembly to write a constitution for Germany. After the constitution had come into force, free elections would be held to select a German parliament and government. The governing coalition greeted the plan with thunderous criticism, charging that it amounted to a swap of freedom for reunification. In early 1960 the SPD scrapped it.

GERMANY, SOLE RIGHT TO REPRESENT (ALLEINVERTRETUNG) see POLICY OF STRENGTH

GERMANY TREATY (DEUTSCHLAND VERTRAG, BONN CONVENTIONS, 1951) see REARMAMENT, GERMAN

GERSTENMAIER, EUGEN (1906-1986). CDU, Member of Bundestag (1949-69), president of Bundestag (1954-69). He was forced to resign his presidency on January 31, 1969, because he had received over $60,000 in reparations payment for his brief and peripheral association with the anti-Hitler Kreisau Circle (q.v.). He had claimed that this had prevented him from receiving a professorship during the Third Reich (q.v.), but the evidence did not back this up. Also damaging was the fact that he had helped steer the law authorizing such payments through the Bundestag, a law from which he personally benefitted.

GESAMTSCHULE see EDUCATION

GESELLSCHAFT (SOCIETY) see GEMEINSCHAFT

GESELLSCHAFT FÜR NEBENBETRIEBE see PRIVATIZATION

GESTALT THEORY see WERTHEIMER, MAX

GESTAPO (GEHEIME STAATSPOLIZEI, SECRET STATE POLICE, NAZI) see HIMMLER, HEINRICH

GLEICHSCHALTUNG. Adolf Hitler (q.v.) and his party enforced a so-called *Gleichschaltung*, an untranslatable German word meaning the destruction or restructuring of all independent groups or institutions so that none could exist without supporting Nazi rule. (See NAZI REPRESSION.)

GLIENICKE BRIDGE. Called the "Bridge of Unity" by GDR (q.v.) authorities, it linked Potsdam with Berlin and was the location for the exchange of dissidents, political prisoners, and spies.

GLOBKE, HANS (1898-1973). CDU state secretary in chancellor's office (1953-63). (See also ADENAUER AND FORMER NAZIS; DENAZIFICATION.)

GLOTZ, PETER (1939-). SPD (q.v.) federal party manager from 1981. A former West Berlin Senator for Education and Science, he was one of the SPD's leading intellectuals and authored many books about politics while remaining politically active.

GLÜCKAUF, ERICH (1903-). SED, from 1971 head of the GDR central committee's Western department.

GNEISENAU, AUGUST WILHELM ANTON COUNT NEIDHARDT VON (1760-1831). This professional soldier served the British as a mercenary in the American Revolutionary War. After making a name in the 1806-07 Prussian (q.v.) campaigns, he joined General Scharnhorst (q.v.) to reorganize and train a new Prussian army, in which he served as General Blücher's (q.v.) deputy. He led the army in the War of Liberation in 1813-14, planned the Prussian invasion of France, and fought in the Waterloo campaign. He was made Field Marshal and count. (See also FRENCH REVOLUTION.)

GODESBERG PROGRAM (1959)   see SOCIAL DEMOCRATIC PARTY OF GERMANY

GOEBBELS, JOSEPH (1897-1945).   Nazi minister for people's enlightenment and propaganda (1933-45). A Rhinelander who received a Ph.D. in Heidelberg in 1920, he was made Nazi (q.v.) leader in Berlin in 1926, put in charge of propaganda in 1929, and entered the Reichstag in 1930. In 1945, he committed suicide after poisoning his wife and six children. In 1992, his diaries were found.

GOERDELER, CARL FRIEDRICH (1884-1945). Mayor of Leipzig (1930-37), a leader in the non-communist resistance to Hitler (q.v.), for which he was executed. (See also RESISTANCE.)

GOETHE, JOHANN WOLFGANG VON (1749-1832). This genius and universal man has the distinction of being the only German after whom an entire epoch has been named. Born in Frankfurt, the son of a patrician, he was influenced by an artistic but serious father and an imaginative, lively mother. As a student of law in Strasbourg, his poetic talent began to unfold. Of all lyric poets, his work is the most powerful and original. His literary diversity over an 82-year period ranges from the turbulent Storm and Stress (q.v.) to the enlightened Classicism (q.v.) to the Romantic. Known mainly as a man of letters, Goethe was a scientist, theater director, administrator in Weimar, and artist. He was interested in mining, economics, architecture, horticulture, and landscape gardening. He was inspired by the many women in his life and by his surroundings. A two-year stay in Italy affected him profoundly. His works include lyric, epic and ballad poetry, drama, novels, and autobiographical writings. His *Faust*, a two-volume tragedy written in verse, best symbolizes the German penchant to overcome the limits of human knowledge while striving for perfection.

GOETHE INSTITUTE. These centers of German culture promote German language and culture throughout the world.

GORBACHEV, MIKHAIL (1931-). General secretary of Soviet Communist Party (1985-90), whose leadership in the Communist world was a precondition for the 1989 Revolution in the GDR. (See also GERMAN DEMOCRATIC REPUBLIC; PARTY OF DEMOCRATIC SOCIALISM.)

GÖRING, HERMANN (1893-1946). Nazi minister president of Prussia (1933-45), air force supreme commander (1935-45), tried at Nuremberg and committed suicide in cell. Göring was a First World War (q.v.) air ace and commanded the famed Richthofen Squadron in 1918. He joined the Nazi (q.v.) party early and was wounded in the 1923 beer hall putsch in Munich. After becoming air minister in 1933, he created and led the Air Force (Luftwaffe) until 1945. After the 1940 military victories, he was made Reichsmarshal. Many other Nazi leaders disliked him because of his ostentation, vanity, and increasing inefficiency and laziness. (See also HITLER'S SEIZURE OF POWER.)

GORLEBEN. A proposed nuclear reprocessing plant in Lower Saxony, made necessary by a 1979 government decision not to license additional nuclear plants until satisfactory arrangements existed for reprocessing and waste management. This plant became the focus of extreme criticism, and even some violence, on the part of Greens (q.v.) and other groups.

GOTHA PROGRAM (1875). In May 1875, two socialist parties which had renounced violent revolution, the General German Workers Union founded in 1963 by Ferdinand Lasalle (q.v.) and the Social Democratic Workers' Party founded in 1869 by August Bebel and Karl Liebknecht (qq.v.), were merged to form the "Socialist Workers' Party of Germany" (SAP). The SPD (q.v.) emerged from this union. But the SAP reappeared and was active in the Weimar Republic (q.v.). One of its best-known members was Willy Brandt (q.v.), who wore this party label as a resistance fighter against the Third Reich (q.v.).

GOTTSCHED, JOHANN CHRISTOPH (1700-1766). A theologian and philosopher during the Enlightenment (q.v.), he is best known for his linguistic reforms which included establishing well-defined genres and dramatic unities based on the French model.

GRABERT, HORST (1927-). SPD, see GUILLAUME AFFAIR

GRADL, JOHANN BAPTIST (b.1904). CDU Bundestag member from the Soviet zone, federal minister for all-German questions (1965-66), chairman of Curatorium Indivisible Germany (q.v.).

GRAND COALITION (1966-1969). In 1966 the FRG's two largest parties formed a "Grand Coalition," with Kurt Georg Kiesinger of the CDU (qq.v.) as chancellor. Although the parliamentary system was operating very smoothly and the war damage and mass poverty had given way to visible prosperity, the major parties' leaders saw economic troubles ahead. The SPD (q.v.) also wanted to participate in such a coalition government in order to demonstrate that it was capable of ruling the FRG.

The Grand Coalition stimulated considerable domestic opposition, especially in 1968 when its majority in the Bundestag passed a series of constitutional amendments and laws granting the government certain emergency powers in times of crisis. Although it argued that any truly sovereign state had to be able to take special measures in times of emergency to defend the democratic order, many West Germans pointed out that similar emergency laws had been misused during the Weimar Republic (q.v.) to undermine democracy. This controversial issue, combined with doubts about American policy in Vietnam, sent thousands of mainly young Germans into the streets. They employed confrontation tactics which they had learned from the civil rights and anti-war movements in the U.S., even using the American terms for these tactics, such as "sit-in" and "go-in." They called themselves the "extra-parliamentary opposition" (APO, q.v.), which they claimed was necessary since the opposition within parliament had sunk to a negligible 5 percent.

Far less controversial in the eyes of young Germans was the Grand Coalition's policy of seeking improved relations with the East. This received a particular push from Foreign Minister Willy Brandt (q.v.) and the crafty minister for all-German affairs, Herbert Wehner (q.v.), both of the SPD. The Kiesinger government took steps toward overcoming the impasse in German reunification (q.v.). It announced that it was prepared to accept the East German regime as a *de facto* government, and it even exchanged letters for the first time with East German leaders on a semi-official basis. It established a trade mission in Prague in 1967, and its diplomatic recognition of Romania in 1967 and Yugoslavia in 1968 indicated that the Hallstein Doctrine, which had required the FRG to break relations with any country (except the Soviet Union) which recognized the GDR, was in fact dead, even if not wiped off the books. On July 8, 1969, Helmut Schmidt (q.v.) told the *Frankfurter Allgemeine Zeitung* that "except for the electoral reform, to which the SPD was not committed from the very beginning, we accomplished every point in the government's declaration." Arnulf Baring called the Grand Coalition the "most important, consequential phase since 1949." The foundation for reforms and renovation in subsequent SPD governments was laid from 1966-69. This was true of domestic politics, as well as policy toward the East (*Ostpolitik*, q.v.) and the GDR (*Deutschlandpolitik*). Important changes were made in the legal system and Basic Law (q.v.). Under Gustav Heinemann's (q.v.) guidance, the penal code was modernized. Protections for the state were loosened. The statute of limitations (q.v.) for atrocities committed during the Hitler years was extended by ten years.

Far more controversial was the extension of the emergency powers (q.v.) the government could wield. In accordance with the Germany Treaty (q.v.) of 1954, the Western powers reserved the right to reclaim their occupation rights in the event of an emergency resulting from an external threat. Since this was an obvious limitation on the FRG's sovereignty, many favored a transfer of those powers to the Bonn government. The debate had raged the entire decade. Early drafts encountered stubborn resistance from critics who feared that they were too similar to powers misused during Weimar and the Third Reich (q.v.). In demonstrations throughout the FRG, opponents hoisted banners: "Emergency Laws Equal Hitler!" and "Nazism Began This Way!" Finally in May 1968 a formula was found that satisfied most lawmakers.

Economic policy was a dramatic success, thanks to Finance Minister Franz-Josef Strauss and Economics Minister Karl Schiller (qq.v.), whose star rose at a dizzying pace in these three years. It involved a mixture of state intervention and planning with the "enlightened market economy." "Medium-term finance planning" set five-year guidelines, while quarterly "concerted actions" brought 75 labor and management leaders together to moderate both union demands for wages and management's demands for profits. The budget was brought under control, and the number of unemployed fell within a year from 700,000 to 200,000. The economy soared out of the doldrums. Within a year, the economic crisis facing the FRG was considered to be over. Being in power enabled the SPD to translate into law some Social Democratic objectives. For instance, unemployment and sickness benefits for workers and employees were put on the same level. Perhaps the most important legislative achievement was the "Law to Promote Economic Stability and Growth." In 1967, a law was adopted providing federal financial support to political parties in order to help free them from undue dependency upon private interest groups. The economic success of this partly-SPD government after the failure of the father of the German "economic miracle," Ludwig Erhard (q.v.), was extremely important for the SPD. Schiller especially had freed the SPD from the nagging doubts about its competence to rule; he became the vote-getter in 1969 who enabled the SPD to rule without the Christian parties.

Although the Grand Coalition was popular with the public, its critics became increasingly vociferous in their opposition. For the first time since Weimar, there were violent clashes in the streets between demonstrators and police. The very formation of a giant coalition that included almost 95 percent of the Bundestag members had contributed to a rising malaise among young West Germans. Even many non-radicals were uneasy that democratic principles might have been violated because opposition seemed to have become ineffective. The only opposition in the Bundestag was the tiny FDP (q.v.). In the minds of young idealists, many of whom discovered a revolutionary Marxist rhetoric at this time, a governing SPD no longer offered an alternative, and the emergency laws helped keep tensions high. The Grand Coalition was not the sole cause of the challenge to the economic and social structure. It had already begun before the government's formation, and in all industrialized democracies thousands of young people went into the streets to protest any form of political "business as usual." In the FRG there was an outcry for the long overdue reform of an autocratic and archaic university system. There were doubts about American policy in Vietnam, and therefore about the wisdom of remaining militarily dependent upon such a power.

GRASS, GÜNTHER (1927-). A contemporary writer originally from Danzig (q.v.), Grass was a committed Social Democrat, who figured prominently in the discussion surrounding reunification. In late 1992 he left the SPD (q.v.) out of protest against its decision to support a change in the Basic Law (q.v.) which would no longer guarantee asylum for every person arriving in Germany. His first novel, *Der Blechtrommel* (*The Tin Drum*), gained him international recognition. Grass uses graphic form and often grotesque characters to write in an imaginative, provocative, sometimes abstruse style. In addition to his plays, novels, essays and short stories, he has produced two volumes of sketches. (See also DENAZIFICATION; ELECTIONS 1969, 1972.)

GREENS (DIE GRÜNEN). In the 1970s, new forms of political organization emerged, such as that of the ecologists, known as the Greens. Such loosely-knit groups understood how to clear the "5 percent hurdle" required to win representation in parliaments at all levels of government. Some are willing to combine in a loose way with each other and to present themselves in elections as "Alternative Lists" or as "Colorful Lists" (*Bunte Listen*). In the 1983 federal elections, the Greens garnered 5.6 percent of the votes and won 27 seats in the Bundestag. In 1987, they raised their totals to 8.3 percent of the votes and 42 seats. In 1990, their eternal in-fighting, rejection of German unity, absence of a positive program, and ambivalence toward taking responsibility in government caught up with them. Grossly misreading the popular mood supporting unity, western Greens adopted the slogan, "Everybody talks about Germany; we talk about the weather!" Failing to unite their parties for the Bundestag elections, western German Greens received only 4.8 percent of the votes in the West and were therefore ejected from parliament, to their shock and dismay. In university towns and large cities, their previous voters deserted them in droves, and they were thrown back to the political fringe. Their spokesman noted sadly: "We fell under the wheels of German unification." An election coalition of eastern German Greens and Alliance 90 (q.v.), a collection of eastern German grassroots groups which organized the 1989 revolution, won 6 percent of the votes in the East (1.2 percent nation-wide) and eight seats under the special election law which applied only to the 1990 elections.

One reason for the Greens' previous success was their early focus on the environmental problem, which most Germans view as having reached crisis proportions and which most polls indicate is the most important issue in Germans' minds. That is why all parties turned their attention to this issue and robbed the Greens of their monopoly on it. From a third to half of the country's forests are said to be dying of pollution, especially acid rain. This widespread concern prompted the federal government to require tighter industrial pollution controls and catalytic converters on new cars by the end of the decade. For example, in 1991 the conservative government passed a law requiring all companies selling in Germany to take back and recycle their packaging. Ecological problems are particularly acute in eastern Germany, where the former Communist rulers showed appalling disregard for the environment.

The Greens created the first new party in over 25 years to find its way into the federal parliament. Their presence affected not only the ability to form stable governments, but also the tone and style of parliamentary government. In the late 1980s, they helped reduce the radicalism which had buffeted the FRG from the mid-1960s to the early 1980s. They often reject any cooperation with the traditional parties, and their programs are most often idealistic and incompatible with those of the established parties. The party itself was split between realists (*Realos*), who favored accepting government posts to achieve the party's goals, and the fundamentalists (*Fundis*), who argued that the party would tarnish its image by ceasing to be an exclusively opposition force and by entering an "arrangement with capitalism." In May 1991, the inevitable occurred: the *Fundis* broke away from the Greens and formed their own "Ecological Left/Alternative List," which vowed to concentrate on strengthening non-parliamentary opposition. It retained the option of contesting elections as well. This split will harm the Greens' electoral chances, while at the same time making the *Realos* more respectable in the eyes of some voters. It is possible that the Greens will be able to stage a political comeback. In January 1993, the western German Greens and eastern German Alliance '90 merged to form a new joint party, the Alliance '90/Greens, with Greens as its abbreviated name.

Leftist parties in Germany can no longer assume that they can easily attract the country's youth, whose attitudes have changed considerably since the late 1960s. Recession and unemployment have concentrated young minds and caused radicalism to give way to conservatism among many young Germans. Succeeding in the existing system is more important than changing it. No longer are political radicals, such as Rudi Dutschke or Petra Kelly (q.v.), the models. Instead, admiration is directed toward young Germans who "made it." Thus, conservative parties, not just the SPD (q.v.) or Greens, have profited from these changes in youth attitudes.

Perhaps more important than the Greens' parliamentary presence was their ability to mobilize hundreds of thousands of persons for mass demonstrations against the Bonn government's defense policy, or against a state government's plans to build a nuclear power or reprocessing plant or to expand the Frankfurt airport. Some feared that it could threaten the democratic regime.

GRIMM BROTHERS, JAKOB (1785-1863) and WILHELM (1786-1859). Both brothers from Hanau studied in Marburg to be librarians and went on to the University of Göttingen together where they wrote their famous book of fairy tales and another on sagas. Although Jakob, as the more original and scholarly of the two, took the lead in the project, Wilhelm was more poetic and a better storyteller. The brothers moved to Berlin where Wilhelm assisted Jakob in writing two volumes of *The History of the German Language* and the greatest contribution to German, the *Deutsches Wörterbuch*, the German equivalent of *The Oxford English Dictionary*. Only four volumes were completed in their lifetime. (See also LIBERALISM.)

GROENER, WILHELM (1867-1939). General and Reichswehr minister (1928-32).

GROSZ, GEORGE (1893-1959). Although this expressionistic painter went through various stages, he is best known for his searing caricatures with animal-like faces. Grosz was a social critic who portrayed vice, poverty, and moral corruption so closely associated with the pre-Nazi period and the Second World War (q.v.). His style changed to "New Objectivity" and he moved to New York in 1933 and began his own art school. On a visit to Berlin, where he intended to return, he fell down some steps and died.

GROTEWOHL, OTTO (1894-1964). Co-founder of SED, minister president of GDR (1949-64). (See also SCHUMACHER, KURT.)

GRÜNDGENS, GUSTAF (1899-1963). This famous actor and later head of the German Theater in Berlin under the Nazis (q.v.) was a victim of the illusion that art can remain free from totalitarian politics.

His most famous role was ironically that of Mephistopheles (1932) from Goethe's *Faust,* who sold himself to the devil. Gründgen's experiences were described in a controversial novel by Klaus Mann (q.v.).

GRUNDSCHULE see EDUCATION

GRÜNEWALD, MATTHIAS (1470-1528). This famous Renaissance (q.v.) painter is best known for *The Isenheim Altar* located in Colmar, France. His interpretation of the Crucifixion is considered one of the best in the history of art. (See also RENAISSANCE.)

GRUPPE 47. This group of writers and critics without a program or statutes met from 1947 to 1967 and played a big part in the literary life of the FRG. Their annual meetings consisted of readings and discussions, and a prize was given to a rising young writer.

GUDERIAN, HEINZ see SECOND WORLD WAR

GUEFFROY, CHRIS. The last East German to be shot trying to cross the Berlin Wall, February 6, 1989. His murderers were tried and convicted in a Berlin court after reunification (q.v.). (See also HONECKER, ERICH.)

GUEST WORKERS (GASTARBEITER) see LABOR

GUILLAUME AFFAIR. Günter Guillaume (1927-) was the son of an SS-trooper and had himself been a member of the Nazi (q.v.) party in 1944-45. That made him an easy Stasi (q.v.) target for recruitment as an agent. After six years of training, he was sent in 1956, along with his wife Christel, as a refugee into West Berlin, and they finally landed in Frankfurt. In 1957, he joined the SPD (q.v.). Because of his diligence, organizational talent, and reputation as a "Juso-eater," he attracted the attention of Georg Leber, who told Willy Brandt (qq.v.) that "I would put my hand into the fire for him." Egon Bahr (q.v.) was not so sure, though, noting in 1969 that Guillaume had worked as a journalist for the East Berlin publishing house Volk und Wissen, often used as a cover for spies. After the 1972 election he was assigned to Brandt as personal aide.

By May 1973 Brandt had grown tired of Guillaume and had asked that he be reassigned, but on May 29, 1973, Interior Minister Genscher (q.v.) informed Brandt that the BfV had evidence that Guillaume was an East German agent. The BfV's chief was Günther Nollau, until 1950 a Dresden lawyer. Nollau recommended that Guillaume be permitted to remain in his position under surveillance and also that he be allowed to accompany Brandt during his summer holiday in Norway. Brandt and Genscher agreed, and the chancellor's state secretary Horst Grabert and office chief Reinhard Wilke (but not Ehmke or Bahr) were informed. Grabert later confessed that it had been a "cardinal error" to use the chancellor as the honey pot for an East German agent.

Guillaume and his wife went to Norway with Brandt. The aide operated the telex machine and had access to all documents transmitted to the chancellor. Foreign Minister Walter Scheel (q.v.) denied that the traffic contained highly sensitive information, such as NATO (q.v.) secrets. When in May 1974 Brandt declared before the Bundestag that Guillaume had seen no secret documents, the CDU (q.v.) floor leader Karl Carstens (q.v.) produced embarrassing evidence that the agent had initialled all the documents sent to Norway, even those marked secret. Even though the BfV got few clues from its ten months of observation, Brandt and Genscher decided on March 1, 1974, to inform the federal prosecutor about Guillaume, which prompted his arrest on April 24. Guillaume's instant confession made the case against him easier. Brandt was deeply disappointed that he could be deceived by a person he had trusted, and he carried his bitterness over to the GDR, which he had dignified through his *Ostpolitik* (q.v.), only to be treated so shabbily in return. Brandt had always been hostile to orthodox Communists, but the SED's (q.v.) fears of him had really been stimulated during his 1970 visit to Premier Willi Stoph (q.v.) in Erfurt, when he was cheered by thousands of East Germans. Guillaume was the SED's means of diminishing the stature of the popular and dangerous Brandt.

Unfortunately for the chancellor, the investigation that followed turned up more than the usual espionage evidence. It uncovered highly personal information about Brandt's private life, including alleged sexual lapses. Brandt had a bad habit of speaking freely in the presence of close aides, such as Guillaume. Neither Guillaume nor his wife talked during the investigation. However, investigators had grilled Brandt's body guard, Ulrich Bauhaus; under pressure, he told all he knew. On April 26, Brandt was informed that investigators were looking into Guillaume's knowledge of "female acquaintances," and on

April 30 Brandt called charges "ridiculous" that Guillaume had "led girls" to the chancellor, a formulation that found its way into the press. Brandt could not make up his mind what to do. The work of the chancellor's office had come to a halt. A public opinion poll revealed that 63 percent of the respondents agreed that the East German spy had done great damage, and 47 percent favored Brandt's resignation. He decided to resign in May 1974. Guillaume and his wife were found guilty in court and served in prison until 1981, when he was exchanged. (See also BRANDT.)

GUSTAVUS ADOLPHUS, GUSTAV II OF SWEDEN (1594-1632) see THIRTY-YEARS WAR

GUTENBERG, JOHANNES (1397/1400-1468). The son of a Mainz patrician family, he invented the movable type for printing in 1436. This new printing process, which revolutionized the world, spread quickly throughout Europe and permitted the relatively fast and cheap publication of books. His most famous book was the Latin-language Gutenberg Bible in 1455, of which he produced 18 copies. It established the groundwork for a wide and intensive theological discussion. (See also LUTHER, MARTIN; RENAISSANCE.)

GUTTENBERG, KARL THEODOR BARON ZU (1921-1972). CSU, parliamentary state secretary in federal chancellor's office (1967-69). Guttenberg was a key figure in establishing and maintaining the Grand Coalition (q.v.).

GYMNASIUM see EDUCATION

GYPSIES see ROMA

GYSI, GREGOR (1948-). PDS chairman (December 1989-January 1993), Member of Bundestag (December 1990-). (See GERMAN DEMOCRATIC REPUBLIC, COLLAPSE; PARTY OF DEMOCRATIC SOCIALISM.)

-H-

HABERMAS, JÜRGEN (1929-). A leading exponent of the critical theory of the "Frankfurt School," a neo-Marxist social theory based on analytical social sciences. Habermas was a professor of philosophy and sociology at the University of Frankfurt, during which time he was one of the intellectual fathers of the student movement and new left (q.v.). In 1971, he became director of the Max-Planck Institute in Starnberg, outside Munich.

HAYDN, JOSEPH (1732-1809). An Austrian composer of symphonies and chamber music.

HAGER, KURT (1912-) see PARTY OF DEMOCRATIC SOCIALISM

HAHN, OTTO see WEIZSÄCHER, CARL FRIEDRICH VON

HALDER, FRANZ (1884-1972). Army chief of staff (1938-42).

HALLSTEIN, WALTER (1901-1982) and HALLSTEIN DOCTRINE. CDU state secretary in foreign office (1951-8), president of EC Commission (1958-67). (See GRAND COALITION.)

HÄNDL, JAKOB (1550-1591). Bohemian composer of masses and other music who lived in Prague.

HANS SEIDEL FOUNDATION see STIFTUNGEN

HANSA LEAGUE. The power and influence of German cities was greatest when they joined together in leagues. The most important was that of the Hansa cities. In 1241, Lübeck and Hamburg forged an alliance in order to protect the land and sea lanes between them from robbers. They were gradually joined by more and more cities along the North and Baltic Sea coasts, and even deep within the interior of Germany, Poland, the Baltic area and Scandinavia. By the time the Hansa League had reached its height in the first half of the 15th century, it embraced such cities as Cologne, Braunschweig, Bremen, Wismar, Rostock, Danzig, Königsberg, Breslau and Cracow. The League had large trading colonies in London, Bruges, Gotland and Novgorod. Seldom did the Hansa cities conduct traditional military warfare; they preferred the far more effective trade war. Not until the end of the 15th century was the Hansa League's dominance over the North and Baltic Sea area broken.

HARDENBERG, FRIEDRICH LEOPOLD VON (NOVALIS) (1772-1801). This former mining administrator and son of a landowner from Thuringia founded the first Romantic (q.v.) school along with Tieck and Schlegel. *Heinrich von Ofterdingen*, one of his best known works, contains the Romantic symbol of the "blue flower."

HARDENBERG, KARL AUGUST PRINCE VON (1750-1822). Born in Essenrode and lawyer and civil servant in Hanover, Hardenberg entered Prussian (q.v.) service in 1790, serving as foreign minister from 1804-06 and chief minister from 1807. He replaced vom Stein (q.v.) as Prussian leader, was fired upon Napoleon's insistence, but resumed his leadership of the government in 1810 as state chancellor. He continued vom Stein's reforms, completing the liberation of the peasants in 1811 and the emancipation of Jews in Prussia in 1812. His diplomatic skill was crucial in the War of Liberation from Napoleon in 1813-14, and he secured Prussia's growth in territory at the Congress of Vienna (q.v.). (See also FRENCH REVOLUTION.)

HARICH, WOLFGANG (1921-). Philosopher and SED reformer. (See GERMAN DEMOCRATIC REPUBLIC.)

HARNACK, ARVID see RED CHAPEL

HARZBURG FRONT (1931). On October 11, 1931, in Bad Harzburg, the Nazis, the Steel Helmets (*Stahlhelm*, a league of front soldiers), and the DNVP, led by Alfred Hugenberg (qq.v.), had totally withdrawn their support from the Weimar Republic (q.v.) and steered an uncompromising confrontation course, and other nationalist groups joined hands in the struggle against the Weimar Republic. Their strength was shown in powerful marches of their paramilitary units and belligerent speeches by Hitler (q.v.) and Hugenberg, who was the chief of a powerful business and press empire and General Director of the film studio Ufa. After Hitler took power in January 1933, Hugenberg and the Stahlhelm leader Franz Seldte sat for a while in Hitler's cabinet, but within a few months all nationalist organizations, including the DNVP, were subjected to *Gleichschaltung* (q.v.) and forced to dissolve.

HASSEL, KAI-UWE VON (1913-). CDU, minister president of Schleswig-Holstein (1954-62), federal minister of defense (1962-66), and of deportees, refugees, and war injured (1966-69).

Helmut Schmidt and Erich Honecker on a winter walk in Döllnsee, GDR, December 1981. (*Source:* GIC).

HAUPTMANN, GERHART (1862-1946). This would-be sculptor won the Nobel Prize for Literature in 1912. He is considered the best German representative of Naturalism (q.v.). His dramas, such as *Die Weber (The Weavers)* and *Bahnwarter Thiel*, show his compassion for the downtrodden and the poor, who are powerless in a hostile world. He was able to represent the landscape, dialect and atmosphere of his native Silesia (q.v.) with great accuracy until he turned fifty and his creativity began to decline. (See also EMPIRE CULTURE.)

HAUPTSCHULE see EDUCATION

HAVEMANN, ROBERT (d. 1982). A respected scientist and long-time Communist, who had been in the same Nazi prison as Honecker (q.v.), Havemann began in the 1960s publicly to criticize the GDR (q.v.) regime's authoritarianism and dishonest claims of democratization. His criticism continued even after he had been removed from his posts and membership in the Academy of Sciences. In 1968, he denounced the Warsaw Pact invasion of Czechoslovakia. In 1977, he was temporarily placed under house arrest. He was also fined for alleged currency violations stemming from his publication of works in the West.

HEARTFIELD, JOHN (1891-1968).   Born Helmut Herzfeld, he anglicized his name during the First World War (q.v.). This was a sign that he was a very unconventional artist and anti-patriot. A Dadaist, nihilist, anti-art artist full of bitter jest, he was one of the originators of photomontage, juxtaposing photos cut from the popular press. Using an economical style, he joined simple images and simple text to convey a poignant message. His favorite targets were the Nazis (q.v.). One of his works shows Hitler (q.v.) in mid-salute, back-handedly receiving banknotes from a man in a suit. The Nazi slogan in the background read: "Millions are behind me." He did not believe in fine art, but only in revolutionary art for the masses. When the Nazis came to power in 1933, he barely escaped from Germany by leaping from the balcony of his Berlin apartment, dodging the SS, and walking across the mountains into Czechoslovakia. He lived in England during the war and emigrated to the GDR (q.v.) in 1950.

HEBBEL, FRIEDRICH (1813-1863).   Despite an early life of poverty and misfortune, Hebbel became one of the best realistic dramatists. His themes deal with the individual who is caught between the old culture and the new and becomes a victim of circumstance. *Mary Magdelena* and *Judith* are two of his best known tragedies.

HECK, BRUNO (1917-) see KIESINGER, KURT GEORG

HECKER, FREDERICK   see AMERICA, GERMAN ATTITUDES TOWARD

HEGEL, FRIEDRICH (1770-1831). Living in Stuttgart, Tübingen, Jena and Berlin, Hegel was a powerful intellectual force in the 19th century. He argued that reality is a living, evolving process. The absolute is universal reason moving through eternity and embodying itself in the actual universe. He believed that thought and being are one. In *Logic* (1817) he elaborated his theory that the universe is rational, as shown by the order seen in the stars, in biology, and in all things.

The work of this philosopher at the University of Berlin had important political implications. His almost encyclopedic work gave rise to at least two contradictory traditions: one supporting authoritarian rule and one supporting revolution. In some of his writings Hegel described the state as an organism which is not a mere instrument in the hands of the citizens, but which grows and has needs of its own. Such growth, he argued, was completely rational; in fact, he maintained that reason reaches its highest perfection in the state. Which state had reached the highest existing perfection? The Prussian (q.v.) state, he answered. A state's power reflects the rationality of the state. "What is rational is actual and what is actual is rational," he wrote. The life of the individual human being has meaning only within the state, he argued. Authoritarian rulers could not have been more pleased with a philosophical doctrine than with this one. (See also MARX, KARL.)

HEIDEGGER, MARTIN (1889-1976).   Trained under Husserl, Heidegger advanced the field of phenomenology as a professor of philosophy at the University of Freiburg. He was also influenced by Kierkegaard and concluded that "concern" is the heart of consciousness and "dread" the basic attitude toward the world. Such dread is concealed by the routine of daily life, but the philosopher must call attention to it. In his *Being and Time* (1927) he argued that the ultimate meaning of those two concepts involves a sense of the significance of conscience, choice, and death.

Heidegger acquired such an enormous reputation in Germany that Leo Strauss, a philosopher who fled Hitler (q.v.) and established an entire school of political philosophy in the U.S., wrote that as soon as Heidegger appeared on the scene, "he stood in its center and began to dominate it. . . . Philosophizing seems to have been transformed into listening with reverence to the incipient *mythoi* of Heidegger." Heidegger's reputation remains tarnished by the fact that, as rector of the University of Freiburg in 1933, he permitted the first steps of Nazi *Gleichschaltung* (q.v.) to take place. He soon retreated from the brutal world of the Third Reich (q.v.) back into his study and never took a public stand against the Nazis. (See also WEIMAR CULTURE.)

HEIDELBERG PROGRAM (1925). SPD party program finally replaced in 1959 by the Godesberg Program (qq.v.).

HEIN, CHRISTOPH (1944-). Hein grew up in Berlin and went to the University of Leipzig. He worked as an author and dramatist for the Volksbühne (People's Stage) in East Berlin. Hein deals with the conflict between the enlightened intellectual and his contemporary who possesses only slight awareness of historical-social developments. *Der Tangospieler* and *Drachenblut* are two of his best known novels.

HEINE, HEINRICH (1797-1856). Son of a Jewish family from Düsseldorf, Heine converted to Protestantism when he found himself disadvantaged in banking, law, and academics. His first effort at prose, *Harzreise*, describes his walking trip through the Harz Mountains. It was the *Buch der Lieder* (*Songbook*), which established his reputation as a poet. He settled in Paris where he first worked as a correspondent. There he remained active in political and literary circles until he became bedridden for eight years and died of syphilitic tuberculosis. Hitler (q.v.) found it impossible to suppress Heine's beautiful poem and song, *Die Lorelei*, and thus ascribed it to an unknown author.

HEINEMANN, GUSTAV (1899-1976). CDU interior minister (1949-50), Heinemann left the CDU out of protest against German rearmament (qq.v.). After founding a short-lived party of his own, the All-German People's Party (GVP, q.v.), he joined the SPD (q.v.) and became justice minister (1966-69) and federal president (1969-74). (See also ALL-GERMAN PEOPLE'S PARTY; GRAND COALITION; PAULSKIRCHE MOVEMENT; REARMAMENT; SOVIET NOTES.)

HEINRICH IV (1050-1106) see GERMAN EMPIRE

HEISENBERGER, WERNER see WEIZSÄCKER, CARL FRIEDRICH VON

HEISER, KLAUS-DIETER see SOCIALIST INITIATIVE

HELSINKI ACCORDS (1975) see SCHMIDT, HELMUT

HENLEIN, KONRAD see SUDETENLAND

HENLEIN, PETER see RENAISSANCE

HERDER, JOHANN GOTTFRIED (1744-1803). A theologian and philosophical leader of the Storm and Stress (q.v.), Herder's main interest was the study of literature. He was a folklorist, literary critic, and translator who helped free German literature from the rigidity of French rules.

HERMLIN, STEPHAN (1915-). Hermlin was a Communist in Dresden who emigrated to England in 1936, took part in the Spanish Civil War, and belonged later to the French army before settling in East Berlin in 1947. His writings and poetry deal with antifascist subjects and the reconstruction of a socialist society. One of his best known collections of stories is *A bendlicht*.

HERRHAUSEN, ALFRED see TERRORIST GROUPS

HERRNSTADT, RUDOLF (1903-1966) see GERMAN DEMOCRATIC REPUBLIC, UPRISING

HERZOG, ROMAN (1934-). CDU, former president of Federal Constitutional Court, elected federal president May 23, 1994.

HERZOG, WERNER (1942-). Poetic New Wave film maker, an eccentric and mystic with a passion for the unusual. A school dropout, he later earned a scholarship to the U.S., but was expelled and made his living smuggling arms from Mexico. His characters are outside the mainstream. Most of his settings are located in hazardous, exotic places.

HESS, RUDOLF (1894-1987). Hitler's deputy in the Nazi (q.v.) Party, he stunned the world when he impulsively flew to Scotland in May 1941, bailing out by parachute, in a ludicrous attempt to persuade the British government to make peace. He was held captive for the rest of the war, tried at the Nuremberg Trials (q.v.), and sentenced to life incarceration in Spandau prison, where he died in 1987. (See also NAZI PARTY; NUREMBERG TRIALS; OVERCOMING THE PAST.)

HESSE, HERMANN (1887-1962). Born in Swabia, the son of a missionary, Hesse's poetry was influenced by a Pietist tradition. His first poems, *Romantic Songs*, were written while he worked in a bookstore in Switzerland, where he eventually became a citizen. A strong pacifist and a student of psychoanalysis, Hesse published several books and was preoccupied with the dual nature of man: the conflicts between intellect and nature, between art and life. *Der Steppenwolf*, written in 1927, was very popular among the hippie generation of the 1970s for its rejection of established norms and its flight into the psychedelic world of drugs. Hesse received the Nobel Prize for Literature in 1946.

HEUSS, THEODOR (1884-1963). FDP, federal president (1949-59). Born in Brackenheim, Heuss studied art history and economics before being drawn into the liberal circle of Friedrich Naumann, whose ideas Heuss adopted. From 1905 to 1912, he was chief writer for Naumann's *Die Hilfe* and then, until 1918, of the *Neckarzeitung*. From 1920 to 1933, he taught at the Political University (Hochschule für Politik) in Berlin, and in 1924-28 and 1930-33 he was a DDP deputy in the Reichstag, grudgingly approving of the Enabling Act (q.v.) in March 1933. In 1945, he became culture minister in Baden-Wurttemberg until 1946 and member of the Land parliament until 1949, when he became the FRG's first president. He advocated the union of all liberal parties in the western zones which culminated in the formation of the FDP (q.v.), of which he became chairman. He played an important role in the Parliamentary Council (q.v.), which produced the Basic Law (q.v.). Heuss was responsible for the fact that the basically symbolic presidency of the FRG gained respect in the eyes of the people, and his foreign visits as president served to enhance the growing respect for the FRG abroad. He consciously emphasized the democratic political and intellectual tradition which had been suppressed by the Nazis (q.v.), and his domestic political emphasis was the harmonizing of political strife.

HEYDRICH, REINHARD (1904-1942). Chief of Reich Main Office for Security (from 1939), deputy Reich Protector of Bohemia and Moravia (1941-42). Himmler's (q.v.) right-hand man, Heydrich was ordered by Göring on behalf of Hitler (qq.v.) to come up with a total plan for the final solution of the "Jewish problem." At the Wannsee Conference (q.v.) on January 20, 1942, Heydrich elaborated his plan before representatives of the various Reich ministries and party offices which would in some way be involved. None of those present raised an objection, and Eichmann (q.v.) was assigned the task of making the bureaucratic and technical preparations. Heydrich was assassinated by resistance fighters in Czechoslovakia, in retaliation for which the village of Lidica was destroyed and all males executed. (See also WANNSEE.)

HEYM, STEFAN (1913-). Heym left Hitler Germany in 1933 for Prague and then the U.S., where he directed a newspaper before joining the American army. Heym rose to the rank of major and was sent back to Germany with the occupation forces. His strong opposition to America's foreign policy and anti-communism prompted him to renounce his American citizenship. He settled in East Berlin in 1951 where he worked as a columnist. Heym's independent, outspoken criticism prevented some of his works from being published in the GDR (q.v.).

HIGH GERMAN see LUTHER, MARTIN

HILDESHEIMER, WOLFGANG (1916-). Born in Hamburg, Hildesheimer fled to England in 1933 and then to Palestine, where he learned to be a carpenter and studied furniture-making and interior design. He also studied drawing and set design in London before deciding to become a writer of short stories, radio plays and biographies. In 1946, he returned to Germany from Palestine to act as an interpreter for the Nuremberg Trials (q.v.).

HIMMLER, HEINRICH (1900-1945). Nazi Chief of SS (1929-45) and of German police (1936-45). Born in Munich, he grew up in a bourgeois, Catholic milieu. He volunteered for military service in 1917, but he was never sent to the front. He joined the Nazi (q.v.) party in 1923 and participated in the Munich Putsch in that year. Hitler (q.v.) made him a member of his protective squad (*Schutzstaffel*--SS, q.v.). In January 1929, he took charge of this squad consisting of about 300 men and built it up to became an elite formation within the Sturmabteilung (SA) (q.v.) functioning as an internal party police troop. As leader of the political police and Gestapo, he was given the task of liquidating the SA on June 30, 1934. As the SS Reich leader, he was directly under Hitler, but his SS was, in practice, an independent organization. All concentration camps (q.v.) were put under his control. From June 1936 he had full command of the entire German police, and he merged the personnel of the Gestapo and police. He became head of Reich administration in 1939 and minister of interior in 1943.

As Reich Commissar for the Strengthening of the German People (*Volkstum*), he conducted a brutal resettlement and "Germanizing" policy in the territories occupied by the Germans. As head of the "Operational Groups" (*Einsatzgruppen*), he organized the terror tactics and the mass murder. Due to the omnipresence and efficiency of his police and terror machine, the Third Reich (q.v.) can be called an "SS-state." Because of his brutal leadership of the Gestapo and atrocities committed under his direction, he acquired a very sinister reputation. In the final months of the war he tried to establish contact with the Western Allies to try to end the war on the Western front and form with those enemies a common front against the Soviet Union. This prompted Hitler to remove him from all his offices. In the uniform of a military policeman, he was captured by British troops on May 21, 1945. When he was recognized, he committed suicide two days later by swallowing a cyanide tablet. (See also RÖHM, ERNST.)

HINDENBURG, PAUL VON (1847-1934). Field Marshall, Weimar president (1925-34). Born into a Prussian military family, he was wounded in the Battle of Königgrätz (q.v.) and in 1871 represented his unit at the proclamation of the German Empire (q.v.) in the Palace of Versailles. He died in August 1934 and was buried at Tannenberg, where he had helped win an important victory in August 1914. (See also FIRST WORLD WAR; WEIMAR REPUBLIC.)

HINTZE, PETER. CDU, former theologian, Hintze was elevated to the post of general secretary of the CDU (q.v.) in 1992, when Volker Rühe (q.v.) became minister of defense.

HISTORIANS' CONTROVERSY (HISTORIKERSTREIT). In the second half of the 1980s a furious debate among intellectuals took place over the basic question of whether the Nazi (q.v.) crimes were unique in history. Those crimes had made it very difficult to be proud of being German, and this absence of pride and identity hampered Germans in the postwar world. The late Andreas Hillgruber, for example, suggested that the collapse of the German nation-state, which had been a barrier against Soviet power in Eastern Europe, was as much of a human tragedy as the Holocaust. Ernst Nolte, in a 1987 book, *Der Europäische Bürgerkrieg, 1917-1945* (*The European Civil War*), argued that Stalinist terror and concentration camps had set a bad example which resulted in Nazi genocide. Many socialist and liberal intellectuals, such as Jürgen Habermas (q.v.), answered the challenge by heaping scathing criticism on conservative historians who dared to relativize or gloss over the singularity of Nazism and especially the Holocaust (q.v.). The debate was bound to be emotional because it touched the sensitive nerves of guilt and atonement, collective and individual responsibility. It showed again how sensitive and difficult the question of national identity is in the FRG. (See also OVERCOMING THE PAST.)

HITLER, ADOLF (1889-1945). Nazi Party leader and Reich chancellor (1933-45). Born in Austria, Hitler lived from 1909 to 1913 in Vienna, where he absorbed anti-Semitic prejudices while trying to make a living as an artist. When the First World War (q.v.) broke out, he went to Bavaria and enlisted in the infantry. He rose to the rank of corporal, was twice awarded the Iron Cross, and was wounded. He began to emerge from the political shadows shortly after the end of the First World War, and he drew around himself a growing circle of enthusiastic admirers. In September 1919, he joined a tiny nationalist group which grew into the energetic, anti-democratic Nazi Party (q.v.). Although he had little formal education, Hitler was a fiery speaker, capable of stirring his listeners with haranguing, emotional tirades. Paranoid, continuously tense and expectant, he was sensitive and suspicious. He had no close relationship with anyone, not even with his mistress, Eva Braun, whom he finally married moments before committing suicide. Untrusting, he always felt that his failures resulted from the enmity or failure of others, even those close to him. He was able, however, to maintain his conduct within nominally acceptable bounds, and some persons considered him to be no more than a "crank." He ruled Germany from 1933-45. (See also HITLER'S SEIZURE OF POWER; NAZI PARTY; NAZI REPRESSION; SECOND WORLD WAR; WEIMAR REPUBLIC.)

Autographed photo of Hitler. (*Source:* SPP.)

HITLER'S SEIZURE OF POWER, 1933. When Heinrich Brüning (q.v.) was dismissed as chancellor in May 1932 because of his inability to muster a parliamentary majority, German politics was dominated by the senile octogenarian, Paul von Hindenburg (q.v.), and three intriguers, Hitler, General Kurt von Schleicher and Baron Franz von Papen (qq.v.). The latter had been the German military attache in Washington during the first part of the First World War (q.v.) who later was expelled from the U.S. for spying. In the twilight of the Weimar Republic (q.v.), many Germans had the impression that there were only two alternatives: the conservatives, with their established position in the army, civil and diplomatic service on the one hand, and Hitler, who stood at the head of a dynamic mass movement on the other. It turned out that Hitler, who had a much clearer idea of what he wanted than did his political opponents, had the advantage. He was no democrat, but he was a populist, whose power was based on the masses, not upon the country's elites. He was in some political trouble because his party had lost two million votes in the parliamentary elections of November 1932. In this last free election in prewar Germany, two out of three Germans voted against Hitler, and most of those who supported him in that election had not approved of all that he was to do in the following 13 years.

Hitler refused to participate in any coalition in which he was not chancellor, and Hindenburg wearily tried every conceivable conservative combination to prevent the chancellorship from going to Hitler, whom he personally despised. But all efforts failed. Von Papen finally persuaded the aged president that he, von Papen, could control the upstart Hitler. So, on January 30, 1933, Hindenburg, backed to the wall, appointed Hitler chancellor in a cabinet containing only three Nazis. Political responsibility usually forces radicals and ideologues to adopt more moderate, practical viewpoints, a historical fact which must have quieted Hindenburg's worries at the time. Hitler came to power by miscalculation, rather than by overwhelming popular demand. His ascension to power was neither inevitable nor a culmination of a thousand years of German history, as he asserted; such an evaluation would honor Hitler far too greatly. In some unsteady situations, such as in 1933, power is like a ripe piece of fruit waiting to be picked by that person who is most ready to act decisively. On January 30, 1933, that person was Adolf Hitler.

For a few weeks, Hitler had to be cautious because he had no parliamentary majority, by coalition or otherwise, and because

Hindenburg, who was still very cool toward him, had not given him permission to exercise emergency powers. But an incident during the night of February 27, 1933, gave Hitler the chance to throw off most of the restraints on his power and put an end to the Weimar Republic (q.v.). On that night the Reichstag was gutted by fire. Controversy still surrounds this incident, but it is probable that the fire was set by the Nazis themselves. Hitler acted "quickly as lightning" (which along with "ice cold" was one of his favorite expressions). He declared that this had been an act of communist violence and won Hindenburg's formal approval the next day to suspend constitutional guarantees for individual and civil liberties.

During the first four weeks of Hitler's chancellorship the courts had dared to reject many of the high-handed methods employed by Hermann Göring's (q.v.) Prussian police force to victimize the Nazis' political opponents. That was no longer possible because Hitler now wielded emergency powers and thereby had the ability to terrorize Germans through instruments of the state. His storm troopers could race through the streets arresting socialists, communists and liberal party leaders, taking sledge hammers to newspaper presses, breaking up all opposition political meetings and terrorizing the entire nation. Neither Hindenburg nor the army resisted these moves.

In this atmosphere of violence and intimidation, the last election of the Weimar Republic was held on March 5, 1933. The Nazis were still unable to receive more than 44 percent of the popular vote. But by scaring and arresting enough members of parliament, Hitler was able to manipulate a majority in the Reichstag in favor of the so-called "Enabling Act" (q.v.), which in effect suspended parliament's power and made Hitler the sole leader of Germany. Only the SPD (q.v.) dared to vote against this. Only a few more steps were necessary to give him full dictatorial power.

HITLER WAVE. This swept the FRG in the 1970s in the form of films, records and photo-articles. It focused on the person of the *Führer* and stimulated a popular cult-like interest in him. The overemphasis of Hitler's personality reached its peak in the filming of Joachim Fest's biography of Hitler.

HITLER YOUTH (HITLERJUGEND--HJ). In their effort to convert the entire German population to their notions of the "National Socialist spirit," the Nazis (q.v.) placed great emphasis on winning the minds of young people. After taking power in 1933, they banned all other youth groups but the Catholic ones, which were somewhat protected by a Concordat (q.v.) signed with the Vatican. Although membership was not required until the Reich Law of December 1, 1936, declared the HJ to be the "state youth," many young Germans were initially attracted to its activities involving camping and sports. Through the "Labor Service" they could go out in the countryside to work on farms or in forests. "Strength through Joy" (q.v.) offered cheap package holidays which included sports and physical fitness. Also, the HJ principle that "youth must be led by youth" appealed to many young persons' yearning for independence. The organization consisted of "German Young People" (boys aged 10 to 14), "Hitler Youth" (boys aged 14 to 18), "Young Girls" (aged 10 to 14), and "Federation of German Girls" (aged 14 to 18). As war came, the HJ's activities were increasingly devoted to military preparation, and in the final months of the war its members were even drafted into service as helpers on anti-aircraft weapons or as soldiers in the Home Guard (*Heimwehr*). In this way, many died a senseless death or became prisoners of war.

As the Hitler Youth became more focused on military preparation, some German youngsters rebelled by forming groups of their own outside the official Nazi youth organization. The Edelweiss Pirates were gangs of young people from working-class families. They hiked, organized sports contests, and went out of their way to lead alternative life styles and show their independence from the stifling strictures of Nazi organization. They sometimes even found their fun in ambushing Hitler Youth groups and beating up on them. It was a source of concern for Nazi leaders to find a way of winning these rebels to their cause. A different form of subculture emerged among children from upper class families--the "Swing movement." They avoided Germanic music, favoring American jazz and music in English. Swing clubs sprang up in many cities. The young people who joined them were apolitical and not necessarily anti-fascist. But they kept themselves aloof from National Socialism. The Edelweiss and Swing subcultures showed that the Nazis were not able to get a complete grip on German society.

HOCHHUTH, ROLF (1931-). This writer's special technique is to use prominent characters in recent history as antagonists (eg. Pope Pius XII or Sir Winston Churchill) against whom he directs accusations. His first two plays, *Der Stellvertreter* and *Soldaten*, deal with man's inhumanity toward man. The construction of his work is imaginative and lively, and the message is so controversial as to invite libel against him. (See also DENAZIFICATION.)

HOEGNER, WILHELM see LAND PRINCES

HÖFER, WERNER (1913-). Werner Höfer was long-time host for the popular Sunday noon discussion among journalists, *Internationaler Frühschoppen*. In 1973 he was awarded the FRG's "Grand Service Cross" (*Grosses Verdienstkreuz*). Although never having denied joining the Nazi Party in March 1933, it was uncovered that he had written countless articles for the Nazi (q.v.) gazette, *12 Uhr Blatt*, during the Third Reich (q.v.). In one writing he had praised the 1943 execution of piano virtuoso Karl-Robert Kreiten, who in private had criticized Hitler and said that the war was lost. That Höfer signed his articles under his own name was a sign that he was considered at that time to have been beyond ideological reproach. (See also DENAZIFICATION.)

HOFFMANN, ERNST THEODOR AMADEUS (1776-1822). This Romantic (q.v.) writer of the fantastic novel can be compared to Edgar Allen Poe, whose subjects and style are similar. Both blend horror and weirdness with scientific realism. Hoffmann was a lawyer and an accomplished musician, who wrote the opera, *Undine*, in addition to many tales and novels.

HOHENLOHE-SCHILLINGSFÜRST, CHLODWIG PRINCE ZU (1819-1901). Imperial chancellor 1894-1900.

HOHENZOLLERN DYNASTY. Tracing its roots to one of Charlemagne's (q.v.) generals, the Count of Zollern in Swabia, this southern German house became the Prussian (q.v.) royal family in 1525 (with the title of "king" in 1701) and the German imperial family from 1871. The last Hohenzollern emperor was Wilhelm II (q.v.), who abdicated and fled to Holland on November 9, 1918. A branch of the family, the Hohenzollern-Sigmaringen, reigned in Rumania from 1866 to 1947. (See also PRUSSIA.)

HOLBEIN, HANS, THE YOUNGER (1497-1543). Although he came from Augsburg, Holbein spent most of his life outside of Germany. A draftsman and portrait painter, he became the court painter for Henry VIII. A considerable number of his portraits, including that of St.

Thomas More, were either destroyed or lost. (See also RENAISSANCE.)

HÖLDERLIN, JOHANN CHRISTIAN FRIEDRICH (1770-1843). Hölderlin spent most of his productive years as a tutor, became insane at the age of 36, and lived on another 37 years. He is considered the most purely Hellenistic of the German poets. One of his best known prose works is *Hyperion*, which deals with a young Greek and his country's struggle against Turkey.

HOLOCAUST. This term refers generally to a great or total destruction, especially by fire. But since Hitler's (q.v.) brutal rampage in Europe, it has come to refer to his policy of massive slaughter, especially the genocide against Jews. To help its citizens learn more about this aspect of the Third Reich (q.v.), the Bonn government decided in 1979 to have the American television mini-series *Holocaust* aired in the FRG, despite criticism of its commercial Hollywood qualities. Because of the fear of how young people might react to it, warnings were given not to watch it alone, and hot lines were set up to deal with emotional crises it could cause. Thousands of schools and universities organized discussions about the series, which enjoyed astonishing audience ratings of about 40 percent. Also, some major German cities in the 1980s followed up with exhibits on the Third Reich which would have been unthinkable earlier.

One way the FRG countered ignorance about the Hitler era since the mid-1960s was to improve the school curriculum dealing with the subject. By the 1990s most teachers had not been adults during the Nazi period and are therefore far less inhibited to talk about all aspects of the past. Some take pupils to concentration camps (q.v.), such as Dachau, which is Germany's fourth most visited site and which attracts about 6,000 school groups each year. Young Germans also have the opportunity to speak with former Jewish inhabitants of their cities, who are invited back to their hometowns for visits and discussions. The effort in the schools is boosted by a greater openness in all German society to discussion dealing with the Nazi era. As fewer and fewer Germans who experienced Hitler as adults are still alive, children no longer need to feel ashamed of their parents' past. Because guilt has become less personalized, it is not so difficult to talk about it. The sudden reappearance of anti-Semitic vandalism in 1992, especially in eastern Germany, where pupils had been taught that the GDR (q.v.)

bore no responsibility for Nazi crimes, again aroused concern inside and outside of Germany that this shameful part of German history has still not been adequately understood. (See also ANTI-SEMITISM; HITLER WAVE; OVERCOMING THE PAST.)

HOLY ALLIANCE see CONGRESS OF VIENNA

HOLY ROMAN EMPIRE see GERMAN EMPIRE

HOME GUARD (HEIMWEHR) see HITLER YOUTH

HONECKER, ERICH (1912-94). General secretary of SED (1971-89), chairman of state council of GDR (1976-1989). Ousted from power on October 18, 1989, he first took refuge in an SED (q.v.) party compound, then in the home of a pastor. In April 1990 his Soviet protectors took him to a military hospital near Berlin. When German authorities issued an arrest warrant and tried to enter the Soviet base to enforce it in March 1991, he was flown to Moscow out of reach of German law. The Kremlin admitted that this had been a "technical violation" of German sovereignty. The FRG tolerated such incidents with little more than bland diplomatic protests because it did not want to antagonize the wounded superpower. An American diplomat put it this way: "The Soviets have done things that are not nice, but the Germans have their eye on the ball, and the ball is a timely troop withdrawal. The German interest is to smooth over any bumps."

Honecker's luck ran out when the Soviet Union collapsed in December 1991, and he fled to the Chilean embassy in Moscow to avoid extradition to Germany to face charges. When the Marxist Allende regime was overthrown in Chile in 1973, the GDR (q.v.) had offered refuge to Chilean leftists, and now it was time to reciprocate. On July 29, 1992, he was forced to return to Germany to face charges of manslaughter, corruption, and breach of trust. The manslaughter charges stem from his having personally supervised the construction of the Berlin Wall (q.v.), which GDR authorities called the "Anti-Fascist Barrier," along which ca. 350 deaths had occurred, although no document had been found in which Honecker personally signed "shoot-to-kill" orders. He was put into the same Moabit jail where he had been imprisoned by the Nazis, and on November 12, 1992, his trial began.

The case against him was tricky because the FRG was prosecuting a man to whom it had given a red-carpet official welcome in 1987 and because he was being tried under the laws of one country (the FRG) for acts committed under the laws of another (the GDR). The arrest of the GDR's former premier, Willi Stoph, defense minister, Heinz Kessler (who was planning to flee to the USSR), and two other SED leaders, Fritz Streletz and Hans Albrecht, was also ordered, and they went on trial with Honecker. As Joachim Gauck (q.v.), director of the agency investigating Stasi (q.v.) files, admitted: "Charges, accusations. The memories, the pain and sadness, the failures--that will last very long. We must face it. We must show ourselves that injustice, and especially injustice in high places, does not pay." Nevertheless, on January 12-13, 1993, all charges against Honecker were dropped, and he was permitted to join his family in Chile. Berlin's Constitutional Court ruled that "it violates respect for human rights to keep in jail an accused person who is suffering from an incurable illness." He was dying of liver cancer. He died an unrepentant Communist May 29, 1994. (See also GERMAN DEMOCRATIC REPUBLIC; HONECKER, FALL OF; PARTY OF DEMOCRATIC SOCIALISM; SOCIALIST UNITY PARTY.)

HONECKER, FALL OF. Because Erich Honecker had no intention of stepping down, he had to be forced to do so in what he later described as a "conspiratorial" purge by his "crown prince," Egon Krenz, and secret police chief Erich Mielke (qq.v.) in a session of the central committee on October 18, 1989. To Honecker's astonishment, all politburo members applauded his "resignation." He was succeeded by Krenz, a typical "apparatchik," whose aim was cautiously to introduce reforms within the framework of "real existing socialism" (a euphemism for Soviet-style communism) and to regain the political initiative and control over East German society. He failed to notice that the country was riven with dissatisfaction, that it was steering toward a political revolution, and that he enjoyed no credibility within the GDR (q.v.). Party members were also skeptical. They did not know whether this change was merely cosmetic or a new policy. They knew quite well that Krenz, although the youngest member on the politburo, was a man from the old elite. At no time was Krenz able to gain the initiative and exercise control over the party and society. Hundreds of thousands gathered at huge demonstrations throughout the country demanding: "Let the Stasi [State Security] work in the factories!" and "Down with the SED!" Thousands of citizens fled the GDR. The party itself was faced with mass desertions. From January to early November 1989 about 66,000 members left the SED, three-quarters of them workers.

The former "leading party" was in a state of disarray; "democratic centralism" broke down, and the SED (q.v.) was on its way to impotence.

HONECKER, MARGOT (1927-). Former culture and education minister in the GDR (q.v.), she fled to the Soviet Union with her husband, Erich (q.v.). When he was returned to Germany in July 1992 to face charges, she fled to Chile, where their daughter lives. She faced an investigation in Germany dealing with her possible links to the GDR's earlier forced adoption program, under which citizens deemed to be politically unreliable were forced to give up their children to politically loyal families.

HORST WESSEL SONG. Written by a young street brawler who became a national hero after his death, this became the official Nazi (q.v.) anthem.

HUBERTUSBURG, PEACE OF (1763) see PRUSSIA

HUGENBERG, ALFRED (1865-1951). Business leader and chairman of DNVP (1928-33), economics minister (1933). (See also GERMAN NATIONAL PEOPLE'S PARTY; HARZBURG FRONT.)

HUGUENOTS see PRUSSIA

HUMBOLDT, ALEXANDER VON (1769-1859). Brother of Wilhelm von Humboldt (q.v.), Alexander was a famous naturalist whose long voyages to South America in the first third of the 19th century not only brought to Europe new species of plants and animals to study but also greater understanding of climate determining currents, such as the Humboldt Current named after him. Living in a time of revolution and counter-revolution, Alexander provided a liberal voice in discussions about authoritarianism and constitutional government. In his honor, a government-funded foundation exists, with headquarters in Bonn-Bad Godesberg and an office in Washington, to enable foreign scholars to do a wide range of research in Germany, especially on natural sciences.

HUMBOLDT, WILHELM VON (1767-1835). A lawyer, diplomat, and intimate friend of Friedrich Schiller (q.v.), Wilhelm reformed the system of higher education in Germany and founded the University of

Berlin (later renamed Humboldt University) in 1810. From 1809 he was Director of the Prussian Administration of Culture and Education. Under his guidance the educational system was taken over by the state, the universal requirement to attend school introduced, and the curriculum revamped. Berlin University became the intellectual center of the growing movement to liberate Prussia from Napoleonic rule. It was also the cradle of the concepts of "academic freedom" and the "unity of teaching and research," which remain key pillars of the German university system today. (See also FRENCH REVOLUTION.)

HUSSERL, EDMUND (1859-1938). Working in Prossnitz and Göttingen, Husserl published *Logical Investigations* in 1901, in which he detached logic from psychology. He is the father of "phenomenology," which posits that objects of thought have an existence independent of the processes by which they are apprehended. Phenomenology avoids the concern with matter and mind because that is outside the pure phenomena of experience. He did not consider his system to be idealistic, materialistic, or metaphysical.

-I-

INDEPENDENT SOCIAL DEMOCRATIC PARTY OF GERMANY (UNABHÄNGIGE SPD--USPD) see COMMUNISM IN GERMANY; SPARTACISTS

INDUSTRY UNION (INDUSTRIE GEWERKSCHAFT--IG). Unions in particular industrial branches, such as IG CHEMIE (Chemistry and Pharmaceuticals), IG DRUCK (Printing), and IG METALL.

INITIATIVE PEACE AND HUMAN RIGHTS see ALLIANCE 90

INNERE FÜHRUNG see BUNDESWEHR and BUNDESWEHR UNIVERSITIES

INTERMEDIATE-RANGE NUCLEAR FORCES (INF). Severe domestic criticism of the FRG's defense policy was unleashed by NATO's "Two-Track Decision" in 1979 to deploy American INF missiles (with a range under 3,000 kilometers) in Europe. Mobile ground-launched Pershing II and Tomahawk missiles capable of reaching targets in the USSR would be deployed in Germany and other

NATO (q.v.) countries if the Soviet Union did not agree in negotiations to remove its mobile SS-20 missiles with multiple warheads, which could reach targets anywhere in Europe. When Moscow refused, deployment of the American missiles began in 1983. Chancellor Helmut Schmidt (q.v.) was the most persistent and influential proponent of the plan, and his government fully supported it, despite bitter opposition by the peace movement (q.v.).

The FRG's key role in having this decision adopted and the domestic reaction to it reveal a unique German dilemma as far as U.S. nuclear weapons are concerned. On the one hand, the FRG has always harbored fears that the United States might disengage its nuclear forces from the defense of the FRG; that is, it fears that the "American guarantee" could be withdrawn. On the other hand, many Germans fear nothing more than that the Americans might just decide to use their nuclear weapons to defend Western Europe after all.

Failure to prevent the Pershing missile deployment in 1983 left the "peace movement" divided and disillusioned. But a consequence of the furious public debate was that the government must pay heed to domestic opinions on defense questions. It must explain to the public far more persuasively the necessity and rationale for the country's defense and for its military collaboration with the NATO and the United States. In 1987 the U.S. and Soviet Union agreed in a landmark treaty to destroy all INF missiles. (See NORTH ATLANTIC TREATY ORGANIZATION; NUCLEAR WEAPONS; OVERCOMING THE PAST; PEACE MOVEMENT.)

INTERZONAL TRADE AGREEMENT (1951). Under the terms of this agreement, the FRG's trade with the GDR (q.v.) was granted preferential treatment. This was only briefly interrupted in 1960 in retaliation for GDR harassment on the transit routes to West Berlin. Such preferences were assured when the FRG joined the EC (q.v.) in 1957 and persuaded its Western European partners to treat East German exports to the FRG or West Berlin as "domestic trade" and therefore free of all tariffs. This economic advantage, which none of the GDR's Communist partners enjoyed, stemmed from the FRG's willingness to pay a high price to maintain contacts between the two Germanys even during times of tension. It was a major reason why the GDR could offer its population the greatest prosperity in the East Bloc.

-J-

JÄCKEL, EBERHARDT see DENAZIFICATION

JÄGER 90 (EUROPEAN FIGHTER) see RÜHE, VOLKER

JAHN, FRIEDRICH LUDWIG (1778-1852) see CARLSBAD ACTS

JAHN, GERHARD (1927-). SPD, minister of justice (1969-74).

JASPERS, KARL (1883-1969). Working in Oldenburg and Heidelberg, Jaspers applied the method of psychopathology to philosophy and advocated giving psychology and history a significant place in the study of philosophy. He attempted to construct a psychological system of world views.

In the 1960s, a skeptical Jaspers leapt into the political arena with a scathing, total critique of the FRG. The spark came from sociologist Ralf Dahrendorf's (q.v.) seminal book, *Society and Democracy in Germany*, whose thesis was that the FRG had completed its road toward normalcy, having abandoned the *Sonderweg* (special path) that had diverted Germans earlier from the path of liberal democracy. The FRG had become Germany's first modern polity in which free, politically mature individual citizens acted rationally and confidently. "The chances of liberal democracy in a German society have never been greater than they are in the German Federal Republic. . . . Authoritarianism of the traditional kind has become impossible in German society."

Jaspers strongly disagreed. He feared that the approaching Grand Coalition (q.v.) by the country's two largest parties could choke off democracy and dissent, especially if it introduced a new emergency law (q.v.). Jaspers, a long-standing nonconformist, lashed back in his 1966 book, *Wohin treibt die Bundesrepublik?* (English title: *The Future of Germany*). In his opinion, nothing had changed since the Weimar Republic (q.v.); he rejected the conclusions of Fritz René Allemann's popular 1956 book, *Bonn ist nicht Weimar* (*Bonn is not Weimar*). Jaspers charged that the FRG's rulers wanted to exclude the people from political decisions, with the Grand Coalition being a deadly step. "We see the possible path: from the party oligarchy to the authoritarian state; from the authoritarian state to dictatorship; from dictatorship to war." Even though the FRG had a parliamentary form of government, "the structure of our state rests on fear of the people, of distrust of the people." Being unconditional and unqualified, his critique was an early example of a new genre of total criticism, and it gave a boost to the re-ideologizing of West German politics in the late 1960s and 1970s.

JCS 1067 see ALLIED OCCUPATION OF GERMANY

JENNINGER, PHILIPP (1932-). Jenninger was CDU (q.v.) Bundestag president, 1984-88. During a Bundestag commemoration of the 15th anniversary of Crystal Night, he tried to explain why Hitler had been able to gain such widespread public support. But this remains an ultra-sensitive subject in Germany which permits no imprecision. He failed to find the right words or intonation and was forced to resign, to the embarrassment to the CDU.

JENS, WALTER (1923-). A writer, translator, literary historian and critic, he held a chair for rhetoric at the University of Tübingen from 1966-88, the first such position since 1829. In 1989, he became director of the Berlin Academy of Arts. He belonged to a group of young literary pacifists, *"Gruppe 47"* (q.v.), and headed West Germany's PEN center. A critic of the FRG's political life and defense policy, he opposed the deployment of American nuclear missles in Germany in the 1980s. He also sheltered American soldiers in his apartment who refused to participate in the 1991 Gulf War.

JEWS IN CONTEMPORARY GERMANY   see ANTI-SEMITISM; GALINSKI, HEINZ; MINORITIES; WANNSEE CONFERENCE

JODL, ALFRED (1890-1946). A General who from 1939 was the Chief of Staff of the Wehrmacht, he advised Hitler (qq.v.) on all strategic and operative questions. He was totally loyal to Hitler. He was found guilty of war crimes at the Nuremberg Trials (q.v.) and was executed on October 16, 1946.

JOHN, OTTO (b. 1909). A participant in the July 20, 1944, plot against Hitler (q.v.), he fled to safety. From 1950-54, he was president of the Federal Office for the Protection of the Constitution (BfV, q.v.). In 1954, he either fled or was kidnapped, and he ended up in East Berlin.

The details remain murky and controversial. He returned to the FRG in 1956, where he was sentenced to four years in prison for treason; he was released in 1958.

JULY CRISIS (1914) see FIRST WORLD WAR

JUNE 2 MOVEMENT see LORENZ, PETER

JÜNGER, ERNST (b. 1895). A writer who was shaped by his experiences at the front in the First World War (q.v.), he was strongly influenced by Friedrich Nietzsche (q.v.). He opposed both parliamentary democracy and the Nazi (q.v.) dictatorship. In the closing years of the Weimar Republic (q.v.), he had a strong influence on students. (See also WEIMAR CULTURE.)

JUNKER. This term was derived from the word, *Jungherr*, meaning young gentleman, those noble sons who served as officer cadets. "Junker" was applied to a class of Prussian (q.v.) estate-owners east of the Elbe River. It produced most of Prussia's top administrators, such as Otto von Bismarck (q.v.), and was the main pool for drawing army officers. They were inclined to be politically conservative and defenders of agrarian interests against liberalism and free trade. (See also FRENCH REVOLUTION.)

-K-

KAFKA, FRANZ (1883-1924). Due to an early death few works of this influential Jewish lawyer-turned-writer from Prague were published in his lifetime. *The Metamorphosis*, *The Trial*, and *The Castle* all deal with man trying to integrate himself in a world which is alienated from God. Kafka's highly symbolic, oblique style of writing makes his work subject to varying interpretations.

KAISEN, WILHELM (1887-1979). SPD, Mayor of Bremen (1945-65). (See also LAND PRINCES.)

KAISER, JAKOB (1888-1961). CDU, minister for all-German affairs (1949-57).

KALKAR. A controversial nuclear fast breeder reactor in Baden-Wurttemberg. In the summer of 1988, the minister president of that Land, Lothar Späth (q.v.), informed the federal government that the Land's two large electricity utilities would no longer help pay to complete the fast breeder.

KANAL, JERZY see ANTI-SEMITISM

KANT, HERMANN (1926-). A recipient of various literary prizes in the GDR (q.v.), Kant's best representative novel is *Die Aula*.

KANT, IMMANUEL (1724-1804). Kant was of Scotch and German ancestry and lived his entire life in Königsberg, from where he never travelled farther than a few miles. He read widely and was an eccentric bachelor his entire life. A professor of philosophy at the University of Königsberg from 1755-97, he also worked in astronomy. He was said to have been so punctual that housewives could set their clocks when he passed on the way to his lectures. He remains one of the giants in the world of philosophy.

His early education emphasized Leibniz's (q.v.) teachings, but he claimed that the works of David Hume jolted him out of his dogmatic slumber. He decided that Leibniz's thought placed too much confidence in human reason and led to dogmatism. By contrast, Hume engendered too little confidence in reason and led to skepticism. Thus, a careful study of the presuppositions, capacities, and limits of human reason was essential. He first proposed this in his 1770 doctoral dissertation, *On the Forms and Principles of the Sensible and Intelligible World*, and brought his analysis to completion in the *Critique of Pure Reason* (1781).

He dealt with the ethical question of what a person ought to do in his *Foundations of the Metaphysics of Morals* (1785) and *Critique of Practical Reason* (1788). He argued that morality consists of actions in accordance with consistent, necessary and universal principles, which are categorical, not conditional. He formulated his "categorical imperative": "Act in such a way that the maxim of your actions can be elevated to a universal law." In other words, one should follow a rule that every other person can also follow, and one should ask for no special privileges. Any double standard is wrong. One should claim no rights which he is not willing to grant to others. This is practical or moral reason. Because man is the rational animal on earth, he must unconditionally respect the humanity of every man. One should never regard humanity as a means to something else, but always as an end in itself.

KAPP, WOLFGANG (1858-1922) and KAPP PUTSCH see WEIMAR REPUBLIC

KÄSTNER, ERICH (1899-1974). This left-wing individualist is best known for his poems, novels, and children's books. His satire against the Nazis (q.v.) resulted in the banning and then burning of his books in 1933. He lived in exile and eventually settled in Munich after the war. His children's books are immensely popular, and many have been made into films. (See also WEIMAR CULTURE.)

KATYN FOREST, MASSACRE AT (1939) see NAZI REPRESSION

KAUTSKY, KARL (1854-1938). Born in Prague, he was a friend of Karl Marx (q.v.). He became well known as a socialist leader at the 1901 Lübeck SPD (q.v.) party congress when he opposed the revisionist ideas of Eduard Bernstein (q.v.), who advocated the gradual achievement of socialism through parliamentary reform. Kautsky was a pacifist and leftist during the First World War (q.v.), who opposed the Bolshevik Revolution in 1917 and the very concept of "dictatorship of the proletariat" as a distortion of true Marxism. After editing a collection of foreign office papers to discredit the Hohenzollern monarchy (q.v.), he moved to Vienna and became recognized as Europe's most incisive social democratic theorist. After the *Anschluss* (q.v.) in 1938, he fled to Holland, where he died.

KEITEL, WILHELM (1882-1946). Chief of Oberkommando der Wehrmacht (OKW), he was sentenced to death at the Nuremberg Trials (q.v.).

KELLER, GOTTFRIED (1819-1890). This Swiss writer and poet spent most of his life in Zürich. His novels *Der grüne Heinrich*, completed in Berlin, and *Kleider Machen Leute (Clothes Make the Man)*, are lively and humorous examples of this representative of Poetic Realism (q.v.).

KELLY, PETRA (1947-1992). A pacifist and environmentalist, she was a founder of the Greens (q.v.). She took the name of her American stepfather, a U.S. Army colonel. She attended high schools and American University in the U.S. and began her political activity in the presidential campaigns of Robert Kennedy and Hubert Humphrey, as well as the anti-Vietnam War protests in the U.S. She brought something of the tactics and fervor of that movement to the Greens. She was intense, hyperactive, extroverted, and a charismatic speaker. She was an important source of encouragement for protest movements in the GDR (q.v.). She coined the expression "anti-party party" to describe the Greens, whom she helped establish. She served in the Bundestag from 1983 to 1990 and became linked with the more pragmatic "*Realos*" within the Green party, although she maintained an independent position. Like Gert Bastian (q.v.), she opposed Green practices, including the rotation of their representatives in the Bundestag. In 1984, she accused the party of trying to create a "dictatorship of incompetence," and in 1990 she charged it with "self-destruction and fruitless, paralyzing infighting." Both she and Bastian became increasingly isolated within the party and reclusive in their private lives. On October 19, 1992, their bodies were found in the house they shared in Bonn. According to the police, Bastian shot Kelly in her sleep and then himself. (See also GREENS.)

KEMPOWSKI, WALTER. (1929-). Originally from Rostock, Kempowski was imprisoned in 1948 and accused of being an American spy. Released in 1956, he began writing six autobiographical novels tracing the history of a bourgeois family from the Kaiser era to the 1950s. His style reflects a sense of the grotesque and a precision of detail. He also writes radio dramas and is active in education reform.

KESSLER, HEINZ see HONECKER, ERICH

KIESINGER, KURT GEORG (1904-1988). CDU, minister president of Baden-Wurttemberg (1958-66), chancellor (1966-69). Known as "King Silver Tongue," who, to use Helmut Schmidt's (q.v.) words, "spoke garlands," Kiesinger loved to discuss scholarly cultural topics and pursue his favorite activities: the "three R's--*Reisen, Reden, Repräsentieren*"(travelling, speaking, representing). He institutionalized a workable way to manage the Grand Coalition (q.v.), in which he served as chancellor. In August 1967, he called Herbert Wehner, Willy Brandt (qq.v.), and future CDU secretary general Bruno Heck together in the small Swabian village of Kressbronn to discuss problems in a pleasant atmosphere of informality and good wines. All future meetings of the "Kressbronn Circle" met in Bonn and included other top leaders, but the informal atmosphere was retained during the Grand Coalition. (See also DENAZIFICATION; GRAND COALITION.)

KINKEL, KLAUS (1936-). FDP, a long-standing colleague and protege of Hans-Dietrich Genscher (q.v.), Kinkel, a Swabian lawyer, was named as head of the Federal Intelligence Service in 1979, where he remained until 1982. He served as parliamentary state secretary in the justice ministry until January 1991, when he became minister of justice in the Kohl (q.v.) government. When Genscher stepped down as foreign minister in May 1992, Kinkel replaced him. He brought a new style to German diplomacy, eschewing the practice of speaking with foggy formulations. (See also SCHWAETZER, IRMGARD.)

KIRCHNER, ERNST LUDWIG (1880-1938). The leader of *Die Brücke* (q.v.), Kirchner evolved from a realist to an expressionist (q.v.). He suffered a breakdown and left the army, settling in Switzerland, where he remained until his death. His post-expressionistic style became more decorative, reflecting the new attitude of the artist toward his environment.

KIRSCH, SARAH (1935-). A GDR (q.v.) poet and feminist writer who at age 42 was asked to leave her country due to her political activity; her poems deal with everyday perceptions and personal experiences.

KLARSFELD, BEATE (1939-). In November 1968 this consummate Nazi-hunter, who resides in France, publicly slapped Chancellor Kurt Georg Kiesinger (q.v.) in the face for his role in Hitler's (q.v.) Reich. (See also DENAZIFICATION.)

KLEIST, HEINRICH VON (1777-1811). Kleist's literary work, his essays and letters are testimony to the inner struggles which dominated his life and prompted his early suicide. His place in literature is between Classicism and Romanticism (qq.v.) because of his pre-occupation with ethics and his interest in the inner workings of the mind.

KLOPSTOCK, FRIEDRICH GOTTLIEB (1724-1803). In his various religious poems, Klopstock glorified religion and nature and also revived interest in his Germanic past with his drama, *The Battle of Hermann*. He is considered a forerunner of the Storm and Stress (q.v.). (See also AMERICA, GERMAN ATTITUDES.)

KLOSE, HANS-ULRICH (1937-). SPD, Hamburg interior minister (1973-74) and mayor (1974-81). He resigned as mayor when his party did not support his efforts to withdraw from nuclear energy projects. He won Herbert Wehner's (q.v.) seat to the Bundestag in 1983 and became SPD treasurer in 1987. In 1991 he was elected chairman of the SPD Bundestag parliamentary group.

KLUGE, ALEXANDER (1932-). As the intellectual lawyer and writer among the New Wave directors, Kluge is considered the "father" of the German New Wave of the 1970s with his theory of realism and the power of the film to activate the audience's imagination.

KNIGGE, ADOLF FREIHERR VON (1752-1796). The "Miss Manners" of his time, Knigge wrote a book of etiquette for self-improvement designed to raise the self-esteem of the middle class.

KNIGHTS, GERMAN ORDER OF. The Crusades, which began at the end of the 11th century, sparked the imagination of a class of persons which had begun to emerge before the 10th century: the knights. Warfare had been revolutionized in such a way that foot soldiers were replaced by well-armed knights who often fought on horseback. Therefore, the high nobility required knights to live in their vicinity or in fortresses or estates which the lords placed at their disposal. Most of the knights in the earlier days were not of noble birth, so they attempted to make up for their humble status by developing certain virtues such as bravery, courage, loyalty and consistency. The highest virtue was moderation in every situation but battle.

One of Friedrich Barbarossa's (q.v.) sons founded a "German Order of Knights" in 1198, whose initial mission was to care for pilgrims and crusaders in the Holy Lands. It soon joined the active military struggles against the Islamic "disbelievers" who had asserted an allegedly unjust claim to the Holy City of Jerusalem. The Order took in both knights, priests and other brothers who could perform useful services, and its uniform was a white cloak with a black cross on it. Their rules were as strict as those in a monastic order. Since they saw themselves as fully dedicated to the service of Christ, they did not marry. They were forbidden to own property, and they swore to maintain absolute loyalty and personal poverty.

Less than a quarter of a century after the Order was founded, its sights were cast in an entirely different geographic direction. A Polish Duke, Conrad of Masovia, asked for the Order's help in 1226 to assist in crushing a hardy tribe of "heathens" called "Prussians." This was a Baltic people related to the Lithuanians and Latvians and regarded by Germans and Poles alike as barbarians. They had no written language, but they had strange customs such as polygamy and placing unwanted babies out to die. The conquest and Christianizing of such a tribe received the blessing of the Pope and the approval of the Holy Roman Emperor. With such encouragement and advancement under the call of "Death to Disbelievers," this conquest was bound to be a cruel one. The Order crossed the Vistula River in 1231 in order to engage the Prussians. Not until 1283 was the bloody job completed and the entire territory from the Vistula to the farthest border of East Prussia (that portion of Prussia east of the Vistula estuary) brought under the Order's control. The struggle had devastated much of the land and almost completely eradicated the Prussian tribe. The remnants were converted to Christianity upon the threat of death and were ultimately absorbed by the German conquerors. Their language disappeared completely, and all that remained of them was the name "Prussia," by which the territory came to be known and which became the official name of the state in 1701.

The German Order created a holy republic over the land, and in 1309 the Order's Supreme Master, who was elected by the other knights, moved his seat from Venice to the fortress of Marienburg in Prussia (now in Poland). From there commands were issued to fortresses and cities throughout the entire area. It became a German-led, rigidly organized land administered by the knights, who since they were forbidden to own property, possess wealth, or marry were more like ascetic civil servants than feudal lords. They directed the systematic colonization of the land and were responsible for the establishment of more than 1,000 villages and 100 cities, including the major ones, Danzig (now Gdansk in Poland), Elbing and Königsberg (now Kaliningrad in Russia). Until well into the 15th century, the history of Prussia is the history of colonization, and in some areas this was more violent than in others. Nowhere were the Slavic or Baltic populations forced to move. Germans, Slavs and Balts lived side-by-side, although in most places the key political and economic positions were occupied by Germans. The nobility and bourgeoisie were predominantly German, but the agricultural population was mixed. This condition continued more or less to exist until Hitler and Stalin launched massive exterminations and expulsions in the 20th century to homogenize the ethnic composition in these areas.

The German Order of Knights reached its pinnacle in the 14th century, but its hold over the area was broken in the 15th century. Poles and Lithuanians attacked Prussia in 1410 and delivered the knights a crushing defeat on a wet and stormy day in the woods of Tannenberg. This was the first major military defeat which the Order had ever suffered. Sensing the way the wind was blowing, many German noblemen sided with the Poles. Only Marienburg remained unconquered, but new battles eventually drove the Order out of all the area except East Prussia, which in 1466 became a tributary of Poland. The Order was compelled to swear loyalty to Poland.

KNIGHTS' REBELLION. There was a rebellion of knights in 1522 led by Franz von Sickingen. Compared to the growing bourgeoisie (middle-upper class), which was becoming more and more prosperous in the cities, the economic importance of that portion of the lower nobility which had also been knighted, such as barons, was steadily declining. Also, armored knights on horseback had become militarily obsolete since Swiss infantry armed with halberds (a wide-shaped axe on a long pole) had learned to decimate their opponents with relative ease. Because of this, Swiss foot soldiers, not knights, became the treasured military mercenaries in half of Europe. The knights had lost most of their income and all justification for existing. Their rebellion was a desperate attempt to turn the clock back in Germany, but it was crushed by the princes. The status of knighthood was thereby eliminated once and for all as a power factor in Europe.

KNOERINGEN, WALDEMAR VON (1906-1971). A Bavarian Social Democrat, he emigrated in 1933. He was chairman of the Bavarian SPD (1947-53), member of the Bundestag (1949-51), and vice-chairman of the SPD (1958-62).

KOHL, HELMUT (1930-). Minister president of Rhineland Palatinate (1969-76), chairman of CDU (1973-), chancellor (1982-). The political and economic success of Kohl, the first German chancellor to have been too young to have played any role in Nazi (q.v.) Germany, helped restore in many citizens an interest and pride in being German. Kohl and his party believe that Germans have atoned enough for the nation's past sins. Kohl frequently speaks of the "Fatherland" and the *Heimat* ("Homeland"). He has also encouraged displays of patriotism and the frequent playing of the national anthem. In Baden-Wurttemberg, school children may be taught all three verses of *Deutschland, Deutschland über Alles*. President Richard von Weizsäcker (q.v.) occasionally deflates such self-satisfaction by reminding Germans of the seamier side of their past, while encouraging them to be proud of what they have accomplished since 1945.

In many ways, Kohl's chancellorship has been a success: both the "peace movement" and the bitter debates over the installation of new American missiles in Germany died down and were muted by arms control treaties and reunification (q.v.). He has maintained close relations with the U.S., Britain, and France while getting along as well with the Soviet Union as his SPD (q.v.) predecessors had. He signalled a strong interest in protecting the environment by creating a ministry of the environment.

He had to take the blame for some embarrassing reversals. In 1985, he persuaded the American president to pay homage to the German war dead buried in a cemetery in Bitburg, without learning in time that SS soldiers were also buried there. The president's visit unleashed a storm of protest among Jewish and veteran groups in the U.S., and both houses of the U.S. Congress passed resolutions imploring the president to reconsider the visit. What had been intended as a gesture of reconciliation and friendship actually revived memories of the Holocaust (q.v.) and the war, and it seriously strained relations between these two friendly nations.

The Kohl government pursued the policy of detente with the GDR (q.v.) and the USSR with as much vigor as had the SPD while in power. Like most West German leaders, Kohl no longer believed that German reunification (q.v.) could be achieved in the present era. In 1987, he stated in Moscow that he personally would never live to see the day when the two Germanys would become one country. Like virtually everybody else, he was taken completely by surprise as the GDR (q.v.) collapsed before his unbelieving eyes, and the elusive German unity fell into his lap.

Lauded in the press as "King Kohl," "happy giant," and "the sun-chancellor at the height of power" after his dramatic federal election victory, Kohl's popularity went into a rapid free-fall in 1991 for several reasons. When Germany's allies launched the Gulf War to end Iraq's occupation of Kuwait, the Bonn government vacillated, while pacifist street demonstrations denounced the allies as "aggressors." Thus, the world saw Germany as an unreliable ally in its first international crisis as a reunified nation. In the wake of widespread fear that Germany would be dragged into the war, voters in Hesse awarded the SPD and Greens (q.v.) a narrow majority in January 1991.

Then, after promising before the 1990 election not to raise taxes to pay for reunification, he decided to introduce one of the largest tax raising measures in German history. He blamed the levy on the contributions Germany had to make to the allied war effort in the Gulf. But his economics ministry admitted that the real reason was the declining economic situation in the East. The powerful president of the central bank (Bundesbank, q.v.), Karl Otto Pöhl, who resigned shortly thereafter, publicly criticized Kohl's management of reunification: "The result is a disaster, as you can see." Dissatisfaction in the East was dramatized by massive street demonstrations there and Kohl's own pelting with eggs when he strolled the streets of Halle. Thus, his credibility suffered, as western Germans remembered his earlier tax pledge, and eastern Germans questioned why Bonn could give billions to the allies to fight a war in the Gulf, but could not pay more to rebuild the shattered economy in the East. He and many others had clearly miscalculated the expenses and problems involved in integrating eastern Germany into the FRG.

The bill for the soaring costs of unity and the tax rise came due in April 1991, when Land elections were held in his native Rhineland-Palatinate. They were viewed as a referendum on his handling of the two Germanys' merger. Pouncing on what it called Kohl's "tax lie," the SPD proclaimed that "One doesn't vote for people who lie!," as one of its posters read. Its reward was 44.8 percent of the votes, while the CDU slid from 45 percent in 1987 to 37.8 percent in 1991. This enabled the SPD to form a governing coalition with the Greens as it had done in Hesse in January. This stinging loss cost the Kohl government its majority in the Bundesrat in Bonn, thereby making it more difficult to get its legislation passed. The chancellor admitted that this election in his own home Land was "personally painful."

Kohl is one of the great survivors of German politics. His sharp instinct for the concerns of middle-class Germans serves him well. He is a skilled administrator with much political experience as former minister president of the Rhineland-Palatinate and as CDU (q.v.) party chairman. Although he was frequently criticized as being a generalist who never actually occupied a ministerial post before becoming chancellor in 1982, he is a superb integrator and is the ultimate politician of consensus who prevaricates until the outline of a possible compromise emerges from the ongoing debate. He was able to maintain close party relations with the CSU, gently woo the FDP (q.v.), and smooth out conflicts within the CDU. He exudes confidence, which is especially important in Germany. Perhaps his greatest skill is as a political survivor despite serious setbacks. His greatest accomplishment is that Germany was reunified under his guidance. (See also CHRISTIAN DEMOCRATIC UNION; OVERCOMING THE PAST.)

KOHL, MICHAEL (1929-1981). SED, director of permanent representation of the GDR (q.v.) in FRG (1974-78). He was known in the FRG because of his extended negotiations with Egon Bahr (q.v.) leading up to the Basic Treaty in 1972. (See also OSTPOLITIK.)

KOKOSCHKA, OSKAR see WEIMAR CULTURE

KOLLWITZ, KÄTHE (1867-1945). Most of her life was spent in Berlin where she was a professor. Her depictions of injustice, poverty, and life in the Berlin slums gained her work the ignoble title of "degenerate art" (q.v.) by the Nazis. Two woodcuts in particular featuring the funeral of the Communist, Karl Liebknecht (q.v.), and another, *Das Proletariat*, express her leftist political sympathies and expressionistic style. Having lost her own son in the First World War (q.v.), death was an inexhaustible theme which appeared in many variations.

KÖNIGGRÄTZ/SADOWA, BATTLE (1866) see BISMARCK, OTTO VON

KONRAD ADENAUER FOUNDATION see STIFTUNGEN

KOPERNICUS, NIKOLAUS see RENAISSANCE

KOTZEBUE, AUGUST VON (1761-1819) see CARLSBAD ACTS

KRANKENKASSEN see FEDERAL HIGHER AUTHORITIES

KRASKE, KONRAD (1926-). Federal Manager of CDU (1958-70), CDU (q.v.) general secretary (1971-73), member of Bundestag (1965-80). After retiring from politics, Dr. Kraske taught political science at the University of Freiburg, where he was well-known and respected for his rapport with and attention to students, something which is rare among professors in Germany.

KREISAU CIRCLE. Anti-Hitler resistance group which formed around Count von Moltke (qq.v.). Meeting at his estate, Kreisau, these regime opponents from all political elements worked on the ethical and moral renewal of Germany after the collapse of Nazi (q.v.) domination. They were devoted to the establishment of a sort of "co-operative society" of European states and ultimately of a European government, which would reduce the significance of the individual European states. Many of its members were executed or incarcerated by the Nazis. (See also DENAZIFICATION; RESISTANCE TO HITLER.)

KRENZ, EGON (1937-). SED (q.v.) General secretary and chairman of state council (October-December 1989). (See GERMAN DEMOCRATIC REPUBLIC, COLLAPSE; HONECKER, FALL; PARTY OF DEMOCRATIC SOCIALISM.)

KRESSBRONN CIRCLE see KIESINGER, KURT GEORG

KREUZZEITUNG PARTY. Co-founded by Bismarck (q.v.), this was on the extreme right of Prussian conservatives.

KRUPP. The Krupp works in Essen was one of Germany's major producers of arms since the middle of the 19th century. It continues to function in Germany today, although it has greatly diversified. (For KRUPP, ALFRED see DENAZIFICATION.)

KÜLZ, WILHELM (1875-1948). Liberal politician, Reich minister of interior (1926-27), mayor of Dresden (1931-33), chairman of LDPD (q.v.) from 1945 to 1948. (See also FREE DEMOCRATIC PARTY.)

KUNERT, GÜNTHER (1929-). In the 1950s this author of poetry, short stories, essays, children's books, and radio and television plays was the most productive writer in the GDR (q.v.). Kunert guest lectured in the U.S. and in England and eventually settled in the FRG.

KYFFHÄUSER, LEGEND OF see BARBAROSSA

-L-

LABOR. An economic handicap for Germany is the supply and cost of labor. For years, the FRG had a shortage of labor and even brought in "guest workers" from southern Europe and Turkey, numbering about four and a half million in the 1990s. While a majority of these guest workers remain indispensable for many sectors of the economy in which few Germans care to work, they present the FRG with immense and potentially explosive problems of social integration which will tax German ingenuity and tolerance for years to come. Also, labor costs in western Germany exceed those in the U.S. and are among the highest in Europe. The average American worker works longer hours and receives 12 days of paid vacation versus 30 for the German. Social benefits applied to each American job are half as high as in the FRG. In the past, productivity was raised to match rising labor costs, but the country's ability to do this in the future is in question, especially given the plunge of productivity in the East. The FRG has some of the highest tax rates in the OECD. Still, the FRG has a higher percentage of its work force in industrial production than in most EC (q.v.) countries. It also is one of the few leading economies in the world to have less than half its jobs in the service sector.

The FRG has a highly skilled labor force. Equally important, it enjoys a high degree of labor peace, despite restlessness among frightened eastern German workers faced with unemployment and retraining, and despite periodic tensions between employers' and employees' groups, which are called "social partners." Both vigorously represent their members' interests. But since the early postwar period, when these groups cooperated closely to help the FRG recover from the war, they have both assumed that they share responsibility for the economy as a whole. The success of this partnership is seen in the facts that strikes are relatively rare and that contracts increased wages above the inflation rate, but not so high that inflation would be seriously stimulated. The latter factor has helped generate and preserve Germany's prosperity.

After reunification, East German unions merged with those in the West. The structure of labor unions (to which about a third of all workers and employees belong) helps to ensure a great measure of labor peace. The 17 major individual trade unions each follow the principle of "one union, one industry." For example, instead of metal workers in the entire country being organized by many different and competing unions, any one of which can paralyze an industry through a strike, all metal workers who wish to be in a union join only one labor negotiating partner, not many. All 17 unions then belong to the German Trade Union Federation (DGB) which, like all individual trade unions, is independent of political parties and religious denominations. The DGB helps to coordinate trade union goals and activities, and it is listened to very carefully by all German governments on labor matters. In addition to the DGB, there are a few other trade union organizations, such as the German Salaried Employees Union (DAG) and the German Civil Servants' Federation (DBB). By law the latter is forbidden to enter collective bargaining and to call strikes.

Unions are on the defensive. They are composed largely of blue-collar workers in a white-collar world, and they are not attracting enough loyalty from young Germans. On the other side of the fence are several hundred employer organizations, many of which are part of a larger umbrella organization called the Federation of German Employers' Associations (BDA), which coordinates fundamental employer interests.

Another institution which helps to ensure labor peace is co-determination (q.v.) (*Mitbestimmung*). In all but the smallest firms, all workers, including foreigners, 18 years or older can elect representatives to a works council, which has many rights, especially in social welfare and personnel matters. Workers in large companies also send representatives to the supervisory councils which are the control organs for the companies' management. Since the 1950s, the exact composition of these supervisory councils has been a hotly debated issue because of its implications for policy-making within the various industrial units. Workers elect half the members in the large mining and steel companies and slightly less than half in other large companies. Despite the many disagreements, co-determination provides a far larger scope for worker participation in decisions made in German firms than in most other countries, including the U.S. It thereby gives labor more responsibility in the firms' policies and serves as an important stabilizing element in the economy and society.

LAFONTAINE, OSKAR (1943-). SPD, mayor of Saarbrücken (1976-86), minister president of Saarland (1986-), SPD chancellor candidate 1990. Lafontaine is a successful young SPD (q.v.) leader in the Saarland, who had once been one of the party's most outspoken leftists. He belongs to a new generation of politicians who did not directly experience Nazism (q.v.) or the division of Europe and whose political outlook was shaped more by the student rebellion of the 1960s. Preparing for the 1990 Bundestag elections, when he carried the SPD banner as its chancellor candidate, he moderated his image. Nevertheless, the SPD suffered badly in the election; voters refused to heed his warning that the reunification (q.v.) of Germany would be far more costly than Helmut Kohl (q.v.) predicted. In 1992 his career suffered a severe setback when he was implicated in a pension scandal in the Saarland. (See also SOCIAL DEMOCRATIC PARTY OF GERMANY.)

LAMBSDORFF, OTTO COUNT VON (1926-). FDP (q.v.), federal minister of economics (1977-84), FDP chairman (1988-), president of Liberal International. (See also FLICK AFFAIR; WENDE.)

LAND (LÄNDER) and STATE (LAND) GOVERNMENT. More than any other country in Europe, with the exception of Switzerland, Germany has decentralized and fragmented political power. Such decentralization is traditional in Germany, which consists of what had been a myriad of states and free cities. The only experience with highly centralized government--the Third Reich (q.v.)--left a bad taste in Germans' mouths. The FRG is now broken down into 16 states (each called a *Land,* plural: *Länder).* Most of these Länder were newly created after 1945, and the five in the former GDR (q.v.), plus unified Berlin, were recreated in 1990. The massive influx of refugees into the Western occupation zones did much to break down the formerly strong particularistic character of the various regions in Germany. But Bavaria has by far retained its own unique character, visually, culturally and politically, more than any other Land. It proudly calls itself the "Free State of Bavaria" and has never formally ratified the Basic Law (q.v.), although it has abided by it since 1949.

Each Land has its own government, the specific form of which is left entirely up to it. The Land constitutions differ considerably in some respects, but they all call for forms of parliamentary government. A government, led by a minister president, is chosen by a unicameral (except in Bavaria) parliament, called a Landtag, elected by proportional representation. Land issues play the dominant role in such Land elections, but since the early 1960s these elections, which are seldom held at the same time as national elections, have increasingly become indicators or bellwethers for citizens' approval of national policies or leaders. Therefore, national

The 16 Länder of the FRG. (*Source:* SPP.)

leaders lend their active support in local campaigns, an important reason why the voter turnout is very high by American standards, averaging about 70 percent since the early 1950s.

In keeping with German tradition and to prevent a single leader or group of leaders in the central government from gathering all strings of power, the founders granted specific exclusive powers to the Länder: education (although the national government does contribute to the financing of universities), law enforcement and internal security (although the central government does maintain an Office for the Protection of the Constitution, roughly equivalent to the FBI in the U.S., and a Federal Criminal Office, which maintains data useful to the Land police authorities), the administration of justice, and mass communications and media. Only in the areas of defense and foreign policy is the national government largely free of the Land governments. As in the U.S., all powers not expressly granted to the national government fall to the Länder. Länder used their powers over regional broadcasting to resist a unified national satellite television policy. Land leaders travel around the globe and conduct their own foreign policy.

Some have even opened offices in Brussels to influence EC (q.v.) policy and seek financial favors. The upper house (Bundesrat), which the Länder dominate, has been used to force the Bonn government to consult with them on any foreign policy deals which affect them. New, small Land-based political parties are complicating the work of the major national parties to win majorities in the Länder. All these trends underscore the fact that regional politics is more significant in the FRG than in any other European country. Almost all important political figures in Bonn rose from a strong base in the Länder.

There are two factors which prevent the Länder from being so diverse as American states: legal uniformity and shared taxation. German law, which was decisively influenced by Roman law and by the Napoleonic Code, was codified in the last three decades of the 19th century. Since the 1950s the criminal code has been in the process of revision. The point is that German law is the same in every Land. In general, the national government wields most of the legislative power while the Land governments wield most of the administrative power. The staffs of most federal ministries are relatively small. Indeed, if one excludes the employees of the Federal Railways and Federal Postal Service, only about 10 percent of public employees work for the national government, whereas roughly a third work for local governments and over half work for the Länder.

LAND PRINCES (LANDESFÜRSTEN). This was the term given to the powerful and effective regional leaders in the western German Länder after 1945. They helped reestablish the regions which had been eclipsed by Prussia (q.v.) during the preceding century. They included Reinhold Maier and Gebhard Müller in the Southwest, Wilhelm Hoegner and Hans Ehard in Bavaria, Karl Arnold and Fritz Steinhoff in the industrialized Rhineland, Max Brauer and Wilhelm Kaisen (q.v.) in Hamburg and Bremen, and Peter Altmeier in the Palatinate.

LANG, FRITZ (1890-1976). Viennese film maker who fled to the U.S. in 1934. He is best known for his film, *Metropolis*.

LARGE GERMAN SOLUTION see REVOLUTION OF 1848

LASSALLE, FERDINAND (1825-1864). Born in Breslau, Lassalle was imprisoned for his agitation for freedom and democracy. He analyzed the concept of private property in *The System of Acquired Rights* and propounded a theory on the historical development of the workers' condition. He was chiefly responsible for the formation of the General German Workers' Union.

LAW ON STABILITY AND GROWTH (1967). During the Grand Coalition (q.v.) from 1966 to 1969, this law assigned to the federal government's budgetary policy a new task of using neo-Keynesian methods to smooth out economic fluctuations. It committed the government to realize full employment, price stability, external equilibrium, and economic growth. The law created the Financial Planning Council (*Finanzplanungsrat*) and the Counter-Cyclical Economic Council (*Konjunkturrat*) to help accomplish these goals. (See also GRAND COALITION.)

LEAGUE OF WEST GERMAN COMMUNISTS (BUND WESTDEUTSCHER KOMMUNISTEN--BWK). The BWK emerged in 1980 from a split in the now defunct Communist League of West Germany (KBW), has its headquarters in Cologne, and counts approximately 300 members, organized in groups in eight Länder. Its efforts to recruit more members failed. It publishes the bi-weekly *Politische Berichte (Political Reports)*, with a circulation of about 1,200 copies. The BWK is the dominant member of the People's Front, whose business office is in the BWK's main office in Cologne. The People's Front, with about 600 members and a bi-weekly *Antifaschistische Nachrichten (Antifascist News*, circulation 600) is an instrument for an alliance of left-extremists. The BWK is willing to cooperate with the DKP (q.v.) and its affiliated or influenced organizations. It condemned the internal movements against Communist regimes in Eastern Europe as "counterrevolution."

LEBENSRAUM (LIVING SPACE). This was a Nazi (q.v.) concept that, because of overpopulation in Germany, the country needed to expand its borders and occupy other territory in order to have the space to develop and prosper. This provided an additional justification for aggressive warfare.

LEBER, GEORG (1920-). SPD, federal minister of transportation, post and communications (1966-72), and of defense (1972-78).

LEBER, JULIUS (1891-1945). SPD (q.v.) and trade unionist member of the Kreisau Circle (q.v.), he was executed for his participation in the July 20, 1944, uprising against Hitler (q.v.).

LEIBL, WILHELM (1844-1900). A very important realist painter whose *Three Women in a Village Church* records three generations of country women in a moment of prayer. This best reflects his sympathy for his subjects and his effort to show the quaintness and honesty of the rural dweller.

LEIBNIZ, BARON GOTTFRIED WILHELM VON (1646-1716). In the little free time he could find from his duties as a public official in Leipzig, Mainz, Paris, and Hanover, Leibniz mastered mathematics and developed logic in new directions, including symbolic logic. He also made discoveries in the theory of knowledge (epistemology), attacking the ideas espoused by John Locke in *Essays on Human Understanding*. In his *New Essays on Human Understanding*, Leibniz presented his view that "there is nothing in intellect which was not first in sense, except intellect itself."

He propounded a metaphysical doctrine, expressed in his 1714 treatise *Monadology*, in which all reality is to be understood in terms of units of force, rather than the inert atoms of materialism. He called these units monads and distinguished between body monads and soul monads, which constitute the scale of reality from the lowest to the highest, God being the monad of monads. Each monad is unique, lives out its own career, is not affected from the outside, and develops its own potentialities from within. Nevertheless, there is some interplay with each other. All are elements in a single system in which each is correlated with the others, just as mathematical variables are functions of each other. There is a logical preestablished harmony among them. Leibniz thought that the universe is the manifestation of Perfect Reason and is therefore the best of all possible worlds.

LEITMOTIV. This is a structural device used in literature involving the repetition of words, phrases or sentences in different contexts to attain various associations. It was originally a music term.

LENZ, SIEGFRIED (1926-). A Wehrmacht deserter who eventually returned to Hamburg to become a journalist, Lenz wrote his first novel in 1950 based on his own experiences as an escapee on the run during wartime. His works are preoccupied with the problem of guilt and the causes of human failure. He has written many short stories, dramas, critical essays, and he is a respected political journalist and broadcaster. His novel, *Deutschstunde*, is considered his best work.

LESSING, GOTTHOLD EPHRAIM (1729-1781). Lessing is considered one of the best literary critics of all time. He broke with the French tradition and created new rules for drama based on the Greek tradition of Aristotle. A Classicist (q.v.) in the purest tradition, he wrote four great plays including the first domestic tragedy (*Miss Sara Sampson*) and the first modern comedy (*Minna von Barnhhelm*), and he introduced blank verse to the German stage with *Nathan der Weise* Lessing's plays illustrated the very points he made in his literary criticism.

LEUSCHNER, WILHELM (1890-1944). SPD, Hesse minister of interior (1928-33), trade unionist and member of the Kreisau Circle (q.v.), he was executed for his participation in the July 20, 1944, uprising against Hitler (q.v.).

LEY, ROBERT see GERMAN LABOR FRONT

LIBERAL DEMOCRATIC PARTY (LIBERALDEMOKRATISCHE PARTEI--LDP) see ALLIANCE OF FREE DEMOCRATS

LIBERAL DEMOCRATIC PARTY OF GERMANY (LIBERALDEMOKRATISCHE PARTEI DEUTSCHLANDS--LDPD) see FREE DEMOCRATIC PARTY

LIBERALISM. This was an expressly political trend, a longing for the previously promised, but largely undelivered, constitutional government and individual freedom. The uprising in Paris in 1830 spread to cities all over Germany and forced the introduction of constitutions in Braunschweig, Hanover, Hesse-Cassel and Saxony. There were further uprisings in 1832. Queen Victoria ascended the British throne in 1837 which nominally included the Hanover crown. The linkage had been established in 1713 when the Hanover monarch George became King of England. Tradition forbade women from ruling Hanover. The new Hanoverian king abolished the constitution, an act publicly opposed by seven prominent professors at the University of Göttingen, including the

Grimm (q.v.) brothers. When the seven were promptly dismissed and given three days to leave the kingdom, loud voices of protest were heard throughout Germany.

It was the reaction to the reestablishment of authoritarian rule in a politically fragmented Germany which gave rise in the early 1830s to the "Young Germany" movement, to which a number of German writers belonged, most notably Heinrich Heine (q.v.) and Ludwig Börne. These young writers were convinced that literary figures should become politically active and socially critical. Their influence was so feared by the authorities that their writings were forbidden by the German Confederation in 1835, and their leading exponents were driven into exile, particularly to Paris.

Like most German intellectuals of their time, these writers saw German nationalism and liberalism as goals which went hand-in-hand. It was in this spirit that Hoffman von Fallersleben wrote a song, "Deutschland, Deutschland über alles," ("Germany, Germany above all others") in the 1840s. The melody had earlier been written by Austrian Joseph Haydn and was a well-known hymn tune in Protestant churches. This song became the national anthem for a united Germany. It is often misunderstood as having been a call for German domination over the whole world. In fact, it was directed against the disunity of Germany. It was a call for placing the goal of a united and democratic Germany above all provincial loyalties and above all inclinations to find one's own happiness in one's own private corner. The final verse, which is the FRG's anthem, sums up the song's message: "Unity and Law and Freedom for the German Fatherland." It was assumed that all these goals were inseparably linked.

LICHTENBERG, GEORG CHRISTOPH (1742-1799). Although he was a math and science professor at Göttingen, Lichtenberg is best known for his short satirical pieces and the many aphorisms (moments of spontaneous insight) he compiled about human nature.

LIEBERMANN, MAX (1847-1935). The characterization and use of light effects apparent in the early impressionist works (*eg. Munich Beer Garden*) of this Jewish painter from Berlin change to a more defined delineation which would classify Liebermann's later works as Early Realism. A humorous and witty man, he was an outspoken critic of Hitler and Nazism (qq.v.).

LIEBKNECHT, KARL (1871-1919). Son of Wilhelm Liebknecht (q.v.), Karl was a Social Democrat who became leader, along with Rosa Luxemburg (q.v.), of the Spartacist League (q.v.), and on January 1, 1919, co-founder of the KPD. He intended to proclaim the new German republic on November 9, 1918, from the balcony of the royal palace where he was speaking, but, informed of this, Social Democrat Philipp Scheidemann (q.v.) rushed to the window of the Reichstag and proclaimed it first. On January 15, 1919, he and Rosa Luxemburg were murdered by right-wing Free Corps, and their bodies were found floating in the Spree River in Berlin. (See also REVOLUTION IN GERMANY.)

LIEBKNECHT, WILHELM (1826-1900). Founder with August Bebel of the Social Democratic Workers' Party in 1869 and a leading SPD (qq.v.) politician in the German Empire.

LIST, FRIEDRICH (1789-1846). A Saxon by birth, this economist was imprisoned for advocating economic and political freedom and sought exile in the U.S. Returning in 1833, he was the first advocate of an all-German railway system radiating from Berlin. More important, he developed a theory of economic protection which emphasized national welfare over the success of an individual enterprise. In *The National System of Political Economy*, published in the year of his death, he argued that it was necessary to impose tariffs during the transition from an agrarian to manufacturing economy although free trade could be introduced later. He influenced the economic rational of the Customs Union (*Zollverein*, q.v.), which imposed increasingly heavy duties on manufactured goods.

LITERATURE, POST-1945. In literature, German writers after 1945 strove to make a clean break with the past. In their writings they tried to come to grips with their nation's experiences under dictatorship, in war and in postwar misery. In the 1950s and 1960s, though, new themes emerged, which focused on the materialism and egotism of a prosperous society. Many German writers became unmistakably political in their writings and, in a few cases, in their public involvement. The best known of such writers in the West are Heinrich Böll and Günter Grass (qq.v.). Böll, who in 1972 became the sixth German to win the Nobel Prize for Literature and who died in 1985, wrote with grace and simplicity. He was an avowed moralist, who was in the forefront of the "peace movement." Grass's German is full, rich and imaginative, and through his fantasy characters he bitterly criticizes the shortcomings of his society. Until late 1992, he was a staunch, if often critical, supporter of the SPD (q.v.). He campaigned actively for the party and even wrote about his electoral activities in a book, *From the Diary of a Snail.*

Much of contemporary western German literature is characterized by anxiety, malaise, self-doubt and social criticism. Many writers show impatience with traditional literary themes and styles, reject fixed criteria, focus sharply and without humor on the individual's problems in society, and above all, criticize their society, which they often view as unjust and hostile to individual freedom and identity. Many see themselves as initiators of resistance to the social order. The predominant picture of western Germany presented in its contemporary literature is that of a sick society.

The public is also very receptive to another kind of critical literature, namely that coming from eastern Germany, where much of the nation's best writing originates. GDR (q.v.) authors like Stefan Heym, Christa Wolf, Ulrich Plenzdorf, and Jurek Becker (qq.v.), were widely published in the West. They were popular enough to disregard the simplicity of "socialist realism" and to criticize certain characteristics of the SED (q.v.) state. Wolf was criticized for withholding some of her criticism of the regime until after the GDR's fall, when she published *Was Bleibt (What Remains)*, written ten years earlier, describing how she had been watched by the secret police.

In addition to their inclination to criticize their own society, western German writers have sought to improve their monetary position within that society. In 1969, they formed the Association of German Writers (VS), which won for writers certain material benefits, such as a law requiring libraries to pay a small fee for every book lent, which goes into a fund to finance such things as writers' supplementary pensions. The VS also has won the possibility for free-lance writers to sell their writings to the mass media at higher prices.

LOCAL GOVERNMENT. The Länder (states) largely finance and set operating rules for local governments in the communities (*Gemeinden*). Local government differs from Land to Land, but all communities have an elected council (*Stadtrat* or *Gemeinderat*). Also, each county (*Kreis*) has an elected council (*Kreistag*) led by an executive official. (See also LAND.)

LOCARNO, TREATIES OF (1925). These resulted from an international conference in Locarno in October 1925. Of the treaties produced, the most important was that which confirmed the inviolability of the Franco-German and Belgian-German borders and the demilitarized zone of the Rhineland. Those three countries signed the treaty, and the British and Italians agreed to guarantee it.

LONDON DEBT AGREEMENT (1953). By signing this agreement, the FRG assumed Germany's prewar debts and began to pay principal and interest on both prewar and postwar obligations totalling more than DM 15 billion.

LORELEI. The rocky promontory on the Rhine upon which, according to legend, sits a seductive beauty who, with her songs, lures sailors to shipwreck on the rocks below. Heinrich Heine's (q.v.) poem of the same name has become a folk song which is always played as the Rhine steamers pass this not-so-ominous spot.

LORENZ, PETER (1922-1987). CDU, president of West Berlin legislature (1975-80). On February 27, 1975, he was kidnapped by terrorists calling themselves the "June 2 Movement." He was released after five jailed terrorists were flown to South Yemen. (See TERRORIST GROUPS.)

LÖWENTHAL, RICHARD (1908-1991, pseudonym Paul Sering). Berlin political science professor and for several decades a leading thinker and theoretician for the SPD (q.v.). (See also FEDERATION OF ACADEMIC FREEDOM.)

LÜBKE, HEINRICH (1894-1972). CDU, federal president (1959-69). First elected president in 1959, the SPD supported his reelection as president in 1964, thus preventing the CDU (qq.v.) from dropping him and nominating a more impressive politician. Willy Brandt (q.v.) expressed the sentiments of many Social Democrats and intellectuals by describing Lübke as a man "with astounding simplicity in thinking and beliefs," whose bumbling speech and behavior spawned many jokes and books containing embarrassing quotations. Lübke had been a conservative proponent of cooperation with the Social Democrats since his days in the Prussian state legislature before 1933 and was the strongest supporter of a grand coalition (q.v.) after 1961. Although the presidential office is chiefly a ceremonial one and is usually not sought by the FRG's top politicians, a presidential election is important because it reflects the political power and climate in the capital. It is always the most powerful man or the emerging majority that steers a presidential election. In 1964, an alliance between the CDU/CSU and SPD was in the air. In historian Arnulf Baring's words, "all presidential elections revolve around the issue of the existing or future federal government." Lübke's reelection was, according to Friedrich Karl Fromme, "an intelligently contrived thread for the netting of the Grand Coalition."

LUDENDORFF, ERICH (1865-1937). A professional soldier, he entered the army in 1882 and had risen to major-general by 1914. After taking part in the invasion of Belgium in August 1914, he was sent to the eastern front as Hindenburg's (q.v.) chief of staff, with whom he shared the glory for the victories at Tannenberg and Masurian Lakes. In August 1916, he became quartermaster general and, together with Hindenburg, dominated German governmental and military policy. He lost his nerve when the Allied powers broke through German lines in France in July and August 1918. He advocated peace talks at the end of September, resigned his post on October 27, and fled to Sweden in disguise. He returned to Germany after the war as an extreme nationalist, and he participated in the Kapp Putsch and Hitler's (q.v.) 1923 putsch in Munich. He ran for president in 1925 and won a paltry 1 percent of the vote. He later broke with Hitler and entered retirement. (See also FIRST WORLD WAR; MUNICH PUTSCH; REVOLUTION IN GERMANY.)

LUFTHANSA see PRIVATIZATION

LUTHER, MARTIN (1483-1586). Martin Luther was the son of a clergyman from Thuringia who was able to save enough money to send his gifted but brooding son to the University of Erfurt to study law. Luther was reportedly shocked by a sudden flash of light and decided instead to become a monk, pastor and professor in Wittenberg. In 1511 he left for a long-awaited voyage to Rome as a firm believer, but he returned to Germany with his faith in the Church badly shaken. His anger and frustration built up as the Roman pontificate devised a method for raising its own revenues by selling to Catholics forgiveness from their sins.

In countries with strong central rulers, such papal financial maneuvers could be resisted, but until 1517 the Church's agents needed not fear resistance in the weak and fragmented Germany. When a papal representative knocked on Martin Luther's door to present the scheme one day, the simmering kettle boiled over. On October 31, 1517, he published his "95 Theses" branding the Catholic Church an insult to God and challenging it to an open debate over fundamental theological issues. It is not certain that he actually tacked this highly explosive writing on the cathedral door at Wittenberg. What is certain, however, is that the Vatican was never the same after this angry monk rolled his weighty stone in its direction.

The Church decided to enter into a three-year debate with Luther, but this merely stimulated the interest which curious and critical Europeans paid to the stream of speeches and writings which poured from Luther's mouth and hand. When the Pope finally decided to silence this troublesome monk, it was too late. Luther merely burned the Papal Bull (writing) in public and defiantly proceeded to the Reichstag in Worms. There he presented his views on April 18, 1521, to Emperor Charles V and to the leading German nobles, clergy and bourgeois. Luther held firmly to his views and asserted that "as long as I am not contradicted by the Holy Scripture or by clear reasoning, I will recant nothing since it is difficult and dangerous to act against one's conscience." In order to protect this renegade with an enormous following in Germany, sympathizers captured him during his journey back to Wittenberg and took him to the Wartburg fortress outside of Eisenach. There he lived for a year under the assumed name of "Junker Jörg" far away from the furious controversies of the day. In 1522, he completed a German translation of the New Testament. This was not the first German translation of the Bible; over 170 handwritten ones had appeared in the Middle Ages, and since the invention of the movable type printing press there had been 14 previous High German (common to southern Germany, Austria and Switzerland) and three Low German (northern Germany) translations. But Luther, the scholar, was able to penetrate deeply into the Greek and "Vulgata" texts and produce a translation, which, as he himself said, forced the prophets and apostles to speak a comprehensible German. Only such a text could enable the Christian to read and understand the Bible on his own, without the guidance or interpretation of the Church. In 1534, he published his final translations of both the New and Old Testaments, which found their way into enthusiastic hands all over Germany. In this way, Luther's German

Martin Luther. (*Source:* SPP.)

became the standardized High German which was spoken by the educated in every corner of Germany. Although a multitude of dialects continue to be spoken in Germany, Luther gave a fractured land a common language, which is essential for any collection of people which hope to be called a nation.

His call for a liberation from the theological confines of Rome unleashed demands for change and other forms of liberation which seriously shook the social structure of Germany. In all of these conflicts, the ultimate victors were the German princes. Some Germans found in Luther's words about the "freedom of a Christian man" a divine justification for their goals and actions. Initially, Luther sympathized with peasants' (q.v.) demands and encouraged the lords to take their pleas seriously. But when bands of rebels began to attack fortresses and churches and to dispatch with bloody swiftness those who wielded earthly authority, he became furious and lashed out against those whom he accused of turning Germany into a battlefield.

When it came to "things belonging to Caesar," Luther did not hesitate to decide in favor of order and princely authority. His reaction to this social revolution and its ultimate cruel suppression had serious consequences for Germany. Peasants remained poor, despised, unfree and without political influence for almost 300 years, until reforms in the wake of the French Revolution (q.v.) finally eliminated the formal chains which had been placed on them. Perhaps more important, Luther's stand left a legacy of freedom in Germany which was interpreted only as inner, purely mental freedom, but not political freedom. Thus, this man who had led the charge against the limits placed on man through Catholic theology actually justified external obedience to the princes and thereby strengthened the hierarchical political order within Germany. This helped to retard the victory of democracy in Germany until the middle of the 20th century. It even allowed some Germans who strongly disapproved of National Socialism after 1933 to remain within a brutal dictatorship, but nevertheless to persuade themselves that they could embark upon an "internal emigration." (See also OVERCOMING THE PAST.)

LUXEMBURG, ROSA (1870-1919). Born in the Russian part of Poland, she became a German citizen in 1895 by marrying a German worker. A brilliant, independent-minded revolutionary, she participated in the failed 1905 revolution in Russia. Returning to Germany, she joined Karl Liebknecht (q.v.) to found the Spartacus League (q.v.).

Because of her vocal opposition to the German war effort, she spent the entire war in prison, but she reentered German politics as soon as the Empire fell in November 1918. Although she was damned in the right-wing press as an agent of Moscow, her "Spartacus Program" differed essentially from Lenin's Bolshevik theory in that it advocated a more democratic communism. She proclaimed that "freedom only for the supporters of the government and for members of a single party" is no freedom at all. Her assertion that "freedom is the freedom of those who think differently" was displayed by GDR (q.v.) dissidents on January 17, 1988, much to the embarrassment of the SED (q.v.) leadership, which had always glorified Luxemburg in its rhetoric. She and Liebknecht were co-founders of the KPD (q.v.) on January 1, 1919, and they led the bloody Spartacist uprising that month, in which they were both captured by Free Corps troops and brutally murdered. This act caused the SPD (q.v.) government, which had ordered the troops to suppress the uprising, to be severely criticized by parts of the working class and served to deepen the gulf between the SPD and the KPD. (See also REVOLUTION IN GERMANY.)

-M-

MACKE, AUGUST (1887-1914). A member of The Blue Rider (*Blaue Reiter*, q.v.) school, Macke rejected his friends' metaphysical views about art. He developed a style which expressed his love of nature and of traditional themes, as well as an insatiable curiosity for life. Influenced by the paintings of Matisse, Macke was very sensitive to color and simple form. Many of his paintings have a poetic quality.

MAGINOT LINE see SECOND WORLD WAR

MAHNCKE, DIETER. CDU, former professor and vice-president of Bundeswehr University (q.v.) Hamburg, Mahncke is a much-published expert on defense and U.S.-German relations. A top aide to former President Karl Carstens (q.v.), Mahncke serves in the planning staff of the defense ministry. He received his Ph.D. in political science from the University of North Carolina and has been a well-known guest professor at several leading American universities.

MAIER, REINHOLD (1889-1971). FDP minister president of Baden-Wurttemberg from 1945 to 1953. (See also FREE DEMOCRATIC PARTY; LAND PRINCES.)

MAIZIERE, LOTHAR DE (1940-). CDU, chairman of CDU in GDR from December 1989, the first and last freely-elected prime minister of GDR (April-October 1990), member of Bundestag (October 1990-), minister without portfolio in Kohl's (q.v.) government for two months until December 1990, and briefly vice-chairman of federal CDU (q.v.) and Brandenburg CDU chairman until pressured to step down in September 1991 because of allegations that he had maintained contacts with the Stasi (q.v.). An interior ministry report exonerated him in February 1991. A concert musician, he practiced law in the GDR and specialized in defending church figures, an activity which, he claimed, necessitated occasional dealings with the Stasi. (See also CHRISTIAN DEMOCRATIC UNION; DENAZIFICATION; REUNIFICATION.)

MANN, HEINRICH (1871-1950). The older brother of Thomas Mann (q.v.), his most famous novel, *Professor Unrat,* was made into the successful film, *Der blaue Engel,* with Marlene Dietrich (q.v.). A pacifist, Heinrich broke with his brother publicly over their political differences. Although he wrote several novels, his excessively sarcastic style prevented him from gaining general recognition. He lived in exile in California where he died while preparing for a position as president of the Academy of Arts in the newly founded GDR (q.v.).

MANN, KLAUS (1906-1949). The son of Thomas Mann (q.v.), Klaus was a drama critic and advisor in Berlin before emigrating to the U.S. in 1936. He worked as a journalist and wrote a novel about Tchaikovsky and a controversial novel, *Mephisto,* based on the actor Gustaf Gründgens (q.v.), his brother-in-law. Overshadowed by his father and disoriented by the changes in his life, he committed suicide.

MANN, THOMAS (1875-1955). Ranked among the master novelists of the 20th century, this author from Lübeck won the Nobel Prize for *Buddenbrooks,* the epic German novel about the rise and fall of a middle-class family. Mann continued to examine the relationship of the artist to himself and to society in his further novels, particularly *Death in Venice* and *The Magic Mountain.* In addition to his many novels, he wrote literary essays, as well as political and historical works with a pervasive irony and intellectual perception for the problems of the Europe of his day. The Nazis (q.v.) revoked his citizenship while he was in Switzerland, the country to which he returned after living 14 years in California, where he had become an American citizen in 1944. *Doktor Faustus*, published in 1947, is his novel and judgment on the Germany of his lifetime.

MANSTEIN, FRIEDRICH ERICH VON (1887-1973) see SECOND WORLD WAR

MARC, FRANZ (1880-1916). The innovator and painter of The Blue Rider (Blaue Reiter, q.v.) school, Marc was born the son of painters and was educated in Munich and Paris. His stylized animal imagery and cubistic planes characterize most of his work. He was killed in the First World War.

MARCH REVOLUTION see REVOLUTION OF 1848

MARIA-THERESIA, EMPRESS OF AUSTRIA (1717-80) see FRIEDRICH II, THE GREAT

MARKETS, LAW ON THE LIBERALIZATION OF (1948). On June 26, 1948, Ludwig Erhard (q.v.) made a determined move toward the social market economy (q.v.) by liberalizing markets and abolishing central planning.

MARLEEN, LILI. A nostalgic song sung by Lala Anderson which was so popular during the Second World War (q.v.) that soldiers on both sides, overcome with emotion, put down their arms at 10 PM when the song was played.

MARNE, BATTLE OF (1914) see FIRST WORLD WAR

MARSHALL PLAN. Secretary of State and ex-armed forces Chief of Staff George C. Marshall (1880-1959) foresaw that Europe would economically stagnate for an unnecessarily long period of time unless massive American aid were poured into the war-ravaged countries. The generous American offer, known as the "Marshall Plan," was even extended to the Soviet Union and what were slowly developing into satellite states which it had occupied militarily. The Soviet Union refused to allow itself or those countries under its domination to accept such assistance.

In July 1947 representatives of 16 European countries receiving Marshall Plan aid declared in Paris that "the German economy should be integrated into the economy of Europe in such a way as to contribute to a raising of the general standard of living. The other nations sought through such economic cooperation to ensure that Germany could not again become an aggressive political enemy. In the next few years West Germans received almost $4 billion in money and supplies from the Marshall Plan. This not only enabled them to rebuild their industrial plants with the most modern tooling, but it established the foundation for West European cooperation, which the Plan required and which culminated in the EC (q.v.). It also introduced a long-range liberalization of European trade and payments, which has been a key to the economic prosperity of many European nations.

MARX, KARL (1818-1883). Marx was born in Trier, the son of a German-Jewish bourgeois family which had accepted Christianity. He married a woman of minor nobility. He was forced to flee Germany in 1843 because of the biting social and political criticism which he wrote in his Cologne newspaper, *Rheinische Zeitung*. As a student of classical philosophy in Berlin and Bonn, he had been attracted to the thinking of Friedrich Hegel (q.v.) who developed a doctrine called the dialectic. This involved the clash of opposites and the development of something entirely new and better. Hegel meant the clash of ideas, but Marx converted this concept of clashing ideas into one of clashing economic forces. The explosive implications of this theory soon became clear. In his London exile he wrote in 1848 the *Communist Manifesto*, which predicted a violent revolution as a result of which the working (proletarian) class would replace the capitalist overlords who owned the land and factories. This powerful tract ended with the words: "Proletarians of the world, rise up; you have nothing to lose but your chains!" Such a rising never came in England or in Germany, but Marxism became and remains a far more significant intellectual and political doctrine in Germany than in the United States. During the 1848 revolution (q.v.) he returned to Cologne, but he fled back to London in 1849 because he faced treason charges. There he spent the rest of his life. He lived some years as a correspondent of a New York newspaper, but he devoted most of his time researching in the British Museum. In 1864, he collaborated in the founding of the International Workingmen's Association, which collapsed in 1876 because of fractious quarrels. His greatest work was *Das Kapital*, the first volume of which was published in 1867, and the final two, thanks to Friedrich Engels (q.v.), after his death in 1885 and 1895.

MARX, WILHELM (1863-1946). Chairman of Center Party (1922-28), Reich chancellor (1923-25).

MARXIST GROUP (MARXISTISCHE GRUPPE--MG). This is a Marxist-Leninist cadre party with a rigidly hierarchical structure, severe discipline, intensive indoctrination and secrecy. Most of its 5,000 members do not publicly acknowledge their affiliation. They and several thousand sympathizers are mainly students and academics, and the focus of their efforts is Bavaria. Their numbers are growing, and members are expected to live together in communes and largely cut off contact with outsiders. It is convinced that trained agitators must spark a class-conscious proletariat to engage in class struggle. It advocates "thoroughly destructive criticism of all existing conditions." It communicates through *MSZ--Marxistische Streit und Zeitschrift-Gegen die Kosten der Freiheit* (Marxist Controversy and Magazine-Against the Costs of Freedom, bi-monthly, 12,000 copies), the *MAZ--Marxistische Arbeiterzeitung* (Marxist Workers' Newspaper, appearing irregularly, circulation about 10,000), the *Marxistische Schulzeitung* (Marxist School Newspaper, about seven issues yearly with almost 7,000 copies), and the *Marxistische Hochschulzeitung* (Marxist University Newspaper, weekly during the semesters with a circulation of about 14,000). The MG has expanded to the point where it now has more members than did the "K-Groups" in their zenith in the 1970s; its publications have a wider distribution than all other groups in the "New Left" category put together. Very active, it normally spurns cooperation with other leftist groups. It scorns Gorbachev's policy of *perestroika* and blames the SED (q.v.) for failing to establish a workable planned economy and for creating anti-communists. The MG rejects any attempt to give socialism a human face and criticized the SED for trying to compete with the West to realize "antiquated humanist ideals of the French Revolution." In its view, the SED got what it deserved.

MARXIST-LENINIST PARTY OF GERMANY (MARXISTISCH-LENINISTISCHE PARTEI DEUTSCHLANDS--MLPD). With about 1,400 members, it has its headquarters in Essen and is organized into 16 districts and approximately 100 local units. It regards itself as the only Marxist-Leninist party in the FRG. Its official organ is *Rote Fahne* (Red Banner), whose weekly circulation is about 7,000; it also publishes a monthly *lernen und kämpfen* (luk--Learn and Fight), with a circulation of 1,500. It participated in the 1987 Bundestag election, winning 13,821 second votes. This zero percent of the total vote indicated how little electoral hope there is for the K-groups and persuaded the MLPD to sit out the 1990 vote. Party spokesman Klaus Vowe argued that the party would have gotten more votes were it not for the "falsification" of the party's arguments by the bourgeois media. After German reunification (q.v.), which the party opposed, the MLPD raised its sword against European unity, which it claims serves the cause of imperialism.

The MLPD has three ineffective affiliated organizations with about 400 members. They are the Marxist-Leninist Workers' Youth Association (AJV/ML) with a press organ, *Rebell,* and a children's group, *Rotfüchse* (Red Foxes), the Marxist-Leninist Pupils' and Students' Association, whose organ is *Roter Pfeil* (Red Arrow), and an active Marxist-Leninist League of Intellectuals.

MASUR, KURT (1927-). Masur has been music director and conductor of the Gewandhaus Orchestra in Leipzig since 1970. Together with two high SED (q.v.) functionaries, he prevented the use of military force against the demonstrators in Leipzig. Later he made the rooms of the Gewandhaus available for "critical dialogue," in which he was prominently involved. Since 1991 he is music director and conductor of the New York Philharmonic Orchestra, while remaining music director in Leipzig. (See also GERMAN DEMOCRATIC REPUBLIC, COLLAPSE; RELIGION.)

MASURIAN LAKES, BATTLE OF (1914) see FIRST WORLD WAR

MATTHÄUS-MAIER, INGRID (1945-). In December 1991, she was elected SPD (q.v.) deputy chairperson of Bundestag parliamentary group.

MAY, KARL (1842-1912). This author of *Winnetou* and *Old Surehand* never set foot in the American West, about which he wrote with incredible accuracy. His Indian stories, narrated in the first person, were the most popular children's books well into the 20th century. May also wrote novels set in the Near East and South America, unusual for someone who never left his country.

McCLOY, JOHN JAY (1895-1989). U.S. high commissioner for Germany (1949-52). (See also INTRODUCTION.)

MECKEL, MARKUS (1952-). SPD, GDR foreign minister (April-September 1990).

MEDIUM-TERM FINANCE PLANNING (MITTELFRISTIGE FINANZPLANNUNG) see GRAND COALITION

MEIN KAMPF see NAZI PARTY

MEINECKE, FRIEDRICH (1862-1954) see BUNDESWEHR

MEINHOF, ULRIKE (1934-1976) see TERRORIST GROUPS

MEINS, HOLGER (1941-1974) see TERRORIST GROUPS

MENDE, ERICH (1916-). FDP until 1970, then CDU (qq.v.) politician. Federal FDP chairman (1960-68), vice-chancellor and minister for all-German affairs (1963-66). (See also POLITICAL PRISONERS; SED-SPD SPEAKER EXCHANGE.)

MENDELSSOHN-BARTHOLDY, FELIX (1809-1847). This child prodigy was the grandson of the writer Moses Mendelssohn. In his brief life he composed five symphonies and three concertos, as well as chamber music and piano pieces.

MENGELE, JOSEF (d. 1979). He was a Nazi doctor who established a center for medical experimentation in the Auschwitz concentration camp (q.v.). He disappeared at the end of the war. In 1992, it was revealed that he had spent about two months in a U.S. prisoner-of-war camp, but he was released by American officials who failed to identify him as the "Angel of Death" from Auschwitz. He lived under an alias on a German farm for four years before fleeing to South America, where he died in 1979 at age 67.

MENZEL, ADOLPH VON (1815-1905). His early art ranged from the famous woodcuts of Frederick the Great (q.v.) to 600 lithographs of Prussian uniforms. As a painter he was a forerunner of Impressionism, creating a sense of atmosphere around his commonplace subjects.

MERBOLD, ULF (1941-) see SPACE PROGRAM

MERKEL, ANGELA (1954-). One of the highest ranking East Germans in the CDU (q.v.), Merkel is minister of women and youth in the Kohl (q.v.) government. She began her political career with the Democratic Awakening citizen's movement in the GDR (qq.v.) and joined the CDU in 1990. She replaced Lothar de Maizière (q.v.) as deputy chair of the CDU when the latter was forced to resign as a result of allegations that he had maintained contacts with the Stasi (q.v.).

MESSERSCHMID, ERNST (1945-) see SPACE PROGRAM

MESSERSCHMITT-BÖLKOW-BLOHM (MBB) see ROCKETS

METTERNICH, KLEMENS WENZEL PRINCE VON (1773-1859). A German from Coblenz in the Rhineland, he fled to Vienna in 1794. He served as an Austrian diplomat in Dresden (1801-03), Berlin (1803-06), and Paris (1806-09) before becoming foreign minister in 1809 and state chancellor in 1821. He was made a prince in 1813. He presided over the Congress of Vienna (q.v.) and was largely responsible for Austria's turning its attention to developing its Italian possessions rather than focusing on Germany. Since he was not an Austrian, he was prevented from exercising influence over domestic policy, once complaining that "I governed Europe sometimes, Austria never." Branded a reactionary politician, he was forced to flee to England during the Revolution of 1848 (q.v.). He returned when the dust settled, but he never regained his political position although he was a respected senior statesman and adviser.

MIELKE, ERICH (1907-). SED, minister of state security (1957-89). On November 12, 1992, Mielke was put on trial in Berlin for his actions as head of the Stasi and his involvement in ordering border guards along the intra-German border to shoot to kill. Earlier in 1992 he had been put on trial on charges that he had committed two murders in 1931 when he was a 23-year-old Communist. On August 9, 1931, two policemen had been shot to death in the center of Berlin and a third injured, allegedly as a KPD (q.v.) act of retaliation for the murder of a party member. Mielke was charged with the murders, but he saved himself by fleeing to the Soviet Union, where he lived until the end of the war, except for 1936-39, when he fought against the Franco forces in the Spanish Civil War. He returned to Germany in 1945. (See also HONECKER, FALL.)

MIELKE, GERD. SPD, a political scientist at the University of Freiburg and nationally-known election analyst for leading German newspapers, Mielke was named in 1992 as Director of Principle, Analysis, and Planning in the office of the Rhineland-Palatinate Minister President Rudolf Sharping.

MIES VAN DER ROHE, LUDWIG (1886-1969). This founding father of modern architecture and master of steel and glass grew up in Aachen, where he was greatly influenced by his hometown architecture and his stone mason father. He went on to become director of *Bauhaus* (q.v.) from 1930 until 1933, when he left Hitler's (q.v.) Germany for the U.S. He was the director of the School of Architecture at the Illinois Institute of Technology for 20 years.

MILITARY SPORTING GROUPS (WEHRSPORTGRUPPEN). When the right-wing NPD (q.v.) faded in the 1970s, a number of these tiny ultra-nationalist terrorist groups emerged like those on the left and similar to "survival groups" in other Western countries. Most were more smoke than fire, spouting rhetoric about reversing moral decay and facilitating national revival and wearing Nazi paraphernalia and waving Hitler (qq.v.) salutes to attract the news media and shock the public. They directed their hatred against guest workers and asylum seekers.

MINISTER PRESIDENT. Head of a Land government. (See also BUNDESRAT; LAND AND STATE GOVERNMENT.)

MINNESANG. This is the formal love poetry of the chivalric age designed to be sung by the poet at court (1180-1220).

MINORITIES AND FOREIGNERS. The FRG was highly successful after 1945 in absorbing and integrating more than 14 million German refugees and expellees from East Germany and the former eastern territories. Now Germany is faced with the very difficult problem of integrating racially and culturally diverse groups of non-Germans. Because of its economic prosperity, political tolerance, liberal asylum laws, and constitutional guarantee of asylum "for persons persecuted on political grounds," it has become a magnet for refugees, although it does not accept as high a percentage of immigrants per capita as does the U.S.

In the 1950s and 1960s, West Germany recruited southern Europeans, particularly Turks, in order to overcome severe labor shortages in low-paying jobs. Foreigners now number about five million, or approximately 6.5 percent of the population, and their numbers are rising because of their far higher birth rate and because members of their families are arriving from their countries of origin to join them. Most foreigners intend to stay in the FRG forever. Relatively few foreign workers accept governmental bonuses to return to their countries. They are especially concentrated in certain large industrial cities, where they often form foreign ghettos in poorer sections of the cities and serve as convenient scapegoats for certain alarming urban ills, most notably, rising crime. For example, foreigners constitute a quarter of Frankfurt am Main's residents. Polls indicate that most Germans believe that the number of foreign residents has become too high. 1991 polls revealed that a third of the population in both parts of Germany feared "too many foreigners," two-thirds believed that immigrants had unfairly taken advantage of the welfare system, 79 percent thought that there should be stronger restrictions on foreigners wishing to live in the FRG. About half the German respondents believed that there is too little tolerance in Germany toward foreigners residing there.

Glasnost (openness) in the Soviet Union seriously affected emigration. In 1989 alone, 377,000 ethnic Germans from Eastern Europe (especially Poland) and the USSR joined 344,000 Germans from the GDR and the steady stream of non-German refugees into the FRG. This was the largest wave of ethnic Germans entering the FRG since 1949, and the influx continued in the 1990s. The sudden outpouring temporarily swamped the procedures and funds. All compete for limited accommodation and employment and, as polls, city elections, and violence show, are testing Germans' patience. About two million Germans remain in the Soviet Union. Many of these also wish to emigrate, even though it is not easy for Soviet Germans to adjust to working and living in a less protective state like the FRG. In a 1991 poll, 52 percent of Germans in the FRG thought restrictions should also apply to ethnic Germans from Eastern European countries, who enjoy an open-door immigration policy. Germany tightened its asylum laws, accepting only 6.4 percent of the applicants in 1991, but 700,000 ethnic Germans from outside of Germany poured into the country in the year following the collapse of the Berlin Wall; many could speak no German.

Almost half of the resident foreigners are Turks, who display a greater resistance to social integration than do other nationalities. This unwillingness to become an integrated part of German society creates particular problems in the schools, where the percentage of foreigners in classes sometimes rises to over 50 percent. Thus, Germans must tackle the problem of bilingualism in the schools, of resultant lowered standards in the classrooms, and of an increasing inclination on the part of German parents to avoid sending their children to schools in which there is a high percentage of foreign children enrolled. This is an extremely delicate problem for a country which tries very hard to be tolerant, compassionate and just. Germans' deep concern about the plight of Turkish guest workers was revealed in 1986-87 by the astonishing high sales (over a million copies) of Günter Wallraff's book, *Ganz Unten* (Rock Bottom), which depicts the difficult lives of Turks in Germany.

Fears that the FRG might become swamped by foreigners persist, and the federal and Land governments have found it necessary to warn against xenophobia, which is strongest in the East, although only about 2 percent of the population there is foreign. The GDR was a more isolated society, so its people had less contact with outsiders. Also, the Communist regime in the GDR had never accepted responsibility for the crimes of the Second World War, so its citizens had not grown up with the same feeling of guilt toward wrongs done to other peoples, such as the Jews, as had people in western Germany. About 100,000 guest workers had been sent there from countries like Angola, Cuba, Vietnam, and Mozambique, and many refused to return to their homelands when the GDR collapsed. It is noteworthy that xenophobia in the East is stronger among young people than among older, whereas the opposite is true in the West. Even more embarrassing for a country with Germany's past was Bonn's temporary decision to halt Jewish immigration from the Soviet Union; 4,000 had entered Germany in

1990, and about 2,500 had arrived in Berlin, which was totally unprepared to receive them. Since Germany had no legal framework for accepting Soviet Jews, some families were told they had to leave Germany immediately. This incensed some members of Germany's 40,000-strong Jewish community (the largest concentration being Berlin with 8,000).

Germany's low-keyed celebration of its first year of reunification (q.v.) was overshadowed by the shock of a frightening upsurge of violent racist attacks in both parts of the country, which were repeated during the second anniversary in 1992. On November 9, 1991, the first anniversary of the Berlin Wall's (q.v) collapse and the 53d anniversary of the Nazi Crystal Night rampage against Jews, the street brawls of several hundred young neo-Nazis (uneducated itinerant thugs who are more like English soccer hooligans than Hitler's ideologists) in eastern Germany stole some of the spotlight from 100,000 demonstrators across the country who marched against racism. Human rights campaigners formed human chains and all-night vigils to protect asylum-seekers from harm. In 1990, 193,000 arrived; in 1991, the number grew to 230,000, roughly half the total of refugees to all of Europe; in 1992, the flood swelled to a half million.

Many Germans, including the Kohl (q.v.) government, partly blame the untenable situation on Article 16 of the Basic Law (q.v.), which grants political asylum to all who claim it. It had been inspired by the fact that many German anti-Nazis had been saved during the Hitler era because they had found asylum in democratic countries and by the fact that thousands of Jews perished because other countries had turned them away. Polls in 1991 showed that 70 percent of Germans favored granting asylum to political refugees, but many believed that this right has been badly abused. Although more than 90 percent of refugees were refused, as many as 40 percent still managed to stay for "humanitarian reasons." Unlike the U.S., Germany has no quota system for legal immigration. The SPD (q.v.) had rejected any alteration of Article 16, but in December 1992 the major parties agreed to scrap the absolute guarantee of political asylum for refugees and bring the country's policy in line with that of other major Western nations. Beginning in 1993, war refugees can remain in Germany only until fighting in their homeland ceases. Those from Third World countries are refused entry, and those coming from countries Germany has declared to be free of political repression are automatically denied asylum. In 1992, the seriousness of the issue was shown by the fact that 17 people were killed and hundreds injured in right-wing extremist attacks. The assimilation of foreigners remains one of the most difficult problems unified Germany faces.

MISCHNICK, WOLFGANG (1921-). Born and raised in Saxony, Mischnick is the long-serving FDP (q.v.) parliamentary group leader (since 1968), federal minister for refugees and war injured (1961-63), deputy FDP party chairman (since 1964). (See also FREE DEMOCRATIC PARTY.)

MITTAG, GÜNTER (1926-). SED, politburo member and central committee secretary for economic affairs. Ousted from power and from the SED (q.v.) in the 1989 revolution, he was subsequently prosecuted for abusing his authority.

MITTELEUROPA (MIDDLE EUROPE). This idea had been born in the 19th century, but it was reintroduced to the German public in the fall of 1915, when the well-known liberal journalist, Friedrich Naumann (q.v.), published his book *Mitteleuropa*. By 1917 more than 137,000 copies had been sold. Naumann argued that the time had come to create a large community of Central European peoples which should include Germans, Hungarians, eastern and western Slavs, and Romanians. Many other smaller peoples could associate themselves with this community, which would be a type of federation, not an empire dominated by a single nation-state. Small nation-states were economically and politically outdated. The creation of such a community would require that narrow nationalism and mutual distrust be replaced by a more liberal understanding of foreign ways and interests and a mutual readiness to cooperate. Only if this could be done could a better and freer future for Europe and Germany emerge from the First World War (q.v.). This idealistic plea was directed against those Germans who advocated naked German annexations and domination. Naumann's idea became particularly compelling after the Second World War (q.v.) and found its culmination, in altered form, in the emergence of the European Community (q.v.).

MITTLERE REIFE see EDUCATION

MODEL GERMANY (MODELL DEUTSCHLAND). This self-confident slogan proclaimed by Chancellor Helmut Schmidt (q.v.)

during the 1976 Bundestag elections symbolized Germany's economic and moral recovery from the Second World War (q.v.) and pride (expressed by Willy Brandt's (q.v.) 1972 slogan: "We can again be proud of being Germans") in having established a stable democracy and economy and a generous social welfare system. (See also ELECTIONS FEDERAL, 1976)

MODROW, HANS (1928-). SED secretary in Dresden (1973-90), minister president of GDR (November 1989-April 1990), member of Bundestag (1990-). He senses that, as a former SED (q.v.) regional chief, he is not wanted in the Bundestag. In 1992, he complained: "These people absolutely don't want you, they want to grind you underfoot." Even though he played a positive role in the GDR's transition from SED rule, he continued to be dogged by allegations that he had been responsible for falsifying election results in May 1989 and that under his watch demonstrators in Dresden were brutally mistreated in early October 1989. (See also GERMAN DEMOCRATIC REPUBLIC, COLLAPSE; and PARTY of DEMOCRATIC SOCIALISM.)

MOELLER VAN DER BRUCK, ARTHUR see WEIMAR CULTURE

MOKE, WERNER, SED see BERGHOFER, WOLFGANG

MÖLLEMANN, JÜRGEN (1945-). FDP, an outspoken, ambitious former economics minister in the Kohl (q.v.) government, Möllemann assumed the additional post of vice-chancellor when Hans-Dietrich Genscher (q.v.) resigned as foreign minister in May 1992. On January 3, 1993, he was forced to resign because of nepotism. He admitted his role in an influence-peddling scheme; he had used his office stationery and own signature to advertise the commercial services of a relative. He was replaced by Günter Rexrodt (q.v.).

MOLTKE, HELMUTH JAMES COUNT VON (1907-1945). Member of Kreisau Circle (q.v.) and a leading head of resistance (q.v.) movement.

MOLTKE, HELMUTH VON (1800-1891). A professional soldier in the Prussian army for 66 years, he became chief of the Prussian general staff in 1857. Collaborating with General von Roon (1803-79) and

Bismarck (q.v.), he re-organized the army from the ground up. He oversaw the strategic planning for the three wars leading up to unification in 1871 and was the first Chief of the Grand German General Staff.

MOLTKE, HELMUTH VON (1848-1916). Nephew of Helmuth von Moltke (q.v.), he was chief of general staff from 1906 until September 14, 1914, when the offensive against France through Belgium became stalled. He was made a scapegoat for the failure to capture Paris and the loss of the Battle at the Marne. (See also FIRST WORLD WAR; SCHLIEFFEN PLAN.)

MOMMSEN, THEODOR see EMPIRE CULTURE

MOMPER, WALTER (1945-). SPD, Mayor of West Berlin in 1989 when Berlin Wall (q.v.) came down.

MORAVIANS see AMERICA, GERMAN ATTITUDES

MORGENTHAU PLAN see ALLIED OCCUPATION

MÖRIKE, EDUARD FRIEDRICH (1804-1875). A less successful pastor than poet, Mörike's craftmanship is marked by a folk song-like quality and a sense of rhythm which account for the fact that over fifty of his poems have been set to music.

MOROCCO CRISES (1905, 1911). In order to try to show the weakness of the newly-formed Anglo-French Entente, Kaiser Wilhelm II (q.v.) landed at Tangier on March 31, 1905, during a Mediterranean cruise, and made a speech in favor of the independence of Morocco, which Britain, France, and Spain wanted to partition. The Germans demanded an international conference, which took place at Algeciras from January to April 1906. A treaty was signed, but the long-range result of this crisis was that it actually strengthened Anglo-French cooperation, to Germany's disadvantage. Another Moroccan Crisis occurred in 1911. (See also EMPIRE, FOREIGN POLICY.)

MÜLLER, ADAM see RECHTSSTAAT

MÜLLER, GEBHARD see LAND PRINCES

MÜLLER, HEINER (1929-). One of the leading dramatists from the former GDR, he received many prizes for his plays. His earlier plays deal with the construction of a socialistic society and its problems. He was the leading dramatist for the "Berliner Ensemble" from 1970-76. *Die Schlacht* and *Germania Tod in Berlin* are two of his best known plays.

MÜLLER, HERMANN (1876-1931). SPD, foreign minister (1919-20), Reich chancellor (1928-30).

MÜLLER, LUDWIG see CONFESSING CHURCH

MÜNCH, WERNER. CDU minister president of Saxony-Anhalt after reunification (q.v.) and in 1992 one of three western Germans to head an eastern German Land.

MUNICH AGREEMENT and CONFERENCE (1938). This agreement was reached among Hitler (q.v.) and the prime ministers of Britain, France, and Italy, ceding to Germany the Sudetenland, which was the western extremity of Czechoslovakia which was inhabited predominantly by Germans and where the main Czech defenses were located. Polish and Hungarian demands for further border adjustments were made at the expense of Czechoslovakia, which thereby lost a third of its population, but received from the parties a worthless guarantee against unprovoked aggression. Czechoslovakia and Russia were not invited to the conference. A year later German troops occupied Bohemia (the Czech portion of the country) and set up a puppet regime in Slovakia. British Prime Minister Neville Chamberlain argued that the agreement had given Europeans "peace in our time," but subsequent events demonstrated the emptiness of those words. Critics then and now argue that such "peace settlements" merely play into the hands of determined bullies like Hitler, who used the respite to prepare better for his total war, which began in 1939. This illusory hope for peace was called an "appeasement policy." (See also THIRD REICH.)

MUNICH MASSACRE (1972). In 1972, Munich hosted the Olympic Games. In order to demonstrate that Germany had changed dramatically since 1936, when Hitler (q.v.) had used the Berlin Olympic Games to impress the world with the dynamism and order he had reintroduced into Germany, the Munich organizers planned minimum security for the athletes. This was a tragic mistake. Eight Arab terrorists kidnapped and then killed 11 Israeli athletes, while German authorities tried in vain to settle the crisis with the least bloodshed possible.

MUNICH PUTSCH (1923). Often referred to as the "Beer Hall Putsch," this was an almost comical attempt by Hitler (q.v.) and his party to overthrow the Bavarian government on November 8-9, 1923, as the first act of a march on Berlin (similar to Mussolini's "March on Rome" in 1922) and declaration of a Nazi (q.v.) state in Germany. It was supported by General Erich Ludendorff (q.v.), but it was badly planned. The police fired on the 2,000 demonstrators and killed 16 of Hitler's followers, who were honored as heros during the Third Reich (q.v.). He was captured and sent to jail, where he dictated *Mein Kampf*. (See also NAZI PARTY.)

MÜNTER, GABRIELE (1877-1962). A companion and former student of Kandinsky, Münter could have been born American had her parents not returned to Germany during the Civil War. This former member of the Blue Rider (*Blaue Reiter*, q.v.) school was considered Germany's most outstanding woman artist of the 1950s. She worked with variations of color and is best known for her vibrant, outlined landscapes and still lifes.

MÜNTZER, THOMAS (ca. 1490-1525) see PEASANTS' REVOLT

-N-

NATIONAL CHURCH (NAZI) see CONFESSING CHURCH

NATIONAL COMMITTEE FOR A FREE GERMANY (NATIONALKOMMITEE FREIES DEUTSCHLAND). On July 12, 1943, this was founded in Moscow as an instrument of the Soviet Union to use patriotic slogans to win the support of conservative elements in Germany. It was disbanded in 1945.

NATIONAL DEMOCRATIC PARTY OF GERMANY (NATIONALDEMOKRATISCHE PARTEI DEUTSCHLANDS --NPD). This ultra-rightist party rose quickly in the wake of economic difficulties and arch-conservatives' disappointment at the CDU/CSU's cavorting with the SPD during the Grand Coalition (q.v.) from 1966 to 1969. The NPD won representation in several Land parliaments and came within a whisker of entering the Bundestag in 1969, having barely fallen short of the 5 percent minimum of votes cast in the entire FRG. The end of the Grand Coalition signalled the demise of the NPD, and most conservative protest voters returned to the CDU/CSU. This was an enormous relief to the major parties. One of the arguments for entering the Grand Coalition had been to create a democratic front against such extremist parties. Bonn was indeed not Weimar; movements of unreconstructed Nazis (q.v.) and other ultra-rightists find it difficult to get a firm foothold on the FRG's democratic terrain.

Taking no chances that there might be a danger of a revival of Nazi sentiment in the FRG, the Bonn government responded to the NPD in several ways. First, it decided to fight politically against neo-Nazi ideas propagated by the NPD in the public arena, rather than having it declared illegal, as was done against the KPD (q.v.) in 1956. The assumption was that if one pushes such thinking underground and does not try to challenge its fallacies in public, the movement would grow rather than die. This calculation proved to be correct: after a rapid rise in the 1960s, when the NPD was able to win as many as 10 percent of the seats in some Land parliaments, it had shrunk to electoral insignificance by the 1990 Bundestag election, although other right-wing parties, such as the Republicans, were doing well in some Land elections. There has been a resurgence of right-wing groups in the 1980s and 1990s due to dissatisfaction against guest workers and immigrants and difficulties in coping with unemployment.

NPD thinking is expressed mainly in the *National Zeitung*, whose circulation is 100,000 and influence minimal. It glorifies Hitler (q.v.). It also supports the notion of the *"Auschwitzlüge"* (Auschwitz lie) put forward by a few American and French scholars that Nazi crimes have been exaggerated. This no doubt helped prompt the SPD government to propose a bill in 1982 (passed in amended form in 1985) making it illegal to propagate lies about Nazi crimes that insult the memory of the Jewish dead. (See also DENAZIFICATION; MINORITIES; PARTIES, RIGHT-WING.)

NATIONAL FRONT see BLOC PARTIES

NATIONAL HOLIDAY. October 3 (Day of German Unity, 1990).

NATIONAL LIBERAL PARTY (NATIONALLIBERALE PARTEI). The right wing of the Liberal Party broke away and formed this new party in 1867. Loyal to Otto von Bismarck (q.v.), it adamantly supported German unification and an energetic German foreign policy. (See also BISMARCK; LIBERALISM.)

NATIONAL PEOPLE'S ARMY (NATIONALE VOLKSARMEE-- NVA) see GERMAN DEMOCRATIC REPUBLIC

NATIONAL SOCIALIST ORGANIZATION OF WOMEN (FRAUENSCHAFT). Like the League of German Girls, this Nazi (q.v.) organization introduced many rural German women to public life. In addition to its ideological retraining function, it permitted women to travel beyond the narrow confines of their village life and mingle with people from other regions and classes. Like the military and labor service, it helped break down the endogamous inter-marriage patterns which had prevailed in the villages.

NATIONAL ZEITUNG see NATIONAL DEMOCRATIC PARTY OF GERMANY

NATIONALISM, GERMAN   see FRENCH REVOLUTION and GERMAN EMPIRE

NATURALISM (1890-1900).   Naturalism is an extreme form of Realism greatly influenced by German socialism. Lacking the aesthetic considerations of Realism, Naturalism dealt with the real issues. Misery, social injustice and capitalistic exploitation explain the unpoetic, depressing and radical portrayal of life in this literature. The naturalists wanted exact documentation and used dialects and vulgar language effectively in their dramas and other works. Limitation of style and the monotony of its themes brought about the decline of Naturalism. Gerhart Hauptmann's (q.v.) *Flagman Thiel, The Beaver Coat* (a comedy), and *The Weavers*, hailed as the first socialistic drama in German literature, are exemplary of this period.

NAUMANN, FRIEDRICH (1860-1919). DDP, Liberal politician and publicist. (See also HEUSS, THEODOR; STIFTUNGEN.)

NAZI PARTY (NATIONALSOZIALISTISCHE DEUTSCHE ARBEITERPARTEI--NSDAP). The Nazi Party had great difficulty gaining political momentum and a significant following during the 1920s. It had first taken shape in the confusion and frustration following the end of the First World War (q.v.) and had aimed its appeal toward the disillusioned and impoverished, first in Austria and shortly afterwards in Germany. Its official name indicated the wide spectrum of groups which it tried to encompass: National Socialist German Workers' Party. Throughout its entire existence, it was not a party which aimed to serve one particular class, as the Communist, Social Democratic or conservative parties tried to do. Instead, the Nazi party was one which attracted the social scrap of all classes. This is why it was and is difficult to put a political label on the party or movement. It was not exactly conservative because it attacked the capitalist economic system and the *status quo*. As a rule, German business leaders did not support the party financially or otherwise until after it had actually come into power in 1933.

In a famous speech before the Industrial Club in Düsseldorf in 1932, Adolf Hitler (q.v.) made it unmistakably clear that German business leaders bore a heavy share of the blame for the 1918 disaster and that business interests would never achieve primacy over political interest in the Third Reich (q.v.). He always kept this promise. Hitler sought many social changes. In many ways he advocated and introduced a revolution (called by many a "conservative revolution") against bourgeois and industrialized society. National Socialist policy and aims were not leftist either. They were blatantly nationalist, a fact which attracted many conservative supporters who abhorred his means of gaining power. Also, he openly attacked the Communist and Social Democratic parties as anti-national and, in the case of the communists, as handmaidens of the Soviet Union. He detested liberalism, democracy, and the Weimar Republic (q.v.), aversions which he shared with the Communists.

Hitler made an almost comical attempt to seize power in Bavaria in 1923 by having his followers "arrest" government leaders in the Munich Bürgerbräu beer hall (now razed). He had hoped this brazen act would set in motion events which would result in the crash of the Weimar Republic. Instead, he was arrested, and there was a highly publicized trial which gave this well-practiced demagogue the opportunity to capture the attention of all Germany and to articulate his attack against the Weimar Republic. He was sent to Landsberg prison for a five-year sentence although he served less than one year. While in prison he produced his rambling, often raving book *Mein Kampf* ("My Struggle"), put into writing by his loyal follower, Rudolf Hess (q.v.).

Hitler's unsuccessful "beer hall putsch" and his imprisonment convinced him that he must try to gain power by means of the ballot box. While in prison, he told a friend: "It will be necessary to pursue a new policy. Instead of working to achieve power by an armed *coup*, we shall have to hold our noses and enter the Reichstag against the Catholic and Marxist deputies. If outvoting them takes longer than outshooting them, at least the result will be guaranteed by their own constitution. Any lawful process is slow . . . . Sooner or later we shall have a majority--and after that, Germany."

Ten years later he accomplished his goal, but it is mistaken to argue that Hitler came to power entirely legally. When the critical elections came in the years 1930-33, he unleashed his two private armies, the *Sturmabteilung* (Storm Division--SA) and *Schutzstaffel* (Protective Troop--SS), to break up other parties' rallies and meetings, to beat up opponents in the streets, to terrorize those who manifested an inclination to vote for another party, and to make other kinds of unnerving demonstrations, such as throwing up blockades around Berlin at election time. No person with democratic convictions and a rudimentary knowledge of the Weimar Constitution could call such tactics "legal."

In the 1920s, Hitler set about to reorganize his party from top to bottom. He divided all of Germany into districts, each called a *Gau* and led by a hard-core Nazi called a *Gauleiter*. These districts were subdivided into circles (each called a *Kreis*) and groups. Such units were also created for Austria, Danzig (q.v.), the Saarland and the Sudetenland, which at the time were not even a part of Germany, but which gave a clue as to what Hitler had in mind for the future. At the top of this party organization was the leader (*Führer*), Hitler himself. Such rule from the top was called the "leadership principle." Until he committed suicide in 1945, Hitler's leadership within the party was only once seriously challenged by a group of military officers who sensed that Germany was committing suicide under the *Führer* during the waning days of the Second World War (q.v.). It is inconceivable that the party would have been so successful without Hitler's powerful will and his ability to coordinate a diverse collection of ambitious Nazis.

Throughout most of the 1920s the Nazi Party found members and votes primarily among fanatical, nationalistic patriots, anti-Semites and social misfits fascinated by militarism. They had a psychological need for rabble-rousing rhetoric which was well supplied by party rallies and a daily reading of the party's newspaper, the *Völkischer Beobachter* ("People's Observer"). But the party was getting nowhere, with 32 parliamentary seats in 1924 and only 12 in 1928. However, after the economic disasters of 1929 and 1930, more and more Germans began to look to the former corporal from Austria, who had gained German citizenship through the back door of Bavarian citizenship only shortly before becoming chancellor of all Germany in 1933. As the novelist Erich Kästner (q.v.) wrote: "People ran after the pied pipers down into the abyss."

In the dark hours of June 30, 1934, known as the "night of the long knives," Hitler had hundreds of potential challengers to his authority within his own party murdered, especially the SA leadership, including Ernst Röhm (q.v.). While his assassination squads were at work, he also eliminated many prominent non-Nazis, such as von Schleicher and some of Franz von Papen's (qq.v.) closest aides, as well as leading authors, lawyers, civil servants, Catholic politicians, and harmless citizens who at some time had caused irritation to one or the other Nazi bosses. Von Papen and Heinrich Brüning (q.v.) escaped by the skin of their teeth. These cold-blooded acts were enough to intimidate most resistance to Hitler inside or outside the Nazi party until his death in 1945.

NAZI REPRESSION. Adolf Hitler (q.v.) and his party enforced a so-called *Gleichschaltung,* an untranslatable German word meaning the destruction or restructuring of all independent groups or institutions so that none could exist without supporting Nazi rule. In March and April 1933 he abolished the federal organization of Germany, and for the first time in its history, Germany became entirely centralized, with governors (*Reichsstatthalter*) carrying out Hitler's policy in the various regions. By June all independent labor unions had been outlawed and a Labor Front was created under the leadership of the invariably intoxicated Robert Ley, with the task of keeping labor under firm control. By July all political parties except the Nazi Party had been abolished, and concentration camps (q.v.) were established, where alleged enemies of the state could be "concentrated" and controlled.

By October, all communications media, including film, were brought under Nazi control. All newspaper editors were required to be Aryans (non-Jewish members of an ancient race to which, according to Nazi doctrine, Germans belonged). They could not even be married to Jews. This was only one of the first of a steadily growing number of measures directed against Jews within Germany, who, according to Nazi ideology, were social parasites who weakened the German nation. Many Jews, including brilliant intellectuals and scientists, began to flee Germany during the ensuing years. One of them was Albert Einstein (q.v.), who came to the United States. These anti-Jewish measures reached a prewar crescendo in the night of November 9-10, 1938, when hundreds of Jewish homes, stores and synagogues were systematically damaged and plundered. The amount of broken glass which this senseless and criminal rampage left gave the event the name of *Kristallnacht* ("Crystal Night"). Although many Germans were sickened by this incident, none dared to resist.

This event increased the tempo of the stampede of Jews from Germany which started in 1933 when all non-Aryans and people who were "no longer prepared to intercede at all times for the National Socialist state" were excluded from the civil service and ultimately from posts in the universities. Many young Germans had streamed into the Nazi student organization and assumed the right to control the lectures and writings of their professors for "un-German" or other politically revealing utterances. Youthful idealism can sometimes have a beneficial effect in politics, but it can also be disastrous. In 1933-34, an estimated 1,684 scholars, including 1,145 professors, were dismissed from the universities. At the universities of Berlin and Frankfurt am Main, about a third of the faculty was fired. In all of Germany the size of the student body fell by about one-third, due largely to the inclusion of Nazi Party membership into the admission procedure.

This policy of *Gleichschaltung* delivered an almost fatal blow to the cultural and intellectual preeminence of Germany. The U.S. benefitted enormously from this self-defeating and short-sighted policy. Before the outbreak of war, approximately 200,000 Germans, half of whom were Jewish, had fled to the U.S. American immigration quota restrictions, which had been tightened during the economic depression of the 1930s, were such that a large portion of the German refugees to the United States were intellectual or cultural leaders who could find sponsors more easily. They were attracted by such universities as the New School for Social Research in New York, Princeton University, the University of Chicago, or to such magnetic cultural centers as Hollywood or New York City.

Even an abbreviated list of those who fled Germany gives an idea of the enormous loss: in addition to scientists Albert Einstein and Edward Teller, in literature practically the entire Mann (q.v.) family (Thomas, Heinrich, Klaus, Erika and Golo), Bertold Brecht (q.v.), Stefan Zweig, Carl Zuckmayer, Alfred Döblin (q.v.), Leon Feuchtwanger (q.v.) and Erich Maria Remarque (q.v.). In film, there were Fritz Lang (q.v.), Marlene Dietrich (q.v.) and Otto Preminger; in theater, Max Reinhardt (q.v.); in music, Arnold Schönberg and Kurt Weil (q.v.); in art, Georg Grosz (q.v.) and Max Ernst (q.v.); in architecture, Walter Gropius and Ludwig Mies van der Rohe (q.v.); in publishing, Frederick Praeger and Kurt Wolff; and in scholarship, Paul Tillich (q.v.), Erich Fromm, Hans Morgenthau, Theodor Adorno (q.v.), Ernst Bloch (q.v.), Leo Strauss (q.v.), Erich Vögelin, Hannah Arendt, Ernst Cassirer (q.v.) and Kurt Riezler (q.v.). By 1938 the New York columnist Dorothy Thompson could claim with justification that "practically everyone whom the world considers to be representative of German culture before 1933 is now a refugee." Some stayed in the United States only until Hitler was defeated, but most stayed for good.

After 1941 Hitler withdrew more and more from public view and spent most of his time in military headquarters. Since his first goal--to dominate Europe--was slipping out of reach, he turned toward a second goal--the eradication of the Jews. His crimes went far beyond what the world had hitherto known and would only be fully discovered at the end of the war. Earlier and contemporary dictators or would-be world conquerors such as Alexander the Great, Napoleon and Stalin, had caused thousands or millions of deaths. But whether one agreed with them or not, they usually had political or military motives for their brutality. Hitler had none. Strictly speaking, his crimes were not war crimes, because his murder campaign of the Jews worked against his political and military objectives. This campaign was not only morally repugnant, but it further sapped the strength of a weakening Germany.

From the time he first began making public speeches, Hitler left no doubt that he was intensely anti-Semitic. He put this in writing in *Mein Kampf* and underscored it with anti-Jewish legislation after coming to power in 1933. On January 30, 1939, the sixth anniversary of his acquisition of power, he spoke publicly of "eradicating the Jewish race in Europe." This actually was another manifestation of his paranoia. His delusion was that the Jews were responsible for Germany's failure in the First World War (q.v.) and also a threat to his current ambitions for Germany.

In mid-1941 Hitler began having Polish and Russian Jews rounded up and shot beside mass graves. At the Wannsee Conference (q.v.) at the outskirts of Berlin on January 20, 1942, the decision was made to extend this policy to Jews in Germany and other occupied countries as well. Special extermination camps were constructed in Treblinka, Sobibor, Maidanek (Lublin), Belzec, Chelmno (Kulmhof) and Auschwitz for this grisly purpose. By the spring of 1942 the "final solution," which of course "solved" nothing but caused the needless death of four to six million innocent people by 1945, was in full swing. This policy was pursued with such single-minded determination that the German war effort itself was hampered. Manpower which was badly needed at the front or in domestic industries was either sent to extermination camps as victims or to SS units or other special military units (called *Einsatzgruppen*) as executors of this policy. Railroad rolling stock was diverted, and rail lines were clogged. Also, this policy of murder prompted the western Allies to declare as a major war aim in January 1943 the "punishment of those persons responsible for these crimes"; the Soviet Union proclaimed the same in November 1943. This new war aim made a compromise peace with Germany unthinkable and prompted Hitler's enemies to demand "unconditional surrender."

How much did the German people know about this ghastly policy at the time? Certainly all Germans of a sound mind knew that their country had adopted an official policy of discrimination against Jews, and all had been informed that their government was "resettling" Jews in the East. However, for a variety of reasons, the regime did not reveal to the German population details about the policy. The most important reason was that Hitler did not trust his own people and suspected that they would not approve. He had noted that most Germans had supported neither the nationwide boycott of Jewish businesses in 1933 nor the "Crystal Night" of 1938. The latter outrage actually produced pity for Jews and shame and irritation (but no more than that) among non-Nazis. Further, in mid-1941 Hitler had to suspend a policy he had introduced publicly in 1939 to eliminate 70,000 to 80,000 patients in convalescent and nursing homes, 10,000 to 20,000 sick and invalids in concentration camps within Germany, all Jewish patients in mental hospitals and about 3,000 children between the ages of three and 13 in orphanages and special schools for the handicapped. One of the major reasons for the suspension was the increasing unrest within the German population and the active opposition of the churches.

Hitler spared the Jews no misery, but he was careful not to allow most Germans to know exactly what was happening to the Jews. The exterminations were conducted in Eastern Europe, outside Germany, and careful precautions were taken not to enable unauthorized persons to witness what was happening within the camps. He even took the special measure, whenever possible, of sending German Jews first to large ghettos such as Theresienstadt in Bohemia, where they were able to write postcards back to Germany for a while before being transported to death camps. Of course, rumors about what was really happening filtered into Germany, but the absence of confirmation enabled anyone to reject the rumors or to remain in doubt if he chose to do so. Most Germans did just that, as did most non-Germans in the other occupied areas. In Germany and in other occupied areas there were persons who took risks by hiding or helping Jews. But nowhere was there the kind of mass uprising which would have been necessary to put an end to that shameful policy. In fact, only the military power of Hitler's enemies brought the Third Reich to its knees.

Hitler's policy of liquidating people whom he considered to be racially inferior was not restricted to the Jews. The Jews were not the only group which fell within his definition of *Untermensch* ("subhuman"). Only about a fifth of the 25,000 Gypsies living in Germany in 1939 survived by 1945, and estimates of the total number of European Gypsies murdered at Hitler's order range up to a half million. In October 1939, German leaders began a five-year campaign to destroy the entire Polish elite and culture. Polish priests, professors, journalists, businessmen and earlier political leaders were systematically liquidated. When one considers that the Soviet Union conducted a similar policy against the Poles in those areas under its domination, most dramatically in the Katyn Forest in 1939, where Soviet forces murdered 10,000 Polish officers and elites and dumped them into mass graves, it is almost miraculous that Poland was able to survive the war as a nation. In the end, Poland had lost about six million countrymen, about half of whom were Jews and not more than 300,000 of whom had fallen in battle.

The treatment of the Russians and of subject peoples under Russian rule was even worse than that of the Poles. German policy in the Soviet Union revealed the extent to which Hitler's racial theories thwarted

Germany's national interests. Many peripheral peoples in the Soviet Union who had never joined it voluntarily greeted invading German soldiers more like liberators than conquerors. A far-sighted German policy to transform these people into allies might have been successful and extremely beneficial to Germany. Instead, Russians and non-Russians were treated with the same brutality. Unlike in Poland, the German Army was involved in the actions directed against the civilian population in the Soviet Union. Soviet prisoners of war were especially mistreated by the Germans. According to German military records, by May 1, 1944, more than five million Russian soldiers had been captured by the Germans, mostly in 1941. However, fewer than two million remained alive. Almost a half million had been executed, 67,000 had fled, and almost three million had died in the camps, mostly of hunger. German mistreatment of the Soviet population helped Stalin unify his people in the war effort against the Germans.

NEUES DEUTSCHLAND. Official SED and later PDS (qq.v.) party organ.

NEURATH, KONSTANTIN BARON VON (1873-1956). Nazi foreign minister (1932-38), Reich protector of Bohemia and Moravia (1939-43).

NEUTRALITY, GERMAN see SOVIET NOTES

NEW CENTER (NEUE MITTE). Concept advanced by Chancellor Willy Brandt after the SPD's (qq.v.) dramatic election victory in 1972 to signal the party's moving toward the political center and curbing the influence of the SPD left. Brandt's successor, Helmut Schmidt (q.v.), developed the notion of "ideological balancer" and used the FDP (q.v.) to contain the assertive left wing in the SPD.

NEW COURSE see GERMAN DEMOCRATIC REPUBLIC, UPRISING

NEW FORUM. A grassroots opposition group in the GDR (q.v.) which was a prime mover in the 1989 revolution and the transformation of the GDR. (See also GERMAN DEMOCRATIC REPUBLIC, COLLAPSE.)

NEW GERMAN CINEMA. This is a collective term for the work of a number of very different directors who grew up in the postwar years and produced films in the late 1960s and 1970s.

NEW LEFT. The term "new left" was coined in the days of the student rebellion of the 1960s when many young people wanted to express their desire for change outside the organized leftist parties. In the 1990s, the New Left is composed of Marxist-Leninists, Trotskyites, anarchists, autonomists and dogmatic revolutionaries, and preaches class struggle. It identifies the proletariat as the essential revolutionary force leading the fight to tarnish the image of the FRG's political order in the eyes of its citizens and to overthrow the bourgeois state and capitalist system. Most advocate establishing a dictatorship of the proletariat culminating in a socialist and ultimately communist order. The autonomous anarchist groups advocate the eradication of the state, to be superseded by a "free" society. Most New Leftists unabashedly advocate using violence to achieve their aims. There are a variety of Marxist-Leninist groups, loosely called "K-groups." (See also COMMUNIST LEAGUE; LEAGUE OF WEST GERMAN COMMUNISTS; MARXIST-LENINIST PARTY OF GERMANY; UNITED SOCIALIST PARTY.)

NEW ORDER. A Nazi (q.v.) term referring to the new German-dominated, racially hierarchical Europe which Hitler (q.v.) sought to create. He boasted that such a New Order would last a thousand years, but it was buried in ashes after only twelve.

NEWSPAPERS AND NEWS MAGAZINES. Germans are relatively well-informed about politics. Roughly 50 percent of all adults read the political coverage in a wide range of daily newspapers. Although the daily sale of newspapers has risen, the total number of independent dailies has declined. More and more newspapers and magazines have become concentrated in publication groups, and the majority of dailies are no longer editorially independent. The largest such group is that controlled by Axel Springer (q.v.), who produced about a quarter of the total national output of daily newspapers. This includes the most widely read daily, the *Bild-Zeitung* (literally "Picture Newspaper"), a sensationalist mixture of conservative politics, crime, sex and gossip, and read by more than a fourth of all adults. The Springer enterprise also publishes one of the four informed, nationally distributed elite newspapers, *Die Welt*. The others are the moderately conservative *Frankfurter Allgemeine Zeitung*, the slightly left of center *Süddeutsche Zeitung* (published in Munich) and the outspoken left-liberal *Frankfurter Rundschau*.

The political party press no longer plays a significant role as it did in the German empire and Weimar Republic (qq.v.), but the CSU puts out its weekly, *Bayernkurier*. Also, the PDS (q.v.) continues to publish the daily *Neues Deutschland*, which has changed greatly from its dogmatic SED (q.v.) days; it reports news more objectively and is free to criticize some PDS policies. All other newspapers in the GDR (q.v.) had been censored and controlled at least indirectly by the Communists. *Berliner Zeitung*, *Freie Presse* (Chemnitz), *Sächsische Zeitung* (Dresden), *Mitteldeutsche Zeitung* (Halle), and *Volksstimme* (Magdeburg) are widely read in eastern Germany. West German publishers bought the East German regional papers and gave them a new look. But none of western Germany's newspapers caught on in the East; only one-eighth of the total circulation are western German products.

There are widely read weeklies. The highly influential *Der Spiegel*, with a circulation of one million, originally modeled itself after America's *Time*. Now it is far more opinionated, investigative, critical and crusading in its reporting. In the words of *The Economist*, it "has probably done more to raise German blood pressure over the years than any other single publication." *Stern*, with sales of 1.4 million, is also investigative (some would say "muck-raking"); since 1983 it has sported a black eye for publishing faked Hitler (q.v.) diaries, for which it had paid a fortune. *Die Zeit* is intelligent and politically moderate, the *Deutsche Zeitung* conservative and Protestant, and the *Rheinischer Merkur* conservative and Catholic.

In 1993, three new weeklies entered the market to challenge the supremacy of the established news magazines. *Focus* has an American-style format and includes short news items and heavy use of graphics and glossy color photos. *Die Woche* also has a color format, shorter articles, and provocative interviews to "organize controversy." *Die Wochenpost*, a serious journal founded in the GDR in 1953 and bought by *Stern* after unification, has been revamped. It emphasizes on-the-spot reporting and includes long articles.

NIEBELUNGENLIED (NIEBELUNGEN SONG). This powerful heroic epic poem from the Middle Ages, whose author is unknown, is the *Beowulf* of German literature.

NIEMÖLLER, MARTIN (1892-1984). Protestant theologian and co-founder of the Confessing Church (q.v.), he was arrested on July 1, 1937, and spent almost eight years in concentration camps (q.v.) before being liberated by German soldiers.

NIETZSCHE, FRIEDRICH WILHELM (1844-1900). Born in Saxony, he studied classical philology in Bonn and Leipzig. He had a professorial chair in Basel, Switzerland, until 1889, when he went mad and spent the final decade of his life staring at the ceiling in Weimar. He was more a poetic than a systematic philosopher. Because he suffered from frequent migraine headaches, he wrote aphorisms; his insights are flashes of intuition expressed in short, pithy and poignant form.

He saw life in terms of a biological urge, which he called the "will to power." Life is a never-ceasing effort to give form to this inner impulse. He was deeply struck by the ancient Greeks' distinction between the "Dionysian" (spontaneous, frenzied) view of life and the "Apollonian" view which stressed the measured and the orderly. In his opinion, the former was superior to the latter, as he presented in *Thus Spake Zarathustra*. Although he admired Schopenhauer (q.v.), Nietzsche was basically an optimist who had hope for a more glorious future. He advocated a liberation of moral standards, which he believed were derived from individuals' will to power. They had to be freed from the leveling tendencies of such morality as Christianity, which favors the "slave morality," the weakest people, the "last man." Heroic people, not the average, should establish life's values. Knowledge is an instrument of survival and should contribute to the power of such heroic people ("Supermen"), who should be able to rule without moral restraints, that is, *Beyond Good and Evil,* as his 1886 work was entitled. Through conflict, the weak should be weeded out or subjugated. To him, ethical systems or ideas are only "horizons" of the philosopher. They are a result of the will to self-realization.

Nietzsche was regarded in his day as a destructive thinker who despised Christianity, humanitarianism, and liberalism. Actually he was an individualist who had no German nationalist sentiments and who regarded the Germans as weak and the Jews as strong. In 1888 he said:

"German spirit: for the past eighteen years a contradiction in terms." Nevertheless, after his death his sister, Elisabeth Förster, edited his writings in such a way, adding her own views, that Pan-German nationalists and Nazis (q.v.) could invoke his quotable formulations to support their causes. (See also EMPIRE CULTURE.)

NIGHT OF THE LONG KNIVES (RÖHM PUTSCH)   see RÖHM, ERNST

NOLDE, EMIL (1867-1956).   He was a well-known German expressionist who was influenced by Matisse in his use of bold color.

NOLLAU, GÜNTHER (1911-)   see GUILLAUME AFFAIR

NORTH ATLANTIC TREATY ORGANIZATION (NATO), CREATION (1949) and FRG ENTRY (1955).   The Cold War froze the division of Germany, but it also provided West Germany opportunities which its crafty first chancellor, Konrad Adenauer (q.v.), knew how to exploit for the benefit of his country and his party. There were intense fears in Western Europe and North America that the Soviet Union sought direct or indirect domination over all of Europe. This fear led to the establishment of NATO on April 4, 1949, several months before the creation of the FRG. When NATO planners began working on plans for defending Western Europe, it was quickly apparent that the necessary forces could not be provided by the Western Allies and smaller West European countries alone. This was especially true since the United States had no intention at that time of permanently maintaining large numbers of American troops in Europe. Western European defense was conceivable only with the help of Germany. In the fall of 1949, the U.S. General Staff drafted a plan for the inclusion of German troops in NATO.

Adenauer listened very carefully to the message which was coming from Western capitals: "No NATO without Germany; no Germany without NATO." He reflected on his country's three principal goals and the best way it could achieve them: 1) West Germans, painfully viewing the plight of their countrymen in East Germany, wanted protection from Soviet domination; 2) they wanted to achieve political and economic recovery after the disgrace, regain fully much of their national sovereignty, create jobs, rebuild their cities, share in international trade and thereby acquire material prosperity and be respected as equals in the Western world, whose values they shared; 3) finally, they wanted their country to be reunified within the German borders of 1937.

The chancellor decided to strike a bargain with the NATO countries. On November 11, 1949, the 31st anniversary of the cease-fire ending the First World War (q.v.), Adenauer announced in an interview with the French newspaper, *L'Est Republicain*, that "if a common Supreme Command could be created, the Federal Republic would be willing at an appropriate time to integrate itself into a European defense system." He presented this decision to his own people as the "politics of necessity," and he stated the issue very simply: "We are faced with a choice between slavery and freedom. We choose freedom." In the years to come, Adenauer was successful in getting an important political advantage for each increase in German activity or responsibility in NATO. He helped to establish the United States as the permanent guarantor of West German security and to counteract the goal which many American leaders had well into the 1950s of withdrawing U.S. troops from Western Europe. He set a course which was never fundamentally changed by his successors in the chancellor's office.

There was, however, a problem with Adenauer's bargain with the West which the opposition Social Democrats could not get out of their minds: how would this Western integration, especially the military part of it, affect the goal of German reunification (q.v.), a goal which most Germans at that time wanted very much and which was an obligation placed on all West German governments by the framers of the Basic Law? Social Democrats strongly sensed at the time that by seeking to achieve the goals of security and recovery through political, economic and military integration with the West, the FRG was greatly reducing the chances that the Soviet Union would permit reunification.

The SPD's (q.v.) order of priorities was almost the complete reverse of Adenauer's. Throughout the 1950s, reunification was its top priority. It was not in principle opposed to reconciliation and integration with the West, nor was it ever opposed to a military defense for Germany, but it believed that the military and economic commitments the FRG had assumed in order to achieve Adenauer's goals would reduce or eliminate the chances that the pieces of Germany would find their way back together again. With the FRG integrated economically in Western Europe, with NATO and Soviet troops facing each other along the Elbe River, and with each part of a divided Germany serving as an essential element in the European balance of power, the Soviet Union would be far less inclined to withdraw its troops from East Germany. This would especially be the case if a reunified Germany were free to join or remain in NATO, as Adenauer always insisted it should be. The SPD feared that the military balance in Europe would require a perpetually divided Germany. Therefore, it showed much greater willingness than the Adenauer government to examine Soviet proposals for reunification and to assume that the Soviets were acting at least partly in good faith.

Adenauer continued to argue that his policy was not hostile to the aim of German reunification. He, like the Social Democrats, sought reunification "in peace and freedom." He argued that in return for the FRG's entering the Western Alliance, the three Western powers had formally committed themselves to seek German reunification. He also cast an eye on the West's greater industrial capability to arm itself quickly, on the high degree of Western political and economic integration in the future, and on the prospects of unrest in Eastern Europe which would be directed against the Soviet Union's tight and self-serving grip on its satellites. He therefore predicted that in time the balance of power would shift in favor of the West, and this shift would make possible negotiations "on the basis of strength" with the Soviet Union. He argued that the Soviets held the key to reunification and would ultimately see themselves compelled to settle the German question on Western terms. This latter element of Adenauer's reunification policy was, as the SPD correctly foresaw, an illusion. With the Soviet Union's acquisition of nuclear weapons, there could be no serious talk of rolling back what Winston Churchill had so aptly named "The Iron Curtain" through demonstrations of military strength.

Adenauer was right, though, in his assessment of what West Germans wanted most and the enormous advantages for his disgraced and impoverished country offered by Western European unity, crowned by the creation of the European Community (EC, q.v.) in 1957: the FRG would be an equal member of such a common market and would derive all the economic benefits which the trade and pooling of raw materials would bring. The position of the SPD, although it appeared to be grounded on the desire of many Germans for reunification, actually caused an erosion of the SPD's domestic political position within the FRG. Social Democrats watched with dismay and bitterness as Adenauer's party grew progressively stronger while the SPD stagnated.

The Soviet Union tried at the last moment to head off the FRG's entry into NATO. On January 25, 1955, it announced an end to the state of war with Germany. In February, it invited a delegation of

Austrian leaders to Moscow and offered them reunification and a withdrawal of all occupation forces if Austria remained militarily neutral and accepted restrictions on the size and equipment of its armed forces. It hoped that an Austrian settlement would be an irresistibly tempting carrot for the Germans. The Paris Treaties were nevertheless accepted by a majority in the Bundestag on February 27, and nothing could prevent them from going into force on May 5, 1955. From this day on, the FRG was a sovereign state, and as such it formally entered NATO on May 9, 1955. Five days later the leaders of eight Communist-ruled Eastern European countries gathered in the Polish capital and signed the Warsaw Pact Treaty. In the years which followed, the FRG became more and more integrated with NATO and made a major contribution to its effectiveness.

NORTH ATLANTIC TREATY ORGANIZATION (NATO), STRATEGY REGARDING GERMANY. NATO strategy is being reexamined in a fundamental way. After the successful allied war effort against Iraq in 1991, NATO adopted a major restructuring to adapt to the post-Cold War era in which the Warsaw Pact and Soviet threat have ceased to exist. No longer is the focus on deterring Soviet aggression by a doctrine of "flexible response" (including the option of using nuclear weapons) or on blunting an all-out Soviet attack on NATO forces concentrated in Germany, necessitating a "forward defense" by "layer-caked" NATO forces along an inter-German border. The future danger might come from undetermined threats to any NATO member state, from Norway to Turkey; they might emanate from non-European countries, such as Iraq against Turkey, or from unknown dangers springing from violent national unrest in Eastern Europe or a disintegrated Soviet Union.

To confront such dangers, NATO is creating a lightly-equipped multi-national rapid-reaction force numbering from 50,000 to 75,000, commanded by British officers and stationed largely in Germany. The main American contribution is air power. Such a force could react to a crisis in a matter of days. It would be backed up by a "base force" of up to five slower-moving but more powerful mobilized corps numbering as many as a half million NATO soldiers and able to move into action in a matter of weeks. This would include several new multi-national divisions and corps; in one such corps, a U.S. combat division will serve in a German-led corps, while in another a German division will be placed into a U.S.-led corps. A further "augmentation force," composed mainly of American units stationed in the U.S., could reinforce NATO within a few months of an outbreak of warfare. Overall NATO command will remain in American hands. This new structure would enable NATO to reduce its armed forces by at least 20 percent and the U.S. to cut its forces in Europe by more than half. Barring an unforeseen development, American forces in Europe will probably shrink to below 100,000 by the end of this century. While insisting that "the Alliance and the presence of U.S. troops in Europe remains indispensable for our security," the Kohl government believes that a common European foreign policy must, in the long run, include a common security and defense policy in some form.

NATO still retains a diminished role for nuclear weapons. Traditionally, FRG governments have always supported a NATO defense strategy which calls for the use of nuclear weapons in the event that an enemy attack could not be stopped by means of conventional arms. Since the FRG refuses to possess nuclear, chemical or biological weapons (although it does possess multi-purpose weapons capable of delivering nuclear warheads), it must rely on its allies, particularly the U.S., to provide the kind of nuclear deterrence which would be necessary to dissuade a potential aggressor from either attacking the FRG in the first place, or from continuing such an attack. To underscore its determination to defend the FRG, the U.S. maintains a drastically declining number of nuclear weapons in the western part of the FRG. Any nuclear strategy has always presented the FRG with a dilemma, however: Germany's defense (and ultimately its very existence as a free country) is dependent upon weapons which are under the exclusive control of foreign, albeit friendly, powers.

This problem was alleviated by dramatic announcements in September 1991 of unilateral American nuclear cuts which were matched by the shaken Soviet Union. The greatest impact was on Europe, where the only targets for tactical nuclear weapons were in countries which are no longer enemies, such as Poland and eastern Germany. Germans, who lived in the midst of the world's heaviest concentration of atomic weapons, were especially delighted, as Helmut Kohl (q.v.) indicated: "President Bush's decision implies that all American short-range nuclear weapons and the nuclear artillery will be removed from German soil. In the name of all Germans I want to thank the President for that." By 1992, all U.S. tactical nuclear weapons had been withdrawn from Europe.

NORTH GERMAN CONFEDERATION (NORDDEUTSCHER BUND) see BISMARCK, OTTO VON

NOSKE, GUSTAV (1868-1946). SPD, defense minister (1919-20), during which time he gained the nickname "Butcher Noske" for his determined suppression of leftist uprisings.

NOVAK, HELGA (1935-). Helga Novak grew up in East Berlin and studied journalism and philosophy in Leipzig. She worked in bookstores and factories in the East until she left with her husband for Iceland in 1961. Her GDR (q.v.) citizenship was revoked in 1966, and she settled in the West. Her poetry and prose reflect a critical social conscience manifested in concrete situations and ordinary individuals.

NOVALIS. This is the pseudonym for Friedrich von Hardenburg (q.v.).

NOVELLE. This refers to a genre of German literature with specific characteristics. The precise meaning is a matter of debate. The term comes from the Italian *Novella* of the 19th and 20th century. It is a story of medium length with a highly artistic form, a clear turning point in the plot, symbolism, and a sharp outline. Its attention to formal composition and the concentration on artistry separates it from a short story (*Erzählung*).

NUCLEAR NON-PROLIFERATION TREATY see ELECTIONS (1969)

NUREMBERG LAWS (1935). These laws deprived Jews of citizenship rights and imposed restrictions on marriages between gentiles and Jews.

NUREMBERG TRIALS. Following the Second World War (q.v.), the German people were largely disgraced and demoralized. Hitler (q.v.) had greatly changed German society, having reduced or eliminated permanently the power and influence which, for example, noblemen, military officers or large Prussian landowners had wielded earlier. Unlike 1918, the collapse of the Third Reich (q.v.) eliminated the nation's entire political elite. In 1945, Stalin favored liquidating with no trials up to 50,000 of the Nazi elite, but the U.S. wanted a trial which would establish new principles and procedures in international law, and it got its way. Germany's highest surviving Nazi leaders were placed on trial in Nuremberg from November 1945 until October 1946, and most were given either death sentences or long prison terms in Spandau Prison in West Berlin. The last prisoner there was Rudolph Hess (q.v.). Blind and crippled, he died in August 1987 at age 93, and the prison was razed. (See also DENAZIFICATION.)

-O-

OBERKOMMANDO DER WEHRMACHT (OKW). This was the supreme Wehrmacht Command during the Second World War (q.v.). The last OKW, General Keitel (q.v.) was sentenced to death at the Nuremberg Trials (q.v.).

OCCUPATION STATUTE. In April 1949, the three Western occupying powers officially ended their military administrations which had governed their zones. Thereafter, ultimate authority over civil affairs were assigned to British, French, and American civilian high commissioners operating within the terms of a three-power Occupation Statute. The commandants of the three Western forces in Germany had authority only over strictly military matters. Since this statute was accepted by the founders of the FRG in May 1949, the new FRG was not a fully sovereign state. The occupation powers retained the last word over foreign and defense affairs, foreign trade, the level of industrial production, reparations, decartelization (qq.v). They could veto any FRG legislation within 21 days, reject any change in the Basic Law (q.v.), and resume their full authority as occupying powers in case of an emergency. In July 1951, the Western powers declared the state of war with Germany to be ended despite the absence of a peace treaty. When the Paris Treaties took effect on May 5, 1955, permitting the FRG to rearm and thereby to become a fully sovereign state, the Occupation Statute lapsed. (See also REARMAMENT.)

ODER-NEISSE LINE. The Oder and Neisse Rivers form the present border between Germany and Poland. The German territory beyond this line before 1937 had amounted to about 44,000 square miles (70,400 sq. km., or 24 percent of Germany's entire land area) and had supplied a large part of Germany's food and coal. After the Second World War (q.v.) most of this area became a part of Poland to compensate Poles for their lands in the East which had been seized by the Soviet Union.

Germany officially relinquished these lands to Poland within weeks after it regained its unity and full sovereignty in 1990. The rest (a part of East Prussia, including the city of Königsberg) remains a part of Russia. (See also OSTPOLITIK.)

OFFICE FOR THE PROTECTION OF THE CONSTITUTION (BUNDESAMT FÜR VERFASSUNGSSCHUTZ--BfV). The Basic Law (q.v.) enjoins the active protection of the democratic constitution so that the post-1945 democracy would not be undermined as was that of the Weimar Republic (q.v.). Therefore, the federal government has a BfV, which is roughly equivalent to the Federal Bureau of Investigation (FBI) in the U.S. without the arrest power. The BfV is under the interior ministry. Each Land also has such an office, called the *Landesamt für Verfassungsschutz--LfV*. The job of these offices is to investigate individuals and groups suspected of attempting to undermine the constitutional system. The BfV publishes an annual report for parliament which lists and describes the activity of extremist groups and assesses trends. (See also LAND GOVERNMENT.)

OFFICE OF MILITARY GOVERNMENT U.S. (OMGUS). All Land leaders and mayors of major cities were removed from office in May 1945, and General Lucius Clay (q.v.) established OMGUS in Frankfurt am Main on October 1, 1945, to convert military government to a civilian operation and separate it from the military structure as quickly as possible. The spectrum of Allied military and local German governments permitted much political activity in the immediate postwar years. (See also ALLIED OCCUPATION.)

OHNE MICH BEWEGUNG (WITHOUT ME MOVEMENT)   see BUNDESWEHR and REARMAMENT

OLLENHAUER, ERICH (1901-1963). SPD party and parliamentary group leader (1952-63). (See also BRANDT, WILLY.)

OPERATIONAL GROUPS (EINSATZGRUPPEN)   see HIMMLER, HEINRICH

ORGANIZATION CONSUL   see ERZBERGER, MATTHIAS

OSSI. Term to describe a German from the eastern part of Germany. (See INTRODUCTION.)

OSSIETZKY, CARL VON (1889-1938). Chief editor of *Die Weltbühne* (1926-33), he was sent by the Nazis to a concentration camp (qq.v.), where he died.

OSTBÜRO (EASTERN BUREAU). This was an SPD (q.v.) organization, with headquarters in West Berlin, which was created to maintain contacts and assistance with the outlawed SPD in the Soviet zone. It was hated by the SED (q.v.). When the SPD wanted to seek a dialogue and cooperation with the SED in order to facilitate *Ostpolitik* (q.v.), there was a dispute between Herbert Wehner (q.v.), who argued for working ties with the SED, and the Ostbüro's director, Stephan Thomas, who was skeptical of cooperation with the SED and who wished to maintain the bureau. After Willy Brandt (q.v.) became chancellor in 1969, the Ostbüro was closed, on the grounds that it was a remnant of the Cold War.

OSTPOLITIK (POLICY TOWARD THE EAST). The Brandt (q.v.) government, which took power in 1969, had no intention of changing the FRG's policy toward the West, but it was determined to conduct a dynamic and innovative policy toward the East. Fundamentally, it decided to overturn two decades of West German foreign policy and to recognize the territorial *status quo* in Europe, including the division of Germany. The word "reunification" (q.v.) was dropped from the government's terminology. The first dramatic step in August 1970 was a German-Soviet treaty in which both states renounced the use of force in Europe. West Germany also declared that it had no territorial claims against any country and that the borders of all European states are inviolable, including the Oder-Neisse (q.v.) line and the border between East and West Germany. This treaty was the first West German recognition of East Germany's international legitimacy. Brandt was correct in commenting that in actual fact, "nothing is lost with this treaty that was not gambled away long ago."

The second step was a German-Polish treaty in late 1970, containing basically the same points as in the German-Soviet treaty, but underscoring the acceptance of the Oder-Neisse frontier. The treaty also provided for normal diplomatic relations, and in a separate accord Poland agreed to grant exit permits for some ethnic Germans living in

Poland. To demonstrate his sincerity in introducing a new era of Polish-German relations, Brandt dropped to his knees in reverence before a monument in Warsaw honoring the Polish Jewish victims who were killed or mistreated by Germany during the Second World War (q.v.). The Poles never forgot this electrifying gesture.

A third step, not involving the FRG directly but strongly encouraged by it, was the Four-Power Agreement on Berlin in 1971. The FRG had linked its ratification of the German-Soviet Treaty to a successful resolution of the Berlin problem. Brandt reasoned that if the FRG was willing to recognize the *status quo* in Europe, the Soviet Union should be willing to recognize the *status quo* in Berlin. The Four-Power Agreement contained the Western Powers' acknowledgment that West Berlin was not a constituent part of the FRG and the Soviet Union's recognition that there were "ties" between the FRG and West Berlin. Further, the FRG would perform consular services for West Berliners and represent them in international organizations and conferences. The Soviet Union also promised that Western transit traffic to and from West Berlin would proceed unimpeded. That was deemed necessary since the East German government had frequently hampered access to the city in order to place pressure on the Bonn government. The Soviet Union admitted that West Berlin was neither located on the territory of the GDR (q.v.) nor was it an entity entirely separate from the FRG.

The last significant step was the Basic Treaty between the two Germanys themselves. Bonn knew that it could not bypass East Berlin despite the fact that the East German regime was defensive, rigid and determined to exact a very high price for any concession. After many months of frustrating negotiations, an agreement was signed in late 1972 and ratified in mid-1973 which normalized the access between the FRG and West Berlin and made it possible for West Berliners to visit both East Berlin and the GDR. By signing the Basic Treaty, the FRG publicly accepted the GDR as a legitimate state and agreed to deal with it as an equal. Yet, Bonn continued to insist that there was only one German nation (even if there were two German states) and that the GDR would not be treated like any other foreign country. To highlight this, the FRG maintained a permanent liaison mission in East Berlin, not an embassy, and Bonn's dealings with the GDR were conducted by the chancellor's office, the ministry of all-German affairs, or a special office in the interior ministry, but not by the foreign office. The official relations between the two Germanys improved as a result of the Basic

Treaty. But the two countries' relationships remained ambiguous and tense, charged with conflict and suspicion.

OTTO I, THE GREAT (912-973). German King and Emperor. see GERMAN EMPIRE

OVERCOMING THE PAST (VERGANGENHEITSBEWÄLTIGUNG). One cannot follow either the "great debates" or current events in the FRG without being constantly reminded of the influence of the Nazi (q.v.) past. The collapse of Hitler's (q.v.) state was the reason for the division of Germany. Any talk of German reunification (q.v.) therefore sparked fears of a renewal of the kind of threat to other European states which had existed before 1945.

The debates over the drafting of a Basic Law (q.v.) (constitution) in the late-1940s were characterized by the determination to create a workable democracy which would, at the same time, make the rise of another Hitler impossible. Adopted exactly four years to the day after the defeat of the Third Reich (q.v.) on May 8, 1945, it reflects several objectives which the founders hoped to achieve after a 12-year nightmare: individual freedom, political democracy, stability (to prevent a repetition of the Weimar experience, which most Germans continue to view in negative terms), built-in safeguards against the emergence of another dictatorship, and links with some aspects of the German political tradition, such as federalism. In contrast to the U.S. Constitution, which has a Bill of Rights tacked on at the end, the West German founders placed in the first 20 articles guarantees for inalienable rights and liberties and the protection of life. Article one opens with the words: "The dignity of man is inviolable." Clearly, the Nazi past had strengthened public sensitivity and awareness of the importance of civil rights.

The founders built in a carefully designed system of checks and balances which was intended to be an insurmountable obstacle to any would-be dictator: a powerful constitutional court which could keep the republic on the democratic path, states with power over the police, education and radio/TV, a powerful upper house through which the states can block important legislation passed by the lower house, an electoral system which keeps small parties (like the Nazi party had been until 1929) out of parliament and makes the formation of stable coalitions possible, a weak indirectly-elected president who could never undermine the authority of parliament, and political parties dignified by the constitution but operating under the requirement to remain democratic or risk being outlawed.

The FRG was the first state in the world to anchor the right to conscientious objection in its constitution. The explosive rearmament (q.v.) debate in the 1950s and the subsequent arms deployment controversies were fueled by a memory of the past. In the 1960s, the introduction of emergency laws, which Hitler had shown could be abused, and the formation of a Grand Coalition (q.v.), which for three years practically eliminated opposition within parliament, were resisted with the Third Reich in mind. That resistance helped give birth to the student rebellion which sought to make up for the missed opportunities in 1945 and get the FRG back on the road to democratic renewal. The state's struggle against terrorism (q.v.) in the 1970s was affected both by the determination not to allow an extremist minority to destroy the democratic state, as had happened in 1933, and by the concern that in restoring order by combatting terrorism, the inalienable rights of all citizens not be trampled in the process by a "police state," just as they had been under Hitler. The FRG did not lose its nerve and overreact when confronted with grisly radical left-wing terrorism, even though Heinrich Böll (q.v.) expressed a different opinion in *The Lost Honor of Katarina Blum,* a film of which was directed by Volker Schlöndorff.

The struggle against the deployment of intermediate-range missiles (INF) on West German soil in the 1980s also invoked the unpleasant past. Critics argued that such weapons were offensive and would convert West Germany from a defensive to an aggressive power and threaten peace, just as the *Wehrmacht* had done. On the other hand, proponents argued that the missiles were essential for deterring a war like the one Hitler had unleashed in Europe. President Richard von Weizsäcker (q.v.) stressed in his famous speech before parliament in May 1985 that "more strongly than before, the last war awakened the longing for peace in the heart of man." To encourage citizens to resist any new Hitler who would come to power by democratic means and then undermine the constitution, the FRG's founders became the first in the world to anchor the right of revolution in the text of the constitution itself. Article 20 of the Basic Law explicitly declares that "all Germans shall have the right to resist any person or persons seeking to abolish the constitutional order, should no other remedy be possible." Opponents of the INF deployment invoked this right and argued unsuccessfully before the Constitutional Court (q.v.) that such missiles endangered life, which, because of the Nazis' total disregard for it, is protected in Article One of the Basic Law.

The very style of foreign and defense policy in the FRG was shaped as an antithesis to the aggressive, belligerent approach during the Third Reich. The FRG's watchwords are conciliation and compromise, rather than threat or confrontation. Its diplomats' instinct was never to get out ahead on any issue and always to have political backing from another country, such as France. The shadow of Nazism creates an almost unanimous aversion to the use of force in international politics. To avoid stimulating fear, it places almost all its troops under NATO (q.v.) command. As one American diplomat remarked, "these people have simply had power politics bred out of them."

Remembering the human suffering their fathers and grandfathers inflicted on Jews and citizens of the Soviet Union, most Germans are reserved in their criticism of those peoples, even when disagreeing with the policies of those states. As Weizsäcker said, "when we think what our Eastern neighbors had to suffer in the war, we will better understand that compensation, detente and friendly relations with these countries remains the central task of German foreign policy." Perhaps the Greens (q.v.) display this aversion to power politics the most assertively: since Hitler was aggressive and militaristic, they are pacifist; since German obedience led to the rise of dictatorship, they are rebellious; since the Nazis exploited the census, a census conducted in 1987 was boycotted. Opponents to the census contended that too many questions were to be asked and that the information obtained could be used by the police and other public bodies, thereby potentially penetrating deeply into the citizen's private life.

Domestic politics reflects a fear of the past. Prodding by allies to reflate the German economy is routinely resisted by politicians, who cite the fact that inflation and unemployment during the Weimar Republic (q.v.) paved the way to Hitler's takeover. Much popular clamoring to tighten up more on refugees pouring into the country and to evict many of the four-and-a-half million foreign "guest workers" in the FRG are usually rejected on the grounds that the new Germany must bend over backwards to respond to human suffering, after all that once had happened. Weizsäcker: "When we remember how those persecuted for their race, their religion and their politics, who were threatened with certain death, often stood before the closed borders of other states, we will not shut the door on those who today are truly persecuted and seek protection among us. . . . We learn from our own history what man is capable of. . . . Our request to young people is this: Do not allow yourselves to be driven into enmity and hatred against other people, against Russians or Americans, against Jews or Turks, against radicals or conservatives, against black or white. Learn to live with one another, not in opposition to one another."

For a couple of decades after the war there was considerable discussion in the FRG about *Vergangenheitsbewältigung*. This explicit discussion is waning because fewer and fewer Germans are still alive who were adults during the Hitler era. The death of Rudolf Hess (q.v.) in Spandau Prison in 1987 was a reminder of how few "big fish" are still around. In the 1990s, two-thirds of Germans had grown up in the post-war era, compared with one-third in the late 1960s. Persons who now are implicated in scandals because of their Nazi pasts are usually ones who could be said to have committed "youth sins."

In an article published in the *German Studies Review* describing the impact of the anti-Nazi resistance movement on the West German rearmament debate, David Clay Large argued that "every nation needs a usable past which can validate its present and inspire faith in its future." Germans have a long and rich history, but it is one of which many are not particularly proud. There have been signs in the FRG of a desire to revive certain national traditions, such as trying again to cut a clear path through the complicated web of German history. The nationwide debate over the meaning of Prussia (q.v.) in Germany's past and present, crowned by several special exhibits in Berlin, whose 750th birthday was celebrated by both Germanies in 1987, indicate that many persons are tapping their canes in the corridors of German history to find more positive possibilities for national identification. Mammoth events focusing on Martin Luther (q.v.), Goethe (q.v.) or the Staufen and Wittelsbach dynasties have taken place.

Chancellor Helmut Kohl (q.v.), who came to power in October 1982, is well suited to the changed times and climate. Born in 1930, he is the first chancellor who was too young to play any part in the Hitler era, including performing military service. He claims to exemplify a new generation of leaders untainted by the past and seeks to appeal to those Germans, including those on the center-left, who want again to feel proud of their country. He uses the word *Vaterland* in his speeches, and his encouragement to play the national anthem more often has helped make it possible to close the day's television programming with its melody. In short, he wants to help produce a "normal patriotism," the kind which is taken for granted in other countries. Germans still show little enthusiasm for such symbols. Nevertheless, national feelings, which were tabu for a long time, do seem to be slightly stronger; it is noteworthy that such feelings were not significantly strengthened by reunification (q.v.) in 1990.

Kohl's efforts to apply total normalcy to relations with other countries have not always succeeded and have revealed that foreign countries still are unwilling to regard the FRG solely as an economically strong, socially just and stable democracy, which is a reliable trading partner and NATO ally. Perhaps the best example was the embarrassing event at Bitburg on May 5, 1985. He had persuaded President Ronald Reagan to pay homage to the German war dead buried in a cemetery in Bitburg, without learning in time that Waffen-SS soldiers were also buried there. The president's visit was supported by three-fourths of all adult West Germans, but it unleashed a storm of protest among Jewish and veteran groups in the U.S. What had been intended as a gesture of reconciliation and friendship actually revived memories of the Holocaust and the war, and it temporarily strained relations between these two friendly countries. *Der Spiegel* spoke of a "cheap self-delusion with which the Germans had stolen away from their unhealthy past so soon after the defeat."

Undoubtedly the most eloquent warning against moving too quickly away from the past was made three days later by President Weizsäcker in his now famous speech before parliament on the occasion of the 40th anniversary of the defeat of the Third Reich. It "is for us Germans no day for celebrations," even if it was "a day that liberated all of us from the inhumanity and tyranny of the National Socialist regime--the end of an aberration in German history." He reminded his fellow citizens of what two-thirds of them already knew as early as 1967 (compared with one-third in 1951): Germany was responsible for the outbreak of the Second World War (q.v.). He spoke to each German who was an adult before 1945 about one of the favorite legends which had comforted them: that even though "the perpetration of this crime [of murdering six million Jews] was in the hands of a few people," nevertheless, "every German was able to experience what his Jewish compatriots had to suffer. . . . Who could remain unsuspecting after the burning of the synagogues. . . ? Whoever opened his eyes and ears and sought information could not fail to notice that Jews were being deported." He continued: "There is no such thing as the guilt or innocence of an entire people. Guilt, like innocence, is not collective but individual. . . . The predominant part of our present population was at that time either very young or indeed not born at all. They cannot acknowledge a personal guilt for acts which they simply did not commit. . . . Yet their forefathers bequeathed them a heavy legacy. . . . All of us, whether guilty or not, whether old or young, must accept the past. We are all affected by its consequences and held responsible for it. . . . It is not a matter of overcoming the past. One can do no such thing. The past does not allow itself to be retrospectively altered or undone. But whoever closes his eyes to the past becomes blind to the present. Whoever does not wish to remember inhumanity becomes susceptible to the dangers of new infection." Fritz Stern, an American historian who had fled from Hitler, was correct when he noted that "the past dominates the present to an extraordinary degree, and the past cannot be erased."

-P-

PACIFISM see REARMAMENT, GERMAN and PEACE MOVEMENT

PAINTING AND SCULPTURE, POST-1945. No post-war German artists have been able to establish a distinguishing German style which is internationally recognized as such. The FRG does have many artists who produce recognized works in styles coming from abroad. This is particularly visible in pop-art and hyperrealism, movements which emanated from the U.S.

PAN-GERMAN LEAGUE. In the age of nationalism in the latter half of the 19th and early part of the 20th centuries, there were many expansionist "Pan" movements bearing names like Pan-American, Pan-Slav, or Pan-German. The latter took the form of an energetic political party which put heavy pressure on the German government to pursue a more aggressive foreign policy. In despair, Chancellor Bethmann Hollweg (q.v.) declared in 1912: "Politics cannot be made with these idiots!" (See also EMPIRE FOREIGN POLICY.)

PAPEN, FRANZ VON (1879-1969). Center Party (q.v.) politician, chancellor (1932). He was tried in Nuremberg after the war and was found not guilty, a judgement which created considerable public consternation at the time. (See HARZBURG FRONT; HITLER'S SEIZURE OF POWER.)

PARAGRAPH 218 see ABORTION and FAMILY

PARLIAMENTARY COUNCIL (PARLAMENTARSCHER RAT). This is the body which wrote the Basic Law (q.v.) in 1948-49. The three Western Allies decided in the summer of 1948 to permit German leaders in their three zones to write a Basic Law and found a West German state. As often the case since 1945, German politics was forced to respond to important political and military developments outside of Germany, especially to tensions between East and West. The council convened in Bonn on September 1, 1948, under the chairmanship of the elderly mayor of Cologne, Konrad Adenauer (q.v.). The SPD (q.v.) and Adenauer's CDU (q.v.) each occupied 27 of the 65 seats. Its work was frequently delayed by the three occupation authorities. Such intervention prompted an irritated SPD leader, Kurt Schumacher (q.v.), to remind the Americans, British and French that "it is as much in your interest as in ours that we get things settled." This was done by May 8, 1949, almost four years to the day since the capitulation of the Third Reich. The occupation powers' rights were in no way affected, and they retained the final authority over such questions as disarmament, demilitarization, reparations, and foreign affairs. The newly founded FRG was seen to be strictly "for a transitional period," and the fundamental document that was adopted was called a Basic Law, not a constitution, a word that might connote something more permanent. The founders wrote into the preamble that they had acted on behalf of those Germans living under Soviet occupation and that "the entire German people is called upon to accomplish, by free self-determination, the unity and freedom of Germany." Thus, West German leaders imposed upon themselves the obligation to bring the two parts of Germany back together. (See also ADENAUER, KONRAD; BASIC LAW; COMMUNISM; SOCIAL DEMOCRATIC PARTY OF GERMANY.)

PARLIAMENTARY GROUP (FRAKTION). All Bundestag deputies belonging to a party which won a certain number of seats in the Bundestag (ca. two dozen) belong to a *Fraktion* of their party, called a "parliamentary party" in Britain. It is the parliamentary groups which distribute key legislative posts, committee assignments and chairmanships, and seats on other executive bodies in the Bundestag. Such distribution is made in accordance with the size of each party's *Fraktion*. Most government funding for administrative and legislative support is given to the parliamentary groups, not to the individual Bundestag members. Each parliamentary group is led by a chairperson, several vice-chairpersons, and an executive committee elected by that body. This leadership directs the party's activities in parliament and maintains strict party discipline on votes, except in cases where moral issues are at stake, such as abortion (q.v.). Individual members are assigned to working groups which deal with specific policy areas. It is in the weekly *Fraktion* meetings that much of the real decision-making in the Bundestag occurs and the party's positions are hammered out.

PARLIAMENTARY STATE SECRETARIES. These positions were introduced in 1967 during the Grand Coalition (q.v.) when there were too few cabinet posts for the leaders of the two largest parties. Each minister is assisted by a parliamentary state secretary who must be a member of the Bundestag. They are nominated by the chancellor, formally appointed by the federal president after the minister concerned has been consulted. Their function is not clearly defined and depends upon the inclinations of the specific ministers to whom they are assigned. In the Bundestag they answer questions for the minister.

PARTIES, POLITICAL. It is crucially important that a person can be elected to the Bundestag only as a member of a political party. In the past, Germans had regarded parties with considerable distrust and disdain. Parties allegedly divided the body politic, and their log-rolling and pursuit of particularist interests had an undignified and illicit air in the eyes of the average German. This condescension before 1945 greatly weakened the prestige of parliament and therefore of democracy. Also, so many parties had seats in the Weimar parliament that it was almost impossible to construct a stable and lasting majority. Therefore, the Basic Law (q.v.), in contrast to the U.S. Constitution, grants political parties official recognition and status, as well as the responsibility to organize the country's political life. Also, any party is required to receive a minimum of 5 percent of the votes cast nationwide in order to win any seats in the Bundestag. In the first election in 1949 many parties won seats, but since 1953 only five parties have been able to accomplish this. The Bundestag is made up of parliamentary groups (q.v., each called a *Fraktion*) which practice a high degree of party discipline; almost nine out of ten votes are straight party votes. Since 1959 the major political parties have received increasing amounts of financial subsidies from the national treasury. Many observers have called the FRG a "party state," and they are largely correct.

No party in Germany which advocates drastic changes in the country's political and economic order has a chance of success in elections; winning votes clearly lie close to the political center. The major parties have always been integration parties--mass organizations with effective means of mobilization. They were largely un-ideological "parties for anybody and everybody." Nevertheless, they were able to offer their members a kind of intellectual and social home. Their role as guarantors of a stable system of government can hardly be exaggerated if one considers that they existed before the FRG was founded in 1949. Their historical legitimacy is therefore prior to that of the state. However, some young Germans turned their backs on these mass-based parties, whose roots reach deeply into the country's social structure; they did not allow themselves to be integrated by these mammoth organizations as easily as before. Instead, they turned more and more to single-issue politics and to the *ad-hoc* groups which sprang into existence around such controversial issues as nuclear energy and unilateral disarmament. New forms of political organization emerged, such as that of the ecologists, known as the Greens (q.v.). Such loosely-knit groups understood how to clear the "5 percent hurdle" required to win representation in parliaments at all levels of government. Some are willing to combine in a loose way with each other and to present themselves in elections as "Alternative Lists" or as "Colorful Lists" (*Bunte Listen*).

PARTIES, RIGHT-WING. The late 1980s and 1990s witness the temporary strengthening of parties on the far right, a development which causes anxiety in both the FRG and abroad. They range from illegal neo-Nazi groups to legal parties which feed on myriad dissatisfactions, including hostility toward immigrants, tight housing, and high unemployment. Some Germans bemoan what they see as a breakdown in law and order caused by the leftist alternative subculture. Indeed, gains on one extreme of the political spectrum seem to foster gains on the other. Founded in Bavaria in 1983, the Republicans are led by Franz Schönhuber, a former Waffen-SS member and popular television talk show moderator. It is not a neo-Nazi party, but it is nationalist. It found a warm reception in western Berlin, where more than 10 percent of the population is foreign; the 150,000 Turks living there constitute the largest Turkish community outside of Turkey and the sixth largest in the world. The Republicans call for repatriation of foreign workers in stages and for tough measures to stem the flow of asylum-seekers into the FRG, noting that "a multiracial society is a red flag to our party." After 1989 the party's fortunes temporarily plummeted. It received only 2.3 percent of the votes and no seats in the 1990 federal elections. Once a refuge for unreconstructed Nazis (q.v.), the National Democratic Party of Germany (NPD, q.v.) is more conservative than the Republicans. Also fishing for votes on the rightist fringe are the German People's Union (DVU), which in 1991 captured an astounding 15 percent of the votes and six seats in Bremen, and the smaller, more militant Free German Workers' Party. In eastern Germany extreme right-wing parties have sprung into existence since reunification (q.v.), such as the German League (Deutsche Liga) and German Alternative (Deutsche Alternative). The latter published a *Brandenburger Beobachter*, that bristled with crude racist propaganda and anti-Semitic cartoons. On December 10, 1992, it became the second neo-Nazi group in two weeks to be banned by the federal government. In the words of Interior Minister Rudolf Seiters, "the disgusting work of these rabble-rousers must be stopped." On December 16, the Kohl (q.v.) government ordered intelligence surveillance of the Republicans to determine whether they fit the legal definition of "anti-democratic," which would permit the government to ban their party also. The chancellor declared: "Germany is a democracy that can defend itself, and we will prove it now."

PARTIES LAW (1967). This is the basis for all legislation dealing with public financing of political parties. The main provision was a formula by which any party which won over 2.5 percent of the vote was given DM 2.5 from public monies for each voter who had voted for the party in the preceding election. The Constitutional Court (q.v.) later lowered the 2.5 percent hurdle to .5 percent in order to give a fair chance to new parties. Also, the amount given to a party per voter was increased twice, first to DM 3.5 and then to DM 5.

PARTY OF DEMOCRATIC SOCIALISM (PARTEI DES DEMOKRATISCHEN SOZIALISMUS--PDS). The SED, DKP, and PDS (qq.v.) all grew out of the Communist Party of Germany (Kommunistische Partei Deutschlands--KPD, q.v.). After ruling the GDR (q.v.) in an authoritarian way for 40 years, the SED faced a fatal crisis in the fall of 1989. It was well on the road to impotence when, on December 8, almost 3,000 SED delegates met to decide the fate of their battered party. The atmosphere was very different from previous congresses. There were no bold letters on the walls proclaiming the triumph of socialism, no fraternal greetings. Nothing was censored, and the frank and critical debates were a sign of the liberated attitude of the rank-and-file. During the first night of debate the atmosphere was so chaotic that it looked as if the congress would split up and fail.

Thanks to Hans Modrow's (q.v.) authority, a new party chairman was elected: Gregor Gysi (q.v.), a marginal party member who won 93.5 percent of the votes. He is a lawyer who had made a name by defending dissidents and the opposition New Forum (q.v.) and by heading the prosecution of former SED leaders accused of corruption. He admitted that a complete break with Stalinism and a new form of socialism were needed and that the SED bore responsibility for plunging

Gregor Gysi (*Source:* PIB.)

the GDR into crisis. He represented a completely new type of party member, and his behavior was unconventional: he was witty and had a magnetic sense of humor, and he stood for the rule of law. After the SED scandals, he seemed to be the right man at the right time. His leftist-inspired intellect attracted the intelligentsia, but not the working class. At his side as vice-chairmen were Modrow, an integrating figure who attracted those who still believed in the idea of socialism but who felt betrayed by the old leadership, and Dresden mayor Wolfgang Berghofer (q.v.), a pragmatist and man of action. After weeks of hesitation, the party decided to rename itself the PDS, in an attempt to escape from the unpopularity of the SED and communism itself.

In the first free elections ever held in the GDR in March 1990, the PDS won only 16% of the votes. In the 1990 federal electoral campaign in the fall the PDS advocated a middle road between the discredited old-style communism in the East and capitalism in the West. Its slogan was "A Liking for the Left," and its leader was the only media star in a very mixed bag of socialists. Gregor Gysi, as a Jew, is a rarity in modern German politics. He declared: "I was already defending political victims when your Kohls and Strausses gave Honecker billions in credits!" He tried to give the party a modern, fresh image, and his followers wore buttons reading in English: "Take it easy Gysi!" As the successor to the SED, which plundered the East German people for 40 years, the PDS was one of the richest parties in Europe, with billions of marks hidden away in secret accounts and assets. Although the Treuhand (q.v.) later limited its access to those resources, it was noticeably well-funded during the 1990 elections, and it ran an extremely professional campaign. Gysi filled halls whenever he appeared in the West, and the visitors were predominantly young people who liked his unconventional and open style and refusal to speak in communist "functionary's Chinese."

For the federal elections it formed a "Left List/PDS," of which it was the senior partner. This alliance garnered only .3 percent of the votes in the West and 11.1 percent in the East, for a total of 2.4 percent nationwide. For this election only, the 5 percent hurdle was waived for new parties, so the PDS was given 17 seats in the Bundestag. Gysi won a directly elected seat in East Berlin's Hellersdorf-Marzahn, a very unusual feat for a candidate from a small party. In the Berlin Land elections, which were also held on December 2, 1990, the PDS captured 1.1 percent of the votes in the western part and 23.6 percent in the eastern, where former SED functionaries and intellectuals are concentrated, for a total of 9.2 percent and 23 seats in the Berlin legislature. Although Germany is united, the PDS will never be more than a regional political force fixated on the former GDR. In future Bundestag elections, when it will have to capture 5 percent of the votes nationwide to win seats, its failure is almost certain. The 1990 federal and Berlin elections made it obvious that the party's downward trend, beginning with the March 1990 GDR elections, was continuing, despite the fact that it garnered enough protest votes to win 30 percent of the votes in the 1992 municipal elections in eastern Berlin.

It is viewed as the heir to the discredited SED and as representative of the interests of former SED members, who make up 90 percent of the PDS's present membership. The antipathy against the party is kept alive by continuing revelations about financial scandals and outrageous Stasi (q.v.) activities, such as its harboring and training former West German terrorists in the GDR. Prosecutors have also issued arrest warrants for former top East German leaders for ordering that persons attempting to escape from the GDR be killed. From 1961 to 1989, about 350 lost their lives this way, including at least 77 in Berlin alone. The PDS lacks acceptance outside the former GDR because of the SED's past. All attempts at renewal remained half-hearted. Its efforts to broaden its appeal to western Germany failed. It is split between a faction which critically regards the past and favors progressive socialist reforms and one which expresses strong anti-capitalist views and evokes a sort of old-time socialist nostalgia. Membership is declining steadily, and in autumn 1991 it dipped below 200,000. Especially young people have left. As a result, pensioners predominate in the rank-and-file. To make matters worse, the other parties seek its demise, and they exclude it from political decision-making. All these internal and external threats to the PDS prevent any form of resurgence. (See also COMMUNISM; ELECTIONS, GDR; GERMAN DEMOCRATIC REPUBLIC, COLLAPSE; SOCIALIST UNITY PARTY OF GERMANY.)

PARZIVAL. This Middle High German epic poem was written by Wolfram von Eschenbach about King Arthur's court in 1210. It tells the story of Parzival from his birth until he becomes the Grail King.

PAUL'S CHURCH (PAULSKIRCHE) MOVEMENT. Social Democrats joined such well-known anti-military advocates as Gustav Heinemann (q.v.) and representatives of the trade unions, universities, and churches in support of an extra-parliamentary movement called the "Paulskirche Movement." This sprang into action on January 29, 1955, and called for an end to German military integration with the West because of the damage it would do to reunification (q.v.). Mass demonstrations took place throughout the FRG. Some were sponsored by the SPD (q.v.), and many of its leaders even supported demands for a plebiscite although the framers of the Basic Law (q.v.) had explicitly forbidden this measure, which had often been so misused in Germany's past.

PAUL'S CHURCH PARLIAMENT see REVOLUTION OF 1848

PAULUS, FRIEDRICH (1890-1957). Commander of Sixth Army captured at Stalingrad in January 1943. Only 6,000 Germans returned.

PEACE MOVEMENT. By the 1980s, the FRG's defense policy was being challenged not only within the established parties, but in public opinion as well. The "peace movement" was an extremely varied group of activists. Its ranks included party members from the SPD and FDP (qq.v.), ecologists, church circles, a multitude of smaller humanitarian groups, a blue ribbon assemblage of intellectuals, well-organized, highly visible but numerically small communist splinter groups and several security experts. The majority of citizens consistently opposed the total withdrawal of U.S. troops from Germany (the largest concentration of American armed forces overseas). Nevertheless, Germans increasingly felt the physical burden of almost a half million allied soldiers on their soil. They called for drastic reductions in bothersome low-level training flights and ground maneuvers, even after the 1991 war in the Persian Gulf. Such calls came in the wake of almost universal revulsion caused by a disaster in August 1988 at an air show at Ramstein Air Base which left 70 persons dead. There have been frequent accidents in the FRG involving NATO (q.v.) aircraft which caused Germans to ask themselves about the blessings of so many foreign troops in their country.

Pacifism can scarcely be detected within the established political parties and institutions. But largely unpolitical pacifist motives inspire the left, church circles, ecology movement and generally young persons who swell the ranks of the "peace movement." Pacifists do not oppose nuclear weapons in Western Europe merely because they are horrified by a possible nuclear war on German soil. More than that, they oppose the very idea of a military defense of their country. No other NATO country has such a large percentage of its population which seeks to avoid compulsory 12-month military service by claiming status as conscientious objectors. This right is anchored in the Basic Law (q.v.), but it was originally intended for a small group of truly conscientious objectors. There are scores of C.O. organizations, and many churches and other groups are active in giving advice about how to apply and successfully argue for such exemption. In 1990, a total of 74,500 young Germans refused military service. Uneasiness over the Gulf War in 1991 caused a three-fold increase in the monthly applications, as 22,000 refused military service in January. What was more dismaying was that more than 60 of the Bundeswehr (q.v.) soldiers deployed to Turkey during the crisis declared their intention to seek C.O. status. An exasperated Turkish President Ozal uttered: "I think Germany has become so rich that it has completely lost its fighting spirit."

Just how little the Bundeswehr is tolerated was revealed in Bremen in 1987, when a monument to the "Unknown Deserter" was publicly displayed. The defense minister rejected explanations that the statue applies only to deserters during the Second World War (q.v.) and argued that it might encourage Germans to avoid military service today. Soldiers in uniform are not accorded automatic respect. In 1986, a female pastor unleashed a national debate when she refused to commence a marriage ceremony until the groom doffed his military jacket and put on a civilian jacket borrowed from a guest. Such would have been unheard of before 1945. But Germany is a different country. In a 1986 poll to determine the most prestigious occupations in the FRG, military officers placed fifteenth, right behind secondary school teachers and just ahead of booksellers. In the total population there is some sympathy for a vaguely articulated pacifism. Yet, few Germans are willing to take a concrete step, such as scrapping the Bundeswehr or withdrawing from NATO to underscore such sentiments.

After intense domestic debates, Germans, by and large, have come to accept military deterrence as a means to maintain peace. But few can accept the notion that the actual use of force is ever justified. There is little room in their minds for a concept of the "just war." For example, the SPD's leader, Björn Engholm (q.v.), stated baldly while the street demonstrations were occurring in January 1991: "There is no just war." Many Germans have persuaded themselves that nobody knows the horrors of war better than they do and that they are therefore particularly sensitive to the victims. This is partly a result of western Germany's efforts for decades to drive home the lessons of two world wars that militarism is wrong and war never pays. This black-and-white message is taught in the schools, propagated in the public media, and expressed on public monuments. Everywhere are "peace museums." The idea that war is always wrong has become a kind of ideology in Germany and prevents many Germans from seeing parallels between Hitler's aggression and that of modern dictators. Such differences of perceptions will continue to make Germany's relations with its NATO allies problematic.

PEACE RESOLUTION (1917) see GERMAN FATHERLAND PARTY

PEASANTS' REVOLT. In 1524-25 an idealistic priest, Thomas Müntzer (ca. 1490-1525), led a futile revolt of poor artisans and day workers against the princes in order to establish a "Christendom of the poor." A far more serious convulsion occurred when thousands of German peasants, primarily in the southern part of Germany, revolted. They rose up against the remnants of serfdom which still bound many of them to the higher nobility. The nobles despised all simple people who worked the land as persons without rights. The peasants resented the steady increase in payments and work days owed to the lords. They demanded protection for fishing and hunting rights, as well as a return to community use of much of the grazing and watering facilities which the lords had simply appropriated for themselves. They demanded a reestablishment of earlier institutions, which had granted them some self-rule. They insisted on a return to "the earlier justice," to German law, rather than Roman law. They preferred the former because the latter denied peasants any freedom whatsoever.

PECHSTEIN, MAX (1881-1955). He was the only painter of *Die Brücke* (q.v.) to gain public success and is considered the most important representative of Expressionism (q.v.). His content was less problematic and intellectual, and his colors less violent.

PEENEMÜNDE see ROCKETS

PEOPLE'S PARTY (VOLKSPARTEI). A broad-based, mass party which encompasses many groups, classes, and interests. The FRG's electoral system, which requires parties to win at least 5 percent of the votes cast in the entire country, forces small parties to combine with larger ones or face extinction. Therefore, the FRG's most important and influential parties are *Volksparteien*.

PEOPLE'S POLICE (VOLKSPOLIZEI, or VOPO). A heavily armed, well-organized East German security force created before either Germany was permitted to maintain military forces. Its functions throughout the GDR's (q.v.) history were heavily political, such as helping secure the border from escapees. Its duties were never limited to the mere maintenance of law and order.

PEOPLE'S POLICE IN BARRACKS (KASERNIERTE VOLKSPOLIZEI--KVP). Shortly after 1945 the first German military units in the Soviet occupied zone were called police, and soon they were housed in military bases. This produced the cadre for the subsequent National People's Army (NVA), which was formed in 1956 by a fusion of the KVP and the People's Police (q.v.). From 1962 on there was conscription in the GDR (q.v.).

PETERSBERG AGREEMENT (1949). This West German agreement with the three Western allied high commissioners permitted the FRG to become a non-voting, associate member of the Council of Europe. This organization, whose seat is in Strasbourg, was intended to facilitate Western Europe's political consolidation. The FRG became a full member in 1951. The agreement was a signal that the Western Allies were willing to work with the FRG as an equal.

PIECK, WILHELM (1876-1960). He joined the SPD (q.v.) in 1895 and the Spartacus League (q.v.) in 1916. After 1919 he was a leading functionary in the KPD (q.v.). He was a member of the Reichstag from 1928 until 1933, when he fled Germany after the arrest of Ernst Thälmann (q.v.). He settled first in France and then in the Soviet Union, where he functioned as the KPD's leader. After the war, he co-founded with Otto Grotewohl the SED (qq.v.), whose chairman he was from 1946-54. He served as president of the GDR (q.v.) from 1949 to 1960. (See also GERMAN DEMOCRATIC REPUBLIC.)

PLANCK, MAX (1858-1938). A physicist in Kiel and Berlin, Planck wrote *On the Elementary Quanta of Matter and Electricity* and *Annalen der Physik IV* (1901). He developed the concept of "quantum," the unit in which energy travels and which is comparable to an atom of matter. His formula was that the magnitude of the quantum of radiant energy of a given frequency is equal to the product of the frequency multiplied by the constant h. This was a path-breaking innovation for interpreting the structure of the physical world. Today he is perhaps best known for the scientific institutes in Germany which bear his name. (See also EMPIRE CULTURE.)

PLENZDORF, ULRICH (1934-). This worker's son was always interested in the theater while growing up in East Berlin. He studied at the Film Institute in Babelsberg and worked as a dramatist, scriptwriter, and author. He deals with the tensions the postwar generation experienced in the GDR's (q.v.) established social order. Perhaps his most well-known work is *The New Sorrows of Young W.*, written in 1969. His work earned him the Heinrich Mann Prize for Literature in 1973.

PLEVAN PLAN see REARMAMENT

PÖHL, KARL OTTO (1929-). Former Bundesbank (q.v.) president. (See KOHL, HELMUT.)

POLAND, GERMAN TREATY WITH (1970), see OSTPOLITIK; GERMAN TREATY WITH (1990), see REUNIFICATION; PARTITIONS OF (1772, 1793, 1795), see PRUSSIA; CORRIDOR see VERSAILLES TREATY. See also ODER-NEISSE LINE.

POLICY OF STRENGTH. The year 1955 demonstrated the spectacular success of Konrad Adenauer's (q.v.) Western policy and the obvious failure of his own German reunification (q.v.) strategy, which had been based upon two assumptions. The first, that the Soviet Union and the U.S. held the keys to reunification, was basically correct. The second was that the balance of power between the East and West would gradually shift in favor of the West and require the Soviet Union to settle the German question on Western terms. Thus, Bonn's policy toward the East had to be one of waiting and of refusing either to recognize the GDR (q.v.) or to deal with it on any official basis. The FRG continued to refuse to recognize the Oder-Neisse (q.v.) line. Also, since the GDR's leadership had not been freely elected, Bonn claimed the right of sole representation of all Germans (*Alleinvertretung*). In 1955, the Adenauer government formulated the Hallstein Doctrine (q.v.), on the basis of which the FRG refused to recognize any government, except the Soviet Union, which officially recognized the GDR. It took over a decade for Bonn to wriggle out of this straight-jacket. But the Soviet Union's awesome military capabilities prevented Bonn's "policy of strength," which had been encouraged by the "roll-back" rhetoric of the first Eisenhower administration, from overcoming Germany's division. Events in Hungary and Poland in 1956 demonstrated that Western military power, even with the FRG's added to the equation, could not inhibit Soviet behavior in its Eastern European empire.

POLITBURO. The leading party and governing body in the SED and GDR (qq.v.). Although it was supposed to be a collegial decision making body, it was increasingly dominated by the party leader, Erich Honecker (q.v.), and the member responsible for the GDR economy, Günter Mittag (q.v.).

POLITICAL PRISONERS PURCHASE (FREIKAUF). The FRG engaged in a practice that many West Germans found seamy and questionable: paying hard cash for the release and resettlement of political prisoners from the GDR (q.v.) and families of persons who had fled to the FRG. Bonn's partner was East Berlin lawyer and authorized agent of the SED (q.v.), Wolfgang Vogel. The practice had been started by Rainer Barzel (q.v.), who had served as minister of all-German affairs for ten months from December 1962. He was a strong advocate within the CDU/CSU (q.v.) of detente, negotiations with the East, and recognition of "the reality of Ulbricht." Publisher Axel Springer (q.v.) had helped Barzel in establishing this prisoner release. Barzel was succeeded by Erich Mende (q.v.), during whose three years more than 4,000 persons had been bought out of East German prisons at a cost of 198 million West German marks. Herbert Wehner (q.v.) expanded the scope of these humanitarian efforts from 1966-69 to include prisoners who had been incarcerated for two decades because of their Nazi past. He paid for the release of 2,000 children whose parents were in the West and arranged for GDR citizens to receive support payments from accounts frozen in the FRG.

Because of Wehner's public insistence that humanitarian issues occupy the forefront of West German politics, the Soviet secret police, KGB, through the SED and Wolfgang Vogel, approached him to secure the release in the FRG of one of its top spies, Heinz Felfe (q.v.). Vogel flew to Wehner in Bonn shortly before Christmas 1968. Wehner was uneasy about the issue and asked Vogel: "What would happen if we do not agree?" Vogel's answer: "Then there will not be any more prisoner releases. . . . Yes that is blackmail. However, I have no other choice." From 1963 to 1989, the year the Berlin Wall (q.v.) fell, 37,775 political prisoners were "bought free" by the FRG at a cost of DM 3.5 billion. Vogel also arranged for a quarter million East Germans to leave the GDR legally. On December 5, 1989, and again on March 13, 1992, Vogel was arrested on charges of collaboration with the Stasi (q.v.), which, prosecutors argued, set up Vogel's law practice and used it for its purposes. Eighteen of his former private clients claimed that he had forced them to sell their property to MfS officers as a condition for emigration. He denied these claims, but not the fact that his trade in people had been very lucrative: Bonn eventually paid him an annual fee of DM 360,000, and he earned up to a million tax-free marks per year defending East German prisoners. The eastern German chairman of the committee investigating the SED's shady financial dealings, Horst

Eylmann, CDU, said: "It is scandalous that the tool of those [the SED] who blackmailed us also represented the other side [the FRG], but still got money from us and then invested it in the West."

POMERANIA (POMMERN). Territory located east of the Oder River and along the Baltic Sea which, like Silesia (Schlesien)--located east of the Neisse River around the city of Breslau (now Wrocklaw), became a part of Poland after the Second World War (q.v.). (See ODER-NEISSE LINE; OSTPOLITIK; REUNIFICATION.)

PONTO, JÜRGEN (1923-1977). Banker murdered by RAF terrorist Susanne Albrecht, who escaped to the GDR (qq.v.) which harbored her until reunification (q.v.) in 1990. (See also TERRORIST GROUPS.)

POTSDAM CONFERENCE (July 1945) see ALLIED OCCUPATION OF GERMANY and DENAZIFICATION

PRESIDENT, FEDERAL (BUNDESPRÄSIDENT). The chief of state is the president. Remembering how the powerful Weimar presidency had overshadowed and, to a certain extent, undermined parliament, the founders decided to grant the president largely ceremonial powers, such as formally naming the chancellor and his cabinet, signing all laws, and appointing and dismissing national civil servants and federal judges. In each case, however, he merely carries out the will of the government or parliament. He could possibly be an important mediator and conciliator in the event of a parliamentary crisis, but that has not yet occurred in the FRG. President Richard von Weizsäcker (q.v.) is a patriarchal Christian Democrat whose style and substance have earned him almost universal respect by transforming the presidency into a post of real authority. He uses the office to describe broadly the direction in which he believes the FRG should go. He spoke out at carefully chosen moments on the meaning of Germany's past, the potential dangers of nuclear power, the importance of trade unions in the society, the significance of German unity, and the need to move the seat of government to Berlin.

In order to prevent the president from claiming a superior role based upon a popular mandate by being directly elected by all the people, the founders decided to have the president selected every five years by a Federal Assembly (*Bundesversammlung*) composed of all members of the Bundestag and an equal number of delegates from the various Land parliaments. The founders decided that no national figure should be elected directly by all voters and that there would be no element of direct democracy (such as initiatives, referenda or plebiscites) at the national level. They did not wish to create a useful tool for a popular demagogue like Hitler (q.v.), who could undermine the authority and responsibility of parliament, the heart of democracy. The president has villas both in Bonn and Berlin, and he spends much more time in Berlin since it became the official capital. (See also LÜBKE, HEINRICH.)

PRESIDIUM OF THE BUNDESTAG see COUNCIL OF ELDERS

PREUSS, HUGO (1860-1925). Co-founder of DDP (q.v.), Reich interior minister (1918-19).

PRIVATIZATION. This is the economic activity of converting state-owned enterprises to private ownership. The FRG has already sold its stakes in such groups as Veba (energy), Volkswagen, Viag (metals and chemicals), and Salzgitter (steel and engineering), but this took 30 years to accomplish. In the Germany of the 1990s the Treuhand (q.v.) is engaged in privatizing thousands of former East German enterprises, while the Kohl (q.v.) government is following the global trend in industrialized democracies of selling off many state-owned businesses. The government also wants the revenue from such sales to help pay the staggering costs of reunification (q.v.). In 1992 it announced the partial privatization of Telekom, the post office's telecommunications corporation, which had been split from the postal service in 1989. It will sell its 53 percent stake in Lufthansa, the German national airline, 49 percent of its stake in the Gesellschaft für Nebenbetriebe, which builds and manages service stations along the *Autobahnen* (interstate freeways), and its 66 percent stake in the Rhein-Main-Donau waterway (q.v.) authority, which manages this maritime link between the Atlantic Ocean and the Black Sea. The federal government also announced that the Federal Railway (*Bundesbahn*), which by 1992 accounted for only 27 percent of goods traffic and 6 percent of passenger traffic, would be sold into private hands, and it turned over its 20 percent share in the German Airbus Company to the Daimler-Benz subsidiary, Deutsche Aerospace AG (DASA), which now controls the 37.9 percent share Germany has in Airbus Industrie, a consortium of German, French,

British, Dutch, and Spanish companies set up in 1967 to develop and build jointly this European airplane.

PROSPERITY, IMPORTANCE FOR DEMOCRACY. The danger that a disappearance of economic success could threaten democratic values applies more or less to all Western countries. But in the case of Germany it applies to a far greater extent. Germany's first real experiment with democracy during the interwar years was rocked from the beginning by staggering economic problems, and the Weimar Republic (q.v.) finally fell in January 1933 in part because of an economic depression which left more than six million Germans out of work. The FRG was able to win and maintain legitimacy in the eyes of its own citizens largely through its almost stunning economic accomplishments. It faces the daunting challenge of absorbing a bankrupt, unproductive socialist economy in its eastern lands, whose people had been deprived of prosperity for four decades. It has proven to be more difficult than expected to stimulate Western investment in the East in order to create jobs and raise the standard of living.

PROTESTANT CHURCH, AND EAST GERMAN REVOLUTION (1989) see RELIGION

PROTESTANT UNION see THIRTY-YEARS WAR

PROTESTANT WORKING CIRCLE (EVANGELISCHER-ARBEITSKREIS). The CDU (q.v.) leadership is predominantly Catholic, but in 1952 the Protestant Working Circle was created within the CDU to safeguard Protestant interests. It was an important base for leading CDU Protestants, such as Gerhard Schröder and Konrad Kraske (qq.v.).

PRUSSIA. An area in the German East which had resisted domination by the Poles was the Elector Principality of Brandenburg, a relatively insignificant, poor and backward territory on the periphery of the German Empire and ruled by a dynasty from southern Germany, the Hohenzollerns (q.v.). Brandenburg and East Prussia had become linked in 1525. Taking advantage of the severe turmoil caused by the Reformation, the last Supreme Master of the German Order (q.v.), Albrecht von Brandenburg-Ansbach from the family of Hohenzollern, simply assumed in 1525 the earthly title of "Duke of Prussia," and in

1660 the last ties which bound East Prussia to Poland were severed. The Hohenzollern dynasty, which had made its residence in Berlin and whose heartland remained Brandenburg, was able to gain control of West Prussia, Pomerania (q.v.) and Silesia (q.v.), and ultimately it acquired huge chunks of territory in the Rhineland and Westphalia as well. From a poor land known derisively as "the sandbox of the Empire" with no raw materials and a population of little over a million persons grew a huge and powerful kingdom ultimately embracing about two-thirds of all Germans and serving as the foundation for the first truly unified German Empire in 1871.

Perhaps more than any other European state, Prussia did not evolve, but was made by the human hand. A series of extraordinarily able rulers in the 17th and 18th centuries enabled Prussia to rise like a meteor to the ranks of the major European powers. From 1640 to 1688, Friedrich Wilhelm, "the Great Elector," laid the cornerstone for a powerful Prussia. He had spent three years in the Netherlands during his youth, and there he had been deeply influenced by the Calvinist dynamism and sense of obligation. He married a woman from the ruling House of Orange. From the Thirty Years War (q.v.) he had drawn the lesson that his state needed to enhance its military prowess. He said: "Alliances are good, but one's own power is even better; one can more safely depend on that." He therefore enlarged the Prussian army from 3,000 to 30,000 soldiers.

He also established an oft-forgotten Prussian tradition which lasted for a century-and-a-half and which was both humanitarian and strengthened Prussia. When the French king invalidated the Edict of Nantes in 1685, which had granted considerable religious and civil liberty to the Huguenots (French Protestants), Friedrich Wilhelm responded with the Edict of Potsdam opening the Prussian gates to the religiously persecuted. More than 20,000 French Huguenots, most of them skilled craftsmen and businessmen, poured into Prussia, and by the year 1700 one out of three residents of Berlin was French. Far from attempting to Germanize these newcomers, foreigners were permitted to retain their own language and customs. The Huguenots built their own schools and churches and powerfully contributed to the arts and to the vibrant economic life of Prussia. Many of the area's greatest names until the present day are of French origin. More than 20,000 Protestants from Salzburg fled the counter-reformation, and in the course of the 18th century there was a steady stream of emigrants and religious refugees to Prussia: Mennonites, Scottish Presbyterians, Jews and sometimes Catholics. In some ways, Prussia in the 18th century was to the persecuted of Europe what America was in the 19th century: a religiously tolerant land which offered opportunities to the talented and hard-working.

Friedrich I ascended to the throne in 1688. He was a well-educated and cultured man who maintained a glittering, but excessively extravagant court. He established another Prussian tradition which is also frequently overlooked today: he turned Prussia, especially Berlin, into a leading home for science and the arts. He founded the Academies of Art and Science. He ordered the building of many edifices, such as the Charlottenburg Palace, which changed the face of Berlin from that of a provincial town to one of the most dignified cities in Europe. He also achieved through patient and skillful diplomacy an important political goal: in 1701 he won the Emperor's approval for the Prussian Elector to bear the title of "king." This was a considerable boost for the prestige of a still poor country on the outskirts of the German Empire (q.v.).

With Friedrich Wilhelm I (so named because his father had not been a king), who was crowned in 1713, Prussia gained a ruler who was capable, but greatly different from his predecessor. What one now most often associates with Prussia was largely due to the new king's influence: the spirit of Spartan simplicity and the conscientious fulfillment of one's obligations to the state, which was to be ruled by the king alone, but for the good of the subjects. As he told his son, "The dear Lord placed you on the throne, not in order to be lazy, but in order to work and to rule his lands well." He discarded the luxurious court life his father had conducted to compete with the glittering courts of France and Austria, and introduced an austere court. He also created a first-rate civil service staffed by duty-conscious, highly respected, but poorly paid officials. His popular name, "the Soldier King," indicates where his primary attention was directed. Although during his entire reign he led his country into only one short war, he poured four-fifths of all state income into the army, whose size he doubled to 70,000 men. The stunningly rapid growth of the Prussian army in size and importance prompted the Frenchman Mirabeau to remark shortly after the death of Friedrich Wilhelm I: "Other states possess an army; Prussia is an army which possesses a state!"

Located in the middle of Europe with a conglomeration of often unconnected territories, no natural frontiers, and a relatively small population, Prussia had to have a strong army to maintain itself in the kind of international setting which prevailed at that time. One could argue the Prussian army was disproportionately large in relation to the country's population and financial strength. But the new army was still considerably smaller than those of Austria, France and Russia, and "militarism" was by no means restricted to Prussia during this "Age of Absolutism." Further, the Prussian army never "possessed" the state. It was the most disciplined army in the world and never made the slightest attempt to rule the state. The army was, without a doubt, first rate. Carlyle once wrote that Prussia had a shorter sword than Austria, France and Russia, but it could draw it out of the sheath much more swiftly. The Prussian army was open to the newest military technology. Also, it became more and more a national army and less and less a mercenary army. Prussia was one of the first countries in the world to learn that its own citizens serve better than the troops of a foreign country. Its discipline and well-planned supply system was also a blessing for the civilian population in those areas where the army operated. In an age of undisciplined armies which "lived off the land," the civilian population was constantly subjected to plunder, murder and rape. Civilians seldom needed to fear such horrors from the new Prussian army.

Friedrich Wilhelm I was interested solely in establishing the best-organized, most modern and efficient state and military in the world. Unlike his father and his son, he was utterly disinterested in art and education. This brought him into violent conflict with his son. The father was a stern ruler wholly absorbed in enhancing his state's power. In 1758 his son, who in 1740 had become King Friedrich II (the Great, q.v.), wrote this about his father: "Books, flutes, writings--if he could ever get his hands on them, they were thrown into the fireplace, and the burning of my books was always accompanied by several blows or by very emphatic rebukes." (See FRIEDRICH II; KNIGHTS, GERMAN ORDER OF; OVERCOMING THE PAST.)

PRUSSIAN WARS AGAINST DENMARK (1864) AND AUSTRIA (1866) see BISMARCK, OTTO VON

PUBLIC SERVICE, TRANSPORT AND TRANSPORTATION UNION (ÖFFENTLICHER DIENST, TRANSPORT UND VERKEHR--ÖTV) see CIVIL SERVICE LAW

PUFENDORF, SAMUEL (1632-1694). A philosopher born in Chemnitz, Pufendorf travelled widely and was imprisoned in Copenhagen, where he was working as a tutor. In prison, he meditated on the writings of Hugo Grotius and Thomas Hobbes and later published his thoughts in *Elements of Universal Jurisprudence*. He made a significant contribution to the understanding of international law by adding to the thought of Grotius and Hobbes on this subject, publishing *On the Law of Nature and of Nations* in 1672. He argued that all knowledge of law flows from three sources--reason, civil statutes, and divine revelation--and results in three disciplines--natural law, civil law, and moral theology. He opposed Hobbes' view that the state of nature is a state of war, arguing instead that the state of nature is one of precarious peace which has to be preserved for the sake of man's survival. The state is a moral person whose will is the sum of the individual wills of citizens. International law conforms with Christianity, is rooted in all nations, and is their common bond. He drew a distinction between ecclesiastical and civil power and developed a theory of tolerance. His views were rejected by the Catholic Church.

-Q-

QUADRIGA. This sculpture atop the Brandenburg Gate (q.v.), which was built from 1788 to 1791 to serve as an entry way to the city, was designed by Christian Bernard Rode and sculpted by Johann Gottfried Schadow (q.v.). The Quadriga is the name for the chariot and four horses driven by Eirene, the goddess of peace, who holds a standard emblazoned with an iron cross and Prussian eagle. Napoleon stole the Quadriga in 1806 and took it to Paris. In 1814, it was returned with Nike, the goddess of victory, holding the reins and standard. The Quadriga was originally conceived as "the gate to peace," but it came to be regarded by some people as a memorial to the victory over Napoleon. Rumors persist that the GDR (q.v.) leaders turned the Quadriga around to face the East, but it has always faced that direction.

QUADRIPARTITE (FOUR-POWER) AGREEMENT (VIERMÄCHTEABKOMMEN--1971) see OSTPOLITIK

-R-

RAABE, WILHELM (1831-1910). A realistic novelist whose writings convey a sense of history and compassion for humanity. Raabe is often compared to Charles Dickens.

RADIO AND TELEVISION. Approximately 85 percent of all Germans watch one of the two half-hour nationally televised daily news programs, and political programs constitute about one-third of all television programming. Radio and television are administered by non-profit public corporations that are financed chiefly by monthly fees paid by those who own televisions or radios and by limited advertising (which does not interrupt television shows). There are about a dozen regional radio-TV corporations, which combine to form the "Association of Public Broadcasting Corporations" (ARD) in the FRG. The ARD sponsors the first TV channel, televised nationally, and the third channel, televised regionally. It also encompasses the two radio corporations, the *Deutschlandfunk*, broadcasting within all of Europe in German and 14 other languages, and the *Deutsche Welle*, transmitting globally on short and medium wave in more than 30 languages.

A second German television channel (*Zweites Deutsches Fernsehen--ZDF*), based in Mainz, transmits nationwide. All channels reach audiences in eastern Germany, where some TV broadcasting stations survived the momentous changes of 1989. In order to ensure that all radio and TV corporations remain politically independent, their legal basis is in Land (q.v.) laws, and they are overseen by broadcasting councils composed of representatives of all important political, ideological, social and religious groups. Although they are duty-bound not to favor any particular political party, their programming and the appointments to their councils and management do sometimes become subject to controversies among the parties.

RADIO IN THE AMERICAN SECTOR (RIAS). Soon after the end of the Second World War (q.v.) the American occupation authorities created this German-language radio station in Berlin. Most East Germans liked to listen to it because of its objective coverage of repression and terror in the GDR (q.v.) and because it broadcast pop music. But the SED (q.v.) and the Soviets were always irritated by RIAS for exactly the same reasons. It continued to operate even after German reunification (q.v.) in 1990.

RAILWAY, FEDERAL (BUNDESBAHN) see PRIVATIZATION

RAINBOW FOUNDATION see STIFTUNGEN

RANKE, LEOPOLD VON (1795-1886). This great historian was born in Thuringia. In his landmark 1824 book, *History of the Roman and German Peoples, 1494-1514,* he made his famous claim that the historian's task is "to narrate events as they had actually happened," a claim he put into practice as Professor of History in Berlin from 1825 to 1872. He founded the science of historical evidence, insisting that the historian must approach his subject free from presuppositions. He thus introduced greater objectivity into the study of history and showed the way to historical research in archives. The product of his wide-ranging interests was 54 books, perhaps the greatest of which was his study of the 16th and 17th century Popes, published between 1834 and 1837.

RAPACKI, ADAM (1909-1970) and PLAN see FIGHT ATOMIC DEATH and GERMANY PLAN

RAPALLO, TREATIES OF (1922). On April 16, 1922, Germany and the Soviet Union established diplomatic relations, renounced financial claims on each other, and pledged economic cooperation. This agreement signalled the end of diplomatic isolation for each country and was a source of concern for the British and French. (See also WEIMAR REPUBLIC.)

RASPE, JAN-CARL (1944-1977) see TERRORIST GROUPS

RATHENAU, WALTER (1867-1922). Born in Berlin, his father was a Jewish industrialist. After studying engineering, Walter became director of the large electrical trust A.E.G. founded by his father. Because of his industrial talents, he was asked to organize Germany's war economy in 1916. He introduced the notion of "war socialism," which subordinated production to state needs and gave the war minister the power to determine all men's work between ages 17 and 60. When the Weimar Republic (q.v.) was created, he became a leading member of the DDP (q.v.). In May 1921, he became minister of reconstruction, and eight months later he became foreign minister. He negotiated financial agreements with France and the U.S. and was mainly responsible for the Rapallo Treaty (q.v.). He was murdered by anti-Semitic nationalists in June 1922. (See also WEIMAR REPUBLIC.)

RAU, JOHANNES (1931-). SPD minister president of North-Rhine Westphalia, Rau is a pragmatic, middle-of-the-road politician whose policies enabled the SPD (q.v.) to win an absolute majority in the 1985 Land election. He refused to consider any coalition with the Greens (q.v.) and advocated the SPD's shift back toward the center. He was chosen as chancellor candidate to lead the SPD in the 1987 Bundestag elections. However, his party strapped him with a left-leaning platform, calling for a total phase-out of nuclear energy, unilateral withdrawal of NATO (q.v.) missiles from Germany, a nuclear-free corridor in Central Europe, the formation of "security partnerships for peace" with communist countries (which were still mightily armed and intact), a cancellation of West German participation in the Strategic Defense Initiative (SDI), a cut in the defense budget, and a restructuring of the Bundeswehr (q.v.) to "render it incapable of offensive action." (See also SOCIAL DEMOCRATIC PARTY OF GERMANY.)

REALISM (1830-1890). Growing industrialization and political and social changes are reflected in the literature of this period which expresses apprehension about a meaningful existence within a new social framework. The age of realism can be subdivided into three groups: "Young Germany" (*Junges Deutschland*) was a group of poets (Heine, q.v., Chamisso) whose writings were in protest against the revolutions of 1830 and 1848. This group was followed by the *Epigonen* or late born ones (Grillparzer, von Platen) who longed for the classicism of Goethe and Schiller (qq.v.) and imitated their heroes. Artistic Realism, the third and most important period, represents poetry, drama, the Novelle (q.v.), and the novel. Lyric poets such as Annette von Droste Hülshoff and Eduard Mörike (qq.v.) wrote about nature, religion and life with astute observation and psychological insight. Friedrich Hebbel's (q.v.) realistic dramas dealt with the powerlessness of man in a heartless cruel world. Wilhelm Raabe, Theodor Storm, and Theodor Fontane (qq.v.) wrote powerful novels and novelles about history, religion, regional conflicts and human behavior. Fontane's *Effi Briest* is an excellent example of psychological realism.

REALOS see GREENS

REALPOLITIK. German for "real politics." Describes a carefully measured, rational policy based on a realistic assessment of a nation's interests, goals, and means. Attributed most frequently to Otto von Bismarck (q.v.).

REALSCHULE see EDUCATION

REARMAMENT, GERMAN. This was a truly explosive issue which dominated West German politics until the FRG's formal entry into NATO (q.v.) in 1955. From the point of view of the Western Allies and the Adenauer (q.v.) government, the major problem was how to place international controls on West German troops. The FRG's future allies, who had fought against Germany only five years earlier, wanted security from West Germany, as well as security for it. Well aware of these fears, which he found entirely justified, and desiring German integration and equal status with the West, Adenauer also stubbornly refused to consider establishing an independent German national army. In an effort to solve this problem, the French had presented the "Pleven Plan" in 1950, calling for the establishment of a European Defense Community (EDC). West German military units would be completely fused with a larger European army, and no German generals would command German corps. The FRG would technically not have NATO status, but it would be included *de facto* since the EDC itself would belong to NATO. The link between the FRG's entry into the EDC and the regaining of West German sovereignty was clear from the very beginning. In 1951, the FRG was permitted to establish a ministry for foreign affairs and to establish diplomatic relations with other states. Also, the *Deutschland Vertrag* (Germany Treaty, also known as the Bonn Conventions) was drafted and was to be signed together with the EDC Treaty. The Bonn Conventions provided for the abolition of the Occupation Statute and Allied High Commission (qq.v.), which formally ruled Germany; they prepared the way for West German sovereignty, with certain restrictions.

The issue of a German military role became acute again, when in 1954, the French National Assembly rejected the EDC, which an earlier French foreign minister had proposed. Surprisingly quickly, however, the foreign ministers of Great Britain, Canada and the U.S. met with the prospective members of the EDC to discuss alternatives. In October, these powers signed the Paris Treaties calling for the direct entry of the FRG into NATO, an end to Germany's occupation status, and the restoration of full German sovereignty. The three Western powers retained their authority on matters relating to German reunification (q.v.), Berlin and a final German peace treaty. In late 1955, Adenauer traveled to the Soviet Union to establish full diplomatic relations and to negotiate a trade treaty and the release of the last German prisoners of war remaining in Soviet hands.

The West German debate over foreign policy remained very polarized. In January 1956, less that a year after the FRG had become a full member of NATO, the first thousand volunteer soldiers entered the Federal Army (Bundeswehr), whose creation the SPD (qq.v.) had opposed. There was a powerful pacifist strain within the SPD which opposed all forms of German rearmament, and this element was part of an emotional mass movement known by the slogan *ohne mich*-- "without me." Because of the recent memories and the direct experience which Germans had with the war, the *ohne mich* movement enjoyed widespread support among the general population. For instance, one opinion survey in 1955 revealed that while 40 percent of the respondents were in favor of a West German army, 45 percent were opposed. Among those respondents identifying themselves with the SPD, only 21 percent were in favor of the army and 71 percent were opposed. Opinion polls also indicated that West Germans were not happy about the stationing of American nuclear weapons on German soil or about the Bundeswehr's (q.v.) acquisition of dual capacity weapons which could fire or deliver nuclear warheads. (See also PEACE MOVEMENT.)

RECHTSSTAAT (STATE OF LAW). This refers to a government which acts in accordance with laws founded in fixed and rational principles which are clearly and publicly stated. This excludes capricious rule. The term was first employed by Adam Müller in 1809, and Baron vom Stein (q.v.) developed the formula that all measures involving the citizen's "liberty and property" require parliament's consent and must be in the form of statutes. This principle was expanded throughout the 19th century although it never included foreign or military affairs. The growing emphasis on law is the reason why legal study was a precondition for entry into the higher civil service, a situation which gave birth to the term "jurist monopoly" and which, to a slightly lesser extent, still exists in Germany today. The 19th century saw the confrontation between monarchy and popular sovereignty, and liberals attempted to replace monarchical with popular government and to establish the citizen's security against the state through a constitution.

Hitler (q.v.) showed that state power in conformity with law could be separated from the moral values which underlay a democratic constitution. In the Third Reich (q.v.) law was separated from justice. He made great efforts to show that each step he took to destroy liberal democracy and individual rights was "legal." An example was the Enabling Act (q.v.) of March 6, 1933, which effectively repealed the Weimar Constitution. After the Second World War (q.v.), the FRG sought to combine justice and law, constitution and morals, in the Basic Law (q.v.). (See also DEMOCRACY ON GUARD; DENAZIFICATION; PRUSSIA.)

RED ARMY FACTION (ROTE ARMEE FRAKTION--RAF). A minority of leftists is quite prepared to disregard the law, property and public order. These groups do not encompass the small band of urban terrorists who belong to such underground groups as the RAF and display precious little regard for the sanctity of life and limb and who have not provoked the kind of extreme reaction they have sought. (See also GERMAN DEMOCRATIC REPUBLIC, COLLAPSE; TERRORIST GROUPS.)

RED BRIGADES see TERRORIST GROUPS

RED CELLS (RZ) see TERRORIST GROUPS

RED CHAPEL (ROTE KAPELLE). This was an anti-Hitler (q.v.) resistance group which was in contact with the Soviet secret service. The Gestapo (q.v.) gave it the name "Rote Kapelle" and was able to destroy it and its members after the war with the Soviet Union began in June 1941. The Gestapo discovered it in 1942 and arrested its leaders, Arvid Harnack and Harro Schulze-Boysen.

REFUGEE PARTY (BUND DER HEIMATVERTRIEBENEN UND ENTRECHTETEN--BHE or GPBHE). Formed after the 1949 Bundestag elections to attract the millions of displaced Germans, this party won 27 seats in the 1953 elections and joined Adenauer's (q.v.) coalition with the CDU/CSU, FDP, and German Party (qq.v.). Like the German Party and most other small parties founded in the early years of the FRG, it disappeared because of its inability to win the required 5 percent of the votes.

REFUGEES AND DISPLACED PERSONS (DP). The expulsion of ethnic Germans began immediately after the cessation of hostilities in 1945 and reached a height in the winter of 1945-46. Those affected were often given 24 hours' notice and were able to take with them only 50 to 60 pounds of baggage apiece. Other Germans fled the Soviet occupation zone in order to escape the kind of authoritarian political order which was being established there. These refugees placed severe strains on the Western occupation authorities and on the previous residents, who were required to share their meager incomes with the often highly unwelcome newcomers in order to distribute the nation's material burdens more fairly. By the time the Berlin Wall (q.v.) was erected on August 13, 1961, approximately 12 million refugees had poured into western Germany. Adding to the refugee problem was that of the DP's, whom the Nazis (q.v.) had brought to Germany to perform forced labor. They numbered about six-and-a-half million persons by the end of the war, and about two million of them refused to return to their homelands in the Soviet Union or in the Baltic states which had been annexed by the USSR. They were fed and clothed largely by the U.S. through the UN Relief and Rehabilitation Administration, but they often occupied jobs and housing which were denied to Germans.

REICHSBANNER. A large SPD (q.v.) political defense formation during the Weimar Republic (q.v.).

REICHSTAG see GERMAN EMPIRE; FIRE (1933) see HITLER SEIZURE OF POWER.

REICHSWEHR (REICH ARMED FORCES). Created after the First World War (q.v.), this armed force was limited by the terms of the Versailles Treaty (q.v.) to 100,000 men. It was later replaced by Hitler's Wehrmacht. (See also BUNDESWEHR UNIVERSITIES; REVOLUTION IN GERMANY; SEECKT, HANS VON; VERSAILLES TREATY.)

REINHARDT, MAX (1873-1943). A Viennese actor who became one of the most prominent theatrical producers in Germany and Austria. He emigrated to the U.S. in 1938.

REINSURANCE TREATY WITH AUSTRIA AND RUSSIA (1887)
see BISMARCK ALLIANCE SYSTEM

RELIGION. Over 80 percent of western Germans belong to Lutheran Protestant or Catholic churches. Protestants and Catholics are divided roughly equally in the western part of the FRG although they are not evenly dispersed throughout the country. In general, the North is predominantly Protestant, whereas the South and the Rhineland are predominantly Catholic. The East was traditionally solidly Protestant; only 5 percent of East Germans are Catholic, compared with 43 percent in the West; 30 percent of East Germans claim to be Protestant, while 62 percent belong to no church. Thus, a united Germany became more Protestant. The churches' hold over the school system has long since been severed, and there are few denominational schools left. Religious instruction is offered in the schools on a voluntary basis and in separate classes for Protestants and Catholics.

There is no clean separation of church and state in the FRG as in the U.S., and both major churches are supported by a church tax which the state collects with the income tax. A person may be excused from paying the tax if he officially leaves the church of which he is a member. Such a step used to bring a person great social or professional handicaps. A doctor or a kindergarten teacher could be denied employment at a church-related hospital or kindergarten because he had formally left his church. But this is the exception today, and more people are formally leaving the churches. By 1992, the number of western Germans unaffiliated with a church had grown to 13 percent, from only 3 percent in 1967. Attitudes sometimes change, however, when it is time for a baptism, wedding, or funeral, or when children are being raised.

The churches, which were the only institutions to survive the Third Reich (q.v.) practically unscathed, have contributed significantly to establishing a moderate and compromising political culture. But questions remain concerning the extent to which they should actively enter the political arena. The Protestant Church is visible in the "peace movement" (q.v.) in both parts of Germany. It was particularly important in the East, where atheism had been officially encouraged by the Communists, but where churches were tolerated if they did not meddle in politics.

Protestants could not agree with the latter stipulation, and their church became a sanctuary for growing oppositional groups in the

1980s; because of this, young people took a new interest in it. In the GDR (q.v.) it opposed the militarization of society through military education in the schools. It advocated a right of conscientious objection which did not exist in the GDR. Under the banner of "Swords to Plowshares," it opposed all countries' arms build-ups. It brought into the limelight the GDR's first massive, organized opposition to the regime by protecting it and providing it with meeting rooms and a forum for all persons interested in a critical dialogue. It supported civil courage to question the regime and urged dissidents to remain in the GDR to build a better country. It made bold and articulate demands for freedom. Perhaps most important, it succeeded in keeping the revolution against the SED (q.v.) regime non-violent. The Leipzig demonstrations every Monday, which broke the back of the regime in the fall of 1989, always began in the Nikolai Church with a "peaceful God's service." It was there on the critical date, October 9, that the call for non-violence, penned by symphony conductor Kurt Masur (q.v.) and five others including clergymen, was proclaimed. In the non-communist government which ruled the last half-year of the GDR's existence, Protestant clergymen were the largest single professional group.

Catholic bishops and priests, especially in Bavaria, have not been above trying occasionally to influence the voting of their parishioners through messages from the pulpit. Yet the strength of religion as an influencing factor in politics and society has declined greatly. It has little bearing on voting, and even the CDU/CSU's (q.v.) policies are not primarily the product of religious considerations. Only about a third of the Catholics and a tenth of the Protestants in the West attend church regularly, and most of those who do have become largely secularized. There are differences in religious beliefs between Germans in the two halves of the country: two-thirds of eastern Germans were either never baptized or left the church, compared with only 7 percent in the West. Also, only 7 percent of eastern Germans say they believe in life after death, compared with half of western Germans.

REMARQUE, ERICH MARIA (1898-1970). Remarque became a journalist after fighting in the First World War (q.v.). In 1929, he published the famous *All Quiet on the Western Front,* which gained worldwide success and later criticism from the Nazis (q.v.) for its brutally realistic and underlying pacifistic treatment of the war. Remarque left Germany in 1938 and spent the rest of his life in the

U.S., where he became a citizen in 1947. (See also WEIMAR REPUBLIC.)

RENAISSANCE. The 15th and early 16th centuries were an age of intellectual awakening. This discovery of man and the world was the focus of humanism and the Renaissance. The latter was an Italian creation of the 14th and 15th century and for Europe signaled an important turning point. It meant an inclination on the part of a few to question all previous religious, scholarly, scientific and political authority which had placed limitations on man. It was a time when Leonardo da Vinci showed that natural science must be based on exact observation and experimentation, when Christopher Columbus dared to cross the ocean to disprove previous theories about the shape of the earth, and when Florentine Niccolo Machiavelli ripped the idealized cloth from politics to show it in its raw, nonethical reality.

Germans were very much a part of this burst of discovery. Nikolaus Kopernicus, a clergyman from Frauenburg in Prussia, showed that the earth was not the center of the universe and was merely one of the many bodies in a much larger planetary system. Martin Behaim constructed the first globe of the earth. Peter Henlein produced the first pocket watch. Berthold Schwarz discovered shooting powder quite by accident and thereby revolutionized warfare. An ingenious goldsmith from Mainz, Johannes Gutenberg (q.v.), developed the first printing press using movable type. This was a prerequisite for taking the written word out of the libraries of the rich, the nobility and the clergy and into the reach of the masses. In art, Albrecht Dürer, Hans Holbein, and Matthias Grünewald (qq.v.) achieved deserved recognition throughout the civilized world. Universities sprouted up all over Germany in this time of inquiry and became important centers of research and learning to the present day.

RENEWERS see GERMAN COMMUNIST PARTY and PARTY OF DEMOCRATIC SOCIALISM

RENGER, ANNEMARIE (1919-). SPD, private secretary to Kurt Schumacher (1945-52), member of Bundestag since 1953, Bundestag president (1972-76) and thereafter Bundestag vice-president. (See also SCHUMACHER, KURT.)

REPARATIONS. High indemnities were imposed on Germany and its allies after the First World War (q.v.). Germany made an initial payment, but in 1922 it suspended payments in the face of disastrous inflation of its currency, prompting an Allied occupation of the Ruhr. In 1924, the Dawes Plan enabled the Germans to receive a loan to pay these reparations, and in 1929 the Young Plan reduced the debt by 75 percent and stretched out payments until 1988. When the economy collapsed in 1931, Germany stopped all payments, having paid only an eighth of the original sum, but having received a fifth of that original sum in the form of loans from Western countries.

Remembering how the requirements for monetary payments had helped undermine the new German democracy after the First World War, the American, British, and Soviet victors agreed at the Potsdam Conference in 1945 that this time reparations would be extracted in the form of machines and industrial equipment, not of money. Since the Western zones were the most industrialized, a portion of the reparations there were to be turned over to the Soviets. In return, the Soviets were to send food to the Western zones from their agricultural zone. Allied tensions quickly developed. The Soviet Union felt justified in dismantling as much industrial equipment as it could, as well as vehicles and rolling stock. Until 1953 it also took up to a fourth of the current production in the remaining industries in its zone and printed money to buy other things it wanted, thereby inflating the German currency and necessitating the currency reform (q.v.). It demanded its full share of industrial shipments from the Western zones although it did not honor its obligation to ship food westward. It became obvious that as Germany's industrial capacity was demolished this way, it was the taxpayers in the countries occupying the Western zones who would have to sustain the population there. Germany would never be able to become self-sufficient, and this fact would also make the development of stable democracy unlikely. In May 1946, the American commandant, Lucius D. Clay (q.v.), ordered that the dismantling of industries cease in his zone, and the French and British followed suit. American policy shifted to aiding the Germans economically, rather than impoverishing them further. (See also GERMAN DEMOCRATIC REPUBLIC, UPRISING; MARSHALL PLAN.)

REPUBLICANS see PARTIES, RIGHT-WING

RESISTANCE TO HITLER. Even during the Second World War (q.v.) there were some symbolic acts of resistance to Nazi (q.v.) rule within Germany. In early 1943 two young Christians in the Catholic youth organization, Hans and Sophie Scholl, brother and sister, passed out flyers on the streets of Munich for a few minutes calling Hitler (q.v.) a tyrant and demanding acts of sabotage in the arms factories before they were whisked away and promptly executed.

The most serious opposition to Hitler came from within the German Army, supported by a unique coalition of aristocrats, civil servants, clergymen from both churches and trade unionists. The German military traditionally had considered itself superior to Nazis, whom it tended to regard as uneducated, rowdy troublemakers. On July 20, 1944, this coalition made a bold attempt to assassinate Hitler, but the bomb placed under the table during a meeting in Hitler's eastern headquarters miraculously failed to harm the Führer seriously when it exploded; Hitler suffered nerve damage to an arm and appeared shaken by the incident. The bomb had been placed there by Colonel Claus Schenk von Stauffenberg, a decorated war hero who had lost an arm and an eye in battle. Assuming that the Nazi leader was dead, the plotters moved to take control of the major governmental and military command centers in Berlin. However, Hitler quickly went on the air to announce that he was alive, and he ordered that the plotters be arrested. Within hours the leaders were executed.

The assassins were prompted to act by information they had of Hitler's grisly extermination policies. When asked about his motive before the "People's Court" following the attempt, Count Yorck von Wartenburg said "I thought about the many crimes," before he was shouted down by the hated chief justice, Roland Freisler (q.v.). But there were other motives as well. Germany was entangled in a war which it could not win, and there was no attempt on the part of Germany's leaders to reach a political settlement. It was characteristic that after the July 20th plot Hitler ordered mass arrests of more than 5,000 former cabinet ministers, mayors, parliamentarians and civil servants (including such important postwar figures as Konrad Adenauer, q.v., and Kurt Schumacher, q.v.), whom the enemy coalition could have viewed as a possible alternative to the Third Reich (q.v.). For Hitler, the only conceivable alternatives were Germany's holding on under his own leadership or facing total destruction. After the war a memorial and museum to the German resistance was created in Berlin's Stauffenbergstrasse. (See also KREISAU CIRCLE; RED CHAPEL.)

RESTITUTION TO JEWS. Under the terms of the Luxembourg Agreement of 1952, the FRG government volunteered to send goods and services worth DM 3 billion to Israel as a way of providing restitution for Nazi (q.v.) persecution and killing of Jews. Several hundreds of millions of additional marks were paid to compensate individual Jews who had been victims of Nazi policies. In 1965 Israel and the FRG established diplomatic relations.

The FRG, which accepted guilt for the crimes committed by the Nazis, paid on its own decision huge sums of money for restitution, totaling more than DM 100 billion by the end of this century. Jewish groups had immediately demanded restitution from the FRG. It is to the credit of first chancellor, Konrad Adenauer (q.v.), and the major parties in the first parliament that, despite severe economic difficulties and a majority of voters who opposed such generous payments, a one-time lump sum to individual Jews who had lost their property was agreed upon quickly at the end of 1951. As a result of a German-Israeli agreement in 1962, reparations (q.v.) in excess of DM 2.5 billion were granted to Israel, while DM 15 billion were paid out directly to individual Jews or their families. In the mid-1950s the FRG also began paying reparations to individuals in most other European countries who could substantiate claims to have been victims of Nazism. Many German organizations, including especially the churches, made private efforts. Sometimes symbolic gestures were just as important in underscoring West German willingness to accept responsibility for the German past. Perhaps the most dramatic example was Chancellor Willy Brandt's (q.v.) dropping to his knees in 1970 at the foot of a memorial to the Jewish dead at the spot where the Jewish ghetto was once located, a gesture which, according to a poll, 48 percent of West German respondents found "overdone." In November 1992, the FRG agreed to make payments to Jews who had been persecuted under the Nazis, but who as citizens of former Communist states in Eastern Europe had received little or nothing. DM 100 million was earmarked for payments between 1993 and 1999. (See also ANTI-SEMITISM; GALINSKI, HEINZ; MINORITIES; WANNSEE CONFERENCE.)

REUNIFICATION OF GERMANY 1989-1990. Germany emerged from the war in 1945 a divided nation. With the FRG firmly planted in the Western alliance after 1955, Bonn's leaders began to look eastward to see how they could improve West Germany's relations with the Soviet Union and its satellites. The construction of the Berlin Wall (q.v.) on August 13, 1961, had made it clear that the two Germanys would not be reunified for a long time. Before August 1961 East and West Berliners could pass freely from one part of the city to the other. But the ugly wall which cut right through Germany's largest city destroyed the last hope of national unity.

From the beginning West Germany's foreign policy was heavily influenced by the fact that Germany was a divided nation in the middle of Europe. After 1955, the FRG did not pursue a determined policy of German reunification, preferring instead to focus on Western economic and military integration, while preventing the legitimization of the status quo in central Europe. Once the U.S. and France began to give the signals for a relaxation of tensions between East and West, culminating in such agreements with the Soviet Union as the nuclear test ban treaty in 1963, German Foreign Minister Gerhard Schröder (q.v.) began a "policy of movement" in the early 1960s. This involved a loosening of the Hallstein Doctrine, which had forbidden West German diplomatic contact with any country (except the Soviet Union) which officially recognized East Germany. The FRG established trade missions in Warsaw, Budapest, Sofia and Bucharest. This policy was an important beginning, but it did not go far enough. The Adenauer and Erhard (qq.v.) governments neither discarded the Hallstein Doctrine altogether, nor recognized the Oder-Neisse border between the GDR (qq.v.) and Poland. They still aimed to isolate the GDR diplomatically.

The FRG had always worked closely with East German officials on practical, day-to-day questions, especially involving economic matters. For instance, the FRG insisted as a condition for its entry into the EC (q.v.) that trade between the two Germanys be conducted as if there were only one Germany. Such free trade was enormously beneficial for the GDR, providing it with an open entry to the EC and serving as a basis for the relatively high economic prosperity in the GDR as compared with other Eastern European countries. Yet, top level political contacts were studiously avoided. In the 1970s, the SPD-FDP (q.v.) governments pursued an active *Ostpolitik* (q.v.) to improve relations with the Communist regimes. The CDU-FDP government, which took power in 1982, continued that approach, culminating in the 1987 state visit to West Germany by GDR leader Erich Honecker (q.v.).

German reunification returned suddenly to Europe's and the superpowers' agenda in 1989, and developments toward it raced faster than any government's ability to react. The rapid collapse of Communist rule left a political vacuum in the GDR (q.v.). Demonstrators in East

German streets unfurled banners bearing "Germany-One Fatherland!" Aware of his constitutional mandate to seek German unity, and wishing to calm the waters and head off right- and left-wing extremists, Helmut Kohl (q.v.) announced on November 28 a ten step plan for reunification, which included humanitarian assistance to refugees, freer travel between the two Germanys, massive economic aid contingent on free elections in the GDR, and ultimately reunification if that is the will of the German people, especially of East Germans. He applied no timetable. To reassure his NATO (q.v.) and EC allies, he stressed that any reunified Germany would be embedded in the Western community of nations and NATO. To those who fear for stability in Europe, which until then had been guaranteed by a divided Germany, he asserted that "freedom does not cause instability." West Germans no longer needed to sacrifice unity for freedom, as they had done since 1949.

In March 1990, the last Communist government, led by Hans Modrow (q.v.), collapsed. East Germans had conducted the only successful revolution in German history, and it was a bloodless one. The pace of the reunification movement quickened with the first free elections in East German history on March 18, 1990. The surprise victor was the conservative coalition, "Alliance for Germany," led by the CDU-East, which won 48 percent of the vote by promising prosperity and union with the FRG. The SPD-East was a distant second. The Communists, running under a new name--Party of Democratic Socialism (PDS, q.v.)--won only 16 percent. As in 1949, Germans turned to the CDU (q.v.) as the party of prosperity and assured democracy. A "grand coalition" of conservatives and SPD formed a government and entered negotiations with the Kohl government to overcome the political, economic, and military obstacles to "One United Germany."

The train was speeding toward unity, and the best the Bonn government could do was to make it an orderly, legal process. There was no time for a transition, no pause to "study the problems." A breathless Kohl, who had said a couple of years earlier in Moscow that he would never live to see German unity, saw a unique opportunity and had announced in February: "We are jumping with a single leap!" He waved aside Social Democrats' calls for a more deliberate process and the demand of many intellectuals for a "better" East Germany treading a "third path" between capitalism and socialism. The next steps toward unity on October 3, 1990, were taken with dizzying rapidity. On July 1, the West German mark was introduced in the GDR in a currency reform without precedent on such a large scale. In a stunning diplomatic breakthrough, Kohl went to the Soviet Union on July 14-16 to get Gorbachev's assurances that he would not stand in the way of German unity and that a united Germany could decide "freely and by itself if, and in which alliance it desires membership"; in other words, Germany would not have to leave NATO in order to be united. Returning to Moscow on September 12, Bonn's leaders joined GDR Prime Minister Lothar de Maizière (q.v.) and the foreign ministers of the four Allied Powers (Poland had observer status) to sign the "two plus four" treaty granting full sovereignty to Germany and suspending the four powers' rights. The CSCE endorsed the agreement in New York on October 1. It went into effect at midnight on October 2, when unity was rung in by a "Liberty Bell" which the U.S. had given to Berlin four decades earlier.

Unity left much unsettled business for a part of Germany in which the economy had to be privatized and in which the secret police, the Stasi (q.v.), supported by 85,000 officers and over a half million informants, had penetrated every niche of GDR society and maintained files on six million persons. Germans were left to wrestle with the problem of what to do with such files, which had been assembled with complete disregard for the individual's privacy. They hold many of the keys to rooting out and punishing those persons who suppressed citizens' freedom, but their misuse could again endanger that freedom. They shed light on the GDR's extensive contacts with and training of terrorist (q.v.) organizations and the sheltering of fugitive West German Red Army Faction (q.v.) killers. They also help Bonn uncover spies who had infiltrated the FRG more thoroughly than had ever been imagined.

Not wishing to announce open season on witch hunts, but wanting to protect the rights of citizens, the government decided in 1991 to allow individuals access to their own files, while threatening journalists with three-year jail terms if they published information from them without permission. This prompted charges of muzzling the press by civil liberty advocates, who called the decision the most serious effort at limiting freedom of the press since the Hitler (q.v.) era and a repetition of earlier times in the FRG, when many prominent Nazis (q.v.) were permitted to resume their careers after 1945 without a review of their histories in well-kept Nazi records. Other former GDR citizens must confront their own troubled past. The legendary former head of East Germany's foreign intelligence service, Markus Wolf, returned to Germany from exile in the Soviet Union and was released on $30,000 bail, a paltry sum for a man who is paid at least that much for interviews with the sensation hungry Western press.

The prelude to the first free all-German elections in almost six decades, scheduled for December 2, 1990, were state elections in the five newly recreated Länder in the East; on October 14 the CDU won in four of them. Therefore, few observers were surprised to see the CDU/FDP coalition win a resounding victory in December and Kohl reap the electoral reward for presiding over the mending of Germany's division. Columbia University historian Fritz Stern noted that "Germany had been given something uncommon: another chance. The century is ending as it began, with a major German lead in Europe based on economic clout, technological advance, and human efficiency and performance...[but] under much more favorable circumstances than in the pre-1914 age of rough-hewn nationalism." Prussia (q.v.) has not been recreated, despite the reburial of Frederick the Great (q.v.) at his beloved Sans Souci Palace in Potsdam outside Berlin and the return of the Prussian eagle and iron cross to the newly-restored statue of the victory goddess atop the Brandenburg Gate (q.v.) in 1991.

Kohl and Foreign Minister Hans-Dietrich Genscher (q.v.) knew that while no European country wanted to thwart German unity, there was uneasiness about the possibility that an economically powerful Germany, 43 percent larger than before and more populous than any country west of Russia, would dominate Europe. Most European leaders were too polite to express these fears publicly. To minimize them, Germany signed landmark treaties with the USSR and Poland. On November 9, it signed a friendship treaty with the Soviet Union which amounted to the closest links the Soviets ever had with any major Western nation. It contains a section affirming that both nations "will refrain from any threat or use of force which is directed against the territorial integrity or political independence of the other side." Neither country would aid an aggressor against the other. Bonn insists that this agreement, ratified in the USSR in March 1991, was aimed at forging a new relationship with the USSR in a way consistent with Germany's obligation to NATO, which is a defensive alliance.

The ink was hardly dry when Germany signed a treaty with Poland on November 14, 1990, fixing their mutual border along the Oder-Neisse line (q.v.). The former German land to the East of this demarcation constituted a third of Poland's territory. Genscher stated bluntly that "we Germans are aware that the treaty does not surrender anything that was not lost long ago as the result of a criminal war and a criminal system." But he also admitted that settling this last major dispute of the war hurt: "For those who have lost their homelands, who suffered expulsion [after 1945], it is an especially painful one." (See also GERMAN DEMOCRATIC REPUBLIC, COLLAPSE; NORTH ATLANTIC TREATY ORGANIZATION, CREATION.)

REUTER, ERNST (1889-1953). He joined the SPD (q.v.) in 1912. As a prisoner of war in Russia, he was admired by Lenin, and he was a people's commissar in the Volga Germany Republic (q.v.). He joined the KPD (q.v.) after his return to Germany in 1918, but he returned to the SPD in 1921 because he could not accept Lenin's requirement that all Communist parties adopt the Bolshevik methods of rule and party organization. In 1931, he was the SPD mayor of Magdeburg. He had a seat in the Reichstag from 1932 to 1933, when he was forced to leave Germany. He became a professor of municipal government at the University of Ankara, Turkey. From 1948 to 1953 he was mayor of West Berlin and a symbol of that city's defiance of Stalin's policy toward Germany and its refusal to be drawn into the Communist order which had been imposed in the Soviet occupation zone.

REVOLUTION OF 1848. The authoritarian German princes seemed to be firmly in their saddles when they were severely shaken in 1848 by a spark of revolution which had started in Sicily and southern Italy and which, as usual, arrived in Germany via France. But the rebels' objectives in Germany and France were different. What many Germans wanted was unity and freedom, things which had already been realized in whole or in part in France a half century earlier. As a student in Bonn, Carl Schurz, wrote in his memoirs, "The word democracy was on all tongues, and many thought it a matter of course that, if the princes should try to withhold from the people the rights and liberties demanded, force would take the place of mere petition." Few Germans wanted a revolution as in France in 1789, but many wanted the traditional authorities to accept more freedom for the people and a constitutional monarchy which would include the principle of popular sovereignty. What specific demands were made became clear very quickly. In frightened response to the spontaneous demonstrations and assemblies in the first week of March 1848, many princes granted freedom of press and assembly, the creation of citizen's militias, jury trials, reform of the electoral system and collaboration in constructing a federal German state.

In Prussia King Friedrich Wilhelm IV (qq.v.) waited a little too long to make concessions. Not until he had been informed that Metternich (q.v.) had been driven out of Austria did he decide to grant Prussia a constitution and to support the move toward a united Germany. An unfortunate incident in the square before the royal palace, where nervous troops fired a volley of shots into a crowd which had presumably assembled to applaud the king's concessions, touched off a rampage of violence in Berlin which was not to be duplicated until the end of the First World War (q.v.). The Prussian troops, which had not engaged in combat since the Battle of Waterloo in 1815, were baffled and quickly demoralized by fighting street battles against snipers who fired from rooftops and from behind barricades and who disappeared into side streets and alleys when regular troops closed in on them. After one day of such fighting, the army was compelled to withdraw from the city, but the king valiantly chose to stay with his "dear Berliners." He was thus a sort of captive of the revolutionaries and was forced to call together bourgeois and intellectual groups to discuss reforms. He later looked back with regret on that humiliating time: "We were on our bellies then." It seemed that the death knell for the loosely-organized group of mainly authoritarian states called Germany had been rung, but time would reveal that the princes had just temporarily lost their nerve.

By the end of March 1848 all German states, including Austria and Prussia, had concluded that there was no alternative to allowing the election of representatives by universal manhood suffrage to a national parliament in order to draft a liberal constitution for a German federation. This first German national parliament convened on May 18 in the Paul's Church in Frankfurt am Main. This has often been called the "parliament of the professors" because of the fact that an overwhelming number of delegates were professors, lawyers or university-educated civil servants who had little practical experience in politics. In typical German scholarly fashion, they spent weeks discussing abstract notions of law, freedom and the state. They had good intentions and produced an admirable document called the Fundamental Rights of the German People. However, they were unable to unite on the question of parliamentary control of royal power. Gradually, their slow, deliberate and discursive work was overtaken by events outside the Paul's Church.

The demands for reform were not quite strong enough to be realized, and the resulting frustration led to outbursts of violence in Vienna, Frankfurt, Berlin and elsewhere which in more and more Germans' eyes discredited the entire reform movement. The reestablishment of firm monarchical control in Vienna stimulated a longing for order in Germany. Suspicions among the states and the classes began to reassert themselves. Nowhere was this more evident than in Prussia, where the king soon began resisting any diminution of his power. The king's disposition was strengthened by a renewal of mob violence in Berlin in June 1848, in which weapons in the state armory were seized and distributed among the rebels. This violence frightened the middle-class citizens and played into the hands of the king. He ordered the troops back into their Berlin barracks in November, an order that ignited more resistance and could be carried out only by force. But this order ended the revolutionary activity in Prussia. Friedrich Wilhelm caught many of his critics off guard by decreeing a constitution. Revised in 1850, this document provided formal safeguards for Prussian subjects' liberties and established a bicameral legislature which was clearly designed to prevent truly innovative action by more radical elements. The upper house was composed mainly of the nobility, and the lower house was elected in a complicated way based on the amount of taxes the citizens paid; two-thirds of the seats were elected by 15 percent of the population which paid two-thirds of the total taxes. This strange electoral system remained a thorn in the side of the Prussian working class and liberal reformers until it was finally abolished in 1918. Despite its many shortcomings, though, this constitution was a step away from absolute government and toward constitutional, parliamentary government in Prussia.

After entirely too much debate, the Frankfurt Parliament made two fundamental decisions. First, the majority recommended a "small German" solution to German unity, with close links to Austria, rather than a "large German" solution under the Habsburgs of Austria. It was decided that it would be nonsense to establish a German nation-state which would include Milan, Venice, Budapest, Prague and Crakow. Second, it offered the German imperial crown to the Prussian king in 1849. Friedrich Wilhelm IV bruskly rejected this gift with the words: "If the thousand-year-old crown of the German nation, unused now for 42 years, is again to be given away, it is I and my likes who will give it!" No doubt, it was not his idea of monarchy to see it based on the sovereignty of the people and offered by lawyers and professors who had been elected by the people. It is possible that he would have accepted it from other princes. But the king was aware that accepting such a crown might have meant war with Austria, which, as later events showed, was not prepared to accept German unity under Prussian domination without a fight. Also, he could neither forget his heritage nor muster enthusiasm for a new state in which the Prussian identity might ultimately disappear. The rejection of the crown sealed the fate of the revolution. Nevertheless, for the rest of the year the king continued to send diplomatic feelers to some other German princes to explore the chances of establishing a form of German unity more to his liking, but these came to nothing. More successful was his troops' suppression of the last acts of rebellion in Saxony in 1849, where they restored the Saxon king to the throne, and during the summer in Baden and the Rhineland-Palatinate, where they crushed a ragtag "people's army" of intellectuals, poets, and professional and amateur revolutionaries. That last victory enabled the king of Wurttemberg to disband the Frankfurt Parliament, which had dwindled to about a hundred die-hards, who had fled to Stuttgart. His comment: "Against democrats only soldiers will do. Adieu!"

The 1848 revolution was over. It has often been said that the Germans' main problem was that they had never had a successful revolution. Of course, as the case of Britain demonstrates, revolutions are not absolutely essential in the establishment of democratic government, as long as reform is possible. However, Germany was to experience too little reform in years to come. Many liberals who had participated in the "March Revolution" became very self-critical after its failure and were convinced that they had to adjust their political objectives much more to the prevailing political conditions. Thus, they became more open to ideas associated with Otto von Bismarck (q.v.), who became the Prussian chancellor a few years later: *Realpolitik* (politics which recognize the hard facts of the world) and the inclination to tone down the demand for freedom if the possibility of national unity is at stake.

REVOLUTION IN RUSSIA AND GERMANY (1917). American entry into the First World War (q.v.) in 1917 made it essential that the Germans eliminate the Eastern front. Because the weapon of war had not worked entirely, they selected another weapon: that of revolution. On March 15, 1917, the Russian Czar abdicated, but to the Germans' surprise, the new government continued the war. Therefore, German leaders decided to transport a group of Russian revolutionaries from their exile in Switzerland through Germany to Scandinavia from where they could return to Russia. This group was composed of Marxists who were known to favor Russian withdrawal from the war. The most prominent was Vladimir Ilyich Lenin. The Germans incorrectly figured that Lenin would be an ideal marionette for Germany since he and his faction-ridden Bolshevik party would presumably be unable to hold power more than a few weeks without German support. Neither the Germans nor Lenin had any concern for each others' interests. As Leon Trotsky wrote in his memoirs: "In the case of Lenin's trip two opposite plans crossed at a definite point, and this point was a sealed [rail] car." The train, which departed from Zurich with 32 Russian revolutionaries, had such high traffic priority that the German Crown Prince's own train was kept on a side track in Halle for two hours until Lenin's train had passed. The group arrived at Petrograd's (now St. Petersburg) Finland Train Station on April 16th and was greeted by thousands of supporters. It cannot be doubted that the transport and subsequent German financial assistance were vital to the Bolsheviks before their seizure of power in Petrograd on November 7, 1917.

Lenin announced Russia's withdrawal from the war, but the Germans imposed an extremely harsh peace treaty upon the new Bolshevik leadership at the Russian border town of Brest-Litovsk in early 1918. The Soviets, as the Bolsheviks had come to be called, were forced to relinquish huge chunks of territory from the Russian Empire. This treaty, along with the reparations demanded of Russia in August, set a most unfortunate precedent. It merely stimulated the Entente's will to resist and reinforced the enemy's moral self-confidence to impose on the Germans nine months later a peace no less dreadful than this one. That moral self-confidence was also strengthened by a weakness which Germany demonstrated during both world wars: its lack of moderation. Without such moderation, no negotiated settlement was possible, only a dictated one. German occupation authorities after 1871 tended to mistreat or try to "Germanize" conquered nations, which could have been potential allies. The highest German diplomat in Russia in the summer of 1918, Kurt Riezler (q.v.), made a bitter comment about his own people: "Never was a *Volk* more capable of conquering the world and more incapable of ruling it!"

REVOLUTION, GERMAN (1918-1919). Early in 1918, the final year of the First World War (q.v.), Hamburg, Leipzig, Cologne, Munich and the heavily industrialized Ruhr area had experienced serious strikes, and in Berlin 200,000 munitions workers struck. Hunger was causing the "home front" to collapse. The average rations for German civilians had been cut to only 1,000 calories per day. Tensions were greatly increased by a worsening of the military situation. Large numbers of fresh American troops began arriving in France in the spring of 1918. Germany's last great offensive was launched on March 21, but the exhausted German troops were unable to cope with the Allied counter-offensive, which began on July 10. On August 8, known to Germans then as "Black Friday," British infantry broke through the German lines at Amiens and threw the German troops in France into a mass retreat. On August 14, General Ludendorff (q.v.) was forced to admit that the war could not be won militarily. On September 29, he communicated to Supreme Headquarters that "the present condition of our army demands an immediate cease-fire in order to avoid catastrophe." On October 3, Hindenburg (q.v.) told the chancellor that "under these circumstances it is necessary to break off the fight in order to spare the German people and its allies needless victims." Despite such calls of desperation at the time, these men and many others had the audacity to claim later that it had been the civilian leadership, especially those who had founded the new Weimar Republic (q.v.), who had "stabbed Germany in the back" by losing their nerve and suing for peace at a time when Germany's armies had allegedly not been defeated in the field. This legend placed an unbearably heavy burden on Germany's postwar democratic leadership.

Its armies retreating, its allies crumbling, its people starving, Germany sent a delegation to seek peace with the Entente. It met French Marshal Foch in a rail car at Compiègne (in which Hitler conducted the French surrender ceremonies almost 22 years later). There Foch delivered undiscussable conditions which Germany could take or leave: the 34 articles included the withdrawal of the German Army from France, Alsace-Lorraine and Belgium to the Rhine, Entente occupation of the left bank of the Rhine and delivery to the Entente of all German submarines and heavy military and transport materials. The disheartened Germans had no alternative but to accept. The war officially ended on November 11, 1918.

Even before the cease-fire could be signed, the German Empire had ceased to exist. Kaiser Wilhelm II (q.v.) simply could not bring himself to abdicate, as the victors had demanded, so Chancellor Max von Baden (q.v.) just announced the Kaiser's abdication on November 9. A short time later, Social Democrat Philip Scheidemann (q.v.) was informed that German communists were about to declare a Republic, so he rushed to the window of the Reichstag building and announced "The Emperor has abdicated . . . Long live the German Republic!" The new SPD chancellor, Friedrich Ebert (q.v.), made no secret of the fact that his emphasis would be on creating order and a parliamentary-democratic political structure in the badly shaken country. But no sooner had the Republic been declared than demands began to be made for a second, more radical revolution. The Polish revolutionary theorist and activist, Rosa Luxemburg (q.v.) remarked sarcastically: "Oh how German this German Revolution is! How proper, how pedantic, how lacking in verve and in grandeur." It was not long before some groups chose to use force against Ebert's government, and Germans witnessed events which threatened the Republic in its infancy. In late 1918, the Communist Party of Germany (KPD, q.v.) was formed, and on the same day the Steel Helmet League, a right-wing para-military organization of disenchanted war veterans, was created. The fatal split in German society which would paralyze and ultimately destroy the Republic continued to widen. The regime found itself in a crisis from which it would never be able to extricate itself.

The communists made two unsuccessful violent attempts to seize power in Berlin. More than a thousand lives were lost in defeating the first attempt on January 6-12, 1919. The second erupted during the first two weeks of March 1919 and caused 2,000 deaths and considerable destruction to the city of Berlin. The government crushed a leftist uprising in Munich in May 1919 with such brutality that many observers accused the new republican government of being "blind in the right eye." That later right-wing strikes against the Republic were not suppressed with equal brutality stemmed from the fact that the Reichswehr (q.v.) and the Free Corps troops, which were hastily assembled to cope with the crises were, on the whole, anti-republican and far more sympathetic to the right; they were never successfully transformed into reliable instruments of the Weimar Republic. To restore and maintain order, the government found itself in the predicament of having no alternative to using troops who were, in the main, unruly, disillusioned freebooters who had become far too accustomed to violence during a war which had severely shaken their sense of values and proportion. Such troops were extremely difficult to control, and the blemish of partiality toward the right was placed on the new Republic itself. (See also WORKERS' AND SOLDIERS' COUNCILS.)

REXRODT, GÜNTER (1941-). A longtime FDP insider who ran Citibank's German operations before joining the Treuhand (q.v.) board in 1991, he was appointed federal economics minister in January 1993.

RHEIN-MAIN-DONAU WATERWAY. This is a 2,175 mile (3,500 kilometer) maritime link between the Atlantic Ocean and the Black Sea via the Rhine, Main, and Danube Rivers. The last canal link was completed in southern Germany in 1992 after 32 years of work and much controversy over whether the environmental and financial costs were justified. There are problems which will prevent it from being lucrative. Although it will boost German-Austrian trade, the narrow, shallow (especially the Danube), and curvy waterway with 59 locks and low clearance under some Danube bridges will prevent many kinds of ships and loaded barges from using it. The locks and twisted course of the Main make traffic much slower than rail and prevent strings of barges from being put together. (See also PRIVATIZATION.)

RHENISH LEAGUE see FRENCH REVOLUTION

RIBBENTROP, JOACHIM VON (1893-1946). A Rhinelander by birth, he was a cavalry officer during the First World War (q.v.) before becoming a wine salesman. In the mid-1920s, he joined the Nazi party and became an SS (qq.v.) leader. He utilized his foreign contacts by maintaining a separate information service which provided foreign intelligence to Hitler outside the foreign office channels. From 1936 to 1938 he was ambassador to the U.K., and from 1938 to 1945 he was foreign minister, giving German foreign policy a specifically Nazi character. He considered his greatest achievement to have been the German-Soviet Pact (q.v.) of 1939. The Tripartite Pact (q.v.) of 1940 was signed under his influence. In the Nuremberg Trials (q.v.) he was found guilty and was hanged in October 1946. (See also SECOND WORLD WAR.)

RIEFENSTAHL, LENI (1902-). This controversial photographer from Berlin studied art, danced with the Russian Ballet, and acted in several German films before opening her own production company in 1931. She filmed, directed and edited five propaganda films for Hitler which more than suggested the superiority of the "Aryan" race. She was best known for *Triumph of the Will* and her film about the 1936 Berlin Olympics. After the Second World War (q.v.) she was blacklisted until 1952, when she returned to film work. Since then she has won recognition for her still photography of the Nuba tribe in the Sudan as well as her underwater photography.

RIESENHUBER, HEINZ (1935-) see SPACE PROGRAM

RIEZLER, KURT (1882-1955). An eminent scholar of classical Greek philosophy, Riezler attracted at age 25 the attention of Kaiser Wilhelm II (q.v.), for whom he wrote speeches. He was soon hired as political adviser to Chancellor Bethmann Hollweg (q.v.). He kept an important diary during the First World War (q.v.) which became a key historical source in examining Germany's policy and war aims during the war. He coordinated Germany's wartime revolutionary policy and helped put Lenin into power in the Soviet Union, where he guided the German mission in 1918. A member of the DDP (q.v.), he supported the Weimar Coalition after the war, but he resigned from public life in protest against the severity of the Versailles Treaty (q.v.). He became president of the University of Frankfurt, but his scorn toward the Nazis (q.v.) led to his dismissal. He was married to the daughter of the painter Max Liebermann (q.v.), and because she was Jewish he accepted a chair at the New School for Social Research in New York, where he taught philosophy until his retirement in 1952. (See also EMPIRE FOREIGN POLICY; SEPTEMBER PROGRAM.)

RIGHT OF REVOLUTION see OVERCOMING THE PAST

RIGHT-WING GROUPS. Some right-wing groups remain in Germany today, but they appear to be more motivated by antiforeigner racism among some working-class youths (but almost no students) or by army unit nostalgia. "Skinheads," who derive morbid pleasure in beating up on isolated foreigners, can be seen in most German cities. Those which commit violent acts, such as the paramilitary "Wehrsportgruppe Hoffmann," are illegal. Authorities permit meetings of former SS members to take place, even though they draw hordes of young protesters who see such events as incompatible with present democracy. These right-wing groups remain on the periphery of German political life; they embarrass the FRG because of its past, rather than endangering it. (See also PARTIES, RIGHT-WING.)

RILKE, RAINER MARIA (1875-1926). This Austrian, born in Prague, is one of the best known German poets in the English-speaking world.

ROCKEFELLER, JOHANN PETER   see AMERICA, GERMAN ATTITUDES

ROCKETS. In 1942, a German rocket was successfully launched at the Peenemünde launch site on the Baltic Sea. This flight, directed by Wernher von Braun, prompted the site commander, Major General Walter R. Dornberger, to declare: "Today the spaceship is born." The next year, on October 3, 1943, von Braun's team fired a rocket outside the earth's atmosphere for the first time. As thousands of British learned, there was a military impetus for these rockets, which gained wartime infamy as the V-2. But their importance for man's future use of outer space is undeniable. Von Braun and most of his scientific team surrendered with their precious documents to the Americans. They were brought by various clandestine ways to White Sands Proving Grounds, where they quickly proceeded to reassemble V-2s from captured equipment. These rockets launched the American space program. Since a few German rocket scientists fell into the hands of the Russians, Germans also played a part in the Soviet Union's nascent space program.

Not everybody is ready to celebrate the work done at Peenemünde. When, in September 1992, German space officials announced plans for a ceremony honoring the 50th anniversary of the testing of the precursor for the V-2 rockets as "the first step into space," there was a storm of protest in Germany and England. Many English found it bad taste to celebrate a rocket which had caused 9,000 casualties between September 1944 and March 1945, and many Germans remembered that 20,000 concentration camp (q.v.) inmates had perished making it. Fearing that the ceremony would resurrect war memories, the German government ordered that it be canceled.

There is another spin-off from Germany's wartime aeronautical research. The German firm, Messerschmitt-Bölkow-Blohm (MBB) in Munich, is working on a space plane named Sänger after the rocket pioneer Eugen Sänger, who conceived of the space plane during the Second World War (q.v.) as a possible means of bombing New York.

Sänger acted as advisor for the MBB's studies on the aircraft for two years until his death in 1964. It would consist of two reusable vehicles, one riding piggyback on the other, and two different kinds of engines, one for the atmosphere and one for space. The larger one, the size of a 747 jumbo jet and looking like a large Concorde, would be powered by turbojet engines using atmospheric oxygen and would take off horizontally from European airports and attain a speed of about six times the speed of sound at approximately 35 kilometers altitude. Then the second stage rocket would ignite and propel the shuttle (called Horus) into space, while the first stage returns to earth and lands at a normal airport (as the second also would after it has performed its mission).

ROCOCO. This style flourished during the early 18th century when feminine rule and influence were exerted in the highest courts of Europe. A reaction against the baroque (q.v.) and the court of Louis XIV, rococo was a lighter, gayer, more decorative type of expression typical in the churches of Austria and Bavaria. In literature elegance and deftness prevailed.

RÖHM, ERNST (1887-1934) and RÖHM PUTSCH (1934). A former officer, he was SA Chief of Staff from 1931 to 1934. The SA had originally been created to maintain order during Nazi (q.v.) events, but it grew to over a million brown-shirted rowdies after Hitler (q.v.) took power in 1933. The SA's leaders saw in their tightly organized units the basis for a new "people's militia," under which even the Reichswehr (q.v.) was to be subordinated. They spoke of a "second revolution." Such talk and plans disturbed Reichswehr leaders, and since Hitler needed the support of the generals for his war plans, he took their side against the social revolutionary ideas of the SA leaders. When the SS (q.v.), which also saw the SA as a challenger to its power, circulated rumors that the SA leaders were planning a putsch, Hitler took that as a pretext to have the entire SA leadership arrested and murdered on June 30, 1934. The Reichswehr remained silent when persons not associated with the SA, such as General Kurt von Schleicher (q.v.), and former Nazi Reich Organization Leader from 1928-32, Gregor Strasser, were assassinated as well. In a Reichstag speech afterwards Hitler complained about the homosexual tendencies of Röhm and other SA leaders. This blow, which Hitler was able to have the senile President

Hindenburg (q.v.) declare as a legal "emergency defense of the state," became known as the "Night of the Long Knives." (See also NAZI PARTY.)

ROHWEDDER, DETLEV (d. 1991). Assassinated chairman of Treuhand. (See also TREUHAND.)

RÖNTGEN, WILHELM KONRAD (1845-1923) see EMPIRE CULTURE

ROLL-BACK see POLICY OF STRENGTH

ROMA (ROMANI) AND SINTI. These are the names which Gypsies in Germany call themselves. The Germans use the word, *Zigeuner*, which comes from a Byzantine word meaning "untouchable." The word "Romani" in their own language means "man." Before the Berlin Wall (q.v.) came down in 1989, about 60,000 Gypsies resided in Germany, divided into two groups. The Romani came from Eastern Europe. Sinti have lived in Germany for centuries and therefore tend to be more affluent and better established. They speak a heavily German-influenced dialect. Both groups seek protection and an expansion of their rights through the Central Council of German Roma and Sinti.

Gypsies have long been the most hated ethnic group in Germany, Hungary, Czechoslovakia and Bulgaria, and in a 1992 poll three in five Germans said they dislike them. This antipathy was heightened by the rapid influx of Gypsies, mainly from Romania, after 1989; by 1992 their numbers had grown to about 200,000. They form a very visible minority. They are often seen outside in large groups, cooking, eating, and sometimes sleeping and (reportedly) relieving themselves in public. Many Germans stereotype them as dirty and criminal, although the German police say there is no evidence that they are responsible for a disproportionate share of crimes committed. In an attempt to defuse a dangerous round of anti-foreigner hatred and violence, the German government signed a treaty with Romania in the fall of 1992 under which Germany would begin deporting to Romania tens of thousands of Gypsies (referred to in the text as "Romanians") who have no legal papers and would pay that country $21 million for job training and other support for resettlement. This prompted a peaceful protest demonstration of 150,000 in Bonn on November 14, 1992, in which speakers denounced the treaty and deportations, calling them dangerous capitulations to right-wing extremists. Beate Klarsfeld (q.v.) called the actions the "worst taken in Germany since the collapse of the Nazi regime." The reference to the Nazis (q.v.) hurt because of the memory of a half million Gypsies who died in Nazi concentration camps.

ROMANS IN GERMANY. Around four centuries B.C., Germanic tribes, which were of Indo-European extraction, began entering from the North and East of what is now Germany and displacing or mingling with the Celtic peoples whom they found there. These tribes were not the only people to be attracted by the soil, rivers and strategic importance of this area in the heart of Europe. In 58 B.C., Julius Caesar led a Roman army which defeated the Germanic tribes in Alsace and in other Germanic areas west of the Rhine River. A keen cultural observer as well a good commander, Caesar wrote the earliest description of the tribes which he had just defeated and thereby sparked the interest and imagination of other Romans who later came to colonize or develop the area.

The Romans extended their frontier eastward toward the Elbe River in 9 B.C., but this expansion survived only two decades. A German chieftain, Arminius (later known to Germans as Hermann) led an army which in 9 A.D. practically decimated the Roman occupation forces during a furious battle in storm and rain in the Teutoburg Forest, which is thought to be located southeast of the present-day city of Bielefeld. The remnants of the Roman forces withdrew westward and southward beyond the Danube and Rhine rivers. Thenceforth, the Romans remained behind their heavily garrisoned frontier stretching from Cologne (Colonia) to Bonn (Bonna) to Augsburg (Augusta Vindelicorum) and all the way to Vienna (Vindobona). Here the Romans built beautiful cities such as Regensburg (Castra Regina) and Trier (Augusta Treverum) with their stone structures, warm air heating underneath the floors, aqueducts, baths, coliseums and even running water in some villas and public buildings. They introduced advanced Roman agricultural methods, a money economy and Roman law, administration and culture. Trier even served temporarily as a seat of the Roman emperor, especially for Constantine the Great from 306-312 A.D. What we now know about the Germanic tribes at that time came to us from Romans such as Tacitus, who in his book *Germania* described the tribes' legends, customs, appearance, morals and political and economic systems. His characterization of these tribesmen as particularly warlike helped launch a cliche about Germans which is by no means an inherent trait nor valid today.

In the latter half of the 2nd century A.D., Germanic tribes began hammering away at the Roman front and, attracted by stories of great wealth in the Italian peninsula itself, actually invaded the heartland of what had become a decadent Roman Empire in the 5th century, causing it to collapse in the West. For centuries the Roman cities were left largely to decay, and much of the legal, administrative and cultural advancements of the past were forgotten. Yet the Romans left their traces in the grammatical structure and some words of the German language, in the German concept of law, and the cities which after the First Crusade in 1095 began to gain significance in Germany again.

Some historians have dated the beginning of German history at 9 A.D., when Arminius defeated the Romans at Teutoburg, but the various German tribes which he led against the Romans certainly felt no common identity among themselves as Germans. There can hardly be a German history without a German people and some kind of German state. It is a mistake to identify Germany with the various tribes which began to enter what is presently Germany before the arrival of the Romans and with those such as the East and West Goths, Vandals, Burgundians and Longobards which swept into the area during the great migrations before and after Roman supremacy. Those migrations almost completely changed the racial make-up of Europe from the 2nd through the 5th centuries A.D. The German nation was formed only very gradually over many centuries through the conquest and integration of a great number of Germanic tribes. Of course, some such as the Angles, some Saxons, the Danes, Swedes and Norwegians never became a part of the German nation. Others were initially conquered, particularly by the larger tribes--the Friesians, Franks and Swabians, Bavarians, Saxons and Thuringers--and ultimately grew into a community larger than any single tribe.

ROMANTICISM (1790-1830). German Romanticism was a continuation of the Storm and Stress (q.v.) and a reaction against the rigidity of Classicism (q.v.). It is best characterized as irrational, passionate, subjective, mysterious, lyrical, and individualistic, and free of limitations in life, literature and morals. The early romantics were the most subjective and individualistic. Notable among them were Dorothea Schlegel, August and Friedrich Schlegel, Hölderlin, Wackenroder, Ludwig Tieck, Heinrich von Kleist, and Friedrich von

Hardenberg (Novalis, qq.v.). Novalis' *The Blue Flower* represented their quest or yearning for the unknown, the flight of the imagination into a fantasy world (thus, the popularity of fairy tales) where a "progressive universal poetry" (Friedrich Schlegel) existed and reality was never to be found. Many romantics suffered from *Weltschmerz* (world grief) or an inability to cope with the world. The period after 1815 is known as the Late Romantic. Representative of this period are poets Joseph von Eichendorff, Heinrich Heine, E.T.A. Hoffmann, master of the fantastic novel, and Austrian dramatist Franz Grillparzer (qq.v.). Richard Wagner's (q.v.) works dealing with the sagas and myths of the German past filled the opera houses of Europe.

Romanticism stressed feelings and was a reaction against the rationality of the Enlightenment (q.v.). The romantic yearned to break all barriers, including those of reason, and sought refuge in the past, in nature, in art or in fantasy. He was drawn to legends and fairy tales, especially following publication by Jakob and Wilhelm Grimm (q.v.) of German fairy tales in the years 1812-1814 and of legends a few years later. Romanticism in art was best portrayed by the painter Caspar David Friedrich (q.v.), whose superb landscape paintings showed the links between man and nature; in music, by Franz Schubert and Carl Maria von Weber. At first Romanticism was not political. But, by the end of the 19th century, it had seeped into the political thinking of many Germans and lent their views an often unrealistic and immoderate air.

ROMMEL, ERWIN (1891-1944). Commander of Afrikakorps (1941-43), suspected by Nazis (q.v.) of complicity in July 20, 1944, plot and forced to commit suicide. (See also SECOND WORLD WAR.)

ROMMEL, MANFRED (1928-). Son of General Erwin Rommel, Manfred became a much-loved and respected CDU mayor of Stuttgart, whose service extended well into the 1990s.

ROON, ALBRECHT VON (1803-1879). Prussian war minister (1859-73) and Prussian minister president (1873).

ROSENBERG, ALFRED (1893-1946). He was the official Nazi (q.v.) philosopher, who attempted to provide scientific evidence for the Nazi race and blood theories. He opened his *The Myth of the Twentieth*

Century with a quote from Goethe (q.v.): "From here and now there begins a new epoch in the history of the world."

ROTE ZORA see TERRORIST GROUPS

ROTH, WOLFGANG (1941-). SPD, federal chairman of Young Socialists (1972-74), member of Bundestag and an SPD (q.v.) economics expert since 1976.

ROUND TABLE DISCUSSIONS (GDR) see PARTY OF DEMOCRATIC SOCIALISM

RÜHE, VOLKER (1942-). A former secretary general of the CDU (q.v.), Rühe became federal minister of defense in April 1992. He had long been one of the best-known German politicians in the U.S., where he had built up a large network of contacts. Americans like his easygoing manner and brilliant English. He demonstrated his decisiveness early in his tenure as defense minister, when he argued successfully that the controversial plans to build the European Fighter Aircraft (Jäger 90) with Britain, Italy, and Spain should be scrapped. The Kohl (q.v.) government cited the high expenses involved and the wish to send a signal that the Bundeswehr (q.v.) was going to be dramatically restructured following the end of the Cold War.

RUHR STATUTE. Upon the urging of France, an international control authority was created for the Ruhr, traditionally Germany's most industrialized region, on April 28, 1949. The BENELUX countries (Belgium, Netherlands, and Luxembourg), France, the U.K., and the U.S. participated. Although the Ruhr region remained a part of German state territory, the control authority was responsible for the most important economic questions. In the Petersberg Agreement (q.v.), Chancellor Konrad Adenauer (q.v.) declared the FRG's willingness to join the authority. Upon the suggestion of French Foreign Minister Robert Schumann that the Germans and French share their coal and steel production, the nations in the control authority (except the U.S. and U.K.), joined by the FRG and Italy, signed the treaty establishing the European Coal and Steel Community (ECSC), which came into effect on June 23, 1952. The ECSC replaced the Ruhr Statute and became one of the pillars for the European Community (EC, q.v.), whose existence officially began on January 1, 1958.

-S-

SAAR, RETURN TO GERMANY (1957). In 1935, this coal-rich region, which had been occupied by France at the end of the First World War (q.v.), reverted to Germany's control as a result of a plebiscite. France annexed it again at the end of the Second World War (q.v.). The SPD (q.v.) and the CDU/CSU (q.v.) gradually adopted the same fundamental position. In 1953, French policy began to shift; France called for a "Europeanization" of the region, an idea Konrad Adenauer (q.v.) had proposed earlier. The SPD strongly rejected this since it fell short of the Saar's full fusion within Germany. Adenauer, whose opinion of the Saar issue was coming much closer to that of the SPD, decided to include the SPD in the search for a solution. On March 21, 1955, seeing that the Saarlanders were growing more and more impatient with French control, Paris granted the Saar political independence, but kept it tied economically to France. However, it was too late for such a half-measure, as was shown by the collapse of the pro-French Social Democratic Party of the Saar (SPS) and the formation of the Democratic Party of the Saar (DPS), which later became the SPD in the Saar. On October 23, 1955, over two-thirds of the Saarlanders voted against any form of "Europeanization" of their region, so on January 1, 1957, the Saar was officially reunited with Germany.

SACHS, HANS (1494-1576). This author from Nuremberg, who was a shoemaker by trade, was one of the most prolific writers of the 16th century. He wrote humorous fables, anecdotes, and tales in verse, as well as over 200 verse plays.

SÄNGER, EUGEN see ROCKETS

SCHABOWSKI, GÜNTER (1929-). SED chief in East Berlin, member of politburo (1984-89), one of leaders responsible for ousting Erich Honecker (q.v.).

SCHACHT, HJALMAR (1877-1970). President of Reichsbank (1923-30 and 1933-39). He was tried in Nuremberg (q.v.) after the war and was found not guilty, a judgment which created considerable public consternation at the time.

SCHACK, ADOLF FRIEDRICH COUNT VON (1815-1894). A talented author of *History of Dramatic History and Art*, he translated Spanish and Portuguese poetry. He was a wealthy diplomat, collector and promoter of the arts, who founded the Schack Gallery in Munich.

SCHADOW, JOHANN GOTTFRIED (1764-1860). Schadow's sculpture was much more realistic and direct compared to his contemporaries, who wavered between Baroque (q.v.) and Neoclassicism. This did not endear him to the Prussian court, however. His work won recognition for the Berlin School throughout Europe.

SCHARNHORST, GERHARD JOHANN DAVID VON (1755-1813). Prussian (q.v.) general who was born near Hanover, in whose army he served from 1793-95 before transferring in 1801 to Prussian duty. Wounded in the 1806-07 campaigns, he was chosen to reorganize the Prussian army, which according to the stipulations of the Peace of Tilsit (q.v.) was limited to 42,000 men. He introduced a new relationship between the soldiers and their officers and improved training methods by introducing short-term enlistments. General Blücher (q.v.) led this army to victory in 1813-15. Scharnhorst died of battle wounds he received in Silesia in May 1813. (See also FRENCH REVOLUTION.)

SCHARPING, RUDOLF (1947-). SPD, minister president of Rhineland-Palatinate. Since June 1993 SPD national chairman and chancellor candidate.

SCHÄUBLE, WOLFGANG (1942-). A top CDU (q.v.) leader, federal interior minister and then leader of CDU parliamentary group (q.v.). Often referred to as Helmut Kohl's (q.v.) heir apparent, Schäuble was consigned to a wheelchair for life as a result of being repeatedly shot by a deranged man during a public appearance in the fall of 1990.

SCHEEL, WALTER (1919-). A Rhinelander born in Solingen, Scheel was a soldier in the Wehrmacht from 1939 to 1945. In 1946, he entered the FDP (q.v.). He served as federal minister for economic cooperation (1961-66). In the SPD-FDP governing coalition, he was vice-chancellor and foreign minister (1969-74), in which capacity he was instrumental in implementing and defending the government's policy of *Ostpolitik* (q.v.). In 1974, he became federal president, defeating the CDU candidate Richard von Weizsäcker (qq.v.) and serving until 1979. (See also FREE DEMOCRATIC PARTY; OSTPOLITIK.)

SCHEIDEMANN, PHILIPP (1965-1939). An SPD (q.v.) leader remembered for declaring the new republic on November 9, 1918, when the Kaiser abdicated and left Germany. In early 1919, he became chancellor in a "Weimar Coalition" government, composed of the SPD, DDP (q.v.), and Center Party (q.v.). The fact that two members of this government signed the Versailles Treaty (q.v.) sparked agitation by right-wing parties, who circulated the "stab in the back legend" that Germany had won the war but had been betrayed by politicians at home. In the Reichstag elections on June 6, 1920, the Weimar Coalition lost its absolute majority, and no coalition of parties ever regained such a majority during the rest of the Weimar Republic (q.v.). (See REVOLUTION IN GERMANY; VERSAILLES TREATY.)

SCHILLER, JOHANN CHRISTOPH FRIEDRICH (1759-1805). Considered the finest German dramatist of his time as well as the most popular poet of the middle class, Schiller's career spans from the emotional Storm and Stress (q.v.) to the sober, rational Classicism (q.v.). His play *Don Carlos* best marks this transition. Schiller spent his last ten years in Weimar where his writing was enriched by his friendship with Goethe (q.v.), which was also marked with rivalry. In addition to nine plays, Schiller wrote historical and philosophical works about the Thirty Years War (q.v.) and Kant (q.v.) and was a history professor at the University of Jena. He died of tuberculosis at age 45.

SCHILLER, KARL (1911-). SPD, professor of public law, federal minister of economics (1966-71), of economics and finance (1971-72). Earlier West Berlin's economic senator and Helmut Schmidt's (q.v.) economics and transport boss in Hamburg. A top SPD (q.v.) vote-getter in the 1969 federal elections, he grew disillusioned with the SPD and joined the CDU (q.v.). He later returned to the SPD. (See also ELECTIONS (1969); GRAND COALITION; SCHMIDT, HELMUT.)

SCHINKEL, KARL FRIEDRICH (1781-1841). Leading Prussian (q.v.) architect and painter designed over 50 buildings in Berlin. Although he produced buildings elsewhere in Germany, his Gothic revival style never became widespread outside of Germany.

SCHIRACH, BALDUR VON (1907-1974). Nazi (q.v.) youth leader of German Reich (1931-40), Gauleiter and Reichstatthalter in Vienna

(1940-45), found guilty in Nuremberg War Crimes Trials (q.v.) of deporting Jews and sentenced to 20 years in prison. (See also HITLER YOUTH.)

SCHLEGEL, AUGUST WILHELM VON (1767-1845). A Romantic (q.v.) philosopher, who together with his brother, Friedrich, published their concepts in *Das Athenäum*. He also translated 17 Shakespearean plays into German.

SCHLEICHER, KURT VON (1882-1934). General, Reich chancellor from December 3, 1932, until Hitler (q.v.) was named to that post on January 30, 1933. Schleicher was President Hindenburg's (q.v.) final attempt to find an alternative to Hitler as chancellor. He was assassinated by the Nazis in the Röhm Putsch (qq.v.) on June 30, 1934. (See also HITLER'S SEIZURE OF POWER.)

SCHLEIERMACHER, FRIEDRICH (1768-1834). Educated by Moravians, this philosopher from Breslau, Halle, and Berlin argued that emotions are the fundamental root of human nature. He praised the critical spirit, but he placed limits on reason; he combined Romanticism (q.v.) with criticism. He elaborated a representation theory of knowledge. In his view, the conceptions which logical criticism rejects are still valid as symbols or aspects of inner experience. Symbols are also seen in religion, art, and science. In ethics, reason and desire govern nature, and will develops gradually through nature and emerges as ethics in man. Each man expresses in an individual way that which is universal. In his *Addresses on Religion* (1799), he argued that religion focuses on the feeling of dependence of the finite on the infinite, of man upon God; religious notions are interpretations of immediate feelings.

SCHLESINGER, HELMUT (1924-). President of the Bundesbank (q.v.). Replaced by Hans Tietmeyer October 1, 1993.

SCHLEYER, HANNS-MARTIN (1915-1977). President of BDA (q.v.), assassinated by RAF (q.v.) terrorists. (See TERRORIST GROUPS.)

SCHLIEFFEN PLAN. Plan of 1905 by Count Alfred von Schlieffen (1833-1913), who served as chief of the German general staff from 1891 to 1905. He produced a military plan designed to meet the danger of a two-front war by means of a German strike at the heart of France instead of a frontal assault on the well-fortified frontier, which extended 150 miles from Switzerland to Verdun. German forces were to be concentrated on the right flank, which would sweep through Luxembourg and Belgium into northern France. Paris would be enveloped, and the French troops would be pushed back toward the Moselle where they would be met by the German left flank. Modified later, this was Germany's operational plan at the outbreak of the First World War (q.v.). Although the plan was logical from the military point of view, it had not been sufficiently thought out politically. The invasion of Belgium brought Britain into the war against Germany. The plan was also poorly executed in August 1914. Only weak German units were to face French forces in eastern France and were to withdraw under attack to tempt French reinforcements to aid in the push toward the German border rather than to defend Paris. But when the French forces in the East were pushed back, General von Moltke (q.v.) sent his own reinforcements there rather than putting Germany's full strength into the push toward Paris. The Germans were thrown back at the Battle of the Marne, and the belligerents settled into bloody and mindless trench warfare for the next four years. (See also FIRST WORLD WAR.)

SCHLÖNDORFF, VOLKER (1939-) see FILM and OVERCOMING THE PAST

SCHMID, CARLO (1896-1979). SPD, urbane and learned professor of public law, vice-president of Bundestag (1949-66 and 1969-72). (See also SOCIAL DEMOCRATIC PARTY OF GERMANY.)

SCHMIDT, HELMUT (1918-). SPD, Hamburg interior minister (1961-65), federal minister of defense (1969-72), of economics and finance (1972-74), chancellor (1974-82). The term "chancellor democracy" lost none of its meaning under Schmidt. Born in 1918, he served as a young officer during the Second World War (q.v.) and rose within the SPD (q.v.) in the 1950s on the basis of his competence in defense matters. As Hamburg's interior minister from 1960-65 and SPD parliamentary floor leader in the Bundestag from 1966 to 1969, he expanded his familiarity with domestic politics. From 1969 to 1972 he was defense minister, and from 1972 until 1974 he simultaneously directed two ministries--economics and finance. He is extremely disciplined and hard-working and expects the same from all those who work under him. He can be impatient and quick-tempered and acquired the nickname, "*Schmidt Schnauze*" (Schmidt the Lip). At the same time he is pragmatic, a quality which sometimes caused him problems with the left wing of his own party. He was able to go quickly to the heart of any question and to master crises (and also lecture others on how to master theirs). He was one of the few world leaders who had a firm grasp of both security and financial problems. As a person, he exuded self-confidence and competence, qualities which western German voters admired greatly. They liked his image as a "doer" (*Macher*). Many credited him with having single-handedly won the parliamentary elections of 1980 for his party and having kept the SPD-FDP coalition alive so long.

As Hamburg's interior minister, Schmidt won acclaim for his decisive leadership during the disastrous flood in 1962. Herbert Wehner drew him and Karl Schiller back to Bonn because Willy Brandt (qq.v.) appeared to be getting tired of his role as SPD leader. The possibility of replacing Brandt was an effective carrot to attract these two competent Social Democrats into the party's work in Bonn. To ensure that Schmidt would devote full attention to his new duties in the country's capital, and perhaps also to ensure that he not become too powerful too soon, Wehner helped sabotage Schmidt's bid in May 1966 to become the head of Hamburg's SPD. Already weakened somewhat by a brief lapse in personal morality in 1961 as well as by his authoritarian manner toward party comrades, Schmidt lost by 37 votes to former mayor Paul Nevermann. With these two men in the SPD's front ranks, Wehner built a brilliant team around Brandt. Schiller was chiefly responsible for the party's election success in 1969, and Schmidt was thereafter the party's strongest vote-getter.

On May 9, 1974, the SPD nominated Schmidt as chancellor. Always a model political manager who had thought for a long time about how he would act as chancellor, he formed his cabinet in five days. It reflected his desire for a more pragmatic policy and included ministers mainly from the party's right. Three left-of-center ministers, Egon Bahr, Horst Ehmke, and Klaus von Dohnanyi (qq.v.), were not reappointed. Bahr replaced Erhard Eppler (q.v.), who resigned as minister of economic cooperation seven weeks later because the Schmidt government announced a cut in Third World aid. This was a bellwether decision that predictably angered the party's left. "German efficiency!" noted Brandt. Kiel political scientist, Werner Kaltefleiter, called it "the most successful change of chancellor in the FRG's history." Konrad Adenauer (q.v.) had vacillated four years before stepping down, and then he made life miserable for his successor, Ludwig Erhard (q.v.), who himself was hacked to pieces by intrigues during his last year in office. Only toward intimates did Brandt confide how difficult it was to take a back seat behind Schmidt and Wehner (q.v.), but he persistently supported them as party chairman. Walter Scheel of the FDP (qq.v.) was elected federal president on May 15, 1974, and the Bundestag confirmed Schmidt as chancellor the next day, with Hans-Dietrich Genscher (q.v.) as his foreign minister and vice-chancellor. Wehner remained as parliamentary party chairman.

Schmidt had little sympathy with theorizing leftist activists, who threatened to polarize and paralyze the party and scare away the SPD's traditional working-class support. Jusos never forgave him for telling them at their 1974 congress that they demonstrated "a crisis of their brain," while he was concerned with the "crisis of the world economy." "I request that you leave the scholastic discussion about superstructure where it belongs: in the seminar or in the study room." They continued to hound him for allegedly abandoning reform and disregarding Social Democratic principles. The chancellor never fully lived down his reputation as "Schmidt the lip" and "knife thrower." His self-image as "the only real leader in the world" irritated other world leaders, especially President Jimmy Carter. Brandt remained party chairman until 1987, thereby sparing Schmidt that added responsibility and double burden. Schmidt left to Brandt the job of dealing with the factional strife within the SPD. Schmidt described his own tense relationship with the SPD: "I am not completely satisfied with my party, and it not with me. But I do not find a better party, and it has no substitute for me. . . . Thus, we must get along with one another." Of course, the "troika's" private tension and criticism continued. SPD Bundestag deputy Ulrich Lohmar noted: "Helmut Schmidt knows everything and most of it better. Herbert Wehner does everything, and the most important alone. Willy Brandt sees all, and looks straight at the future."

The Schmidt era was stamped by the oil crisis of 1973-74, which created fear of future economic limits. Schmidt and his successor, Helmut Kohl of the CDU (qq.v.), departed from grandiose visions painted by Brandt. Schmidt's watchwords were "concentration" and "continuity." He spoke of "stability" instead of "reform." Any remaining reform goals were few in number and restricted to practical projects that could be financed in a setting of economic recession, could be accepted by an increasingly critical FDP coalition partner, and was agreeable to an upper house in which the CDU/CSU had a majority. Wehner agreed: "There are times in which it is crucial to defend what has already been achieved so that it will not be damaged or washed away and so that one can start building again as soon as the storm has passed by." There were some important reforms during the Schmidt years, including improvements in pensions and social security, marriage and divorce laws, penal laws for homosexuals, and environmental protection. A co-determination (q.v.) bill was enacted in 1976 that required equal representation of employees and owners on supervisory boards of all companies employing more than two thousand persons. Since one seat was reserved for "managerial personnel," the unions charged that the balance was still tipped toward the owners. Nevertheless, the FRG found itself in the forefront of labor participation in management. The government did not try to bring about major shifts in income. In a nation extremely skittish about economic down-swings since the Weimar Republic (q.v.), such talk of "stability" sounded good in voters' ears. The chancellor had a keen ear to the ground. There was no consensus for reform in the electorate. But many idealistic Social Democrats resented Schmidt's efforts to preserve the currency's stability and limit the growth of the welfare state to match declining tax revenues. They branded Schmidt and the SPD mere appendages of the establishment and either fought them inside the party or left the SPD altogether.

Energy and related economic problems increasingly replaced the *Ostpolitik* (q.v.) focus of the government. Schmidt did travel to Eastern Europe, including the GDR (q.v.) in 1981. He continued the "policy of small steps" toward the GDR, which sought to improve living standards, increase trade by granting interest-free credit to the GDR, and normalize relations between the two states. The FRG was a prime mover and signatory in the Helsinki (CSCE) Accords in 1975, which forbade border changes except by peaceful means and which called for the free movement of people and ideas between East and West. Schmidt met with GDR leader Erich Honecker (q.v.) at the conference in Helsinki. There was little opposition to Schmidt's *Ostpolitik*, either from the FDP or the opposition CDU/CSU, and the latter parties continued it after the SPD fell from power in 1982. But Schmidt's attention became more directed toward the West and away from the East. His emphasis was to maintain what had already been achieved, and to preserve or reestablish the economic health and military security of Western Europe. His ability to protect the economy, and his own image of confidence, dynamism, and expertise helped change the FRG's image in the world to match his own. During his chancellorship West Germany's weight in NATO and the EC (qq.v.) grew noticeably. His statement in 1969 as defense minister still applied: "Clear judgment for the possible is the most important quality for German policy--pitched as it is between the two Super Powers."

Plagued by continual dissension within the SPD and recurrent coalition crises with the FDP, the Schmidt government collapsed in 1982, when the Free Democrats switched partners and enabled the CDU, led by Helmut Kohl, to take power. The following year, voters confirmed this *Wende* (change, q.v.) by giving the new CDU/CSU-FDP coalition government a solid endorsement in the Bundestag elections. The Kohl (q.v.) government set about tackling the problems of unemployment and the emotionally charged deployment of American Pershing and cruise missiles on German soil. The Schmidt government had agreed to do the latter in the 1979 NATO "Twin-track" decision, which was designed to counter a renewed Soviet nuclear missile threat. (For his government's fall, see WENDE.)

SCHMITT, CARL (b. 1888). He was a conservative legal expert in the Weimar Republic (q.v.). He did not support the Republic and was the best known of the competent political theorists who developed elaborate justifications for the emerging Third Reich (q.v.). But he did not enthusiastically support the Nazi (q.v.) regime, and by 1936 the Nazis no longer acknowledged him as an authoritative interpreter of their ideology. Nevertheless, his insights were often cited by persons skeptical of or cynical toward liberal democracy. (See also WEIMAR CULTURE.)

SCHNUR, WOLFGANG (1944-). Co-founder of Democratic Awakening (q.v.) on December 16-17, 1989, of which he was president from December 1989 to March 1990, when forced to step down because of allegations of earlier cooperation with the Stasi (q.v.).

SCHOLL, HANS (1918-43) and SOPHIE (1921-43) see RESISTANCE TO HITLER

SCHÖNHUBER, FRANZ (1923-) see PARTIES, RIGHT-WING

SCHOPENHAUER, ARTHUR (1788-1860). Schopenhauer rejected the optimism of idealists like Hegel (q.v.) and elaborated a pessimistic philosophy. It is said that he scheduled his lectures at the University of Berlin at the same time as Hegel's in order to force students to choose between the two opposing views. The main inspiration for him was Kant's (q.v.) analysis of the role of will. He accepted the notion that in both man and the universe will is the "thing-in-itself," a view that he explained in his classic 1819 study, *The World as Will and Idea*. The will can objectify itself in phenomena, and the universe is idea. Since no one person can comprehend the entire "world will," an individual considers the world to be his own idea. Schopenhauer does not argue that the will is rational. Looking at nature and life, he saw no evidence that there was a rational process at work. Instead, he saw life as a blind purposeless impulse, as confusion rather than order. People like Hegel, who saw underlying rationality in the universe, were victims of wishful thinking. Life is desire which can never be satisfied; its essence is restlessness and movement.

Any thinking man will be pessimistic because he will never find satisfaction in life. Although one can never totally escape from this pessimism, there are three places to turn for temporary solace. One is art and music, in which both eternal ideas and the restless movement of life can be combined; but one cannot live every moment of his life in artistic ecstasy. A second is sympathy, which subordinates individualism, minimizes conflict, creates a degree of unity among men, and forms the basis for ethics. The third is to renounce the very will to live. This does not mean suicide, which results from dissatisfaction with present conditions, but a complete indifference to living. None of these are final solutions because any solace they provide will be dashed again, and man will be cast back into pessimism.

SCHRÖDER, GERHARD (1910-1989). CDU, federal minister of interior (1953-61), of foreign affairs (1961-66) and of defense (1966-69).

SCHULZE-BOYSEN, HARRO (1909-1945). A leader of resistance group Red Chapel (q.v.). (See also RESISTANCE.)

SCHUMACHER, KURT (1895-1952). Never in SPD (q.v.) history did one person so dominate the party as did Kurt Schumacher until his death on August 20, 1952. In many respects, the direction he established endured for decades after his passing and helped establish the character of the party. In other respects, his policies were not in step with the direction in which his country and his people were moving and had to be altered later in order to enable the party to win enough votes to govern the country. Schumacher opposed all forms of totalitarianism as inherently evil, asserting that "every kind of reservation *vis-à-vis* the idea of democracy means the greatest imaginable danger for the German future" and that "democracy is the state, and the state which can live in Europe is democracy, and we reject every other form." In his commitment to democracy, he was entirely oriented toward the political values of the Western Allies and of the smaller democratic nations in Western Europe. Very early he had cast off any thoughts of Germany playing a politically neutral, intermediary role between East and West. He maintained publicly that "the whole German people in thought and deed belong to the West." This democratic commitment, along with his charisma and determination, is an important reason why such diverse personalities as Willy Brandt, Waldemar von Knöringen, Willy Eichler, Karl Schiller, Carlo Schmid, and Herbert Wehner (qq.v.), who would not have been prototypical Social Democrats before 1933, were drawn to the SPD after 1945.

Because of his aim to establish a democratic order, he opened the SPD's doors to young ex-Nazis, especially from the Hitler Youth (qq.v.) and the Waffen-SS. Schumacher saw great dangers for German democracy if such persons, who had been too young to form independent opinions during the Third Reich (q.v.), were not persuaded of the necessity and desirability of Western liberal democracy and were not brought into the democratic movement. Schumacher had seen a democracy collapse in the 1920s and 1930s partly because the youth had not been persuaded to support it. At the same time, Schumacher was utterly convinced that those who had suffered most in their opposition to Nazi terror had now come to the SPD, which therefore had the sole moral right and obligation to take complete political command of the new Germany. This conviction strengthened his obstinate refusal to share power with any other party, even though some SPD leaders at the state level had taken a more independent course and had entered governing coalitions with other parties. An SPD that could not rule the new Germany alone would remain in unyielding opposition to the government.

Schumacher's commitment to democracy and individual rights and his determination for the SPD to rule the new Germany made a clean break with the Communists necessary. His major challenger for SPD leadership in all of Germany was Otto Grotewohl (q.v.), who in mid-June 1945 had created a "central committee of the SPD" in Berlin and had proclaimed the goal of reshaping Germany on the basis of working-class unity. The KPD (q.v.), no doubt hoping to be the most dynamic element within an all-German working-class movement, warmly greeted Grotewohl's proclamation. However, Schumacher stuck to his principle stated on May 6, 1945: there could be no cooperation with the KPD because of the latter's entirely different way of viewing ideas and the political world and because of its close attachment to the Soviet Union; the SPD must refuse to become the "autocratically manipulated instrument of any foreign, imperial interest." He was able to point to developments in the Soviet zone to strengthen his point. In January 1946, he stated: "If that which we are experiencing in the Eastern Zone were actually socialism, then European humanists could pronounce the death sentence of socialism." Only truly independent parties could join forces, but German Communists had become "Russian patriots," for whom Germany and socialism had become secondary matters. Because they used brute force to suppress democracy, Schumacher called them "nothing but twin copies of National Socialists varnished with red." This characterization is doubly devastating, given his description of Nazism: "the permanent appeal to the swine [*Schweinhund*] in man, which for the first time in German politics succeeded in the complete mobilization of human stupidity."

Schumacher's SPD showed little interest in ideological or theoretical questions. It was far more involved in grappling with the immediate practical problems Germans faced in the postwar years. Nevertheless, Schumacher's economic thinking and interpretation of that setting had been shaped by Marxism, to which "we owe more strength, more insights, and more weapons than every other scholarly and sociological method in the world." Schumacher assumed that Germans had become such an impoverished people that most had sunk into a proletarian mass which hated capitalism. He thought that there was a "latent proletarian revolution" present in Germany and that a class struggle was forming in which the enlarged working class would emerge victorious. He also assumed that capitalism was unjust and incapable of rebuilding Germany and that German capitalists had been responsible for Hitler's (q.v.) takeover of power and therefore ultimately for the devastating war. He called for widespread nationalization of banks, insurance companies, and heavy industry. These calls found much support among the German population, the French and British governments, who were in the process of nationalizing much of their own industry and banks, and American authorities. The SPD's chief competitor in the political arena, the CDU (q.v.), also adopted in February 1947 its Ahlen Program which called for state ownership of much of the economy.

Under Schumacher foreign policy occupied an important place in SPD politics for the first time. He was an emphatic patriot. He always insisted that since the SPD encompassed the "other Germany" which had opposed Hitler and had suffered greatly as a result, Germany under its leadership had a right to determine its own fate and to take its place as an equal member in the community of nations. "We [Social Democrats] fought the Nazis . . . before anyone else in the world bothered about them," and later "we opposed the Nazis at great cost when it was still fashionable for the rest of the world to vie for their goodwill." His highest goal was the reunification (q.v.) of Germany within its 1937 borders on the basis of self-determination. This meant that his party rejected both the Oder-Neisse (q.v.) line as the permanent border between Germany and Poland and France's claims to the Saar (q.v.) area. The SPD also demanded that Berlin remain the capital of Germany. His party's insistence upon reunification prompted it to oppose the FRG's rearmament (q.v.) and partial integration into a united Europe. The SPD's fixation on national unity lasted throughout the 1950s. In general, Schumacher's foreign policy objectives could not be achieved under the conditions that prevailed in Europe during his lifetime. He could not communicate effectively with the occupying powers and put himself in their shoes. Therefore, he could never understand their attitudes or behavior. His economic objectives were, in some important ways, unrealistic and increasingly out of step with the aspirations of his own countrymen. The stubborn pursuit of his economic goals also contributed to the widespread impression in the FRG that the Social Democrats were not qualified to rule in Bonn and to the party's disheartening electoral setbacks. Under Schumacher, the SPD's domestic and foreign policies were inflexible and out of touch.

SCHUMANN, ROBERT (1810-1856). A composer during the Romantic era (q.v.) with a lively imagination, Schumann's marriage in 1840 was inspiration for the outpouring of new songs set to poems. Most famous among these is *Liederkreis*, twelve poems by Eichendorff (q.v.). He also set poems by Burns and Byron to music. He became director of music for the city of Dresden until he committed himself to an mental institution.

SCHURZ, CARL (1829-1906) see AMERICA, GERMAN ATTITUDES and REVOLUTION OF 1848

SCHUSCHNIGG, KURT VON (1897-1977) see ANSCHLUSS

SCHWAETZER, IRMGARD. FDP (q.v.) minister for regional planning and urban development in the Kohl (q.v.) cabinet. She almost became Germany's first female foreign minister following the resignation of Hans-Dietrich Genscher (q.v.) in May 1992, but her nomination was overturned by the FDP parliamentary group, which led to the appointment of Klaus Kinkel (q.v.).

SCHWARZ, BERTHOLD see RENAISSANCE

SECOND WORLD WAR. By the spring of 1939, Britain and France had already allowed Germany to become the dominant power in Europe. Hitler's (q.v.) greatest mistake was that he cast this enormous accomplishment away by leading Germany into war. After 1938 he had no further diplomatic victories. From 1939 to 1941 he led Germany to dazzling successes, but all were of a military nature. With relative ease his newly created army (*Wehrmacht*) overran part of Poland, Denmark, Norway, Holland, Belgium, Luxembourg, Yugoslavia and Greece. The most miraculous victory was the victory over France. Most German generals shuddered at the thought of attacking France, remembering the failure of the 1914 advance and the four-year war of attrition which had sapped Germany's strength and will. But Hitler had great faith in the tank warfare tactics developed by General Heinz Guderian and in the brilliant strategic plan devised by General Friedrich Erich von Manstein. He also recognized the most important factor: France was unwilling to fight a sustained war. In six weeks, Germany had rolled into France via a flank attack around its famed Maginot line of supposedly impregnable fortresses.

By the summer of 1940, Germany controlled Europe from the Arctic Circle to the Pyrenees and from the Atlantic Ocean to the Soviet Union. If Hitler had made a generous peace offer to France, he might have destroyed Britain's and other countries' will to resist, but Hitler never thought of such a possibility. He could not grant a magnanimous peace because, as he himself later wrote, the victory of the stronger always involved "the destruction of the weaker or his unconditional subservience." He had a knack for seeing the weakness in his enemies, but he was unable to build anything lasting. Also, because he considered himself to be infallible and irreplaceable, he insisted on doing everything quickly; he could not plant anything which required time to grow. Based upon his writings and actions, one can say with reasonable certainty that Hitler sought to establish German hegemony in Europe and direct domination over the Soviet Union, which along with the older European powers' overseas colonies, would occupy the bottom of Hitler's power pyramid. Above them would be the rest of the European countries, divided into Germanic lands bordering on Germany, servant peoples, such as the Poles, and satellites and quasi-independent states. On top would be an all-powerful Germany. This German-dominated order would place Hitler in a good position later to struggle against America and Japan for world domination. That he did not accomplish this ambitious goal was due in large measure to serious mistakes which he himself made after such stunning successes.

In 1940, he launched an aerial attack against Britain which left rubble piles throughout the country, but which also inspired heroic action in what Prime Minister Winston Churchill called Britain's "finest hour." While still involved in this furious struggle, violating the treaty whereby Germany and Russia had split up Poland between them, Hitler unleashed his armies against the Soviet Union in mid-1941, against the advice of his generals, thereby creating a two-front war which had been such a nightmare for Germany during the First World War (q.v.). The attack was launched too late, so in a repeat of Napoleon's humiliation, "General Winter" saved the weaker Russians. Cold weather and snow closed in on the German troops, many of whom had not been issued proper winter equipment. After initial victories against an enemy which Hitler had grossly underestimated, the German advance ground to a halt. Hitler saw his dreams of grandeur buried under Russian snow and ice.

In the midst of this truly desperate situation, Hitler compounded his difficulties even further. On December 7, 1941, Japan attacked the U.S. fleet at Pearl Harbor in Hawaii, and the U.S. responded by declaring war on Japan, but not on Germany. Germany had no treaty obligation with Japan, but inexplicably and without conferring with anyone, Hitler declared war against the U.S. Germany had no military means for conducting military operations against the Americans, but this step decisively tipped the scales in favor of his opponents and ultimately sealed Germany's defeat. Thereafter, he had no idea how to extricate Germany from ruin. For example, he could not follow up on General Erwin Rommel's (q.v.) victories in North Africa in the summer of 1942, and, of course, he excluded the very idea of a political settlement. His only order was "Hold at all costs!" In 1942, Germany began losing territory in the East, especially after a disastrous defeat at Stalingrad in early 1943.

By the fall of 1944, enemy armies were advancing on Germany from the East and West. More and more Germans saw the hopelessness of the situation and began to regard conquest by the Western Allies as liberation. But Hitler did not share this secret war aim of many ordinary people. He personally assumed command of the German forces. Then he had unleashed a torrent of powerful rockets (q.v.) on London and its suburbs using technology only recently developed. These attacks by what he called his "wonder weapons" merely served to harden even more the determination of the British and their American ally. Disregarding warnings from military advisers that the Red Army was poised for a massive strike from the East, Hitler ordered his last military offensive against the Western Allies in the Belgian Ardennes Forest in late 1944. The element of surprise and extremely bad weather which kept Allied aircraft grounded for a few days helped the Germans gain initial success and stop the Western powers' advance on Germany. However, once American and British air power could be brought into action, the German offensive was halted, and by the first week of January the German forces were being decimated or rolled back. As some of Hitler's generals had warned, the Red Army crashed through the German line in the East, and in one violent movement pushed from the Vistula to the Oder Rivers. Because Hitler had squandered his last reserves in the Ardennes offensive, he had nothing left to stop the Russian advance.

Hitler's decisions which had slowed down the Western Allied advance and favored a rapid Russian advance into the heart of Germany had unfortunate consequences for postwar Germany. In the first half of February 1945, President Roosevelt, Prime Minister Churchill and General Secretary Stalin met in Yalta in the Crimea to discuss the postwar control of Germany and to divide Germany into zones of occupation. The lines which they drew were heavily influenced by the calculations of where exactly the Allied armies would be in Germany at the end of the war. At the time, it appeared that Russian troops would be somewhat farther within Germany than was actually the case when hostilities ceased. However, based on the decisions made at Yalta, U.S. troops had later to be pulled back from Saxony and Thuringia, which were within the designated Soviet zone. Also, the collapse of cooperation among the four Allies after the war left the temporary line drawn between the Soviet zone of occupation and the zones of the Western Allies as the line of division between East and West Germany until 1990.

Seeing enemy armies advancing within his own country's territory and with no hope of stopping them, any rational and responsible leader with a concern for his own citizens would have done anything to salvage whatever would be necessary for their survival. Hitler was not such a leader. In late 1941, he had made a chilling statement to the Danish and Croatian foreign ministers: "If ever the German people is no longer sufficiently strong and willing to sacrifice its own blood for its existence, then it should fade away and be destroyed by another, stronger power. . . . In that situation, I will lose no tears for the German people." On March 18 and 19, 1945, he gave two orders which demonstrated that he had not changed his mind and that he now thought it was time to carry through with the end of Germany. He ordered all Germans in areas threatened by the invasion forces in the West to leave their homes and set out on what could only have been a death march eastward. The following day he gave the so-called "Nero order": "to destroy all military, transport, communications, industrial and supply facilities as well as anything of value within the Reich which could be used by the enemy for continuing his struggle either immediately or in the foreseeable time." When Albert Speer (q.v.), his trusted confidant and munitions minister, objected to this policy, which would have completely eliminated the Germans' ability to survive after defeat, Hitler answered "ice-coldly": "If the war is lost, then the people will be lost also . . . In that case the people will have shown itself as the weaker, and the future would belong solely to the strengthened Eastern people. Whoever survives this struggle would be the inferior ones anyway since the superior ones have already fallen."

Hitler himself chose not to be among the survivors. On April 30, 1945, a few hours before his underground bunker in Berlin was captured by Soviet troops, he stuck a pistol in his mouth and pulled the trigger. Speer and others did their best to prevent Hitler's orders from being carried out. But their effect was that most Germans, at least in the western part of Germany, did view the enemy occupation of Germany as a liberation. While the occupation forces expected to find a nation of fanatic Nazis on their hands, they found instead a shell-shocked, seriously disillusioned people who had been far more thoroughly "denazified" by Hitler's treatment of Germany in the closing months of the war than the carefully planned denazification (q.v.) and reeducation program would otherwise ever have been able to accomplish. The occupation powers interpreted the Germans' passivity and willingness to cooperate as typical German servility, but it was rather a reflection of the extent to which Germans felt themselves to have been deceived and betrayed by Hitler.

SECURITY SERVICE (SICHERHEITSDIENST--SD). A Nazi party institution under the SS (q.v.). A prominent member was Adolf Eichmann (q.v.). (See also HEYDRICH, REINHARD.)

SED-SPD SPEAKER EXCHANGE (1966). In early 1966, the SPD entered dramatic negotiations with the SED (qq.v.) concerning an exchange of speakers. This prospect was sensational and captured the imagination of the German public. The *Stuttgarter Zeitung* wrote on April 16: "Brandt, Wehner and Erler in Chemnitz [then Karl-Marx-Stadt]. Now that is a prospect over which the political fantasy can richly explode! . . . Because Herbert Wehner has been burned by a thousand Communist fires, no one has the right to fan suspicions of the party's change of course." People spoke of an "all-German spring." SPD-KPD relations had been bad since their rupture during the First World War (q.v.) and had grown worse. The reasons were the revolutions in 1918-19 and 1923, the inability to cooperate in the face of Hitler's (q.v.) rise, the KPD's (q.v.) attacks against the SPD as "social fascists," the competition in the resistance, and finally the forced merger of the two parties in the GDR (q.v.) in 1946 and rapid suppression of the SPD as an independent political force in the GDR. The exchange dominated the SPD's Dortmund conference in June, at which the SPD crossed the Rubicon by formally renouncing the ban against contacts between the two states. The goal should now be to help the GDR's citizens have a better life, and Willy Brandt (q.v.) stressed that this was possible through coexistence.

The new SPD policy line was greeted enthusiastically by many academics and intellectuals, who were frustrated by the stalemate in the East. For instance, the Protestant Church had called in October 1965 for a recognition of the Oder-Neisse (q.v.) border. All-German Minister Erich Mende (q.v.) was interested, and in February 1966 his ministry proposed that the FRG focus on national unity and lessen the importance of winning back territory lost after the war. There was considerable thinking in all parties about how to bring movement into the FRG's relationship with the East. It came to nothing, largely because many influential politicians opposed such a move at that time. On July 14, the day when Wehner, Brandt, and Erler (qq.v.) had been scheduled to appear in Chemnitz, all three made their prepared speeches on West German radio and television. It was Erler's last public appearance before his death.

SEDAN, BATTLE OF (1870) see FRANCO-PRUSSIAN WAR

SEEKT, HANS VON (1866-1936).   Supreme Commander of Reichswehr (1920-26). From 1919 to 1926 he was responsible for the secret German army build-up, thereby getting around the Versailles Treaty's (q.v.) disarmament clauses. The German army trained with, and received supplies from, the Soviet Union. In Germany he was a powerful figure and was willing to use the Reichswehr (q.v.) against revolutionaries of both the right and left. Friction with Hindenburg (q.v.) led to his resignation in October 1926. It was his long-term planning which later enabled Hitler (q.v.) to transform rapidly the 100,000-man Reichswehr into the conscript army which performed so well in the early part of the war.

SEGHERS, ANNA (1900-1983).   This is the pseudonym of Netti Radvanyi, an avid Marxist who had to leave Hitler's (q.v.) Germany. After fleeing occupied France and spending time in exile in Mexico, she returned to the GDR (q.v.) as a firm supporter of the system. Concerned with social justice, her novels and short stories deal with war, refugees, and fascism. *The Seventh Cross* (1942) and *Transit* (1944) are two of her well-known works.

SEITERS, RUDOLF (1937-).   CDU interior minister in Helmut Kohl's (qq.v.) government. Resigned July 4, 1993.

SELDTE, FRANZ see HARZBURG FRONT

SEPTEMBER PROGRAM. On September 9, 1914, the chancellor's adviser, Kurt Riezler (q.v.), wrote this famous program which combined elements of all the various demands from military, governmental, journalistic, and business circles concerning war aims in France, Belgium, Luxembourg, the Netherlands, Central Africa, and, most importantly, *Mitteleuropa* (q.v., a middle European economic union under German hegemony). In the 1960s, the document was discovered in the chancellery archives in Potsdam by Hamburg historian Fritz Fischer, who saw in the document clear proof of his theory presented in *Griff nach der Weltmacht* that Bethmann Hollweg (q.v.), who initialed the draft, did have war aims for which Germany unleashed the First World War (q.v.) in the first place and which the government consistently pursued throughout the war. The "Fischer controversy" raged for years in Germany, as his supporters staunchly defended his position that Germany had indeed been responsible for the outbreak of the war. Other documents found subsequently in the Potsdam Archives, as well as Riezler's own diaries, which were published in 1973, revealed weaknesses in Fischer's thesis. The September Program, which had been marked "provisional," had not been written in the expectation of a rapid victory and contained maximum demands in case Germany had suddenly to enter negotiations. Negotiators always have a "fall-back position," which represents what they actually hope or expect to achieve in the talks. However, Fischer did not attempt to determine what that fall-back position would be. Despite the fact that Fischer's thesis had weaknesses, he raised important questions and stimulated a furious debate which enlarged scholars' understanding of the First World War.

SERFDOM see FRENCH REVOLUTION

SEVEN-YEARS WAR (1756-1763) see PRUSSIA

SEYSS-INQUART, ARTHUR (1898-1946). Austrian Nazi (q.v.) who was Reich Commissar for the Netherlands (1940-45). (See also ANSCHLUSS.)

SICKINGEN, FRANZ VON see KNIGHTS' REBELLION

SILESIA (SCHLESIEN). Territory east of the Neisse River around the city of Breslau (now Wrocklaw) which, like Pomerania--located to the north of it and east of the Oder River--became a part of Poland after the Second World War (q.v.). (See also FRIEDRICH II THE GREAT; ODER-NEISSE LINE; REUNIFICATION.)

SIMMEL, GEORG   see EMPIRE CULTURE

SINTI   see ROMA

SMALL GERMAN SOLUTION   see REVOLUTION OF 1848

SOCIAL DEMOCRATIC PARTY OF GERMANY (SPD). The SPD is a traditional working-class party which is the only one in the FRG having had a continuous existence since before the German Empire (q.v.). In the Weimar Republic (q.v.) it was one of the regime's staunchest supporters, and during the Third Reich (q.v.) its leaders either found themselves in concentration camps (q.v.) or went into exile. After the war it fully expected to become Germany's governing party under the leadership of Kurt Schumacher because of its former opposition to the Nazis (qq.v.), but its leaders badly misread the voters' minds. Gripped by poverty, West Germans were less interested in the SPD's socialist solutions than they were in the prosperity which its opponents promised and actually produced. Also, Social Democrats focused on strong national policy directed against all four occupation powers and especially aimed toward German reunification (q.v.). This proved to be far less appealing than Adenauer's (q.v.) policy of winning West German sovereignty, international respect and military security through military and economic integration with the West.

In order to break out of the "one-third ghetto" (winning only a third of the votes) within the electorate and to attract more Catholic and middle-class voters, the SPD changed its program at the party congress in Bad Godesberg in 1959. It cast off the Marxist ballast in its party program and made the basic decision not to challenge the capitalist order in a fundamental way, but instead to seek to correct its flaws through social reform. The following year the party's chief strategist, Herbert Wehner (q.v.), announced in the Bundestag that the SPD would accept Adenauer's (q.v.) foreign policy of integration with the West. Having become in theory as well as in fact a mass social reform party anchored in the democratic West, and with a new young chancellor candidate, Willy Brandt (q.v.), who remained the party's chairman until 1987, the party began attracting increasing numbers of middle-class voters. These included gains among civil servants, white-collar employees in industry and the service sector, and especially youth; these groups soon gained a far greater share of the party's leadership positions than workers. This opening of the party to the middle class was crucial to the SPD's gaining power in 1969, but it also converted the SPD into a broad-spectrum party whose main problem became that of unifying such diverse groups behind a common leadership. Since 1945, the party refused to cooperate with the communists, but there were and are many voices within the party which think that it must also dissociate itself from a minority of leftist ideological members. Brandt was pressured to resign the party chairmanship in 1987, not merely because he had shown bad judgment in appointing as party spokesperson a young woman who was neither an SPD party member nor a West German citizen. More important, moderates within his badly divided party blamed him for tolerating and encouraging the party's leftward drift, which had alienated many voters.

After the 1980 elections, in which it won 42 percent of the vote, the party temporarily lost popularity. In an effort to reunify the party, Hans-Jochen Vogel (q.v.), an experienced former justice minister and mayor of Munich and West Berlin with a reputation as a hard worker and conciliator, was chosen as chancellor candidate in 1983 and as party chairman in 1987. Nevertheless, in the 1983 elections, it won only 38.2 percent of the votes and 193 seats. Some party analysts became even more convinced that this was due to those on the leftist fringe of the party who scared off traditional supporters like workers and trade unionists. The SPD entered the 1987 elections with a new chancellor candidate, Johannes Rau (q.v.), minister president of the largest land, North-Rhine-Westphalia. The elections again revealed the extent to which the SPD had deteriorated since the 1970s. It won only 37 percent of the vote and 186 seats, the SPD's worst showing since 1961.

In 1990, the SPD picked as its chancellor candidate its biggest vote-getting provincial politician, Oskar Lafontaine (q.v.), minister president of the Saarland and earlier one of the party's most outspoken leftists. He belongs to a new generation of politicians who did not directly experience Nazism (q.v.) or the onset of the Cold War. His political outlook was significantly shaped by the student rebellion of the 1960s, and his politics are post-industrial, post-materialist "new politics" emphasizing environmental issues. He was brought up in a divided Germany and showed no emotions toward the idea of a united country, to which he derisively referred as a "provisional entity" until the nation-state became superfluous. He hated words like "fatherland," and on the occasion of Germany's unity at midnight October 2 to 3, 1990, he alone among political leaders refused to sing the national anthem. He was unable to notice, let alone tap, the emotions released by the opening of the Berlin Wall (q.v.). This antagonized many of his party comrades, including former chancellors Brandt and Schmidt (q.v.). In his campaign, during which he was almost killed when a deranged women slit his throat with a butcher knife, he harped on the problems and costs associated with reunification (q.v.) and was perceived as a prophet of doom. His message was depressing, and his leftist themes did not interest German voters in 1990, especially those in eastern Germany, who wanted prosperity within the FRG. *Die Zeit* called him "the wrong man at the wrong time," and the electoral disaster proved this. The SPD dropped to 33.5 percent of the vote and 239 seats. Its 35.7 percent in the West was well below its 1987 performance, and its 24.3 percent in the East, which had been the party's electoral fortress before Hitler's takeover, was shocking. It got the votes of only a fourth of East German workers. Lafontaine tried to console his dejected comrades by claiming that the youth had been behind the party, but that was a fiction; it won only 38 percent of young voters, many of whom had deserted to the Greens (q.v.).

Having led the SPD back into the "one-third ghetto" from which it had worked so long to escape, Lafontaine fled to the Saar and left his party to rebuild itself. He was weakened even further in 1992 as a result of his implication in a pension scandal. Because Lafontaine refused to become party chairman, Vogel was replaced by Björn Engholm (q.v.), urbane man with a labor union background and a pragmatic, moderate brand of social democracy. In May 1993, he resigned and was replaced by Rudolf Scharping (q.v.), who shares his moderate, unideological approach to politics. The party's prospects are not bad, given Kohl's postelection unpopularity and difficulties, the SPD's string of victories in Land elections, and the growing dissatisfaction in the East, where voter volatility is high. (See also ELECTIONS; SCHUMACHER, KURT; SED-SPD SPEAKER EXCHANGE.)

SOCIAL DEMOCRATIC VOTERS' INITIATIVE see ELECTIONS, FEDERAL (1972 AND 1976)

SOCIAL DEMOCRATIC WORKERS' PARTY (SOZIALDEMOKRATISCHE ARBEITERPARTEI--1869). A forerunner of the SPD (q.v.). (See LASSALLE, FERDINAND; LIEBKNECHT, WILHELM.)

SOCIAL FASCISTS see SED-SPD SPEAKER EXCHANGE

SOCIAL MARKET ECONOMY (SOZIALMARKTWIRTSCHAFT). This guiding economic principle of the FRG combines a free market approach with a commitment to the social welfare of its citizens. It helped West Germany become prosperous in contrast to its counterpart in East Germany. It was also crucially important for social peace within Germany and, more important, for democracy.

SOCIALIST INITIATIVE (SOZIALISTISCHE INITIATIVE--SI). Since 1990, the minuscule Socialist Initiative (SI) is heir to the defunct Socialist Unity Party of West Berlin (SEW). SI publishes a quarterly magazine *Konsequent* (Consistent), with a circulation of 2,500. The dramatic changes which occurred in the GDR (q.v.) and the rest of Europe in the fall of 1989 surprised and overwhelmed the SEW, which had historically been totally servile to and dependent upon the discredited SED (q.v.). Before folding almost immediately, its *Neue Zeitung* (New Newspaper, earlier *Die Wahrheit*) asserted in October 1989 that "the times today call for new thinking, new acting--nothing remains static."

In the wake of the political hurricane which blew down the Berlin Wall (q.v.) on November 9, 1989, 40 percent of the SEW members stormed out of the party, and its entire politburo and secretariat resigned. One of its leaders, Klaus-Dieter Heiser, emphasized that "the process of renewal within the SEW was accelerated by the development in the GDR." He admitted that in the past, the SEW had idealized the achievements and situation in the GDR and had therefore been blind to the growing alienation between the people and the leaders of the SED and the state. "We had believed that the collective human rights developed in socialism were to be valued above individual human rights, such as freedom of movement, which had been fought for in the bourgeois revolution." The SEW had to struggle to survive in a city which became very different.

Under chaotic circumstances, a party congress on April 28-29, 1990, sealed the SEW's fate. The 250 elected or self-appointed delegates, representing no more than 1,600 total party members, transformed the SEW into the SI, whose ideological manifesto parroted that of the PDS (q.v.). However, the SI was unable to establish a durable alliance with the PDS, which decided to expand its own organization into West Berlin and the rest of the FRG. The SI was able neither to field its own candidates in the first all-Berlin elections on December 2, 1990, nor to help enlarge the vote of the PDS in the western part of Berlin. The PDS will be the major communist political force in Berlin for several years into the 1990s, while the SI will remain irrelevant. (See also COMMUNISM IN GERMANY.)

SOCIALIST PARTY OF THE SAAR (SPS) see SAAR

SOCIALIST REICH PARTY (SOZIALISTISCHE REICHSPARTEI--SRP) see CONSTITUTIONAL COURT; DEMOCRACY ON GUARD; GERMAN REICH PARTY; PARTIES, RIGHT-WING

SOCIALIST UNITY PARTY (SOZIALISTISCHE EINHEITSPARTEI DEUTSCHLANDS--SED). The SED, DKP, and PDS (qq.v.) all grew out of the Communist Party of Germany (Kommunistische Partei Deutschlands--KPD). The KPD had been officially founded on December 31, 1918, by left-wing Spartacists, who had broken away from the SPD (q.v.) following the Bolshevik revolution in Russia a year earlier. After the Second World War, the KPD was the first party to be legalized on June 11, 1945. It toned down its revolutionary rhetoric and advocated the creation of an "anti-fascist democratic order" and a popular front.

Local elections in Berlin in 1945 demonstrated that the Communists could not expect to out-poll the SPD (q.v.), to say nothing of gaining a majority of Germans' votes in a free election. Also, 82 percent of SPD members from the three Berlin Western sectors voted in March 1946 against an immediate union with the KPD (q.v.). The Soviet occupation authorities refused to allow Social Democrats in their sector to vote. Instead, they permitted the KPD in April 1946 to sponsor a Unity Party Congress in the Admiral Palace in East Berlin at which the KPD and SPD in the Soviet Zone of Germany were combined into the Communist-dominated Socialist Unity Party of Germany (SED). The Communists exerted much pressure and sometimes outright force to get many Social Democrats to accept such unification. Some Social Democrats favored the formation of the SED, noting that the common suffering during the Nazi (q.v.) dictatorship had created in the minds of many German socialists a dream of a political unity of the working class. The disastrous fighting between the SPD and KPD at critical periods during the Weimar Republic (q.v.) had strengthened some Socialists' longing for the older party that had existed before splitting into Communist and Social Democratic parties during the chaotic and bloody aftermath of the First World War (q.v.). The Soviet occupation authorities and KPD leaders wanted to manipulate this longing. Because of bitter opposition to such merger by leading Social Democrats in the Western zones, especially Kurt Schumacher (q.v.), no unification took place in the West. They prevented the SPD in the Western zones from being embraced or infiltrated by the Communists.

The establishment of the SED had important effects on Schumacher's SPD. The predominantly Protestant eastern part of Germany had always been the SPD's stronghold. Schumacher found it "an enormous tragedy" that his party had to struggle for power in that region which had always been most hostile to the SPD. But the rapid neutralization of the SPD in the Soviet zone by the SED put an end to the cooperation between Social Democrats and Communists in many West German cities. There was scarcely any disagreement within the SPD over the termination of such collaboration since all hopes of being able to work together with the Communists as equal partners had been dashed. Social Democrats had already learned years earlier about the purely tactical nature of the KPD's offers of cooperation, and the SPD observed a policy of maintaining a sharp line between itself and German Communist parties and of refusing all domestic political collaboration between Social Democratic and Communist parties.

The SED monopolized rule over the GDR (q.v.) for 40 years. In the late 1980s it faced its greatest ideological challenge: the Soviet policy of *perestroika* and *glasnost*, which ultimately undermined the basic principles of a post-Stalinist party like the SED. It became split into conservative hardliners and "renewers" (reformers). The seeds for such a development had already been sown during the 1970s when the party was confronted with the effects of the Helsinki process of detente. Among the rank-and-file party members problems such as human rights, the free exchange of information, non-restricted travel to the West, and demands for greater pluralism were discussed more and more openly. After people had experienced the initial fruits of detente, they wanted more.

When Gorbachev came to power in March 1985, he attacked corruption and self-serving privileges within the party and advocated intra-party democracy, openness, and the reconstruction of society. This indirect challenge to the SED's structure and understanding was enthusiastically welcomed by most SED members, above all by intellectuals. But the party leadership, Erich Honecker (q.v.) and the politburo, favored only Gorbachev's policy of arms reduction and improving relations with the U.S. When it was clear that Gorbachev would not use military force to rescue the SED regime and that he would no longer treat the GDR (q.v.) as a strategic ally, dramatic change became only a matter of time.

The SED leadership recognized this threat and rejected the relevance of *glasnost* and *perestroika* for the GDR and SED. Lacking any appropriate response to Soviet policy, SED politburo member, Kurt Hager, drew a now-infamous analogy to *perestroika*: one need not change his wallpaper merely because his neighbor does so. SED leaders were confident they could diminish the impact of *perestroika* in the GDR by disciplining party members. In November 1988 Honecker banned the widely-read Soviet monthly digest *Sputnik,* which published frank articles on Stalinism, which at that time was not a matter of public discussion in the GDR. Since no explanation was given, many intellectuals believed that they had been humiliated and treated with arrogance. Open opposition within the SED was impossible because of autocratic cadre selection, party discipline, and the control commission. However, in 1988 about 11,000 of the 2.3 million members were thrown out of the party, and by October 1989 the number had risen to 18,000. They were the ones who allegedly "opposed the party's main strategy, denied the GDR's successes, constantly complained and grumbled, or betrayed the party." The SED was clearly in crisis.

Dissatisfaction among the population and party members grew steadily. Since the party leadership was unable to respond to all these problems and questions, they censored the media even more, falsified the local election results in May 1989, and praised the brutal military suppression of the Chinese students' protest on Tienanmen Square in June 1989. East Germans were dismayed. After Hungary dismantled its security installations on the border with Austria on May 2, 1989, thousands of GDR citizens fled to West Germany illegally via Austria.

Party members were irritated and confused, and their leaders were impotent to stem their own rapid decline in authority. Many of the rank-and-file were embittered at the failure and arrogance of Honecker and the politburo and could no longer accept the party line. In July and August 1989 alone, about 14,000 members left the party. The fact that the SED had ceased to exist as a tightly-knit unit was crucial for the

1989 peaceful revolution in the GDR. Many party members felt betrayed and ashamed. Others sprang into action and forced the leadership to undertake decisive measures. On October 18, 1989, Honecker was replaced by Egon Krenz (q.v.), who tried in vain to present himself as a reformer. On November 8, 1989, for the first time ever, a spontaneous mass demonstration of about 10,000 party members, among them many intellectuals, took place in Berlin while the central committee met. The crowds demanded an extraordinary party congress to elect a new leadership. Within just two months, from mid-October to mid-December 1989, about 600,000 members left the SED. One of the few survivors was Hans Modrow (q.v.), the former head of the Dresden party branch and one of the few leading Communists untainted by corruption and scandals. He was elected prime minister on November 13. Together with the "Round Table," which represented the new parties and movements in the GDR, he prevented the country from slipping into chaos.

On December 1, 1989, the SED was forced to eliminate the Communists' monopoly on power from the GDR constitution. Two days later the entire discredited politburo and central committee under Krenz's leadership stepped down. The SED's collapse constituted more than just its own demise as a state party; it marked the historical decline of a certain type of party. Within the SED and other post-Stalinist parties there were no mechanisms for enabling the party to rejuvenate itself through reform. The state party's failure necessarily entailed the collapse of the whole system because socialism was based on it. This was a precondition for the peaceful revolution in the GDR. The SED was outpaced by Gorbachev's changes and could not handle the worsening situation. It had to concede political pluralism. Within weeks it was dead and was replaced by the Party of Democratic Socialism (PDS, q.v.). (See also COMMUNISM; GERMAN DEMOCRATIC REPUBLIC; PARTY OF DEMOCRATIC SOCIALISM; SCHUMACHER, KURT.)

SOCIALIST UNITY PARTY OF WEST BERLIN (SEW)   see COMMUNISM IN GERMANY; SOCIALIST INITIATIVE

SOCIALIST WORKERS' PARTY (SOZIALISTISCHE ARBEITERPARTEI--SAP) see GOTHA PROGRAM

SOLOMAN, ERNST VON see DENAZIFICATION

SONTHEIMER, KURT (1928-). Munich political science professor, whose books analyze the FRG's political culture. (See also FEDERATION OF ACADEMIC FREEDOM.)

SOVIET MILITARY ADMINISTRATION IN GERMANY (SMAD). In the immediate post-1945 years this was the most powerful political force in the eastern zone of occupation. (See ALLIED OCCUPATION.)

SOVIET NOTES OF 1952. The Soviet Union sent a note on March 10, 1952, to the three Western Allies, followed by three additional exchanges until September 23, 1952. These notes, whose goal was to prevent West German entry into the Western alliances, unleashed hopes in the minds of some Germans and bitterness in the minds of others that a unique opportunity to achieve German unity had been neglected and missed. For decades the memories of this debate over the Soviet notes continued to resurface in controversies over the political costs of the FRG's NATO (q.v.) membership.

The Soviet note of March 10 called for a unified Germany extending as far eastward as the Oder-Neisse line (q.v.). An all-German government could be formed, and "democratic rights" would be guaranteed to all German people. Only organizations inimical to democracy and to the maintenance of peace would be prohibited from operating within Germany. All occupation troops would be withdrawn from Germany within a year's time, and no foreign military bases would be permitted on German soil thereafter. The Germans would be forbidden from entering any kind of coalition or military alliance directed against any power that had fought against Germany. Germany would be permitted to maintain a number of its own military forces "which are necessary for the country." Finally, a peace treaty would be signed with Germany. It is impossible to say whether Stalin was seriously contemplating a change in Soviet policy toward Germany. It is possible that Stalin might have considered sacrificing the division of Germany in return for German neutrality and a political order that would enable German Communists to exert some influence upon the central government. But this by no means eliminated the potential dangers that such a settlement might have entailed.

On March 25, after consulting with Adenauer (q.v.), the three Western Allies rejected the Soviet note on several grounds. One of the most important was the absence of any reference to free elections in all parts of Germany. The Western Allies and Adenauer insisted that free elections precede the formation of an all-German government. The terms "democracy" and "democratic," which Soviet leaders understood differently than in the West, were left undefined. Adenauer wanted four-power talks dealing with Germany's future to be postponed until the EDC Treaty and Bonn Conventions had been signed and ratified. His brusk rejection of the note was in some respects a mistake since the initiative had awakened hopes and expectations among the SPD (q.v.), some respected journalists, and the West German population. Even some Christian Democrats thought their government should probe this initiative. It helped deepen the gap that divided the government from the parliamentary opposition. Some SPD parliamentarians even pressed for mass extra-parliamentary action to demand negotiations on the Soviet note.

Although many Germans wanted to see their country reunified in the near future and were not enthusiastic about creating an army in Germany, the concept of neutrality enjoyed very little sympathy in the minds of most West Germans. It was rejected by the SPD since at least 1947, the CDU/CSU (q.v.), German industry and trade unions, the Catholic Church (though the Lutheran Church was divided on the issue), and the overwhelming majority of the German press. It was supported only by Gustav Heinemann's (q.v.) "Emergency community for peace in Europe," by the extreme right, and by the Communists, as well as by a small number of respected journalists such as Paul Sethe, Karl Silex, and Rudolf Augstein (q.v.). The idea of neutrality implied a turning away from the West, to which most West Germans believed they belonged; it created imponderable foreign policy and military risks. Adenauer's course promised security from the Soviet Union and profitable economic cooperation with the West. It offered a European identity to replace the national one that had been compromised during the Third Reich (q.v.). He also held out the promise of reunification through a policy of strength (qq.v.). The SPD could not come up with an alternative. The opposition was unable to explain convincingly how the security needs of both the FRG and the USSR could be brought into harmony. The SPD wanted four-power negotiations to arrange free elections in Germany, but it was silent on whether it would have accepted the specific demands that the USSR made in its notes. The Soviet Union would not have accepted free elections and the withdrawal of its troops without important concessions that the SPD was unwilling to accept at that time: direct negotiations between the FRG and the GDR, the formation of an un-elected all-German government, or the recognition of the Oder-Neisse line. On May 26 and 27, 1952, the FRG signed the Bonn Conventions and the EDC Treaty, and the Bundestag ratified them. On September 23, 1952, the exchange of four-power notes on the subject of German unity stopped.

SOVIET RECOGNITION OF GDR AND FRG   see NORTH ATLANTIC TREATY ORGANIZATION, CREATION

SOVIET UNION, 1970 GERMAN TREATY WITH, see OSTPOLITIK; 1990 GERMAN TREATY WITH, see REUNIFICATION.

SPACE PROGRAM.   Germany has great economic prowess, considerable technological capabilities, and a significant conventional military force. As a country whose economy depends upon a high level of technology, the FRG cannot turn its back on the exploration and utilization of space. As in all democracies with highly vocal publics, German proponents of space exploration must constantly respond to criticism that the costs are not justified, given other human needs, that a manned program is dangerous, wasteful and unnecessary, that non-American partners will have too little control in cooperative ventures, and that what is billed as "peaceful" research could ultimately be used for military purposes. The cost of space activity is prohibitively expensive for a single nation, and this makes cooperation and division of labor essential. An official from the ministry of research and technology (BMFT) put it bluntly: "If you ask me, we are all condemned to cooperate."

In 1989, an agency was created to ensure a long-term, coherent concept, conduct international negotiations which effectively represent German interests, and execute projects with industrial management methods--the German Space Agency (Deutsche Raumfahrt Agentur--DARA). Like NASA headquarters in the U.S., this unified agency coordinates all space activities. DARA is incorporated, which means that it is not a government agency, although it is 100 percent government-owned; a special law gives it the right to act on behalf of the government on space affairs. Certain ministries are still involved although DARA has assumed most of their earlier functions. The main partner is the BMFT, which provides most of the funds for DARA. The foreign ministry plays a role because technology involved in international trade or agreements is an important foreign policy issue, the post ministry because of communications satellites, the transportation ministry because of satellite weather observation, and the defense ministry because of military surveillance.

The technical arm and major advisor to the BMFT is the German Aerospace Research Establishment (DLR, formerly DFVLR), which is a private non-profit organization with its headquarters in Bonn. This is Germany's largest major research establishment. It has a space control center in Oberpfaffenhofen (near Munich), various institutes in Braunschweig, Göttingen and Stuttgart, and an astronaut training facility in Cologne, which trains all astronauts for the European Space Agency (ESA). In 1986, it announced four new openings for astronauts to fly with the delayed second German Spacelab mission (D-2). It was flooded by applications from 1,438 men and 349 women for a flight which would not take place before late 1991. The Challenger disaster had obviously not discouraged Germans from space travel; in 1977, only about 700 had applied for the D-1 mission. In March 1992, a German astronaut flew on a Russian mission to the MIR space station. About half of the DFVLR's budget comes from the BMFT, while the Länder provide 6 percent, and third parties account for another third. The FRG's military space effort is small, but that it exists is revealed by the fact that 12 percent of its funds in the late 1980s came from the ministry of defense, which has no research institutes of its own.

The FRG gained valuable experience in cooperating with NASA through the Spacelab, a reusable laboratory for space, which was built as a result of an FRG initiative under the overall aegis of ESA in 1983; 55 percent of the DM 1.7 billion costs were borne by the FRG. In the first Spacelab venture in 1983, the German physicist Ulf Merbold was on board the 11-day flight during which 72 scientific experiments were conducted. The Spacelab was given to NASA to pay the transportation costs but was chartered back to ESA in 1985 to conduct D-1 (for Deutschland 1), the first manned space mission scientifically guided and supported outside the U.S. or Soviet Union. Command was exercised by the DFVLR ground control center in Oberpfaffenhofen, FRG. Two of the eight crew members were Germans: Ernst Messerschmid and Reinhard Furrer of DFVLR. During this seven-day flight, 74 experiments dealing with biological science and materials research were conducted. Spacelab proved that important research could be done with the help of manned space flights. Also, it showed the U.S. what German technology could do.

Numerous private institutes and universities also engage in space research. Examples include the Berlin Space Institute, founded in 1987, which conducts basic research under weightless conditions and offers private firms the opportunity for experiments in space; it is privately financed but has a cooperative agreement with Berlin's Free University. Also in Berlin is the Aeronautics Institute of the Technical University. On the occasion of Berlin's 750th birthday in 1987, it sent a mini-satellite made by a private Bremen firm to an altitude of 45 kilometers on board a high-altitude research balloon launched from the Swedish space flight control center in Kiruna. From the same site in 1987, the Max Planck Institute for Nuclear Physics in Heidelberg launched a research rocket to a height of 60 kilometers with instruments on board to examine trace gases which could possibly destroy the ozone layer. Finally, the smallest of three satellites launched by the first Ariane 4 flight in June 1988 had been designed and built by Marburg University's central electronics laboratory. Named Oscar 13 (for Orbiting Satellite Carrying Radio) and designed for use by ham radio enthusiasts all over the globe, its DM 1.5 million costs were paid by the BMFT.

The FRG has many incentives for its space program. They include German scientific and economic needs; humanitarian goals, such as environmental protection, help in catastrophes or verification of arms control agreements; German influence on shaping concepts for the future European space travel infrastructure; and the development of a technological base in Germany. But the federal government does not hide the fact that political motives are foremost. BMFT Minister Riesenhuber responded to German critics of his space program by saying that "you cannot express in money what we are winning for the integration of Europe, for the partnership with the U.S. and the challenge to our industries to achieve top performance." He even added that "peace results from common effort, not just from the avoidance of war. Thus, space travel is also a contribution to the securing of peace."

There are various political dimensions to the FRG's space program: prestige, European unity and bilateral cooperation with France and the U.S. The non-official but authoritative Society for Foreign Policy in Bonn concluded in a major report that "the political position of a state, its influence, its image within the international community will essentially depend upon whether it has the capability and the will to gain access to space." It is thus not surprising that one of the most energetic supporters of the FRG's space program was former Foreign Minister Genscher (q.v.). Referring to space endeavor, he stated unequivocally that "if we don't do it now, we will be forever dependent." Because of Germany's preference since 1945 to play a low-profile, modest role in the world, German critics are particularly apt to attack costly efforts which smack of national prestige. Riesenhuber admits that the FRG should not embark upon such a large-scale program solely on this basis. But he is willing publicly to assert that "in the real world the image of a country, perhaps even a part of its self-image, is based on its ability to achieve top performance in science and technology." In a high-level report describing the FRG's three-prong approach--a purely national program, a contribution to the European effort and cooperation with the U.S.--German space officials and scientists from industry and the universities stressed that the FRG's national program does not spring from "national renaissance" or "chauvinism." Nor is there a large military component, unlike in France and the UK. Its space program is embedded in European cooperation and the goal of European autonomy in space, with an openness to wider international cooperation. The report concluded that within European space activities, the role of the FRG will inevitably become stronger "in accordance with its political and economic weight." (See also ROCKETS.)

SPANISH SUCCESSION (1870) see FRANCO-PRUSSIAN WAR

SPARTACISTS (LATER KPD). In 1916, the SPD (q.v.), torn by the question of how to react to the ongoing First World War (q.v.), split into the majority Social Democratic Party, which supported continuing the war, and the leftist Independent Social Democratic Party (USPD), which opposed it. The Spartacus League was to the left of the Independent Social Democrats. On January 1, 1919, the Spartacists formally left the USPD and formed the KPD (q.v.). (See also COMMUNISM; REVOLUTION IN GERMANY.)

SPÄTH, LOTHAR (1937-) see CHRISTIAN DEMOCRATIC UNION

SPEER, ALBERT (1905-1981). An architect and Nazi (q.v.) armaments minister (1942-45), he was sentenced at the Nuremberg Trials (q.v.) to 20 years in Spandau Prison. After his release he published diaries and was one of the few leading Nazis who showed any regret and contrition for what he had done. (See also SECOND WORLD WAR.)

SPEIDEL, HANS (1897-1984). In 1944, chief of General Rommel's (q.v.) general staff, he belonged to the resistance (q.v.) movement and was arrested. He survived the war, and in 1951 he joined the "Blank Office" (q.v.). From 1957-63, he was the NATO (q.v.) supreme commander for Central Europe.

SPENGLER, OSWALD (1880-1936). Spengler's book, *The Decline of the West*, was a book rich with documentation and mystical ideas about such things as "race beauty," "voice of the blood," and "cosmic force." His ideas were used by the Nazis (q.v.) and other anti-democrats as evidence of the bankruptcy of the old world and the need to create a new one by heroic means. (See also WEIMAR CULTURE.)

SPIEGEL AFFAIR (1962). An ever-weakening CDU/CSU-FDP (qq.v.) government stumbled in October 1962 over a major incident that put the 13-year democracy to a severe test. It sparked a wave of protests and outcries of police-state methods in a land where the memories of such were still fresh. Rudolf Augstein (q.v.), publisher of the well-informed investigative weekly news magazine, *Der Spiegel*, his assistant editor, Conrad Ahlers (q.v.), and nine others, including the magazine's defense correspondent, were jailed under suspicion of treason. Ahlers' arrest in fascist Spain with the help of dictator Francisco Franco's police was particularly distasteful. The German police searched the offices and private residences of *Der Spiegel* and confiscated an entire issue of the magazine. The journalists were alleged to have used illegally obtained classified documents from the defense ministry to write an article criticizing the government's security policy. But there was widespread suspicion that their "crime" was to have criticized the government. At first, Konrad Adenauer and Defense Minister Franz-Josef Strauss (qq.v.) denied any complicity. But investigations revealed that they had not only been involved in the decisions which preceded the arrests, but had not informed the FDP justice minister. The "*Spiegel* Affair" so infuriated the Free Democrats that they left the government and refused to reenter it until Strauss was removed.

Many Germans had vivid memories of the Weimar Republic (q.v.), in which numerous citizens had not had democratic attitudes and sentiments despite the fact that Germany had a democratic constitution. Many in 1962 believed that this affair was proof that democracy had not yet become firmly established in the FRG. In the end, West German democracy proved to be quite resilient. All charges against the arrested were ultimately dropped as groundless. Widespread public protests quickly placed the Adenauer government on the defensive, and unintimidated journalists in all media uncovered the facts that left Strauss no alternative to resignation. Unlike in the Weimar Republic, intellectuals came to the rescue of democracy. The FRG's free institutions seemed strong, and Strauss' forced resignation demonstrated that no person was above the law. Strauss was not banished permanently from politics, even though he had been temporarily driven back to Munich. But he remained a *bête noire* for many Social Democrats.

SPITZWEG, CARL (1808-1885). A pharmacist turned painter, Spitzweg is probably the best representative of the Biedermeier (q.v.) period. With affectionate satire he painted scenes of cute, old-fashioned, amiable men and women: the *Bookworm* balancing on a ladder while searching for a book or the man sitting in bed with an umbrella as the rain drips through the roof.

SPONTIS. This is a shortened form for "those who act spontaneously." *"Chaoten"* ("chaotics") are "those who act chaotically," and "autonomists" are "those who act on their own authority." These terms are applied to some protestors who confront police in conflicts over urban squattings or who travel around the FRG and abroad to participate in violent street battles with police over the construction of nuclear energy and missile sites or airport runway expansions. For them, taking part in violence and getting arrested are exhilarating experiences, regardless of whether they have any prospect of achieving anything worthwhile by their actions.

SPÖRI, DIETER (1943-). SPD, deputy minister president and economics minister of Baden-Wurttemberg following June 1992 elections. (See also TEUFEL, ERWIN.)

SPRINGER, AXEL (1912-1985). Approximately 60 percent of readers of daily newspapers in western Germany read those published by the Springer publishing company, the flagship being *Bild-Zeitung*. Springer was passionately engaged in the great political debates of the postwar era, and his papers attacked left-wing politics and accommodation with the Soviet Union and Eastern Europe as a sellout of German interests. He was critical of the SPD-FDP (q.v.) ruling coalition from 1969-82, and his publishing company was a favorite target of leftist student radicals in the late 1960s and early 1970s. (See also MEDIA; POLITICAL PRISONERS.)

SS (SCHUTZSTAFFEL, PROTECTIVE SQUADS). In January 1929, Heinrich Himmler (q.v.) took charge of this organization, which had been created to protect Hitler (q.v.) and which consisted of about 300 men. Himmler built it up to become an elite formation within the SA (q.v.) functioning as an internal party police troop. Since he commanded the political police and Gestapo (q.v.), he was given the task of liquidating the SA on June 30, 1934. As the SS Reich leader, he was directly under Hitler, but his SS was, in practice, an independent organization. Due to the omnipresence and efficiency of his police and terror machine, the Third Reich (q.v.) can be called an "SS-state." In addition to SS units which specialized in police work and terror, there were elite military units, called "Waffen-SS" (Weapons-SS), to which normal conscripts could be assigned. (See also HIMMLER, HEINRICH; NAZI PARTY; THIRD REICH.)

STAB-IN-THE-BACK LEGEND (DOLCHSTOSSLEGENDE) see REVOLUTION IN GERMANY

STABREIT, IMMO (1933-). German ambassador to the U.S. since November 1992, when he replaced Jürgen Ruhfus, who had served since 1987.

STANDING CONFERENCE OF MINISTERS PRESIDENT. This meets once or twice a year and brings together all Land ministers president with the federal chancellor. Below this level are other joint meetings of federal and Land ministers which assemble more frequently and have created secretariats, committees and subcommittees.

STASI (MINISTERIUM FÜR STAATSSICHERHEIT--MFS). SED domination of the GDR (qq.v.) was tightened through a pervasive state security police (Stasi) which spied on the citizenry and stifled dissent. It was staffed by 85,000 officers and supported by over a half million informants. It penetrated every niche of GDR society and maintained files on six million persons. After reunification (q.v.) Germans were left to wrestle with the problem of what to do with such files, which had been assembled with complete disregard to the individual's privacy. In

1992, eastern Germans were granted access to their own files. They hold many keys to rooting out and punishing those persons who suppressed citizens' freedom. They shed light on the GDR's extensive contacts with and training of terrorist (q.v.) organizations from many nations and the sheltering of fugitive West German Red Army Faction (q.v.) killers. The files also help Bonn uncover spies who had infiltrated the FRG more thoroughly than had ever been imagined. (See also GERMAN DEMOCRATIC REPUBLIC; REUNIFICATION.)

STATE SECRETARY. This is the senior civil service rank. The larger ministries have two state secretaries, the smaller only one. They are political appointees of the ruling parties and are a part of the government.

STATUS OF FORCES AGREEMENTS. When the Germany Treaty was signed in 1954, the three Western Allies proposed that their troops remain in Germany on the basis of separate deployment agreements with the FRG government. These status of forces agreements are periodically revised.

STATUTE OF LIMITATIONS (VERJÄHRUNG). The statute of limitations for murder freed war criminals from answering for their barbarity during the Third Reich (q.v.) after 20 years. In 1969, it was extended ten years, and in 1979 it was abolished altogether, permitting newly discovered Nazi (q.v.) crimes to be prosecuted. (See also DENAZIFICATION.)

STAUFEN DYNASTY see BARBAROSSA

STAUFFENBERG, CLAUS SCHENK COUNT VON (1907-1944) see RESISTANCE

STEEL HELMET LEAGUE (STAHLHELM) see REVOLUTION IN GERMANY

STEIN, HEINRICH FRIEDRICH KARL REICH BARON VOM UND ZUM (1757-1831). Prussian reformer and statesman, Stein was born near Nassau and educated at Göttingen. He entered the Prussian (q.v.) civil service in 1780 and was made chief minister in October 1807 following the Prussian humiliation at Tilsit (q.v.). In 14 months as chief minister, he introduced a political and social revolution. He issued an edict emancipating the serfs, encouraged land reform, and introduced reforms in central and municipal government administration. Because of French intrigues, he had to flee to Austria in December 1808. In 1812, he travelled to St. Petersburg and served the Czar until Napoleon's fall, acting as administrator of the freed German lands from 1813 to 1814. At the Congress of Vienna Metternich (qq.v.) rejected his plan for a political union of German states. (See also FRENCH REVOLUTION.)

STEINER, JULIUS (1924-), CDU see WIENAND AFFAIR

STEINER, RUDOLF see WALDORFSCHULE

STEINHOFF, FRITZ see LAND PRINCES

STEINHOFF, JOHANNES (1913-). He was a Second World War (q.v.) flying ace, during which he received severe burns on his face. After the war he became a Bundeswehr (q.v.) general, Inspector of Air Force (1966-71), chairman of NATO Military Committee (1971-73).

STIFTUNGEN (FOUNDATIONS). The major political parties receive annual government grants to maintain party foundations. They are research and educational organizations, which maintain archives and sponsor research, seminars, and speeches. The SPD (q.v.) has the Friedrich Ebert Foundation, the CDU (q.v.) the Konrad Adenauer Foundation, the FDP (q.v.) the Friedrich Naumann Foundation, and the CSU (q.v.) the Hans Seidel Foundation. All have their central offices in Bonn (later Berlin), and all maintain an office in Washington, D.C. The Constitutional Court (q.v.) ruled in 1986 that the Greens (q.v.) are also entitled to such a foundation. As of the early 1990s, they had not been able to agree on what form such a foundation should take, but they have proposed to establish a loose grouping of party institutes with the name Rainbow Foundation.

STOLPE, MANFRED (1939-). SPD (q.v.), a politician and official in the Protestant Church administration in the GDR (q.v.). In the first Land elections in eastern Germany, held two weeks after reunification (q.v.), he emerged as the only Social Democratic minister president. He headed an SPD-led government in Brandenburg. Like many eastern

German leaders, he is dogged by the fact that he had met frequently with the Stasi (q.v.) before reunification and in 1978 was awarded the GDR's Order of Merit in a clandestine Stasi safe-house. He did not deny his regular meetings with the Stasi, but he claimed that they were a part of the Church's efforts to help East Germans persecuted by the GDR authorities.

STOLTENBERG, GERHARD (1928-). CDU, federal minister of scientific research (1965-69), from 1971 minister president of Schleswig-Holstein, minister of finance and later of defense in Kohl (q.v.) cabinet (1982-92).

STOPH, WILLI (1914-). SED, GDR chairman of council of ministers (Prime Minister 1964-73 and 1976-89), chairman of state council (1973-76). After reunification (q.v.) he was charged for crimes committed by the GDR. (See GERMAN DEMOCRATIC REPUBLIC; GUILLAUME AFFAIR; HONECKER, ERICH; OSTPOLITIK.)

STORM AND STRESS (STURM UND DRANG or GENIEZEIT) (1760-1785). This short-lived movement can be best understood in a literary historical sequence as a reaction against the Enlightenment (q.v.) and a preparation for the Classic and Romantic (qq.v.) periods. It is characterized by young rebellious thinkers who challenged the existing political and social order. Freedom of expression was their primary concern. They passionately promoted a revolution in thought, feeling, and style which marked the beginning of modern literary consciousness. Johann Gottfried Herder (q.v.) was their philosophical leader. Goethe's (q.v.) two works, *Gotz von Berlichingen* (1773) and *The Sorrows of Young Werther* (1774), and Schiller's (q.v.) *The Robbers* (1781) are most representative of the Storm and Stress.

STORM, THEODOR WOLDSON (1817-1888). A lawyer most of his life, Storm's lyrical poetry and short stories sprang from personal experience, thus making him one of the greatest writers of the Age of Realism (q.v.). *Der Schimmelreiter* (*The Rider of the White Horse*) is considered the best of the over 50 Novellen (q.v.) which he wrote. Expelled from his beloved Schleswig-Holstein for political reasons, he used this area as a background for many of his stories, which revolve around heredity, environment, and the forces of nature which are seldom overcome.

STRAUSS, FRANZ-JOSEF (1915-1988). Chairman of CSU (1961-88), federal minister without portfolio (1953-55), for atomic questions (1955-56), for defense (1956-62), for finance (1966-69), Bavarian minister president (1978-88). After many federal ministerial posts, Strauss insisted on being the CDU/CSU's (q.v.) chancellor candidate because he was convinced that there was a conservative majority in all the FRG, just as in Bavaria. In 1980, he threatened to take his party out of the long-standing cooperative arrangement with the CDU if he were not backed as the chancellor candidate. Although he was a highly intelligent, experienced and colorful political figure, who fit the Bavarian political landscape like a mountain goat in the high Alps, he was widely mistrusted outside of Bavaria. He often came off as too strong and ambitious. Also, as defense minister he had ordered a raid of the main office of *Der Spiegel* in 1962 on the grounds that the editors had acquired and published secret documents. This was widely viewed as overreaction and left him in the minds of many Germans as an impulsive man not completely committed to democracy and the rule of law. He hurt the political fortunes of the CDU/CSU, which lost the 1980 elections. (See also CHRISTIAN DEMOCRATIC UNION; ELECTIONS (1969 and 1980); GRAND COALITION; SPIEGEL AFFAIR.)

STRAUSS, LEO see HEIDEGGER, MARTIN; NAZI REPRESSION

STRAUSS, RICHARD (1864-1949). Strauss was a distinguished conductor and considered one of the best opera composers of the early 20th century. He wrote music for the orchestra. His illustrative orchestral works were intended to convey visual and literary impressions. One of his famous works is *Der Rosenkavalier*. (See also EMPIRE CULTURE.)

STREIBL, MAX (1932-). CSU, Bavarian minister president following Franz-Josef Strauss (q.v.). Replaced 1993 by Edmund Stoiber.

STREICHER, JULIUS (1885-1946). Nazi Gauleiter in Franken (1928-40), editor of the magazine *Der Stürmer*. A raving anti-Semite, he was sentenced to death at the Nuremberg Trials (q.v.).

STREIM, ALFRED see DENAZIFICATION

STRELETZ, FRITZ see HONECKER, ERICH

STRENGTH THROUGH JOY. This was a leisure time organization created by the Nazis (q.v.) within the German Work Front. It was somewhat effective as a propaganda means for the Nazis, especially during the years 1933-39, when an impressive and fun program of free-time activities was offered. (See also HITLER YOUTH.)

STRESEMANN, GUSTAV (1878-1929). A leader of the National Liberal Party and after First World War the Deutsche Volkspartei (DVP, the "People's Party," qq.v.), chancellor (1923), foreign minister (1923-29). Born in Berlin, he entered the Reichstag in 1906. During the First World War he was a vocal nationalist, a strong advocate of German annexations, and a parliamentary mouthpiece of the High Command. When the war ended, he became convinced that Germans must work with the Western powers and "fulfill" the obligations to carry out the terms of the Versailles Treaty (q.v.). Serving as chancellor from August to November 1923, he was foreign minister until his untimely death in October 1929. His greatest successes were the Treaty of Locarno (q.v.) in 1925 and the acquisition by Germany of a seat in the League of Nations and a permanent seat on the Council in 1926. He scaled down the reparations (q.v.) bill, and shortly before his death he persuaded the victorious powers to evacuate the Rhineland. In 1926, he was awarded the Nobel Prize for Peace. (See also WEIMAR REPUBLIC.)

Gustav Stresemann. (*Source:* GIC, New York)

STRITTMATTER, ERWIN (1912-). This former waiter, zookeeper and chauffeur became a writer and lives in the former GDR (q.v.) with his poet wife, Eva. His novel, *Ole Bienkopp*, is a good example of his "socialistic village novel."

STUDENT REBELLION (1968) see OVERCOMING THE PAST

STURMABTEILUNG (STORM DIVISION--SA). Originally created to maintain order during Nazi (q.v.) events, it grew to over a million brown-shirted rowdies after Hitler (q.v.) took power in 1933. Its leaders saw in their tightly organized units the basis for a new "people's militia," under which even the Reichswehr (q.v.) was to be subordinated. They spoke of a "second revolution." When the SS (q.v.), which also saw the SA as a challenger to its power, circulated rumors that the SA leaders were planning a putsch, Hitler took that as a pretext to have the entire SA leadership arrested and murdered on June 30, 1934. (See NAZI PARTY; RÖHM, ERNST.)

STUTTGART CONFESSION OF GUILT. In October 1945, Protestant Church leaders met in Stuttgart and declared that their church shared the German people's guilt for the Third Reich (q.v.) and its crimes. Although this was resented by many Germans because of the implication of collective guilt (q.v.), it won admiration abroad. It launched a new era of political Protestantism which erased the sharp line between church and state and encouraged the Church's involvement in politics. This new attitude became very important in postwar Germany, as the peace movements (q.v.) in both parts and the 1989 revolution in the GDR (q.v.) demonstrated. (See also CONCORDAT; CONFESSING CHURCH.)

SUDETENLAND. The Sudetenland had been a part of Austria-Hungary, assigned to Czechoslovakia after the First World War (q.v.). It contained three million German-speakers in 1919. By and large content to be a part of Czechoslovakia until 1933, many Sudeten Germans were attracted to the Nazi-financed Sudeten German Party, led by Konrad Henlein, which launched an active campaign against the Czech state. In 1945, the area reverted back to Czech control, and the German-speaking inhabitants were expelled. (See also MUNICH AGREEMENT.)

SURREALIST MOVEMENT see ERNST, MAX

SÜSKIND, PATRICK (1949-). The son of a writer, he studied history in Munich and southern France. Süskind began writing short stories very early and had successful scripts for television and the stage. *Das Parfum*, his most successful book, was translated into many languages. Ignoring the press and public, Süskind prefers to live reclusively in Munich and Paris.

SÜSSMUTH, RITA (1937-). CDU, president of the Bundestag.

SWING MOVEMENT see HITLER YOUTH

-T-

TACITUS, PUBLIUS CORNELIUS (ca. 55-120 A.D.) see INTRODUCTION and ROMANS IN GERMANY

TANNENBERG, BATTLE OF (1914) see FIRST WORLD WAR

TAXATION. The national government and the Länder try to coordinate their policies through such advisory bodies as the *Konjunkturrat* (economic council) and *Finanzplanungsrat* (finance planning council). But the central government cannot order the Länder to follow its policy, largely because it has no monopoly on taxing power. According to the Basic Law (q.v.), the living standards in all states must be uniform. This became a very problematic requirement after reunification (q.v.) in 1990, which linked a prosperous West with a pauperized East. Thus, the complicated taxation system in the U.S., which permits the per capita tax receipts in some states to be three or four times as high as in other states, was not found in the FRG, at least not before reunification. Whereas in the U.S. prior to the Second World War (q.v.) the states were virtually financially independent, in the FRG the question has been how to divide common tax revenues. The financial relations between the national government and the states is extremely complicated, but it involves roughly the following: federal payments to poorer states, the sharing of common tax revenues, payments by richer states (such as North Rhine-Westphalia and Baden-Wurttemberg) to poorer ones (such as Schleswig-Holstein and the new

Länder in the East), intergovernmental grants and subsidies, and federal payments to states for administrative services rendered.

Individual and corporate income taxes, the biggest source of revenue, is divided in a way that the national government gets 40 percent, the states get 40 percent and the cities 20 percent. Thus, there is no need for a German citizen to file two different income tax returns. However, the states receive only a third of the second biggest source, the Value Added Tax (VAT). This tax means what its title literally says: if, for example, parts from several companies are used to make an automobile, a tax is imposed on the value added to the parts after they have been assembled to manufacture the car. Bonn gets all taxes on gasoline and alcohol, the Länder all on car taxes, and the cities all property taxes.

In short, Bonn receives about 55 percent of all taxes, but makes less than 45 percent of all expenditures, including national defense. The states, on the other hand, spend more than they receive, and Bonn must make up the difference. No one is entirely satisfied with the present tax system, but as yet no one has found an acceptable alternative to the continuous haggling over the distribution of revenues. In 1986, the Constitutional Court (q.v.) demanded a fairer equalization of payments between richer and poorer states. In 1990, the controversy flared up again, as the cash-strapped new Länder in the East clamored for a full share of the pie. Some politicians in both parts advocated tax breaks for eastern Germans during the difficult transition.

In the Bonn government a "dynamic tension" exists between the separate ministries of economics and of finance, which are usually guided by members of different parties within the governing coalition. They receive expert advice from the FRG's five leading economic research institutes and from the government's own council of economic advisers, known as the "five wise men." To help maintain stability are two government banks. One is the Bundesbank (q.v.), and the other is the Kreditanstalt für Wiederaufbau (Loan Corporation for Reconstruction). The latter was founded in 1948 to channel Marshall Plan (q.v.) funds and now helps finance German trade, foreign aid and domestic investment. Owned 80 percent by Bonn and 20 percent by the Länder, it receives funds from both the budget and the capital market to help provide long-term investment capital on favorable terms for small and medium-size companies, environmental protection, hard-hit sectors such as shipbuilding, and regional development.

TELEKOM see PRIVATIZATION

TELEVISION see RADIO

TELTSCHIK, HORST (1940). He served for a while as Helmut Kohl's (q.v.) top adviser for foreign and security affairs. Unlike his predecessors, he was ambitious and conscious of his power and did not keep a low, bureaucratic profile. Thus, the problem of rivalry between the national security adviser and the foreign minister, so familiar in Washington, became important in Bonn as well. He left politics to work for the Bertelsmann publishing company.

TERRORIST GROUPS. Deadly and destructive terrorist actions continue although their numbers continued to decline into the 1990s. The hard core, command level (*Kommandobereich*) of the Red Army Faction (RAF, q.v.) is composed of about 20 underground killers, approximately the same number as in the mid-1970s. They engage in political assassinations and dramatic bombings. On November 30, 1989, RAF assassins killed Deutsche Bank chairman Alfred Herrhausen by a remote-controlled bomb. The RAF, which murdered more than 20 West German business and political leaders since the early 1970s, claimed that changes in Europe require a "new chapter" for the "revolutionary movement." The leading figures associated with the RAF are Andreas Baader and Ulricke Meinhof (whose partnership became known as the "Baader-Meinhof Band"), Holger Meins, Gudrun Ensslin, Jan-Carl Raspe, and Susanne Albrecht. Most of these killers committed suicide in West German prisons, but Albrecht, along with other RAF terrorists, was found in eastern Germany after the collapse of the GDR (q.v.). It was revealed that the SED (q.v.) leadership permitted RAF terrorists to be trained, supplied, and harbored in the GDR.

Closely supporting the RAF terrorists is a second echelon of "RAF militants," numbering approximately 250 persons. Recruited from the anti-imperialist resistance circles, they handle logistics for the command level, such as documents, vehicles, weapons, explosives and secret housing. These militants reportedly do engage in violent actions against material targets, but not against human beings. A further echelon is composed of "RAF sympathizers," who number around 2,000. They engage in propaganda and public relations for the terrorists and assist those who are in prison. Herrhausen's murder was, according to an RAF letter, partly to support a 1989 hunger strike by faction members in prison who demanded an end to isolation and the right to be housed together. That strike had also been supported by Italian Red Brigades.

As was proven in 1987, when French police captured four leaders of Action Directe in a farm near Orleans, the RAF maintains close political collaboration with like-minded foreign terrorist groups, such as Action Directe in France, the Fighting Communist Cells in Belgium, the Red Brigades in Italy, and GRAPO in Spain, despite serious setbacks in 1987. The RAF failed to mobilize a Western European guerilla movement and therefore reportedly shifted from a strategy of shattering the "military-industrial complex" to one directed against the "European world power." This call also failed to elicit a response, as large-scale operations with other terrorist organizations failed to materialize.

The Red Cells (Rote Zellen; RZ), their female affiliate--Rote Zora and various "autonomist groups" also launch terrorist attacks. The RZ find themselves in basic ideological agreement with the RAF's "socialist revolutionary and anti-imperialist" aims. The various other groupings and individuals lumped together as "autonomists" also choose their victims in the same basic way as the RAF and RZ and apply the same rationale for their attacks as is expressed in the "letters taking responsibility" sent by the RAF and RZ. The common characteristics of all these groups are hatred of the political, social and economic systems of the FRG and a rigorous readiness to use violence, no matter what it may cost in life and limb.

TEUFEL, ERWIN (1939-).   Following the June 1992 Baden-Wurttemberg Land elections, when the CDU lost its majority and right-wing parties made dramatic gains, the CDU and SPD (qq.v.) formed a governing coalition, with Teufel (CDU) as minister president and Dieter Spöri (SPD) as deputy minister president and economics minister.

THÄLMANN, ERNST (1886-1944).   From 1925 until his arrest by the Nazis in 1933, he was the chairman of the KPD (qq.v.). He steered the party onto the Stalinist course. In 1925 and 1932, he ran for Reich president. He spent 11 years in concentration camps before dying in Buchenwald in 1944.

THEATER, POST-1945.   German theater thrives today, thanks partly to massive state subsidies. Only about a fifth of western Germany's 300 theaters are privately owned, but many persons argue that state support enables more artistic guidance, rather than commercial ambitions. Several dramatists have won international recognition, such as Heinar Kipphardt, Franz Xaver Kroetz, Martin Walser (q.v.), and Peter Weiss (q.v.). Rolf Hochhuth's (q.v.) play, *The Representative,* dealing with Pope Pius XII's attitude toward Hitler's (q.v.) extermination of the Jews stirred up much impassioned discussion after the war and gives an idea of how Germans searched their souls to understand their recent past. The works of several East German authors, such as Peter Hacks and Ulrich Plenzdorf (q.v.), were played with much success on western stages. East Germany succeeded in maintaining a high standard of theater. Bertold Brecht (q.v.) had returned there after wartime exile in the U.S. and provided an important impetus to it. After 1989, eastern German theater has been able to become more experimental.

THIERSE, WOLFGANG (1943-). The most influential East German Social Democrat in the Bundestag, he was elected deputy chairman of the SPD's (q.v.) Bundestag parliamentary group (q.v.) in December 1991. He had once been employed by the GDR's (q.v.) ministry of culture, but he was fired when he protested the expulsion of dissident singer Wolf Biermann (q.v.) from the GDR in 1976. He later worked in the Academy of Sciences. During the 1989 revolution in the GDR, he joined the New Forum (q.v.), but in early 1990 he switched to the SPD.

THIRD REICH. A senile President Paul von Hindenburg (q.v.) died on August 2, 1934, and Adolf Hitler (q.v.) simply combined the offices of president and chancellor and declared himself the absolute *Führer* of party and state. He then required that the nation give retroactive approval of this unconstitutional act in a plebiscite, a favorite maneuver of dictators whereby one may vote "yes" or "no" under the watchful eyes of party henchmen. Despite intimidation measures, five million Germans voted "no" to this act. Hitler then proceeded to require all officers and soldiers to take an oath of allegiance, not to Germany but to him alone. Many German officers had grave misgivings about taking such an oath. But Hitler's shrewd treatment of the army gradually eliminated it as an immediate threat to his power, although high-ranking officers would later prove to be his most daring, though ill-fated, foes.

By fall 1934, Hitler had become the undisputed leader of a dictatorial state which he called the "Third Reich." This name was used to remind Germans that he had created anew a Germany worthy of the two earlier German empires: the one created by Charlemagne (q.v.) in 800 and the one formed by Otto von Bismarck (q.v.) in 1871. His path to power had been washed by blood and strewn with corpses. Many of his subjects had been driven through fear to passivity. Yet, in 1939, he could claim with justification that he ruled a people which generally supported him. How was this possible? In the first half of his 12-year rule he was able to achieve certain things which many Germans and non-Germans alike regarded as miraculous. His accomplishments confused and disarmed his opponents, who in 1933 were still the majority within Germany. But their numbers had dwindled considerably by 1938, even if most of them did not actually become Nazis (q.v.).

Before 1933, Hitler had shown himself to be an unparalleled organizer and hypnotic speaker, but few Germans expected him actually to succeed in conducting the complex affairs of state. Before he came to power, he remained largely in the realm of fuzzy generalities. For example, he made no concrete suggestions on how to combat the problem of unemployment. After coming to power, he quickly inflicted a heavy dose of terror on the German people. Indeed, that his rule always rested in part on terror indicated that the whole German people never entirely embraced National Socialism. But terror gradually declined and remained at a level just sufficient to keep the population in a state of fear without driving them into desperate resistance. His orchestration of terror within Germany and his skillful use of his own undeniable charisma were psychological masterpieces from which all would-be dictators could learn.

What were his specific accomplishments? By far his most important and popular was his dealing with the economic crisis. In early 1933, there were more than six million Germans out of work; by 1936, Germany had achieved full employment without creating inflation. Germans had been put to work building an admirable network of superhighways known as *Autobahnen,* as well as other public works. Industries were given tax relief, and the government's financial leaders, especially Dr. Schacht (q.v.), channeled investments to desperately needy economic sectors and successfully manipulated government funds and the money supply so that the economy would not be choked for lack of money. Also, Hitler revitalized the arms industry in Germany. This provided an important stimulus for the economy, but it should be noted that most of Germany's unemployed found jobs in civilian industries, not in arms industries. In the three years after Hitler had assumed power in Germany, the country's GNP and national income had doubled, and Germans had begun to enjoy a modest prosperity. Within Germany the mood had changed from hopelessness to confidence in the future. Of course, the facts should not be overlooked that by 1939 many Germans had become soldiers and approximately 300,000 were in concentration camps (q.v.). Hitler's economic performance was so successful that many persons in and out of Germany gained the impression that this man could indeed perform wonders. Others in countries all over Europe began to see totalitarianism, cooperation with and imitation of Germany as attractive.

A second accomplishment was that he accelerated a process which had begun several decades earlier in Germany, namely the breaking down of class differences. The Nazis were officially in favor of this. They did not speak of a "classless society," as do communists, but of "community" (*Volksgemeinschaft*). This latter term had become very attractive to many Germans who were sick and tired of conflict and who wanted to see central authority established in Germany. "Community" as interpreted by the Nazis required a high degree of social mobilization of youth, women, farmers and other groups. In fact, Germans were expected to become so active in politically dominated groups that they could not possibly go their own way and be individually free. Still, in the Third Reich there was much upward and downward mobility, mixing of classes and open opportunity for the talented, as long as they were not Jewish or openly critical of the new political order. It is incorrect to describe Hitler's rule as "class rule" because no one social group dominated the party and state. For that reason, it is technically incorrect to call National Socialism fascism, which in southern Europe meant upper class domination over the other social classes and groups, all bundled together and cemented by artificially produced mass enthusiasm. No social groups fared badly in Hitler's Reich. Yet it would be wrong to argue that Hitler eliminated class conflict entirely. Despite the rapid economic recovery, the problems between capital and labor, big and small business, or industry and agriculture were not solved. But the important fact is that there was less social inequality in Germany during the Third Reich than there had been before, and both East and West Germany greatly profited from and continued this process after 1945.

A third accomplishment which won the admiration of many of his countrymen was Hitler's rapid rearmament of Germany. In January 1933, Germany had a 100,000-man army without an air force and modern weapons. By 1938, it had a conscript army and was the strongest military power in Europe. Hitler also made the significant decision, against the advice of many military experts, to integrate armored units with other combat forces. This later proved quite successful in overrunning most of Western Europe. The military buildup may have been a curse for the rest of Europe, but it was approved by many Germans, who saw it as a means for revising the despised Versailles Treaty (q.v.).

A fourth accomplishment was a string of almost stunning diplomatic and military victories. Until 1942, Hitler had always been a master of recognizing when houses of cards were about ready to collapse and then acting decisively while others wavered. He had the instinct of a buzzard which told him when to swoop in on that which had been already dying. He had seen when the Weimar Republic (q.v.) had reached the end of its road, and Hitler merely gave it the *coup de grace*. He also could see that the international system which had emerged from Versailles was collapsing. At that conference, one of the four pre-1914 great European powers, Austria-Hungary, had been destroyed, and another, Russia, had been excluded from the victorious coalition. The United States refused to help enforce the Treaty, so only Britain and France remained to hold the dictated settlement together. In the course of the 1920s Britain grew tired of its role and began to seek a policy of moderation and accommodation toward Germany. French leaders did not favor such a policy of appeasement, but France had become so weakened by pacifism and political division from within that it could no longer oppose Germany energetically. Hitler violated the Locarno Treaty (q.v.) in 1936 and remilitarized the Rhineland. In March 1938, Germany swallowed up Austria through the Anschluss (q.v.), facing virtually no opposition from it or any other country. Six months later, Germany obtained French and British approval at a conference in Munich for Germany's absorption of the Sudetenland (q.v.), the predominantly German-speaking western part of Czechoslovakia. Hitler's appetite was whetted, so in 1939 he declared Bohemia (capital: Prague) and Moravia to be German protectorates, and German troops occupied the Memel area. He had marched his troops a long way while the rest of Europe slept, but when his troops entered Prague, Britain woke up and resigned itself to the bitter fact that it would have to prepare for war against Germany. France reluctantly agreed.

THIRTY-YEARS WAR.   The Peace of Augsburg by no means permanently settled the religious question in Germany. A Catholic counter-reformation, set in motion in Rome and supported by the Hapsburg emperors, heated tensions between German Protestants and

Catholics, who formed a Protestant Union and Catholic League in 1608 and 1609 respectively. All that was needed was a spark in Bohemia to ignite an almost indescribably destructive "Thirty-Years War" on German soil which ravaged this weak and divided land from 1618 until 1648. In the early years of the war the Catholic states, particularly Austria and Bavaria, won brilliant victories, penetrating northern Germany to the Baltic Sea and reconverting by the sword many Germans to Catholicism. Catholic successes stemmed largely from strong internal friction within the Protestant camp between Lutherans and Calvinists and from extraordinarily capable generals, Tilly and the dashing and overly ambitious Wallenstein. These initial successes under Hapsburg leadership prompted other European powers to enter the war. It was soon obvious that this war was not primarily a religious struggle for the souls of Germans. Fearing Hapsburg control over a strategically important part of the Baltic Sea, and noting suspiciously a Hapsburg alliance with Catholic Poland, the Danish king, Christian IV, and then the Swedish king, Gustavus Adolphus, took over leadership of the Protestant cause. They received financial support from England and Holland. More importantly, the Swedish king was able to receive aid from Catholic France, which was always determined to prevent the Habsburgs from growing too strong, especially when in control of Spain as well as Austria.

Germany was crisscrossed by marauding foreign armies which lived off the land in a manner summarized by Wallenstein: "The war must feed the war." No door, wall or fortress could protect the civilian population from the armies which cut wide swaths through the countryside and cities, followed by hordes of often disease-ridden camp followers, and leaving a trail of wreckage, ashes and corpses behind them. Ironically, some of the powerful, comforting and assertive Lutheran hymns were written during this devastation. An example of how arbitrary such destruction could be was Rothenburg ob der Tauber, today one of Germany's most beautifully intact medieval cities. Field Marshal Tilly offered in 1631 to spare the town and its leaders only if one of the city councilmen could drink about a gallon of wine in one draw. The elderly mayor stepped forward and accomplished this incredible feat, thereby saving his city and colleagues.

Who won this 30-year nightmare? A quick glance at the Treaty of Westphalia in 1648 gives the answer. Sweden took control of the city of Wismar, the Dukedom of Bremen-Verden (except the city of Bremen), the islands of Rügen, Usedom and Wollin, and part of

Pomerania (q.v.), thereby depriving Germany of the outlets to the sea via the Elbe, Weser and Oder rivers. France got most of Alsace, the cities of Metz, Toul, Verdun, Breisach and the Rhine, and achieved protector status over ten German imperial cities. Germany's western border, which had existed since the 9th century, was thus fundamentally altered. Switzerland and the Netherlands were granted full independence from Germany. The German princes' official right to determine the religious beliefs of all their subjects was withdrawn, at least in theory. But the German princes were granted full sovereignty within their own territories, including the right to make treaties with foreign powers. The proviso that these treaties could not be directed against the emperor or the Empire remained valid only on paper. Germany was left with almost 2,000 sovereign states ranging from the large territories of Brandenburg, Austria, Saxony and Bavaria, and 83 free and imperial cities (including Hamburg and Frankfurt am Main), to countless ecclesiastical and other small units, some of which included as few as about 2,000 inhabitants. The map of Germany now looked more than ever before like the face of a child with measles. At a time when centralizing, centripetal forces were at work in England and France, centrifugal forces were prevailing in Germany, throwing it farther and farther away from national unity. There could no longer be any serious talk of "imperial politics"!

Germany was left breathless, devastated and demoralized from the plunder and destruction. In some areas such as Wurttemberg, the Palatinate, Thuringia and Mecklenburg, two-thirds of the inhabitants had been eradicated, and overall losses in Germany ranged from a third to a half of the total population. The total population dropped from about 20 million to 10-14 million. Thus, Germany, which at the beginning of the 17th century had the largest number of inhabitants in all of Europe, fell behind the population of France for the next century and a half and behind that of Russia to the present day. It was more than a century before it reached its pre-1618 level. In addition to human deaths, 1,600 cities and 18,000 villages had been totally demolished, and livestock, farmland and the rest of the economic infrastructure had been left in shambles. In comparative terms, the destruction to Germany was far greater in 1648 than in 1945. One could say that only an atomic war could produce comparable damage today.

THOMAS, STEPHAN see OSTBÜRO

THREE CLASS ELECTORAL SYSTEM, PRUSSIAN. Since May 30, 1849, Prussia (q.v.) had a bicameral parliament in which the upper house, the Herrenhaus, consisted of the nobility and princes of the royal family, and a lower house was elected by the people. But the distribution of seats was made as follows: The population was divided into three tax classes, and each of these classes received the same number of electors in an electoral college which would elect the deputies. The class which paid the top third of total taxes (but constituted only about 4 percent of the population) elected a third of the electors. The class paying the next third of taxes (constituting 12 to 14 percent of the population) elected a third of the electors. The class paying the lowest third of the taxes (making up some 82 percent of the population) elected the final third. This electoral system remained in force until 1918 and was a constant thorn in the side of Social Democrats and liberals, who resented the advantage it gave to those with higher incomes. (See also BISMARCK, DOMESTIC POLICY; REVOLUTION OF 1848.)

THREE EMPERORS' CONFERENCES (1872-78). Wilhelm I of Prussia, Franz Josef of Austria, and Alexander II of Russia met several times and, in effect, renewed the principles of the Holy Alliance. These meetings were important initial steps in Bismarck's (q.v.) foreign policy and a prelude to the Three Emperors' League in 1881, which stipulated that if a fourth power attacked Germany, Austria, or Russia, the two remaining powers would adopt a policy of "benevolent neutrality."

TIECK, LUDWIG (1773-1853). Tieck's desire to become an actor was never realized. Instead he became one of the most prominent Romantics (q.v.). He wrote short stories, fairy tales, and novels, and he translated *Don Quixote.* He was appointed dramatic advisor to the court in Dresden and was eventually appointed reader to the king of Prussia. He edited and published the works of Novalis and Kleist (qq.v.).

TIETMEYER, HANS. Bundesbank (q.v.) president since 1993.

TILL EULENSPIEGEL. Till is the subject of a very popular 16th century folktale enjoyed by peasants and artisans. He is a practical joker who uses his innocence to disarm his victims, who are members of the governing class.

TILLICH, PAUL (1886-1965). Tillich fled Germany and occupied professorships in New York and at Harvard University. Considered by many as the most important figure in the resurgence of religious thought during his lifetime, he expounded neo-orthodoxy, a defense of supernaturalism which had been greatly influenced by Kierkegaard. He elaborated his views in *Systematic Theology, Love, Power, and Justice*, and *Biblical Religion and the Search for Ultimate Reality*; both were published in the 1950s.

TILLY, JOHANN G. GRAF VON (1559-1632) see THIRTY-YEARS WAR

TILSIT, TREATIES and PEACE OF (July 8, 1807). Secret agreement signed by Napoleon and Czar Alexander on a raft in the Niemen River, this ended the war between Russia and France. Russia accepted French dominance in central and western Europe, the reduction of Prussia (q.v.) to half its size, and the creation of a Kingdom of Westphalia. Russia respected the terms of this agreement until the end of 1810, and it was formally ended with Napoleon's invasion of Russia, in which many German troops served in his army, on June 24, 1812. (See also FRENCH REVOLUTION.)

TIRPITZ, ALFRED VON (1849-1930). Grand admiral and politician, he argued that a blue-water fleet was essential for Germany's standing as a colonial power and as a bargaining chip in dealing with Britain. Such a fleet would not need to be the world's strongest, but it would have to be such that the risks of confronting it would be too great for any power to dare. He argued that a policy of naval armament would in the long run force Britain to reach a rapprochement with Germany and guarantee for Germany complete political and military equality. Chancellor Bethmann Hollweg (q.v.) and the army disagreed, but the Kaiser backed Tirpitz. He served as naval minister from 1897 to 1916 and built up the German high seas fleet. After the outbreak of war in 1914 Tirpitz was frustrated that his fleet could not engage the enemy. Since his calls for unrestricted submarine warfare were ignored until 1917, he resigned in March 1916. After the war he represented the Nationalists in the Reichstag from 1924 to 1928. (See also EMPIRE FOREIGN POLICY.)

TISCHBEIN, JOHANN HEINRICH WILHELM (1751-1823). "Goethe" Tischbein's career in art was diversified and influenced by many styles, but he is best known for his two portraits of Goethe (q.v.). He restored and copied the masters and painted many portraits at the Court of Berlin, as well as landscapes and historical scenes.

TÖNNIES, FERDINAND (1855-1936). Working in Odenswort and Kiel, Tönnies was influenced by Schopenhauer's (q.v.) notion of the will. He focused mainly on social philosophy, and in his *Community and Society* (1887) he argued that community living is group life in which individuals are linked to each other organically, by a generic will. By contrast, social life is more individualistic and mechanistic than organic. He noted an irresistible tendency toward the mechanization of life which would destroy community life and lead to a society of free activity carried on by the intellect. Modern socialism would not restore communal living, but it would create a situation in which more individuals would have the same rights. (See also EMPIRE CULTURE.)

TÖPFER, KLAUS (1938-). Environmental minister in cabinet of Helmut Kohl (q.v.). (See also BROKDORF.)

TREITSCHKE, HEINRICH VON (1834-1896). Born in Dresden and educated in Bonn and Leipzig, this German historian taught at many universities, including Berlin and Heidelberg. From 1871 to 1888 he was a Conservative member of the Reichstag, and he supported the policies of Bismarck (q.v.). A patriot and admirer of power politics, he sought in his *History of Germany in the Nineteenth Century*, of which he completed five volumes by the time of his death, to demonstrate that Prussian (q.v.) domination of the German states was a historical necessity. (See also EMPIRE CULTURE.)

TREUHAND (TRUST AGENCY). To help guide the transition from an unproductive socialist economy to a modern capitalist one after reunification (q.v.) in 1990, a Trust Agency (*Treuhand*) holding company was established. With a staff of 3,000 by mid-1991, its job after unity was to try to privatize at reasonable prices and as quickly as possible the huge empire of former East German state assets, consisting of more than 8,000 companies, 60 percent of the forests, and 35 percent of the farmland. It also had to divide up state assets among the various levels of government, distribute liquidity cash, supervise the restructuring of companies not yet fit for sale, and prevent the creation of monopolies. No agency could accomplish such a massive task easily. It assumed from the start that a third of the companies could be privatized quickly, another third only after considerable restructuring, and a final third would have to go under. Some flagship East German companies were allowed to fail when the right kind of buyers could not be found, such as the Interflug airline and the Wartburg automobile manufacturer.

The Trust Agency's work went painfully slowly. By 1992 over 4,000 companies had been sold (95 percent to western German companies), and 435 had been closed. When large street demonstrations took place in the spring of 1991, the Trust Agency was instructed to shift its emphasis to making companies viable which were not ready for sale, while still officially aiming to transfer ownership of the eastern German economy to private hands. This amounted to massive infusions from Bonn's treasury, including from a German Unity Fund, to keep the companies afloat and to save jobs. But this assistance could not prevent the Trust Agency from becoming a scapegoat for the downturn in the eastern economy and for capitalism's slow start. Amid mounting protests against unemployment and soaring costs for rent, energy, and transportation, its chairman, Detlev Rohwedder, was assassinated in his Düsseldorf home. His violent death eliminated the last hopes that the merger of two unequal parts into one harmonious whole could be done without upheaval.

TRIPARTITE PACT. This was a diplomatic effort in 1940 and 1941 to establish cooperation in the form of a "New Order" in Europe and a "Greater East Asia." The first signatories were Germany, Italy, and Japan at Berlin on September 27, 1940, but they were joined in time by Hungary, Romania, Slovakia, Bulgaria, and Croatia, the latter being a puppet state of Germany. Yugoslavia also signed it on March 25, 1941, but its government was overthrown two days later. The signatories pledged to help each other if any one of them were attacked by a country not already in the war when the pact was made. It was understood that this pledge was intended to operate particularly against the U.S.

TRIPLE ALLIANCE. On May 20, 1882, Otto von Bismarck (q.v.) concluded this secret alliance of Germany, Austria-Hungary, and Italy.

The terms were that if any one or two of them were attacked by two enemy powers, all three would be obligated to go to war. For Germany this provided a guarantee against French revenge after the Franco-Prussian War (q.v.). When combined with the Reinsurance Treaty (q.v.) with Russia, Bismarck's treaty system secured Germany's position on the continent until the Triple Entente (q.v.) took shape in 1907.

TRIPLE ENTENTE (1907). After Bismarck (q.v.) was dismissed as chancellor in 1890, Germany allowed his carefully constructed treaty system to become unravelled. France, Russia, and England saw an opportunity to settle their differences. This was especially desirable because of bellicose German behavior. The Triple Entente counterbalanced the Triple Alliance by offering mutual assistance by the three signatories in case of war with any of the Central Powers (Germany and Austria-Hungary). Its conclusion left Europe divided into two armed camps, and peace rested on a delicate balance of power.

TRIZONIA (1949). In April 1949, the French began merging their occupation zone with those of the Americans and British. The result was Trizonia, a semi-state which included all of postwar Germany except Berlin, the Soviet zone, and the Saarland (q.v.). It was dissolved a month later with the foundation of the FRG.

TROIKA see SCHMIDT, HELMUT

TROTSKYIST GROUPS. About 15 Trotskyist groups and circles, some only in certain regions, grew by 1990 to a total of about 800 members. Advocating "permanent revolution" and the "dictatorship of the proletariat," they decry "real existing socialism" in Communist-ruled countries as "bureaucratic" or "revisionist decadence." They saw the collapse of Communist regimes as confirmation of this ideology. Unlike most other Marxist groups, they interpreted the opening of the Berlin Wall (q.v.) as a good opportunity to establish the "unity of the German working class" and a "red council republic in Germany." To this end, some of them expanded their activities into the eastern part of Germany. The League of Socialist Workers (BSA), with headquarters in Essen, is the German section of the International Committee of the Fourth International in London. Together with its Socialist Youth League, it counts fewer than 100 members, and its weekly organ, *Neue Arbeiterpresse* (New Workers' Press) advocates a general strike for overthrowing the government. The smaller Trotskyist groups, such as the Trotskyist League of Germany (TLD), which publishes the weekly *Spartakist*, the International Socialist Workers' Organization (ISA), which is centered in Cologne and publishes the monthly *Sozialistische Arbeiterzeitung* and *Internationale Tribüne*, the International Communist Movement, the Socialist Workers' Group (SAG), headquartered in Hanover and publisher of the monthly *Klassenkampf*, and the Posadistic Communist Party, protest against animosity directed toward foreign workers in the FRG and advocate revolutionary struggles in the Third World.

TROTT ZU SOLZ, ADAM VON (1909-1944). A German diplomat and specialist in Asian affairs, he engaged in resistance activities during the Hitler era in collaboration with Baron Ernst von Weizsäcker (qq.v.) of the Foreign Office. He made three trips to Britain in the eight months before the outbreak of war and was in close contact with resistance leaders within Germany, such as General Ludwig Beck and Carl Goerdeler (q.v.). In November 1939, he travelled to the U.S. to try to win President Roosevelt's support for German resistance (q.v.) groups. His mission failed, despite the fact that Heinrich Brüning (q.v.), who was teaching at Harvard University, was able to get a memorandum about this read at a high level, and the White House had reportedly shown lively interest in it. This episode was merely one of many examples of how little Allied support was ever given to the German resistance. Trott himself met a cruel fate. On August 26, 1944, he was hanged by the Nazis (q.v.) for his prominent role in the anti-Hitler resistance.

TROTTA, MARGARETHE VON (1942-). An actress turned film director, she wrote the screenplay and directed *The Lost Honor of Katharina Blum*. She has made several other films which have given her the reputation of one of Germany's best directors. She was married to film director Volker Schlöndorff (q.v.).

TUCHOLSKY, KURT (1890-1935). Critical journalist and author whose books were burned on May 10, 1933 (q.v.). (See WEIMAR CULTURE.)

TWIN-TRACK DECISION (DOPPELBESCHLUSS, 1979) see INTERMEDIATE-RANGE NUCLEAR FORCES; PEACE MOVEMENT; SCHMIDT, HELMUT

TWO-GERMANY POLICY OF SOVIET UNION. By mid-1955 it had become clear that Adenauer (q.v.) had succeeded in achieving political and economic recovery through integration with the West and that the SPD's (q.v.) policy of giving German unity the highest priority had failed. It is by no means certain that the USSR would have permitted a form of German reunification (q.v.) acceptable to the Bonn government and to most West Germans if the FRG had chosen not to join with the West. It could always have blocked all efforts to unite the two parts of Germany plus the lost territories East of the Oder-Neisse (q.v.) line by continually insisting on more guarantees. Especially after the Geneva summit conference in July 1955, it had become clear that the Soviet Union was not prepared to accept German reunification on any terms other than its own. This placed the SPD in a dilemma since its conceptions of a reunified Germany and the necessary steps to achieve it differed greatly from those of the USSR.

The Soviet Union now openly favored a two-Germany policy and the status quo in Central Europe, and Soviet Premier Nikita Khrushchev spoke on July 26, 1955, for the first time of "two German states." If the Soviet Union could not keep a unified Germany weak and compliant, it insisted at least that it remain divided. As a result, the Soviet Union signed a treaty with the GDR (q.v.) in September 1955, granting it sovereignty. From September 9 to 13, 1955, Adenauer was invited to Moscow to work out details for diplomatic relations and a trade treaty between the USSR and the FRG. Both German states began playing more important roles in their respective blocs, and each superpower accepted its German ally's demands for solving the German question. At the Four-Power foreign ministers' conference in Geneva from October 27 to November 16, 1955, Soviet Foreign Minister Nikolai Bulganin announced that German reunification was now a matter which the two German states would have to sort out between themselves. Soviet leaders also embarked on a two-decade quest to obtain formal recognition from the FRG and NATO (q.v.) for its hegemony over the GDR and Eastern Europe.

-U- and -V-

UHLAND, LUDWIG (1787-1862). Uhland is one of the founders of German literary and philological studies. He wrote ballads and Romantic poetry and was very interested in medieval literature and German legend. He was a professor of German at Tübingen and also served as a Liberal representative to parliament in 1848.

ULBRICHT, WALTER (1893-1973). SED general secretary (1950-71), chairman of state council (1960-73). Ernst Thälmann's (q.v.) arrest shortly after Hitler's takeover of power in 1933 was the signal for Walter Ulbricht's bid for leadership of the KPD (q.v.). He took part in the resistance (q.v.) against Hitler and spent the war years in the Soviet Union. He returned to Germany on the heels of the Red Army in 1945 and guided the construction of a GDR (q.v.) modeled after and almost totally servile to the Soviet Union. Under his direction, the Berlin Wall (q.v.) was erected in 1961. Because he opposed the policy of *Ostpolitik,* which the Kremlin leaders supported, Ulbricht was removed from effective control in 1971 and was replaced by Erich Honecker (q.v.). (See also GERMAN DEMOCRATIC REPUBLIC; SOCIALIST UNITY PARTY OF GERMANY.)

Walter Ulbricht. (*Source:* GIC, New York.)

UNCONDITIONAL SURRENDER OF GERMANY. This was the Allies' demand in both world wars that Germany surrender without attaching any conditions to that surrender whatsoever.

UNITED SOCIALIST PARTY (VEREINIGTE SOZIALISTISCHE PARTEI--VSP). Born from the 1986 merger of the Communist Party of Germany-Marxist Leninist (KPD, earlier known as KPD-ML) and the Trotskyist Group International Marxists (GIM), the VSP, with about 400 members, has its headquarters in Cologne. Its biweekly publication,

Sozialistische Zeitung (Socialist Newspaper, circulation 2,500), replaced the KPD's earlier *Roter Morgen* (Red Morning) and the GIM's *Was Tun* (What To Do) in 1986. Its youth group is the Autonomous Socialist Youth Group (ASJG). It opposed German unity, and after the collapse of the GDR (q.v.), the VSP asserted that socialism remains "a real utopia," even though it exists nowhere.

UNIVERSITY RECTORS' CONFERENCE (HOCHSCHULREKTORENKONFERENZ). Standing commission of university presidents that makes recommendations on educational policy.

UNSERE ZEIT see GERMAN COMMUNIST PARTY (DKP)

V-1 AND V-2 see ROCKETS

VALUE ADDED TAX (UMSATZSTEUER--VAT) see TAXATION

VERFREMDUNGSEFFEKT. This term refers to the theatrical device of alienation used in Brecht's (q.v.) Epic Theater in which the spectator is detached from the reality on the stage by means of various devices which will make him a more critical viewer.

VERNUNFTREPUBLIKANER (COMMON-SENSE REPUBLICAN). The disastrous First World War (q.v.) and collapse of the empire convinced some Germans that a more democratic republic was a necessity and the only alternative, even though they had not yet come to believe entirely in democracy itself. They supported the new republic for pragmatic reasons. The great number of such common-sense republicans and of other Germans who renounced the republic altogether led some observers to describe the Weimar Republic (q.v.) as a "democracy without democrats."

VERSAILLES TREATY. The necessity of fulfilling the highly unpopular task of signing a peace treaty after the First World War (q.v.) caused the coalition of the Weimar Republic's (q.v.) supporters to lose its parliamentary majority in 1920, which it never regained. The first major problem with the Versailles Treaty was the manner in which it was written. In contrast to all previous peace settlements in Europe, the vanquished (in this case, the Germans) were not included in the negotiations. If the Germans had been included, perhaps they would have felt some responsibility for the Treaty, but as it was, it represented a dictated peace towards which the Germans never felt any moral obligation to subscribe to its terms. The settlement had a strong whiff of "victor's justice." Prior to American entry into the conflict, President Woodrow Wilson had proposed a "peace without victory" and later issued a written document containing "Fourteen Points" as a basis for European peace which contained very lofty language. The Germans later accepted the text, but it faded into the background at Versailles as French Prime Minister Georges Clemenceau virtually dictated the terms of what turned out to be an attempt at revenge. Little did he know that he was helping sow the seeds of disaster, particularly in the mind of a wounded Austrian corporal, Adolf Hitler (q.v.).

When the terms were forwarded to Berlin in mid-May 1919, with the warning that non-acceptance would result in an immediate resumption of hostilities, the Germans could hardly believe their eyes. They had expected to lose all territory conquered during the war, as well as Alsace-Lorraine, but they also lost a tenth of their prewar population and an eighth of their territory. The city of Danzig (q.v.) and the province of Posen were ceded to Poland, and a narrow corridor was cut right through West Prussia to connect these areas with Poland. Worse, the coal-rich Saar (q.v.) region was placed under League of Nations and French control for 15 years. Combined with the loss of practically all its merchant marine fleet, this made it far more difficult for Germany to pay the shockingly high reparations (q.v.) demanded of it. The Rhineland was occupied by Allied soldiers and was to be demilitarized permanently. Germany's high seas fleet was to be turned over to the Allies, a requirement which prompted the Germans to scuttle all their naval ships, which had been interned at Scapa Flow in the Orkney Islands north of Scotland in mid-1919. The future German Army was to be restricted to 100,000 career officers and men with no military aircraft, tanks or other offensive weapons. Perhaps worst of all, Article 231 of the treaty placed sole responsibility for the outbreak and therefore for all destruction of the war on the shoulders of Germany and its allies. This article had been written by a young American diplomat, John Foster Dulles, as a compromise to the French, who had wanted to annex the Rhineland and require even higher reparation payments from Germany. But Dulles had to admit later that "it was the revulsion of the German people from this article of the Treaty which, above all else, laid the foundation for the Germany of Hitler." For the next quarter of a century Hitler never ceased railing against the weak Weimar government and the wickedness of the Versailles Treaty.

The document made a mockery of many of Woodrow Wilson's Fourteen Points, such as "open covenants openly arrived at," freedom of the seas, the "impartial adjustment of all colonial claims," and of course the self-determination of nations. The victors permitted this latter right only where people wanted to detach themselves from Germany, such as in northern Schleswig and part of Upper Silesia (q.v.). Wherever an area's population wanted to join Germany, such as Austria or northern Bohemia, no referendum was permitted. Such hypocrisy stimulated within Germany cynicism toward both the Treaty and any German government which would sign it. Of course, Germany's harsh policy toward a collapsing Russia at Brest-Litovsk had provided a disastrous precedent. Nevertheless, Germany's shortsightedness in 1918 could not reasonably be invoked to justify an equally shortsighted Allied policy a year later. Chancellor Scheidemann (q.v.) said to the National Assembly in 1919, "Which hand would not wither up which put itself and us into these bonds?" The Treaty was a millstone around the neck of the new republic. It not only helped create a deep division in German society; it seriously hampered the normalization of Germany's relations with the outside world. It could only be maintained by force, but the United States quickly withdrew from Europe's military affairs, and Britain and France gradually lost the will to enforce it energetically. One day a spell-binding demagogue would be able to untie the "fetters of Versailles" right before the eyes of a weary and lethargic Europe and reap much applause within Germany for doing this.

VOGEL, BERNHARD (1932-). CDU. Brother of former SPD leader, Hans-Jochen Vogel (q.v.), Bernhard was minister president of Hesse and chairman of the CDU-affiliated Konrad Adenauer Foundation. When Josef Duchac was compelled to resign as minister president of Thuringia in January 1992, following a crisis of confidence arising from his political activities in the GDR (q.v.), Vogel was elected to take his place.

VOGEL, HANS-JOCHEN (1926-). Federal minister of justice (1974-81), chairman of SPD (q.v.) Bundestag Fraktion (1983-91), chairman of SPD (1987-91). An experienced former justice minister and mayor of Munich and West Berlin with a reputation as a hard worker and a conciliator, Vogel was chosen as SPD chancellor candidate in 1983 and as party chairman in 1987. Under his guidance, the SPD became more unified and moved more closely to the center in domestic politics, where the winning votes are. In October 1991, he announced his resignation after nine years as chairman of the SPD parliamentary group (q.v.). He also served as national SPD chairman for four years before passing that post on to Björn Engholm (q.v.) in 1991. (See also SOCIAL DEMOCRATIC PARTY OF GERMANY.)

VOGEL, WOLFGANG see POLITICAL PRISONERS

VOGELWEIDE, WALTHER VON DER (ca.1168-ca.1228). The aristocracy in medieval Germany was a warrior class, which developed an elaborate code of chivalry and honor. This inspired vernacular Middle High German literature around the end of the 12th century from the pens of such authors as Walther von der Vogelweide, who praised the experiences and ethos of the knightly class. The writers of secular lyric poetry, known as Minnesang (q.v.), described such sentiments as unattainable love for noble women beyond their reach.

VOIGT, KARSTEN DIETRICH (1941-). SPD, federal chairman of Young Socialists (1969-72), member of Bundestag since 1972 and one of the SPD's (q.v.) top foreign policy specialists.

VOLGA GERMANS. From 1764-74 this oldest group of German settlers in Russia moved to the shores of the Volga River during the reign of Catherine II. From 1924-41 they had an "Autonomous Socialist Soviet Republic of Volga Germans." Following Germany's invasion of Russia in 1941, Stalin ordered their resettlement to Siberia where many of them remain today. About one-and-one-half million Germans live in the Soviet Union, and after Mikhail Gorbachev came to power in 1985, thousands of them have been permitted to emigrate to Germany.

VOLK UND WISSEN see GUILLAUME AFFAIR

VÖLKISCHER BEOBACHTER see NAZI PARTY

VOLKSGEMEINSCHAFT. This was a term used by the Nazis (q.v.) to describe their racial community. Their chief domestic goal was to create out of a German people weakened by divisions of class, ideology, and religion, a new and unified "national community" based on blood and racial ties and infused with a common view of the world. This would provide the morale for Germany's bid for world domination. The citizens of this community would be *Volksgenossen* ("national comrades"), who were expected to be of Aryan race, genetically healthy (*erbgesund*), efficient, and ideologically and politically reliable, which included active participation in Nazi organizations and repeated gestures to express their loyalty, such as the Hitler (q.v.) salute.

-W-

WACKENRODER, WILHELM HEINRICH (1773-1798). He was the son of a highly placed civil servant and a good friend of Tieck (q.v.) with whom he wrote his principal work, *Outpourings of an Art-loving Monastic,* 1797. This contribution enhanced the Romantics' (q.v.) enthusiasm for medieval German art and culture.

WAGNER, RICHARD (1813-1883). Considered one of the geniuses of German culture, Wagner's career as a composer is not without controversy. He was a revolutionary, liberal, art theorist, conductor, poet, anti-Semite, and chauvinist. His political involvement forced him to spend many years abroad where he wrote several of his most famous operas. Ludwig II invited him to Munich in 1866 and built him an opera house (*Festspielhaus*) in Bayreuth (q.v.) where his works were performed. Many of his operas glorify the German Middle Ages, their legends and mysticism, and thus endeared his works to Hitler (q.v.). *The Ring, Lohengrin,* and *Parzival* are among his most famous works.

WAIGEL, THEO (1939-). Chairman of CSU (1988-), federal finance minister in the Kohl (q.v.) government.

WALDORFSCHULE. This school was founded in 1919 by a Stuttgart cigarette magnate named Waldorf. It was the model for the anthroposophical methods of education taught by the Swiss pedagogue Rudolf Steiner, its first head.

WALLENSTEIN, GENERAL see THIRTY-YEARS WAR

WALLRAFF, GÜNTER see MINORITIES

WALSER, MARTIN (1927-). This former member of "Gruppe 47" (q.v.) is known for his novels and plays and is a severe and sarcastic critic of contemporary society and authority.

WANDERJAHRE (WANDER YEARS). During the 19th and first half of the 20th centuries, many young German males, particularly from working-class backgrounds, "wandered" far from their hometowns working for several years in various places before returning home to settle down.

WANDERVÖGEL (WANDERING BIRDS). This was a generally middle-class and anti-Marxist youth movement in Imperial Germany which cast off the stuffy restraints of bourgeois society by wearing loose-fitting casual clothing, hiking and camping, and trying to return as close to nature as possible. Critical of the establishment, parliamentary politics, the prevailing educational system, and what they saw as pervasive materialism, they nevertheless tended to be both nationalistic and anti-Semitic, since Jews were identified with the greedy moneymaking class in their society.

WANDLITZ see GERMAN DEMOCRATIC REPUBLIC

WANNSEE CONFERENCE. On January 20, 1942, 15 officials of the Third Reich (q.v.) met in the Wannsee area of Berlin and drew up a plan systematically to exterminate European Jewry. The elegant villa in which the meeting took place is now a permanent memorial to the millions of Jews who perished at the hands of the Nazis (q.v.). (See also HEYDRICH, REINHARD; NAZI REPRESSION.)

WAR OF THE AUSTRIAN SUCCESSION see FRIEDRICH II, THE GREAT

WARSAW PACT TREATY see NORTH ATLANTIC TREATY ORGANIZATION

WARTBURG see LUTHER, MARTIN

WARTENBURG, YORCK VON see RESISTANCE TO HITLER

WEBER, MAX (1864-1921). A student of law and economics and professor at the University of Heidelberg, Weber critically examined the economic theories of his time and attempted to show the influence of Protestant ethical teaching on what he called the "capitalist spirit." In his *Collected Essays on the Sociology of Religion* (1920) he wanted, more generally, to uncover the religious roots of the rationale of modern culture. The medium for most of his essays was the *Archiv für Sozialwissenschaften* (Journal of Social Science), which he founded. He developed a theory of "chance" of realizing expectations, as well as the concept of "ideal type," by which he judged individual complexes. He argued that empirical science is not concerned with how humans ought to act, but with how they can and will act.

His encyclopedic works were a prodigious attempt to explore and explain the twists and turns of Western history, in contrast to the societal and cultural patterns of other parts of the world. To do this, he developed a set of social and political concepts and a method of analysis which allowed room for human meanings and motivations. His work has been subjected to a variety of criticism, but contemporary scholars cannot ignore this man whose breadth, erudition, and richness of suggestion have perhaps never been surpassed.

One of his main fears in the modern age was bureaucracy. Like his protégé, Robert Michels, Weber foresaw the rapid growth of bureaucracies which could suffocate autonomous individuals, freedom, and liberalism. The solution, in his view, was a "plebiscitarian leader-democracy," in which great charismatic leaders would rise above the bureaucratic structures and, regardless of the goals they seek, be followed willingly and unconditionally, within the framework of a democratic constitution. This charismatic leader could rise above bureaucratic pettiness. This was a potentially dangerous doctrine. Although for himself he chose the values of liberal democracy, freedom, and the Enlightenment (q.v.), his notion of populist leaders who could cast off restraints helped legitimize the rise of anti-democratic authoritarian leaders. His theory did not distinguish between democratic leaders, such as Konrad Adenauer (q.v.), and despots, such as Hitler (q.v.) or Mussolini. Weber had not experienced fascism and assumed that the charismatic leader, legitimated by plebiscites, would be benign. His death in 1920 prevented him from seeing and experiencing this danger in his own lifetime. (See also EMPIRE CULTURE.)

WEDEKIND, FRANK (1864-1918). The son of an actress and a doctor, Wedekind was secretary for a circus before turning to literature, acting and play writing. As a cabaret artist and a writer, he used risqué satire, and his works were controversial and considered immoral. His aim was to shock his middle-class audience. (See also EMPIRE CULTURE.)

WEHNER, HERBERT (1906-1990). Deputy SPD chairman (1958-73), federal minister of all-German affairs (1966-69), chairman of SPD Bundestag Fraktion (1969-82). By the time he died on January 19, 1990, Wehner had become a symbol of the twists and turns, the highs and lows of a half century of German history. In the 1920s, he was an anarchist and Communist firebrand determined to destroy the Weimar Republic (q.v.). In the 1930s, he was a top KPD (q.v.) leader, head of the Communists' illegal resistance network within Germany, and the Comintern's chief analyst for German affairs in Moscow during Stalin's purges. In the 1940s, he was arrested and imprisoned in Sweden, broke with communism (q.v.), and found his way to the FRG and the SPD (q.v.). In the 1950s, he ascended to the top leadership of the SPD, prodded his party to change in order to gain power, and worked tenaciously for German unity. In the 1960s, he was the architect of the Grand Coalition (q.v.) and the most powerful man in West German politics after Konrad Adenauer's (q.v.) retirement in 1963. In the 1970s, he held his party together to show that it could be trusted to rule. And, in the 1980s, his life's work collapsed as the SPD returned to opposition in 1982.

His contemporaries placed him on a pedestal. He became a legend in his own time, stemming from his adventuresome past, his political accomplishments over a long period of time, his tactical virtuosity, and his aloofness that prevented people from discovering the "real Wehner." The saying was that "only Wehner knows what Wehner wants." He usually got what he wanted, and after the dust settled and the complaining stopped, most people admitted that he had been right. The fact that everybody came to know that nourished his legend and added to his power. Everyone listened when he spoke, and even when he was wrong, they ran his statements through their minds over and over again trying to understand what he had meant. There were very few others in Bonn who could get a political ball rolling by making a single statement. As changeable and unpredictable as he was, people believed that he did nothing by accident and that everything was a tactical move.

Herbert Wehner (*Source*: Friedrich Ebert Stiftung)

He had a whole arsenal of tactics ranging from soft, kind words, to terrifying verbal eruptions. Perhaps his most intimidating weapon was silence. Rudolf Augstein (q.v.), who considered him to have been the most significant politician in German postwar history, wrote that Wehner "could silence people flat against the wall and right out of the room."

One television interviewer introduced Wehner by recalling Wild West films that show a herd of wild horses. And then one spots a single horse that does not allow itself to be caught, so finally one decides to let it run free. Wehner did not object to the comparison. He was indeed one of a kind and was so puzzling as a political figure because there was no one else like him. When he left the political stage in 1983, he was the oldest parliamentarian active in West Germany's founding years. The FRG was being ruled by the postwar generation, and the majority of citizens had no memory of the Third Reich (q.v.). Wehner came from an entirely different era. He had had the most adventuresome and intriguing political socialization of anyone in the Bundestag; he had come out of the cold.

When he appeared, he stepped out of German history. Half his political life took place before 1945. Like Adenauer, with whom he was often compared, he had been shaped by Weimar. He was a Social Democrat whose roots plunged into the history of the working class movement. He experienced Weimar's sharp class dichotomy between proletarians and capitalists and the after-pains of Bismarck's (q.v.) anti-Socialist laws. When he died, the SPD party journal, *Vorwärts*, wrote that he was "the personification of Social Democracy's primeval force that must have driven our party through its long tradition." Unlike most postwar politicians, he had never studied at the university, nor had he even attended the Gymnasium. He had seen Germany's first democratic republic driven into a corner and destroyed by people like himself. He went through a purgatory of struggle, war, near-death, and survival. There was no normalcy in the first half of his life. He was a victim of Germany's past; CSU Chairman Theo Waigel (q.v.) wrote that Wehner's "life was a German fate, torn between ideologies and powers, often disappointed, but not resigned, bitter but hopeful." Wehner went to Bonn in 1949 to try to help his nation overcome that past. The vast majority of those he encountered in building the new republic had been associated in one way or the other with National Socialism. A former Communist in their midst was discomforting, and only through aggressiveness could he carve out a place for himself in this new democracy.

Wehner fit no political category. He defied the usual cliches and flaunted the tabus. There was too much about him to which people were unaccustomed in contemporary Germany. He seemed always to wear a mask, and whoever tried to get close to him for a better look could count on his distrust. Unable to describe him precisely, observers attached labels: "apparatchik," "Bolshevik," "Stalinist," "tool of Moscow," "tool of reaction," "class enemy," "Uncle Herbert," "puritanical strongman," "helmsman," "coachman," "king-maker," "king-murderer," "chief strategist." Wehner said that such terms are the things "to which one is exposed who has not led an entirely normal life and who has not had enough time to explain it to everybody in sufficient detail." (See also ADENAUER, KONRAD; BRANDT, WILLY; POLITICAL PRISONERS; SCHMIDT, HELMUT; SOCIAL DEMOCRATIC PARTY OF GERMANY.)

WEHRBEAUFTRAGTER see BUNDESWEHR OMBUDSMAN

WEHRMACHT see SECOND WORLD WAR

WEHRSPORTGRUPPE HOFFMANN see RIGHT-WING GROUPS

WEILL, KURT (1900-1950). This German-born American composer wrote the music for *The Threepenny Opera* in 1928 with Bertold Brecht (q.v.). Weill wrote his short satirical operas in a modern style. He and his actress wife, Lotte Lenya, left Hitler's (q.v.) Germany and in 1938 settled in the U.S., where he continued to write musicals and operas.

WEIMAR COALITION see WEIMAR REPUBLIC

WEIMAR CONSTITUTION see DEMOCRACY ON GUARD and WEIMAR REPUBLIC

WEIMAR CULTURE. The Weimar Republic (q.v.) was a period of extraordinary cultural achievement, although the roots of "Weimar culture" no doubt were planted during Imperial Germany. It was a time in which the Mann brothers, Thomas and Heinrich, Gerhard Hauptmann, Bertold Brecht, Kurt Tucholsky, Erich Kästner, Gottfried

Benn (qq.v.), and Oskar Kokoschka were reaching huge audiences and producing works which in some ways supported the new political order.

Still, many writers continued to capture the attention of those whose ideals had been crushed by the fall of the empire and the loss of the war and who could not view civilian life in the new democratic republic as a satisfactory replacement. Erich Remarque's (q.v.) novel, *The Road Back*, portrayed a disillusioned returning soldier, who asked: " . . . what are we doing here? Look about you: look how flat and comfortless it all is. We are a burden to ourselves and others. Our ideals are bankrupt, our dreams are kaputt, and we wander around in this world of rotten opportunists and speculators like Don Quixotes in a foreign land." Such feelings were intensified by the immensely popular battle-front novels by authors such as Ernst Jünger (q.v.), Werner Beumelburg and Edwin Erich Dwinger, which called for a return to heroic virtues. Some of Germany's most respected academic minds, such as Martin Heidegger and Carl Schmitt (qq.v.) focused on the shortcomings of liberalism and democracy. Also, many anti-liberals were able to sooth their consciences by reading such bestsellers as Oswald Spengler's (q.v.) *The Decline of the West*, which decried the Weimar Republic (q.v.) and the alleged death of culture in the materialist West, and Arthur Moeller van der Bruck's *The Third Reich*, which called for a new and better political and social order.

For the first time in its history, Germany had a city which was not only the political, but also the cultural and intellectual center of the country. In fact, Berlin in the 1920s equalled or even surpassed Paris as the cultural center of Europe. Painters, writers, dramatists and filmmakers from all over Europe found Berlin to be the most stimulating place to work and live, and entertainers like Marlene Dietrich (q.v.) and American-born Josephine Baker found wildly enthusiastic audiences there. However, some Germans were repelled by the experimentalism in art, sexuality and lifestyles which were being practiced in Berlin, and they rejected the city as a center of decadence. In fact, one of the first things to be swept out of Germany when the Nazis (q.v.) came to power was the Weimar culture.

WEIMAR REPUBLIC. In the spring of 1919 delegates to a National Assembly met in Weimar, a city chosen because it lay outside the storm of revolution which raged in Berlin and because of its association with the humanists Goethe and Schiller (qq.v.), who had lived and worked there. This assembly, whose venue gave the new Republic its name, had three tasks: to form a government of Germany, to sign a peace treaty, and to draft a new constitution. It legitimized the "Weimar Coalition," composed of the SPD, Center, and German Democratic (qq.v.) parties, which had ruled Germany since the November Revolution of 1918. It was unfortunate that national humiliation coincided with the birth of the first democracy in Germany. When at last it had adopted the political organization extolled by the victorious Allies, it had become an international outcast. The new German constitution reflected a democratic spirit. The delegates sought to accomplish what the delegates of the Frankfurt Assembly had tried to do in 1848: to combine liberty with national unity and strength. It guaranteed basic individual rights and created a strong lower house of parliament (Reichstag) which had the right to initiate legislation. It also maintained certain traditional German political institutions, such as a federal form and a strong presidency elected every seven years (as a republican substitute for a strong Kaiser).

The Weimar constitution did include several weaknesses. In order to give parliamentary representation to as many different groups as possible, it established the proportional representation electoral system. The unfortunate result was not only that anti-republican splinter groups, such as the Nazi Party (q.v.), could publicize their causes in parliament, but the large number of parties which could win seats made the formation of a majority almost impossible. The result was predictable: parliamentary instability and ultimately paralysis. A second weakness was the provision for initiatives and referenda. While such instruments of direct democracy often appear progressive, they can frequently be manipulated by enemies of the democratic order, as Hitler (q.v.) did after 1933. The third mistake was the inclusion of emergency powers in Article 48, which could be invoked in the event that "public order and safety be seriously disturbed or threatened." This article was later used to circumvent parliament and thereby to undermine the democratic intentions of the framers. On the whole, this constitution was an admirable document, but the German nation was too divided on fundamental political values to be able to live by it. To be respected and observed, a constitution must fit a nation and a society well. If it does not, then it will ultimately be cast off like an ill-fitting garment.

The Weimar Republic experienced continuous crisis. The population had been impoverished by the long war and postwar chaos. The government saw no other way of keeping up its reparations (q.v.) payments than to borrow money abroad and produce new money as fast as it could be turned out by the printing presses. The devastating result was inflation. At the beginning of 1922, the German mark was worth only one-fiftieth of its prewar value; one year later it was worth one ten-thousandth. In 1914, the U.S. dollar had been worth 4.2 marks; in 1923, it was worth 25 billion marks! The hero in Erich Remarque's (q.v.) novel, *Three Comrades*, gave an idea of what this meant in personal terms: "In 1923 I was advertising chief of a rubber factory. I had a monthly salary of 200 billion marks. We were paid twice a day, and then everybody had half an hour's leave so that he could rush to the stores and buy something before the next quotation of the dollar came out, at which time the money would have lost half its value." There finally was a currency reform in 1923 in which one new mark (Rentenmark) was equal to a trillion old marks. But this dizzying inflation had already had the effect of a second revolution in Germany. It had financially wiped out millions of Germans and had spread fear and cynicism throughout the land, which merely weakened the Republic further.

The Republic was continuously battered from the left and the right. During the night of March 12-13, 1920, Free Corps troops marched on Berlin, singing military songs and flying the black-red-white flag of Imperial Germany. On their helmets was a popular Free Corps symbol: the swastika, the distorted cross which was also the Nazis' chief symbol. The troops faced no armed resistance since the majority of generals in Berlin refused to allow their soldiers to fire on former comrades from the front. The leader of the coup d'état was Wolfgang Kapp, who had grown up in the United States. He installed himself as chancellor and forced the government to flee the city. But a general strike called by the government before departing was observed by virtually all groups in Berlin: socialist labor unions, radical leftist militants, shopkeepers and the government ministries. Factories, schools, banks and stores were closed, streetcars and buses ceased running, and water, electricity and gas were shut off. This resistance finally forced Kapp and his supporters to flee Berlin only five days later. Almost immediately after the Kapp effort, the communists staged disorders in Berlin, Münster and the Ruhr area, especially Düsseldorf. Former Finance Minister Matthias Erzberger (q.v.), who had signed the Versailles Treaty (q.v.), was gunned down in the Black Forest in 1921 by a right-wing squad, and the following year Foreign Minister Walter Rathenau (q.v.) was felled by assassins' bullets. The next day, Chancellor Joseph Wirth declared in the Reichstag, where Rathenau's body lay in state: "The enemy is on the right!" He was correct. Although the radical left tried to destroy the Republic, the right presented a greater danger, primarily because it was so well-placed in the civil service, the judicial system and the army.

The year 1923 saw the suppression of an attempted coup d'état by the Nazis in Munich (q.v.) and of communist disorders in Hamburg, Saxony and Thuringia. It also saw the French military occupation of the Ruhr area, Germany's industrial heartland. The German government temporarily suspended all reparations payments and called upon Rhinelanders to practice passive resistance by refusing all cooperation with the French, but this form of retaliation merely meant more hunger and inflation for Germans. The French action was partially a reaction to Germany's signing the Rapallo Pact (q.v.) with the Soviet Union in 1922, calling for a normalization of political and trade relations between the two countries. The two armies began to maintain secret contacts with each other, and German officers started training in Russia with weapons which the Versailles Treaty (q.v.) forbade: tanks, airplanes and submarines. The Soviet Union was also an international outcast at the time and was seeking some support against the Western Allies.

That the storm over the Ruhr finally blew over was the work of the man who became chancellor for a few months in August 1923 and who served as foreign minister until his untimely death in October 1929: Gustav Stresemann (q.v.). Before and during the First World War (q.v.), Stresemann had been a fervent nationalist who had strongly advocated German expansion. But he was one of those persons who had learned from Germany's past and who had concluded that its future was best served by cooperating with the West, not by fighting it. Like Konrad Adenauer (q.v.) after the Second World War (q.v.), he helped to restore Germany's position in the world without having much military power at his disposal. However, unlike Adenauer's policy, Stresemann's foreign policy failed to win much domestic support and legitimacy for the Weimar Republic. Stresemann ended passive resistance in the Ruhr, and he set out to reach an international agreement which would enable Germany to pay its reparations. In 1924, the American banker Charles Dawes led a committee of experts which drew up a plan to regulate German reparations payments and to channel foreign credit into Germany to stimulate its recovery. This plan set the stage for a remarkable increase in German living standards and wages in the second half of the 1920s. The results were so promising that five years later the Young Plan, also of American origin, sought even further economic stimulation by scaling down the payments scheduled in the Dawes Plan. The overall result was that more than 25 billion marks worth of foreign capital was poured into Germany, mainly from the United States. This inflow of capital actually exceeded the outflow of reparations payments from Germany. Thus, in the long run, the payments did not have as adverse an economic effect on Germany as agitators constantly charged.

Stresemann also reached out to France. In the Locarno Treaty (q.v.) of 1925 Germany agreed to recognize the permanence of its borders with France and Belgium, to foreswear (with France and Belgium) the use of force against each other except in self-defense, to submit any disputes to arbitration or conciliation, and finally to enter the League of Nations, which Germany did in 1926. Although Germany did not recognize the permanency of its eastern borders, it agreed to seek their modification only by peaceful means. It underscored this commitment by signing in 1926 a pact of friendship, the Berlin Treaty, with the Soviet Union. The foreign minister's main focus remained on the West, though. His cooperation with the British and French leaders created considerable enthusiasm in Europe and greatly cooled tensions for the rest of the decade, which because of its increasing prosperity, optimism and cooperation was known as "the golden twenties." The second half of the 1920s was a time of relative political stability, thanks not only to Stresemann's influence, but also to another event: the election in April 1925 of Field Marshal Paul von Hindenburg (q.v.), the "Wooden Titan" and "Hero of Tannenberg," as president of the Republic. At the time, many democrats threw up their hands in despair that such a man who was mentally embedded in the imperial past could become the highest political leader in Germany. But he actually took seriously his pledge to defend the Weimar constitution. With this war hero in the presidential palace as a kind of substitute monarch, many German conservatives began for the first time to accept the legitimacy of the Republic and to tone down their attacks against it.

Two things brought the "golden years of the twenties" to an end. First, Stresemann died of a stroke in late 1929. He had been the only leader who had made parliamentary government work acceptably well, had brought about compromise between labor and capital, and had enabled Germany to take an equal place among the nations of the world. His death was an untimely tragedy for a nation entering a grave crisis, for he was the only leader who could have successfully competed with Hitler (q.v.) for control of Germany's destiny. Only ten days after his death came the second blow to the Republic: the American stock market collapsed, and overnight the chief source of credit for Germany dried up. Germany was thrown into a fatal economic crisis.

By 1930 the Weimar Republic was practically dead, although it limped on for another three years. Heinrich Brüning (q.v.) became chancellor and attempted to master the economic crisis by reducing government spending rather than trying to stimulate the economy through decisive government economic programs. This policy earned him the name "hunger chancellor." He had no parliamentary majority. The SPD sometimes supported him grudgingly in the absence of any acceptable alternative, but Brüning was compelled to resort to the emergency powers granted in Article 48 of the Weimar Constitution, which had been designed originally to enable the president to "restore public safety and order" in times of crisis. Article 48 was never intended to enable a president or chancellor to rule for long periods of time semi-independently of the parliament, as all chancellors did during the imperial time and which all did again after March 1930.

When the Reichstag voted its no confidence for the government for this violation of the constitution, Brüning dissolved parliament and called for new elections for September 1930. He disregarded all warnings that elections in the middle of such an economic depression and widespread unemployment could only benefit the extremist parties of the left and right. After all, unemployment had risen from 1.37 million in 1929 to 3.15 million in 1930. Such warnings were absolutely correct. The Communist Party increased its number of seats in the Reichstag from 54 to 77, and the Nazi Party grew from 12 members to 107, thereby becoming the second largest party after the SPD. The Nazis were thereafter in a position to hammer away at the Republic through parliamentary obstruction. Unemployment continued to rise to over 6 million in 1932, while production by 1932 had fallen to barely half the 1929 level. Such economic desperation and governmental paralysis gave a man with a small, socially unpolished minority of followers, but with great demagogical skill and the power to sway the frightened masses, the chance he had awaited for a decade. (See also HITLER'S SEIZURE OF POWER; REVOLUTION IN GERMANY; WEIMAR CULTURE; WORKERS' AND SOLDIERS' COUNCILS.)

WEISS, PETER (1916-1982). Weiss fled Hitler's (q.v.) Germany in 1934 for Sweden, where he became a citizen in 1945 and joined the

Communist Party there in the 1960s. He worked as a graphic artist and in film production before beginning to write in mid-life. He is considered the best representative of the documentary theater with his play on Marat Sade.

WEIZSÄCKER, CARL FRIEDRICH VON (1912-). A physicist, philosopher, and peace activist, Weizsäcker learned from the physicist, Werner Heisenberger, about the far-reaching scientific revolution brought about by the quantum theory of the atom. He became so engrossed in the philosophical consequences of this revolution that he came to prefer philosophy to physics. Nevertheless, as a brilliant physicist, he found that he had considerable influence within the prestigious scientific "Uranium Association" for atomic research. After Otto Hahn's discoveries concerning the splitting of the atom, Weizsäcker became convinced that the atomic bomb, even in Hitler's (q.v.) hands, would make future wars impossible. He later admitted that "only by the grace of God" was this early opinion of his not realized, and he spent much of the rest of his life opposing nuclear weapons. He became a radical pacifist, and when the possible arming of the Bundeswehr (q.v.) with nuclear weapons was discussed in 1956, he joined Hahn and other nuclear scientists to formulate the sensational manifesto of the "Göttingen Eighteen," who demanded that the FRG voluntarily renounce the possession of nuclear weapons. In 1970, his efforts culminated in the establishment of the Max Planck Institute for Research of the Living Conditions of the Politico-Scientific World, located in Starnberg outside Munich. It concentrates on such topics as the dangers of atomic war, the destruction of the environment, and the North-South conflict. Weizsäcker spent the final years of his working life completing his principal philosophical work, *Zeit und Wissen* (Time and Knowledge). He sought to find the unity between science, political morality, and religious experience. He is the brother of President Richard von Weizsäcker (q.v.). (See also PEACE MOVEMENT)

WEIZSÄCKER, ERNST FREIHERR VON (1882-1951). State secretary in foreign office (1938-1943). He was a naval officer during the First World War (q.v.), and after the war he transferred to the foreign office. From then on his family was on the move continuously, from Copenhagen to Basel, the Hague and Berlin. After Hitler (q.v.) came to power in 1933, von Weizsäcker was a state secretary who formed a cohesive anti-Ribbentrop group within the foreign office. This group attempted to establish and maintain contact with Britain, the U.S., and other major powers. He was regularly able to send high level messengers to these powers in an effort to achieve the twin objectives of restoring peace and overthrowing the Hitler regime, objectives which he regarded as inseparably linked. Accused after the war of supporting Hitler's foreign policy, he was defended in court by his son, Richard (q.v.). (See also RESISTANCE TO HITLER; TROTT ZU SOLZ, ADAM VON.)

WEIZSÄCKER, RICHARD FREIHERR VON (1920-). One of Germany's most prominent Christian Democrats, Weizsäcker was mayor of West Berlin from 1981-84. In 1984 he was elected federal president and gave new importance and dignity to that office. He sometimes publicly criticized the chancellor from his own CDU (q.v.), Helmut Kohl. He will probably be best remembered as a "conscience of the nation," who could always find the right words to remind his countrymen of their moral responsibilities stemming from the past and the need to show tolerance toward foreigners who came to Germany to find refuge or work. (See also DENAZIFICATION; OVERCOMING THE PAST; PRESIDENT.)

WELS, OTTO (1873-1939). Chairman of SPD (1931-39). Exiled during the Second World War (q.v.).

WENDE (CHANGE--1982). The term "*Wende*" was widely used in Germany to describe the dramatic collapse of the SED (q.v.) regime in the GDR and the reunification (q.v.) of Germany. However, it was first coined in 1982 to describe the change of power in Bonn from the Social Democrats to the Christian Democrats. Some Social Democrats, such as Herbert Wehner and Helmut Schmidt (qq.v.), had always been wary of the "unreliable" FDP (q.v.), and that party's disloyalty seemed to confirm their suspicion. Since 1981 the two coalition partners had clashed continually on how to cope with the worsening economic recession, differences that had ideological roots. On September 10, FDP Economics Minister Count von Lambsdorff (q.v.) delivered what Peter Glotz (q.v.) termed the "divorce certificate," calling for reduced financial help for the unemployed and handicapped, an elimination of assistance for mothers staying home with their babies and for pupils receiving state scholarships, a liberalization of the rental law, and tax concessions for entrepreneurs to stimulate investment. On September 15, Schmidt and SPD cabinet members discussed the impending break with the FDP and decided to offer the CDU/CSU (q.v.) new elections. On September 17, the four Free Democrats in the cabinet resigned when Schmidt ordered them to respect the coalition's program to which they had agreed.

Schmidt's plan was to remain chancellor in a minority government and then, as Brandt (q.v.) had done in 1972, bring about a vote of no confidence that he would intentionally lose. That would open the way to new elections in which the disloyal FDP could be punished, and voters, who would be offended by the shabby treatment of the SPD (q.v.), might give the Social Democrats an absolute majority. The plan was a long shot, but the risks were great. The problem was that the FDP and the CDU/CSU leader, Helmut Kohl (q.v.), had already forged a plan of their own. The FDP's decision had infuriated many of its party members, and within a few months a third left the FDP; it clearly required time to stabilize itself before facing the voters. Helmut Kohl agreed, realizing that his government needed them. Therefore, he rejected the SPD's request for immediate elections and called instead for a "constructive vote of no confidence": first a vote to demonstrate no confidence in the existing chancellor, and then a vote for a new chancellor. The date was set for October 1, 1982. In the parliamentary debates that preceded the vote, Rainer Barzel (q.v.) hammered at rising unemployment and budget deficits, which had stimulated public opposition to SPD rule and helped weaken the SPD-FDP alliance. Kohl narrowly won the first successful constructive vote of no-confidence in the FRG's history. He became chancellor on the same day, October 1, 1982, thereby ending 13 years of SPD rule.

WENDERS, WIM (1945-). Communication in all forms and the American colonization of the subconsciousness of postwar Germans are recurrent themes in Wenders' films. After mixed success in America, he returned to Germany and produced his masterpiece, *Wings of Desire*, which is considered one of the ten best films of the 1980s.

WERBELLINSEE MEETING (1981). In December 1981, Chancellor Helmut Schmidt and SED chief Erich Honecker (qq.v.) met in Werbellinsee, outside Berlin in the GDR (q.v.). Although the meeting was not held in the GDR's capital and thus was below the protocol level of a state visit, Schmidt affirmed the GDR's "sovereignty and statehood." The meeting signalled a growing mutual accommodation between the two German governments. (See also SCHMIDT, HELMUT.)

WERTHEIMER, MAX (1880-1943). One of the founders of Gestalt psychology, he rejected the notion of distinct psychic units suggested by analytic psychology and associationalism. In contrast, Gestalt psychology establishes the importance of configuration on all levels of experience. Parts receive their importance and character from the whole. He worked in Frankfurt am Main and Berlin, but he left for New York.

WESSI. Term to describe a German from the western part of Germany. (See also INTRODUCTION.)

WESTPHALIA, TREATY OF (1648) see THIRTY-YEARS WAR

WHITE ROSE see RESISTANCE TO HITLER; SCHOLL, HANS

WIELAND, CHRISTOPH MARTIN (1733-1813). The son of a minister, Wieland studied in Tübingen and became a professor in Erfurt. He switched to journalism, and his publications were influential in spreading the ideals of the Enlightenment (q.v.). He translated 22 plays of Shakespeare into German. His *Agathon* is considered one of the best examples of the Enlightenment (q.v.). His work is not considered original, but his expressive prose introduced qualities into German which had formerly been attributed to French.

WIENAND, KARL (1926-) and WIENAND AFFAIR. He was manager of the SPD (q.v.) parliamentary group (qq.v.) (1967-74), from which he was forced to resign because of a vote-buying scandal. A failed constructive vote of no-confidence against Chancellor Willy Brandt (q.v.) took place on April 27, 1972. The results stunned Rainer Barzel (q.v.), who would have become chancellor. He had thought he had lined up the support he needed, but he had received only 247 votes, two shy of the absolute majority. At least two Christian Democrats had obviously voted against the motion. Herbert Wehner's (q.v.) aide, Karl Wienand, later said that the opposition had persuaded five deputies to defect, but that he had succeeded in luring one of them back and secretly recruiting four CDU/CSU (qq.v.) deputies to support the government. Not until June of the following year did information begin coming to light about what had happened. A CDU deputy, Julius Steiner, claimed that Wienand had bought his abstention for DM 50,000. The claim was supported by SPD Hans-Joachim Baeuchle, but it was never proven. Steiner's credibility was questioned because of his dissolute personal life and his later admission to having been in the pay of the East German Stasi (q.v.). The result was a long investigation that ultimately led to Wienand's resignation from the Bundestag in 1974 and had the potential of ending Herbert Wehner's career. (See also BRANDT.)

WILHELM I (1797-1888). King of Prussia 1861-1888, German Kaiser 1871-1888. (See also BISMARCK, OTTO VON.)

WILHELM II (1859-1941). The young, inexperienced and impetuous Wilhelm II became Kaiser in 1888. The new ruler hoped to become popular by canceling the Anti-Socialist Law, introducing some domestic reforms, and conducting an energetic German foreign and colonial policy. Noting that Bismarck (q.v.) had wholly different ideas, he fired the "Iron Chancellor" in 1890. He was then free to take the lead over a people enthusiastic about the prospects for Germany's future. The Kaiser, who was rather intelligent and superficially interested in many different things, but who was unable to focus his attention on anything very long, was boastful about Germany's power. He also had a way, as one of his biographers noted, of approaching every issue with an open mouth. Although in actual crises the young Kaiser tended to be cautious, he seemed to many non-Germans to represent a restless country with more power than it could use well. He abdicated at the end of the First World War (q.v.) and lived out the rest of his life in Holland. (See also BISMARCK, OTTO VON; BÜLOW, BERNHARD; EMPIRE FOREIGN POLICY.)

WILKE, REINHARD (1929-) see GUILLAUME AFFAIR

WILLY-NICKY TELEGRAMS. Wilhelm II (q.v.) refused to renew the Reinsurance Treaty (q.v.) with Russia and Austria-Hungary, but he bent over backwards to retain close, friendly relations with Czar Nicholas II. He maintained affectionate correspondence with Nicholas in English for over two decades preceding the outbreak of war in 1914. Both rulers nourished the illusion that their personal relations could hold their nations together while the diplomatic situation deteriorated.

WINCKELMANN, JOHANN JOACHIM (1717-1768). He was the son of a poor cobbler who fell in love with Greek antiquity and managed to acquire a university education. He became the greatest Hellenist and archeologist of the century and wrote a monumental book on the history of classical art. His works extolling the originality and perfection of the Greeks greatly influenced Goethe (q.v.).

WINDELBAND, WILHELM (1848-1915). A historian of philosophy, Windelband developed a philosophy which focused on the theory of value. Philosophy is concerned with values, whereas science deals with facts. Philosophy is not merely descriptive, but is normative. That is, it involves what "ought" to be. In his *History and Natural Science*, published in 1894, he differentiated between natural science, which involves generalizations, and history, which deals with important individuals and events as unique occurrences.

WINDHORST, LUDWIG (1812-1891) see CENTER PARTY

WINZER, OTTO (1902-1975). SED, GDR foreign minister (1965-75).

WIRTH, JOSEPH (1879-1956). Center Party, chancellor (1921-22). (See also WEIMAR REPUBLIC.)

WISCHNEWSKI, HANS-JÜRGEN (1922-). SPD, federal minister for economic cooperation (1966-68), federal manager of SPD (1968-72), from 1974 parliamentary state secretary and minister in foreign ministry and state minister in the federal chancellor's office. Known as "Ben-Wisch" for the skill with which he performed special tasks, such as liberating passengers from a high-jacked Lufthansa plane in Mogadishu, Somalia, he was the top trouble-shooter for the SPD governments of Brandt and Schmidt (qq.v.).

WITTIG, PETER. A contemporary diplomat in the foreign office, where he rose to be a top aide to Foreign Minister Hans-Dietrich Genscher (q.v.). An expert on the Fabian movement in Britain, Dr. Wittig taught political science at the University of Freiburg before serving as culture attache in Madrid and as political officer in Germany's U.N. mission in New York.

WOHMANN, GABRIELE (1932-). Born in Darmstadt in 1932, she studied music and languages in Frankfurt and taught a few years before devoting herself to writing. She has published novels, poetry, and short stories, as well as radio and television plays. She concentrates on the outsider and his inability to communicate.

WOLF, CHRISTA (1929-). Born and schooled in what is now Poland, Wolf moved to East Germany in 1945 where she studied and worked as a magazine editor. Although her work includes essays, film scripts, open letters, stories and tales, she is best known for her novels which are a voice of social realism. In 1976, she was one of the intellectuals who protested when Wolf Biermann (q.v.) was prevented from returning to the GDR (q.v.). Her speech at the mass demonstration at the Berlin Alexander Platz on November 4, 1989, found worldwide attention. (See also LITERATURE.)

WOLF, FRIEDRICH (1888-1953). This former physician became a member of the Communist Party. He was on the run from 1933 until 1945, when he finally settled in East Berlin. One of the few talents who was able to defy Brecht's (q.v.) Epic Theater, his plays counted on the empathy and emotions of his audience and dealt with historical, political and social issues. He served as the first GDR (q.v.) ambassador to Poland in 1951.

WOLF, MARKUS (1923-). Legendary East German spymaster and model for novelist John le Carre's Soviet spy Karla, Wolf headed the foreign service of the GDR's Stasi (qq.v.) secret police for 33 years. He controlled the GDR's foreign agents, electronic surveillance, border controls, and investigative department. He was once known as the man without a face because Western intelligence agencies could not even obtain a photo of him. After the demise of the GDR, he fled to the USSR, where he had spent his boyhood years during the war. When the Soviet Union itself collapsed, Russia denied him further refuge. Therefore, he returned to Germany in 1991, turned himself over to Bonn authorities, and was released on $30,000 bail, a paltry sum for a man who was being paid at least that much for each interview he granted to the sensation-hungry Western press. In 1992, he was charged with spying and treason. (See also REUNIFICATION.)

WOMEN FOR FREEDOM (FRAUEN FÜR DEN FRIEDEN)   see
BOHLEY, BÄRBEL

WOMEN'S LEAGUE. An independent eastern German party which
sprang into existence upon the collapse of Communist rule in the GDR
(q.v.). Together with the Greens (q.v.), it received almost 2 percent of
the votes in the March 18, 1990, GDR (q.v.) elections. There was also
a Democratic German Women's League (DFD), which captured only
.33 percent of the votes.

WONDRATSCHEK, WOLF (1943-). He is important as a poet and
short story writer who represents the German pop culture of the 1970s
in a style characterized by brevity. Using sparse sentences, curt phrases,
and often mixing languages, he gives a series of impressions of basic
human situations. He is originally from Rudolstadt in the former GDR
(q.v.).

WORKERS' AND SOLDIERS' COUNCILS (ARBEITER- UND
SOLDATENRÄTE). The goal of leftist revolutionaries after the First
World War (q.v.) was the establishment of a "council republic," in
which all state power would be wielded by so-called "Workers' and
Soldiers' Councils." These would be the source of supreme
governmental power and would elect a central council. The economy
would be nationalized. These councils sprang into existence in the
chaos of the collapsing empire during the final weeks of the war. On
November 10, 1918, the assembly of Berlin councils approved the
provisional government of the SPD and Independent Social Democrats
(USPD) but created a control organ which was supposed to share the
ruling power. However, this organ played no major role because most
councils favored Friedrich Ebert's (q.v.) plan to hold elections for a
National Assembly which would write a democratic constitution and
establish a parliamentary democracy. In 1919, leftist revolutionaries
rose up in various parts of Germany, including Bremen, Braunschweig,
and Bavaria, demanding council republics, but they were suppressed by
force. These events and the reaction to them alienated part of the
working class from the SPD (q.v.) rulers, who were seen as responsible
for such suppression. (See also REVOLUTION IN GERMANY and
WEIMAR REPUBLIC.)

WÖRNER, MANFRED (1934-). The CDU's (q.v.) defense expert in the Bundestag for many years, he served as Helmut Kohl's (q.v.) first defense minister. In 1988, he was appointed NATO (q.v.) general secretary and was reappointed in 1992. He is the first German ever to hold this position, and his appointment was an important symbol of the FRG's postwar political rehabilitation. (See also NORTH ATLANTIC TREATY ORGANIZATION.)

WOSSI. A derogatory term for a West German who seeks his fortune by working in eastern Germany after reunification (q.v.) in 1990.

-Y-

YALTA CONFERENCE (February 1945) see SECOND WORLD WAR

YOUNG GERMANY see LIBERALISM

YOUNG GIRLS (JUNGMÄDEL) see HITLER YOUTH

YOUNG, OWEN D. (1874-1962) and YOUNG PLAN (1929). U.S. economist. (See WEIMAR REPUBLIC.)

YOUNG SOCIALISTS (JUSOS) see SCHMIDT, HELMUT

-Z-

ZABERN AFFAIR (1913). In the small Alsatian town of Zabern, a young German lieutenant struck with his sword a local shoemaker who refused to make way for him on the street. This sparked clashes between soldiers and townspeople and exacerbated antagonism between German liberals and Prussian militarists. The result was that the Prussian military's image was somewhat tarnished.

ZAISSER, WILHELM see GERMAN DEMOCRATIC REPUBLIC, UPRISING

ZEPPELIN, COUNT FERDINAND VON (1838-1917). A balloon enthusiast, he constructed his first inflated airship ("blimp") in 1900. In 1908, a 12-hour flight over Switzerland was a sensation. In 1909, he created the world's first airline company, which flew 100,000 miles without a casualty in the first five years. Zeppelins were used primarily as reconnaissance crafts by both sides in the First World War (q.v.), but in February 1915 one crossed the North Sea and bombed Yarmouth, followed by raids on London the next summer. They were so vulnerable to air defenses, though, that such raids were halted after a mass attack on London ended in disaster in November 1917. Zeppelins were used from 1928 to 1937 to provide trans-Atlantic air service, but this ceased when the "Hindenburg" zeppelin burned while landing in Lakehurst, NJ, on May 6, 1937. Zeppelins went out of service in 1940. (See also AMERICA; GERMAN ATTITUDES.)

ZERO HOUR (STUNDE NULL). Germany's collapse in 1945 was complete. Fears that a bloodbath would occur and that "self-justice" would be practiced proved to be unfounded. The Nazi (q.v.) organizations disintegrated overnight, and the Germans were politically apathetic in the face of a formidable struggle to survive. For the first time since the Napoleonic wars, fighting had taken place in all parts of the nation, and all of Germany was occupied by foreigners who became total rulers for a while. People spoke of the *Stunde Null* or "Zero Hour," when the edifice had to be rebuilt from the foundation up. (See also ALLIED OCCUPATION; DENAZIFICATION.)

ZILLE, HEINRICH (1858-1929). Zille is best known for his drawings of the common people of Berlin whom he portrayed in a gently satirical style which well suited his publications: *Lustige Blätter*, *Jugend*, and *Simplissimus*. He worked as a draftsman and lithographer.

ZIMMERMANN, ARTHUR and TELEGRAM see FIRST WORLD WAR

ZINN, GEORG AUGUST (1901-1976). SPD, minister president of Hesse (1950-69).

ZWEITES DEUTSCHES FERNSEHEN (ZDF) see RADIO AND TELEVISION

BIBLIOGRAPHY

INTRODUCTION

An enormous body of literature exists on Germany for several reasons. It has a rich and fascinating history and culture which scholars cannot resist studying and writing about. It is the most populous European nation west of Russia, and its central geographic position and economic preponderance in Europe give it an importance that cannot be ignored. It is a country in the throes of dramatic change, especially since the collapse of the German Democratic Republic in 1989 and the reunification in 1990. This means that much of what had been thought and written about Germany must be reassessed and described.

This bibliography attempts to take account of the changes that are occurring and the rethinking which is taking place. Because of the sheer magnitude of available literature, this is, of necessity, a selected bibliography. It is largely restricted to books, and priority has been given to English-language sources. However, because this book is aimed at the scholar as well as the general reader, German language books have been included if they are particularly important or if they fill a gap which is not covered sufficiently by English-language sources. Works by the same author in the same section are listed in chronological rather than alphabetical order to display the development of the author's work. Emphasis is placed on recent sources, but works produced earlier cannot be ignored and are therefore included. Also, the bulk of entries are secondary literature; however, one section contains numerous autobiographies and memoirs. Finding one's way to the right sources in such a multitude of literature is not easy. Therefore, we begin with research guides, bibliographies, and journals dealing with German subjects. The general reader can also refer to the general sources listed at the beginning of the two sections on history and the Federal Republic of Germany that follow. Finally, because this dictionary is not restricted to contemporary politics, sections are also provided on Germany's history, economy, and culture.

RESEARCH GUIDES AND BIBLIOGRAPHIES

Braunthal, Gerard and Jeffrey M. Tenenbaum. *A Select Bibliography of English-Language Books on German History and Politics*. Amherst, MA: Occasional Papers Series, Western European Studies, 1992.

The Columbia Dictionary of European Political History Since 1914. 2nd ed. by John Stevenson. New York: Columbia University Press, 1992.

Detweiler, Donald S. and Ilse G. Detweiler. *West Germany*. World Bibliographical Series, Vol. 72. Oxford: Clio Press, 1987. [Annotated]

Edgington, Peter. *The Politics of the Two Germanies: A Guide to Sources and English-Language Materials*. Ormskirk, England: Hesketh, 1977.

Faulhaber, Uwe K. and Penrith B. Goff. *German Literature: An Annotated Reference Guide*. New York: Garland, 1979. [Section XIII includes references to books on history and politics.]

Germanistik. Internationales Referatenorgan mit bibliographischen Hinweisen. (Quarterly). Tübingen: Max Niemeyer Verlag.

Der Grosse Bildatlas zur deutschen Geschichte. Von Karl dem Grossen bis zur Wiedervereinigung. Munich: Bertelsmann Lexikon Verlag, n.d.

Hansel, Johannes. *Bücherkunde für Germanisten*. Studienausgabe, 7th rev. ed. Berlin: Erich Schmidt Verlag, 1978.

Kimmich, Christoph M., ed. *German Foreign Policy, 1918-1945. A Guide to Research and Research Materials*. Revised ed. Wilmington, Del: Scholarly Resources, 1991.

Krewson, Margrit B. *The German-speaking Countries of Europe: A Selected Bibliography*. Washington, D.C.: Library of Congress, 1985.

Merritt, Anna J., and Richard C. Merritt, comps. *Politics, Economics, and Society in the Two Germanies, 1945-75: A Bibliography of English Language Works*. Urbana: University of Illinois Press, 1978.

Paul, Barbara Dotts. *The Germans after World War II: An English-language Bibliography*. Boston: G.K. Hall, 1990.

Press and Information Office of the Federal Government. *Von der Spaltung zur Einheit. 1945-1990. (From Division to Unity, 1945-1990. An Illustrated German Chronical).* Text in German, French and English. Bonn, 1992.

Price, Arnold H., comp. *East Germany: A Selected Bibliography.* Washington, D.C.: Library of Congress, 1967.

Price, Arnold H. *The Federal Republic of Germany: A Selected Bibliography of English-Language Publications.* 2nd rev. ed. Washington, D.C.: Library of Congress, 1978.

Rees, Philip. *Biographical Dictionary of the Extreme Right since 1890.* New York: Harvester Wheatsheaf, 1990.

Reunified Germany. Two annotated bibliographies, one of English-language sources and one of books in German. Chicago: The Goethe Institute Chicago Library, 1992.

Richardson, Larry L. *Introduction to Library Research in German Studies: Language, Literature and Civilization.* Boulder, CO: Westview, 1984.

Sykes, J.B. and W. Scholze-Stubenrecht. *The Oxford Duden German Dictionary.* Oxford: Oxford University Press, 1990.

Wallace, Ian. *East Germany: The German Democratic Republic.* World Bibliographical Series, Vol. 77. Santa Barbara, CA: Clio Press, 1987. [Annotated]

JOURNALS AND PERIODICALS

Aussenpolitik. German Foreign Affairs Review. English quarterly edition. Hamburg: Interpress Verlag.

Central European History. Published by Humanities Press International for the Conference Group for Central European History of the American Historical Association. Department of History, University of California, Riverside.

Colloquia Germanica. Published for the University of Kentucky's Department of Germanic Languages and Literature by Francke Verlag, Bern.

Debatte. A New Journal for the New Germany. Published twice yearly by Berg Publishers, Oxford (UK) and New York.

German Brief. Published by the *Frankfurter Allgemeine Zeitung* and available from European Business Publications, Darien, CT.

German Comment. Published by Fromm Verlag for the Konrad Adenauer Stiftung.

German History. The Journal of the German History Society, UK. Published by Oxford University Press.

German Life and Letters. Oxford (UK) and Cambridge, MA: Blackwell Publishers.

German Politics. Published by Frank Cass for the Association for the Study of German Politics, UK.

German Politics and Society. Published by the Center for European Studies, Harvard University.

The German Quarterly. A journal devoted to the study of German published by the American Association of Teachers of German. Cherry Hill, NJ.

German Studies Review. Published by the German Studies Association, Arizona State University, Tempe.

The Germanic Review. Edited by the Department of Germanic Languages of Columbia University.

Historische Zeitschrift. Munich: R. Oldenbourg Verlag.

Politics and Society in Germany, Austria and Switzerland. The Journal of the Institute of German, Austrian and Swiss Affairs at the University of Nottingham, UK.

Scala. A bi-monthly magazine in five languages with stories of general interest on Germany, published by the Frankfurter Societäts-Druckerei, P.O. Box 100801, 6000 Frankfurt am Main.

Vierteljahreshefte für Zeitgeschichte, FRG.

The Week in Germany. A weekly publication of the German Information Center, 950 Third Avenue, New York, NY 10022.

HISTORY

GENERAL SOURCES

Bade, Klaus J., ed. *Population, Labour and Migration in 19th and 20th Century Germany.* Oxford: Berg, 1987.

Balfour, Michael. *West Germany. A Contemporary History.* New York: St. Martin's, 1982.

Balfour, Michael. *Germany. The Tides of Power.* New York: Routledge, 1992.

Bark, Dennis L. and David R. Gress. *A History of West Germany.* 2 vols. 2nd rev. ed. Cambridge, MA: Basil Blackwell, 1993.

Barraclough, Geoffrey. *The Origins of Modern Germany.* New York: Capricorn Books, 1963.

Benz, Wolfgang. *Deutschland seit 1945. Entwicklungen in der Bundesrepublik und in der DDR.* Munich: Verlag Moos & Partner, 1990.

Berghahn, Volker. *Modern Germany.* 2nd ed. Cambridge: Cambridge University Press, 1987.

Böhme, H. *An Introduction to the Social and Economic History of Germany. Politics and Economic Change in the 19th and 20th Centuries.* Oxford: Basil Blackwell, 1978.

Bruck, W.F. *Social and Economic History of Germany from William II to Hitler, 1888-1938: A Comparative Study.* Oxford: Oxford University Press, 1938. Reprint. New York: Russell & Russell, 1962.

Cahnman, Werner J. *German Jewry: Its History and Sociology. Selected Essays.* Ed. and intro. Joseph B. Maier, Judith Marcus, and Zoltan Tarr. New Brunswick and Oxford: Transaction Publishers, 1989.

Calleo, David P. *The German Problem Reconsidered: Germany and the World Order, 1870 to the Present.* Cambridge: Cambridge University Press, 1978.

Carr, William. *A History of Germany 1815-1985.* 4th ed. New York: Edward Arnold, 1991.

Craig, Gordon A. *The Politics of the Prussian Army, 1640-1945.* Oxford: Oxford University Press, 1964.

Craig, Gordon A. *From Bismarck to Adenauer: Aspects of German Statecraft.* Rev. ed. New York: Harper & Row, 1965.

Craig, Gordon A. *Germany 1866-1945.* Oxford: Oxford University Press, 1981.

Craig, Gordon A. *The Germans.* With a New Afterword. New York: Penguin, 1992.

Detweiler, Donald S. *Germany: A Short History.* 2nd ed. Carbondale: Southern Illinois University Press, 1989.

Diemer, Gebhard and Eberhard Kuhrt. *Kurze Chronik der Deutschen Frage.* Munich: Olzog, 1991.

Epstein, Klaus. *The Genesis of German Conservatism.* Princeton: Princeton University Press, 1966.

Evans, Ellen Lovell. *The German Center Party, 1870-1933: A Study in Political Catholicism.* Carbondale: Southern Illinois University Press, 1981.

Evans, Richard J. *The Feminist Movement in Germany, 1894-1933.* Beverly Hills, CA: Sage, 1976.

Feuchtwanger, E.J., ed. *Upheaval and Continuity. A Century of German History.* Pittsburgh: University of Pittsburgh Press, 1974.

Fischer, Fritz. *From Kaiserreich to Third Reich: Elements of Continuity in German History.* Trans. by Roger Fletcher. London: Allen & Unwin, 1986.

Freund, Michael. *Deutsche Geschichte von den Anfängen bis zur Gegenwart.* Munich: Goldmann, 1981.

Fulbrook, Mary. *A Concise History of Germany.* Cambridge: Cambridge University Press, 1990.

Fulbrook, Mary. *The Divided Nation: A History of Germany, 1918-1990.* Oxford: Oxford University Press, 1992.

Gay, Ruth. *The Jews of Germany. A Historical Portrait.* New Haven: Yale University Press, 1992.

Gerschenkron, Alexander. *Bread and Democracy in Germany.* Ithaca: Cornell University Press, 1989.

Gordon, John C.B., ed. *German History and Society.* Vol 2: 1918-1945. New York: St. Martin's, 1992.

Herwig, Holger H. *Hammer or Anvil? Modern Germany 1648-Present.* Lexington, MA: D.C. Heath, 1994.

Hildebrand, Klaus. *German Foreign Policy from Bismarck to Adenauer: The Limits of Statecraft.* Trans. by Louis Willmot. London: Unwin Hyman, 1989.

Hillgruber, Andreas. *Germany and Two World Wars*. Cambridge: Harvard University Press, 1981.

Hoffmeister, Gerhardt and Frederic Tubach. *Germany: 2000 Years*. Vol. 3. New York: Ungar, 1986.

Holborn, Hajo. *A History of Modern Germany, 1840-1945*. 3 vols. New York: Knopf, 1959-1969. [Vol. 3: 1840-1945]

Hughes, Michael. *Nationalism and Society: Germany 1800-1945*. London: Edward Arnold, 1988.

Iggers, George, ed. *The Social History of Politics. Critical Perspectives in West German Historical Writing*. Oxford: Berg, 1986.

Jacob, Herbert. *German Administration since Bismarck: Central Authority versus Local Autonomy*. New Haven: Yale University Press, 1963.

James, Harold. *A German Identity, 1770-1990*. New York: Routledge, Chapman, and Hall, 1989.

Jarausch, Konrad H. and Larry Eugene Jones, eds. *In Search of a Liberal Germany. Studies in the History of German Liberalism from 1789 to the Present*. Oxford: Berg, 1990.

Jones, Larry Eugene and James N. Retallack, eds. *Between Reform, Reaction and Resistance. Studies in the History of German Conservatism from 1789 to 1945*. Oxford: Berg, 1993.

Kisch, Herbert. *From Domestic Manufacture to Industrial Revolution*. Oxford: Oxford University Press, 1989.

Knodel, John E. *Demographic Behavior in the Past: A Study of Fourteen German Village Populations in the Eighteenth and Nineteenth Centuries*. Cambridge: Cambridge University Press, 1988.

Knowlton, James and Truett Cates, translators. *Forever in the Shadow of Hitler? The Dispute about the Germans' Understanding of History:*

Original Documents of the Historikerstreit. Atlantic Highlands, NJ: Humanities Press, 1993.

Koch, H. W. *A Constitutional History of Germany in the Nineteenth and Twentieth Centuries.* London: Longmans, 1984.

Kocka, Jürgen, ed. *Bürgertum im 19. Jahrhundert: Deutschland in europäischen Vergleich.* Munich: Deutscher Taschenbuch, 1988.

Krockow, Christian Graf. *Die Deutschen in ihrem Jahrhundert. 1890-1990.* Reinbek: Rowohlt, 1990.

Laqueur, W. *Young Germany. A History of the German Youth Movement.* London: Routledge & Kegan Paul, 1962.

Longerich, Peter, ed. *"Was ist des Deutschen Vaterland?": Dokumente zur Frage der deutschen Einheit, 1800 bis 1990.* Munich: Piper, 1990.

Manchester, William. *The Arms of Krupp. 1587-1968.* New York: Bantam Book, 1970.

Mann, Golo. *The History of Germany since 1789.* New York: Praeger, 1968.

Martell, Gordon. *Modern Germany Reconsidered 1870-1945.* New York: Routledge, 1992.

Meyer, Henry Cord. *Mitteleuropa in German Thought and Action 1815-1945.* The Hague: Martinus Nijhoff, 1955.

Miller, Susanne and Heinrich Potthoff. *A History of German Social Democracy from 1848 to the Present.* Oxford: Berg, 1986.

Moses, John A. *Trade Unionism in Germany from Bismarck to Hitler, 1869-1933.* 2 vols. Totowa, NJ: Barnes & Noble, 1982.

Moss, George L. *The Crisis of German Ideology: Intellectual Origins of the Third Reich.* New York: Grosset & Dunlap, 1964.

Mosse, George E. *Fallen Soldiers: Reshaping the Memory of the World Wars.* Oxford: Oxford University Press, 1990.

Müller, Helmut M. *Schlaglichter der deutschen Geschichte.* Bonn: Bundeszentrale für politische Bildung, 1988.

Orlow, Dietrich. *A History of Modern Germany 1870 to the Present.* Englewood Cliffs, NJ: Prentice-Hall, 1987.

Owen, Francis. *The Germanic People. Their Origin, Expansion and Culture.* New York: Dorset Press, 1990.

Pachter, Henry M. *Modern Germany: A Social, Cultural and Political History.* Boulder, CO: Westview, 1978.

Pasley, M. *Germany: A Companion to German Studies.* 2nd ed. London: Methuen, 1982.

Pinson, Koppel. *Modern Germany: Its History and Civilization, 1871-1918.* 2nd ed. New York: Macmillan, 1966.

Pulzer, Peter. *The Rise of Political Anti-Semitism in Germany and Austria.* Cambridge: Harvard University Press, 1988.

Questions on German History. Ideas, Forces, Decisions--From 1800 to the Present. Bonn: German Bundestag Press and Information Center, 1984.

Raff, Diether. *A History of Germany: From the Medieval Empire to the Present.* Oxford: Berg, 1988.

Reinhardt, Kurt. *Germany: 2000 Years.* Vols. 1 and 2. New York: Ungar, 1986.

Ritter, Gerhard. *The Sword and the Scepter.* 4 vols. Coral Gables, FL: University of Miami Press, 1969-1973.

Rosenberg, Arthur. *Imperial Germany: The Birth of the German Republic.* Boston: Beacon Press, 1964.

Rürup, Reinhard. *Germany and the Rise of Bourgeois Society.* Cambridge: Harvard University Press, 1988.

Ryder, A.J. *Twentieth Century Germany: From Bismarck to Brandt.* New York: Columbia University Press, 1973.

Sheehan, James J. *German Liberalism in the Nineteenth Century.* Chicago: University of Chicago Press, 1978.

Sheehan, James J. *German History, 1770-1866.* Oxford: Oxford University Press, 1990.

Snyder, Louis L. *Basic History of Modern Germany.* Huntington, NY: Krieger, 1980.

Taylor, A.J.P. *The Course of German History: A Survey of the Development of Germany Since 1815.* 6th ed. NY: Capricorn, 1962.

Todd, Malcolm. *The Early Germans.* Oxford: Blackwell, 1992.

Verheyen, Dirk. *The German Question: A Cultural, Historical, and Geopolitical Exploration.* Boulder, CO: Westview, 1991.

MEDIEVAL GERMANY

Arnold, Benjamin. *German Knighthood 1050-1300.* Oxford: Clarendon Press, 1985.

Arnold, Benjamin. *Princes and Territories in Medieval Germany.* Cambridge: Cambridge University Press, 1991.

Barraclough, Geoffrey. *The Origins of Modern Germany.* Oxford: Basil Blackwell, orig. 1946, reissued 1988.

Burleigh, Michael. *Prussian Society and the German Order.* Cambridge: Cambridge University Press, 1984.

Chazan, Robert. *European Jewry and the First Crusade.* Berkeley: University of California Press, 1987.

Du Boulay, F.R.H. *Germany in the Later Middle Ages.* London: Athlone Press, 1983.

Fleckenstein, J. *Early Medieval Germany.* Oxford: North-Holland, 1978.

Fuhrmann, H. *Germany in the High Middle Ages.* Cambridge: Cambridge University Press, 1986.

Geary, Patrick J. *Before France and Germany: The Creation and Transformation of the Merovingian World.* Oxford: Oxford University Press, 1988.

Gillingham, J. *The Kingdom of Germany in the High Middle Ages.* London: The Historical Association, 1971.

Haverkamp, Alfred. *Medieval Germany, 1056-1273.* 2d. ed. Trans. by Helga Braun and Richard Mortimer. Oxford: Oxford University Press, 1992.

Leuschner, J. *Germany in the Later Middle Ages.* Oxford: North-Holland, 1979.

Leyser, K. *Medieval Germany and its Neighbours, 900-1250.* London: Hambledon Press, 1982.

McKitterick, Rosamond. *The Carolingians and the Written Word.* Cambridge: Cambridge University Press, 1989.

Stuard, Susan Mosher. *Women in Medieval History and Historiography.* Philadelphia: University of Pennsylvania Press, 1987.

Tacitus. *Agricola, Germany, Dialogue on Orators.* New York: The Library of Liberal Arts/ Bobbs-Merrill Co., 1967.

GERMANY, 1500-1648

Bak, J. ed. *The German Peasant War of 1525.* London: Frank Cass, 1976.

Benecke, G. *Society and Politics in Germany 1500-1800.* London: Routledge and Kegan Paul, 1974.

Blickle, Peter. *The Revolution of 1525. The German Peasants' War from a New Perspective.* Trans. by Thomas A. Brady, Jr. and H.C. Erik Midelfort. New Haven: Yale University Press, 1985.

Brendler, Gerhard. *Martin Luther. Theology and Revolution.* Trans. by Claude R. Foster, Jr. Oxford: Oxford University Press, 1991.

Carsten, F.L. *Princes and Parliaments in Germany.* Oxford: Clarendon Press, 1959.

Dickens, A.G. *The German Nation and Martin Luther.* Glasgow: Collins (Fontana), 1976.

Fichtner, Paula Sutter. *Protestantism and Primogeniture in Early Modern Germany.* New Haven: Yale University Press, 1989.

Hsia, R. Po-Chia. *The Myth of Ritual Murder: Jews and Magic in Reformation Germany.* New Haven: Yale University Press, 1988.

Karant-Nunn, Susan C. *Zwickau in Transition, 1500-1547: The Reformation as an Agent of Change.* Columbus, OH: Ohio State University Press, 1987.

Kouri, E.I. and Tom Scott, eds. *Politics and Society in Reformation Europe: Essays for Sir Geoffrey Elton on his Sixty-Fifth Birthday.* New York: St. Martin's, 1987.

Robisheaux, Thomas. *Rural Society and the Search for Order in Early Modern Germany.* Cambridge: Cambridge University Press, n.d.

Roper, Lyndal. *The Holy Household: Woman and Morals in Reformation Augsburg.* Oxford and New York: Clarendon Press, 1989.

Scott, Tom. *Freiburg and the Breisgau: Town-Country Relations in the Age of Reformation and Peasants' War.* Oxford: Clarendon Press, 1987.

Scott, Tom and R.W. Scribner, eds. *The German Peasants' War: A History in Documents.* Atlantic Highlands, NJ: Humanities Press, 1991.

Scribner, R.W. *The German Reformation.* London: MacMillan, 1986.

Scribner, R.W. *Popular Culture and Popular Movements in Reformation Germany.* London: Hambledon Press, 1987.

Scribner, R. and G. Benecke. *The German Peasant War 1525: New Viewpoints.* London: George Allen and Unwin, 1979.

GERMANY, 1648-1815

Abulafia, David. *Frederick II. A Medieval Emperor.* Oxford: Oxford University Press, 1992.

Beiser, Frederick C. *Enlightenment, Revolution, and Romanticism. The Genesis of Modern German Political Thought, 1790-1800.* Cambridge: Harvard University Press, 1992.

Berdahl, Robert M. *The Politics of Prussian Nobility. The Development of a Conservative Ideology, 1770-1848.* Princeton: Princeton University Press, n.d.

Blanning, T.C.W. *Reform and Revolution in Mainz, 1743-1803.* Cambridge: Cambridge University Press, 1974.

Blanning, T.C.W. *The French Revolution in Germany.* Oxford: Oxford University Press, 1983.

Bruford, W. *Germany in the Eighteenth Century.* Cambridge: Cambridge University Press, 1935.

Carlyle, Thomas. *History of Friedrich II of Prussia Called Frederick the Great.* Edited with introduction by John Clive. Chicago: University of Chicago Press, 1969.

Carsten, F.L. *The Origins of Prussia.* Oxford: Clarendon Press, 1954.

De Staël, Madame. *De L'Allemagne*. 2 vols. Paris: Garnier-Flammarion, 1968, first published in 1810.

Duffy, Christopher. *Frederick the Great. A Military Life*. New York: Routledge, 1988.

Fulbrook, Mary. *Piety and Politics: Religion and the Rise of Absolutism in England, Württemberg and Prussia*. Cambridge: Cambridge University Press, 1983.

Haffner, Sebastian. *The Rise and Fall of Prussia*. London: Weidenfeld and Nicolson, 1980.

Hampson, N. *The Enlightenment*. Harmondsworth: Penguin, 1968.

Hellmuth, Eckhart. *The Transformation of Political Culture. England and Germany in the Late Eighteenth Century*. Oxford: Oxford University Press, 1990.

Horn, D.B. *Frederick the Great and the Rise of Prussia*. New York: Perennial Library, 1964.

Hubatsch, W. *Frederick the Great*. London: Thames and Hudson, 1975.

Ingrao, C. *The Hessian Mercenary State. Ideas, Institutions and Reform under Frederick II 1760-1785*. Cambridge: Cambridge University Press, 1987.

La Vopa, Anthony J. *Grace, Talent and Merit: Poor Students, Clerical Careers, and Professional Ideology in Eighteenth-Century Germany*. Cambridge, New York, New Rochelle, Melbourne, Sydney: Cambridge University Press, 1988.

Lindemann, Mary. *Patriots and Paupers*. Oxford: Oxford University Press, 1990.

Parker, G., ed. *The Thirty Years War*. London: Routledge and Kegan Paul, 1984.

Pedlow, Gregory W. *The Survival of Hessian Nobility, 1770-1870.* Princeton: Princeton University Press, 1988.

Porter, R. and M. Teich, eds. *The Enlightenment in National Context.* Cambridge: Cambridge University Press, 1981.

Raeff, M. *The Well-ordered Police State.* London: Yale University Press, 1983.

Ritter, Gerhard. *Frederick the Great.* Berkeley: University of California Press, 1968.

Rosenberg, H. *Bureaucracy, Aristocracy, Autocracy.* Boston: Beacon Press, 1966.

Saine, Thomas P. *Von der Kopernikanischen bis zur Französischen Revolution: Die Auseinandersetzung der deutschen Frühaufklärung mit der neuen Zeit.* Berlin: Erich Schmidt, 1987.

Scott, H.M., ed. *Enlightened Absolutism: Reform and Reformers in Later Eighteenth Century Europe.* London: Macmillan, 1990.

Vann, J.A. *The Making of a State: Württemberg 1593-1793.* London: Cornell University Press, 1984.

Vierhaus, R. *Germany in the Age of Absolutism.* Cambridge: Cambridge University Press, 1988.

Whaley, J. *Religious Toleration and Social Change in Hamburg, 1529-1819.* Cambridge: Cambridge University Press, 1985.

GERMANY, 1815-1871

Bowman, Shearer Davis. *Masters and Lords. Mid-Nineteenth Century U.S. Planters and Prussian Junkers.* Oxford: Oxford University Press, 1993.

Gispen, Keis. *New Profession, Old Order. Engineers and German Society, 1815-1914.* Cambridge: Cambridge University Press, 1990.

Hamerow, T.S. *Restoration, Revolution, Reaction.* Princeton: Princeton University Press, 1966.

Hamerow, T.S. *The Social Foundations of German Unification, 1858-1871.* Princeton: Princeton University Press, 1969.

Hinners, Wolfgang. *Exil und Rückkehr: Friedrich Kapp in Amerika und Deutschland.* Stuttgart: Akademischer Verlag, 1987.

Howard, Michael. *The Franco-Prussian War. The German Invasion of France, 1870-1871.* New York: Routledge, 1981.

Krieger, Leonard. *The German Idea of Freedom. History of a Tradition From the Reformation to 1871.* Chicago: University of Chicago Press, 1957.

Liberles, Robert. *Conflict in Social Context: The Resurgence of Orthodox Judaism in Frankfurt am Main, 1838-1877.* Westport, CT: Greenwood, 1985.

Lüdtke, Alf. *Police and State in Prussia, 1815-1850.* Trans. by Pete Burgess. Cambridge: Cambridge University Press, 1989.

Moran, Daniel. *Toward the Century of Words: Johann Cotta and the Politics of the Public Realm in Germany, 1795-1832.* Berkeley and Los Angeles: University of California Press, 1990.

Mosse, W.E. *Jews in the German Economy: The German-Jewish Elite 1820-1835.* Oxford: Oxford University Press, 1987.

Ohles, Frederick. *Germany's Rude Awakening. Censorship in the Land of the Brothers Grimm.* Kent, OH: Kent State University Press, 1992.

Paret, Peter and Daniel Moran, eds. *Carl von Clausewitz: Historical and Political Writings.* Princeton: Princeton University Press, n.d.

Pedlow, Gregory W. *The Survival of the Hessian Nobility, 1770-1870.* Princeton: Princeton University Press, n.d.

Prelinger, Catherine M. *Charity, Challenge and Change: Religious Dimensions of the Mid-Nineteenth Century Women's Movement in Germany.* Westport, CT: Greenwood, 1987.

Schleunes, Karl A. *Schooling and Society: The Politics of Education in Prussia and Bavaria, 1750-1900.* Oxford: Berg, 1989.

Schulze, Hagen, ed. *Nation-Building in Central Europe.* Oxford: Berg, 1987.

Schulze, Hagen. *The Course of German Nationalism. From Frederick the Great to Bismarck 1763-1867.* Cambridge: Cambridge University Press, 1991.

Sorkin, David. *The Transformation of German Jewry, 1780-1840.* Oxford: Oxford University Press, 1990.

Sperber, Jonathan. *Popular Catholicism in Nineteenth-Century Germany.* Princeton: Princeton University Press, 1984.

Sperber, Jonathan. *Rhineland Radicals: The Democratic Movement and the Revolution of 1848-1849.* Princeton: Princeton University Press, 1991.

EMPIRE, 1871-1918

Adams, Carole Elizabeth. *Women Clerks in Wilhelmine Germany.* Cambridge: Cambridge University Press, 1989.

Albisetti, James C. *Schooling German Girls and Women: Secondary and Higher Education in the Nineteenth Century.* Princeton: Princeton University Press, 1989.

Barkin, Kenneth D. *The Controversy over German Industrialization.* Chicago: University of Chicago Press, 1970.

Berghahn, Volker. *Germany and the Approach of War.* London: Longmans, 1984.

Berghahn, Volker R. *Germany, 1871-1914. Economy, Society, Culture and Politics.* Oxford: Berg, 1993.

Berghahn, Volker R. and Wilhelm Deist, eds. *Rüstung in Zeitalter der wilhelminischen Weltpolitik: Grundlegende Dokumente 1890-1914.* Düsseldorf: Droste, 1988.

Bismarck, Otto von. *Gedanken und Erinnerungen.* Munich: Wilhelm Goldmann, 1989.

Blackbourn, David. *Populists and Patricians: Essays in Modern German History.* Boston: Allen & Unwin, 1987.

Blackbourn, David and G. Eley. *The Peculiarities of German History.* Oxford: Oxford University Press, 1984.

Blackbourn, David and Richard J. Evans, eds. *The German Bourgeoisie: Essays on the Social History of the German Middle Class From the Late Eighteenth to Early Twentieth Century.* New York: Routledge, 1991.

Bucholz, Arden. *Moltke, Schlieffen and Prussian War Planning.* Oxford: Berg, 1991.

Cecil, Lamar. *Wilhelm II--Prince and Emperor, 1859-1900.* Chapel Hill: University of North Carolina Press, 1990.

Coetzee, Marilyn Shevin. *The German Army League: Popular Nationalism in Wilhelmine Germany.* Oxford: Oxford University Press, 1990.

Doerries, Reinhard R. *Imperial Challenge. Ambassador Count Bernstorff.* Chapel Hill: University of North Carolina Press, 1989.

Dukes, Jack R. and Joachim Remak. *Another Germany. A Reconsideration of the Imperial Era.* Boulder, CO: Westview, 1987.

Erdmann, Karl Dietrich, ed. *Kurt Riezler. Tagebücher, Aufsätze, Dokumente.* Göttingen: Vandenhoeck & Ruprecht, 1972.

Evans, Richard J. *Society and Politics in Wilhelmine Germany.* London: Croom Helm, 1978.

Evans, Richard J. *Death in Hamburg: Society and Politics in the Cholera Years, 1830-1910.* Oxford: Clarendon Press, 1987.

Evans, Richard J. *Rethinking German History: Nineteenth-Century Germany and the Origins of the Third Reich.* London: Allen & Unwin, 1987.

Evans, Richard J. *Proletarians and Politics: Socialism and the Working Class in Germany before the First World War.* New York: St. Martin's, 1991.

Farrar, L. L., Jr. *The Short-War Illusion: German Policy, Strategy & Domestic Affairs August-December 1914.* Santa Barbara: Clio, 1973.

Feldman, Gerald D. *Army, Industry and Labour in Germany, 1914-1918.* Oxford: Berg, 1991.

Feldman, Gerald D. *The Great Disorder. Politics, Economics, and Society in the German Inflation, 1914-1924.* Oxford: Oxford University Press, 1993.

Fischer, Fritz. *Griff nach der Weltmacht. Die Kriegszielpolitik des kaiserlichen Deutschland 1914/1918.* 3rd ed. Düsseldorf: Droste, 1964. Published in English as *Germany's Aim in the First World War.* London: Chatto and Windus, 1967.

Fischer, Fritz. *Krieg der Illusionen. Die deutsche Politik von 1911 bis 1914.* Düsseldorf: Droste, 1969.

Fischer, Fritz. *World Power or Decline. The Controversy over Germany's War Aims in the First World War.* London: Weidenfeld and Nicolson, 1975.

Gall, Lothar. *The White Revolutionary.* Trans. by J.A. Underwood. 2 vols. London: Allen & Unwin, 1968-1987.

Gatzke, Hans W. *Germany's Drive to the West. A Study of Germany's Western War Aims During the First World War.* Baltimore: Johns Hopkins Press, 1950.

Gordon, J.C.B., ed. *German History and Society. Vol. 1: 1870-1920.* Oxford: Berg, 1985.

Guttmann, Barbara. *Weibliche Heimarmee: Frauen in Deutschland 1914-1918.* Weinheim: Dt. Studien, 1989.

Haffner, Sebastian. *The Ailing Empire: Germany from Bismarck to Hitler.* Trans. by Jean Steinberg. New York: Fromm International Publishing Corporation, 1989.

Herwig, Holger H. *"Luxury" Fleet: The Imperial German Navy, 1888-1918.* London: Ashfield Press, 1987.

Jarausch, Konrad H. *The Enigmatic Chancellor: Bethmann Hollweg and the Hubris of Imperial Germany.* New Haven: Yale University Press, 1973.

Jarausch, Konrad H. *Students, Society and Politics in Imperial Germany. The Rise of Academic Illiberalism.* Princeton: Princeton University Press, n.d.

John, Michael. *Politics and the Law in Late Nineteenth-Century Germany.* Oxford: Oxford University Press, 1989.

Kennan, George F. *The Decline of Bismarck's European Order. Franco-Prussian Relations 1875-1890.* Princeton: Princeton Univ. Press, 1979.

Kennedy, Paul M. *The Rise of the Anglo-German Antagonism 1860-1914.* London: The Ashfield Press, 1980.

Kennedy, Paul M. *The Rise and Fall of the Great Powers.* New York: Random House, 1987.

Kocha, Jürgen. *Facing Total War: German Society 1914-1918.* Trans. by Barbara Weinberger. Oxford: Berg, 1984.

Kohut, Thomas A. *Wilhelm II and the Germans. A Study in Leadership.* Oxford: Oxford University Press, 1991.

Lamberti, Marjorie. *State, Society, and the Elementary School in Imperial Germany.* Oxford: Oxford University Press, 1989.

Lentin. *Lloyd George, Woodrow Wilson and the Guilt of Germany: An Essay in the Prehistory of Appeasement.* Baton Rouge: Louisiana State University Press, 1985.

Lerman, Katherine Anne. *The Chancellor as Courtier; Bernhard von Bülow and the Governance of Germany, 1900-1909.* Cambridge: Cambridge University Press, 1990.

Lidtke, Vernon L. *The Outlawed Party: Social Democracy in Germany, 1878-1890.* Princeton: Princeton University Press, 1966.

Long, James W. *From Privileged to Dispossessed: The Volga Germans, 1860-1917.* Lincoln: University of Nebraska Press, 1988.

Luebke, Frederick C. *Germans in Brazil: A Comparative History of Cultural Conflict During World War I.* Baton Rouge: Louisiana State University Press, 1987.

Medlicott, W.N. *Bismarck and Modern Germany.* New York: Perennial Library, 1965.

Mitchell, Allan. *Revolution in Bavaria 1918-1919: The Eisner Regime and the Soviet Republic.* Princeton: Princeton University Press, 1965.

Mitchell, Allan. *The German Influence in France after 1870. The Formation of the French Republic.* Chapel Hill: University of North Carolina Press, 1979.

Mitchell, Allan. *Victors and Vanquished. The German Influence on Army and Church in France after 1870.* Chapel Hill: University of North Carolina Press, 1984.

Mitchell, Allan. *The Divided Path. The German Influence on Social Reform in France After 1870.* Chapel Hill: University of North Carolina Press, 1991.

Nichols, J. Alden. *The Year of the Three Kaisers: Bismarck and the German Succession, 1887-1888.* Champaign: University of Illinois Press, 1987.

Pflanze, Otto. *Bismarck and the Development of Modern Germany.* 3 vols. Princeton: Princeton University Press, 1963.

Remak, Joachim. *The Gentle Critic: Theodor Fontane and German Politics, 1848-1898.* Syracuse: Syracuse University Press, 1964.

Retallack, James N. *Notables of the Right: The Conservative Party and Political Mobilization in Germany, 1876-1918.* Boston: Unwin Hyman, 1988.

Ringer, Fritz K. *The Decline of the German Mandarins: The German Academic Community, 1890-1933.* Cambridge: Harvard University Press, 1969.

Rose, Paul Lawrence. *German Question-Jewish Question: Revolutionary Antisemitism in Germany from Kant to Wagner.* Princeton: Princeton University Press, 1992.

Schöllgen, Gregor. *Escape into War? The Foreign Policy of Imperial Germany.* Oxford: Berg, 1990.

Schorske, Carl E. *German Social Democracy 1905-1917: The Development of the Great Schism.* Cambridge: Harvard, 1955.

Sheehan, James J. *Imperial Germany.* New York: New Viewpoints, 1976.

Showalter, Dennis E. *Tannenberg: Clash of Empires.* Hamden, CT: Archon, 1991.

Smith, Woodruff D. *Politics and the Sciences of Culture in Germany.* Oxford: Oxford University Press, 1991.

Stern, Fritz. *Gold and Iron: Bismarck, Bleichröder, and the Building of the German Empire.* New York: Random House, 1979.

Stürmer, Michael. *Bismarck: Die Grenzen der Politik.* Munich: Piper, 1987.

Taylor, A.J.P. *Bismarck: The Man and the Statesman.* New York: Random House, 1967.

Thomas, Donald E. Jr. *Diesel Technology and Society in Industrial Germany.* Tuscaloosa: University of Alabama Press, 1987.

Thompson, Wayne C. *In the Eye of the Storm. Kurt Riezler and the Crises of Modern Germany.* Iowa City: University of Iowa Press, 1980.

Veblen, Thorsten. *Imperial Germany and the Industrial Revolution.* Ann Arbor, MI: University of Michigan Press, 1968, first printed 1915.

Volkov, Shulamit. *The Rise of Popular Antimodernism in Germany. The Urban Master Artisans, 1873-1896.* Princeton: Princeton University Press, 1978.

Weber-Kellermann, Ingeborg. *Frauenleben im 19. Jahrhundert: Empire u. Romantik, Biedermeier, Gründerzeit.* Munich: Beck, 1988.

Wehler, Hans-Ulrich. *The German Empire 1871-1918.* Oxford: Berg, 1985.

Weiss, Sheila Faith. *Race Hygiene and National Efficiency: The Eugenics of Wilhelm Schallmeyer.* Berkeley: University of California Press, 1987.

Wertheimer, Jack. *Unwelcome Strangers.* Oxford: Oxford University Press, 1991.

Wheeler-Bennett, John W. *Brest-Litovsk, The Forgotten Peace March 1918.* London: Macmillan, 1956.

Williamson, John G. *Karl Helfferich 1874-1924: Economist, Financier, Politician.* Princeton: Princeton University Press, 1971.

Young, Harry F. *Prince Lichnowsky and the Great War.* Athens: University of Georgia Press, 1977.

Zeman, Z.A.B., ed. *Germany and the Revolution in Russia 1915-1918: Documents from the Archives of the German Foreign Ministry.* Oxford: Oxford University Press, 1958.

WEIMAR REPUBLIC, 1919-1933

Abraham, David. *The Collapse of the Weimar Republic: Political Economy and Crisis.* 2nd ed. New York: Holmes & Meier, 1987.

Adams, Henry M. and Robin K. *Rebel Patriot: A Biography of Franz von Papen.* Santa Barbara: McNally and Loftin, 1987.

Barnouw, Dagmar. *Weimar Intellectuals and the Threat of Modernity.* Bloomington: Indiana University Press, 1988.

Bessel, Richard and E.J. Feuchtwanger, eds. *Social Change and Political Development in Weimar Germany.* Totowa, NJ: Barnes & Noble, 1981.

Braunthal, Gerard. *Socialist Labor and Politics in Weimar Germany: The General Federation of German Trade Unions.* Hamden, CT: Archon Books, 1978.

Breitman, Richard. *German Socialism and Weimar Democracy.* Chapel Hill: University of North Carolina Press, 1981.

Bridenthal, Renate, Anita Grossmann, and Marion Kaplan, eds. *When Biology Became Destiny: Women in Weimar and Nazi Germany.* New York: Monthly Review Press, 1984.

Broszat, Martin. *Hitler and the Collapse of Weimar Germany.* Oxford: Berg, 1991.

Caplan, Jane. *Government Without Administration: State and Civil Service in Weimar and Nazi Germany.* Oxford: Clarendon Press, 1989.

Carr, Edward Hallett. *German-Soviet Relations Between the Two World Wars, 1919-1939.* Baltimore: Johns Hopkins Press, 1951.

Carsten, F.L. *The Reichswehr and Politics, 1918-1933.* Oxford: Clarendon Press, 1966.

Diephouse, David J. *Pastors and Pluralism in Württemberg 1918-1933.* Princeton: Princeton University Press, 1987.

Evans, Richard J., ed. *The German Unemployed: Experiences and Consequences of Mass Unemployment from the Weimar Republic to the Third Reich.* New York: St. Martin's, 1987.

Eyck, Erich. *A History of the Weimar Republic.* 2 vols. New York: Athenaeum, 1970.

Fink, Carole, Alex Frohn, and Jürgen Heideking, eds. *Genoa, Rapallo, and European Reconstruction in 1922.* Cambridge: Cambridge University Press, 1991.

Fout, John C. ed. *Politics, Parties, and the Authoritarian State: Imperial Germany, 1878-1918.* New York: Holmes & Meier, 1991.

Fritzsche, Peter. *Rehearsals for Fascism: Populism and Political Mobilization in Weimar Germany.* Oxford: Oxford University Press, 1990.

Fromm, Erich. *The Working Class of Weimar Germany: A Psychological and Sociological Study.* Cambridge: Harvard University Press, 1984.

Gay, Peter. *Weimar Culture: The Outsider as Insider.* New York: Harper & Row, 1968.

Gilbert, Martin. *Britain and Germany between the Wars*. London: Longmans, 1964.

Gordon, Harold. *The Reichswehr and the German Republic, 1919-1926.* Princeton: Princeton University Press, 1957.

Gordon, J.C.B., ed. *German History and Society. Vol. 2: 1918-1945.* Oxford: Berg, 1989.

Guttsman, Wilhelm Leo. *Workers' Culture in Weimar Germany: Between Tradition and Commitment.* Oxford: Berg, 1990.

Halperin, S. William. *Germany Tried Democracy: A Political History of the Reich from 1918 to 1933.* Hamden, CT: Archon, 1963.

Herf, Jeffrey. *Reactionary Modernism: Technology, Culture and Politics in Weimar and the Third Reich.* Cambridge: Cambridge University Press, 1984.

Hermand, Jost. *Die Kultur der Weimarer Republik.* Frankfurt am Main: Fischer, 1989.

Hiden, J. *The Weimar Republic.* Harlow: Longman, 1974.

Holt, John. *German Agricultural Policy, 1918-1934.* Chapel Hill: University of North Carolina Press, 1936.

Hughes, Michael L. *Paying for the German Inflation.* Chapel Hill: University of North Carolina Press, 1988.

Hunt, Richard N. *German Social Democracy, 1918-1933.* New Haven: Yale University Press, 1964.

Jablonsky, David. *The Nazi Party in Dissolution. Hitler and the Verbotzeit, 1923-1925.* Portland: Frank Cass, 1989.

James, H. *The German Slump.* Oxford: Clarendon Press, 1986.

Jones, Larry Eugene. *German Liberalism and the Dissolution of the Weimar Party System, 1918-1933*. Chapel Hill: University of North Carolina Press, 1988.

Jonge, Alex de. *The Weimar Chronicle. Prelude to Hitler*. New York: New American Library, 1978.

Kent, Bruce. *The Spoils of War: The Politics, Economics, and Diplomacy of Reparations, 1918-1932*. Oxford: Clarendon, 1989.

Kershaw, Ian, ed. *Weimar: Why Did German Democracy Fail?* New York: St. Martin's, 1990.

Kolb, Eberhard. *The Weimar Republic*. London: Hutchinson, 1988.

Kruedener, Jürgen Baron von, ed. *Economic Crisis and Political Collapse: The Weimar Republic, 1924-1933*. Oxford: Berg, 1990.

Laqueur, Walter. *Weimar. A Cultural History 1918-1933*. New York: Capricorn Books, 1976.

Lebovics, Herman. *Social Conservatism and the Middle Classes in Germany, 1914-1933*. Princeton: Princeton University Press, 1969.

Lee, Marshall and Wolfgang Michalka. *German Foreign Policy 1917-1933: Continuity or Break?* Oxford: Berg, 1987.

Lyth, Peter J. *Inflation and the Merchant Economy. The Hamburg Mittelstand 1914-1924*. Oxford: Berg, 1990.

Maehl, William H. *The German Socialist Party: Champion of the First Republic, 1918-1933*. Philadelphia: American Philosophical Society, 1986.

Malone, Henry O. *Adam von Trott zu Solz. Werdegang eines Verschwörers, 1909-1938*. Berlin: Siedler, 1986.

Morgan, J.H. *Assize of Arms*. Oxford: Oxford University Press, 1946.

Morris, Benny. *The Roots of Appeasement. The British Weekly Press and Nazi Germany during the 1930s.* Portland: Frank Cass, 1991.

Mosse, George L. *Germans and Jews: The Right, the Left, and the Search for a "Third Force" in Pre-Nazi Germany.* New York: Fertig, 1970.

Nicholls, A. *Weimar and the Rise of Hitler.* 2nd ed. London: Macmillan, 1979.

Orlow, Dietrich. *Weimar Prussia, 1918-1925. The Unlikely Rock of Democracy.* Pittsburgh: University of Pittsburgh Press, 1985.

Orlow, Dietrich. *Weimar Prussia, 1925-1933. The Illusion of Strength.* Pittsburgh: University of Pittsburgh Press, 1991.

Pore, Renate. *A Conflict of Interest: Women in German Social Democracy, 1919-1933.* Westport, CT: Greenwood, 1981.

Ratliff, William G. *Faithful to the Fatherland: Julius Curtius and Weimar Foreign Policy.* (American University Studies, Series IX History, Vol. 62.) New York: Peter Lang, 1990.

Stachura, Peter D. *Nazi Youth in the Weimar Republic.* Santa Barbara, CA: Clio Books, 1975.

Stachura, Peter D. *The Weimar Republic and the Younger Proletariat: An Economic and Social Analysis.* New York: St. Martin's, 1989.

Stachura, Peter D. *Political Leaders in Weimar Germany. A Biographical Study.* New York: Simon & Schuster, 1993.

Turner, Henry Ashby, Jr. *Stresemann and the Politics of the Weimar Republic.* Princeton: Princeton University Press, 1963.

Waite, Robert G.L. *Vanguard of Nazism: The Free Corps Movement in Postwar Germany 1918-1923.* New York: Norton, 1969.

Webb, Steven B. *Hyperinflation and Stabilization in Weimar Germany.* Oxford: Oxford University Press, 1989.

Wheeler-Bennett, John W. *The Nemesis of Power: The German Army in Politics, 1918-1945.* 2nd ed. London: Macmillan, 1964.

Willett, J. *The New Sobriety: Art and Politics in the Weimar Period, 1917-33.* London: Thames and Hudson, 1978.

Williamson, David G. *The British in Germany, 1918-1930.* Oxford: Berg, 1991.

Winkler, Heinrich August. *Der Weg in Katastrophe: Arbeiter und Arbeiterbewegung in der Weimarer Republik 1930-1933.* Berlin/Bonn: Verlag J.H.W. Dietz, 1987.

THIRD REICH AND NATIONAL SOCIALISM, 1933-1945

Adler, Jacques. *The Jews of Paris and the Final Solution: Communal Response and Internal Conflicts, 1940-1944.* Oxford: Oxford University Press, 1987.

Allan, William Sheridan. *The Nazi Seizure of Power. The Experience of a Single German Town 1930-1935.* New York: New Viewpoints, 1973.

Avraham, Barkai. *Nazi Economics: Ideology, Theory, and Policy.* New Haven: Yale University Press, 1990.

Aycoberry, P. *The Nazi Question.* London: Routledge and Kegan Paul, 1981.

Baird, Jay W. *To Die for Germany: Heroes in the Nazi Pantheon.* Bloomington: Indiana University Press, 1990.

Balfour, Michael. *Withstanding Hitler.* London: Routledge and Kegan Paul, 1988.

Baranowski, Shelley. *The Confessing Church, Conservative Elites, and the Nazi State.* Lewiston, NY: The Edwin Mellen Press, 1987.

Barkai, Avraham. *Nazi Economics. Ideology, Theory and Policy.* Trans. by Ruth Hadass-Vashitz. New Haven: Yale University Press, 1990.

Barnett, Victoria. *For the Soul of the People. Protestant Protest Against Hitler.* Oxford: Oxford University Press, 1992.

Bar-On, Dan. *Legacy of Silence.* Cambridge: Harvard University Press, n.d.

Bauman, Zygmunt. *Modernity and the Holocaust.* Ithaca: Cornell University Press, n.d.

Bessel, Richard, ed. *Life in the Third Reich.* Oxford: Oxford University Press, 1987.

Bloch, Michael. *Ribbentrop.* New York: Crown Press, 1992.

Bracher, Karl Dietrich, Wolfgang Sauer, and Gerhard Schulz. *Die nationalsozialistische Machtergreifung.* Cologne: Westdeutscher Verlag, 1960.

Bracher, Karl Dietrich. *The German Dictatorship: The Origins, Structure, and Effects of National Socialism.* New York: Praeger, 1970.

Brandt, Willy. *In Exile: Essays, Reflections and Letters, 1933-1947.* Philadelphia: University of Pennsylvania Press, 1971.

Breitman, Richard. *The Architect of Genocide: Himmler and the Final Solution.* New York: Knopf, 1991.

Broszat, Martin. *The Hitler State.* London: Longman, 1981.

Browning, Christopher R. *Fateful Months. Essays on the Emergence of the Final Solution.* New York: Holmes & Meier, 1991.

Browning, Christopher R. *The Path to Genocide. Essays on Launching the Final Solution.* Cambridge: Cambridge University Press, 1992.

Browning, Christopher R. *Ordinary Men: Reserve Police Battalion 101 and the Final Solution in Poland.* Scranton: Harper Collins, 1992.

Bull, H. ed. *The Challenge of the Third Reich.* Oxford: Clarendon Press, 1986.

Bullock, Alan. *Hitler: A Study in Tyranny.* Rev. ed. New York: Harper & Row, 1963.

Burdick, Charles B. *An American Island in Hitler's Reich: The Bad Neuheim Internment.* Menlo Park, CA: Markgraf Publications, 1987.

Burleigh, Michael. *Germany Turns Eastwards.* Cambridge: Cambridge University Press, 1990.

Burleigh, Michael and Wolfgang Wipperman. *The Racial State. Germany 1933-1945.* Cambridge: Cambridge University Press, 1991.

Carr, William. *Hitler: A Study in Personality and Politics.* London: Edward Arnold, 1978.

Childers, Thomas. *The Nazi Voter: The Social Foundations of Fascism in Germany, 1919-1933.* Chapel Hill: University of North Carolina Press, 1983.

Childers, Thomas and Jane Caplan, eds. *Reevaluation of the Third Reich.* New York: Holmes & Meier, 1992.

Corni, Gustavo. *Hitler and the Peasants. Agrarian Policy of the Third Reich, 1930-1939.* Oxford: Berg, 1990.

Crankshaw, Edward. *Gestapo: Instrument of Tyranny.* London: Putnam, 1956.

Crome, Len. *Unbroken: Resistance and Survival in the Concentration Camps.* London: Schocken, 1989.

Dagrelle, Leon. *Hitler: Born at Versailles.* Costa Mesa, CA: Institute for Historical Review, 1987.

Deutsch, Harold C. *The Conspiracy Against Hitler in the Twilight War.* Minneapolis: University of Minnesota Press, 1968.

Edinger, Lewis. *German Exile Politics.* Berkeley: University of California Press, 1956.

Ericksen, Robert P. *Theologians Under Hitler. Gerhard Kittel, Paul Althaus, and Emanuel Hirsch.* New Haven: Yale University Press, 1985.

Feig, Konnilyn. *Hitler's Death Camps. The Sanity of Madness.* New York: Holmes & Meier, 1991.

Fest, Joachim C. *Hitler.* New York: Random House, 1975.

Fischer, Conan. *The German Communists and the Rise of Nazism.* New York: St. Martin's, 1991.

Fleming, G. *Hitler and the Final Solution.* London: Hamish Hamilton, 1975.

Flood, Charles Bracelen. *Hitler: The Path to Power.* New York: Houghton Mifflin, 1990.

Freeden, Herbert. *The Jewish Press in the Third Reich.* Oxford: Berg, 1992.

Freeman, M. *Atlas of Nazi Germany.* London: Croom Helm, 1987.

Friedlander, Saul, ed. *Probing the Limits of Representation--Nazism and the "Final Solution".* Cambridge: Harvard University Press, 1991.

Gellately, Robert. *The Gestapo and German Society: Enforcing Racial Policy 1933-1945.* Oxford: Oxford University Press, 1990.

Gilbert, Martin. *The Holocaust.* London: Collins, 1986.

Giles, Geoffrey J. *Students and National Socialism in Germany.* Princeton: Princeton University Press, 1985.

Gillingham, John. *Industry and Politics in the Third Reich: Ruhr Coal, Hitler and Europe.* New York: Columbia University Press, 1985.

Gordon, Sarah. *Hitler, Germans, and the "Jewish Question".* Princeton: Princeton University Press, 1984.

Graml, H., et al. *The German Resistance to Hitler.* London: Batsford, 1970.

Grosshans, Henry. *Hitler and the Artists.* New York: Holmes & Meier, 1991.

Grunberger, R. *A Social History of the Third Reich.* Harmondsworth: Penguin, 1971.

Haffner, Sebastian. *The Meaning of Hitler.* Cambridge: Harvard University Press, 1983.

Hale, Oron J. *The Captive Press in the Third Reich.* Princeton: Princeton University Press, 1964.

Hamilton, Richard F. *Who Voted for Hitler?* Princeton: Princeton University Press, 1982.

Hart, B.H. Liddell. *The German Generals Talk.* New York: William Morrow, 1948.

Hayward, N.F. and D.S. Morris. *The First Nazi Town.* New York: St. Martin's, 1988.

Hiden, J. and J. Farquharson. *Explaining Hitler's Germany.* London: Batsford, 1983.

Hilberg, Raul. *The Destruction of the European Jews.* Rev. ed. 3 vols. New York: Holmes & Meier, 1985.

Hirschfeld, Gerhard and L. Kettenacker, eds. *The 'Führer State': Myth and Reality.* Stuttgart: Klett-Cotta, 1981.

Hirschfeld, Gerhard and Patrick Marsh, eds. *Collaboration in France: Politics and Culture during the Nazi Occupation, 1940-1944.* Oxford: Berg, 1989.

Hitler, Adolf. *Mein Kampf.* Trans. by Ralph Manheim. Boston: Houghton-Mifflin, 1971.

Hoffmann, Peter. *The History of the German Resistance, 1933-1945.* Cambridge: Harvard University Press, 1977.

Hoffmann, Peter. *German Resistance to Hitler.* Cambridge: Harvard University Press, 1988.

Jarman, Thomas L. *The Rise and Fall of Nazi Germany.* New York: Signet/ New American Library, 1961.

Kater, Michael H. *Doctors under Hitler.* Chapel Hill: University of North Carolina Press, 1990.

Kele, Max. *Nazis and Workers: National Socialist Appeals to German Labor, 1919-1933.* Chapel Hill: University of North Carolina Press, 1972.

Kershaw, Ian. *Popular Opinion and Political Dissent in the Third Reich.* Oxford: Clarendon Press, 1983.

Kershaw, Ian. *The Nazi Dictatorship.* London: Edward Arnold, 1985.

Kershaw, Ian. *The "Hitler Myth": Image and Reality in the Third Reich.* Oxford: Clarendon Press, 1987.

Klein, Burton H. *Germany's Economic Preparations for War.* Cambridge: Harvard University Press, 1959.

Klemperer, Klemens von. *German Resistance Against Hitler. The Search for Allies Abroad, 1938-1945.* Oxford: Oxford University Press, 1992.

Koch, H.W. *In the Name of the Volk: Political Justice in Hitler's Germany.* New York: St. Martin's, 1989.

Kogon, Eugen. *The Theory and Practice of Hell: The German Concentration Camps and the System Behind Them.* New York: Berkeley, 1950. Reprint. New York: Octagon Books, 1973.

Koonz, Claudia. *Mothers in the Fatherland: Women, the Family, and Nazi Politics.* New York: St. Martin's, 1987.

Kropat, Wolf-Arno. *Kristallnacht in Hessen: Der Judenpogrom von November 1938.* Wiesbaden: Komm. Gesch. Juden, 1988.

Laqueur, Walter. *The Terrible Secret.* Harmondsworth: Penguin, 1980.

Large, David Clay, ed. *Contending with Hitler: Varieties of German Resistance in the Third Reich.* Cambridge: Cambridge University, 1992.

Lewy, Guenter. *The Catholic Church and Nazi Germany.* London: Weidenfeld & Nicolson, 1964.

Lochner, Louis P. *Tycoons and Tyrants: German Industry from Hitler to Adenauer.* Chicago: Regnery, 1954.

Longerich, Peter. *Propagandisten im Krieg: Die Presseabteilung des Auswärtigen Amtes unter Ribbentrop.* Munich: R. Oldenbourg Verlag, 1987.

Maier, Charles S. *The Unmasterable Past: History, Holocaust, and German National Identity.* Cambridge: Harvard University Press, 1988.

Maier, Klaus A., Horst Rohde, Bernd Stegemann, and Hans Umbreit. *Germany and the Second World War. Vol II: Germany's Initial Conquests in Europe.* Oxford: Oxford University Press, 1991.

Manstein, Peter. *Die Mitglieder und Wähler der NSDAP 1919-1933: Untersuchungen zu ihrer schichtmäßigen Zusammensätzung.* New York: Peter Lang, 1988.

Marrus, Michael R. *The Holocaust in History.* Hanover: University Press of New England, 1987.

Maser, Werner. *Hitler's Letters and Notes.* New York: Harper & Row, 1974.

Mason, Tim. *Social Policy in the Third Reich. The Working Class and the 'National Community', 1918-1939.* Trans. by John A. Broadwin. Oxford: Berg, 1992.

Mayer, Milton. *They Thought They Were Free. The Germans 1933-45.* Chicago: University of Chicago Press, 1955.

McKale, Donald M. *Curt Prüfer: German Diplomat from the Kaiser to Hitler.* Kent, OH: Kent State University Press, 1987.

McKale, Donald M., ed. *Rewriting History: The Original and Revised World War II Diaries of Curt Prüfer, Nazi Diplomat.* Kent, OH: The Kent State University Press, 1988.

Meinecke, Friedrich. *The German Catastrophe: The Social and Historical Influences which Led to the Rise and Ruin of Hitler and Germany.* Boston: Beacon, 1963.

Merkl, Peter H. *Political Violence under the Swastika. 581 Early Nazis.* Princeton: Princeton University Press, 1975.

Middlebrook, Martin. *The Berlin Raids: R.A.F. Bomber Command Winter 1943-44.* Also *The Schweinfurt-Regensburg Mission: American Raids on 17 August 1943.* Both New York: Penguin, 1990.

Mierzejewski, Alfred C. *The Collapse of the German War Economy, 1944-1945: Allied Air Power and the German National Railway.* Chapel Hill: University of North Carolina Press, 1988.

Milfull, John. *Why Germany? National Socialist Antisemitism and the European Context.* Oxford: Berg, 1992.

Mitchell, Otis C. *Hitler's Nazi State: The Years of Dictatorial Rule, 1934-1945.* New York: Peter Lang, 1988.

Mommsen, Hans. *From Weimar to Auschwitz.* Princeton: Princeton University Press, 1991.

Mosse, George L. *Masses and Man: Nationalist and Fascist Perceptions of Reality.* Detroit: Wayne State University Press, 1987.

Mühlberger, Detlef. *Hitler's Followers: Studies in the Society of the Nazi Movement.* New York: Routledge, 1991.

Müller, Ingo. *Hitler's Justice: The Courts of the Third Reich.* Trans. by Deborah Lucas Schneider. Cambridge: Harvard University Press, 1991.

Müller, Klaus-Jürgen. *The Army, Politics and Society in Germany 1933-1945.* New York: St. Martin's, 1987.

Mulligan, Timothy. *The Politics of Illusion and Empire: German Occupation Policy in the Soviet Union, 1942-1943.* New York: Praeger, 1988.

Naumann, Bernd. *Auschwitz.* New York: Frederic A. Praeger, 1966.

Neumann, Franz. *Behemoth: The Structure and Practice of National Socialism, 1933-1944.* 2nd ed. with new appendix. New York: Octagon Books, 1963.

Nicosia, Francis R. and Lawrence D. Stokes, eds. *Germans Against Nazism. Noncompliance, Opposition and Resistance in the Third Reich.* Oxford: Berg, 1990.

Noakes, Jeremy and Geoffrey Pridham, eds. *Nazism.* 3 vols. Exeter: Exeter Studies in History, 1983, 1984, 1988.

Noakes, Jeremy and Geoffrey Pridham, eds. *Nazism 1919-1945: A Documentary Reader: Vol. 3: Foreign Policy, War and Racial Extermination.* Atlantic Highlands, NJ: Humanities Press International, 1988.

Nolte, Ernst. *Der europäische Bürgerkrieg, 1917-1945: Nationalsozialismus und Bolschewismus.* Berlin: Propyläen, 1987.

Orlow, Dietrich. *The History of the Nazi Party, 1919-1933.* 2 vols. Pittsburgh: University of Pittsburgh Press, 1969, 1973.

Overy, R. *The Nazi Economic Recovery, 1932-38.* London: Macmillan, 1982.

Pehle, Walter H., ed. *November 1938: From 'Kristallnacht' to Genocide.* Oxford: Berg, 1991.

Peterson, Edward N. *The Limits of Hitler's Power.* Princeton: Princeton University Press, 1969.

Peukert, D. *Inside Nazi Germany.* London: Batsford, 1987.

Phayer, Michael. *Protestant and Catholic Women in Nazi Germany.* Detroit, MI: Wayne State University Press, 1990.

Proctor, Robert N. *Racial Hygiene: Medicine under the Nazis.* Cambridge: Harvard University Press, 1988.

Reiche, Eric G. *The Development of the SA in Nürnberg, 1922-1934.* Cambridge: Cambridge University Press, 1986.

Reinhardt, Klaus. *Moscow: The Turning Point?* Oxford: Berg, 1992.

Remak, Joachim, ed. *The Nazi Years--A Documentary History.* Englewood Cliffs, NJ: Prentice Hall, 1969.

Rempel, Gerhard. *Hitler's Children: The Hitler Youth and the SS.* Chapel Hill: University of North Carolina Press, 1989.

Ritter, Gerhard. *The German Resistance: Carl Goerdeler's Struggle against Tyranny.* New York: Praeger, 1958.

Roberts, Geoffrey. *The Unholy Alliance: Stalin's Pact with Hitler.* Bloomington: Indiana University Press, 1989.

Rosenberg, Alan and Gerald E. Myers, eds. *Echoes from the Holocaust: Philosophical Reflections on a Dark Time.* Philadelphia: Temple University Press, 1988.

Rothbrust, Florian K. *Guderian's XIXth Panzer Corps and the Battle of France: Breakthrough in the Ardennes, May 1940.* New York: Praeger, 1990.

Rothfels, Hans. *The German Opposition to Hitler: An Appraisal.* 2nd ed. Chicago: Regnery, 1963.

Rückerl, Adalbert. *NS-Verbrechen vor Gericht.* Heidelberg: C. F. Müller, 1982.

Ruhl, Klaus-Jörg. *Unsere verlorenen Jahre: Frauenalltag in Kriegs- u. Nachkriegszeit 1939-1949 in Berichten, Dokumenten u. Bildern.* Darmstadt: Luchterhand, 1985.

Schoenbaum, David. *Hitler's Social Revolution: Class and Status in Nazi Germany.* Garden City: Doubleday, 1966.

Schulte, Theo. *The German Army and Nazi Policies in Occupied Russia.* Oxford: Berg, 1990.

Schumann, Willy. *Being Present. Growing up in Hitler's Germany.* Kent, OH: The Kent State University Press, 1992.

Schweitzer, Arthur. *Big Business in the Third Reich.* Bloomington: Indiana University Press, 1965.

Scobie, Alex. *Hitler's State Architecture: the Impact of Classical Antiquity.* University Park: Pennsylvania State University Press, 1990.

Sereny, Gitta. *Into that Darkness: An Examination of Conscience.* New York: Random House, 1983.

Shirer, William L. *Berlin Diary. The Journal of a Foreign Correspondent 1934-1941.* New York: Alfred A. Knopf, 1941.

Shirer, William L. *The Rise and Fall of the Third Reich: A History of Nazi Germany.* New York: Simon & Schuster, 1960.

Shirley, Dennis. *The Politics of Progressive Education--The Odenwaldschule in Nazi Germany.* Cambridge: Harvard University Press, 1992.

Simpson, William. *Hitler and Germany. Documents and Commentary.* Cambridge: Cambridge University Press, 1991.

Smelser, Ronald. *Robert Ley: Hitler's Labour Front Leader.* Oxford: Berg, 1988.

Smith, Arthur L., Jr. *Hitler's Gold. The Story of the Nazi War Loot.* Oxford: Berg, 1989.

Smith, Bradley F. *The Road to Nuremberg.* New York: Basic Books, 1981.

Smith, Woodruff D. *The Ideological Origins of Nazi Imperialism.* Oxford: Oxford University Press, 1986.

Snell, John L., revised by Allan Mitchell. *The Nazi Revolution. Hitler's Dictatorship and the German Nation.* Lexington, MA: D.C. Heath, 1973.

Snyder, Louis L., ed. *The Third Reich, 1933-1945: A Bibliographical Guide to German National Socialism.* New York: Garland, 1987.

Speer, Albert. *Inside the Third Reich: Memoirs.* New York: Macmillan, 1970. Reprint. New York: Collier Books, 1981.

Speier, Hans. *German White-Collar Workers and the Rise of Hitler.* New Haven: Yale University Press, 1987.

Spiegelman, Art. *Maus: A Survivor's Tale.* 2 vols. New York: Pantheon, 1991.

Stachura, Peter, ed. *The Shaping of the Nazi State.* London: Croom Helm, 1978.

Stachura, Peter, ed. *The Nazi Machtergreifung.* London: Allen and Unwin, 1983.

Steiger, Rudolph. *Armour Tactics in the Second World War. The Panzer Army Campaigns of 1939-41 in German War Diaries.* Oxford: Berg, 1991.

Steinberg, Jonathan. *All or Nothing: The Axis and the Holocaust 1941-1943.* New York: Routledge, 1990.

Stephenson, J. *The Nazi Organization of Women.* London: Croom Helm, 1981.

Stieg, Margaret F. *Public Libraries in Nazi Germany.* Tuscaloosa: University of Alabama Press, 1992.

Stoakes, Geoffrey. *Hitler and the Quest for World Dominion. Nazi Ideology and Foreign Policy in the 1920s.* Oxford: Berg, 1987.

Stroop, Juergen. *The Stroop Report: The Jewish Quarter of Warsaw Is No More!* New York: Pantheon, 1979.

Sykes, Christopher. *Tormented Loyalty: The Story of a German Patriot who Defied Hitler.* (Adam von Trott zu Solz). New York: Harper & Row, 1969.

Syndor, Charles W. Jr. *Soldiers of Destruction. The SS Death Head Division, 1933-1945.* Princeton: Princeton University Press, 1990.

Szepansky, Gerda. *"Blitzmädel", "Heldenmutter", "Kriegerwitwe": Frauenleben im 2. Weltkrieg.* Frankfurt am Main: Fischer, 1986.

Taylor, Telford. *Sword and Swastika: Generals and Nazis in the Third Reich.* New York: Simon & Schuster, 1952.

Trevor-Roper, H.R. *The Last Days of Hitler.* 6th ed. Chicago: University of Chicago Press, 1992.

Troller, Norbert. *Theresienstadt: Hitler's Gift to the Jews.* Trans. by Susan E. Cernyak-Spatz. Chapel Hill: University of North Carolina Press,1991.

Turner, Henry Ashby, Jr., ed. *Nazism and the Third Reich.* New York: Quadrangle Books, 1972.

Turner, Henry Ashby, Jr. *German Big Business and the Rise of Hitler.* Oxford: Oxford University Press, 1985.

Turner, Henry Ashby, Jr., ed. *Hitler--Memoirs of a Confidant.* New Haven: Yale University Press, 1985.

Vassiltchikov, Marie. *The Berlin Diaries, 1940-1945.* New York: Random House, 1988.

Von Klemperer, Klemens. *German Resistance Against Hitler: The Search for Allies Abroad, 1938-1945.* Oxford: Oxford University Press, 1992.

Walker, Mark. *German National Socialism and the Quest for Nuclear Power, 1939-1949.* Cambridge: Cambridge University Press, 1990.

Weinberg, Gerhard L. *The Foreign Policy of Hitler's Germany: Starting World War II, 1937-1939.* Chicago: University of Chicago Press, 1980.

Weindling, Paul. *Health, Race and German Politics between National Unification and Nazism, 1870-1945.* Cambridge: Cambridge University Press, 1989.

Weingartner, James J. *Crossroads of Death: The Story of the Malmedy Massacre and Trial.* Berkeley: University of California Press, 1979.

Wette, Wolfram, Hans-Erich Volkman, Wilhelm Deist, and Manfred Messerschmidt. *Germany and the Second World War. Volume I: The*

Build-Up of German Aggression. Oxford: Oxford University Press, 1990.

Whealey, Robert H. *Hitler and Spain: The Nazi Role in the Spanish Civil War, 1936-1939.* Lexington: University Press of Kentucky, 1989.

Ziegler, Herbert F. *Nazi Germany's New Aristocracy: The SS-Leadership, 1925-1939.* Princeton: Princeton University Press, 1988.

Zitelmann, Rainer. *Adolf Hitler: Eine politische Biographie.* Göttingen: Muster-Schmidt, 1989.

ALLIED OCCUPATION, 1945-1949

Almond, Gabriel A., ed. *The Struggle for Democracy in Germany.* New York: Russell & Russell, 1965.

Botting, Douglas. *From the Ruins of the Reich. Germany 1945-1949.* New York: New American Library, 1986.

Broszat, Martin, Klaus-Dietmar Henke, and Hans Woller, eds. *Von Stalingrad zur Währungsreform: Zur Sozialgeschichte des Umbruchs in Deutschland.* Munich: R. Oldenbourg, 1989.

Buscher, Frank M. *The U.S. War Crimes Trial Program in Germany, 1946-1955.* New York: Praeger, 1989.

Clay, Lucius D. *Decision in Germany.* New York: Doubleday, 1950.

Clay, Lucius D. *The Papers of General Lucius D. Clay.* Vol. 1, Jean Edward Smith, ed. Bloomington, IN: Indiana University Press, 1974.

Davidson, Eugene. *The Death and Life of Germany: An Account of the American Occupation.* New York: Knopf, 1959.

Davidson, Eugene. *The Trial of the Germans: An Account of the Twenty-two Defendants before the International Military Tribunal at Nuremberg.* New York: Macmillan, 1966.

Davidson, W. Philips. *The Berlin Blockade.* Princeton: Princeton University Press, 1958.

de Zayas, Alfred M. *Nemesis at Potsdam: The Anglo-Americans and the Expulsion of the Germans.* Rev. ed. London: Routledge, 1979.

Diefendorf, Jeffry M. *In the Wake of War. The Reconstruction of German Cities After World War II.* Oxford: Oxford Univ. Press, 1993.

Dulles, Allen W. *The Marshall Plan.* New York: St. Martin's, 1992.

Ebsworth, Raymond. *Restoring Democracy in Germany: The British Contribution.* London: Stevens, 1961.

Farquharson, John F. *The Western Allies and the Politics of Food. Agrarian Management in Postwar Germany.* Oxford: Berg, 1985.

Freymond, J. *The Saar Conflict, 1949-1955.* London: Stevens, 1960.

Gimbel, John. *A German Community under American Occupation: Marburg, 1945-52.* Stanford: Stanford University Press, 1952.

Gimbel, John. *The American Occupation of Germany: Politics and the Military.* Stanford: Stanford University Press, 1968. Also, *Science, Technology, and Reparations: Exploitation and Plunder in Postwar Germany.* Stanford: Stanford Univ. Press, 1990.

Gollancz, Victor. *In Darkest Germany.* Hinsdale, IL: H. Regnery, 1947.

Hearnden, Arthur, ed. *The British in Germany.* London, 1978.

Kuklick, Bruce. *American Policy and the Division of Germany: The Clash with Russia over Reparations.* Ithaca: Cornell Univ. Press, 1972.

Litchfield, Edward H. et al. *Governing Postwar Germany.* Ithaca: Cornell University Press, 1953.

Maier, Charles, ed. w. Günter Bischof. *The Marshall Plan and Germany.* Oxford: Berg, 1991.

German newspapers are sold in Aachen for the first time since end of war, June 1945. (*Source:* GCML)

U.S. soldiers distributing food in Badersdorf, December 1945. (*Source:* GCML)

Merritt, Anna J. and Richard L. Merritt. *Public Opinion in Occupied Germany: The OMGUS Surveys, 1945-1949*. Urbana: University of Illinois Press, 1970.

Morgenthau, Henry, Jr. *Germany Is Our Problem*. New York: Harper and Brothers, 1945.

Nettl, J.P. *The Eastern Zone and Soviet Policy in Germany*. New York: Hippocrene Books, 1977.

Noelle-Neumann, Elisabeth and Renate Köcher. *Die verletzte Nation*. Stuttgart: Deutsche Verlags-Anstalt, 1987.

Peterson, Edward N. *The American Occupation of Germany: Retreat to Victory*. Detroit: Wayne State University Press, 1977.

Peterson, Edward N. *The Many Faces of Defeat. The German People's Experience in 1945*. New York: Peter Lang, 1990.

Rodnick, David. *Postwar Germans: An Anthropologist's Account*. New Haven: Yale University Press, 1948.

Sanford, Gregory W. *From Hitler to Ulbricht: The Communist Reconstruction of East Germany 1945-46*. Princeton: Princeton University Press, 1983.

Schwarz, Thomas A. *America's Germany: John J. McCloy and the Federal Republic of Germany*. Cambridge: Harvard University, 1991.

Sharp, Tony. *The Wartime Alliance and the Zonal Division of Germany*. Oxford: Clarendon Press, 1975.

Smith, Jean Edward. *Lucius D. Clay: An American Life*. New York: Holt, 1990.

Snell, John N. *Wartime Origins of the East-West Dilemma over Germany*. New Orleans: Hauser Press, 1959.

Stares, Paul. *Allied Rights and Legal Constraints on German Military Power.* Washington, D.C.: Brookings Institution Occas. Paper, 1990.

Tent, James F. *Mission on the Rhine: Reeducation and Denazification in American-Occupied Germany.* Chicago: University of Chicago, 1982.

Turner, Ian D., ed. *Reconstruction in Postwar Germany. British Occupation Policy and the Western Zones, 1945-1955.* Oxford: Berg, 1989.

Willis, F. Roy. *The French in Germany, 1945-1949.* Stanford: Stanford University Press, 1962.

Wolfe, Robert, ed. *Americans as Proconsuls: United States Military Government in Germany and Japan, 1944-1952.* Carbondale, IL: Southern Illinois University Press, 1984.

GERMAN DEMOCRATIC REPUBLIC AND COMMUNISM

Abraham, Richard. *Rosa Luxemburg. A Life for the International.* Oxford: Berg, 1989.

Allen, Bruce. *Germany East. Dissent and Opposition.* Concord, MA: Black Rose Press, 1991.

Bahne, Siegfried. *Die KPD und das Ende von Weimar.* Frankfurt am Main: Campus, 1976.

Bahro, Rudolf. *The Alternative in Eastern Europe.* London: New Left Books, 1978.

Bahro, Rudolf. *From Red to Green.* New York: Routledge Chapman & Hall, 1984.

Baring, Arnulf M. *Uprising in East Germany: June 17, 1953.* Ithaca: Cornell University Press, 1972.

Baylis, Thomas. *The Technical Intelligentsia and the East German Elite.* Berkeley: University of California Press, 1974.

Bell, David S. *Western European Communists and the Collapse of Communism.* Chapter on Germany by Heinrich Bortfeldt and Wayne C. Thompson. Oxford: Berg, 1993.

Bentley, Raymond. *Research and Technology with the Former GDR.* Boulder, CO: Westview, 1992.

Bortfeldt, Heinrich. *Von der SED zur PDS. Wandlung zur Demokratie?* Bonn: Bouvier, 1992.

Bronner, Stephen Eric. *Rosa Luxemburg: A Revolutionary for Our Times.* New York: Columbia University Press Morningside Edition, 1987.

Bryson, Phillip J. and Manfred Melzer. *The End of the East German Economy. From Honecker to Reunification.* New York: St. Martin's, 1992.

Buber, Margarete. *Under Two Dictators.* London: Victor Gollanz, 1949.

Childs, David, ed. *Honecker's Germany.* London: Allen & Unwin, 1985.

Childs, David. *The GDR: Moscow's German Ally.* 2nd ed. New York: Harper Collins Academics, 1988.

Childs, David, Thomas A. Baylis, Erwin L. Collier, and Marilyn Rueschemeyer. *East Germany in Comparative Perspective.* London: Routledge, 1989.

Dennis, Mike. *German Democratic Republic: Politics, Economics and Society.* New York: Columbia University Press, 1988.

Duhnke, Horst. *Die KPD von 1933 bis 1945.* Cologne: Kiepenheuer & Witsch, 1972.

Edwards, G.E. *GDR Society and Social Institutions.* London: Macmillan, 1985.

Fischer, Ernst. *An Opposing Man.* London: Allen, 1974.

Fischer, Ruth. *Stalin and German Communism.* Cambridge: Harvard University Press, 1948.

Forster, Thomas M. *The East German Army: The Second Power in the Warsaw Pact.* Boston: Allen & Unwin, 1980.

Freyberg, Jutta von. *Sozialdemokraten und Kommunisten.* Cologne: Rugenstein, 1973.

Fricke, Karl Wilhelm. *Zur Menschen- und Grundrechtssituation politischer Gefangener in der DDR.* Cologne: Verlag Wissenschaft und Politik, 1986.

Gay, Peter. *The Dilemma of Democratic Socialism. Eduard Bernstein's Challenge to Marx.* New York: Collier Books, 1962.

Geber, Margy, ed. *Studies in GDR Culture and Society, 8 Selected Papers from the Thirteenth New Hampshire Symposium on the German Democratic Republic.* New York and London: University Press of America, 1988.

Gedmin, Jeffrey. *The Hidden Hand. Gorbachev and the Collapse of East Germany.* Lanham, MD: AEI, 1992.

Gerber, Margy et al., eds. *Studies in GDR Culture and Society: Selected Papers from the Fourteenth New Hampshire Symposium on the German Democratic Republic.* Lanham, MD: University Press of America, 1989.

Gillen, Eckhart and Rainer Haarmann. *Kunst in der DDR.* Cologne: Kiepenheuer u. Witsch, 1990.

Goeckel, Robert F. *The Lutheran Church and the East German State: Political Conflict and Change under Ulbricht and Honecker.* Ithaca: Cornell University Press, 1990.

Gross, Babette. *Willi Münzenberg.* E. Lansing: Michigan State University Press, 1974.

Grunenberg, Antonia. *Aufbruch der inneren Mauer: Politik und Kultur in der DDR 1971-1990*. Bremen: Ed. Temmen, 1990.

Hacker, Jens. *Deutsche Irrtümmer. Schönfarber und Helfershelfer der SED-Diktatur im Westen*. Berlin: Verlag Ullstein, 1992.

Hamilton, Richard F. *The Bourgeois Epoch: Marx and Engels on Britain, France, and Germany*. Chapel Hill: University of North Carolina Press, 1991.

Hangen, Welles. *The Muted Revolution: East Germany's Challenge to Russia and the West*. New York: Knopf, 1966.

Hanhardt, Arthur M., Jr. *The German Democratic Republic*. Baltimore: Johns Hopkins Press, 1968.

Hay, Julius. *Born 1900. Memoirs*. LaSalle, IL: Open Court, 1975.

Helwig, Gisela, ed. *Die letzten Jahre der DDR: Texte zum Alltagsleben*. Cologne: Wissenschaft und Politik, 1990.

Heym, Stefan. *5 Tage im Juni* (novel). Frankfurt am Main: Fischer Taschenbuch, 1990, first published 1974.

Holzweissig, Gunter. *Militärwesen in der DDR*. Berlin: Holzapfel, 1985.

Hopf, Helmuth and Brunhilde Sonntag. *Im Osten nichts Neues? : Zur Musik der DDR*. Wilhelmshaven: Noetzel, 1989.

Iggers, Georg, ed. *Marxist Historiography in Transformation. New Orientations in Recent East German History*. Trans. by Bruce Little. Oxford: Berg, 1991.

Institut für Geschichte der Arbeiterbewegung. *In den Fängen der NKWD*. Berlin: Dietz, 1991.

Ketzel, Eberhard. *DDR-Wirtschaft: Befunde, Probleme, Perspektiven*. Stuttgart: Deutsche Sparkassenverlag, 1990.

Klier, Freya. *"Lüg Vaterland" Erziehung in der DDR.* Munich: Kindler, 1990.

Kolinsky, Eva, ed. *Youth in East and West Germany.* London: Association for Modern German Studies, 1985.

Krisch, Henry. *German Politics under Soviet Occupation.* New York: Columbia University Press, 1974.

Krisch, Henry. *The German Democratic Republic: The Search for Identity.* Boulder, CO: Westview, 1985.

Kuhrt, Eberhard and Henning von Löwis. *Griff nach der deutschen Geschichte: Erbaneignung und Traditionspflege in der DDR.* Paderborn: Ferdinand Schöningh, 1988.

Legters, Lyman H., ed. *The German Democratic Republic: A Developed Socialist Society.* Boulder, CO: Westview, 1978.

Lehmann, Hans Georg. *Chronik der DDR, 1945/49 bis heute.* Munich: C.H. Beck, 1987.

Leonhard, Wolfgang. *Child of the Revolution.* Chicago: Henry Regnery, 1958. Originally published as *Die Revolution entlässt ihre Kinder.* Cologne: Kiepenheuer und Witsch, 1955.

Leonhard, Wolfgang. *Das kurze Leben der DDR: Berichte und Kommentare aus 4 Jarhzehnten.* Stuttgart: Deutsche Verlags-Anstalt, 1990.

Leptin, Gert and Manfred Melzer. *Economic Reform in East German Industry.* Oxford, 1978.

Lippmann, Heinz. *Honecker and the New Politics of Europe.* New York: Macmillan, 1972.

Löw, Konrad, ed. *Beharrung und Wandel: die DDR und die Reformen des Mikhail Gorbatschow.* Berlin: Duncker u. Humblot, 1990.

Ludz, Peter C. *The GDR from the Sixties to the Seventies.* Harvard Center for International Affairs: Occasional Papers in International Affairs, no. 26, November 1970.

Ludz, Peter C. *The Changing Party Elite in East Germany.* Cambridge: MIT Press, 1972.

Mallinckrodt, Anita M. *The Environmental Dialogue in the GDR: Literature, Church, Party, and Interest Groups in the Socio-Political Context.* Lanham, MD: University Press of America, 1987.

Mayenburg, Ruth von. *Blaues Blut und Rote Fahnen.* Vienna: Fritz Molden, 1969.

Mayenburg, Ruth von. *Hotel Lux.* Munich: C. Bertelsmann, 1978.

McAdams, A. James. *East Germany and Detente: Building Authority after the Wall.* Cambridge: Cambridge University Press, 1985.

McAdams, A. James. *Germany Divided. From the Wall to Reunification.* Princeton: Princeton University Press, 1993.

McCauley, Martin. *Marxism-Leninism in the German Democratic Republic: The Socialist Unity Party (SED).* New York: Barnes & Noble Books, 1979.

McCauley, Martin. *The German Democratic Republic Since 1945.* London: Macmillan, 1983.

Millar, Peter. *Tomorrow Belongs To Me.* Bloomsbury, 1992.

Mitter, Armin and Stefan Wolle, eds. *Ich liebe euch doch alle! Befehle und Lageberichte des MfS Januar-November 1989.* Berlin: Basis Druck, 1990.

Phillips, Ann L. *Soviet Policy toward East Germany Reconsidered: The Postwar Decade.* Westport, CT: Greenwood, 1986.

Phillips, Ann L. *Seeds of Change in the German Democratic Republic: The SED-SPD Dialogue.* American Institute for Contemporary German Studies Research Reports #1. Washington, D.C.: AICGS, 1989.

Przybylski, Peter. *Tatort Politbüro. Die Akten Honecker.* Berlin: Rowohlt, 1991.

Rudzio, Wolfgang. *Die Erosion der Abgrenzung: Zum Verhältnis zwischen der demokratischen Linken und Kommunisten in der Bundesrepublik Deutschland.* Opladen: Westdeutscher Verlag, 1988.

Rueschemeyer, Meyer and Christiane Lemke, eds. *The Quality of Life in the German Democratic Republic: Changes and Developments in a State Socialist Society.* Armonk, NY: M.E. Sharpe, 1989.

Sandford, Gregory W. *From Hitler to Ulbricht: The Communist Reconstruction of East Germany, 1945-46.* Princeton: Princeton University Press, 1983.

Scharf, C. Bradley. *Politics and Change in East Germany.* Boulder, CO: Westview, 1984.

Shaffer, Harry G. *Women in the Two Germanies: A Comparative Study of a Socialist and a Non-Socialist Society.* New York: Pergamon Press, 1981.

Smith, Duncan. *Walls and Mirrors: Western Representations of Really Existing German Socialism in the German Democratic Republic.* Lantham,MD: University Press of America, 1988.

Smith, Jean Edward. *Germany beyond the Wall.* Boston: 1969.

Solberg, Richard W. *God and Caesar in East Germany: The Conflicts of Church and State in East Germany since 1945.* New York: Macmillan, 1961.

Sontheimer, Kurt and Wilhelm Bleek. *The Government and Politics of East Germany.* New York: St. Martin's, 1976.

Starrels, John M. and Anita M. Mallinckrodt. *Politics in the German Democratic Republic.* New York: Praeger, 1975.

Stasi Intern: Macht und Banalität. Ed. by Bürgerkomitee Leipzig. Leipzig: Forum, 1991.

Steele, Jonathan. *Inside East Germany: The State that Came In From the Cold.* New York: Horizon Books, 1977.

Thomaneck, J.K.A. and James Mellis, eds. *Politics, Society and Government in the German Democratic Republic: Basic Documents.* New York: St. Martin's, 1989.

Tudor, H. and M. Tudor, eds. and trans. *Marxism and Social Democracy: The Revisionist Debate 1896-1898.* Cambridge: Cambridge University Press, 1988.

Von Beyme, K. and H. Zimmermann, eds. *Policymaking in the German Democratic Republic.* Aldershot: Gower, 1984.

Wawryzn, Lionhard. *Der Blaue. Das Spitzelsystem der DDR.* Berlin: Verlag Klaus Wagenbach, 1991.

Weber, Hermann, ed. *DDR: Dokumente zur Geschichte der Deutschen Demokratischen Republik 1945-1985.* Munich: Deutscher Taschenbuch Verlag, 1986.

Weber, Hermann. *Die DDR 1945-1986.* Munich: Oldenbourg, 1988.

Weber, Hermann. *"Weisse Flecken" in der Geschichte. Die KPD-Opfer der Stalinschen Säuberungen und ihre Rehabilitierung.* Frankfurt am Main: ISP-Verlag, 1989.

Weber, Hermann. *DDR. Grundriss der Geschichte. Die abgeschlossene Geschichte der DDR. 1949-1990.* Hanover: Fackelträger Verlag, 1991.

Wilkening, Christina. *Staat im Staat: Auskünfte ehemaliger Stasi-Mitarbeiter.* Berlin: Aufbau Verlag, 1990.

Woods, R. *Opposition in the GDR under Honecker, 1971-85.* London: Macmillan, 1986.

Wroblewsky, Clement. *"Da wachste eines Morgens uff und hast 'nen Bundeskanzler": wie DDR-Bürger über ihre Zukunft denken.* Hamburg: Rasch u. Röhring, 1990.

Zieger, Gottfried. *Die Haltung von SED und DDR zur Einheit Deutschlands 1949-1987.* Cologne: Verl. Wiss. u. Pol., 1988.

THE FEDERAL REPUBLIC

GENERAL SOURCES

Alleman, Fritz Rene. *Bonn ist nicht Weimar.* Cologne: Kiepenheuer & Witsch, 1956.

Ardagh, John. *Germany and the Germans: After Unification.* New Rev. ed. New York: Penguin Books, 1991.

Atlantic Brücke. *Civil Liberties and the Defense of Democracy against Extremists and Terrorists: A Report on the West German Situation.* Freiburg: Rombach, 1980.

Bailey, George. *Germans: The Biography of an Obsession.* Rev. ed. New York: Free Press, 1991.

Balfour, Michael. *West Germany: A Contemporary History.* New York: St. Martin's, 1982.

Baring, Arnulf. *Machtwechsel. Die Ära Brandt-Scheel.* Stuttgart: Deutsche Verlags-Anstalt, 1982.

Berghahn, Volker R. *Modern Germany: Society, Economy and Politics in the Twentieth Century.* 2nd ed. Cambridge: Cambridge University Press, 1987.

Betz, Hans-Georg. *Postmodern Politics in Germany. The Politics of Resentment.* New York: St. Martin's, 1991.

Beyer, Rolf A. *Deutschland Heute. Politik - Wirtschaft - Gesellschaft. Ein Studien- und Arbeitsbuch zur Deutschen Landeskunde.* Oxford: Berg, 1989.

Beyme, Klaus von. *Die politische Elite in der Bundesrepublik Deutschland.* Munich: Piper, 1977.

Beyme, Klaus von. *The Political System of the Federal Republic of Germany.* New York: St. Martin's, 1983.

Beyme, Klaus von and Manfred Schmidt. *Policy and Politics in the Federal Republic of Germany.* London: Gower, 1985.

Bloch, Ernst. *Heritage of Our Times.* Oxford: Oxford University Press, 1991.

Bölling, Klaus. *Republic in Suspense: Politics, Parties, and Personalities in Postwar Germany.* New York: Praeger, 1964.

Bulmer, Simon and William Paterson. *The Federal Republic of Germany and the European Community.* London: Allen & Unwin, 1987.

Burdick, Charles, Hans-Adolf Jacobsen, and Winfried Kudszus, eds. *Contemporary Germany: Politics and Culture.* Boulder, CO: Westview, 1984.

Conradt, David P. *The German Polity.* 5th ed. New York: Longman, 1992.

Dalton, Russell J. *Politics in Germany.* 2nd ed. New York: Harper Collins, 1993.

Derbyshire, Ian. *Politics in Germany from Division to Unification.* New York: Chambers Kingfisher Graham Publishers, 1992.

Detwiler, Donald S. and Ilse E. Detwiler. *West Germany: The Federal Republic of Germany.* Santa Barbara: Clio Press, 1987.

Diem, Aubrey. *The New Germany: Land, People, Economy.* Waterloo, ON: Media International, 1991.

Edinger, L. *West German Politics.* New York: Columbia University Press, 1986.

Eich, Hermann. *Germans.* New York: Stein and Day, 1980.

Ellwein, Thomas, et al, eds. *Ploetz. Die Bundesrepublik Deutschland.* Freiburg: Ploetz, 1985.

Ellwein, Thomas. *Die Bundesrepublik seit den sechziger Jahren.* Munich: Deutscher Taschenbuch Verlag, 1989.

Esche, Falk, ed. *Handbuch der deutschen Bundesländer.* Frankfurt am Main: Campus, 1990.

Fout, John C., ed. *German Women in the Nineteenth Century.* New York: Holmes & Meier, 1984.

Fulbrook, Mary. *The Two Germanies 1945-1990.* Atlantic Highlands, NJ: Humanities Press, 1992.

Gelpel, Gary L., ed. *Germany in a New Era.* Indianapolis: Hudson Institute, 1993.

Geschichte der Deutschen: 1949-1990. Eine Chronik zu Politik, Wirschaft und Kultur. Frankfurt am Main: Insel, n.d.

Golay, John F. *The Founding of the Federal Republic of Germany.* Chicago: University of Chicago Press, 1958.

Goldman, Guido, Andrei Markovits, Lily Gardner Feldman, and Diane Kent, eds. *German Politics and Society.* Issues 16 and 17. Cambridge: Harvard University Press, 1989.

Grosser, Alfred. *Germany in Our Time: A Political History of the Postwar Years.* New York: Praeger, 1971.

Hancock, M. Donald. *West Germany: The Politics of Democratic Corporatism.* Chatham, NJ: Chatham House, 1989.

Herbst, Ludolf and Constantin Goschler, eds. *Wiedergutmachung in der Bundesrepublik Deutschland.* Munich: R. Oldenbourg, 1989.

Hillgruber, Andreas. *Deutsche Geschichte 1945-1986 : die "deutsche Frage" in der Weltpolitik.* Stuttgart: Kohlhammer, 1989.

Hiscocks, Richard. *The Adenauer Era.* Philadelphia: Lippincott, 1966. Reprint. Westport, CT: Greenwood, 1975.

Hoffmann, Alexander. *Die neuen deutschen Bundesländer.* Stuttgart: Bonn Aktuell, 1991.

Hoffmann-Lange, Ursula, ed. *Social and Political Structures in West Germany: From Authoritarianism to Postindustrial Democracy.* Boulder, CO: Westview, 1991.

Hofmann-Göttig, J. *Emanzipation mit dem Stimmzettel, 70 Jahre Frauenwahlrecht in Deutschland.* Bonn: Verlag Neue Gesellschaft, 1986.

Horne, Alistair. *Return to Power: A Report on the New Germany.* New York: Praeger, 1956.

Humphreys, Peter J. *Media and Media Policy in West Germany: The Press and Broadcasting since 1945.* Oxford: Berg, 1990.

Iggers, George G. *The Social History of Politics.* New York: St. Martin's, 1987.

Jacobeit, Sigrid and Wolfgang Jacobeit. *Illustrierte Alltagsgeschichte des deutschen Volkes.* 2 vols. Vienna: Globus, 1986-87.

Katzenstein, Peter J. *West Germany's Internal Security Policy. State and Terrorism in the 1970s and 1980s.* Ithaca: Cornell University, 1991.

Kistler, Helmut. *Die Bundesrepublik Deutschland. Vorgeschichte und Geschichte 1945-1983.* Bonn: Schriftenreihe der Bundeszentrale für politische Bildung, 1985.

Klessmann, Christoph. *Die doppelte Staatsgründung. Deutsche Geschichte 1945-1955.* Bonn: Schriftenreihe der Bundeszentrale für politische Bildung, 1986.

Klessmann, Christoph. *Zwei Staaten, eine Nation: Deutsche Geschichte 1955-1970.* Göttingen: Vandenhoeck and Ruprecht, and Bonn: Schriftenreihe der Bundeszentrale für politische Bildung, 1988.

Koch, Karl. *West Germany Today.* London: Routledge, 1989.

Kolinsky, Eva, ed. *The Federal Republic of Germany: The End of an Era.* Oxford: Berg, 1991.

Kolinsky, Eva, ed. *The Federal Republic of Germany. Innovation and Continuity at the Threshold of the 1990s.* Oxford: Berg, 1991.

Kommers, Donald P. *The Constitutional Jurisprudence of the Federal Republic of Germany.* Durham: Duke University Press, 1989.

Laqueur, Walter. *Germany Today: A Personal Report.* London: Weidenfeld & Nicolson, 1985.

Lilge, Herbert. *Deutschland 1945-1963.* Hanover: Verlag für Literatur und Zeitgeschehen, 1967.

Livingston, Robert Gerald, ed. *West German Political Parties.* German Issues 4. Washington, D.C.: American Institute for Contemporary German Studies, 1986.

Loewenthal, Nessa P. *Update Federal Republic of Germany.* Yarmouth: Intercultural Press, 1990.

Lützeler, Paul Michael, ed. *Western Europe in Transition. West Germany's Role in the European Community.* Baden-Baden: Nomos, 1986.

Marsh, David. *The Germans: The Pivotal Nation. A People at the Crossroads.* New York: St. Martin's, 1990.

Marshall, Barbara. *The Origins of Postwar German Politics.* London: Routledge, 1988.

Mattox, Gale A. and Bradley Shingleton, eds. *Germany at the Crossroads. Foreign and Domestic Policy Issues.* Boulder, CO: Westview, 1992.

Merkl, Peter H. *The Origins of the West German Republic.* Oxford: Oxford University Press, 1965.

Merkl, Peter H., ed. *The Federal Republic at Forty.* New York: New York University Press, 1989.

Nipperday, Thomas. *Thinking about Germany.* Oxford: Berg, 1990.

Paterson, William E. and Gordon Smith. *The West German Model: Perspectives on a Stable State.* London: F. Cass, 1981.

Paterson, William E. and David Southern. *Governing Germany.* New York: W. W. Norton, 1991.

Rosenzweig, Peter, ed. *Von Brandt, Willy bis Weigel, Theo: Daten zur Person. 200 Politiker aus West und Ost.* Berlin: Verlag der Nation, 1990.

Rotfeld, Adam Daniel and Walther Stutzle. *Germany and Europe in Transition.* Oxford: Oxford University Press, 1991.

Schweitzer, Carl-Christoph and Detlev Karsten, eds. *The Federal Republic of Germany and EC Membership Evaluated.* New York: St. Martin's, 1990.

Smith, Gordon, William E. Paterson, Peter H. Merkl, and Stephen Padgett, eds. *Developments in German Politics.* Durham: Duke University Press, 1992.

Stares, Paul B., ed. *The New Germany and the New Europe.* Washington D.C.: Brookings, 1992.

Stern, Susan, ed. *Meet United Germany.* 2 vols. Frankfurt am Main: Frankfurter Allgemeine Zeitung, Handbook 1991/2.

Turner, Henry A. *The Two Germanies since 1945.* New Haven: Yale University Press, 1987. Revised edition: *Germany from Partition to Reunification.* New Haven, 1992.

Wallach, H.G. Peter and George K. Romoser, eds. *Politics in the Mid-Eighties.* New York: Praeger, 1985.

Watson, Alan. *The Germans.* London: Thames Methuen, 1992.

Weidenfeld, Werner and Karl-Rudolf Korte. *Die Deutschen. Profil einer Nation.* Stuttgart: Klett-Cotta, 1991.

BIOGRAPHIES, AUTOBIOGRAPHIES, MEMOIRS, INTERVIEWS

Adenauer, Konrad. *Memoirs 1945-1959.* London: Weidenfeld and Nicolson, 1965.

Adenauer, Konrad. *Memoirs 1945-1953.* Chicago: Henry Regnery, 1966.

Adenauer, Konrad. *Erinnerungen.* 4 vols. Frankfurt am Main: Fischer, 1967-1970.

Alexander, Edgar. *Adenauer and the New Germany: The Chancellor of the Vanquished.* New York: Farrar, Straus and Cudahy, 1957.

Andert, Reinhold and Wolfgang Herzberg. *Der Sturz. Erich Honecker im Kreuzverhör.* Berlin/Weimar: Aufbauverlag, 1990.

Apel, Hans. *Bonn, den... Tagebuch eines Bundestagsabgeordneten.* Cologne: Kiepenheuer & Witsch, 1972.

Apel, Hans. *Der Abstieg.* Stuttgart: Deutsche Verlags-Anstalt, 1990.

Appel, Reinhard. *Gefragt: Herbert Wehner.* Bonn: Berto Verlag, 1969.

Barzel, Rainer. *Auf dem Drahtseil.* Munich: Droemer Knaur, 1978.

Barzel, Rainer. *Geschichten aus der Politik.* Frankfurt am Main: Ullstein, 1987.

Binder, David. *The Other German. Willy Brandt's Life and Times.* Washington, D.C.: New Republic Book Company, 1975.

Bölling, Klaus. *Bonn von aussen betrachtet.* Stuttgart: Deutsche Verlags-Anstalt, 1986.

Borkowski, Dieter. *Erich Honecker.* Munich: Bertelsmann, 1987.

Brandt, Willy, and Richard Löwenthal. *Ernst Reuter.* Munich: Kindler, 1957.

Brandt, Willy. *People and Politics. The Years 1960-1975.* Boston: Little, Brown, 1976.

Brandt, Willy. *Links und Frei. Mein Weg 1930-1950.* Hamburg: Hoffmann und Campe, 1982.

Brandt, Willy. *My Life in Politics.* New York: Penguin, 1992.

Brecht, Arnold. *The Political Education of Arnold Brecht. An Autobiography 1884-1970.* Princeton: Princeton University Press, 1970.

Bronner, Stephen Eric. *Rosa Luxemburg. A Revolutionary for Our Times.* New York: Columbia University Press, 1987.

Carr, Jonathan. *Helmut Schmidt: Helmsman of Germany.* London: Weidenfeld & Nicolson, 1985.

Chickering, Roger. *Karl Lamprecht. A German Academic Life (1865-1915).* Atlantic Highlands, NJ: Humanities Press, 1993.

Draht, Viola Herms. *Willy Brandt.* Radnor, PA: Chilton, 1975.

Dutschke, Rudi. *Mein langer Marsch. Reden, Schriften und Tagebücher aus zwanziger Jahren.* Reinbek: Rowohlt, 1980.

Eppler, Erhard. *Einsprüche. Zeugnisse einer politischen Biographie.* Freiburg: Dreisam, 1986.

Freudenhammer, Alfred and Karlheinz Vater. *Herbert Wehner. Ein Leben mit der Deutschen Frage.* Munich: Bertelsmann, 1978.

Gall, L. *Bismarck: The White Revolutionary.* London: Allen & Unwin, 1985.

Gaus, Günther. *Staatserhaltende Opposition oder Hat die SPD kapituliert? Gespräche mit Herbert Wehner.* Reinbeck bei Hamburg: Rowohlt Taschenbuch, 1966.

Gehlen, Reinhard. *The Service. The Memoirs of General Reinhard Gehlen.* New York: Popular Library, 1972.

Gerstenmaier, Eugen. *Streit und Friede hat seine Zeit. Ein Lebensbericht.* Frankfurt am Main: Propyläen, 1981.

Glotz, Peter. *Kampagne in Deutschland. Politisches Tagebuch 1981-1983.* Hamburg: Hoffmann und Campe, 1986.

Guttenberg, Karl Theodor Freiherr von und zu. *Fussnoten.* Stuttgart: Seewald, 1971.

Hamilton, Nigel. *The Brothers Mann.* London: Secker & Warburg, 1978.

Honecker, Erich. *Aus meinem Leben.* Berlin: Dietz, 1981.

Hutchinson, Peter. *Stefan Heym, The Perpetual Dissident.* Cambridge: Cambridge University Press, 1992.

Jahn, Gerhard, ed. *Herbert Wehner, Wandel und Bewährung.* Frankfurt am Main: J.H.W. Dietz Nachf., 1968.

Jahn, Gerhard, ed. *Herbert Wehner. Beiträge zu einer Biographie.* Cologne: Kiepenheuer & Witsch, 1976.

Jahn, Gerhard, ed. *Herbert Wehner Zeugnis.* Cologne: Kiepenheuer & Witsch, 1982.

Kessler, Harry Graf. *Tagebücher 1918-1937.* Frankfurt am Main: Im Insel, 1961.

Kiesinger, Kurt Georg. *Dunkle und helle Jahre. Erinnerungen 1904-58.* Ed. by Reinhard Schmoechtel. Stuttgart: Deutsche Verlags-Anstalt, 1989.

Koch, Peter. *Willy Brandt.* Berlin: Ullstein, 1988.

Krause-Burger, Sibylle. *Helmut Schmidt. Aus der Nähe gesehen.* Düsseldorf: Econ, 1980.

Krone, Heinrich. *Aufzeichnungen zur Deutschland- und Ostpolitik 1959-1969.* In Rudolf Morsey and Konrad Repgen, eds. *Veröffentlichungen der Kommission zur Zeitgeschichte.* Reihe B: Forschungen, Band 15. Mainz: Matthias-Grünewald, n.d.

Kühn, Heinz. *Aufbau und Bewährung.* Hamburg: Hoffmann und Campe, 1981.

MacDonogh, Giles. *A Good German. Adam von Trott zu Solz.* Woodstock, NY: The Overlook Press, 1992.

McGhee, George. *At the Creation of a New Germany. From Adenauer to Brandt. An Ambassador's Account.* New Haven: Yale University Press, 1989.

Mende, Erich. *Von Wende zu Wende. 1962-1982.* Munich: Herbig, 1986.

Oberndörfer, Dieter, ed. *Kurt Georg Kiesinger. Die Grosse Koalition 1966-1969.* Stuttgart: Deutsche Verlags-Anstalt, 1979.

Prittie, Terence. *Konrad Adenauer, 1876-1967.* London: Stacey, 1972.

Prittie, Terence. *Willy Brandt: Portrait of a Statesman.* New York: Schocken Books, 1974.

Renger, Annemarie. *Fasziniert von Politik.* Stuttgart: Seewald, 1981.

Runge, Irene and Uwe Stelbrink. *Gregor Gysi: "Ich Bin Opposition".* Berlin: Dietz, 1990.

Schabowski, Günter. *Das Politbüro. Ende eines Mythos. Eine Befragung.* Edited by Sieren, Frank, and Ludwig Koehne. Hamburg: Rowohlt, 1990.

Scheidemann, Philipp. *Memoiren eines Sozialdemokraten.* Dresden: Carl Reissner, 1928.

Schmid, Carlo. *Erinnerungen.* Munich: Scherz, 1979.

Schmidt, Helmut. *Menschen und Mächte.* Berlin: Siedler, 1987. English translation by Ruth Hein: *Men and Powers--A Political Retrospective.* New York: Random House, 1990.

Schmidt, Helmut. *Die Deutschen und ihre Nachbarn.* Berlin: Siedler, 1990.

Schmidthammer, Jens. *Rechtsanwalt Wolfgang Vogel. Mittler zwischen Ost und West.* Hamburg: Hoffmann und Campe, 1987.

Scholz, Günther. *Herbert Wehner.* Düsseldorf: Econ, 1986.

Schroeder, Karsten. *Egon Bahr.* Rastatt: Arthur Moewig, 1988.

Seebacher-Brandt, Brigitte. *Ollenhauer--Biedermann und Patriot.* Berlin: Siedler, 1984.

Soell, Hartmut. *Fritz Erler--Eine politische Biographie.* 2 vols. Bonn-Bad Godesberg: J.H.W. Dietz, 1976.

Soell, Hartmut. *Der junge Wehner. Zwischen revolutionärem Mythos und praktischer Vernunft.* Stuttgart: Deutsche Verlags-Anstalt, 1991.

Speer, Albert. *Spandau. The Secret Diaries.* New York: Macmillan, 1976.

Stachura, Peter P. *Political Leaders in Weimar Germany. A Biographical Study.* New York: Simon & Schuster, 1993.

Stern, Carola. *Ulbricht.* New York: Praeger, 1965.

Sternburg, Wilhelm von. *Adenauer. Eine deutsche Legende.* Frankfurt am Main: Athenäum, 1987.

Stirtz, Maria. *Heinrich von Brentano.* Darmstadt: J.G. Bläschke, 1970.

Strauss, Franz Josef. *Die Erinnerungen.* Berlin: Siedler, 1989.

Terjung, Knut, ed. *Der Onkel. Herbert Wehner in Gesprächen und Interviews.* Hamburg: Hoffmann und Campe, 1986.

Thompson, Wayne C. *In the Eye of the Storm. Kurt Riezler and the Crises of Modern Germany.* Iowa City: University of Iowa Press, 1980.

Thompson, Wayne C. *The Political Odyssey of Herbert Wehner.* Boulder, CO: Westview, 1993.

Uschner, Manfred. *Egon Bahr. Ein Leben für Deutschland.* Berlin: Dietz, 1991.

Vosske, Heinz. *Walter Ulbricht. Biographischer Abriss.* Berlin: Dietz, 1984.

Weymar, Paul. *Adenauer: His Authorized Biography.* New York: Dutton, 1957.

Wighton, Charles. *Adenauer: A Critical Biography.* New York: Coward-McCann, 1964.

Wischnewski, Hans-Jürgen. *Mit Leidenschaft und Augenmass.* Munich: Bertelsmann, 1989.

THE EXECUTIVE

Chaput de Saintonge, Rolland A.A. *Public Administration in Germany: A Study in Regional and Local Administration in Land Rheinland-Pfalz.* London: Weidenfeld & Nicolson, 1971.

Dönhoff, Marion Gräfin. *Foe into Friend: The Makers of the New Germany from Konrad Adenauer to Helmut Schmidt.* London: Weidenfeld & Nicolson, 1982.

Dyson, Kenneth H.F. *Party, State and Bureaucracy in Western Germany.* Beverly Hills: Sage, 1978.

Johnson, Nevil. *Government in the Federal Republic of Germany: The Executive at Work.* London: Pergamon Press, 1973.

Koerfer, Daniel. *Kampf ums Kanzleramt. Erhard und Adenauer.* Stuttgart: Deutsche Verlags-Anstalt, 1987.

Prittie, Terence. *The Velvet Chancellors: A History of Post-War Germany.* London: Frederick Müller, 1979.

Richard von Weizsäcker im Gespräch mit Gunter Hoffmann und Werner A. Perger. Frankfurt am Main: Eichborn, 1992.

Schmidt, Helmut. *Helmut Schmidt: Perspectives on Politics.* Edited by Wolfram F. Hanrieder. Boulder, CO: Westview, 1982.

Schoenbaum, David. *The Spiegel Affair.* Garden City, NY: Doubleday, 1968.

Sternburg, Wilhelm von, ed. *Die deutschen Kanzler von Bismarck bis Schmidt.* Königstein/ Ts: Athenäum, 1985.

PARLIAMENT, COURTS, PUBLIC POLICY, FEDERALISM AND LOCAL GOVERNMENT

Blair, Philip M. *Federalism and Judicial Review in West Germany.* Oxford: Clarendon Press, 1981.

Braunthal, Gerard. *The West German Legislative Process: A Case Study of Two Transportation Bills*. Ithaca: Cornell University Press, 1972.

Bulmer, Simon, ed. *The Changing Agenda of West German Public Policy*. Aldershot, England: Gower, 1989.

Burkett, Tony and S. Schuettemeyer. *The West German Parliament*. London: Butterworths, 1982.

Burns, Rob and Wilfried van der Will. *Protest and Democracy in West Germany: Extra-Parliamentary Opposition and the Democratic Agenda*. New York: St. Martin's, 1988.

Dorondo, D.R. *Bavaria and German Federalism*. New York: St. Martin's, 1992.

Gunlicks, Arthur B. *Local Government in the German Federal System*. Durham: Duke University Press, 1986.

Hallet, Graham. *The Social Economy of West Germany*. New York: St. Martin's, 1973.

Hattenhauer, Hans. *Zwischen Hierarchie und Demokratie*. Karlsruhe: C.F. Müller, 1971.

Hucko, Elmar M., ed. *The Democratic Tradition. Four German Constitutions*. Oxford: Berg, 1989.

Jeffrey, Charlie and Peter Savigear, eds. *German Federalism Today*. New York: St. Martin's, 1991.

Katzenstein, Peter. *Policy and Politics in West Germany: The Growth of a Semi-sovereign State*. Philadelphia: Temple University Press, 1987.

Kirchof, Paul and Donald P. Kommers. *Germany and Its Basic Law*. Baden-Baden: Nomos 1993.

Kommers, Donald P. *Judicial Politics in West Germany: A Study of the Federal Constitutional Court*. Beverly Hills, CA: Sage, 1976.

Kommers, Donald S. *The Constitutional Jurisprudence of the Federal Republic of Germany.* Durham: Duke University Press, 1990.

Livingston, Robert and Uwe Thaysen, eds. *The Congress and the Bundestag: A Comparison.* Boulder, CO: Westview, 1988.

Loewenberg, Gerhard. *Parliament in the German Political System.* Ithaca: Cornell University Press, 1966.

Mayntz, Renate and Fritz W. Scharpf. *Policy-making in the German Federal Bureaucracy.* New York: Elsevier, 1975.

McWhinney, Edward. *Constitutionalism in Germany and the Federal Constitutional Court.* Leyden: Sythoff, 1962.

Pinney, Edward L. *Federalism, Bureaucracy, and Party Politics in Western Germany: The Role of the Bundesrat.* Chapel Hill: University of North Carolina Press, 1963.

Safran, William. *Veto-Group Politics: The Case of Health-Insurance Reform in West Germany.* San Francisco: Chandler, 1967.

Stone, Deborah A. *The Limits of Professional Power: National Health Care in the Federal Republic of Germany.* Chicago: University of Chicago Press, 1980.

Thaysen, Uwe, et al., eds. *The U.S. Congress and the German Bundestag. Comparisons of Democratic Processes.* Boulder, CO: Westview, 1990.

Trossmann, Hans. *The German Bundestag: Organization and Operation.* Darmstadt: Neue Darmstädter Verlagsanstalt, 1965.

Wells, Roger H. *The States in West German Federalism: A Study of Federal-State Relations, 1949-1960.* New York: Bookman Associates, 1961.

Westphalen, Raban Graf von, ed. *Parlamentslehre. Das parlamentarische Regierungssystem im technischen Zeitalter.* Munich: Oldenbourg, 1993.

POLITICAL PARTIES, INTEREST GROUPS, ELECTIONS

Apel, Hans. *Die deformierte Demokratie. Parteienherrschaft in Deutschland.* Stuttgart: Deutsche Verlags-Anstalt, 1991.

Bölling, Klaus. *Die letzten 30 Tage des Kanzlers Helmut Schmidt. Ein Tagebuch.* Hamburg: Spiegel-Buch, 1982.

Bouvier, Beatrix W. *Zwischen Godesberg und Grosse Koalition.* Bonn: Dietz Nachf., 1990.

Braunthal, Gerard. *The Federation of German Industry in Politics.* Ithaca: Cornell University Press, 1965.

Braunthal, Gerard. *The West German Social Democrats, 1969-1982: Profile of a Party in Power.* Boulder, CO: Westview, 1983.

Burkett, Tony. *Parties and Elections in West Germany: The Search for Stability.* New York: St. Martin's, 1975.

Burns, Rob and Wilfried Van Der Will. *Protest and Democracy in West Germany: Extra-parliamentary Opposition and the Democratic Agenda.* New York: St. Martin's, 1988.

Capra, Fritjof and Charlene Spretnak. *Green Politics: The Global Promise.* New York: Dutton, 1984.

Cerny, Karl H., ed. *Germany at the Polls: The Bundestag Elections of the 1980's.* Durham: Duke University Press, 1990.

Chalmers, Douglas A. *The Social Democratic Party of Germany: From Working-Class Movement to Modern Political Party.* New Haven: Yale University Press, 1964.

Childs, David. *From Schumacher to Brandt: The Story of German Socialism, 1945-1965.* Oxford: Pergamon Press, 1966.

Conradt, David P. *The West German Party System: An Ecological Analysis of Social Structure and Voting Behavior, 1961-1969.* Beverly Hills, CA: Sage, 1972.

Cullingford, E.C.M. *Trade Unions in West Germany.* Boulder, CO: Westview, 1977.

Dalton, Russell J. *Citizen Politics in Western Democracies: Public Opinion and Political Parties in the United States, Great Britain, West Germany, and France.* Chatham, NJ: Chatham House, 1988.

Dalton, Russell J., ed. *The New Germany Votes. Reunification and the Creation of a New German Party System.* Oxford: Berg, 1993.

Dominick, Raymond H., III. *The Environmental Movement in Germany. Prophets and Pioneers, 1871-1971.* Bloomington, IN: Indiana University Press, 1992.

Edinger, Lewis J. *Kurt Schumacher: A Study in Personality and Political Behavior.* Stanford: Stanford University Press, 1965.

Fisher, Stephen L. *The Minor Parties of the Federal Republic of Germany: Toward a Comparative Theory of Minor Parties.* The Hague: Nijhoff, 1974.

Fletcher, Roger, ed. *Bernstein to Brandt. A Short History of German Social Democracy.* New York: Edward Arnold, 1987.

Frankland, E. Gene and Donald Schoonmaker. *Between Protest and Power: The Green Party in Germany.* Boulder, CO: Westview, 1992.

Graf, William D. *The German Left since 1945.* Cambridge: Oleander Press, 1976.

Heidenheimer, Arnold J. *Adenauer and the CDU: The Rise of the Leader and the Integration of the Party.* The Hague: Nijhoff, 1960.

Hülsberg, Werner. *The German Greens: A Social and Political Profile.* London: Verso/ Methuen, 1988.

Jesse, Eckhard. *Elections: The Federal Republic of Germany in Comparison.* Trans. by Lindsay Batson. Oxford: Berg, 1990.

Kaase, Max and Klaus von Beyme, eds. *Elections and Parties.* Beverly Hills, CA: Sage, 1978.

Kitschelt, Herbert. *The Logic of Party Formation: The Structure and Strategy of the Belgian and West German Ecology Parties.* Ithaca: Cornell University Press, 1989.

Kitzinger, Uwe W. *German Electoral Politics: A Study of the 1957 Campaign.* Oxford: Clarendon Press, 1960.

Kolinsky, Eva. *Parties, Opposition, and Society in West Germany.* New York: St. Martin's, 1984.

Kolinsky, Eva, ed. *The Greens in West Germany: Organisation and Policy Making.* Oxford: Berg, 1989.

Langguth, Gerd. *The Green Factor in German Politics: From Protest Movement to Political Party.* Boulder, CO: Westview, 1986. Originally published as *Der Grüne Faktor: Von der Bewegung zur Partei?* Osnabrück: Fromm, 1984.

Markovits, Andrei S. *The Politics of the West German Trade Unions: Strategies of Class and Interest Representation in Growth and Crisis.* Cambridge: Cambridge University Press, 1986.

Markovits, Andrei S. *The German Left. Red, Green, and Beyond.* Oxford: Oxford University, 1994.

Marks, G. *Unions in Politics.* Princeton: Princeton University, 1989.

Michels, Robert. *Political Parties: A Sociological Study of the Oligarchical Tendencies of Modern Democracy.* New York: Collier Books, 1962, first published in 1915.

Müller-Rommel, Ferdinand, ed. *New Politics in Western Europe: The Rise and Success of Green Parties and Alternative Lists*. Boulder, CO: Westview, 1989.

Nagle, John D. *The National Democratic Party: Right Radicalism in the Federal Republic of Germany*. Berkeley: University of California Press, 1970.

Niedermayer, Oskar. *Innerparteiliche Partizipation*. Opladen: Westdeutscher Verlag, 1989.

Oberndörfer, Dieter and Gerd Mielke. *Stabilität und Wandel in der westdeutschen Wählerschaft. Das Verhältnis von Sozialstruktur und Wahlverhalten im Zeitraum von 1976 bis 1987.* Freiburg: Arnold-Bergstraesser-Institut, 1990.

Oberndörfer, Dieter, Gerd Mielke, and Ulrich Eith, eds. *Die Bundesrepublik im Umbruch. Analysen zur ersten gesamtdeutschen Bundestagswahl 1990.* Freiburg: Arnold-Bergstraesser-Institut, 1992.

Padgett, Stephen and Tony Burkett. *Political Parties and Elections in West Germany: The Search for a New Stability.* London: C. Hurst, 1986.

Papadakis, E. *The Green Movement in West Germany.* New York: St. Martin's, 1984.

Parness, Diane L. *The SPD and the Challenge of Mass Politics. The Dilemma of the German Volkspartei.* Boulder, CO: Westview, 1991.

Preece, Rodney J.C. *"Land" Elections in the German Federal Republic.* Harlow: Longmans, 1968.

Pridham, Geoffrey. *Christian Democracy in Western Germany: The CDU/CSU in Government and Opposition, 1945-1976.* New York: St. Martin's, 1977.

Rohe, Karl, ed. *Elections, Parties and Political Traditions: Social Foundations of German Parties and Party Systems, 1867-1987.* Oxford: Berg, 1990.

Rosolowky, Diane. *West Germany's Foreign Policy: The Impact of the Social Democrats and the Greens.* Westport, CT: Greenwood, 1987.

Schellenger, Harold K. *The SPD in the Bonn Republic: A Socialist Party Modernizes.* The Hague: Nijhoff, 1968.

Schmidt, U. *Zentrum oder CDU. Politischer Katholizismus zwischen Tradition und Anpassung.* Opladen: Westdeutscher Verlag, 1987.

Schonauer, Karlheinz. *Die ungeliebten Kinder der Mutter SPD. Die Geschichte der Jusos von der braven Parteijugend zur innerparteilichen Opposition.* Bonn: n.p., 1982.

Smith, Gordon. *Democracy in Western Germany: Parties and Politics in the Federal Republic.* New York: Holmes & Meier, 1979.

Spotts, Frederic. *The Churches and Politics in Germany.* Middletown, CT: Wesleyan University Press, 1973.

Stöss, Richard. *Politics against Democracy: Right-wing Extremism in West Germany.* Oxford: Berg, 1992.

ECONOMY AND LABOR

Altmann, Norbert, Christoph Köhler, and Pamela Meil, eds. *Technology and Work in German Industry.* Boulder, CO: Westview, 1991.

Arndt, Hans-Joachim. *West Germany: Politics of Non-Planning.* Syracuse: Syracuse University Press, 1966.

Bellon, Bernard P. *Mercedes in Peace and War: German Automobile Workers, 1903-1945.* New York: Colombia University Press, 1990.

Berghahn, Volker R. *The Americanization of West German Industry, 1945-1973.* New York: Peter Lang, 1986.

Berghahn, Volker R. and Detlev Karsten. *Industrial Relations in West Germany*. Oxford: Berg, 1988.

Boarmann, Patrick M. *Germany's Economic Dilemma: Inflation and Balance of Payments*. New Haven: Yale University Press, 1964.

Braun, Hans-Joachim. *The German Economy in the Twentieth Century: The German Reich and the Federal Republic*. London: Routledge, 1990.

Braunthal, Gerard. *The Federation of German Industry in Politics*. Ithaca, NY: Cornell University Press, 1972.

Bulmer, S. *The Domestic Structure of European Community Policy-Making in West Germany*. New York: Garland, 1986.

Christ, Peter. *Kolonie im eigenen Land. Die Treuhand, Bonn und die Wirtschaftskatastrophe der fünf neuen Länder*. Hamburg: Rowohlt, n.d.

Deppe, Frank, ed. *Geschichte der deutschen Gewerkschaftsbewegung*. Cologne: Pahl-Rugenstein, 1989.

Erhard, Ludwig. *Prosperity through Competition*. 3rd rev. ed. New York: Praeger, 1962.

Fichter, Michael. *Labour Unions in West Germany*. Oxford: Berg, 1989.

Fukui, Haruhito, Peter H. Merkl, Hubertus Müller-Groeling, and Akio Watanabe, eds. *The Politics of Economic Change in Postwar Japan and West Germany*. New York: St. Martin's, 1992.

Geary, Dick. *Aspects of German Labour 1871-1933*. New York: St. Martin's, 1992.

Germany's Business Leaders, 1400-1917. The Rudolf Mosse Collection from the Leo Baeck Institute. Frederick, MD: University Publications of America, n.d.

Germany's Top 300 [Corporations]. Frankfurt am Main: Frankfurter Allgemeine Zeitung Information Services, 1991.

Giersch, Herbert, et al. *The Fading Miracle. Four Decades of Market Economy in Germany.* Cambridge: Cambridge University Press, 1992.

Graf, William D., ed. *The Internationalization of the German Political Economy.* New York: St. Martin's, 1992.

Grant, W., C. Whitston, and W. Paterson. *Government and the Chemical Industry: A Comparative Case Study of Britain and West Germany.* Oxford: Clarendon, 1989.

Grebing, Helga. *The History of the German Labour Movement.* London: Oswald Wolff, 1969.

Hardach, K. *The Political Economy of Germany in the Twentieth Century.* Berkeley: University of California Press, 1980.

Hayes, Peter. *Industry and Ideology. I.G. Farben in the Nazi Era.* Cambridge: Cambridge University Press, 1987.

Herbert, Ulrich. *A History of Foreign Labor in Germany, 1880-1980.* Trans. by William Templer. Ann Arbor: University of Michigan Press, 1990.

Holbik, Karel, and Henry A. Myers. *Postwar Trade in Divided Germany: The Internal and International Issues.* Baltimore: Johns Hopkins Press, 1964.

Holbik, Karel, and Henry A. Myers. *West German Foreign Aid, 1956-1966: Its Economic and Political Aspects.* Boston: Boston University Press, 1968.

Jungblut, Michael. *Wirtschaftswunder ohne Grenzen. Wohlstand diesseits und jenseits der Elbe.* Stuttgart: Deutsche Verlags-Anstalt, 1990.

Katzenstein, Peter J., ed. *Industry and Politics in West Germany: Toward the Third Republic.* Ithaca: Cornell University Press, 1989.

Kennedy, Ellen. *The Bundesbank: Germany's Central Bank in the International Monetary System.* New York: Council on Foreign Relations Press, 1991.

Knott, Jack H. *Managing the German Economy: Budgetary Politics in a Federal State.* Lexington, MA: Lexington Books, 1981.

Knusel, Jack L. *West German Aid to Developing Nations.* New York: Praeger, 1968.

Kramer, Alan. *The West German Economy 1945-1955.* Oxford: Berg, 1991.

Leaman, Jeremy. *The Political Economy of West Germany, 1945-1985: An Introduction.* New York: St. Martin's, 1988.

Liedtke, Rüdiger. *Wem gehört die Republik. Die Konzerne und ihre Verflechtungen. Namen, Zahlen, Fakten.* Frankfurt: Eichborn, 1991.

Markovits, Andrei S., ed. *The Political Economy of West Germany: Modell Deutschland.* New York: Praeger, 1982.

Markovits, Andrei S., ed. *The Politics of the West German Trade Unions.* Cambridge: Cambridge University Press, 1986.

Marsh, David. *The Bundesbank: The Bank That Rules Europe.* London: Heinemann, 1992.

Peacock, Alan and Hans Willgerodt, eds. *German Neo-Liberals and the Social Market Economy.* Boulder, CO: Westview, 1989.

Pfaff, Lucie. *The American and German Entrepreneur: Economic and Literary Interplay.* New York: Peter Lang, 1989.

Roseman, Mark. *Recasting the Ruhr, 1945-1958. Manpower, Economic Recovery and Labour Relations.* Oxford: Berg, 1991.

Schneider, Michael. *A Brief History of the German Trade Unions.* Bonn: Dietz, 1991.

Schuchman, Abraham. *Co-determination: Labor's Middle Way in Germany*. Washington, D.C: Public Affairs Press, 1957.

Sinn, Gerlinde. *Jumpstart*. Cambridge: MIT Press, 1993.

Smith, Owen. *The West German Economy*. London: Croom Helm, 1983.

Smyser, W.R. *The Economy of United Germany. Colossus at the Crossroads*. New York: St. Martin's, 1992.

Spiro, Herbert J. *The Politics of German Codetermination*. Cambridge: Harvard University Press, 1958.

Stolper, Gustav. *German Economy, 1870-1940*. New York: Reynal & Hitchcock, 1940.

Stolper, Gustav, Karl Häuser and Knut Borchardt. *The German Economy: 1870 to the Present*. New York: Harcourt, Brace & World, 1967.

Streeck, Wolfgang. *Industrial Relations in West Germany: A Case Study of the Car Industry*. New York: St. Martin's, 1984.

Thelen, Kathleen A. *Union of Parts. Labor Politics in Postwar Germany*. Ithaca: Cornell University Press, 1991.

Wallich, Henry C. *Mainsprings of German Revival*. New Haven: Yale University Press, 1955.

Welfens, Paul J.J., ed. *Economic Aspects of German Unification*. Berlin: Springer Verlag, 1992.

FOREIGN POLICY

Artner, Stephen J. *A Change of Course. The West German Social Democrats and NATO, 1957-1961*. Westport, CT: Greenwood, 1985.

Baranovsky, Vladimir and Hans-Joachim Spanger. *In from the Cold. Germany, Russia, and the Future of Europe.* Boulder, CO: Westview, 1992.

Bathurst, Maurice E. and John L. Simpson. *Germany and the North Atlantic Community: A Legal Survey.* New York: Praeger, 1956.

Bergner, Jeffrey T. *The New Superpowers. Germany, Japan, the United States and the New World Order.* New York: St. Martin's, 1991.

Brandt, Willy. *The Ordeal of Coexistence.* Cambridge: Harvard University Press, 1963.

Brandt, Willy. *A Peace Policy for Europe.* New York: Holt, Rinehart and Winston, 1969.

Buhler, Phillip A. *The Oder-Neisse Line. A Reappraisal Under International Law.* New York: Columbia University Press, 1990.

Bulmer, Simon and William Paterson. *The Federal Republic of Germany and the European Community.* London: Allen & Unwin, 1987.

Chubin, Shahram. *Germany and the Middle East.* New York: St. Martin's, 1992.

Clemens, Clay. *Reluctant Realists: The Christian Democrats and West German Ostpolitik.* Durham: Duke University Press, 1989.

Conant, James B. *Germany and Freedom: A Personal Appraisal.* New York: Capricorn Books, 1962.

Deutsch, Karl Wolfgang, and Lewis J. Edinger. *Germany Rejoins the Powers.* Stanford: Stanford University Press, 1959.

Deutschkron, Inge. *Bonn and Jerusalem: The Strange Coalition.* Philadelphia: Chilton Book Co., 1970.

Drath, Viola Herms, ed. *Germany in World Politics.* New York: Cyrco Press, 1979.

Dulles, Eleanor L. *One Germany or Two: The Struggle at the Heart of Europe.* Stanford: Hoover Institution Press, 1970.

Feldman, Lily Gardner. *The Special Relationship between West Germany and Israel.* Boston: Allen & Unwin, 1984.

Freund, Gerald. *Germany between Two Worlds.* New York: Harcourt, Brace, 1961.

Friend, Julius W. *The Linchpin: French-German Relations, 1950-1990.* Washington Paper 154. Westport: Praeger, 1991.

Fritsch-Bournazel, Renata. *Confronting the German Question: Germans on the East-West Divide.* Oxford: Berg, 1988.

Fritsch-Bournazel, Renata. *Europe and German Reunification.* Rev. 2nd ed. Oxford: Berg, 1992.

Gaffney, John and Eva Kolinsky, eds. *Political Culture in France and West Germany. A Contemporary Perspective.* London: Routledge, 1991.

Gillingham, John. *Coal, Steel and the Rebirth of Europe, 1945-1955.* Cambridge: Cambridge University Press, 1991.

Griffith, William. *The Ostpolitik of the Federal Republic of Germany.* Cambridge: MIT Press, 1978.

Grosser, Alfred. *Western Germany.* London: Allen & Unwin, 1955.

Hacke, Christian. *Weltmacht wider Willen: Die Aussenpolitik der Bundesrepublik Deutschland.* Stuttgart: Klett-Cotta, 1989.

Haftendorn, Helga. *Security and Detente: Conflicting Priorities in German Foreign Policy.* New York: Praeger, 1985.

Haglund, David G. *Alliance Within the Alliance? Franco-German Military Cooperation and the European Pillar of Defense.* Boulder, CO: Westview, 1991.

Hanrieder, Wolfram F. *The Stable Crisis.* New York: Harper & Row, 1970.

Hanrieder, Wolfram F., ed. *West German Foreign Policy: 1949-1979.* Boulder, CO: Westview, 1980.

Hanrieder, Wolfram F. *Germany, America, Europe: Forty Years of German Foreign Policy.* New Haven: Yale University Press, 1989.

Hartmann, Frederick H. *Germany between East and West: The Reunification Problem.* Englewood Cliffs: Prentice-Hall, 1965.

Heisenberg, Wolfgang, ed. *German Unification in European Perspective.* London: Brassey's, 1991.

Hendricks, Gisela. *Germany and European Integration. The Common Agricultural Policy: An Area of Conflict.* Oxford: Berg, 1991.

Kaiser, Karl. *German Foreign Policy in Transition: Bonn between East and West.* Oxford: Oxford University Press, 1968.

Kirchner, Emil J. and James Sperling, eds. *The Federal Republic of Germany and NATO.* New York: St. Martin's, 1991.

Krippendorf, Ekkehart and Volker Rittberger, eds. *The Foreign Policy of West Germany: Formation and Contents.* Beverly Hills, CA: Sage, 1980.

Kulski, Wladyslaw W. *Germany and Poland: From War to Peaceful Relations.* Syracuse: Syracuse University Press, 1976.

Lafontaine, Oskar. *Deutsche Wahrheiten: die nationale und die soziale Frage.* Hamburg: Hoffmann und Campe, 1990.

Laird, Robbin F. *The Soviets, Germany, and the New Europe.* Boulder, CO: Westview, 1991.

Landauer, Carl. *Germany: Illusions and Dilemmas.* New York: Harcourt, Brace and World, 1969.

Lankowski, Carl. *Germany and the European Community.* New York: St. Martin's, 1992.

Laqueur, Walter. *Russia and Germany. A Century of Conflict.* New Brunswick, NJ: Rutgers University Press, 1990.

Lee, Marshall M. and Wolfgang Michalka. *German Foreign Policy 1917-1933: Continuity or Break?* Oxford: Berg, 1987.

McCarthy, Patrick. *France-Germany, 1983-1993.* New York: St. Martin's, 1993.

Merkl, Peter H. *German Foreign Policies, West and East: On the Threshold of a New European Era.* Santa Barbara: ABC-Clio Press, 1974.

Merkl, Peter H. *German Unification in the European Context.* University Park: Pennsylvania State University Press, 1993.

Minnerup, Günther. *German Question.* New York: St. Martin's, 1992.

Montgomery, John. *Forced to be Free: The Artificial Revolution in Germany and Japan.* Chicago: University of Chicago Press, 1957.

Moreton, N. Edwina, ed. *Germany between East and West.* Cambridge: Cambridge University Press, 1987.

Morgan, Roger P. *West Germany's Foreign Policy Agenda.* Beverly Hills, CA: Sage, 1978.

Nawrocki, Joachim. *Die Beziehungen zwischen den beiden Staaten in Deutschland.* 2. ergänzte Auflage. Berlin: Gebr. Holzapfel, 1988.

Paterson, William E. *The SPD and European Integration.* Lexington, MA: Lexington Books, 1974.

Pfetsch, Frank R. *West Germany: Internal Structures and External Relations: Foreign Policy of the Federal Republic of Germany.* New York: Praeger, 1988.

Pittman, Avril. *From Ostpolitik to Reunification. West German-Soviet Political Relations since 1974.* Cambridge: Cambridge University Press, 1992.

Planck, Charles R. *The Changing Status of German Reunification in Western Diplomacy, 1955-1966.* Baltimore: Johns Hopkins Press, 1967.

Plock, Ernest D. *East German-West German Relations and the Fall of the GDR.* Boulder, CO: Westview, 1992.

Rabinbach, Anson and Jack Zipes, eds. *Germans and the Jews since the Holocaust.* New York: Holmes and Meier, 1986.

Remak, Joachim, ed. *War, Revolution and Peace: Essays in Honor of Charles B. Burdick.* Lanham, MD: University Press of America, 1987.

Rosolowsky, Diane. *West Germany's Foreign Policy: The Impact of the Social Democrats and the Greens.* Westport, CT: Greenwood, 1987.

Schweigler, Gebhard. *West German Foreign Policy: The Domestic Setting.* New York: Praeger, 1984.

Schweitzer, Carl-Christoph and Detlev Karsten, eds. *Federal Republic of Germany and EC Membership Evaluated.* New York: St. Martin's, 1991.

Simonian, H. *The Privileged Partnership: Franco-German Relations in the European Community 1969-84.* Oxford: Clarendon, 1985.

Sodaro, Michael J. *Moscow, Germany, and the West from Khrushchev to Gorbachev.* Ithaca: Cornell University Press, 1990.

Sowden, J.K. *The German Question 1945-1973.* London: Bradford University Press, 1975.

Speier, Hans and W. Phillips Davison, eds. *West German Leadership and Foreign Policy.* Evanston, IL: Row, Peterson, 1957.

Steininger, Rolf. *The German Question: The Stalin Note of 1952 and the Problem of Reunification.* New York: Columbia University Press, 1990.

Stent, Angela. *From Embargo to Ostpolitik.* Cambridge: Cambridge University Press, 1981.

Strauss, Franz Josef. *The Grand Design: A European Solution to German Reunification.* New York: Praeger, 1966.

Szaz, Zoltan Michael. *Germany's Eastern Frontiers: The Problem of the Oder-Neisse Line.* Chicago: Regnery, 1960.

Tilford, Roger, ed. *The Ostpolitik and Political Change in Germany.* Lexington, MA: Lexington Books, 1975.

Uschner, Manfred. *Die Ostpolitik der SPD.* Berlin: Dietz, 1991.

Vali, Ferenc A. *The Quest for a United Germany.* Baltimore: Johns Hopkins Press, 1967.

Verheyen, Dirk. *The German Question. A Cultural, Historical and Geopolitical Exploration.* Boulder, CO: Westview, 1991.

Verheyen, Dirk and Christian Søe, eds. *The Germans and Their Neighbors.* Boulder, CO: Westview, 1993.

Wessels, Wolfgang and Elfriede Regelsberger, eds. *The Federal Republic of Germany and the European Community: The Presidency and Beyond.* Bonn: Europa Union, 1988.

Whetten, Lawrence L. *Germany's Ostpolitik: Relations between the Federal Republic and the Warsaw Pact Countries.* Oxford: Oxford University Press, 1971.

Whetten, Lawrence L. *Germany East and West.* New York: New York University Press, 1980.

Willis, F.R. *France, Germany and the New Europe 1945-63.* Oxford: Oxford University Press, 1965.

Windsor, Philip. *Germany and the Western Alliance.* London: International Institute for Strategic Studies, 1981.

Wiskemann, Elizabeth. *Germany's Eastern Neighbours: Problems Relating to the Oder-Neisse Line and the Czech Frontier Regions.* Oxford: Oxford University Press, 1956.

Wolffsohn, Michael. *West Germany's Foreign Policy in the Era of Brandt and Schmidt, 1969-1982.* Frankfurt am Main: Lang, 1986.

Wolffsohn, Michael. *Ewige Schuld? 40 Jahre Deutsch-Jüdisch-Israelische Beziehungen.* Munich: Serie Piper, 1988.

DEFENSE POLICY

Abenheim, Donald. *Reforging the Iron Cross: The Search for Tradition in the West German Armed Forces.* Princeton: Princeton University Press, 1989.

Bastian, Gert. *Frieden schaffen!* Munich: Kindler, 1983.

Boutwell, Jeffrey. *The German Nuclear Dilemma.* Ithaca: Cornell University Press, 1990.

Brauch, Hans Günter, ed. *Star Wars and European Defense.* New York: St. Martin's, 1987.

Cioc, Mark. *Pax Atomica: The Nuclear Defense Debate in West Germany during the Adenauer Era.* New York: Columbia University Press, 1988.

Drummond, Gordon D. *The German Social Democrats in Opposition, 1949-1960. The Case Against Rearmament.* Norman: Oklahoma University Press, 1982.

Enders, Thomas. *Die SPD und die äussere Sicherheit: Zum Wandel der sicherheitspolitischen Konzeption der Partei in der Zeit der Regierungsverantwortung 1966-1982.* Melle: Ernst Knoth, 1987.

Fischer, Alexander, ed. *Wiederbewaffnung in Deutschland nach 1945.* Berlin: Duncker & Humblot, 1986.

Gress, David. *Peace and Survival. West Germany, the Peace Movement, and European Security.* Palo Alto, CA: Hoover Institution, 1985.

Haglund, David G. and Olaf Mager. *Homeward Bound? Allied Forces in the New Germany.* Boulder, CO: Westview, 1992.

Hancock, M. Donald. *The Bundeswehr and the National People's Army: A Comparative Study of German Civil-Military Polity.* Denver: University of Denver Press, 1973.

German civilians salute U.S. national anthem, July 4, 1945. (*Source:* SPP).

Chancellor Adenauer visits some of the first Bundeswehr soldiers, January 1956. (*Source:* PIB).

Bundeswehr officers in the 1990's. (*Source:* SPP).

Herf, Jeffrey. *War by Other Means: Soviet Power, West German Resistance, and the Battle of the Euromissiles.* New York: Free Press, 1991.

Isby, David C. and Charles Kamps, Jr. *Armies of NATO's Central Front.* London: Jane's, 1985.

Kelleher, Catherine McArdle. *Germany and the Politics of Nuclear Weapons.* New York: Columbia University Press, 1975.

Kirchner, Emil J. and James Sperling. *The Federal Republic of Germany and NATO.* New York: St. Martin's, 1992.

Laird, Robbin F. *Strangers and Friends: The Franco-German Security Relationship.* New York: St. Martin's, 1989.

Lowry, Montecue Judson. *The Forge of West German Rearmament. Theodor Blank and the Amt Blank.* New York: Peter Lang, 1990.

Macgregor, Douglas A. *The Soviet-East German Military Alliance.* Cambridge: Cambridge University Press, 1989.

McGeean, Robert. *The German Rearmament Question: American Diplomacy and European Defense after World War II.* Urbana: University of Illinois Press, 1971.

Menges, Constantine C. *The Future of Germany and the Atlantic Alliance.* Washington, D.C.: American Enterprise Institute, 1991.

Moller, Bjorn. *Resolving the Security Dilemma in Europe. The German Debate on Non-Offensive Defence.* London: Brassey's, 1991.

Mushaben, Joyce. *The Post-Postwar Generations: Changing Attitudes Toward Nationalism and Security in West Germany.* Boulder, CO: Westview, 1994.

Paret, Peter. *Understanding War--Essays on Clausewitz and the History of Military Power.* Princeton: Princeton University Press, 1992.

Reed, John A., Jr. *Germany and NATO.* Washington, D.C.: National Defense University Press, 1987.

Richardson, James. *Germany and the Atlantic Alliance: The Interaction of Strategy and Politics.* Cambridge: Harvard University Press, 1966.

Schmidt, Helmut. *Defense or Retaliation: a German View.* New York: Praeger, 1962. Originally published as *Verteidigung oder Vergeltung.* Stuttgart: Seewald, 1961.

Schmidt, Helmut. *The Balance of Power: Germany's Peace Policy and the Super Powers.* London: William Kimber, 1971. Originally published as *Strategie des Gleichgewichts.* Stuttgart: Seewald, 1969.

Smith, Arthur L., Jr. *Churchill's German Army: Wartime Strategy and Cold War Politics, 1943-1947.* Beverly Hills and London: Sage Publications, 1977.

Speier, Hans. *German Rearmament and Atomic War: The Views of German Military and Political Leaders.* Evanston, IL: Row, Peterson, 1957.

Szabo, Stephen F. *The Changing Politics of German Security.* New York: St. Martin's, 1990.

Szabo, Stephen F., ed. *The Bundeswehr and Western Security.* New York: St. Martin's, 1990.

Thompson, Wayne C. and Marc D. Peltier. "The Education of Military Officers in the Federal Republic of Germany." *Armed Forces and Society.* Vol. 16, No. 4, Summer 1990.

U.S. War Department. *Handbook on German Military Forces.* Baton Rouge: Louisiana State University Press, 1990.

GERMANY AND THE UNITED STATES OF AMERICA

Adams, Willi Paul and Knud Krakau, eds. *Deutschland und Amerika: Perzeption und historische Realität.* Berlin: Colloquium, 1985.

Amlinger, Lore, ed. *Germany and the United States: Changing Perceptions--Danger and Hope; the University of Virginia and Roanoke College Symposium 1985.* Stuttgart: Heinz, 1987.

Barkai, Avraham. *The German-Jewish Immigration to the United States 1820-1914.* New York: Holmes & Meier, 1991.

Benseler, David P., Walter F. Lohnes, and Valters Nollendorfs, eds. *Teaching German in America. Prolegomena to a History.* Madison: University of Wisconsin Press, 1988.

Berghahn, Volker R. *The Americanization of German Industry, 1945-1973.* Cambridge: Cambridge University Press, 1986.

Bortfeldt, Heinrich. *Washington Bonn-Berlin. Die USA und die Deutsche Einheit.* Bonn: Bouvier, 1993.

Burns, Arthur F. *The United States and Germany: A Vital Partnership.* New York: Council on Foreign Relations, 1986.

Coffey, Joseph I. and Klaus von Schubert, with Dieter Dettke, James R. Golden, and Gale A. Mattox. *Defense and Detente: U.S. and West German Perspectives on Defense Policy.* Boulder, CO: Westview, 1989.

Cooney, James A., Gordon Craig, Hans Peter Schwartz, and Fritz Stern, eds. *The Federal Republic of Germany and the United States: Changing Political, Social, and Economic Relations.* Boulder, CO: Westview, 1984.

Droege, Heinz, Fritz Münch, and Ellinor von Puttkamer. *The Federal Republic of Germany and the United Nations.* New York: Carnegie Endowment for International Peace, 1967.

Ermarth, Michael, ed. *America and the Shaping of German Society 1945-1955.* Oxford: Berg, 1993.

Espich, Horst. *Die Entwicklung des England- und Amerikabildes in den 'sozialistischen' Staaten unter besonderer Berücksichtigung der Englischlehrwerke der SBZ, DDR.* Frankfurt am Main: Lang, 1987.

Friedrich, Wolfgang-Uwe, ed. *Die USA und die Deutsche Frage: 1945-1990.* Frankfurt am Main: Campus, 1991.

Gaida, Burton C. *"USA--DDR": politische, kulturelle und wirtschaftliche Beziehungen seit 1974.* Bochum: Brockmeyer, 1989.

Gatzke, Hans W. *Germany and the United States. "A Special Relationship?"* Cambridge: Harvard University Press, 1980.

Gilhoff, Johannes. *Jürnjakob Swehn, der Amerikafahrer.* Munich: Deutscher Taschenbuch, 1986.

Glaser, Wolfgang. *Americans and Germans: A Handy Reader and Reference Book.* Trans. by Christopher Baker. Munich: Gräfelfing, 1986.

Greffrath, Matthias, ed. *Die Zerstörung einer Zukunft: Gespräche mit emigrierten Sozialwissenschaftlern.* Frankfurt am Main: Campus, 1989.

Heilbut, Anthony. *Kultur ohne Heimat: deutsche Emigranten in den USA nach 1930.* Berlin: Quadriga, 1987.

Helbich, Wolfgang. *"Alle Menschen sind dort gleich...": d. dt. Amerika-Auswanderung im 19. u. 20. Jh.* Düsseldorf: Schwan, 1988.

Helbich, Wolfgang, Walter D. Kamphoefner and Ulrike Sommer, eds. *Briefe aus Amerika: Deutsche Auswanderer schreiben aus der Neuen Welt, 1830-1930.* Munich: C.H. Beck, 1988.

Herzstein, Robert E. *Roosevelt and Hitler: Prelude to War.* New York: Paragon House, 1989.

Hodge, Carl C. and Cathal J. Nolan, eds. *Shepherd of Democracy? America and Germany in the Twentieth Century.* Westport, CT: Greenwood, 1992.

Jonas, Manfred. *The United States and Germany: A Diplomatic History.* Ithaca, NY: Cornell University Press, 1985.

Junker, Detlef. *Kampf um die Weltmacht: d. USA u.d. Dritte Reich 1933-1945.* Düsseldorf: Schwan, 1988.

Kirschbaum, Erik. *The Eradication of German Culture in the United States 1917-1918.* Stuttgart: Heinz, 1986.

Knauer, Sebastian. *Lieben wir die USA? Was d. Dt. über d. Amerikaner denken.* Hamburg: Gruner und Jahr, 1987.

Körner, Gustav Phillip. *Das deutsche Element in den Vereinigten Staaten von Nordamerika 1818-1848.* Frankfurt am Main: Lang, 1986.

Krampikowski, Frank. *Amerikanisches Deutschlandbild und deutsches Amerikabild in Medien und Erziehung.* Baltmannsweiler: Pädagogischer Verlag, 1990.

Krohn, Claus-Dieter. *Wissenschaft im Exil: deutsche Sozial- und Wirtschaftswissenschaftler in den USA und den New School for Social Research.* Frankfurt am Main: Campus, 1987.

Lentz, Andrea. *Aspekte des Deutschlandbildes in der amerikanischen Presse während der zweiten Hälfte der sozial-liberalen Koalition 1977-1982.* Münster: Lit, 1989.

Luebke, Frederick C. *Germans in the New World: Essays in the History of Immigration.* Chicago: University of Chicago Press, 1990.

Mahncke, Dieter, ed. *Amerikaner in Deutschland. Grundlagen und Bedingungen der transatlantischen Sicherheit.* Bonn: Bouvier, 1991.

Markham, Sara. *Workers, Women and Afro-Americans: Images of the United States in German Travel Literature from 1923 to 1933.* New York: Lang, 1986.

Martin, Jay. *Permanent Exiles: Essays on the Intellectual Migration from Germany to America.* New York: Columbia University Press, 1986.

Mattox, Gale A. and John H. Vaughan, Jr., eds. *Germany Through American Eyes: Foreign Policy and Domestic Issues*. Boulder, CO: Westview, 1989.

Morgan, Roger P. *The United States and West Germany, 1945-1973: A Study in Alliance Politics*. Oxford: Oxford University Press, 1974.

Müller, Emil-Peter. *Antiamerikanismus in Deutschland: zwischen Care-packet u. Cruise Missile*. Cologne: Deutscher Institut, 1986.

Muller, Steven and Gerhard Schweigler, eds. *From Occupation to Cooperation: The United States and United Germany in a Changing World Order*. New York: Norton, 1992.

Nadel, Stanley. *Little Germany: Race, Ethnicity, Religion and Class in New York City, 1845-1880*. Urbana and Chicago: University of Illinois Press, 1990.

Ninkovich, Frank A. *Germany and the United States. The Transformation of the German Question since 1945*. Boston: Twayne Publishers, 1988.

Osterle, Heinz D. *Bilder von Amerika: Gespräche mit deutschen Schriftstellern*. Münster: Englisch Amerikanische Studien, 1987.

Ott, Ulrich. *Amerika ist anders: Studien zum Amerika-Bild in deutschen Reiseberichten des 20. Jahrhunderts*. Frankfurt am Main: Lang, 1991.

Pommerin, Rainer. *Der Kaiser und Amerika: Die USA in der Politik der Reichsleitung 1890-1917*. Cologne: Böhlau, 1986.

Pond, Elizabeth. *Beyond the Wall. Germany's Road To Unification*. Washington, D.C.: Brookings, 1993.

Quandt, Siegfried and Gerhard Schult, eds. *Die USA und Deutschland seit dem Zweiten Weltkrieg*. Munich: Schöningh, 1985.

Rossmeiss, Dieter, ed. *Demokratie von aussen: amerikanische Militärregierung in Nürnberg 1945-1949.* Munich: Dt. Taschenbuch, 1988.

Schöberl, Ingrid. *Amerikanische Einwandererwerbung in Deutschland 1845-1914.* Stuttgart: Franz Steiner, 1990.

Schröder, Hans-Jürgen, ed. *Confrontation and Cooperation. Germany and the United States in the Era of World War I, 1900-1924.* Oxford: Berg, 1992.

Schroeder, Adolf E. and Carla Schula-Geisberg. *Hold Dear, As Always: Jette, a German Imigrant Life in Letters.* Trans. by Adolf E. Schroeder. Columbia: University of Missouri Press, 1988.

Schwartz, Thomas Alan. *America's Germany: John J. McCloy and the Federal Republic of Germany.* Cambridge: Harvard University Press, 1991.

Seppain, Helene. *Contrasting U.S. and German Attitudes to Soviet Trade, 1917-1991.* New York: St. Martin's, 1992.

Smyser, W.R. *Restive Partners: Washington and Bonn Diverge.* Boulder, CO: Westview, 1990.

Srubar, Ilja, ed. *Exil, Wissenschaft, Identität: d. Emigration dt. Sozialwissenschaftler 1933-1945.* Frankfurt am Main: Suhrkamp, 1988.

Stephan, Alexander, ed. *Exil: Literatur und die Künste nach 1933.* Bonn: Bouvier, 1990.

Stuecher, Dorothea Diver. *Twice Removed: The Experience of German-American Women Writers in the 19th Century.* New York: Peter Lang, 1990.

Tolzmann, Don Heinrich. *The Cincinnati Germans after the Great War.* New York: Peter Lang, 1987.

Treverton, Gregory F. *The Dollar Drain and the American Forces in Germany.* Athens: Ohio University Press, 1978.

Trommler, Frank, ed. *Amerika und die Deutschen: Bestandsaufnahme einer 300 jährigen Geschichte.* Opladen: Westdeutscher Verlag, 1986.

Trommler, Frank, ed. *Germanistik in den USA: Neue Entwicklungen und Methoden.* Opladen: Westdeutscher Verlag, 1989.

Wander, Karl Friedrich Wilhelm. *Auswanderungs-Katechismus: e. Ratgeber für Auswanderer, besonders für diejenigen, welche nach Nordamerika auswandern wollen.* Frankfurt am Main: Lang, 1988.

Weigelt, Klaus, ed. *Das Deutschland- und Amerikabild: Beiträge zum gegenseitigen Verständnis beider Völker.* Melle: Knoth, 1986.

Wellenreuther, Hermann, ed. *German and American Constitutional Thought. Contexts, Interactions and Historical Realities.* Oxford: Berg, 1990.

Wellenreuther, Hermann and Claudia Schnurmann, eds. *Die Amerikanische Verfassung und Deutsch-Amerikanisches Verfassungsdenken. Ein Rückblick über 200 Jahre.* Oxford: Berg, 1991.

Wessel, Daisy. *Bild und Gegenbild die USA in der Belletristik der SBZ und der DDR.* Opladen: Leske u. Budrich, 1989.

Willet, Ralph. *The Americanization of Germany, 1945-1949* (Studies in film, television, and the media). New York and London: Routledge, 1989.

Zink, Harold. *The United States in Germany, 1945-1955.* Princeton: Van Nostrand, 1957. Reprint. Westport, CT: Greenwood, 1974.

BERLIN

Ambrose, Stephen E. *Eisenhower and Berlin, 1945: The Decision to Halt at the Elbe.* With a new introduction. New York: Norton, 1986.

Balfour, Alan. *Berlin: The Politics of Order, 1737-1989.* New York: Rizzoli, 1990.

Bark, Dennis L. *Agreement on Berlin.* Washington, D.C.: American Enterprise Institute for Public Policy Research, Stanford, CA: Hoover Institute on War, Revolution and Peace, 1974.

Borneman, John. *After the Wall. East Meets West in the New Berlin.* New York: Basic Books, 1992.

Catedal, Honoré M., Jr. *The Diplomacy of the Quadripartite Agreement on Berlin. A New Era in East-West Politics.* Berlin: Berlin Verlag, 1977.

Catedal, Honoré M., Jr. *A Balance Sheet of the Quadripartite Agreement on Berlin: Evaluation and Documentation.* Berlin: Berlin Verlag, 1978.

Clare, George. *Before the Wall. Berlin Days 1946-1948.* New York: E.P. Dutton, 1990.

Davison, W. Phillips. *The Berlin Blockade: A Study in Cold War Politics.* Princeton: Princeton University Press, 1958.

Dulles, Eleanor L. *The Wall: A Tragedy in Three Acts.* Columbia: Institute of International Studies, University of South Carolina, 1972.

Elkins, T.H. and B. Hopmeister. *Berlin: Spacial Structure of a Divided City.* London and New York: Methuen, 1988.

Friedrich, Otto. *Before the Deluge. A Portrait of Berlin in the 1920's.* New York: Avon, 1972.

Friedrich, Thomas. *Berlin Between the Wars.* New York: Vendome Press, 1991.

Gelb, Norman. *The Berlin Wall.* London: Michael Joseph, 1986.

Gottlieb, Manuel. *The German Peace Settlement and the Berlin Crisis.* New York: Paine-Whitman, 1960.

Haxthauser, Charles W. and Heidrun Suhr, eds. *Berlin: Culture and Metropolis.* Minneapolis: University of Minnesota Press, 1990.

Hertz, Deborah. *Jewish High Society in Old Regime Berlin.* New Haven and London: Yale University Press, 1988.

Keithly, David M. *Breakthrough in the Ostpolitik.* Boulder, CO: Westview, 1986.

Keller, John W. *Germany, the Wall and Berlin: Internal Politics during an International Crisis.* New York: Vantage Press, 1964.

Le Tissier, Tony. *The Battle of Berlin 1945.* New York: St. Martin's, 1988.

Liang, Hsi-Huey. *Berlin Before the Wall. A Foreign Student's Diary with Sketches.* New York: Routledge, 1990.

Mander, John. *Berlin: Hostage for the West.* Baltimore: Penguin Books, 1962.

Merritt, Richard L. and Anna J. Merritt, eds. *Living with the Wall: West Berlin, 1961-1985.* Durham: Duke University Press, 1985.

National Security Archive. *The Berlin Crisis 1958-1962.* Alexandria: Chadwyck-Healey, 1992.

Nelson, Daniel J. *Wartime Origins of the Berlin Dilemma.* University, AL: University of Alabama Press, 1978.

Paret, Peter. *The Berlin Secession: Modernism & Its Enemies in Imperial Germany.* Cambridge: Harvard University Press, 1980.

Reinfrank-Clark, Karin and Arno Reinfrank. *Berlin: Two Cities under Seven Flags: A Kaleidoscopic A-Z.* New York: Oswald Wolff, 1987.

Rimmer, Dave. *Once Upon a Time in the East.* North Pomfret, VT: Fourth Estate, 1992.

Schick, Jack M. *The Berlin Crisis, 1958-1962*. Philadelphia: University of Pennsylvania Press, 1971.

Shears, David. *The Ugly Frontier*. New York: Knopf, 1970.

Slusser, Robert M. *The Berlin Crisis of 1961*. Baltimore: Johns Hopkins University Press, 1969.

Smith, Jean E. *The Defense of Berlin*. Baltimore: Johns Hopkins Press, 1963.

Speier, Hans. *Berlin Divided: The Anatomy of Soviet Political Blackmail*. New York: Praeger, 1961.

Sutterlin, James S. and David Klein. *Berlin: From Symbol of Confrontation to Keystone of Stability*. Westport, CT: Praeger, 1989.

Tent, James F. *The Free University of Berlin: A Political History*. Bloomington, IN: Indiana University Press, 1988.

Wetzlaugh, Udo. *Die Allierten in Berlin*. Berlin: Arno Spitz, 1988.

Wyden, Peter. *Wall. The Inside Story of Divided Berlin*. New York: Simon & Schuster, 1993.

Zimmer, Dieter. *Das Tor*. Stuttgart: Deutsche Verlags-Anstalt, n.d.

GERMAN REVOLUTION OF 1989 AND GERMAN REUNIFICATION

Angepasst oder mündig? Briefe an Christa Wolf im Herbst 1989. Afterword by Jan Hofmann. Frankfurt am Main: Luchterhand Literatur Verlag, 1990.

Ash, Timothy Garton. *The Magic Lantern: The Revolution of '89 Witnessed in Warsaw, Budapest, Berlin and Prague*. New York: Random House, 1990.

Brandt, Willy. *"...was zusammengehört": Reden zu Deutschland.* Bonn: Dietz, 1990.

Dahrendorf, Ralf. *Reflections on the Revolution in Europe.* New York: Random House, 1990.

Darnton, Robert. *Berlin Journal 1989-1990.* New York: Norton, 1991.

Förster, Peter and Günter Roski. *DDR zwischen Wende und Wahl: Meinungsforscher analysieren den Umbruch.* Berlin: Links Druck Verlag, 1990.

Fritsch-Bournazel, Renata. *Europe and German Unification.* Oxford: Berg, 1992.

Glaessner, Gert-Joachim. *The Unification Press in Germany. From Dictatorship to Democracy.* New York: St. Martin's, 1992.

Glaessner, Gert-Joachim and Ian Wallace, eds. *The German Revolution of 1989: Causes and Consequences.* Oxford: Berg, 1992.

Gragner, Wolf-Jürgen. *Leipzig im Oktober: Kirchen und alternative Gruppen im Umbruch der DDR.* Berlin: Wichern, 1990.

Grosser, Dieter, ed. *German Unification: The Unexpected Challenge.* Oxford: Berg, 1992.

Hancock, M. Donald and Helga Welsh, eds. *German Unification. Process and Outcomes.* Boulder, CO: Westview, 1992.

Heiling, Gerhard K., Thomas Büttner, and Wolfgang Lutz. *Germany's Population: Turbulent Past, Uncertain Future.* Washington, D.C.: Population Reference Bureau, n.d.

Heym, Stefan. *Auf Sand Gebaut.* Munich: Bertelsmann, 1990.

Heym, Stefan and Werner Heiduczek, eds. *Die sanfte Revolution: Prosa, Lyrik, Protokolle, Erlebnisberichte, Reden.* Leipzig: Kiepenheuer, 1990.

James, Harold and Marla Stone. *When the Wall Came Down. Reactions to German Unification.* New York: Routledge, 1992.

Jarausch, Konrad H. *Uniting Germany. Documents and Debates, 1944-1993.* Trans. by A. Brown and B. Cooper. Oxford: Berg, 1994.

Jaspers, Karl. *Freiheit und Wiedervereinigung: über Aufgaben deutscher Politik.* Munich: Piper, 1990.

Keithly, David M. *The Collapse of East German Communism. The Year the Wall Came Down.* New York: Praeger, 1992.

Krenz, Egon. *Wenn Mauern fallen: die friedliche Revolution. Vorgeschichte-Auflauf-Auswirkungen.* Vienna: Neff, 1990.

Lasky, Melvin. *Voices in a Revolution.* New Brunswick, NJ: Transaction, 1992.

Marcuse, Peter. *A German Way of Revolution. DDR-Tagebuch eines Amerikaners.* [In German]. Berlin: Dietz, 1990.

Menge, Marlies. Forward by Christa Wolf. *"Ohne uns läuft nichts mehr": die Revolution in der DDR.* Stuttgart: Deutsche Verlags-Anstalt, 1990.

Philipsen, Dirk. *We Were the People: Voices from East Germany's Revolutionary Autumn of 1989.* Durham, NC: Duke University Press, 1992.

Rein, Gerhard, ed. *Die Opposition in der DDR: Entwürfe für einen anderen Sozialismus; Texte, Programme, Statuten von Neues Forum, Demokratischer Aufbruch, Demokratie Jetzt, SPD, Böhlener Plattform und Grüne Partei in der DDR.* Berlin: Wichern, 1989.

Rotfeld, Adam Daniel and Walter Stutzle, eds. *Germany and Europe in Transition.* Oxford: Oxford University Press, 1991.

Schäuble, Wolfgang. *Der Vertrag. Wie ich über die deutsche Einheit verhandelte.* Ed. by Dirk Koch and Klaus Wirtgen. Stuttgart: Deutsche Verlags-Anstalt, n.d.

Stolpe, Manfred. *Den Menschen Hoffnung geben.* Berlin: Wichern, 1991.

Szabo, Stephen F. *The Diplomacy of German Unification.* New York: St. Martin's, 1992.

Wallach, H.G. Peter and Ronald A. Francisca. *United Germany: Past, Politics, Prospects.* Westport, CT: Greenwood, 1992.

Wolf, Christa. *Reden im Herbst.* Berlin: Aufbau Verlag, 1990.

POLITICAL THOUGHT AND CULTURE

Anchor, Robert. *Germany Confronts Modernization. German Culture and Society, 1790-1890.* Lexington, MA: D.C. Heath, 1972.

Aschenheim, Steven E. *The Nietzsche Legacy in Germany 1890-1990.* Berkeley, CA: University of California Press, 1992.

Baker, Kendall L., Russell Dalton, and Kai Hildebrandt. *Germany Transformed: Political Culture and the New Politics.* Cambridge: Harvard University Press, 1981.

Becker, Jillian. *Hitler's Children: The Story of the Baader-Meinhof Terrorist Gang.* Rev. ed. London: Panther, 1978.

Beetham, D. *Max Weber and the Theory of Modern Politics.* London: Allen & Unwin, 1974.

Beiser, Frederick C. *The Fate of Reason. German Philosophy from Kant to Fichte.* Cambridge: Harvard University Press, 1987.

Berg-Schlosser, Dirk and Ralf Rytlewski. *Political Culture in Germany.* New York: St. Martin's, 1992.

Bracher, Karl Dietrich. "Gleichschaltung of the Universities," in *The German Dilemma: The Throes of Political Emancipation*. London: Weidenfeld and Nicolson, 1974.

Braunthal, Gerard. *Political Loyalty and Public Service in West Germany: The 1972 Decree against Radicals and its Consequences*. Amherst: University of Massachusetts Press, 1990.

Brubaker, Rogers. *Citizenship and Nationhood in France and Germany*. Cambridge: Harvard University Press, 1992.

Bruford, Walter Horace. *The German Tradition of Self-Cultivation: Bildung from Humboldt to Thomas Mann*. London: Cambridge University Press, 1975.

Bunn, Ronald F. *German Politics and the Spiegel Affair: A Case Study of the Bonn System*. Baton Rouge: Louisiana State University Press, 1968.

Burdick, Charles, Hans-Adolf Jacobsen, and Winfried Kudszus. *Contemporary Germany: Politics and Culture*. Boulder, CO: Westview, 1984.

Burns, Robert and Wilfried van der Will. *Protest and Democracy in West Germany: Extra-Parliamentary Opposition and the Democratic Agenda*. New York: St. Martin's, 1988.

Campbell, Joan. *Joy in Work, German Work: The National Debate, 1800-1945*. Princeton: Princeton University Press, 1989.

Childs, David and Jeffrey Johnson. *West Germany: Politics and Society*. New York: St. Martin's, 1981.

Chytry, Josef. *The Aesthetic State: A Quest in Modern German Thought*. Berkeley: University of California Press, 1989.

Clausewitz, Carl Von. *On War*. Edited and translated by Howard, Michael and Peter Paret. Princeton: Princeton University Press, 1976.

Dahrendorf, Ralf. *Society and Democracy in Germany.* Garden City, NY: Doubleday Anchor, 1967.

Dahrendorf, Ralf and Gina Thomas, eds. *The Unresolved Past: A Debate in German History.* New York: St. Martin's, 1991.

Doering, Herbert and Gordon Smith, eds. *Party Government and Political Culture in Western Germany.* New York: St. Martin's, 1982.

Eley, Geoff. *Reshaping the German Right--Radical Nationalism and Political Change after Bismarck.* Ann Arbor: University of Michigan Press, 1990.

Eley, Geoff, gen. ed. *Social History, Popular Culture, and Politics in Germany.* Ann Arbor: University of Michigan Press, 1990.

Evans, Richard J. *In Hitler's Shadow: West German Historians and the Attempt to Escape from the Nazi Past.* New York: Pantheon, 1989.

Farias, Victor. *Heidegger and Nazism.* Philadelphia: Temple, 1989.

Ferry, Luc and Alain Renaut. *Heidegger and Modernity.* Chicago: University of Chicago Press, 1990.

Freundlieb, Dieter and Wayne Hudson. *Reason and Its Other. Rationality in Modern German Philosophy and Culture.* Oxford: Berg, 1993.

Gilman, Sander L., ed. *Conversations with Nietzsche. A Life in the Words of His Contemporaries.* Trans. by David J. Parent. Oxford: Oxford University Press, 1991.

Goldman, Harvey. *Max Weber and Thomas Mann: Calling and the Shaping of the Self.* Berkeley: University of California Press, 1988.

Habermas, Jürgen, ed. *Observations on "The Spiritual Situation of the Age": Contemporary German Perspectives.* Cambridge: MIT Press, 1984.

Hamilton, Peter, ed. *Max Weber. Critical Assessments.* 2 sets of 4 vols. each. New York: Routledge, 1991 and 1992.

Hancock, M. Donald. *West Germany: The Politics of Democratic Corporatism.* Chatham, NJ: Chatham House Publishers, 1989.

Hartmann, Heinz. *Authority and Organization in German Management.* Princeton: Princeton University Press, 1959.

Hoffmann-Lange, Ursula, ed. *Social and Political Structures in West Germany: From Authoritarianism to Postindustrialism.* Boulder, CO: Westview, 1991.

Holborn, Hajo. "German Idealism in the Light of Social History," in *Germany and Europe: Historical Essays.* Garden City: Doubleday, 1971.

Holton, Robert J. and Bryan S. Turner. *Max Weber on Economy and Society.* New York: Routledge, 1991.

Holub, Robert C. *Jürgen Habermas. Critic in the Public Sphere.* New York: Routledge, 1991.

Howard, Michael. *Clausewitz.* Oxford: Oxford University Press, 1988.

Hughes, H. Stuart. *Consciousness and Society. The Reorientation of European Social Thought 1890-1930.* New York: Vintage Books, 1961.

Inglehart, Ronald. *The Silent Revolution.* Princeton: Princeton University Press, 1977.

Jaspers, Karl. *Hoffnung und Sorge: Schriften zur deutschen Politik, 1945-1965.* Munich: Piper, 1965.

Jaspers, Karl. *Wohin treibt die Bundesrepublik? Tatsachen-Gefahren-Chancen.* Munich: Piper, 1966. English title: *The Future of Germany.* Chicago: University of Chicago Press, 1967.

Jay, Martin. *The Dialectical Imagination: A History of the Frankfurt School and the Institute of Social Research, 1923-1950.* Boston: Little, Brown, 1973.

Klemperer, Klemens von. *Germany's New Conservatism: Its History and Dilemma in the Twentieth Century.* Princeton: Princeton University Press, 1968.

Kohn, Hans. *The Mind of Germany. The Education of a Nation.* New York: Harper Torchbooks, 1960.

Koolen, Harry and Mary J. Meyer. *Society and Political Culture: West Germany and United States, Characteristics and Comparisons.* Amherst, MA: Occasional Papers Series, Western European Studies, 1985.

Krieger, Leonard. *The German Idea of Freedom: History of a Political Tradition.* Boston: Beacon Press, 1957.

Lewis, Rand C. *A Nazi Legacy: Right Wing Extremism in Postwar Germany.* Westport, CT: Praeger, 1991.

Mann, Philip. *Hugo Ball: An Intellectual Biography.* Leeds, England: Institute of Germanic Studies, University of London, 1987.

Mann, Thomas. *Thomas Mann's Addresses Delivered at the Library of Congress, 1942-1949.* Washington: Library of Congress, 1963.

McLellan, David. *Karl Marx.* New York: Penguin Books, 1976.

Meinecke, Friedrich. *Cosmopolitanism and the National State.* Transl. by Robert B. Kimber. Princeton: Princeton University Press, 1963.

Mommsen, Wolfgang J. *The Age of Bureaucracy. Perspectives on the Political Sociology of Max Weber.* New York: Harper Torchbooks, 1974.

Mommsen, Wolfgang J. *Max Weber and German Politics, 1890-1920.* Trans. by Michael Steinberg. Chicago: University of Chicago Press, 1984.

Mosse, George L. *The Nationalization of the Masses. Political Symbolism and Mass Movements in Germany from the Napoleonic Wars Through the Third Reich.* Ithaca: Cornell University Press, n.d.

Muller, Jerry Z. *The Other God that Failed--Hans Freyer and the Deradicalization of German Conservatism.* Princeton: Princeton University Press, 1991.

Neumann, Erich Peter and Elisabeth Noelle-Neumann. *The Germans: Public Opinion Polls, 1947-1966.* Allensbach am Bodensee: Verlag für Demoskopie, 1967.

Noelle-Neumann, Elisabeth. *The Germans: Public Opinion Polls, 1967-1980.* Westport, CT: Greenwood, 1981.

Parkes, K. Stuart. *Writers and Politics in West Germany.* London: Croom Helm, 1986.

Petzet, Heinrich Wiegand. *Encounters and Dialogues with Martin Heidegger, 1929-1976.* Transl. and ed. by Parvis Emad and Kenneth Malz. Chicago: University of Chicago Press, 1993.

Piper Verlag. *Historikerstreit.* Munich: Piper, 1987.

Rist, Ray C. *Guest Workers in Germany: The Prospects for Pluralism.* New York: Praeger, 1978.

Ritter, Gerhard. *The German Problem: Basic Questions of German Political Life, Past and Present.* Trans. by S. Burkhardt. Columbus: Ohio State University Press, 1965.

Roberts, Julian. *The Logic of Reflection. German Philosophy in the Twentieth Century.* New Haven: Yale University Press, 1992.

Rubanowice, Robert J. *Crisis in Consciousness: The Thought of Ernst Troeltsch.* Gainesville: University of Florida Press, 1982.

Russell, Peter. *The Divided Mind: A Portrait of Modern German Culture.* Essen: Die Blaue Eule, 1988.

Safranski, Rüdiger. *Schopenhauer and the Wild Years of Philosophy.* Trans. by Ewald Osers. Cambridge: Harvard University Press, 1990.

Schaff, Lawrence A. *Fleeing the Iron Cage: Culture, Politics and Modernity in the Thought of Max Weber.* Berkeley: University of California Press, 1989.

Stark, Gary D. and Bede Karl Lackner, eds. *Essays on Culture and Society in Modern Germany.* College Station, TX: Texas A&M University Press, 1982.

Schweigler, Gebhard. *National Consciousness in Divided Germany.* Beverly Hills, CA: Sage, 1975.

Stern, Fritz. *The Politics of Cultural Despair: A Study in the Rise of the Germanic Ideology.* Berkeley: University of California Press, 1961.

Stern, Fritz. *The Varieties of History: From Voltaire to the Present.* New York: Random House, 1973.

Stern, Fritz. *The Failure of Illiberalism: Essays on the Political Culture of Modern Germany.* Chicago: Chicago University Press, 1975.

Stern, Fritz. *Dreams and Delusions.* New York: Knopf, 1987.

Tauber, Kurt P. *Beyond Eagle and Swastika: German Nationalism since 1945.* 2 vols. Middletown, CT: Wesleyan University Press, 1967.

Thayer, Charles W. *The Unquiet Germans.* New York: Harper, 1957.

Trumpbour, Jack. *The Dividing Rhine.* Oxford: Berg, 1989.

United States Information Agency. *The West German Successor Generation: Their Social and Political Values.* Washington, D.C.: USIA, 1984.

Weizsäcker, Richard von. *Speeches for Our Time.* German Issues 10. Washington, D.C.: American Institute for Contemporary German Studies, 1992.

Wiggershaus, Rolf. *Die Frankfurter Schule: Geschichte, Theoretische Entwicklung Politische Bedeutung.* Munich: Carl Hanser, 1987.

Williams, Arthur. *Broadcasting and Democracy in West Germany.* Bradford, England: Bradford University Press, 1976.

Wolin, Richard. *The Politics of Being: The Political Thought of Martin Heidegger.* New York: Columbia University Press, 1990.

SOCIETY AND SOCIAL INSTITUTIONS

Berding, Helmut. *Moderner Antisemitismus in Deutschland.* Frankfurt am Main: Suhrkamp, 1988.

Beuys, Barbara. *Familienleben in Deutschland: neue Bilder aus der deutschen Vergangenheit.* Hamburg: Rowohlt, 1990.

Boehncke, Heiner and Harald Wittich, eds. *Buntesdeutschland. Ansichten zu einer multikulturellen Gesellschaft.* Hamburg: Rororo, 1991.

Cocks, Geoffrey and Konrad H. Jarausch, eds. *German Professions, 1800-1950.* Oxford: Oxford University Press, 1990.

Frevert, Ute. *Women in German History. From Bourgeois Emancipation to Sexual Liberation.* Oxford: Berg, 1989.

Fritzsche, Peter. *A Nation of Fliers: German Aviation and the Popular Imagination.* Cambridge: Harvard University Press, 1991.

624 ■ *Bibliography-Society*

Greive, Hermann. *Geschichte des modernen Antisemitismus in Deutschland.* Darmstadt: Wiss. Buchges., 1988.

Gugel, Guenther. *Ausländer, Aussiedler, Übersiedler: Fremdenfeindlichkeit in der Bundesrepublik Deutschland.* 3d rev. ed. Tübingen: Verein für Friedenspädagogik, 1991.

Hearnden, Arthur. *Education in the Two Germanies.* Oxford: Oxford University Press, 1974.

Hearnden, Arthur. *Education, Culture, and Politics in West Germany.* Oxford: Oxford University Press, 1976.

Humphreys, Peter J. *Media and Media Policy in West Germany. The Press and Broadcasting since 1945.* Revised and updated. Oxford: Berg, 1993.

Jarausch, Konrad H. *The Unfree Professions: German Lawyers, Teachers, and Engineers, 1900-1950.* Oxford: Oxford University Press, 1990.

Kolinsky, Eva. *Women in Contemporary Germany. Life, Work and Politics.* 2nd rev. ed. Oxford: Berg, 1992.

Krejci, J. *Social Structure in Divided Germany.* London: Croom Helm, 1976.

Liebersohn, Harry. *Fate and Utopia in German Sociology, 1870-1923.* Cambridge: MIT Press, 1988.

McClelland, Charles E. *The German Experience of Professionalization.* Cambridge: Cambridge University Press, 1991.

Mommsen, Wolfgang, ed. *The Emergence of the Welfare State in Britain and Germany.* London: Croom Helm, 1981.

Neuhaus, R. *Social Security: How it Works in the Federal Republic of Germany.* Bonn: Friedrich Ebert Stiftung, 1979.

Oppenheim, A.N. *Civic Education and Participation in Democracy.* Beverly Hills and London: Sage, 1977.

Petrat, Gerhardt. *Schulerziehung: ihre Sozialgeschichte in Deutschland bis 1945.* Munich: Ehrenwirth, 1987.

Pritchard, Rosalind M.O. *The End of Elitism? The Democratization of the West German University System.* Oxford: Berg, 1991.

Rippley, LaVern. *Of German Ways.* New York: Barnes & Noble, 1980.

Rueschemeyer, Dietrich. *Lawyers and Their Society.* Cambridge: Harvard University Press, 1973.

Ruh, Ulrich. *Religion und Kirche in der Bundesrepublik Deutschland.* Iudicium Verlag, 1990.

Watts, Meredith W., Arthur Fischer, Werner Fuchs, and Jürgen Zinnecker. *Contemporary German Youth and Their Elders: A Generational Comparison.* Westport, CT: Greenwood, 1989.

Weber-Kellermann, Ingeborg. *Die deutsche Familie: Versuch einer Sozialgeschichte.* Frankfurt am Main: Suhrkamp, 1989.

Weiss, Sheila Faith. *Race Hygiene and National Efficiency: The Eugenics of Wilhelm Schallmeyer.* Berkeley: University of California Press, 1987.

LITERATURE

Bausinger, Hermann. *Folk Culture in a World of Technology.* Trans. by Elke Dettmer. Bloomington: Indiana University Press, 1990.

Bennett, Benjamin. *Modern Drama and German Classicism. Renaissance from Lessing to Brecht.* Ithaca: Cornell University Press, 1986.

Bithell, Jethro. *Germany: A Companion to German Studies.* London: Methuen, 1955.

Blackall, Eric A. *The Novels of the German Romantics.* Ithaca: Cornell University Press, 1983.

Bottigheimer, Ruth B. *Grimm's Bad Girls and Bold Boys: The Moral and Social vision of the Tales.* New Haven: Yale University Press, 1987.

Bronner, Stephen Eric and Douglas Kellner, eds. *Passion and Rebellion: The Expressionist Heritage.* New York: Columbia University Press, 1988.

Bullivant, Keith. *Realism Today: Aspects of the Contemporary West German Novel.* Oxford: Berg, 1987.

Bullivant, Keith, ed. *The Modern German Novel.* Oxford: Berg, 1987.

Bullivant, Keith, ed. *After the 'Death' of Literature. West German Writing of the 1970s.* Oxford: Berg, 1989.

Bullivant, Keith. *The Future of German Literature.* Oxford: Berg, 1993.

Burkhard, Marianne and Jeanette Clausen, eds. *Women in German Yearbook 4: Feminist Studies and German Culture.* Lanham, MD: University Press of America, 1988.

Burwick, Frederick. *The Haunted Eye: Perception and the Grotesque in English and German Romanticism.* Heidelberg: Carl Winter, 1987.

Case, Sue-Ellen, ed. *The Divided Home/Land--Contemporary German Women's Plays.* Ann Arbor: University of Michigan, 1992.

Chapple, Gerald, Frederick Hall, and Hans Schulte, eds. *The Romantic Tradition. German Literature and Music in the Nineteenth Century.* Lanham, MD: University Press of America, 1992.

Clausen, Jeanette and Helen Cafferty, eds. *Women in German Yearbook 5: Feminist Studies and German Culture.* Lanham, MD: University Press of America, 1989.

Constantine, David. *Hölderlin*. Oxford: Clarendon Press, 1988.

Di Napoli, Thomas. *The Children's Literature of Peter Hacks*. New York: Peter Lang, 1987.

Dow, James R. and Hannjost Lixfeld, eds. *German Volkskunde: A Decade of Theoretical Confrontation, Debate, and Reorientation 1967-1977*. Bloomington: Indiana University Press, 1986.

Durrani, Osman, ed. *German Poetry of the Romantic Era. An Anthology*. Oxford: Berg, 1986.

Emmerich, Wolfgang. *Kleine Literaturgeschichte der DDR*. Expanded ed., 1989.

Finney, Gail. *Women in Modern Drama: Freud, Feminism, and European Theater at the Turn of the Century*. Ithaca: Cornell University Press, 1989.

Franke, Konrad. *Die Literatur der Deutschen Demokratischen Republik*. Kindler's Literatur Geschichte der Gegenwart. Munich: Kindler, 1974.

Frederiksen, Elke, ed. *Women Writers of Germany, Austria and Switzerland: An Annotated Bio-Bibliographical Guide*. Westport, CT: Greenwood, 1989.

Friederich, Werner P. *History of German Literature*. New York: Barnes & Noble, 1961.

Garland, Henry. *A Concise Survey of German Literature*. Coral Gables, FL: University of Miami Press, 1971.

Garland, Henry and Mary Garland. *The Oxford Companion to German Literature*. Oxford: Clarendon Press, 1976.

Guthrie, John. *Annette von Droste-Hülshoff: A German Poet between Romanticism and Realism*. Oxford: Berg, 1989.

Hardin, James, ed. *German Fiction Writers, 1914-1945.* Detroit: Gale Research Company, 1987.

Hardin, James. *Dictionary of Literary Biography: Volume 66: German Fiction Writers, 1885-1913 Part I: A-L.* Detroit: Gale Research Co., 1988.

Heinemann, Marlene E. *Gender and Destiny: Women Writers and the Holocaust.* Westport, CT: Greenwood, 1986.

Helwig, Gisela, ed. *Die DDR-Gesellschaft im Spiegel der Literatur.* Cologne: Verlag Wissenschaft und Politik, 1986.

Herd, E.W. and August Obermayer, eds. *A Glossary of German Literary Terms.* Dunedin, NZ: University of Otago, 1983.

Hewitt, Nicholas, ed. *The Culture of Reconstruction: European Literature, Thought and Film, 1945-50.* New York: St. Martin's, 1989.

Hill, Claude. *Zweihundert Jahre Deutscher Kultur.* New York: Harper & Row, 1966.

Hilliard, Kevin. *Philosophy, Letters, and Fine Arts in Klopstock's Thought.* London: Institute of Germanic Studies, 1987.

Hilscher, Eberhard. *Gerhard Hauptmann: Leben und Werk.* Frankfurt am Main: Athenäum, 1988.

Hoffmann, Hilmar and Heinrich Klotz, eds. *Die Kultur unseres Jahrhunderts.* 3 vols. Düsseldorf: Econ, 1987-1989.

Hofstetter, Eleanore O. and Michael T. O'Pecko. *The Twentieth-Century German Novel: A Bibliography of English-Language Criticism, 1945-1986.* Metuchen, NJ: Scarecrow Press, 1989.

Hohendahl, Peter Uwe. *Building a National Literature: The Case of Germany, 1830-1870.* Ithaca: Cornell University Press, 1989.

Houlgate, Stephen. *Hegel, Nietzsche, and the Criticism of Metaphysics.* Cambridge: Cambridge University Press, 1986.

Jackson, David Arthur. *Theodor Storm: The Writer as Democratic Humanitarian.* Oxford: Berg, 1992.

Jelavich, Peter. *Munich and Theatrical Modernism: Politics, Playwriting, and Performance, 1890-1914.* Cambridge: Harvard University Press, 1985.

Jennings, Michael W. *Dialectical Images: Walter Benjamin's Theory of Literary Criticism.* Ithaca: Cornell University Press, 1987.

Johnston, Otto W. *The Myth of a Nation--Literature and Politics in Prussia under Napoleon.* Columbia, SC: Camden House, 1989.

Kane, Martin, ed. *Socialism and the Literary Imagination. Essays on East German Writers.* Oxford: Berg, 1991.

Keele, Alan F. *Understanding Günter Grass.* Columbia: University of South Carolina Press, 1988.

Kluge, Friedrich. *Etymologisches Wörterbuch der deutschen Sprache.* 22nd. ed. Berlin: Walter de Gruyter, 1989.

Koepke, Wolf. *Johann Gottfried Herder.* Boston: Twayne, 1987.

Koepke, Wolf and Michael Winkler, eds. *Exilliteratur 1933-1945.* Darmstadt: Wissenschaftliche Buchgesellschaft, 1989.

Kuhn, Anna and Barbara D. Wright, eds. *Playing for Stakes. German-Language Drama in Social Context.* Oxford: Berg, 1992.

Lawson, Richard H. *Franz Kafka.* New York: Ungar, 1987.

Lederer, Herbert. *Handbook of East German Drama, 1945-1985/ DDR Drama Handbuch.* New York: Peter Lang, 1987.

Mann, Klaus. *Mephisto.* Trans. by Robyn Smith. New York: Penguin, 1983.

Martini, Fritz. *Deutsche Literaturgeschichte von den Anfängen bis zur Gegenwart.* Stuttgart: Alfred Kröner, 1977.

Mauser, Wolfram and Helmtrud. *Christa Wolf "Nachdenken über Christa T."* Munich: Wilhelm Fink, 1987.

McCormick, Richard W. *Politics of the Self: Feminism and the Postmodern in West German Literature and Film.* Princeton: Princeton University Press, 1991.

McGlathery, James M., ed. with Larry Danielson, Ruth E. Lorbe, and Selma K. Richardson. *The Brothers Grimm and Folktales.* Urbana: University of Illinois Press, 1988.

Michael, Friedrich and Hans Daiber. *Geschichte des deutschen Theaters.* Frankfurt am Main: Suhrkamp, 1989.

Mueller, Roswitha. *Bertolt Brecht and the Theory of Media.* Lincoln: University of Nebraska Press, 1989.

Müller, Harald, ed. *DDR-Theater des Umbruchs.* Frankfurt am Main: Eichborn, 1990.

Mullen, Inga E. *German Realism in the United States: The American Reception of Meyer, Storm, Raabe, Keller and Fontane.* New York: Peter Lang, 1988.

Nehamas, Alexander. *Nietzsche: Life as Literature.* Cambridge: Harvard University Press, 1985.

Ostwald, Thomas. *Karl May: Leben und Werk.* 4th ed. Braunschweig: Graff, 1977.

Pasley, Malcolm. *Germany, A Companion to German Studies.* London: Methuen, 1972.

Perraudin, Michael. *Heinrich Heine: Poetry in Context. A Study of Buch der Lieder.* Oxford: Berg, 1989.

Peucker, Brigitte. *Lyric Descent in the German Romantic Tradition.* New Haven: Yale University Press, 1987.

Pfefferkorn, Kristin. *Novalis: A Romantic's Theory of Language and Poetry.* New Haven: Yale University Press, 1988.

Reid, James H. *Heinrich Böll: A German For His Time.* Oxford: Berg, 1988.

Reid, James H. *Writing without Taboos. The New East German Literature.* Oxford: Berg, 1990.

Richards, David G. *The Hero's Quest for the Self: An Archetypal Approach to Hesse's Demian and Other Novels.* Lanham, MD: University Press of America, 1987.

Rilke, Rainer Maria. *The Sonnets to Orpheus.* Columbia, SC: Camden House, 1989.

Roberts, David and Philip Thomson, eds. *The Modern German Historical Novel. Paradigms, Problems and Perspectives.* Oxford: Berg, 1991.

Röhrich, Lutz. *Folktales and Reality.* Trans. by Peter Tokofsky. Bloomington: Indiana University Press, 1991.

Roper, Katherine. *German Encounters with Modernity: Novels of Imperial Berlin.* Atlantic Highlands, NJ: Humanities Press, 1991.

Schmidt, Henry J. *How Dramas End--Essays on the German Sturm und Drang, Büchner, Hauptmann, and Fleisser.* Ann Arbor: University of Michigan Press, 1992.

Schmiedt, Helmut. *Karl May: Studien zu Leben, Werk und Wirkung eines Erfolgsschriftstellers.* Frankfurt: Athenäum, 1987.

Schrader, Bärbel and Jürgen Schebera. *The "Golden" Twenties: Art and Literature in the Weimar Republic.* Trans. by Katherine Vanovitch. New Haven: Yale University Press, 1988.

Sebald, W.G., ed. *A Radical Stage: Theatre in Germany in the 1970s and the 1980s.* Oxford: Berg, 1988.

Sharpe, Lesley. *Friedrich Schiller. Drama, Thought and Politics.* Cambridge: Cambridge University Press, 1991.

Sheppard, Richard, ed. *New Ways in Germanistik.* Oxford: Berg, 1990.

Spaethling, Robert. *Music and Mozart in the Life of Goethe.* Columbia, SC: Camden House, 1987.

Stahl, E.L. and W.E. Yuill. *German Literature of the Eighteenth and Nineteenth Centuries.* Vol. 3. London: Cresset, 1970.

Stephens, Anthony. *Heinrich von Kleist.* Oxford: Berg, 1992.

Tatar, Maria. *The Hard Facts of the Grimms' Fairy Tales.* Princeton: Princeton University Press, 1990.

Udoff, Alan, ed. *Kafka and the Contemporary Critical Performance: Centenary Readings.* Bloomington: Indiana University Press, 1987.

Vivian, Kim, ed. *A Concise History of German Literature to 1900.* Charlotte, VT: Camden House, 1992.

Waldeck, Marie-Luise. *The Theme of Freedom in Schiller's Plays.* Stuttgart: Hans-Dieter Heinz Akademischer Verlag, 1986.

Weisinger, Kenneth D. *The Classical Facade: A Nonclassical Reading of Goethe's Classicism.* University Park: Pennsylvania State University Press, 1988.

Wetzel, Christoph. *Lexikon der Autoren und Werke.* Stuttgart: Klett, 1986.

Williams, Arthur, Stuart Parkes, and Roland Smith, eds. *Literature on the Threshold. The German Novel in the 1980s.* Oxford: Berg, 1990.

Wilson, Katharina M. and Frank J. Warnke, eds. *Women Writers of the Seventeenth Century.* Athens: University of Georgia Press, 1989.

Zimmermann, Harro. *Freiheit und Geschichte: F.G. Klopstock als historischer Dichter und Denker.* Heidelberg: Carl Winter, 1987.

Ziolkowski, Theodore. *German Romanticism and its Institutions.* Princeton: Princeton University Press, 1990.

Zipes, Jack. *The Brothers Grimm: From Enchanted Forests to the Modern World.* New York: Routledge, 1988.

ART

Adam, Peter. *Art of the Third Reich.* New York: H.N. Abrams, 1992.

Barron, Stephanie, ed. *"Degenerate Art:" The Fate of the Avantgarde in Nazi Germany.* New York: Harry N. Abrams, 1991.

Benz, Richard. *Die deutsche Romantik. Geschichte einer geistigen Bewegung.* Leipzig: Philipp Reclam, 1937.

Christensen, Carl C. *Art and the Reformation in Germany.* Athens: Ohio University Press, 1979.

Dube, Wolf Dieter. *Expressionismus in Wort und Bild.* English title *Expressionists and Expressionism.* Trans. by James Emmons. New York: Skira, 1983.

Eberle, Matthias. *World War I and the Weimar Artists: Dix, Grosz, Beckmann, Schlemmer.* Trans. by John Gabriel. New Haven: Yale University Press, 1985.

Flavell, M. Kay. *George Grosz. A Biography.* New Haven and London: Yale University Press, 1988.

Greenberg, Allan Carl. *Artists and Revolution: Dada and the Bauhaus, 1917-1925.* Ann Arbor: University of Michigan Research Press, 1979.

Haftmann, Werner. *Verfremdte Kunst: bildende Künstler d. inneren u. äusseren Emigration in d. Zeit d. Nationalsozialismus.* Cologne: DuMont, 1986.

Hepp, Corona. *Avantgarde: moderne Kunst. Kulturkritik u. Reformbewegungen nach d. Jahrhundertwende.* Munich: Deutscher Taschenbuch, 1987.

Hess, Hans. *George Grosz.* New Haven: Yale University Press, 1985.

Hutchison, Jane Campbell. *Albrecht Dürer: A Biography.* Princeton: Princeton University Press, 1990.

Hütt, Wolfgang. *Deutsche Malerei und Graphik 1750-1945.* Berlin: Henschelverlag Kunst und Gesellschaft, 1986.

Kane, Martin. *Weimar Germany and the Limits of Political Art: A Study of the Work of George Grosz and Ernst Toller.* The Hutton Press, 1987.

Lewis, Beth Irwin. *George Grosz.* Princeton: Princeton University Press, 1991.

Lützeler, Heinrich. *Deutsche Kunst: Einsichten in d. Welt u. in d. Menschen. Von d. Frühzeit bis zur Gegenwart.* Bonn: Bouvier, 1987.

Makela, Maria. *The Munich Secession--Art and Artists in Turn-of-the-Century Munich.* Princeton: Princeton University Press, 1990.

Neidhart, Hans Joachim. *Deutsche Malerei des 19. Jahrhunderts.* Leipzig: Seemann, 1990.

Pohl, Edda. *Die ungehorsamen Maler der DDR: Anspruch und Wirklichkeit d. SED-Kulturpolitik, 1965-1979.* Berlin: Oberbaum, 1979.

Rogoff, Irit, ed. *The Divided Heritage: Themes and Problems in German Modernism.* Cambridge: Cambridge University Press, 1991.

Roh, Franz. *Geschichte der deutschen Kunst von 1900 bis zur Gegenwart*. English title *German Art in the 20th Century*. Transl. by Catherine Hutter. Greenwich, CT: New York Graphic Society, 1968.

Steinweis, Alan E. *Art, Ideology, and Economics in Nazi Germany. The Reich Chambers of Music, Theater, and the Visual Arts*. Chapel Hill: University of North Carolina Press, 1993.

Stephan, Alexander, ed. *Exil: Literatur und die Künste nach 1933*. Bonn: Bouvier, 1990.

Uhr, Horst. *Masterpieces of German Expressionism at the Detroit Institute of Arts*. New York: Hudson Hills, 1982. Also *Lovis Corinth*. Berkeley: University of California Press, 1990.

Vogt, Paul. *Geschichte der deutschen Malerei im 20. Jahrhundert*. Cologne: DuMont, 1989.

Watkin, David and Tilman Mellinghoff. *German Architecture and the Classical Ideal*. Cambridge: MIT Press, 1987.

Zalampas, Sherree Owens. *Adolf Hitler: A Psychological Interpretation of His Views on Architecture, Art and Music*. Bowling Green, OH: Bowling Green State University Popular Press, 1990.

MUSIC

Boomgaarden, Donald R. *Musical Thought in Britain and Germany during the Early Eighteenth Century*. New York: Peter Lang, 1987.

Brody, Elaine. *The Music Guide to Austria and Germany*. New York: Dodd, Mead, 1975.

Chorley, Henry Fothergill. *Modern German Music*. London: Smith, Elder, 1954.

Cirillo, Nancy R., Marion S. Miller, and Leroy R. Shaw, eds. *Wagner in Retrospect: A Centennial Reappraisal*. Amsterdam: Editions Rodopi, 1987.

Geissmar, Berta. *Two Worlds of Music.* New York: Creative Age, 1946.

May, Ernest and George Stauffer, eds. *Bach as Organist: His Instruments, Music and Performance Practices.* Bloomington: Indiana University Press, 1986.

Meyer, Michael. *The Politics of Music in the Third Reich.* New York: Peter Lang, 1991.

Müller, Ulrich and Peter Wapnewski, eds. *Wagner Handbook.* Transl. by John Deathridge. Cambridge: Harvard University Press, 1992.

Polk, Keith. *German Instrumental Music of the Late Middle Ages.* Cambridge: Cambridge University Press, 1992.

Schonzeler, Hans-Hubert. *Of German Music: A Symposium.* London: O. Wolff, 1976.

Solomon, Maynard. *Beethoven Essays.* Cambridge: Harvard Univ., 1988.

Sonntag, Brunhilde and Helmuth Hopf, eds. *Im Osten nichts neues? Zur Musik der DDR.* Wilhelmshaven: Florian Noetzzel, 1989.

Stuckenschmidt, Hans Heinz. *Germany and Central Europe.* New York: Holt, Rinehart and Winston, 1971.

FILM

Berghaus, Günter, ed. *Theater and Film in Exile: German Artists in Britain, 1933-1945.* New York: Oswals Wolff, Berg, 1989.

Corrigan, Timothy, ed. *The Films of Werner Herzog: Between Mirage and History.* New York: Methuen, 1987.

Cziffra, Geza von. *Es war eine rauschende Ballnacht: e. Sittengeschichte d. dt. Films.* Berlin: Ullstein, 1987.

Elsaeser, Thomas. *New German Cinema--A History.* New Brunswick, NJ: Rutgers University Press, 1989.

Frieden, Sandra, Richard W. McCormick, Vibeke R. Petersen, and Laurie Melissa Vogelsang, eds. *Gender and German Cinema. Feminist Interventions.* 2 vols. Oxford: Berg, 1993.

Helt, Richard C. and Marie E. *West German Cinema Since 1945* and *West German Cinema, 1985-1990.* Metuchen: Scarecrow, 1987, 1992.

Kaes, Anton. *From Hitler to Heimat--The Return of History as Film.* Cambridge: Harvard University Press, 1989.

Kolker, Robert P. and Peter Beicken. *The Films of Wim Wenders. Cinema as Vision and Desire.* Cambridge: Cambridge Univ., 1993.

Murray, Bruce. *Film and the German Left in the Weimar Republic.* Austin: University of Texas Press, 1990.

Pflaum, Hans Günther. *Germany on Film: Theme and Content in the Cinema of the Federal Republic of Germany.* Transl. by Richard C. Helt and Roland Richter. Detroit: Wayne State University Press, 1990.

Plummer, Thomas G., ed. et al. *Film and Politics in the Weimar Republic.* New York: Holmes & Meier, 1982.

Rentschler, Eric, ed. *German Film and Literature: Adaptations and Transformations.* New York: Methuen, 1986.

Rentschler, Eric. *West German Film Makers on Film: Visions and Voices.* New York and London: Holmes and Meier, 1988.

Riess, Curt. *Das gab's nur einmal: d. grosse Zeit d. dt. Films.* Berlin: Ullstein, n.d.

Sandford, J. *The New German Cinema.* Totowa: Barnes & Noble, 1980.

Santner, Eric L. *Stranded Objects, Mourning, Memory and Film in Postwar Germany.* Ithaca: Cornell University Press, 1990.

Willet, John. *The Theatre of the Weimar Republic.* New York and London: Holmes and Meier, 1988.

Map of Germany, 1937, 1949-1990, and 1990. (*Source:* SPP).

CHANCELLORS AND GOVERNING COALITIONS IN THE FRG

1949-1953, Konrad Adenauer, CDU (CDU/CSU, FDP, DP)

1953-1957, Konrad Adenauer, CDU (CDU/CSU, FDP, DP, BHE)

1957-1961, Konrad Adenauer, CDU (CDU/CSU, DP)

1961-1963, Konrad Adenauer, CDU (CDU/CSU, FDP)

1963-1965, Ludwig Erhard, CDU (CDU/CSU, FDP)

1965-1966, Ludwig Erhard, CDU (CDU/CSU, FDP)

1966-1969, Kurt-Georg Kiesinger, CDU (CDU/CSU, SPD)

1969-1972, Willy Brandt, SPD (SPD, FDP)

1972-1974, Willy Brandt, SPD (SPD, FDP)

1974-1976, Helmut Schmidt, SPD (SPD, FDP)

1976-1980, Helmut Schmidt, SPD (SPD, FDP)

1980-1982, Helmut Schmidt, SPD (SPD, FDP)

1982-1983, Helmut Kohl, CDU (CDU/CSU, FDP)

1983-1987, Helmut Kohl, CDU (CDU/CSU, FDP)

1987-1990, Helmut Kohl, CDU (CDU/CSU, FDP)

1990-, Helmut Kohl, CDU (CDU/CSU, FDP)

Note: Election years are bold.

ABOUT THE AUTHORS

WAYNE C. THOMPSON is Professor of Political Science at the Virginia Military Institute (VMI) and a specialist on German politics and history. A graduate of the Ohio State University, he spent an undergraduate year at the University of Göttingen on a university exchange scholarship. After serving three years in Germany with the U.S. Army as an interpreter and liaison person with the German army and police, he received his M.A. and PhD. in government at Claremont Graduate School. He wrote his dissertation in Germany as a Fulbright, Woodrow Wilson, and German Academic Exchange scholar. He has been an Alexander von Humboldt fellow and guest professor at the University of Freiburg im Breisgau. Among his books are *Kurt Riezler and the Crises of Modern Germany* (Iowa City: University of Iowa Press, 1980); *The Political Odyssey of Herbert Wehner* (Boulder, Colo.: Westview Press, 1993); and the annually updated *Western Europe* and *Canada* volumes in the World Today Series (Harpers Ferry, WV: Stryker-Post Publications). He created and administers a cadet exchange between VMI and the Universities of the Federal Armed Forces in Hamburg and Munich.

SUSAN L. THOMPSON is a Professor of German at Mary Baldwin College, Staunton, Virginia, specializing in German language and culture. A graduate of Ohio State University, she earned a Diploma of the German Language at the University of Freiburg im Breisgau and an M.A. in German Literature at the University of Massachusetts. She has a variety of German teaching experiences in the U.S. and abroad. She has lived approximately nine years in Germany, where she frequently guides study tours with her husband, Wayne.

JULIET S. THOMPSON is a graduate of Davidson College, where she was admitted to the Delta Phi Alpha German honorary society and was awarded top honors in German competency by the Goethe Institute. She is a Ph.D. candidate and Presidential Fellow in International Studies at Old Dominion University, Norfolk, Virginia. She has lived several years in Germany, where she attended the Gymnasium. She edited with Wayne C. Thompson *Margaret Thatcher: Prime Minister Indomitable* (Boulder, Colo.: Westview Press, 1994) and collaborated with Steven W. Guerrier and Wayne C. Thompson in the editing of *Perspectives on Strategic Defense* and *Space: National Programs and International Cooperation* (Boulder, Colo.: Westview Press, 1987, 1989).